CW00543772

Remaking the Chinese City

中西皮鞋莊
承辦軍裝

Remaking the Chinese City

Modernity and National Identity, 1900–1950

Edited by Joseph W. Esherick

University of Hawai'i Press
Honolulu

Printed in the United States of America
04 03 02 01 00 5 4 3 2 1

Library of Congress Cataloging-in-Publication Data
Remaking the Chinese city: modernity and national identity, 1900–1950
/ edited by Joseph W. Esherick.
p. cm.
Includes bibliographical references and index.
ISBN 0–8248–2148–3 (cloth : alk. paper)
1. Cities and towns—China—History—20th century. 2. China—
Civilization—20th century. I. Esherick, Joseph.
HT147.C48R46 1999
307.76' 0951—dc21 99–27948
CIP

University of Hawai'i Press books are printed on acid-free paper and meet the guidelines for permanence and durability of the Council on Library Resources.

Designed by David Alcorn, Alcorn Publication Design,
Red Bluff, California

Printed by The Maple-Vail Book Manufacturing Group,
York, Pennsylvania

Frontispiece: Changsha street scene, 1930s. Paved streets, rickshaws, uniformed police, electric power lines, and a sign *(left)* advertising Chinese and Western leather shoes mark this as a typical commercial street of republican China. Photo courtesy of the Library of Congress.

Contents

List of Illustrations

Maps

Figures

千枝麗秀榮華

Preface

In a nation of peasants, Chinese cities have not always received the attention they deserve. For many years, the history of modern China was dominated by the narrative of peasant-based communist revolution. The question to be answered was how Mao Zedong and the Chinese Communist Party rose to power and led China down a revolutionary path that included mobilizing millions of peasants into communes and sending officials and intellectuals to learn from the peasantry during the Cultural Revolution. The anti-urban bias of Mao's revolution tended to relegate urban history to a subordinate role in the grand narrative of modern China. But now Mao's revolution is itself a relic of history. With Chinese cities entering the new millennium as vibrant centers of economic, social, and cultural change, it is time to seek the origins of this renewed urban vitality by looking back to the transformation of urban space and society in the first half of the twentieth century.

Our understanding of Chinese cities has advanced substantially in recent years, but to date the coverage has been uneven. The late imperial city has been elegantly analyzed, with a rich volume of essays edited by G. William Skinner and two seminal volumes on Hankou by William Rowe. For the twentieth century, with the notable exception of books by David Buck on Jinan and Gail Hershatter on Tianjin, urban history has been marked by a singular focus on Shanghai. In recent years, excellent studies have been published on Shanghai capitalists, workers, students, native-place associations, rural immigrants, gangs, prostitutes, municipal government, and police. Shanghai is now quite well understood, but it is not clear that China's largest city and economic center can represent the full diversity of China's modern urban experience. What remains to be examined is the history of other early twentieth century cities. This volume, which was conceived in a conference titled "Beyond Shanghai: Imagining the City in Republican China," aims to fill that gap.

A modern city was a city of light. Here, a lamplighter ignites one of the gas lamps that preceded electricity. City unknown, late nineteenth century. Photo courtesy of the Library of Congress.

The essays collected here are not, however, just designed to fill a gap in modern China studies. They seek to address, in a comparative way, issues that affected modern cities everywhere. In particular, the process of urban reform involved a quest for modernity that was remarkably uniform across the globe. Everywhere, urban reformers sought clean, healthy, safe, orderly, efficient, productive cities. But if Chinese sought a modernity much like any other, they also sought to preserve a distinctive national identity. Indeed, modernization was not only an end in itself, it was also a means to preserve the nation, and preserving the nation meant preserving those things that made one Chinese. Modernity and nationalism, sometimes working in tandem, sometimes coming in conflict, are two forces that have dominated modern history. This book is about their interaction in Chinese cities in the first half of this century.

As noted above, this volume began with a conference titled "Beyond Shanghai." Held at the University of California at San Diego in September 1996, it was entirely sponsored by various units of that institution. I would like to take this opportunity to express my thanks to the Hwei-chih and Julia Hsiu Endowment for Chinese Studies, the Humanities Center, the Council on East Asian Studies, the Department of History, the Graduate School of International Relations and Pacific Studies, and the Chinese Studies Program for their generous support. Julie Broadwin and James Cook efficiently recorded the conference discussion as rapporteurs; my UCSD colleagues Richard Madsen and Paul Pickowicz served as session chairs; Nancy Chadwick assisted with logistics; and James Holston, Emily Honig, and Susan Glosser offered extremely helpful advice and criticism as commentators. Without the generous and talented assistance of all of these people, we would not have had the lively and productive intellectual exchanges that made this project possible.

As the conference essays were transformed into chapters for this book, all of us benefited from the advice and criticism of our fellow contributors and of two anonymous referees for the press. At the University of Hawai'i Press, Patricia Crosby and Masako Ikeda served as helpful and supportive editors and Susan Biggs Corrado as a most competent copy-editor. Most of the maps for this volume were prepared with great care and expertise by Dick Gilbreath, director of cartography, Department of Geography, University of Kentucky, with the support of the office of the Vice Chancellor for Research and Graduate Studies of the University of Kentucky. Maps for David Buck's essay were prepared by the University of Wisconsin-Milwaukee Cartography Lab, and for Charles Musgrove's by Joce Lin. For most of the illustrations, we are indebted to the Prints and Photographs Division of the Library of Congress. I would like to thank all of these individuals and institutions for their assistance.

Finally, as editor, let me express my gratitude to all of the contributors for their prompt, patient, and helpful participation in every stage of this process, and to my own graduate students for leading me away from rural rebels and revolutionaries to join this interesting and educational excursion into urban history.

Chapter 1

Modernity and Nation in the Chinese City

Joseph W. Esherick

In all developing countries (and many developed ones) there is an intricate dialectical relationship between modernity and national identity. On the one hand, nationalism is very much a product of the modern age, the result of economic and political forces that have made the nation-state the social unit within which a people acquires wealth, power, and international recognition.[1] Modernity and nationalism are inseparably linked. On the other hand, there is always a certain tension between what Clifford Geertz called the "search for identity," which looks back to history and the past, and the forward-looking "demand for progress."[2] This tension is particularly acute in Asia and Africa, where the "modernity" that is the mark of progress has been defined (and often imposed) by the imperialist powers of the West—the very powers against which the new nations have struggled for their place in the world.

By and large, the struggle for (and between) nation and modernity has taken place in cities. In any society, the city is the locus of the modern. In the discourse of the early twentieth century, the "modern" city was always set against the "backward" countryside. If a nation was to modernize, the cities had to take the lead. In China in this period, with a vast countryside and a weak central government, the city also proved to be a manageable social and political unit for significant modernizing efforts. For that reason, the urban reforms that are the subject of this volume were arguably the most successful Chinese efforts at modernization in the early twentieth century. But the city was also the site of the schools, press, associations, and civil and military state organs most engaged in defining, promoting, and protecting the nation.

In studies of urban life, the tension between modernity and identity is often expressed as the conflict between time and place. In the words of one critic, much social science theory holds that in the modern era "time conquers space."[3] With the "internationalization of daily life" in the cities, a set of institutions and practices associated with modern life (from movies to weekends, Coca-Cola to street lights, newspapers to factory production) spreads across the globe. There is a consequent tendency for the common aspects of modernity to eclipse the differences of local cultures. Through the never-ceasing change brought on by capitalist production, a new world is created in which, in Marx's memorable words, "all that is solid melts into air."[4] The constant change represented by modernity is both liberating and disorienting, bringing both empowerment and anxiety. As a consequence, one of the key problems of urban modernization is the need to construct and preserve structures and sites that will have the permanence of place and the comfort of identity. This volume is about that effort in China: the twentieth-century attempt to construct cities that would be both modern and Chinese.

The Chinese tradition of urban planning is as old and distinguished as any on earth. Classical texts describe the proper rectilinear form of the royal city, and successive dynasties built their capitals and regional administrative cities with ever closer attention to the classical models. With exceptions dictated by local topography, cities were carefully oriented to the cardinal directions and surrounded with high walls that by the late imperial period were usually faced with brick or stone. Gates with elaborate guard towers cut through the walls at regular intervals, and wide avenues led from the gates to set the framework for a north-south, east-west grid of streets. Within the walls, the city was horizontal, with only an occasional temple or government office rising slightly above a standard one- or (at most) two-story roofline. Until the modern era, Chinese cities were the largest and most populous in the world, and early European travelers marveled at their prosperity and order.[5]

Given this glorious history of urban planning, it is somewhat ironic that in the modern era both Chinese and foreign observers saw Chinese cities as dirty, disorderly, unhealthy, and inefficient places in need of fundamental reform. The early twentieth century, from the last decade of the Qing dynasty (1644–1911) through the republican era (1912–1949), saw a major effort to remake Chinese cities. Walls were torn down; streets were straightened, widened, and paved; first rickshaws and then tramways and buses speeded transport; public utilities provided water, electricity, and telephone service; new regulations promoted public health and safety, and newly organized police took to the streets to enforce them; parks and squares and athletic fields provided new public spaces; new buildings housed the functional ministries and bureaus of an increasingly interventionist state; department stores introduced new forms of commercial culture and anchored downtown developments served by the new transport; theaters, cinemas, coffeehouses, dance halls, hotels, and brothels established new modes of popular and elite entertainment; a lively press fed news and opinion, rumor and gossip, fashion and fantasies to an eager urban reading public; by the mid-1920s, radios began to appear in upper-class homes; railways, banks, and telecommunications linked the major cities in a national urban network; and for the first time, municipal governments were formed to administer cities as social and political entities separate from their rural hinterlands.

Alongside these efforts to make the city modern were efforts to keep it Chinese, or to preserve its local character. Place still struggled against time. We see this in attempts to protect historic sites and to reconfigure them to fit the requirements of modern tourism; to build modern buildings that would preserve Chinese forms; to construct modern monuments that would commemorate the nation's history; and to configure new social and ritual spaces for the celebration of China's present. Above all, Chinese identity survived in the small habits of daily life: in domestic spaces and the life of alleys; in food and family and neighborhood; in the little places of local history and memory that survived in any Chinese city.

Modern Urban Types

The walls and low houses, the rectilinear streets lined with shops, the narrow alleys where most people lived, and the architectural form of public buildings both religious and secular were sufficiently similar across China that an eighteenth-century European observer could remark that "there is almost no difference between the majority of towns of China, so that it is almost enough to have seen one to get an idea of all others."[6] Like so many outsiders' generalizations, the observation reveals both a blindness to subtle distinctions and a useful comparative insight. But however uniform eighteenth-century Chinese cities may have been, by the twentieth century such generalizations would have been impossible. By then, a number of distinct urban types had emerged.

Some cities, like Shanghai, were **treaty ports**: commercial entrepôts opened to foreign trade by treaty with the Western powers and Japan, and usually including concession areas governed under foreign consular authority where Chinese sovereignty was severely constrained. Tianjin, Canton (Guangzhou), and Hankou in the tri-city complex of Wuhan were other important treaty ports, and each is discussed in this volume. With their foreign concessions and commercial functions, treaty ports were a distinct Chinese urban type. They were nodes of Western (and Japanese) power and influence. Foreign consular jurisdiction in the concessions provided a degree of autonomy from the fiscal and political reach of the Chinese state. This autonomy attracted a great deal of Chinese economic, political, journalistic, and cultural activity. Much of China's modern industry, virtually all modern banking, most major newspapers, publishers, and film studios were located in the concession areas. These factors lent a distinctly modern and cosmopolitan flavor to treaty port life, but also marked these cities as centers of imperialist power and alien cultural influence.[7]

From the late nineteenth century, the Western enclaves in Shanghai (as well as the British colony in Hong Kong) offered accessible examples of order and progress that Chinese reformers sought to emulate. From the stand-

Map 1. China during the republican era. Map shows major cities and railroads built by 1949. Based on a map in *The Cambridge History of China,* vol. 13: *Republican China,* 1912–1949, Part 2.

point of Chinese urban reformers, the concessions provided a model and a challenge for their own modernizing agenda—especially in the areas of hygiene, public works, and policing. At the same time, the fragmented sovereignty of the treaty ports made comprehensive planning difficult and citywide mobilization of resources impossible. Divided sovereignty also made it far easier for prohibited or regulated activity (prostitution, gambling, dance halls, narcotics) to flee from one jurisdiction to another. Especially in Shanghai, fragmented sovereignty encouraged the growth of criminal gangs as a necessary institution to enforce contracts across jurisdictional boundaries.[8]

The prominence of the concession areas gave the treaty ports a distinctive urban morphology that Linda Johnson has called a "dual city." The concession areas generally faced the water, were oriented to commerce, and featured central business districts dominated by Western colonial and neoclassical architecture. The Chinese areas were oriented to a status-hierarchy centered on the official yamen and a City-God temple.[9] Even the residential architecture differed in the two areas, as windows faced the street in concession houses, while the Chinese city's housing presented a honeycomb pattern in which streets and alleys were lined by walls, and the houses faced interior courtyards.[10]

If the treaty ports represented one distinctly modern urban form, their primary urban counterpoint was the administrative center, especially the **capital city**. The classical morphology of these cities has been well described in the literature: cardinal orientation, rectilinear streets and walls, fortified gates, focus on the palace or official yamen, internal division into distinct quarters, market areas away from the center and near gates.[11] A recent study has shown Qing dynasty Beijing to have been one of the most intensively policed cities in the world, with one police officer for every thirty residents and some 1,219 Inner City street gates confining residents to their own neighborhoods at night and facilitating social control.[12] This great visibility of street-level policing stood in direct contrast to the invisibility of imperial power, confined behind the walls of the Forbidden City.

The republican capitals sought a dramatic break from this imperial mold. Each of them is discussed in this volume: the early Republic's capital in Beijing (1911–1928), the Nationalists' capital in Nanjing (1927–1937, 1945–1949), and the wartime capitals in Wuhan and Chongqing. In Beijing, imperial spaces were transformed into public parks. In Nanjing, the model was international and favored building a new capital city, as in Washington, D.C., or the more recent capitals in Canberra or Ankara: wide streets, open vistas, monumental public buildings, Western architecture (with Chinese "hats"), and windows that opened official structures to the public—although walls seem to have kept the view more from the inside out than vice-versa. In Wuhan and Chongqing there was less attempt to construct lasting structures or monuments lest the wartime capitals come to symbolize more than a temporary retreat from Japanese-occupied Nanjing and the coast. In all cases there was a particular concern to structure the capital to impress not just the citizens of the Republic, but foreign visitors as well—a concern that was not uniquely Chinese, as one also sees it in Hitler's contemporaneous plans for Berlin or Mussolini's for Rome.[13] Inherent to the search for national identity was the quest for international recognition: "one aim is to be noticed," Geertz observed, as "being somebody in the world."[14] Since international recognition and approval came especially to those who proved their modernity, this quest for recognition produced another inherent link between national identity and modernity: one gained respect as a nation and people only by being modern.

The final capital city treated in this volume is Changchun, which as Xinjing (New Capital) became the seat of the Japanese puppet regime called Manchukuo. The plans for Xinjing were the most grandiose of any of China's twentieth-century capitals. With plenty of open space to work with, the Japanese designed a city of broad boulevards, extensive parks and green spaces, large plazas for parades, a modern subway, and impressive public buildings. Here was a true colonial capital, with a foreign look as pronounced as the other new cities of the northeast, Harbin and Dairen (Dalian). But Changchun also provides a comparative foil with which to look back at the Chinese plans for Nanjing and Beijing.

Treaty ports and capitals, cities of commerce and of

administration, cosmopolitan cities and distinctly Chinese ones—these are familiar dichotomies in the study of modern Chinese urbanism. They have been expressed most clearly in discussions of the distinctive styles of Shanghai and Beijing, the fast-paced cosmopolitan metropolis famous for money making, modern women, and vice, and the old capital, which had become a depository of cultural tradition.[15] But these are not uniquely Chinese dichotomies, for new nations the world over built capitals in the interior to escape the polluting influence of commerce and colonial culture in their leading ports: Ankara (vs. Istanbul) in Turkey, Islamabad (vs. Karachi) in Pakistan, New Delhi (vs. Calcutta and Bombay) in India, Brasilia (vs. Rio) in Brazil, Canberra (vs. Sydney) in Australia, Abuja (vs. Lagos) in Nigeria, and even Washington, D.C. (vs. New York) in the United States. In every case, the new capital was designed to express a distinctive national identity, against the cosmopolitan (or colonial) modernism of the ports.[16] For all their importance, however, ports and capitals do not encompass the full range of urban experience in modern China.

A third type of city, especially on the level of contemporary consciousness, was the **interior city**. In many ways this was a distinctly modern urban type, because it emerged out of contrast to the rapidly modernizing coast. Before the era of treaty ports, there was no fundamental difference between coastal and interior cities. In the twentieth century, however, and especially during the War of Resistance against Japan (1937–1945), when so many coastal Chinese fled inland, the interior city was invariably characterized as backward, dirty, unhealthy, conservative, and lacking the cultural and material marks of modernity. We see this in Lee McIsaac's description of the "downriver" people's accounts of wartime Chongqing (see chapter 11), but very similar images emerged when refugees from Japan's 1932 attack on Shanghai fled to cities like Yangzhou,[17] and they pervade such popular novels as Ba Jin's *Family* and Mao Dun's *Rainbow*.[18]

Before the war with Japan, there was never a national effort for long-term development of the interior—and nothing even remotely similar to the Brazilian project to recenter the nation on Brasilia,[19] or the efforts that created Ankara and Islamabad. Only wartime necessity spurred such an effort, and cities like Chongqing, Chengdu, Kunming, Guilin, Lanzhou, and Luoyang saw their populations rapidly increase by 50 to 100 percent as the war brought an influx of soldiers, students, and industrial workers. The war also brought buses, autos, and paved streets, with all the reordering of urban space that those changes entailed.[20] The wartime industrialization of the interior was continued as a policy of the People's Republic of China (PRC), as many of these same cities were targeted for industrial development beginning with the First Five-Year Plan.[21] Despite significant romanticization of the rural interior by novelists like Shen Congwen or academics in the folklore movement, there was little discussion of a distinctive role for China's interior cities. Instead, these cities were routinely measured by the unattainable standards of the coast, and especially Shanghai.[22] This certainly spoke to the importance of Shanghai in defining the modern for Chinese cities, but it also trapped the interior cities in a discourse that would always hold them up (or down) as "backward."

Liping Wang (see chapter 7 of this volume) reveals a fourth type of city, the **tourist city**. In the PRC, after 1949, such cities would be designated "cultural cities," recognized and supported for their supposed preservation of the physical vestiges of China's cultural tradition.[23] In the republican era such cities were rare but important, because here more than anywhere a conscious effort was made to create a distinctly Chinese urban landscape. Hangzhou and Suzhou were certainly the most famous, but as Madeleine Dong shows (see chapter 8), Beijing also assumed this role after 1928, when it was renamed Beiping and ceased to be the capital. Such cities are interesting both for the deliberate "invention of tradition" involved in the promotion of tourism, and for the particular effects of this commodification of the city itself. Tourism required a careful combination of modern conveniences (railroads, buses, hotels, restaurants, and souvenir and photo shops) with cultural sites that could be presented as historically authentic.

David Buck (see chapter 5) introduces a fifth type of city, the **railway city**. Railroads unquestionably affected most major Chinese cities, breaking through walls and recentering certain activities around railway stations. The train station always attracted hotels, urban transport, and some shops, and frequently faced a public square with some civic monument. Public rituals of welcome and farewell for important political figures were staged (and photographed) at the station. This happened in any city served by trains, but cities like Changchun, Shijiazhuang, Zhengzhou, or Xuzhou really owed their existence to the railroad. Located at major railway junctions, these cities were new (or vastly expanded) communities built almost from the ground up. In the northeast, the Japanese-run South Manchurian Railway Company planned and built much of Changchun. As company towns, these cities bore important formal and functional similarities to railway towns elsewhere, especially North America.

It is symptomatic of the pace and shape of China's economic development that one of the most distinctly modern urban types, the **industrial city**, was scarcely seen in republican China. After 1949, any number of cities could be classified as industrial cities, especially the eighteen cities targeted for industrial development in the First Five-Year Plan. Cities that in the republican era were primarily railway cities (Changchun, Shijiazhuang, Zhengzhou, Baotou) are prominent on this list, which also includes more purely industrial centers like Anshan, Luoyang, Taiyuan, and Lanzhou—most of which got their start under the Japanese in Manchukuo or during the war against Japan. In the early twentieth century, China's industrial production was concentrated in the treaty ports. Shanghai (with 31 percent of the factories in 1937) dominated industrial production,[24] and Tianjin was north China's industrial center. But these treaty ports were primarily centers of trade, finance, and services, and they cannot really be classed as industrial cities. The closest approximation to purely industrial cities in this era were mining cities such as Tangshan in Hebei, site of the Kailuan coal mine (with seven mines and 42,000 miners), the Qixin cement company, and a railway shop. Tangshan was clearly an industry town, and the massive enterprises also supported schools, hospitals, bathhouses, and company housing.[25] But in the republican era, such a city was notable mostly for being so exceptional.

A final urban type would be **frontier cities**, which have been described elsewhere by Piper Rae Gaubatz. Especially along China's northwestern frontier, these cities had a number of distinctive features. Built largely by Han administrators, they rigorously adhered to the rectilinear ideal for administrative centers, but they also tended to be divided into dual cities, separated along clear ethnic lines. In Inner Mongolia this division was usually between a Han commercial city and a Manchu garrison; in the northwest, between a Han administrative center and a walled Muslim suburb.[26] We see something of this duality in the northeast as well, with Russian settlements in Harbin and Japanese settlements in Changchun and the southern Manchurian cities providing an intriguing colonial variation on this dual city theme—a variation with obvious parallels to treaty ports.

Modern Chinese cities differed from their imperial predecessors not only by being more diverse in function and morphology, but also by virtue of the new urban hierarchies in which they were embedded. In the imperial era, Chinese cities were conceived as part of a unitary hierarchy of county, department, prefectural, and provincial capitals all oriented toward the Son of Heaven in the imperial center. This hierarchy was represented in bureaucratic chains of command, official rituals, and the successive levels of the examination system. At every level, uniform systems of architectural, behavioral, and visual symbolism expressed the unity of the imperial system. But in the modern era, the treaty ports (and especially Shanghai) challenged the centrality of the political centers, and a new developmental hierarchy was created between the modern coast and the "backward" interior.

It is tempting to analyze this new development in terms of the dichotomy between cosmopolitan treaty ports and self-consciously Chinese political centers—the urban expression of the dual struggle for modernity and national identity—but this would be too simple. Modern means of communication linked all of these cities into a single system, and political, economic, and cultural elites moved easily between them by rail or steamship. Although modern capitalism required a greater separation of economic and political spheres than prevailed under the empire, the modern state required close ties to the new industrial and financial powers. Thus the Guomindang moved the national capital from Beijing to Nanjing in 1927, in large part to be closer to the economic center in Shanghai. In the realm of culture, Beijing opera was promoted as "national theater," but none rose to star status in the modern era without successful tours to the new theaters of Shanghai.[27] Foreigners may have regarded Shanghai as the cosmopolitan "Paris of the East," but the city's Chinese residents (in addition to their taste for Beijing opera) were hungry enough for Chinese history and culture to be the mainstay of the culture-garden tourist industry in Hangzhou. Despite the underlying tensions between modernity and national identity, the two were inextricably linked, and that linkage was fundamental to the structure of modern Chinese urbanism.

The Modernist Project

Despite the great diversity of modern urban types, there was remarkable uniformity in the modernist agenda of China's urban reformers. This uniformity reflected the universal characteristics of modernity, but it was also the product of a common model: city planning in the West and Japan, and the visible examples of the new urban order in Hong Kong and the treaty port concessions. When the late Qing reformer Kang Youwei first visited Hong Kong in 1879, he was impressed by "the elegance of the buildings of the foreigners, the cleanliness of the streets, the efficiency of the police."[28] These, of course, were exactly the areas where urban reform began in the West. A concern for public health (and its effect on industrial productivity) led the way. In England, the 1842 *Sanitary Report* of the utilitarian civil servant Edward Chadwick and subsequent research linking the cholera epidemics of 1848–1849 and 1853–1854 to polluted water supplies provided the key impetus for systematic efforts in public hygiene and town planning.[29] In Paris, Baron Haussmann's formula involved broad boulevards and impressive vistas, building codes to regulate the public faces of new apartments, a safe water supply, and sewers so hygienic they could become a tourist attraction.[30]

It has been said that the Revolution of 1848 made Haussmann's reforms in Paris possible as "the discourse of salubrity, cleansing, aerating, movement" became infused with political meaning.[31] Political crisis was similarly crucial in China. The hygienic reforms in Tianjin, described in this volume, were set off by the foreign occupation of 1900–1901. The Revolution of 1911 brought fundamental reform to Hangzhou and Beijing; new regimes initiated urban reform in Canton and Chengdu in the 1920s; and the rise of the Guomindang after 1927 was critical to the reorganization of Nanjing and urban reform in Shanghai. Across the country, revolution provided the opportunity to sweep away the physical as well as the political corruption of the old order and to create a new, clean, and efficient urban environment.

The Nationalist revolution of the 1920s created a special opportunity for new, young, technically trained people to take up ambitious agendas for urban reform. Many of these men had been trained abroad, where universities and professional associations promoted urban planning under the influence of men like Le Courbusier, Lewis Mumford, and Frederick Osborn. Such foreign-trained architects and engineers, and some American advisers as well, were particularly important in the plans for urban renewal in the Guomindang strongholds of Canton, Shanghai, and Nanjing.[32] In the new Shanghai municipal government, the technical bureaus responsible for hygiene, education, public works, and public utilities were led by new men with technical university training, often acquired abroad.[33] On the southeast coast, overseas Chinese returned to Xiamen (Amoy) to provide the capital, expertise, and political will to lead an aggressive urban modernization.[34]

In city after city we see the same menu of reforms, and often the same sequence. The first task was usually to tear down the city walls, invariably building a wide, paved ring road where the wall had stood, a road often traveled by tramways. In Canton, the task of tearing down the walls was contracted to the tramway company in exchange for its right to the route. The object of this effort was invariably to ease the flow of commerce, the same dynamic that brought down the walls of European cities.[35] It expressed as much as anything the triumph of a new discourse of economic development over old concerns for security, and a shift from controlling to facilitating the movement of goods and people.

Fig. 1. Commercial street in Chinese section of Changchun (see map 8), late Qing. Rain could turn streets into a quagmire. Note electric lines and street lights, early signs of modernization. Shop at far left belongs to British American Tobacco. A Japanese photo courtesy of Library of Congress.

This same concern for mobility is seen in efforts to widen, straighten, and pave the main urban thoroughfares. In all Chinese cities, the press of population and the proliferation of shops and stalls in the commercialized economy of late imperial China had gradually narrowed the wide boulevards of the original urban plans. In north China especially, dirt roads with centuries of accumulated dust and debris became impassable quagmires in the rainy season (see fig. 1). In the early Republic, the encroaching stalls and storefronts were cleared away, producing straight paved thoroughfares. The macadamized streets permitted the introduction of the rickshaw, a new vehicle that spread rapidly throughout China at this time; and in the 1920s and 1930s, the larger cities would add tramways and bus lines.[36]

Public hygiene was a concern everywhere: clean water, regular night-soil collection, public toilets, garbage disposal, rat control—an intensive effort to make cities look and smell clean.[37] Ruth Rogaski (see chapter 3) has described the effort in Tianjin. The concern for public health led to vaccination programs and quarantines to prevent epidemics, the registration and examination of prostitutes to control venereal disease, and health exams in schools to ensure a healthy future citizenry. The control of narcotics, especially opium, was motivated as much by a concern for a strong and healthy China as a desire to check criminal activity.

In order to carry out this more intrusive surveillance and disciplining of public behavior, cities across China organized uniformed police as one of the first steps toward reforming urban society. In many ways the police were the visible face of municipal reform, "street-level bureaucrats," to use David Strand's term, "pioneer agents of the modern Chinese state."[38] Their responsibilities went well beyond crime control, as they collected taxes to support their operations and fund municipal government; protected public health by inspecting food vendors and guarding against spitting, urinating, or defecating in public; and promoted public morality by enforcing regulations to control narcotics, gambling, prostitution, and begging. As such, the police served as "domestic missionaries"[39] promoting (and prohibiting) a wide range of public behavior with an intrusiveness never before seen, even in the closely policed imperial capital. Under the authoritarian Nationalist regime after 1927, their responsibilities expanded to include censorship, inspection of the mails, and political control. Their power was such that Frederic Wakeman, in his study of the Shanghai police, has associated them with what he calls "municipal autocracy."[40]

To carry out and direct this effort at urban reform, new institutions were needed. Under the empire, cities were not separate administrative units. At best they were seats of counties or prefectures whose responsibilities included a substantial rural hinterland. Most large cities and provincial capitals were divided between two separate counties, as in Canton, described in chapter 2. In the treaty ports, the fragmented sovereignty of foreign concessions further impeded an integrated urban administration. Coordinated efforts at urban planning and reform required new institutions of municipal government *(shizheng)*. Such institutions were first formed in Beijing in the early Republic and authorized by national regulations of 1919. Canton, under the Guomindang, initiated its own model of municipal government in 1921. Other cities followed suit in the 1920s, in the context of a broad national discussion of municipal governance in professional journals and lobbyist associations.[41]

With the institutions of municipal government in place, the Nanjing Decade (1927–1937) of Guomindang rule was a period for grandiose plans in many cities. The Nationalist project for a new capital in Nanjing is discussed by Charles Musgrove in this volume (see chapter 9); Christian Henriot and Kerrie MacPherson have described the plans for an entirely new civic center in the Greater Shanghai Project.[42] But in both of these cases, fiscal constraints blocked completion of the grand plans. Urban renewal had its greatest success when circumstances presented the authorities with relatively cost-free solutions, as in Hangzhou where the 1911 Revolution freed up for development the choice lakefront property that had previously been occupied by the Manchu garrison.

Urban renewal is an exceptionally costly enterprise. The most successful urban renewal project in history, Haussmann's transformation of Paris, was achieved only with complex deficit financing. Increased revenues generated by economic expansion following each stage of the decades-long process helped refinance the continuously rolled over debt until the sum reached 2.5 billion francs in 1870, interest charges ate up 44 percent of the municipal budget, and the popular outcry brought Haussmann down.[43] Shanghai's urban renewal was also financed by debt, but especially after the destructive Japanese attack of 1932, even China's richest city could not generate adequate revenues to carry out its grand plans.[44] With the national budget dedicated to the military priorities of fighting the Communists and preparing for war against Japan, even less progress was made on building the new capital in Nanjing.

One consequence of the financial weakness of the new municipal administrations was the delegation of many modernizing projects to private (and often foreign) enterprise. Public utilities (of which water and electricity were the most important) were almost always provided by private companies—and usually run by foreigners. Balancing the public interest and the logic of profit-making companies was a constant struggle—a struggle often complicated by the conflict between concerns for modernization and concerns for national sovereignty.[45]

The New City Landscape

The reorganization of urban space was a fundamental part of the modernist agenda. In Beijing, imperial ritual sites were turned into public parks.[46] Trees were planted along major streets for shade and aesthetic effect on the model of the "City Beautiful" movement. A modern set of public buildings was deemed essential to a modern citizenry, so that cities everywhere built public libraries, museums, auditoriums, exhibition halls, and sports stadiums. Spaces were cleared for public squares, and patriotic and revolutionary monuments were erected—although rarely to significant public acclaim. More popular were the new sites of urban entertainment: theaters, cinemas, dance halls, amusement centers, coffeeshops, restaurants, and hotels.

By the republican era, most major city streets were lit at night, first by gas, later by electricity. Shanghai, of course, led the way in lighting its streets, permitting lively entertainment districts and a reputation as the "city without night."[47] Well-lit streets became one of the classic marks of modernity as the "city of light" conquered darkness and the enlightened city made public places safe to stroll at all hours of day and night.[48]

One characteristic of the late imperial Chinese city was the absence of a clear center. Neighborhoods were the primary focus of identity. Separate neighborhoods each had their own religious association, for worship of the Lord of the Earth *(tudi gong)*.[49] Most shopping for everyday goods was done from itinerant peddlers or at neighborhood markets. Major markets tended to be located at city gates, or even outside the walls. At important trading centers like Shanghai or Canton, the main commercial districts were located outside the city walls. Here were warehouses and markets for interregional trade, and also the native banks and *huiguan* (native place associations), which catered to the economic, political, and cultural needs of the mercantile community.[50]

The twentieth-century city almost invariably had a center, an identifiable "downtown" whose defining feature was retail commerce. Michael Tsin has described this process for Canton (see chapter 2), which forsook the old commercial district in the west to transform the official core into a downtown with department stores and terminals for the buses and tramways that brought customers. Hangzhou transformed the former Manchu garrison into a New Business District (Xin shichang), a center of tourism and commerce that supplanted the old commercial district around City-God Hill. Chongqing and Wuchang also built New Business Districts, which seem to have been a favorite idea of city planners of the early Republic. Throughout the country Shanghai's Nanjing Road in the international concession was the model that all strove to emulate: a wide, clean, orderly center of commerce and entertainment, with department stores, hotels, restaurants, and upscale cinemas.[51]

Downtowns were not the only new centers of the modern city. Railway stations and the plazas that faced them were another center of shops, hotels, and civic rituals. Parks, described in this volume by Madeleine Dong (chapter 8), contained not only places for fresh air and relaxation, but also museums and athletic fields that made them important centers for entertainment, the education of citizens, and political demonstrations. What is most striking and important about all of these centers is that their defining structures—department stores, railway stations, hotels, cinemas, public parks, and museums—were all creations of the modern city, new institutions that brought anonymous strangers together in new ways, creating new social connections for the modern metropolis.

Such centers would not have been possible without the modern means of transport that facilitated movement beyond one's own neighborhood. Increased mobility—the circulation of goods and people—was one of the defining characteristics of the modern city anywhere. Modernity entails movement, crossing social and physical space.[52] In China, the rickshaws, trams, and buses that followed the paving of main arteries facilitated this social and economic circulation. They made downtowns possible.

Urban Identity, Urban Behavior

The new mobility was inter-urban as well. Without it, Hangzhou's development as a tourist city was unthinkable. The steamships and especially the trains linking China's major cities in the republican era also helped produce a class of people that was distinctly urban, but not necessarily tied to any particular city. Brett Sheehan (see chapter 4) has illustrated this phenomenon in his analysis of modern bankers, who were as mobile as money could make a man. But the same could also be said of the entertainment and, to some degree, the intellectual elite, which moved easily between Beijing, Tianjin, Shanghai, and Canton—and brought their urban lifestyles to Chongqing, Chengdu, and Kunming in the interior during the war.

Other modern means of communication linked China's twentieth-century cities, helping to create a modern culture that was distinctly urban. Motion pictures were perhaps most important, a medium confined to the cities and by and large devoted to urban subjects (in part because the most popular movies were made in Hollywood). Movies were the classic modern medium, because they allowed people to imagine alternative futures.[53] But the print media were also important, and here Shanghai journals dominated a national market made possible by the postal service and rail and steamboat transportation. These media particularly addressed an audience of "petty urbanites" *(xiao shimin),* but they were urbanites who could live in virtually any Chinese city.[54]

The conventional wisdom has long held that there was no sharp cultural distinction between urban and rural in traditional Chinese culture, but instead an "urban-rural continuum."[55] More recent voices have contested this view, positing an "autonomous urban culture" in the late imperial period,[56] a culture expressed in novels and in urban merchant or literati lifestyles of bookstores and antique shops, brothels and teahouses—a lifestyle quite divorced from the life of the soil. I am personally more inclined to accept the latter view, but whatever the case in late imperial China, there is little doubt that in the modern period the urban-rural gulf was palpable and real.[57]

As cities modernized, the modern became associated with the cities. If "peasant" (*nong*) was not a pejorative term in imperial China, the modern term "country bumpkin" (*tu baozi*) most assuredly was. From the viewpoint of the city, peasants were "backward," superstitious, and conservative. The difference between urban and rural was visible everywhere. City people dressed differently: many men forsook long gowns for Western suits, uniforms, or the new Sun Yat-sen outfits after the mid-1920s; women wore skirts and blouses or *qipao* (themselves a modern invention) that men from the countryside found shockingly revealing. Women bobbed their hair or had permanents; men greased theirs and combed it back, or covered their heads with fedoras. Young men and women lived by themselves, or with friends and colleagues, or in company dormitories. Living apart from their families they had unprecedented freedom, which found expression in their social and sexual lives.[58]

Work in the city also implied a different sense of time. The city worked by the solar calendar, the seven-day week, and the twenty-four-hour day. Working by the clock both disciplined and sped up the pace of life, but the workweek produced weekends and time for leisure activities, which tended to be distinctly urban: the cinema or shopping, excursions to a park, museum, racecourse, or sporting event; for the less wholesome: a visit to a casino, dance hall, or brothel; or simply gathering to eat and drink with friends. On special occasions the weekend might afford a vacation to some tourist site—by train, on schedule.[59]

The new urban lifestyle obviously entailed new freedoms, and young people in particular welcomed the variety of diversions and opportunities for self-expression that urban life provided. These freedoms were not restricted to middle- and upper-class men. In Shanghai, working-class women from the cotton mills saved their meager earnings to dress up and go to the movies, the opera, or window-shopping with their friends—some even leaving their families to live with coworkers for the greater freedom it brought.[60] But as theorists from Marx to Weber have recognized, modernity is a "condition that at once empowers people and constrains them."[61] Some of these constraints were legal. As community sanctions became less effective in the anonymous city, the police enforced new restrictions on public behavior. Vagrancy, hawking without a license, obstructing traffic, improper dress, littering, spitting, urinating, and "disturbing the peace" became punishable offenses.

In one of the enduring images of Ba Jin's novel, *Family*, proper upper-class women in the conservative "premodern" city of Chengdu could move in public only in closed sedan chairs.[62] As the modern city opened up streets and public spaces to women, reordering gender relations required a host of new regulations. Guidebooks introducing visitors to the new disciplines of urban life recorded the new rules in detail. One Tianjin guidebook of 1911 listed 125 regulations related to public behavior, including regulations against men and young women riding together on rickshaws or entering bathhouses hand in hand, or against young men "gathering around and joking when women and girls go in and out of schools and factories."[63] When it became acceptable and popular for women to attend the opera, most cities had regulations requiring separate entrances for women and seating in the balcony.

It was not just official regulations that trained people to the new modes of urban behavior. The new, mobile, anonymous conditions of modernity themselves engendered new ways of behaving. In a memorable short essay, Lu Xun describes how women "accustomed to life in Shanghai" adopt manners that are "both provocative and wary, seductive and on the defensive . . . friendly yet hostile to the opposite sex" as a way to deal with salesmen and other strangers in the department stores and boutiques of the city. This gradual transformation of public behavior affected men as well:

> If you live in Shanghai, it pays better to be smart than dowdy. If your clothes are old, bus conductors may not stop when you hail them, park attendants may inspect your tickets with special care, and the gate-keepers of big houses or hotels may not admit you by the main door. That is why some men do not mind living in dingy lodgings infected with bedbugs, but insist on pressing their trousers under the pillow each night so that the creases are sharp the next day.[64]

Beyond Shanghai

By citing Lu Xun on Shanghai customs I am of course succumbing to the common convention that takes Shanghai as the representation of the modern Chinese city. As noted in the preface, this volume had its origins in a conference titled "Beyond Shanghai." The intent was to gather a group of studies on cities beyond Shanghai to present the full range and diversity of the urban experience in modern China.

But going beyond Shanghai cannot mean ignoring Shanghai. Shanghai may not have been, as the famous subtitle of Rhoads Murphey's 1953 book described it, "The Key to Modern China," but it was certainly the dominating urban presence on the national landscape. G. William Skinner has argued compellingly that late imperial China did not have a single integrated urban system, but a set of nine regional urban systems.[65] Central to his argument was the lack of a single dominant economic and population center for the entire country. But certainly on the economic front, all that had changed by the 1930s: Shanghai's economic dominance was now unchallenged (except, perhaps, in the Japanese-dominated Manchukuo). In the 1930s, Shanghai was estimated to employ 43 percent of China's industrial workers and produce 51 percent of the country's industrial production.[66] The statistics provided by Sheehan on the financial front are even more impressive. In 1935, of China's twenty-three largest banks, those headquartered in Shanghai controlled 97.9 percent of the capital.

Shanghai's dominance was not simply economic; its cultural influence was enormous. China's major publishing houses, like the Commercial Press, were located in Shanghai. The important newspapers and journals with a national circulation were published in Shanghai. The new movie industry was almost exclusively based in Shanghai studios, and the advertising industry naturally established its base in China's premier commercial center. Only Beijing could rival Shanghai as a center of universities and intellectual life.[67] Shanghai's modern culture industry made the city both a model and a magnet. When the hero of Ba Jin's best-selling novel *Family* finally escapes his hometown, he immediately heads for Shanghai, where "all that was new was developing."[68] Those who could not go to Shanghai imitated its style, as in Tianjin, where a 1921 guidebook dolefully noted that "everything follows Shanghai,"[69] or in Kunming, where the wartime expansion of the city produced a "Shanghai-style main business road with four- and five-storied buildings and Western-style architecture."[70]

As a result of its tremendous economic and cultural influence, Shanghai was a city with a "significance well beyond its own limits."[71] We see this most strikingly in Lee McIsaac's description of wartime Chongqing (see chapter 11), where the measures that "downriver" people held up to judge the new capital's progress toward modernity were all derived from Shanghai: "big mansions, cinemas, coffeehouses, western eateries, shiny cars and buses and neon lights." One might have expected Chongqing, as the new national capital, to be compared to Nanjing, but that was not the case. Only Shanghai was a proper standard of modernity.

There was hardly a city that was not linked in some way to Shanghai. Hangzhou's rise as a tourist city was predicated on the proximity of Shanghai and its new middle class—a middle class that wished to escape the Westernized treaty port for a taste of "authentic" Chinese culture. Tianjin's banks and bankers were closely linked to Shanghai and its financial elite. Much of Beijing's modern identity as a city of tradition and culture was constructed in explicit contrast to the crass commercialism of Shanghai culture.

A Place for History

The examples of Beijing and Hangzhou remind us that Shanghai, despite all its influence, was still not China. In the contestation between modernity and Chinese identity, Shanghai certainly represented modernity—but the modern Chinese city still had to find a place for China, a place for history. Even in Shanghai, when the new Civic Center was planned, the architects of the first plan were chided for their failure to adapt "traditional Chinese architecture to modern city planning."[72]

The desire to combine national stylistic motifs and modern construction materials has been a constant theme in the architecture of emerging nations. It has been most conscious and explicit in the designing of national capitals where planners have sought to "define a sense of national identity by careful manipulation of the built environment."[73] Charles Musgrove examines Chinese efforts to do this in chapter 9 of this volume. But a century ago, Louis Sullivan enunciated the canonical principle of modern architecture: "form follows function."[74] As a result, the form of most modern buildings has been dictated by their modern functions, and national identity has largely been relegated to their ornamentation, and especially their roofs.[75] Indeed, the rhetoric of such design schemes often portrays a distinct dichotomy between national forms appealing to aesthetic sensitivities and local sentiment and modern structures representing universal rational principles.[76]

In general, republican China was not terribly successful in constructing monuments to celebrate the nation's recent history. Dong (chapter 8) describes the futile efforts to commemorate revolutionary heroes in Beijing, and McIsaac (chapter 11) describes the quick collapse of the "Spiritual Fortress" monument in Chongqing. The one unquestioned success was the Sun Yat-sen Memorial in Nanjing, with its impressive park-like extramural setting and the reflected glory of the nearby tomb of the first Ming emperor.[77] But, as Musgrove shows, fiscal considerations frustrated plans to locate the national government at the foot of the memorial, although a massive sports stadium was built there and hosted a hugely successful 1933 national games.[78] To the extent that national identity was fostered through new construction, it was in such efforts as sports stadiums for athletic meets to display the new, strong national body, in public educational sites like the museums and libraries, or in the many modern theaters built for traditional drama performances—especially for Beijing opera, which in the Nationalist era assumed a new identity as "National Theater" *(guoju)*.[79]

National identity was promoted in China's cities through the preservation and representation of historic sites. Chapters 7 and 8 of this volume show this most clearly. In Hangzhou there was a great deal of "invention of tradition" in the construction of this historical playground for the middle class of modern Shanghai. In Beijing, once the Manchu emperor had been expelled, there were plenty of imperial palaces and parks to amuse and edify the citizens of the republic—and remind them of the nation's glorious past. In these cities, urban leaders vigorously promoted historical preservation as part of their urban renewal strategy and marketed their cities as tourist sites where modern China could meet its past.

Above all, however, Chinese identity was preserved and promoted in smaller and less public ways. If public architecture (except for the roofs) was largely Western, vernacular architecture and interior decorating maintained much of its Chinese flavor. There was perhaps a sense in which many Chinese were modern in public and Chinese at home (much as the cliché describing imperial scholar-officials as Confucian at work and Daoist off duty). Certainly in the small spaces of home and alley and neighborhood—away from the main streets and the bright lights—there was ample place for history and Chinese identity in China's modern cities.

Organization

This volume is organized into three main parts: The Modernist City, Tradition and Modernity, and City and Nation. We begin with five views of the modernist city. Michael Tsin's essay on Canton (chapter 2) introduces the new spatial order of the modernist city. In a discussion ranging from streets to statistics, sanitation to social surveys, parks to department stores, Tsin explores the dual logic of emancipation and discipline, which the modernist project entailed. In the new city created under the Guomindang in the 1920s, he sees a new political rationality, predicated on a new spatial order, which enabled "the imaginary of an enclosed, rational and ordered regime."

From Canton, we turn to two chapters on Tianjin. In chapter 3 Ruth Rogaski examines public hygiene in this north China treaty port and the new social discipline brought by the effort to clean up the sights and smells of the city. In the "hyper-colony" of Tianjin, with the divided sovereignty created by the concessions, controlling disease vectors was a difficult task, but the treatment of the city as a "medicalisable object" (in Foucault's terms) was taken up with energy. The result was new and more intrusive forms of social control to ensure clean water and sanitary waste disposal.

While protecting public health required new monitoring of urban behavior, Brett Sheehan, in chapter 4, writes about another source of "behavioral urbanism": the cosmopolitan professionalism of bankers—a group that symbolized the status bestowed by money in the modern Chinese city. He argues persuasively that just as banks and their branches linked Chinese cities together economically, bankers formed networks and moved in social circles that gave them a distinctly urban identity—but an identity not tied to any particular city. Interestingly, however, a concern for rural credit in the 1930s led banks and bankers to try to reestablish links to the countryside, at precisely the same time that writers and intellectuals were showing a new interest in rural matters—no doubt influenced by the growing communist insurgency among the peasantry.

From these coastal treaty ports we turn to a quite different site of colonial power in David Buck's history of Changchun (chapter 5). Buck charts the northeastern city of Changchun through three stages of development: as frontier town, railway city, and utopian capital. From a frontier trading center in northern Manchuria, it grew with the development of the railway, first by the Russians, then by the Japanese. As a railway town, it displayed elements similar to North American railway cities, with streets in a regular grid and separate residential and commercial districts; but it also, given the colonial planners, evinced a dual-city morphology similar to China's treaty ports. The final stage, as utopian capital city, is described in telling detail. We see the links to contemporary utopian schemes in the role of Japanese planners who had studied with Le Courbusier, but also the attempt to create a distinctive "Developing Asia" style of Japanese colonial architecture that would combine modernist functionalism with Asian tradition. The axial streets, broad plazas, and large ceremonial spaces give Changchun a unique colonial modernist look among China's cities, and Buck skillfully excavates this forgotten history of a utopian colonial capital.

In the final chapter of part I, Kristin Stapleton documents the important fact that modernist urban reform was not confined to coastal treaty ports or colonial capitals. Her discussion of the warlord Yang Sen's urban renewal effort illustrates the extent to which the 1920s campaign for more activist urban administration and construction was truly national in scope. With professional journals and such lobbyist associations as the road builders, municipal administration advocates pressed for better and cleaner streets, sewers, toilets, parks, and trees—all of which significantly transformed even a distant interior city like Chengdu. The arbitrary authoritarianism of Yang Sen's efforts made his tenure in Chengdu quite short, but the reformist project he initiated was continued with energy after his departure.

Part II includes three chapters on Tradition and Modernity. Liping Wang opens with chapter 7, on the tourist city of Hangzhou. Hangzhou's urban landscape was radically transformed after the 1911 Revolution, as the former Manchu garrison was remade into a New Business District along the shore of West Lake. In the culture garden constructed along the lake, tradition and modernity were simultaneously created for the benefit of tourists from Shanghai's new middle class. But at the same time that Hangzhou was promoting an elite tradition of cultural sightseeing, it was neglecting and suppressing the old ritual and commercial center around City-God Hill. While a cultured past was carefully reconstructed for urban tourists, a popular religious tradition that formerly linked city and countryside in annual spring pilgrimages was suppressed.

In chapter 8 Madeleine Dong describes the republican elite of Beijing, the former imperial capital, seeking to redefine the city as a cultural foil to the Westernized money-oriented Shanghai. Like Hangzhou, Beijing sought to project an image of "Chineseness," especially after it ceased to be the national capital in 1928 and began systematically promoting tourism—although in this case a tourism designed especially for foreigners. The result was the commodification of the city, with "Chinese tradition" on display. In the effort, the past was able to survive, not as part of a meta-narrative of the nation, but as "things"—scattered material forms that resisted the erasure of local identities by universal industrial time.

From Beijing's attempts to preserve the historic sites of an old capital we turn, in chapter 9, to Charles Musgrove's analysis of the Guomindang's effort to create a new capital in Nanjing. Here, foreign-trained architects and engineers and American advisers worked to create a modern capital by international standards. The concern for large public spaces and dramatic vistas represented unequivocal breaks in Chinese thinking about capital cities. But in its architecture, the new capital sought to create a "modernity with Chinese characteristics"—buildings whose basic form was shaped by modernist functional considerations, but adorned with aesthetic and symbolic elements (especially roofs) expressing continuity with Chinese tradition.

Part III focuses on City and Nation and treats China's two wartime capitals. When Japan invaded China proper in 1937, the national government was forced to flee inland. Unwilling to signal an abandonment of the coast by any effort to establish more than temporary capitals in Wuhan and Chongqing, the Guomindang made few efforts to remake the physical structure of these cities. Both cities had seen some transformation in the 1920s and 1930s (more in Wuhan than Chongqing), but they were most notable for the transformation of their political cultures and their efforts to symbolize the nation.

Wuhan, described by Stephen MacKinnon in chapter 10, had a unique revolutionary tradition as the city where the 1911 Revolution began and where the left Guomindang established its government in 1927. In 1938, this tri-city commercial and industrial metropolis became China's capital at an unprecedented moment of tolerance and political diversity in the first year of national resistance to Japan. MacKinnon describes the remarkable agglomeration of cultural figures from China and around the world—writers, dramatists, journalists, cinematographers, doctors—who joined the city's politicians, students, and industrial workers to create a unique moment in China's history. As "China's Madrid," Wuhan came to symbolize not just the nation, but the active imagination of a new political future for China.

In chapter 11, Lee McIsaac describes wartime Chongqing, the final stop of the Guomindang as it moved its capital up the Yangzi, ever deeper into the interior. She describes the striking bifurcation of the city's image: dirty, rat-infested, and "backward" where it fronted the river, but modernizing in the conventional ways (cleaning streets, expelling beggars and prostitutes) in the upper city atop the rocky bluffs. The facade of modernization was especially important to present to foreign visitors. But the domestic effect, with "downriver" outsiders in charge of modernizing municipal governance, constructed a dichotomy between the modern coast and the backward interior. While the magnetism of the national government attracted people from across the country to Chongqing and made the city a microcosm of the nation, the symbolic dichotomy between modern leaders and a "backward" city inevitably divided the population.

Chapters 12 and 13 were written as commentaries on the ten preceding chapters. Jeffrey Wasserstrom has provided a view from Shanghai—that all-important and much-studied symbol of China's urban modernity. Shanghai was a city that no other Chinese city could ignore. In one way or another, the residents and leaders of other cities envied, imitated, guarded against, studied, and criticized the Shanghai model. Many of the chapters in this volume have explored the multifarious practical and imaginary ways in which particular cities related to Shanghai. Wasserstrom reflects on these chapters by exploring the various ways in which "Shanghai exceptionalism" has been conceived—in particular the multivalent notion that "Shanghai is not China." He examines the various ways in which Shanghai has been compared and contrasted to other Chinese cities; and he concludes by suggesting that one reason such comparison is so difficult is because there were, in fact, so many Shanghais. This very multiplicity of Shanghais made it much like other modern cities: London, New York, or Los Angeles. Indeed, we might suggest, the multiplicity of Shanghais was but another aspect of its modernity.

To conclude the volume, David Strand both comments on the preceding chapters and looks forward to the next stage of research on modern China's cities. Reflecting on the diverse manifestations in Chinese cities of this era, he explores the interaction of new technologies and old habits, of urban imaginings and material culture, of resistance to change and emerging urban hybrids. In a challenging and provocative essay, he suggests that despite the shortcomings and failures of urban reform and the agenda left incomplete by a state still too weak to order and discipline the city, the twentieth-century Chinese urban experience played a central role in shaping the imagined future for China.

Part I
The Modernist City

Chapter 2

Canton Remapped

Michael Tsin

The ordering of space has always been intrinsic to the business of government. Spatial regulation serves to manipulate the visual representation of power, define the site of its application, and enable its circulation.[1] Thus Julius Caesar was said to have wanted change in the form of government to begin with changes in the circus.[2] More recently, cartography has been an instrument in the hands of European colonial administrators in their quest to remake the world since the sixteenth century.[3] In China, the classic *Zhou li* provided detailed instructions on how to construct a capital city. Arthur Wright suggested long ago how the blueprint from *Zhou li* on urban planning could be tied to what he called the "Han synthesis." The latter included the notion of "centralism," that is, "the centrality of the emperor in the world of men and the centrality of China, the Central Kingdom, in the universe."[4] It is surely not coincidence that the Ming (1368–1644) as well as the Qing (1644–1911) governments, in their attempts to restore the centralism of the Han, more closely followed the classical plan for their capital than their immediate predecessors. In the late imperial period, the "imperial city" *(huangcheng)* was literally "centered" in the layout of the capital. The plan was to establish the locus of the government on the person of the sovereign, whose gaze as well as might were deemed to reach far and wide from his literally elevated position in the capital.[5]

With the focus on the sovereign and his court, the construction of provincial cities was of rather less symbolic significance than that of the dynastic capital. To be sure, efforts were made to follow, at least to some extent, the capital plan in the provinces, but many provincial cities, particularly in the central and southern regions, were not even square or rectangular in shape. In the late nineteenth century the walls of five out of the eighteen provincial capitals, including Canton (Guangzhou), bore no relationship to the ideal rectangle.[6] Still, even with its rather irregular morphology, the provincial and prefectural yamen in Canton were located, as in the case of many other administrative seats, close to the center of the walled city: as the physical emblem of the centrality of political authority; but late imperial cities also offered us a glimpse of the nature of dynastic governmental power beyond the symbolic. As the architectural historian Liang Sicheng wryly observed, the foremost concern of the late imperial planners was the centering of dynastic government, with scant regard for the problems of communication and integration. While the plan for late imperial cities was often clear in its demarcation of areas for different purposes, its raison d'être bore little resemblance to the discipline of "urban planning" that emerged in Europe in the nineteenth century.[7]

The dynastic regimes operated, of course, at a time prior to the institutionalization of the need—and of the belief in the possibility—for the government to manage and regulate the realm's human and material resources *as an interconnected totality.* For the dynasties, the art of government dealt rather with the mechanism for ensuring a stable and proper order. It was thus imperative for governmental power to be perceived as awesome and encompassing, capable of granting rewards and inflicting punishment, but in practice it need not penetrate to the level of everyday local domains. People were recorded as tax-paying units and as providers of labor service. They were exhorted to dress, behave, and worship according to their station and to refrain from heterodox activities, even though the actual mechanism for everyday enforcement was lacking. Above all, they were not regarded as constituent parts of an aggregate (be it the "population," the "people," or "society") exhibiting its own internal regularities and dynamics, and which must therefore be dissected, analyzed, and expressed in precise

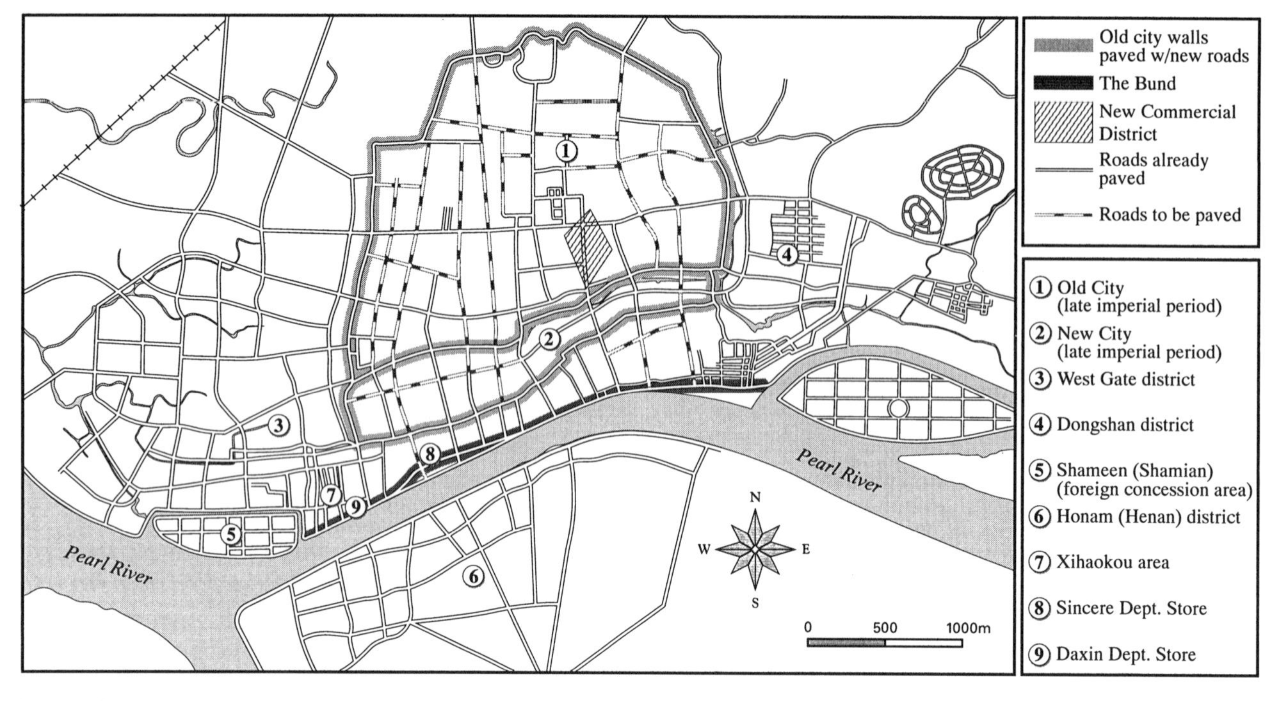

Map 2. Canton, ca. 1925. Based on maps in *Guangzhoushi jingque da ditu* (1925) and *Guangzhoushi xupi malu luxiantu* (1929).

statistical terms in order for the government to function effectively.[8] In terms of urban planning, then, integration was less important than the selected strategic locations of the apparatus of government. Dynastic governmental power was marked, in other words, more by its imposing representation than by its circularity.

This chapter is an exploration of the articulation of a new form of governmental power in early republican China, as seen through the prism of the reordering of space in Canton. It was in Canton that a group of modernist elites, most of whom were associated with the Guomindang, first tried to put into practice a new mode of governance in the form of a municipal government in 1921. Canton went on to become the base of the Guomindang's self-styled Nationalist Revolution in the mid-1920s, and of its national government *(guomin zhengfu)* after the latter was proclaimed in 1925. The model of government instituted in Canton would later be applied to other parts of the country and, at least in theory, to the "nation" at large in the wake of the Guomindang's "reunification" of the polity in 1928. It is interesting to note, for instance, that the Shanghai mayor Huang Fu pointed to Canton as the example for his own administration of China's largest city in 1927.[9]

To understand the change in spatial regulation and its relation to the nature of governance in the early Republic, one must, however, situate it within the larger context of the modernist project of the elites. The term "modernist" is used here to denote a set of discursive and material practices that stemmed from a particular worldview: a specific constellation of ideas associated with European thought since about the eighteenth century, usually referred to as the Enlightenment. Central to this worldview are the notions of the power of reason inherent in each individual subject, the unlimited possibilities of scientific knowledge, man as an active and rational agent in the making of the world and its future, the cult of progress, and the ultimate knowability of all the intricate processes at work in both the human and the physical worlds.[10]

Translated into political practice, this belief in the power of human reason and capacity to order the world meant that the legitimacy of government was no longer grounded in Heaven or in the divine. Rather, it was now invoked in the name of the "people" or "society." Hence Hannah Arendt once remarked that the modern age was signaled by "the rise of the social."[11] Benjamin Schwartz reminds us that modern polities of very different stripes share the common claim of deriving their sovereignty from the "people."[12] Moreover, it is central to the modernist credo, with its focus on human mastery, that space is "to be shaped for social purposes and therefore always subservient to the construction of a social project."[13] Command over one's physical environment is thus vital to reshaping a material base from which new political and social practices can be articulated. Indeed, the past can be physically discarded, its social forms literally remade. If "creative destruction" is truly a critical tenet of the culture of modernity,[14] a large segment of the political and intellectual elites in early republican China was amply qualified to be labeled "modernist," as they were undoubtedly afflicted with this Dionysian impulse.

Late Imperial Canton

What struck most observers, particularly those from the West, about late imperial Canton was its physical appearance. One enthusiastic, if somewhat exasperated, late nineteenth century visitor described the city as "one labyrinth of lanes bordered by houses and shops running in every direction. . . . So narrow are the thoroughfares that one seems to be passing for hours through the interior of some mammoth establishment, where, in endless succession, wares of all varieties are exposed for sale, and where manufacturers and producers of the same may be seen at their work." He exclaimed, with apparent delight, that "[t]here was shouting and calling; Laughing and scolding! What a singular Chinese Babel!!"[15] Not everyone, needless to say, viewed the seeming disorder with the same fascination. Arriving at the southern metropolis in 1866, the Reverend John Turner was more appalled by the "low shabby-looking houses stretching away for miles" and "[t]he prevalence of foul odours." "The shops were mostly poor, with open fronts," he added, but even he conceded that "some of the richer merchants' places of business were gorgeous with fantastic designs."[16]

Fig. 2. Canton street, ca. 1880. A range of shops, from money-changers to mat-and-padding retailers, lines this typically compact street. Photo courtesy of Library of Congress.

It is clear that the visitors' reports covered not only the walled city, or Guangzhoucheng. Indeed, it is likely that their impressions were shaped by a view of the areas outside the wall. Walled cities in late imperial China usually had substantially populated areas outside their gates, and these were often developed even before space within the walls had been saturated.[17] Canton was by no means the only urban center in which one found more vibrant and congested surroundings outside rather than inside the walls. In fact, it is often difficult to determine what exactly was referred to as the city of Canton in the late Qing. The city had no clear boundaries of its own.[18] It did not constitute an autonomous administrative unit. Jurisdiction over Canton was divided between two counties, Panyu and Nanhai, the boundary between which ran right down the middle of the walled area. Nor was this division of the city purely administrative. The authors of a Panyu gazetteer explained why there should be a separate body for each half of the city to prepare for local self-government in the last years of the Qing. The people of Panyu and Nanhai, the authors wrote, despite their common place of habitation, had very different customs, values, and habits *(fengqi jishu xishang yiyi).*[19]

Not only did late Qing Canton lack territorial and administrative integrity as a city, there was also little difference in the realm of material life that separated Canton from its surroundings. As F. W. Mote argues persuasively in his study of Nanjing during the early Ming, "Neither the city wall nor the actual limits of the suburban concentration marked the city off from the countryside in architectural terms. Nor did style of dress, patterns of eating and drinking, means of transportation, or any other obvious aspect of daily life display characteristic dichotomies between urban and rural."[20] Elsewhere he suggests that "[a] city's people [in Ming and Qing China] probably had no sense of themselves as forming a cohesive and self-perpetuating urban group."[21] That was undoubtedly the case in late Qing Canton. The creation of a discrete "urban" entity and identity for Canton was to be an early republican phenomenon.

Although the city had long grown beyond the confines of the walls, that sixteen-gate construction, which averaged twenty-five feet in height and between fifteen and twenty-five feet in width, was nonetheless an imposing presence.[22] While the foundation for part of the wall was laid during the medieval period, the complete six-mile circumference, like so many such structures in China, was not constructed until the Ming. The wall was extended around 1377 to connect what were then three different parts of the city. A new section of the wall was added in 1565, with the additional enclosed part acquiring the label of New City (Xincheng), in contrast to the Old City (Laocheng). Both the outer and inner walls were reportedly kept in good repair throughout the Qing period.[23]

One of the reasons the "suburb" came to be the dominant feature of the city's landscape was because the center of trade and commerce was located to the west of the walled city, in an area known as West Gate (Xiguan) in the Qing. Indeed, to most inhabitants of late Qing Canton, the walled city represented the "official" section of the metropolis. After all, a large number of yamen, ranging from the county to the provincial level, were clustered within the walls. They were surrounded with the standard gentry institutions such as Confucian temples, various official "religious" establishments, or scholarly academies, including the famous Xuehai Academy. The official flavor of the walled city was undoubtedly reinforced with the establishment of the bannerman garrison: a section of the city demarcated for the Qing banner troops and their families. Its distinctive large dwelling quarters set these symbols of Qing rule apart. In sharp contrast to the rest of Canton, the streets within the bannerman district were wide. The houses, mostly built of adobe, bore the distinguishing mark of having broad black lines around the doorways. "The general appearance," according to an observer, "is like that of northern cities."[24]

The physical division between officials and others in Qing Canton, however, should not be exaggerated. There was no restriction on people going in or out of the walled city, and no special privilege was accorded to people inside the walls on the basis of their residence. There were obviously shops and itinerant vendors operating within the walls. Not only was there a stratum of so-called gentry-merchants that moved easily between different circles, there were also institutions such as the Wenlan Academy, where the official elite and local notables from the West Gate area mixed freely. Still, it is also clear that, almost without exception, nonofficial organizations ranging from the long-standing native-place associations to the philanthropic institutions of the late Qing were all found outside the walls. Little wonder that when a group of philanthropists *(shanshi)* petitioned for the establishment of a *fangbiansuo*—a kind of shelter for the homeless and the needy—in West Gate during the epidemic of 1894, they stated that although there was already a similar institution inside the walls, people in West Gate were fearful that they were too far removed from it because of the barriers imposed by the walls.[25]

From the perspective of the exercise of governmental power, however, the division as symbolized by the wall did not in itself pose a problem for the dynasty. Officials were content that life in the communities outside the walls had developed a certain rhythm of its own and that local notables, such as the leaders of the Nine Charitable Halls (Jiushantang), served as the mediators between the government and the populace. The imperial bureaucrats would make sure that their authority was visible and that their blessing was always sought, but they were not in the business of consistently reconstituting the fabric of the social. West Gate, famous for its unfathomable network of narrow lanes, was a source of loans, contributions, and revenues, but the working of its economic and social processes was left largely to its own devices. To the officials, the populace, or *min,* were simply the subjects of the sovereign; they had yet to become *qunzhong* (the masses, or the people) or *shehui* (society). Constituents of *qunzhong* or *shehui* could be classified and arranged into separate segments, reformulated in different combinations, and disciplined to become productive members of the body politic. They were "the subject of needs, of aspirations, but [they were] also the object in the hands of the government."[26] In fact, the metamorphosis of *min* into *qunzhong* or *shehui* in the political discourse would coincide with the emergence of other notions such as *jingji* (the economy),[27] all of which pointed to the possible regulation of economic and social processes as a total system. To achieve this purpose, however, a different spatial imaginary would be required for the exercise of governmental power. That was to be the domain of a *modern* government.

On Urban Planning

One of the most vocal advocates for urban planning in early republican China was Sun Fo [Sun Ke] (1891–1973). Son of the Guomindang founder Sun Yat-sen, the younger Sun was to become the first mayor of the newly created municipality of Canton (Guangzhoushi) in 1921. Having left for Hawai'i at the age of five, Sun Fo studied at the University of California and at Columbia before returning to China in 1916. In perhaps his most famous publication, a substantial article titled "On Urban Planning" *(Dushi guihua lun),* which appeared in late 1919, he exalted the virtue of utilizing scientific knowledge for the purpose of urban planning. Urban planning, Sun Fo wrote, includes everything that has to do with the construction of a city: the network of roads, the location of commerce, the choice of parks and fairgrounds, the facilities of public institutions, the management of water supply and sewage, and the construction of factories and housing.[28]

At first glance, that did not sound so different from the concern for an orderly urban environment in the *Zhou li.* A telling indication of what was new in Sun Fo's vision, however, can be detected in his evaluation of the state of urban planning in different countries. Sun Fo was particularly effusive in his praise of planners in Germany. German planners not only cater to the current needs of their cities, he said, but have already mapped out the expansion of their capital, Berlin, with details of streets and buildings, for the next hundred years.[29] As a committed modern planner, Sun Fo shared with his counterparts elsewhere a vision of control over *the future* through the use of "scientific" knowledge and methods. It allowed them, as David Harvey puts it, to design long-term schemes for "social engineering and rational planning, and the institutionalization of rational systems of social regulation and control" through the ordering of space.[30]

The attainment of such objectives, however, required the institution of a set of mechanisms for the production of a new kind of knowledge. Sun Fo pronounced that "investigation" *(diaocha)* and "survey" *(celiang)* constitute essential tools for urban planning. The scope of investigation, he wrote, should cover every aspect of society and the economy. It must contain all the facts that can be put in statistical form *(yi tongji de xingshi biaolie).* To construct an urban center, investigation should be made on the population in the area, the different occupations of the residents, the nature and quantity of local products, and the amount and variety of present and future trade. In addition, surveys must be conducted on the topography of the site, its links to water and land transportation, the distance from other centers of population, and the degree of difficulty in facilitating water supply. It is clear that Sun Fo saw critical linkages in these different sets of data. Again, the emphasis is on procuring accurate statistics, which in turn requires a well-equipped official organization as well as detailed and thorough investigation.[31]

Urban planning, according to Sun Fo, has three major objectives. First, it must prepare the city for the communication needs of the future. It should address the issue of port facilities and their connection to railroad networks to facilitate the transportation of goods and commodities. Similarly, to ease the movement of people within the city, the street plan must be put together in such a way as to avoid the potential congestion created by the many different modes of transportation available in a modern urban center, and to allow sidewalks for the flow of pedestrians. Second, reforms must be made in the sanitary conditions *(weisheng)* of Chinese cities so that they could be fit for human living. Western countries, Sun Fo wrote, have developed systematic methods, through the use of sewers and manual collection, to dispose of their human and material waste in order to prevent the spread of disease—something that had not been properly taken care of in China. Echoing the Reverend Turner's observations of Canton, Sun Fo suggested that the result was a foul odor and bad sanitary conditions, which are both unseemly and uncivilized.

Third, as few Chinese cities historically possessed open public areas,[32] Sun Fo suggested the construction of recreational facilities for the people. There should be two types of public parks: type one would be located outside the city, preferably a wide area adorned with plantations and man-made embellishments, which would provide the people with a refuge from the urban milieu and a sense of nature's wonders. Type two would be found in the most densely populated center of a city and provide a small amount of open ground for quick relaxation and, as Sun Fo stated, "an opportunity to breathe some fresh air." Together with other facilities such as theaters, cinemas, fairgrounds, and concert halls, they would constitute new public arenas as the locus of urban life outside of work, where residents would congregate for entertainment or for assembly and public lectures.[33]

Sun Fo's vision offers a glimpse of the dual logic of the modernist project: emancipation and discipline. The city was seen as a distinct economic unit, as reflected by his emphasis on communication networks and on the assiduous collection of data on society and the economy. The government, armed with such knowledge and in the name of the "people," would exercise its power in a more immediate and direct manner than that of the dynastic regime. Government regulation of sanitary conditions could, of course, result in better living environments, but it was also a step toward intervention in the most intimate details in the conduct of people's lives.[34] Similarly, the creation of public areas was, to some extent, genuinely "democratizing." Still, one should not lose sight of the fact that it was also part of the mechanism through which the government produced the opposition between "city" and "country" and sought to regulate the work and leisure time of the residents. It is beyond the scope of this chapter to examine the complex negotiation of this dual logic of modernist governments. Suffice it to reiterate that the spatial regulation of a city was aimed not only at the (re)construction of the physical infrastructure. It had more ambitious goals: to transform the *conditions* in which people ordered their everyday lives, by reaching into the realms of their daily practices, right down to the level of hygiene and patterns of entertainment. It was meant, in short, to be instrumental in the production of disciplined members for the body politic.

Toward Modernity

The city inherited by Sun Fo and his associates when Sun first assumed the mayoralty in 1921 had not remained unchanged in the late Qing and early Republic. Although often piecemeal and ad hoc, various measures were taken in the last years of the dynasty to "modernize" the infrastructure of the metropolis, in particular under the general rubric of the so-called "New Policy" reforms. In 1904, for instance, the then governor-general Cen Chunxuan authorized the addition of 12,000 feet to the Bund, which had hitherto stretched a mere 120 feet along the Pearl River. In effect this provided a new thoroughfare, albeit one located at the fringe of the urban landscape, for a city best known for its web of narrow crisscrossing lanes.[35] The insolvency of the Qing government, however, meant that it often had to turn to nonofficial sources to support even tentative steps toward the renovation of the city. The establishment of the waterworks is a good example. The project was created in 1905 by Cen Chunxuan with an initial capitalization of 1.2 million taels to be shared evenly between the government and private sources. Much of the nongovernment funding initially came from Shanghai.[36] As the cost of construction increased, however, another three hundred thousand taels were raised from the private sector. Three years after the founding of the Republic in 1912, the dire financial condition of the republican government in Canton led to the sale of the official share of the waterworks to investors, most of whom were from the local merchant community. A completely private enterprise, named the Canton Waterworks Company, thus came into existence.[37]

In much the same vein, the late Qing authority succeeded in putting together a sum of 1.5 million yuan in 1909 to purchase Canton's first electric lighting plant from the British, who had installed it in 1901. Two-thirds of the amount was raised from private investors, in part through the issuing of shares with an initial value of ten yuan each. As with the waterworks, the initial capitalization was found to be inadequate and was raised to three million yuan in 1919. At the same time, all the government shares were sold, again mostly to merchant holders.[38]

While there was much talk of further renovation of the city by the government in the early years of the Republic, the effort was seriously hampered by both the shortage of funds and political instability. A further impetus for change was provided by the émigré community, many of whose members were supporters of the anti-Qing movement. With the establishment of the Republic, they were quite eager to invest in the city they had left decades earlier. Many involved themselves in trade or founded small industrial enterprises in the "suburb" of Honam (South of the River). But the most conspicuous sign of their investment was that quintessential symbol of modernist representation: the department store.[39] Cen Chunxuan's extension of the Bund finally bore fruit in 1912. The Sincere (Xianshi) Company, which had begun its operation in Hong Kong at the turn of the century, opened its first store in China on the western section of the Bund—known as Changdi—in Canton. It was founded by a group of émigré investors from Australia, led by Ma Yingbiao (1864–1944). Ma started his career as a young farm hand in Australia, converted to Christianity, then made his mark as an entrepreneur in fin de siècle Hong Kong with his "set pricing" *(buerjia)* in the retail trade.[40] The organization of the department store stood in stark contrast to the earlier commercial world of Qing Canton. The latter was protean, unruly, and chaotic, while the former, with its world of goods, was enclosed, rational, and ordered.[41] There was no doubt where "progress" lay. In the words of Guo Le, another émigré who came back from Australia and founded the Yongan Company, his aim in establishing the department store was "to introduce the foreign art of commerce to the motherland and to raise the level of commercial expertise of our compatriots in order to catch up quickly [with the West]."[42]

Sincere became an instant landmark of the metropolis: mecca to the residents of the city and its surrounding areas with its exhibition of an often bewildering range of commodities, which were nevertheless always divided into neatly arranged categories. Its system of management was borrowed directly from its Western (and Japanese) counterpart, with its clear bureaucratic hierarchy and division of labor mixed with a strong dosage of "paternalism" designed to engender unswerving loyalty to the company.[43] The Sincere store was five stories. Towering by the standards of the day, it featured, in addition to an impressive array of merchandise, an open-air amusement park on its top floor, which carried regular performances of opera, acrobatics, and movies.[44] The store proved to be a prime attraction. The company, moreover, had constructed an equally imposing building next to the store to run as a hotel. Indeed, the western section of the Bund was said to have become almost a replica of the famous Nanjing Road of Shanghai.[45] With its new stores, cinemas, and other avenues of entertainment, the area was transformed into an urban magnet for the rich, the curious, and the unsavory.

Sincere, however, did not bask in the glamour of being Canton's sole department store for long. Its success soon attracted a neighbor farther west on the Bund: the Daxin Department Store, another émigré concern housing itself within a seven-story building that also came with a rooftop entertainment park.[46] Daxin opened in 1916 and was located on the section of the Bund where the western end of Changdi adjoined the southern tip of the West Gate area. The area was referred to by the local inhabitants as Xihaokou, and it was reputedly the liveliest part of town.[47] Indeed, both Sincere and Daxin were, to borrow the description of Michael Miller, a combination of the monumental, the theatrical, and the fantastical. Like the Bon Marché, which was touted as "one of the sights of Paris" in the nineteenth century,[48] Sincere and Daxin became attractions in their own right for the city of Canton.

Despite developments along the Bund, Canton remained something of a nightmare for the modern urban planner. In fact, at first glance, the establishment of the department stores seemed simply to have shifted the center of commerce back to near where it was during the Ming, that is, to the south of the walled city. Local governmental authority was still fragmented, and the city remained congested and difficult to get around. It was not until a comprehensive restructuring of the city was undertaken, including the demolition of the city walls, that the geography of Canton could be truly recast.

Ironically, when the first concrete step was finally taken to reconstruct the city, it might have been for reasons other than the creation of a more "progressive" city or the production of a new form of governmental power. Canton was in the grips of the so-called old "Guangxi clique" when a new municipal council *(shizheng gongsuo)* was set up in October of 1918,[49] giving the city its own governmental authority and freeing it from the dual hold of Panyu and Nanhai Counties. Although the official purpose of the municipal council was to "modernize" the city, many members of the government then were probably more interested in a share of the wealth than in the welfare of the city. The council was headed by Yang Yongtai, who, perhaps not coincidentally, was also the director of the treasury of the provincial authorities dominated by the clique.[50] Yang Yongtai's chief lieutenants at the council were Wei Bangping and Cao Ruying. Both were career military men, with Wei best known for his role, as head of the police, in suppressing the students and the press in Canton during the May Fourth movement of 1919.[51] By claiming jurisdiction over municipal affairs, the council could monopolize matters ranging from the sale of "public properties" (such as land belonging to the bannermen or temples) to the imposition of various fees and levies. Functions assumed by the municipal authority could also be farmed out to merchants and others for profit. Even the renovation of the city was lucrative business, as it involved more opportunities for appropriating land and property.[52]

Fig. 3. Constructing new roads in Canton, ca. 1910. Photo courtesy of Library of Congress.

Accordingly, a contract for the demolition work was concluded between the new municipal council and the Canton Tramways Syndicate,[53] the latter being a private company that put up financing for the project. It took three years for the walls—the physical and symbolic barrier to the integration of the city—to be torn down completely, and in their place was over 67,000 feet of wide, if not exactly well-paved, streets. In what can be described as a local version of "Haussmannization," a new network of avenues and a new downtown were created.[54] As in Paris, there was considerable resistance from the city's inhabitants, particularly those merchants whose livelihood was threatened by the changes.[55] Meanwhile, as early as 1921 the Canton Tramways Syndicate began to operate about twenty gasoline buses, covering a stretch of over ten miles linking West Gate to Dongshan in the east through what was the old walled city, although the buses were described by a contemporary as "very clumsy large bod[ies] on small chassis."[56]

Together with construction in other parts of the city, there were by 1922 about 137,000 feet of new roads in Canton.[57] Two to three hundred automobiles made their appearance, but in the mid-1920s it was the thousands of rickshaws that became the "favorite among the people of Canton" as a mode of transportation.[58]

The Reordering of Canton

It was, then, not until the ousting of the old "Guangxi clique" by the forces of Chen Jiongming in October 1920 that a proper municipal government was established for Canton. A new Office of Municipal Administration (Shizheng ting) was put into place with Sun Fo as mayor. Chen Jiongming (1878–1933), who was once described by a British military attaché as "one of the two most able soldiers" in China of the early 1920s (the other being Wu Peifu),[59] is an enigmatic figure. It was his capture of Canton that allowed Sun Yat-sen and his recently renamed Chinese Nationalist Party (Zhongguo guomindang) to regain a viable base, at least until Chen Jiongming's falling out with Sun in 1922. Chen Jiongming was trained with a classical education before graduating from the new Guangdong Academy of Law and Government in 1908. He was also a vocal member of the Guangdong Provincial Assembly during the late Qing. During his tenure as governor of Guangdong in 1920–1922, Chen Jiongming's initiatives included bringing the prominent radical Chen Duxiu to Canton as well as trying to institute local elections. It was he who backed Sun Fo in the latter's effort to put a new municipal structure in place.[60]

The direction of the new municipal government can be detected in an early contest between Chen Jiongming and Sun Fo on the one side and the provincial assembly on the other. Citing the promotion of "democratic" practices *(minzhi)* as a reason, the assemblymen objected to vesting most of the power in the executive branch of the municipal administration, and particularly to the direct appointment of the mayor by the governor. In the administrative plan, the mayor and the heads of various bureaus were to constitute the executive commission *(xingzheng weiyuanhui)*. It would be advised by a consultative board *(canshihui)*, consisting of ten appointees of the governor, ten directly elected representatives, and ten representatives of the different segments of society *(jie)*, such as business, labor, and education.[61] In a reply to the objections of the assembly (which was issued in the name of Chen Jiongming but almost certainly drafted by Sun Fo), Chen went to some length in arguing the merits of different forms of municipal government. There are three different types: council *(shihui)*, commission *(weiyuan)*, and managerial *(jingli)*. Using the United States as an example, Chen Jiongming maintained that the municipal council system would only result in corruption and the domination of the government by unprincipled politicians, as in New York City of the past. Consequently, American cities adopted the commission system, he wrote, but had in recent years further progressed to a managerial system of governance. After all, municipal government deals only with administrative matters *(chunshu shiwu xingzhi)*; thus it is hard to achieve the best result without unified authority.[62] In other words, in the true spirit of a modernist, Chen Jiongming (or Sun Fo) made an eloquent case for the centralization of power in the name of "efficiency."

The city that Sun Fo took over in 1921 was already quite a different entity from the one of a couple of years earlier. Guangzhou *cheng* had been transformed into Guangzhou *shi;* the walled city had been changed to the city-market, that is, the city as a locus of consumption and exchange. Symbolizing this transformation was the new centrally located commercial district, found at the heart of the old walled city, around what used to be the "official" quarter at the junction of Yonghan beilu (now Beijing lu) and Hui'ai lu (now Zhongshanlu), in a section popularly known as Shuangmendi. Two of the earliest tenants of the new district were, as might be expected, branch stores of Sincere and Daxin. Opened in the early 1920s, they were reportedly even more glamorous than their main outlets on the Bund. The Sincere branch, known as Hui'ai shangdian, was billed as one of the largest enterprises in south China, while the Daxin branch was housed nearby in a recently constructed five-story building.[63]

There were also new-style general stores—miniature department stores—that dealt in an assortment of products, many of which were Western-style goods *(yanghuo)*.

Defying the codes of the old commercial establishment where every trade was supposedly restricted to its own quarter,[64] these new retailers stocked a range of goods under one roof. Mimicking the practice of department stores, the merchandise was clearly categorized, labeled, and priced, with emphasis on efficient service. Also ubiquitous at Shuangmendi were bookstores, many of which were branches of chains, catering to a growing audience whose interests ranged from Western political philosophy to the latest romance novels.[65] All of this was made possible, of course, by the expansion of the market created by a more integrated city. In fact, the Shuangmendi section quickly became the nodal point of a new transport system, from which bus and rickshaw routes were to spread throughout the city. As rickshaws were the most popular mode of transportation, their operations, ranging from fares and designated stops to the cleanliness of the vehicle and the manners of the pullers, were all regulated by the municipal government.[66]

A modern city, however, was not just a center of consumption; it was also a place of industrial production. The new central commercial district was to be flanked by "outlying areas," particularly those to the east and across the river, which served as the sites for the growing number of industrial enterprises in the city.[67] With the development of communications, as a municipal government report later put it, the country would then be able to supply the city directly with its produce, while the city would then sell its industrial products directly to the country. The aim was to get rid of the mediation of greedy and unprincipled merchants. Indeed, whenever possible, the report stated, major public-interest enterprises should be operated by the municipal government. The waterworks, for instance, was incorporated into the structure of government.[68]

Despite Chen Jiongming's claim, then, the power of the municipal government extended far beyond administrative matters. In fact, like most modern governmental authorities, the first order of business of the new Office of Municipal Administration in 1921 was to claim and consolidate all the territories supposedly under its jurisdiction—that is, to define the material form of the entity it claimed to govern.[69] A surveying commission was constituted to map and demarcate the boundaries of the new entity: the municipality of Canton. After all, a map, as has been noted, "may not just function as a medium; it could well be the creator of the supposed reality."[70] It was stipulated that "areas already deemed to be part of the Canton municipality cannot secede *(tuoli)* to form their own autonomous *(duli)* entity."[71] The new government, headed by Mayor Sun Fo, consisted of six bureaus with responsibilities ranging from public utilities to education. Interestingly enough, all six heads of bureau were returned students from the United States, Japan, and Europe, as were reportedly (perhaps with some exaggeration) over 80 percent of the section chiefs and their immediate subordinates.[72]

To underscore the need of the new administration to manage with "unified authority," all of the old yamen were earmarked for demolition. A new building, which would house all of the different branches of the administration and be known as the Municipal Administration Offices (Shizheng heshu), was to be constructed as the nerve center *(zhongshu)* of government.[73] Such physical centralization of authority, in the view of one contemporary commentator, constituted an "unprecedented new system" of governance.[74] More important, the centering of the government here was not just to provide an elevated position for the ruler to project his gaze and might (although the old yamen were derided for their decay); rather, it was a nodal point from which governmental power was meant to circulate and penetrate into the very fabric of the social and economic formations of the entity under its jurisdiction.

Thus, for instance, the municipality was divided into twelve wards for the purpose of policing. The police force consisted of about 4,500 members.[75] Since the population of the municipality, as a new government survey discovered in 1923, was 801,646,[76] that would translate into a ratio of about one police officer for every 180 residents, which was higher than, say, mid-nineteenth century London (one for every 350).[77] In addition to the standard duties of maintaining order, the police were entrusted with the task of acting as the guardian of the inhabitants' morality and of closing down unlicensed enterprises.[78] The police were to become, to use the apt words of Robert Storch, "domestic missionary."[79] Moreover, as befitting a modernist administration, a special bureau had been established for the maintenance of health standards (an undertaking that hitherto tended to fall under the purview of the police). The city was divided, for regulatory purposes, into six districts by the Bureau of Health. Rules and codes were enacted to regulate the use of the new public areas, as an elaborate hierarchy of functionaries was organized to inspect and license public establishments.[80] Even more revealing was the jurisdiction of the Bureau of Education. The development of a more integrated city, while allowing the government to institute new forms of management, also led to the unchecked growth of unregulated entertainment. The educational mission of the bureau was thus broadly defined: in addition to being the regulator of the schools, the bureau was also the overseer of the general conduct and welfare of "society." It thus had the authority to shut down theaters, cinemas, and various venues of public entertainment. It also took on the responsibility to operate municipal charities and to supervise nonofficial philanthropic organizations.[81]

The attempt to create a new public arena also provided the opportunity for the construction of new facilities to "educate-and-reform" *(ganhua)* the city's residents. The government was to build a public theater for the purpose of "social education" and raising "consciousness."[82] Also outside the formal schools, public lecture series were organized to "enlighten" the city's inhabitants. Topics included, for example, "Science and Superstition" and "Principles of Science." The Bureau of Education apparently also tried to organize courses on child-rearing, family education, and hygiene for women, but were forced to abandon those plans for lack of funds.[83]

Instead of regarding the constitution of these disciplinary regimes as simply a threat to civic autonomy, it might be more instructive to analyze them as an integral part of a governmental effort to produce a specific form of social body that could be effectively harnessed by the authorities. As Timothy Mitchell puts it, "Power relations do not simply confront [the] individual as a set of external orders and prohibitions. His or her very individuality, formed within such institutions, is already the product of those relations."[84] It is in this sense that the raison d'être of modern government is to engage in "the management of population in its depths and its details."[85] The reconstruction of Canton opened up the possibility of a new spatial order to enable governmental authority to entertain such aspirations.

Historians have long been accused, not without justification, of privileging time over space. The rash of urban construction that took place in early twentieth century China has in the past often been celebrated as examples of the successful remodeling of medieval cities in the name of "modernization," or regarded as little more than a footnote to the grand narrative of China's transition to the modern world. This chapter does not pretend to have addressed the many aspects of urban reconstruction during the republican period. It does, however, suggest, by using Canton as an example, that a new spatial order, such as that envisioned by Mayor Sun Fo and his associates, was an intrinsic part of the institution of a new political rationality, a political rationality that is central to the culture of modernity of our time.

The new order allowed the government to re-imagine Canton as a discrete entity, with clear boundaries and its own social and economic regularities, which could be uncovered with "scientific" knowledge and were thus amenable to systematic manipulation and intervention. For the next decade, the municipal government, with the help of institutions such as universities and banks, would carry out numerous detailed "investigations" in Canton: on social conditions, trade performance, wage index, price series, and so on. Similar exercises were conducted in many other parts of the country at the same time. A close examination of the impact of such instruments of a modernist government is the subject for another study. Suffice it to say, however, that they could not have been carried out in the absence of a new kind of spatial order: one that *enabled* the imaginary of an enclosed, rational, and ordered regime.

Chapter 3
Hygienic Modernity in Tianjin

Ruth Rogaski

> **"Work to create a *wenming, weisheng* city!"**
>
> government slogan painted on wall, Tianjin, 1996

> **"The West considers *weisheng* to be the original principle of government."**
>
> Tianjin government regulations, 1907

For Tianjin's contemporary municipal authorities, the concept of modernity is best captured by two closely related words: *wenming,* meaning "civilized," and *weisheng,* usually translated as "clean." In its frequent juxtaposition with *wenming,* however, the meaning of *weisheng* goes far beyond clean. It is a word that invokes images of the laboratory and the microscope, the smell of disinfectant, the white-coated authority of the scientist-administrator. *Weisheng* suggests a harmony of interests between public space and private behavior, presided over by an enlightened and effective government. A *weisheng* city is free of odors, dust, and harmful bacteria; its streets are ordered and lined with greenery. City residents who practice *weisheng* do not excrete or expectorate in public places, refrain from littering, and maintain a healthy distance between themselves and other individuals. With its complex allusions to science, order, and government authority, *weisheng* may best be translated as "hygienic modernity," a major cornerstone of the twentieth-century urban ideal.

This chapter explores the translation, contestation, and negotiation of hygienic modernity that took place in the unique treaty-port environment of early-twentieth-century Tianjin.[1] Although a late comer to treaty-port status compared to Shanghai, in many ways Tianjin went on to become the ultimate treaty port, the site of as many as nine different foreign concessions. If in addition to the various concessions we also include consideration of the Chinese who lived under both foreign and native administrations, then Tianjin becomes a remarkable site to study the intersections of imperialism, disease, and indigenous society.

In this chapter I am primarily concerned with tracing the ways in which hygienic modernity altered the built environment and the human landscape of Tianjin. At the same time, I wish to explore how the people living within this changing landscape understood the meaning of *weisheng.* In the early twentieth century, *weisheng* emerged both as a powerful discourse of Chinese inadequacy and an essential "skill" necessary for joining the ranks of the modern. Yet the evidence from Tianjin indicates that the meaning of *weisheng* was far from being fixed. As Tianjin's residents interpreted and shaped the practice of hygienic modernity, they subtly altered the meaning of urban modernity itself.

The Shaping of Hygienic Modernity

If we wish to formulate a definition of what "the modern" means in the context of the twentieth-century city, then one core element must be the administration of space and populations in order to eliminate dirt and prevent disease. Concern for health and hygiene was certainly not a new phenomenon in urban administration: it was evident in the plans of cities as diverse as those of ancient Rome or Tang dynasty China.[2] However, a major disjunction in the relationship between the body, the urban environment, and the state took place in late eighteenth century Europe. After the Enlightenment, the city became, in the words of Michel Foucault, a "medicalisable object," a malleable organic entity subject to scientific management, containing a population subject to scientific surveillance. New state-mandated collection of detailed census data revealed disturbingly high mortality rates and gave new insights into patterns of epidemic disease. Armed with this numerically precise way of understanding the urban environment, physicians, bureaucrats, and scientists devised techniques aimed at producing a healthier populace for the benefit of the nation.[3]

This link between health and the nation became a major rationale for the reformations of the Euro-American urban landscape in the nineteenth century. It was Hausmann's obsession with salubrity, combined with the nationalist vision of Louis Napoleon, that motivated the transformation of Paris. Government surveys of health and disease among the laboring classes set the stage for nationwide urban reforms in England. New York's massive nineteenth century park, aqueduct, and sewer projects reflected in part the city's anxiety over preserving health in the face of rapid industrialization and the massive influx of immigrants. To an unprecedented degree, health was invoked through the establishment of boundaries—boundaries between different urban functions, and boundaries between different urban populations. By the late nineteenth century the functioning of sewers, the salubrity of water, the banishment of odors, and the regulation of the population during times of epidemic disease were hailed as hallmarks of urban modernity.[4]

The nineteenth-century rise of state intervention in matters of health coincided with the rise of European imperial expansion.[5] Even though the major surveys, policies, and projects associated with urban public health in Europe had their genesis as late as the mid- to late nineteenth century, for many Western observers the government administration of hygiene had not only become a central emblem of modernity; it had also become an essential quality of Western civilization, an elemental characteristic that distinguished West from East.[6] Scholars have argued that manifestations of European modernity and bourgeois identity were themselves the product of imperial experience. Ann Laura Stoler has shown how the bourgeois concerns of bodily discipline and hygiene were primarily a product of European efforts to bolster their identity and distinguish themselves from Oriental others. Paul Rabinow and Gwen Wright have traced the antecedents of continental French modernity in architecture to the experimental manipulations of urban space in Morocco and Vietnam. Brenda S. A. Yeoh has shown how British theories of municipal public health considered in London and Manchester were used to reconstruct the "contested space" of colonial Singapore. Colonial cities served as the ultimate "laboratories of modernity" during this time, with hygiene constituting a major part of the experiment.[7]

In spite of the power of hygienic modernity to transform urban space and urban behaviors, it did not achieve a seamless hegemony, nor should it be seen as a monolithic entity. In Europe and the United States, sanitarians and scientists debated the importance of what was evolving into the "germ theory of disease" throughout the late nineteenth century, while local populations evaded or resisted the sanitary efforts of progressive urban reformers.[8] In the colonies, public health administration was shaped by the complex debates going on in the metropole and the actions of indigenous actors in each colonial locale. David Arnold, in his seminal work on public health in India, reminds us that imperial medicine was constantly engaged in dialectical interaction with a broad array of indigenous groups, including doctors of traditional Aryuvedic medicine, progressive Indian reformers, and poor Hindu pilgrims. Yeoh has detailed how different elements in Singapore's Chinese community reinterpreted and reshaped British plans for a sanitary city. The impulse of hygienic modernity to rearrange space, monitor populations, and change individual behaviors was mediated by the negotiation of medical knowledge at the local level.[9]

Disease and the Urban Environment in China

Despite the large amount of scholarship on Chinese cities in recent years, many questions still remain about the Chinese perception of the relationships among the body, disease, and the urban environment prior to the advent of European influence. At first glance, there is little evidence in the historical record that indicates the urban environment was considered particularly insalubrious. This does not mean that cities in late imperial China did not include a variety of provisions for health and sanitation. Officials and local gentry funded charitable clinics and old-age homes. Garbage and human waste were constantly recycled by legions of private scavengers and night-soil dealers. In most major walled cities, drainage of wastewater was accomplished through a system of moats and canals maintained by government officials and local elites.[10] For example, an early nineteenth century literati poet felt inspired to extol the virtues of Tianjin's drainage system in the following verse:

> *The excellence of Tianjin!*
> *Everywhere a land of lakes and rivers.*
> *In the East Marsh, lotus flowers blossom in masses of white,*
> *By the North River, reeds bend yellow to the sky,*
> *The ocean tide ebbs and flows far beyond the city.*
>
> *The excellence of Tianjin!*
> *Planned on a fine model,*
> *With neat square fields for the early rice.*
> *At the Four Gates one can still see*
> *The city's drainage "calabashes."*[11]

These two stanzas are taken from a series of one hundred poems that wonderfully capture the sights and sounds of old Tianjin. Even though he is describing a massive walled city of a quarter million people, in the poet's vision there seems to be no great distinction between the urban and the rural environment. Taken as a whole, these poems portray Tianjin as a Chinese landscape painting, an unfolding panorama with multiple points of perspective, accented with painterly conventions of gently swaying reeds and mist-shrouded rivers. Hoi polloi composed of itinerant vendors, day laborers, and uncouth shoppers crowd together on the streets, but these crowds are signs of prosperity and happiness, not a cause for anxiety about contagion, dirt, or disease. Water is present through the city, but its natural flows are captured and wisely utilized in symmetrical rice paddies. Wastes are channeled from the well-designed drainage system at the four corners of the city and into the Hai River, where ocean tides finally sweep the impurities out to sea (see map 3). In this vision of the city, there is little sense of bodies being at odds with the environment, no indication that the chaotic commingling of people, water, and air might produce disease.

There is evidence that some Chinese medical practitioners in the Qing held a view of epidemic pathogenesis very similar to the Western miasmatic view of disease, a view that saw the urban environment as a prime contributor to illness. In her pioneering work on the plague in nineteenth-century China, Carol Benedict notes that some medical practitioners, particularly those associated with the Warm Factor school, located the origin of epidemics in the harmful *qi* that arose from dirt, stagnant water, and crowded, airless conditions. These practitioners urged people to leave the city for the open spaces of the countryside when an epidemic threatened.[12] Some Chinese scholars have even proudly claimed that the writings of the Warm Factor school anticipated Western theories of pathogenesis—including the germ theory of disease—by several centuries.[13] Far more relevant to our discussion is the recent work by Bridie Andrews on the "selective assimilation" of Western medical ideas and practices in early twentieth century China. Using tuberculosis as an example, Andrews has demonstrated how Chinese made sense of the germ theory of disease by comparing it to (and merging it with) the concept of disease-causing "worms" *(chong)* found in traditional Chinese medicine. Rather than search in Chinese history for the antecedents (or lack thereof) to Western concepts of disease, it is more fruitful to imagine how similar concepts within Chinese medicine may have shaped understanding of certain concepts from the West, resulting in a creative, shifting synthesis in knowledge and practice.[14]

On the whole, it is possible to conclude that Chinese medical concepts in the late nineteenth century did not privilege any one theory regarding the relationship between the environment and disease. It is important to note that this was also the case in Western medical thought and practice of the time. Bruno Latour's description of nineteenth-century European hygienists' claims—"Illness can be caused by almost anything . . . contagion, the soil, the air, overcrowding. Nothing must be ignored, nothing dismissed"—would also be a fitting characterization of the state of Chinese medicine at the same historical juncture.[15] In addition to elements such as pestilent *qi* or malevolent *chong,* there were many other explanations for the origin of disease within Chinese medicine and popular belief, including the harmful effects of unseasonable weather, immoderate diet, and the presence of evil spirits. Disease was just as likely to be associated with these factors as with any element of the urban environment. This multi-

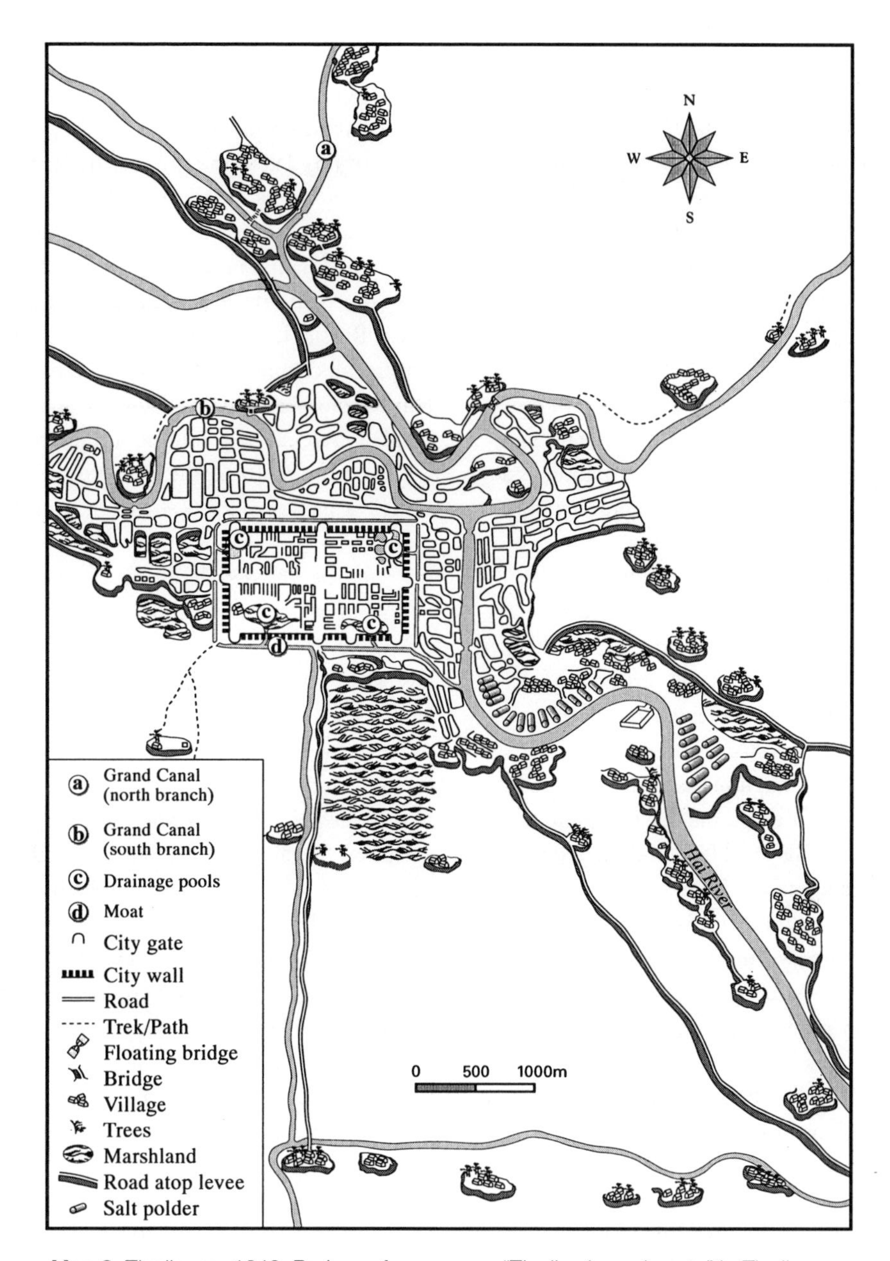

Map 3. Tianjin, ca. 1846. Redrawn from a map, "Tianjin chengxiang tu" in *Tianjin jianshi* (1987).

plicity of explanations provided a rich vocabulary from which Chinese shaped their understandings of Western medical notions in the twentieth century.[16]

The momentous events of 1900—the Boxer Uprising and the subsequent occupation of the city by the International Expeditionary Force—signaled the beginning of Tianjin's twentieth-century transformation. These events, although earth shattering in their own right, did not result in an immediate disjunction in Chinese conceptions of health and disease. Instead, they created conditions that became the basis for a long-term reconfiguration of life in the city, including the relationship between the body and the urban environment. The humiliating defeat of the Boxers, the occupation of the Chinese city, and the creation of multiple sites of imperialism in Tianjin coincided with the introduction of a new discourse of health and disease, one that emphasized Chinese hygienic inadequacy as it altered the urban landscape.

The Emergence of a Hyper-Colony

During the first two decades of the twentieth century, Tianjin was the location of as many as nine foreign settlements. I characterize Tianjin's unique situation as a "hyper-colony," a status that had several important implications for the career of hygienic modernity in the city.[17] First, Tianjin's status as a hyper-colony placed Chinese elites and nonelites alike under the gaze—and sometimes the control—of multiple imperial powers. As a result, there were multiple actors within Tianjin who utilized the discourse of hygiene as a symbol of foreign superiority and a marker of Chinese inadequacy. At the same time, the close juxtaposition of so many foreign settlements within one urban space dramatically influenced the self-representations of the imperial powers at the local level and offered the Chinese a view of several variant models of urban modernity. Finally, in contrast to colonial cities, the presence of a "native-administered" area within the city provided some groups in Tianjin society with a physical and symbolic space from which they tested and reshaped the dictates of the new regime.

Tianjin was originally opened to foreign settlement by the 1860 Conventions of Peking, signed by the Qing after British and French forces occupied Beijing and burned the summer palace. Soon after the signing of the treaty, Great Britain and France established Tianjin's first foreign concessions side by side along the south bank of the Hai River. In the 1890s these concessions were joined by the Japanese and German settlements, creating a two-mile-long row of foreign outposts along the Hai.[18] For the fewer than two thousand foreign residents living downriver from Tianjin's massive walls, the Chinese city and its "native" concerns seemed far away. It was not until the Boxer Uprising of 1900 that Tianjin was transformed into a hyper-colony, a chaotic crossroads of Chinese and foreigners and a booming showcase of imperialism.

In July 1900, the International Expeditionary Force *(baguo lianjun)* of over twenty thousand soldiers landed in Tianjin and occupied the city. The foreign powers took advantage of Tianjin's occupation to establish new concessions or expand those already existing. Between 1900 and 1902, Russia, Italy, Belgium, and the Austro-Hungarian Empire all claimed settlements on the north bank of the Hai River. Great Britain, France, Germany, and Japan expanded their existing holdings on the south bank by over 200 percent. By 1902, the total area of the foreign concessions was eight times the size of the original walled city (see map 4).[19]

In the first decades of the twentieth century Tianjin became, both visually and politically, an urban hyper-colony, an exaggerated version of what Timothy Mitchell has called "world-as-exhibition."[20] In the age of empire, Mitchell argues, the European city became "a place of discipline and visual arrangements . . . the organization of everything and everything organized to represent, to recall like the exhibition some larger meaning." Tianjin after 1900 was home to eight different empires, and each empire proclaimed its presence through distinctive arrangements of space and edifice. By the 1920s, Tianjin's multiple "colonies" stood together as a Disneyland-like exhibition of world architectures and design, including the Japanese Concession's Daiwa Park, with its imposing wooden torii arch, the filigreed balconies of the Italian Concession's villas, and the British municipal council's Gordon Hall, a stylized medieval castle with exaggerated parapets and massive towers (see figs. 4–6).[21]

The last element of this hyper-colonial configuration, although it lasted only two years, had a tremendous impact on Tianjin's future: the Tianjin Provisional Government, or TPG, a "colonial" government set up to control the walled Chinese city and its immediate environs (excluding the concessions) after the siege of Tianjin. The TPG was a council made up of representatives from each of the nations in the International Expeditionary Force. Intense rivalries between these imperial powers militated

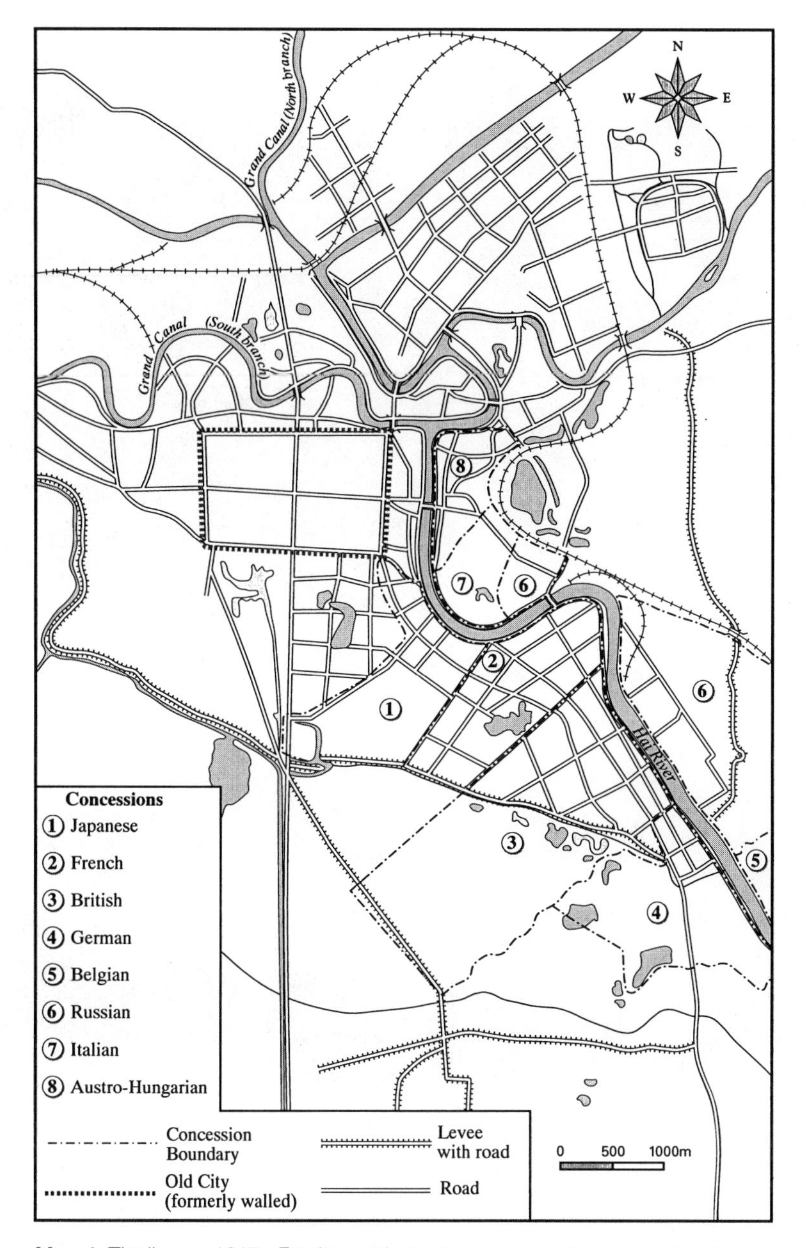

Map 4. Tianjin, ca. 1917. Foreign settlements occupy both banks of the Hai River southeast of the former walled city, on land that had previously contained swamps and salt polders. After 1902, the Qing built a new commercial and administrative area to the northeast of the old city. Map courtesy of the Tianjin Academy of Social Science.

against any attempt at long-term cooperation, and the eight nations relinquished the administration of the Chinese city to Yuan Shikai and the Qing government in the summer of 1902.[22] After reversion, the Chinese city remained under Chinese rule until the Japanese occupation in 1937, creating yet another zone of administration, "exhi-

***Figs. 4 – 6**. Tianjin as "hyper-colony"*

Fig. 4. Gordon Hall, the gothic home of the British concession municipal government, Tianjin. Photo courtesy of the Tianjin Academy of Social Sciences.

Fig. 5. Tuscan-style villa in Italian concession, Tianjin. Photo courtesy of the Tianjin Academy of Social Sciences.

Fig. 6. Torii at the entrance of a public park in Japanese concession, Tianjin. Photo courtesy of the Tianjin Academy of Social Sciences.

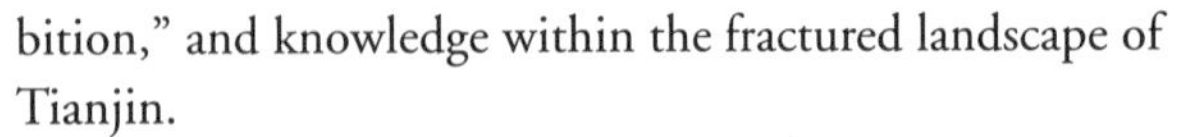

bition," and knowledge within the fractured landscape of Tianjin.

Thus early-twentieth-century Tianjin represented a unique "laboratory of modernity," an urban space where imperial powers consciously represented their advancements not only before an indigenous gaze, but also before an implied audience of other rival European and Asian empires. Distinctions between concessions, and particularly between the concessions and the Chinese city, were consciously marked by boundaries of architecture, politics, and, most important for our discussion, boundaries of hygiene. Each concession undertook its own administration of hygienic modernity, seeking solutions for the provisioning of water, the removal of waste, and the prevention of disease behind its own borders. However, this impulse to create distinct hygienic boundaries within Tianjin was constantly thwarted by human and organic elements that resisted containment. Movements of the rapidly burgeoning Chinese population were beyond the control of concession administrations.[23] While humans circulated freely through the city, so, too, did water. Like water, disease moved through space, oblivious to political divisions.

Perhaps the most serious threat to the hygienic security of concession boundaries came in the summer of 1902, when a devastating cholera epidemic swept through all the enclaves of Tianjin. Foreigners focused their anxiety on the imagined threat to health posed by the population of the Chinese city—and on the threat posed by the Chinese within their midst. Suspicions of Tianjin's indigenous water, air, and climate were coupled with fears of the Chinese who dared to mingle with Europeans in the Victoria Gardens, or the Chinese servants who were responsible for boiling the tea water in foreign households.[24] Anxiety over the concession boundaries' porousness to disease figured prominently in the negotiations to return the native city to Qing rule. High on the list of prerequisites for reversion was the demand that Qing administration adopt measures to enforce hygienic modernity in their sector of Tianjin. Without such administration, foreigners intimated, the Chinese would remain a backward people, incapable of coexisting independently with representatives from more "advanced" civilizations. Any perceived failure to halt the spread of disease in the native city could be used by foreigners to justify the extension of concession borders to encompass areas deemed unsanitary.[25]

The desire for political autonomy compelled Qing authorities to incorporate a new conception of public health into their urban administration. The Chinese word used to describe this conception was *weisheng,* an ancient term that by the turn of the century had taken on radically new meanings. In the first decades of the twentieth century some Chinese embraced *weisheng* as a central marker of Chinese deficiency and a cornerstone of urban modernity. Others questioned this formulation of *weisheng* and critiqued elements that they deemed antithetical to Chinese culture. While *weisheng* became a major rationale for numerous changes in the city's environment, the specific meaning and practice of the term continued to be created and contested at many levels of Tianjin society.

The Genesis of *Weisheng*

The new order of hygienic modernity brought to Tianjin after 1900 is perhaps best represented by the words and work of Tsuzuki Jinnosuke, a bacteriologist who was dispatched to Tianjin in 1902 by the Japanese Imperial War Board to investigate the deadly cholera epidemic that was ravaging the city. Tsuzuki was one of many young Japanese who had studied in Germany under the foremost medical scientists of the late nineteenth century, including Rudolf Virchow and Robert Koch. Newly versed in Western science, they returned to their native country to establish hospitals, laboratories, and a national public health system.[26] By the turn of the century many of these scientists and physicians joined in the service of Japan's expanding Asian empire.

Tsuzuki trained his German-made microscopes on Tianjin's rivers and cesspools and determined that drinking water collected from the Hai River was the major cause of the cholera epidemic. In his report on Tianjin published in a German medical journal, Tsuzuki bluntly concluded *"Der Prophylazis sind die Chinesen unzugänglich"* (the Chinese are incapable of enacting [sanitary] prevention), and warned that in terms of public health, foreigners must be exceedingly suspicious of the Chinese city and the people in it. Although his experiments pinpointed the waterborne bacteria vector of Tianjin's common gastrointestinal disorders, Tsuzuki nonetheless sternly warned foreign residents to limit direct contact with Chinese people if they wished to avoid contracting disease. In addition, he prescribed that each foreign settlement establish a special constabulary to enforce strictly sanitation, vaccination, and quarantine once their national armies had withdrawn from the city. Tsuzuki was convinced that public and private hygiene were markers of modern civilization and was equally convinced that the Chinese were deficient in both.[27]

Had Tsuzuki published his report in Chinese or

Japanese, he would have used the same two Chinese characters to describe his concern over germs, Chinese inferiority, and proper municipal administration: 衛 (Chinese *wei,* Japanese *ei:* to guard, to protect) and 生 (Chinese *sheng,* Japanese *sei:* life). The original meaning of *weisheng* was far removed from Tsuzuki's world of microscopes and sanitary police. The word first appears in the ancient Taoist text, the *Zhuangzi,* in a passage that emphasizes the importance of following the way of nature in order to maintain health.[28] For the next two millennia of Chinese imperial history, *weisheng* was associated with techniques the individual could employ to preserve and strengthen his or her own health—whether it was eating the correct foods, taking the appropriate health-giving herbal medicines, or practicing breathing exercises and calisthenics designed to channel vital energy through the body.

Beginning in the 1870s, the meaning of *weisheng* underwent a major transformation in Meiji Japan. Nagayo Sensai, a German-educated government administrator and practitioner of Western medicine, is credited with using the term *"eisei"* as the official translation for a combination of German concepts, including *Hygiene, Sanitats-wesen,* and *Gesundheitsplfege*—all terms that related to the state-directed management of health. [29] Under his leadership, the name of the Japanese Medical Affairs Bureau (Imu kyoku; Chinese Yiwu ju) was changed to Eisei kyoku (Chinese Weisheng ju), a name that is now usually translated as the Sanitary Bureau.[30] Rather than just overseeing medical education and practice, as the original name suggested, Nagayo argued that this newly reconfigured Eisei kyoku (or Eisei Bureau) should "encompass all facets of life, whether great or small, that could possibly endanger human existence," including epidemic control, water supply, and urban sanitation.[31] In his 1903 autobiography Nagayo expressed pride that the term he had coined, *"eisei,"* had become widespread throughout Japan, where it was not only used to describe the medical duties of the state to its people, but was also used in restaurants and households to indicate that objects such as eating utensils and drinking vessels were germ-free.[32]

The transformed meaning of *weisheng* does not seem to have made inroads into China until the Qing defeat in the Sino-Japanese War. This does not mean that Chinese observers were unaware of the formulations of hygienic modernity taking place in foreign concessions and in the British colony of Hong Kong before this time. In Tianjin, Qing administrators viewed the public health and sanitation functions of the French and British concessions with a combination of admiration and suspicion. Impressed by the cleanliness of Tianjin's British Concession, one retired official went so far as to publish a poem praising the virtues of municipal garbage collection, calling it an expression of an enlightened "Kingly Way" *(wang dao).* On the other hand, during an interview in Tianjin, Li Hongzhang expressed concern over reports he had received detailing the measures undertaken by the British during the 1894 Hong Kong plague epidemic. He found the government enforcement of quarantine and the use of potent chemical disinfectants to be particularly unwise and disruptive, and the treatments used by foreign doctors on Chinese patients abusive and absurd.[33] For Li and other Qing officials, the state should not and could not interfere so directly in the lives of its people. Qing statecraft held that during health crises such as epidemics, the proper public role of the government and gentry was to distribute free food and medicine, provide burial services, attend to epidemic-fighting religious rituals, and publicize important medical information.[34] In addition, elites were to admonish individuals to follow the traditional precepts of disease prevention, such as eating foods right for the season and practicing a moderate lifestyle, a collection of knowledge popularly known as *weisheng.*

The appearance of a different type of *weisheng* in Tianjin can be dated to 1895, in a report carried by Tianjin's first Chinese language newspaper, *Zhibao.* Edited by some of Tianjin's progressive elites, *Zhibao* published editorials on modernization (including Yan Fu's first essays on society and evolution), while its news reports kept readers up-to-date on the battles of the Sino-Japanese War. One article reported on the activities of the Japanese army's Eisei ko (Sanitation/Epidemic Prevention Section; Chinese Weisheng ke) during the Japanese conquest of Taiwan. The newspaper accounts noted that hundreds of doctors and nurses from the Weisheng ke were frantically attempting to quell the epidemics that were decimating the Japanese army ranks, but their methods were sadly ineffective. The report went on to criticize the Japanese army's ignorance of the true principles of *weisheng*. As even the lowliest Taiwanese native understood, the article read, the best way to avoid disease in Taiwan's climate was to practice sexual abstinence during hot weather. It was the rapacious libidos of the Japanese soldiers that rendered them susceptible to Taiwan's deadly tropical miasmas.[35]

This account indicates that Tianjin's elites recognized that by the late nineteenth century the Japanese claimed to be practicing a new form of *weisheng*. However, they were unclear as to its exact content, skeptical about its efficacy, and did not hesitate to apply their own interpretation to the word based on their understanding of Chinese medical theory. For even these progressive, Western-leaning elites, *weisheng* had not yet become "hygienic modernity," a centerpiece of true civilization and a mark of Chinese inferiority. It was only after 1900 that Tsuzuki's vision of hygienic modernity—the product of Euro-American administration, European laboratories, and Japanese bureaucrats—was introduced directly to Tianjin by the foreign occupation government. The process of understanding and reinterpreting *weisheng* in Tianjin continued, even as its regime was being enforced.

Administering Hygienic Modernity

This section considers the work of three different "public health" administrations in Tianjin: the TPG's Bureau Sanitaire, the New Policy-era Chinese Weisheng Bureau, and the Japanese Concession's Eisei Bureau. I have chosen to maintain the French, Chinese, and Japanese-language names for these administrations rather than translate them all as Sanitary Bureau or Public Health Bureau. This somewhat awkward device reminds us that the definition of "public health" held by early twentieth century administrators differed significantly from our own contemporary understanding. More important, it suggests that the function of these bureaus was not fixed, but was interpreted, mediated, and contested in different ways by the people who were the object of their policies.

The TPG's Bureau Sanitaire—Enforcing Hygienic Behavior

The TPG changed many things in Tianjin, but perhaps no aspect of this regime changed the lives of Tianjin residents as profoundly as the TPG's Bureau Sanitaire. The personnel and policies of the bureau reflected an international faith in hygienic modernity as a centerpiece of urban administration.

The name of the bureau not only reflects the fact that French was the official language of the TPG; it also represents the prestige that French medical science had gained in the West—and among Westerners in Tianjin—by the late nineteenth century. The bureau was directed by the French physician Rene Depasse, a professor at Tianjin's Beiyang Medical School and one-time personal physician to Li Hongzhang. French physicians attached to the Beiyang Medical School at this time were also responsible for founding Tianjin's Pasteur Institute, which grew to become one of the premier laboratory facilities in North China. In spite of the French domination of the Bureau Sanitaire, adherents of hygienic modernity from all TPG nations were represented under its roof. The bureau owed its existence in part to the Japanese expeditionary army commander, Colonel Fukushima Yasumasa, who insisted that a public health bureau would be as essential to the preservation of social order in the Chinese city as a police force. While the administration was predominantly French, the work of the bureau was carried out by a combination of Japanese, Sikh, German, and Chinese personnel.[36]

The Bureau Sanitaire performed many functions that by today's standards seem to be quite outside the purview of public health. One of the greatest changes in Tianjin's appearance during this time was the destruction of the city wall, brought about in great part by the bureau's desire to eliminate the "unsanitary" dwellings and stagnant water that collected along the wall's perimeter.[37] The bureau also managed all aspects of poor relief, an arrangement that provided a ready source of labor for the bureau's tasks. In a form of welfare reform new to Tianjin, the bureau rounded up the homeless, clothed them in uniforms marked with the characters *weisheng*, and put them to work cleaning the city streets in return for their daily bread. Depasse brought other European advancements in hygiene to Tianjin, including public toilets, the burning of unclaimed corpses (without burial rites, a practice that many Chinese found particularly objectionable), and the establishment of government-inspected brothels for all foreign troops.[38]

The bureau also attempted to influence directly the customs and behaviors of Chinese families and individuals in ways never contemplated by the Qing government: it intervened in the rituals relating to death previously managed by families and native place associations by demanding licenses for coffins and official permission to move bodies out of the city limits.[39] Failure to notify the TPG of a death in a family resulted in a sentence of hard labor. Even intimate functions such as excretion were also regulated. Working-class residents and out-of-town travelers who had previously used the convenience of open fields were forced at gunpoint to defecate in public toilets constructed by the TPG. The far-reaching regulations of the Bureau Sanitaire eventually touched the lives of all of Tianjin's classes. Even merchants and degree holders who lapsed in their observation of hygienic modernity were forced to carry pails of sewage for the bureau under the watchful eye of armed Sikh guards.[40]

In spite of the intrusiveness of the occupation government, the Chinese response to TPG rule was not necessarily one of united resistance. Some policies, such as the random burning of corpses, seem to offend deeply the sensibilities of elites and nonelites alike.[41] On the other hand, TPG rule offered many elites a welcome opportunity to incorporate new information into their definition of "modern civilization." For example, Yan Xiu, the founder of Nankai University, frequently contemplated the hygienic benefits of Western clothing and Western-style houses during this time.[42] Hua Xuelan, a member of the prestigious Hua clan of Tianjin salt merchants (who later became a pioneer in the field of chemistry), did note seeing chain gangs on sanitation duty being led through city streets by foreign soldiers during the occupation, but let the incidents pass without much comment. Hua was more likely to remark favorably on the utility of other TPG services, such as the new municipal garbage collection and the remarkable maintenance of a no-spitting, single-file ticket line at the Tianjin train station.[43] Behind the observations of these and other similar-minded Tianjin elites lay an implicit understanding of *weisheng* as both a cornerstone of modernity and a marker of Chinese inadequacy, if not inferiority.

Other Tianjin elites were far more suspicious of the new reign of hygienic modernity and boldly formulated their own definitions of an urban *weisheng* appropriate for the Chinese people. One such synthesis was developed by Ding Zilang, an outspoken commentator on Tianjin's turn-of-the-century political scene and one of the city's best-known doctors of traditional Chinese medicine. Ding Zilang maintained that traditional Chinese practices of *weisheng*, including the ingestion of the proper medicinal foods and maintenance of a moderate lifestyle, were far superior to what he deemed to be the intrusive and harmful attributes of the Bureau Sanitaire's version of *weisheng*. Ding Zilang was particularly critical of the role that germ theory played in the new public health administration. He claimed that a fixation on germs caused the Bureau Sanitaire foolishly to neglect other obvious pathogenic factors such as weather, eating habits, and lifestyle—elements that lay beyond the control of the government. Moreover, Ding Zilang held that the harsh quarantine and epidemic control procedures motivated by the germ theory constituted an attack on the Chinese race. In a conspiratorial tone, Ding Zilang claimed that the quarantine procedures mandated by foreigners in Tianjin during the cholera epidemic of 1902 not only violated Confucian principles of filial piety (by separating family members from each other), but also killed more Chinese than the disease itself.[44]

At the same time, Ding Zilang embraced other aspects of hygienic modernity, particularly the TPG's efforts to reconfigure urban space for the purpose of preventing disease. The destruction of the city wall, the creation of orderly food markets, the construction of public toilets, and the government-administered removal of rubble and garbage all met with his approval. For Ding Zilang, what marked Chinese inadequacy was not a lack of *weisheng*, but rather a lack of public morals and cooperative spirit *(gong de)*. Actions of the government that encouraged citizens to be aware of their common environment became important elements in Ding Zilang's reinterpretation of *weisheng*, a reinterpretation that he publicized broadly through newspaper articles, public lectures, and his own medical practice.[45]

The newly introduced discourse on *weisheng* provided Chinese elites with a central theme for a critique of traditional Chinese urban administration—and Chinese personal habits. Some, like Ding Zilang, explored alternative definitions of *weisheng* and rejected some of its more intrusive "modern" elements. Others, demoralized by the Boxer debacle, saw the occupation of Tianjin as an opportunity to create a new Chinese city based on Western models, with hygienic modernity as a core element. Ultimately, the occupation of Tianjin made adoption of Western models a political necessity. Before it would turn over (nonconcession) Tianjin to the Qing, the TPG demanded that native authorities adopt two new aspects of urban administration: a Police Bureau to keep order and a Sanitary Bureau to control the outbreak of contagious disease.[46]

The New Policy Weisheng Bureau—Altering Urban Space in the Name of the Public

Tianjin's New Policy-era Weisheng Bureau was a direct inheritor of the TPG Bureau Sanitaire. During its ten-year existence (1902–1911) this Chinese-administered body further impressed upon Tianjin's citizens the power and meaning of the term *"weisheng."* While it aspired to continue the Bureau Sanitaire's work of altering the private hygiene habits of Tianjin's populace, in fact the Weisheng Bureau was more effective in altering the function and appearance of the city's public spaces. Sanitation crews carted off garbage and swept streets, imbuing the urban landscape with an orderly profile and clean line. More lines were drawn as the Weisheng Bureau moved tallow makers, dye boilers, and abattoirs away from the city center, separating the filth of petty industries from residential and business environments. As it changed the shape and character of the city, the Weisheng Bureau, together with the people of Tianjin, began to shape a new hybrid rhetoric of *weisheng:* a rhetoric that employed elements of traditional Chinese medicine, traces of germ theory, and invocations of the public interest.

The Weisheng Bureau preserved the influence of French medicine from the Bureau Sanitaire. Depasse passed away in 1902, but his role as director of public health in Tianjin was taken over by one of his Chinese students, Qu Yongqiu. A native of Panyu County in Guangdong, Qu Yongqiu had come to Tianjin as a young man to study at the Beiyang Medical School under the patronage of Li Hongzhang. He remained in Tianjin after graduation and became an instructor at the Viceroy's Medical School, as the Beiyang institution was then known.[47] His colleagues in instruction at the school were a mix of physicians from south China and France. Qu Yongqiu shared duties at the Weisheng Bureau with his Cantonese and Fujianese colleagues, while French doctors from the school and the French army served in advisory roles.

For the leaders of the Weisheng Bureau, germ theory had become a central part of hygienic modernity and the major justification for their interventions into Chinese society. *Weisheng* regulations from 1907 cite bacteria *(duchong)* as the disease-causing element in unboiled water, untreated night soil, tainted meat, and rotting fruit. The bureau was also concerned with eliminating germs from the tea water of Tianjin's residents, although their recommendations would have been unintelligible to all but Tianjin's elites. Regulations urged residents to drink only tap water that had been boiled for exactly twenty-four minutes in order to ensure a germ-free beverage, yet only a small portion of Tianjin's Chinese population used *zilai shui* (tap water) or possessed a watch. Yet while they adhered to the foreign "gospel of germs" to justify their work, the bureau's French-trained doctors could also utilize Confucian rhetoric to convey the gravity of their public health pronouncements. In cautioning against the dangers of eating bacterially contaminated foodstuffs, the bureau invoked the citizen's duty to the Son of Heaven: "With regard to food and drink that can harm man, are there any outside of the categories [designated by the four characters] of rotten and unclean? By not eating unclean things, one truly obeys the spirit of the Sacred Edict *(sheng xun).*"[48]

The Weisheng Bureau consciously combined the novel discourses of Western science with traditional appeals to enlightened public interest when justifying its more intrusive policies against private businesses. This was vividly demonstrated in 1906, when the bureau attempted to move all dye manufacturers out of the city, citing the industry's production of noxious chemicals and smoke. In its initial complaint, the Weisheng Bureau represented itself as striving for the public interest *(gong)* while the dye manufacturers pursued selfish desires for self-enrichment *(si)* at the expense of the city's health.[49] In response, the companies offered to erect tall chimneys to take the smoke high into the air, where it would be dispersed by the winds. The Weisheng Bureau marshaled the voice of scientific authority to counter this suggestion. Chemists in the West, they argued, had recently proven in scientific experiments that smoke produced by the dye manufacturing process was of a density that did not allow it to rise in the air. Because of this unavoidable principle of nature, the chimneys proposed by the manufacturers would be useless. The combined force of hygienic modernity *(weisheng),* chemistry *(huaxue),* and public interest *(gong)* proved effective: these businesses were eventually forced to move their operations away from the populated areas of the city.[50]

There is evidence that some constituencies in Tianjin welcomed the Weisheng Bureau's interventions but possessed different conceptions of what actually caused disease in the urban environment. In 1907, the newspaper *Dagong bao* published an open letter to the bureau from several Tianjin residents that complained about the pestilent miasma *(yiqi)* emanating from a slaughterhouse in their neighborhood. According to the petitioners, the slaughterhouse accumulated the carcasses of cows and sheep, emitting such a stench that everyone who neared it had to hold their noses and cross to the opposite side of the street. They claimed that this *yiqi* had entered the noses of the residents and had already caused two people to die from epidemic fevers *(wenyi)* in recent months, while a third woman was just barely clinging to life. They called upon the Weisheng Bureau to remove this miasmatic danger to the *public* health *(weisheng),* much as it might remove a noxious tallow maker or a careless night soil drier.[51]

This coexistence of different conceptions of pathogenesis—in this case, germs and miasmas—was not unusual for the turn of the century, whether in the United States, Europe, or Asia. The existence of a decade of *weisheng* administration in Tianjin did not displace previously held beliefs about health and illness. However, the public petition in the *Dagong bao* indicates that by the early twentieth century some residents associated *weisheng* with a new conception of urban space and public responsibility. In their eyes, the Weisheng Bureau's function was to relocate certain insalubrious urban functions to other locales in the city, creating separate zones for residence and industry. Through this process of negotiation and interpretation, hygienic modernity would eventually change the face of Tianjin, although different elements in the city held different understandings about the whys and wherefores of the change.

During the chaotic warlord period that engulfed China after the 1911 Revolution, the Chinese-administered Weisheng Bureau experienced a period of decline. However, in subsequent decades hundreds of thousands of Chinese encountered other forms of hygienic modernity in Tianjin's foreign concessions. To understand the formation of concession sanitary arrangements and how these were in turn shaped by concession residents, let us examine the foreign settlement that had the largest Chinese population and also left behind the most thorough documentation—the Japanese Concession.

The Japanese Concession Eisei Bureau—Science and the Persistence of Shit

Hygienic modernity was a centerpiece of administration in the Japanese Concession since the founding of the settlement government in 1908. In the marketplace of imperialism that was Tianjin, *eisei* administration was one way that the Japanese sought to distinguish themselves from the Chinese in European eyes and at the same time confirm their status as a "civilized" people.[52] The Eisei Bureau combined the expertise of Japanese laboratory science with the coercive force of the Japanese military, providing Tianjin with a highly specific, highly interventionist model of hygienic modernity. In spite of this commitment to efficient scientific administration, the Eisei Bureau quickly discovered that it had to negotiate its methods with the lowly likes of the night soil carriers who removed the concession's daily accumulation of human waste. The Eisei Bureau's failure to replace human labor with sanitary technology indicates that even the city's humblest denizens had a hand in shaping the meaning and practice of hygienic modernity.

Japanese experience with hygienic modernity had a profound impact on the development of health technologies in China. Many in China first learned of the precepts of Western medicine through Japanese translations of European texts. In the early twentieth century, thousands of Chinese traveled to Japan to experience firsthand this new model of Asian modernity. An entire generation of Chinese physicians, scientists, and public health administrators received training in Japanese universities. They returned to China to serve in warlord armies, private clinics, and numerous municipal public health administrations. In addition, Japanese pharmaceuticals marketed in shops throughout China brought a cache of hygienic modernity to areas far beyond the coastal cities.[53]

Japan's medical influence was particularly strong in Tianjin, which was home to both a large Japanese Concession and the North China headquarters of the Japanese Imperial Army. Japanese doctors provided medical training and medical care at several of Tianjin's Chinese hospitals, including the Beiyang Army Medical School founded by Yuan Shikai. The large number of Chinese doctors trained abroad in Japan who came to Tianjin to practice were widely known as the city's *Ri pai* (Japanese school). Most important for our discussion, the Japanese Eisei Bureau figured prominently in Tianjin's response to epidemic disease throughout the first decades of the twentieth century, culminating in the harsh reign of a Japanese-enforced hygienic modernity under the occupation of the city during the War of Resistance (1937–1945).

To accomplish hygienic modernity in their enclave, the Eisei Bureau drew on the expertise of civilian medical personnel and frequently enlisted the help of the Japanese North China army, whose headquarters were located in Tianjin just south of the Japanese Concession boundary. Cooperation between civilian and military authorities was especially close when epidemics threatened the Japanese Concession. First, the widespread network of the Japanese army in China helped provide local authorities with accurate reports on the progress of disease down railway lines from Manchuria or up the coast from Hong Kong and Shanghai. When disaster threatened, the Japanese army medical laboratory could quickly produce enough vaccines for the concession's Japanese and Chinese populations. The biological assays necessary to pinpoint the cause of infectious disease were entrusted to scientists from the Imperial Army. These same military doctors led the Eisei Bureau's emergency committees in times of public health crises.[54]

Given his combination of German scientific education, experience in China, and connections to a powerful military authority, it is not surprising that the head of the Eisei Bureau, Dr. Fukuda, was elected by European representatives to head Tianjin's first All-Concession Epidemic Committee in 1911. The committee had been formed to decide on a united strategy against the devastating plague that had descended on Tianjin from Manchuria.[55] The Western Concession representatives proposed a ban on any Chinese movement into the foreign concessions and suggested using military force to effect such a quarantine.[56] Fukuda protested, arguing that it would be impossible to cut off all traffic between the Japanese Concession and the Chinese populations on its border. He called for the use of "scientific methods" of surveillance and education to stem the plague and argued that crude military methods would only harm Tianjin's business and anger the Chinese. In the end, no agreement was reached, and each settlement left the meeting to deal with the plague in its own way.

The Japanese authorities were confident that their scientific methods could track individual residents and pinpoint carriers of disease without shutting down concession commerce and society. First the Japanese issued passes to all Chinese residents of the concession who had to travel beyond the concession borders. All Chinese entering the concession borders from the Chinese city had to undergo chemical disinfection with a potent carbolic acid spray and inspection for any signs of plague infection. Suspected cases were immediately isolated and tested for plague bacteria. Within the concession, a hygiene committee was set up on every street to conduct rat-catching contests and facilitate door to door inspections by the combined forces of the Eisei Bureau, the police department, and the Imperial Army. The entire population of the concession was required to attend a series of compulsory lectures on *eisei/weisheng* given by the head of the army hospital and the municipal bacteriologist.[57]

After the plague threat passed, the Japanese Settlement Corporation applauded the success of its scientific methods. The French, British, and German concessions had used their police forces to cut off all traffic with the Chinese, an action that was denounced by the Chinese Chamber of Commerce and had serious repercussions for business within those concessions. The Japanese allowed traffic across their borders to continue, but while a total of seventy-three plague deaths were reported in the bordering Chinese city, the Japanese Concession suffered only one death.[58] The Japanese policy in part reflected the strength of business interests in the Japanese Concession, but more important, the policy reflected the determination of Japanese colonial scientists and administrators to bring other Asian groups in the embrace of hygienic modernity. Epidemic management in Tianjin reflected Japan's growing confidence in its ability to enforce hygienic modernity in its colonies—a confidence that was the result of a combination of bacteriological expertise, a far-flung network of military intelligence, and the unhesitating use of police intervention. The successful deployment of scientific administration techniques in Tianjin echoed Japanese government efforts to turn Taiwan, the southern Manchurian leased territory, and the new colony of Korea into "hygienic zones," safe for Japanese colonization and economic activities.[59]

The Japanese administration of hygienic modernity, so effective in the face of public health emergencies like the 1911 plague, hit a snag when it came to one of the bureau's most basic everyday tasks: the removal and disposal of the concession's excreta. In Tianjin, one of the most telling conflicts between the forces of hygienic modernity and elements of Chinese society took the form of a clash between Japanese Concession authorities and the night soil carrier guilds of the city. The struggle pitted the advanced engineering expertise of imperial organizations like the Southern Manchurian Railway Company against the plyers of that humble but ancient trade of hauling feces. In the end, neither side could claim victory. Far from being an example of the hegemony of hygienic modernity, the sewer system that evolved in Tianjin represented a compromise between indigenous techniques and new technologies—a negotiation that took place not in scholars' studies but at the level of the street.

One characteristic of hygienic modernity is the use of clean and predictable technology to eliminate potentially unhygienic and unpredictable human factors from the provisioning of essential urban services. Perhaps the best example of this is the introduction of waterworks and sewers as a replacement for water carriers and night soil collectors. Prior to the introduction of these technologies, Tianjin's daily street scene included thousands of men who deftly pushed carts and wheelbarrows in and out of alley traffic, their splashing buckets filled with either drinking water from the Grand Canal or night soil and urine from the city's myriad chamber pots (see fig. 7). The logic of hygienic modernity would replace this ubiquitous human presence with a network of pipes running silently and invisibly beneath city streets, efficiently conveying water to private homes and discreetly removing wastes.[60] The use of pipes to provide clean water and remove waste is not only an example of how technology could alter habits of daily life and change the physical configuration of the city; it also demonstrates how hygienic modernity had the potential to change the *human* landscape of the city as well.

Fig. 7. Tianjin water carriers, ca. 1900. Photo courtesy of Library of Congress.

The Japanese Concession began installing sewer pipes under its main thoroughfares as early as 1908. The construction proved to be quite a challenge, since the concession was located on low-lying swampland with abysmal drainage. Just as drainage was accomplished in one section of the concession, development in areas across the border in the Chinese city would send water and sewage backing up into the concession's business and residential districts. Finally the concession enlisted (at considerable expense) the help of engineers from the Southern Manchurian Railroad Company to solve the problem. By 1929, the Settlement Corporation had laid a pipe network of over ten kilometers under all the concession's streets.[61]

But as this construction progressed, both Chinese and Japanese residents in the concession continued to contract with Chinese carriers to haul away the waste from private chamber pots and latrines. The situation was untenable in the eyes of the Eisei Bureau, who felt that the members of the night soil guild were an unruly lot, ignorant of germ theory and ill qualified to perform a task so central to the realization of hygienic modernity. Moreover, they were "the lowest sort of characters" who often extorted extra money from households, used foul speech, and worked at an extremely slow pace.

Still, it proved impossible to eliminate the night soil men. Even as the concession invested public funds to build a sewer system, the majority of private households did not have indoor plumbing. The expense of purchasing and installing such equipment, as well as the additional expense of water fees and maintenance, limited the number of households that could flush directly into the underground drainage system. As late as 1928, only eight hundred out of the concession's four thousand households had indoor flush facilities. Of those eight hundred households, over one hundred still used the night soil service, because, it was explained, "many Chinese women still retained the habit of using chamber-pots."[62] Any attempt by the authorities to do away with the guilds resulted in work slowdowns or stoppages that were extremely dangerous to the public health.

Finally, in the 1920s, the concession authority founded a Sanitation Section (Japanese Hojōka; Chinese Baojing ke), a compromise between the interests of the Chinese night soil carriers and the interests of hygienic modernity. The concession provided a monopoly contract for certain groups of night soil carriers who in turn agreed to work under the supervision of Japanese sanitary inspectors. Every morning, the Sanitation Section workers continued to remove the contents of the previous evening's chamber pots, even from households that possessed flush toilets. The economics of the concession, the lifestyles of concession residents, and the strength of the Chinese laborer's organization guaranteed the presence of the night soil man on Tianjin's streets.

Conclusion

By the 1920s the idea of *weisheng* had made major contributions to the transformation of Tianjin. *Weisheng* was a driving force that brought down the city wall, moved its cemeteries, and filled in acres of its famed "watery landscape." *Weisheng* furthered the distinctions between different neighborhoods as elites lobbied the government to move petty industries and workshops out of more "upscale" commercial and residential areas. Even the establishment of a water treatment system resulted in a radical transformation of major symbolic importance in Tianjin. In 1904, the new waterworks company razed a former mansion that had once hosted the Qianlong emperor and replaced it with a modern water plant that included a sixty-thousand-gallon capacity coal-fueled steam pump, three huge settling ponds, and two slow-filtration tanks. The company then established its headquarters in the northwest corner of the old city, across the street from the City God Temple. Photographs of the City God Temple from the early twentieth century show the water company's 110-foot high water tower dominating the sky above the former center of ritual life in imperial Tianjin.[63]

Weisheng not only transformed the built environment of Tianjin; it altered the human landscape of the city as well. The once ubiquitous presence of water and night soil carriers on Tianjin's streets was reduced (but not eliminated) by the construction of sewers and water pipes beneath the city's streets. Although not detailed in this chapter, the appearance of Western-style dress on Tianjin's streets also had its hygienic element as progressive voices extolled the healthful virtues of narrow sleeves (which prevented chilling breezes from entering in), form-fitting pants (which allowed for more vigorous movements than scholars' gowns), and, of course, unbound feet (although the hygienic counsel against high heels for the most part went unheeded).[64]

Another important aspect of *weisheng*'s impact on the human landscape of China's cities should not be overlooked: there is evidence that improvements in sanitation, vaccination, and personal hygiene may actually have begun to reduce urban mortality rates in certain neighborhoods by the 1920s.[65] In neighborhoods afforded the advantages of hygienic modernity, the streets would echo with the laughter of more children who had survived the contagious diseases of infancy, watched over by more grandmothers and grandfathers whose lives had been extended simply by drinking treated water. At the same time, other neighborhoods neglected by the water company and government bureaus were branded as *bu weisheng,* and the poor health of the residents blamed on a lack of personal hygienic behavior.[66]

The transformative power of hygienic modernity in the early twentieth century—its ability physically to alter cities, its use in defining class and ethnicity, its employment as a marker of national identity and national status—was evident not only in China, but in numerous other places around the world, as a glimpse into the histories of any of the eight nations that occupied Tianjin in 1900 would reveal. Yet as the great 1900 watershed for imperialism in China worked its transformative power on Tianjin, the meaning and practice of modernity was being reinterpreted and reshaped in unique ways in the alleys and residences of the city—within scholars' studios, in the back rooms of pharmacies, and in the daily lives of the common people. *Weisheng,* the word from an ancient Taoist text, continued to embody other practices of hygiene, other ways of conceptualizing the body, even as it came to symbolize a modern regime of bacteria, microscopes, and medical police. Although for some Chinese and foreign observers *weisheng* represented that which China lacked in its quest for modern civilization, at the same time it could also embody a vision of hybrid modernity, one that combined technologies that reduced disease and death with technologies that maintained the autonomy of the Chinese and the dignity of the individual.

Chapter 4

Urban Identity and Urban Networks in Cosmopolitan Cities

Banks and Bankers in Tianjin, 1900–1937

Brett Sheehan

By the 1930s, modern banks and the bankers who ran them had become recognizable icons of modern, cosmopolitan Chinese cities.[1] Leftist writers such as Mao Dun and the playwright Cao Yu gave bankers a prominent role in their criticisms of urban China. The role of bankers as a specifically urban elite type was nowhere clearer than in Cao Yu's popular play, *Sunrise* (1936). In it, Cao Yu paints a tableau of urban elites and the poor they mercilessly oppress. This sordid and cruel city life is set against the wholesomeness of Fang Dasheng, a liberal activist who comes from the countryside to see his childhood sweetheart, Chen Bailou. In the city Fang Dasheng meets a variety of unsavory elite types: the gangster, the society matron, the gigolo, the obsequious returned student, and the banker. The banker, Pan Yueting, is especially prominent. He pays Chen Bailou's many bills (for her luxury hotel room, beautiful clothes, cosmetics, etc.); he finds a job in his bank for the society matron's gigolo; and he deals regularly with the gangster, who eventually ruins Pan Yueting by manipulating speculation in government bonds. If for Cao Yu the gangster represented the epitome of urban power, the banker represented the archetype of urban wealth. In the words of Cao Yu's society matron, he was "to quote a modern phrase . . . a 'unique unprecedented first-class type.'" Later, when "little creature"—a sixteen-year-old orphan who had been sold to the gangster—is derided for rejecting her suitor, another character states, "She's got it into her head that she's going to stay a virgin, won't sell at any price. . . . I suppose [her] father's a bank manager? Or does he run a gold mine?"[2]

Banks and bankers played central roles in how Chinese in the republican period imagined cities, making them ideal subjects for a study of what it meant to be urban in this period. We need not accept the explicit critique of urban life by a Cao Yu or a Mao Dun to understand that, by the 1930s, banks and the men who ran them were a powerful and evocative symbol of the urban in popular consciousness. As Wen-hsin Yeh has noted, among petty urbanites in Shanghai, "banking . . . meant glitter and glamour." The modern bankers' associations were among the most powerful business organizations in Chinese cities.[3]

Just as the characters in Cao Yu's *Sunrise* are quite consciously drawn as "types" rather than real people, the city in which they live is, too, a type. As Joseph M. S. Lau states,

> Though the locale of the play is not given, one can, however, still make out from the stage directions and the identities of the characters that the action must have taken place in one of China's cosmopolitan cities like Shanghai or Tientsin [Tianjin], for only a city like one of these could have hosted such a diverse range of characters as banker, courtesan, returned student from America, child prostitute, gangster, gigolo, etc.[4]

In fact, Cao Yu later revealed that the location he intended was none other than Tianjin, where he grew up and had gone to school.[5] As such, Tianjin is an appropriate place to begin studying this particular type of cosmopolitan city. Tianjin was the financial center of north China, with banks and bankers in abundance. It was also linked closely to the other cosmopolitan cities of China: Beijing, Hankou, Nanjing, and especially Shanghai.

Bankers made appropriate figures for Cao Yu's criticism and for Shanghai petty urbanites' admiration because their power, access to capital, and "glamorous" lifestyle typified the way Chinese imagined cosmopolitan cities during the republican period. Cities, however, represented much more than just a set of behaviors and an abstract quality of imagined "urbanity," what might be called "behavioral urbanism." Cities were also nodes in larger structures of urban and urban-rural systems. As indicated by the modern Chinese word for city, *chengshi,* cities were defined both by their walls *(cheng)* and what went on inside them, and also by the market *(shi)* that connected cities to their hinterlands and to other cities.[6] I take my cue from Jan deVries when he says that we should seek to understand cities "in the context of urbanization rather than the context of urban history [of individual cities]."[7] I have not completely abandoned the idea of looking at the history of individual cities, but I will attempt to go one step further and examine one city—Tianjin—as both an arena for urban behavior and a node in a larger urban system.

The individual contributions of cities must be understood in relation to their collective function and vice versa. As urban systems, cities need to be understood, following deVries, in terms of the decision making "of people and their migration patterns; of the controllers of capital and their investment behavior; of the state and its political decisions."[8] To deVries' list of decision-making realms I would add culture and its media of transmission and influence within urban systems. Understanding cities as arenas for particular urban behavior is equally complicated and requires the study of people, capital, politics, and culture under the specific local conditions of many different cities. I will limit myself to examining supralocal urban systems and local urban behavior in two different spheres—banks as organizations and bankers as an elite group. Both were important facets of the economic and social linkages among cities in republican China, and both played important roles in shaping the behavior and imagination of urban residents. In terms of deVries' decision-making realms, my discussion of banks and bankers reflects primarily on people and capital, although government influence (including war and invasion) and the development of a culture of professionalism affected those decision-making realms dramatically.

The following discussion uses Tianjin as a case study to take up the relationship between city and urban system in regard to banks and bankers from the founding of the first Chinese modern bank at the very end of the nineteenth century to the Japanese invasion of 1937. I emphasize the relationship of Tianjin to other higher central places as defined by the networks of bank branches, the movements of bank capital, and the behavior of elite bankers.[9] I call these higher level urban places "cosmopolitan" for two reasons. First, "cosmopolitanism" by definition indicates openness to the outside, and flows of bank capital and banking elites show the patterns of openness among cities. Second, "cosmopolitan" points to certain characteristics that republican-period Chinese identified with modern cities. The presence of foreigners and foreign companies marked cosmopolitanism, but so did public parks, movie theaters, and, of course, modern banks—because they represented openness to the foreign, the new, and the modern in regard to the ordering of urban space and the patterns of urban behavior.

During the early republican period, China had no one dominant city that served as the focus of elite banker networks and bank capital flows. Following the pattern of the late imperial period, China's system of higher-level urban places was relatively decentralized. Bank capital and banking elites circulated in a more diffused pattern among China's capital city (Beijing), treaty ports (especially Shanghai and Tianjin), and even a few inland cities (most notably Chongqing).[10] In the 1900–1928 period, bank offices, bankers, and bank capital were concentrated in Beijing, Tianjin, and Shanghai, with no city completely dominant. After the Guomindang moved the capital to Nanjing in 1928, bank offices and flows of bankers and bank capital shifted south to concentrate in Tianjin, Shanghai, and the new capital of Nanjing. After the Japanese invaded Manchuria in 1931, north China became less attractive as a banking center, and by the eve of the war in 1937 Shanghai had become completely dominant as the center of bankers and bank capital. As the conditions that made Tianjin attractive for the concentration of bank capital changed, its relationship to other cities—its "cosmopolitanism"—changed as well. Tianjin was not Shanghai, but neither was it "beyond" Shanghai, and its identity as a cosmopolitan city was a combination of its own unique, local circumstances and its inseparable relationship to Shanghai and the other cities of China.

Like the cosmopolitan urban networks in which they circulated, China's elite bankers had an urban identity that was diffuse and unfocused on particular cities. Their behavior and forms of organization cannot be explained either in terms of simple native-place ties or in terms of attachment to the cities in which they lived and worked. Bankers in China's cosmopolitan cities had primarily urban, not local, identities. To paraphrase R. E. Pahl's classic conceptualization of behavioral urbanism, bankers were in and of the city, but not in or of any particular city.[11] By the 1930s, China's perceived rural crisis threw this diffuse urban identity into sharp focus, and China's cosmopolitan bankers began exploring a new relationship between city and countryside. This new relationship never matured, however, as the Japanese invasion in 1937 cut short bankers' efforts to include "saviors of the countryside" as part of their urban and cosmopolitan identities.

The richness of the ambiguities in the relationship between local urban area and supralocal urban network in early twentieth-century urban China is as much in the details as in the overall patterns. Before I move on to discuss the larger issues as seen from Tianjin, I first present a brief description of one bank, the Jincheng Bank (one of Tianjin's largest privately owned banks), and one banker, its founder, Zhou Zuomin. His life, the structure of his bank, and its sources of capital show how the local and supralocal intertwined in China's network of cosmopolitan cities. The rocky waters of republican politics influenced the sources of capital for Jincheng Bank, directed that capital to the safety of treaty-port Tianjin, and ultimately drove Jincheng to relocate to Shanghai in the 1930s. Likewise, Zhou Zuomin's own career path led him from one cosmopolitan city to another as he negotiated the constant political changes.

The Tale of Jincheng Bank and a "Tianjin Banker" Who Lived in Beijing

Like most banks with general offices in Tianjin, Jincheng Bank was founded in the years after Yuan Shikai's death. Established in 1917, Jincheng Bank would go on to become one of the largest and most influential banks in republican China. Its president was Zhou Zuomin, the son of an impoverished Jiangsu literati. Born in Huai'an, Jiangsu, in 1884, Zhou Zuomin spent his early years at the Tan Family Foreign Languages School in Huai'an. He went with one of his teachers to Guangdong, where, in 1906, he was awarded a scholarship to study in Japan, but he returned to China without finishing his studies when the scholarship was cut off. Back in China, he went to work at a law school in Nanjing as a translator, and after the 1911 Revolution he was one of a number of returned students from Japan drafted to work in Sun Yat-sen's short-lived provisional government in Nanjing. After Sun Yat-sen resigned as president in favor of Yuan Shikai, Zhou Zuomin landed on his feet and went to work for the Finance Ministry in Beijing.[12]

Zhou Zuomin soon transferred to the Communications Ministry, where he went to work for the Bank of Communications, and became recognized as a member of the communications clique. When asked to open a Bank of Communications branch in Wuhu, Anhui, Zhou Zuomin made the acquaintance of the Anhui military governor, Ni Sichong, and his military supplies officer, Wang Zhilong. Ni Sichong was an Anhui native who had trained in the Beiyang Army at Xiaozhan near Tianjin, and Wang Zhilong was a native of Tianjin with a somewhat obscure merchant background.

In 1917, Ni Sichong and Wang Zhilong financed the founding of Jincheng Bank in Tianjin and chose Zhou Zuomin as bank president. Although there were more than seventeen stockholders, ten people supplied 470,000 yuan out of a 500,000 yuan total initial capitalization, and 280,000 yuan came from Ni Sichong and Wang Zhilong.[13] Jincheng Bank was spectacularly successful and solicited more capital from ever-larger groups of shareholders in 1919, 1922, and 1927, growing to seven million yuan in paid-in capital. As more shareholders were brought in, the share ownership of Ni Sichong and Wang Zhilong dropped from more than half of the shares in 1917 to only 16 percent in 1927. By then, the total number of shareholders had grown to more than five hundred.[14] Zhou Zuomin took advantage of the dilution in the power of the major shareholders and became chairman of the board in 1929. The cosmopolitanism of Jincheng Bank as represented by the number and diversity of its shareholders allowed Zhou to distance himself from his initial warlord backers.

In the 1920s, Jincheng Bank formed a strategic alliance with three other banks, forming a group popularly referred to as the "Northern Four Banks," even though one of the banks was located in Shanghai. The four banks comprising the partnership show the intercity reach of bank and banker networks. Jincheng Bank and Continental (Dalu) Bank had headquarters in Tianjin, the Salt (Yanye) Bank in Beijing, and the China and Southsea Bank (Zhongnan) in Shanghai. The desire to issue paper money acted as catalyst for their alliance, and none of the northern banks involved was authorized by the government to issue paper money. The Shanghai-based China and Southsea Bank, run by Zhou Zuomin's fellow provincial and former colleague from the Bank of Communications, Hu Bijiang, did have a license to print money, and the four banks pooled their resources to do so.[15]

In addition to capital from shareholders and printing money, banks also raised funds locally by soliciting deposits from residents of the cities in which they had branches. The Northern Four Banks began a small deposit association, and Jincheng Bank itself actively sought personal savings accounts, which provided the bank with a great source of funding, but once landed Zhou Zuomin in jail. The warlord Feng Yuxiang required frugality among his troops, and Zhou Zuomin arranged for them to open savings accounts at Jincheng Bank. After Feng Yuxiang lost to the Fengtian armies, Jincheng Bank deposit books were discovered in the pockets of all of Feng's soldiers. Zhou Zuomin was arrested by a Fengtian general but was released within a day after Jincheng Bank agreed to make a large loan to the new warlord government in Beijing.[16] This incident is not just indicative of the dangers of warlord China; it also shows the important role of banks in redefining the place of the individual in society. "Depositor at Jincheng Bank" joined family, native place, and occupation as a mark of identity for Feng Yuxiang's soldiers.

The changing political climate in China provided opportunities as well as dangers, and Zhou Zuomin succeeded in adapting Jincheng Bank to the successive political regimes. Zhou Zuomin personally capitalized on the success of Jincheng Bank to become head of the Beijing Bankers' Association and, later, vice president (1920) and president (1926) of the Beijing Chamber of Commerce. After 1928, Zhou Zuomin was active on a number of Nationalist government committees, although, unlike another Tianjin colleague, Wu Dingchang (head of another one of the Northern Four Banks), he never held a cabinet-level position with the Nationalist government. Before the Japanese invasion in 1937, trade between China and Japan and the Japanese-occupied northeast became increasingly important. Jincheng Bank pursued a strategy of employing branch managers who had studied in Japan, and at one time its managers were presidents of the bankers' associations in Beijing, Hankou, and Tianjin. In 1935, Zhou Zuomin moved the headquarters of Jincheng Bank from Tianjin to Shanghai, where, after 1937, he found refuge in the foreign concessions. Later, he served on the Chinese Economic Commission under the Wang Jingwei puppet regime. After the war he was arrested by the Nationalist government on the charge of collaboration but was released after paying a substantial fine. After the Communist victory in 1949, Zhou Zuomin, who had left for Hong Kong, returned to China to run the bank until the government dissolved it in the early 1950s.

This brief history of Jincheng Bank and its founder, Zhou Zuomin, nicely illustrates the close relationship between the local and supralocal in Tianjin banking. Jincheng Bank's general office lay in Tianjin, but its largest shareholder was Ni Sichong, a Beiyang militarist and Anhui native who lived in Anhui at the time of his initial investment. Its second largest shareholder, Wang Zhilong, was a Tianjin native who had contacts with both the Tianjin merchant community and several Beiyang warlords. Zhou Zuomin, a Jiangsu native who had studied abroad and returned to a career in government and state banking, was president. Even though the bank was headquartered in Tianjin, Zhou Zuomin did not live there; instead, he stayed in Beijing, becoming prominent in the Beijing Bankers' Association and the Beijing Chamber of Commerce. Jincheng Bank was one of the Northern Four Banks, one of which was headquartered in Shanghai in the south. When Jincheng issued paper money, it was not in its own name, but under the name of its Shanghai partner. Finally, the bank moved its headquarters to Shanghai as Tianjin's importance as a financial center declined and the

Japanese presence in Manchuria made north China less hospitable. Jincheng Bank's national network of branches and alliances and Zhou's Zuomin's national network of friends and fellow provincials allowed the bank to prosper throughout the chaos and constant political changes of republican China, and Zhou managed an extraordinary balancing act from one regime to the next.

Jincheng Bank may have been a Tianjin bank, but its activities and those of its president were hardly limited to Tianjin. Jincheng Bank's backing, which crossed regional and native-place boundaries, and its national operations indicated the importance of supralocal connections. To examine this topic in more depth, let us turn to banks as organizations and their relationships to urban systems.

Banks and Urban Systems

The Chinese began founding modern banks at the end of the nineteenth century, after the 1895 Treaty of Shimonoseki, which G. William Skinner sees as a "turning point in China's urban development." Skinner argues that, prior to 1895, the Qing government carefully designed administrative boundaries to divide up economic cores, especially the lower Yangzi, for purposes of control.[17] The branch structures of China's modern banks and their sources of capital do not fit neatly into either Skinner's periodization or his picture of discrete economic and administrative systems. The administrative initiatives and new institutional structures that set the stage for the creation of modern banks date to the self-strengthening period at least several decades before 1895, and they served to unite economic cores and link them together. In addition, unlike the framework of Skinner's analysis, the organizational structures and sources of capital of modern banks cannot easily be classified as either administrative or economic.

The state played a central role in the development of Chinese modern banking from its inception, and government officials (both in their official capacities and as private investors) made some of the key decisions about the relationships between bank capital and networks of bank branches. As such, banks serve as an important example of how urban systems changed in the latter half of the nineteenth century and into the twentieth century, under the mutual influence of state-sponsored modernizing economic institutions and the growing importance of treaty ports as urban centers.

Urban Systems and Bank Branch Structures

In order to examine the relationship between urban networks and bank organizations, I use two measures: the number of bank offices in a given city and the rank of those offices in bank administrative hierarchies. Judged by the links created by the supralocal structures of modern banks, cities like Beijing, Tianjin, and Shanghai had large numbers of highly ranked bank offices. Other cities were relatively cosmopolitan, based on either the large number of bank offices that linked them to supralocal networks (Hankou and Nanjing) or by the relatively high ranking of those offices in bank hierarchies (Chongqing, Xiamen, Guangzhou). Changes in hierarchy, in particular, clearly show the shift away from the north and the northeast after the Manchurian incident in 1931.

Chinese banking in Tianjin began only around the turn of the century, and at that time Tianjin had already functioned for centuries as a node in many important supralocal systems like the Grand Canal, the Changlu salt gabelle, and the branch networks of Shanxi native banks *(piaohao)*.[18] Salt merchants, the long-distance traders who shipped goods along the Grand Canal, and Shanxi native bankers all had access to capital and local business connections; salt merchants and Shanxi native bankers had close relationships with government officials as well, but for the most part these were not the supralocal systems that came into play in the development of Tianjin banking. Instead, modern banking in Tianjin grew from the rise of Tianjin as north China's most important treaty port and trading center following its opening in 1860 and from the organizations and networks related to the self-strengthening and New Policies reforms. These institutions and networks included the administration of Li Hongzhang (Zhili governor-general, 1870–1895), the Bank of China, the Bank of Communications, and the Beiyang Army, overseen by Yuan Shikai in his administration over Tianjin as Zhili governor-general (1901–1907). Networks and organizations related to Li Hongzhang played a particularly important role by linking Tianjin to the Jiangnan region and especially to Shanghai, where Li had established a number of self-strengthening organizations during his tenure as Jiangsu governor.

The first Chinese-owned modern bank in Tianjin was a branch of the Commercial (Tongshang) Bank of China, established there in 1898.[19] The Commercial Bank, founded in Shanghai by Li Hongzhang's protégé, Sheng Xuanhuai, was one of many self-strengthening organizations founded in the late nineteenth century under official or semi-official sponsorship that linked Tianjin more closely to Shanghai. After Li Hongzhang moved his office as Zhili governor-general and commissioner of north China ports to Tianjin, he installed a telegraph line between the two cities to help him handle his diplomatic duties. While in Tianjin he kept an active interest in the self-strengthening enterprises he had founded in Shanghai and with the Jiangnan elite who provided his financial backing. Steamship links between the two cities increased rapidly from the 1870s to the 1880s, outpacing steamship links between Shanghai and either Ningbo or Hankou.[20]

The Shanghai-Tianjin connection was not the only axis of growth for modern banks. State banks during the first decade of the twentieth century began in Beijing and expanded southward to Tianjin and Shanghai. In 1905 the Board of Revenue in Beijing, in cooperation with private shareholders, established its own bank, Hubu Bank (later Da Qing Bank and after 1911 reorganized as the Bank of China), which became China's largest modern bank. As a subsidiary of the central government, the Hubu Bank located its headquarters in Beijing, then quickly opened branches first in Tianjin and then a month later in Shanghai. Hubu Bank did not open branches in other cities like Hankou and Jinan until nearly a year later.[21]

Beijing, the national capital, and Tianjin and Shanghai, China's two largest treaty ports, became the core of an urban system of modern bank branches in the early twentieth century. In addition to being treaty ports, Tianjin and Shanghai both had the advantage of being international financial centers (home to foreign banks and nodes in an international financial system) in their own right. By 1905 Shanghai and Tianjin were the eighth- and ninth-largest international banking centers in the world (ranked just behind number seven, Hong Kong).[22] Although Chinese modern banks from the beginning had only cursory financial relationships with foreign modern banks, which preferred to work with Chinese native bankers, the large foreign banking presence in both cities could not be ignored. Shanghai and Tianjin's status as world-class financial centers added prestige and cachet to the newly founded Chinese banks, which were closely patterned on foreign models.

Up to 1937, at least fifty-seven banks would have one or more offices in Tianjin, and new branches were opened in Tianjin until the mid-1930s. This level of activity made Tianjin second to Shanghai in terms of numbers of bank offices, although by the 1930s it was a distant second. After the Nationalist government moved the capital from Beijing to Nanjing in 1928, Beijing declined in importance as a banking center, while Shanghai and Nanjing grew. The Japanese invasion of Manchuria in 1931 reinforced this trend, leading to Shanghai's complete dominance of the domestic financial markets and to Tianjin's relative decline. In 1931, five new banking offices were opened in Tianjin and six in Shanghai. In the next two years no new bank offices were opened in Tianjin, although activity continued briskly in Shanghai, with six new offices in 1932 and fifteen in 1933. The move of the government from the north to the south and the Japanese invasion of Manchuria did not jeopardize Tianjin's position as China's second most important banking city, but it did amplify Shanghai's lead. Even more important, Nanjing joined the key Beijing-Tianjin-Shanghai nexus, which focused increasingly on Shanghai.[23]

By 1936 Tianjin had a total of 66 bank offices, compared to Shanghai's 182, Beiping's 59, and Nanjing's 53. These four cities, which made up the core of China's cosmopolitan urban network, had 360—or nearly one quarter—of the 1,496 bank offices in China. Other cosmopolitan cities like Hankou (33 offices), Chongqing (26), Qingdao (23), Guangzhou (22) and Hangzhou (21) had much smaller scales of activity, but together were home to another 8 percent of China's bank offices.[24]

Each of the bank offices in Tianjin was only one

node in larger supralocal bank organizations linking the cities and towns of China—especially the cities of the eastern coast—in a complex web of financial and personnel transactions. Banks ranked these nodes in hierarchical order, depending on their own structures and strategies. At the top, each bank had a headquarters or general office. Below that were branches in various important cities, and below them sub-branches and suboffices.[25] In table 4.1, I show how China's twenty-three most important banks ranked their offices in a number of cities in 1931 and 1936. I show the percentage of important banks that classified their highest-ranking office in a given city as a branch or higher. In the interests of brevity, I have included only cities in which more than 60 percent of the offices of these banks were branch level or higher in either 1931 or 1936.[26]

Table 4.1
Hierarchy of Branches of China's 23 Most Important Banks

	% of bank offices branches or above		Number of banks with offices in the city	
City	**1931**	**1936**	**1931**	**1936**
Shanghai	100	100	23	23
Tianjin	100	100	15	15
Chongqing	100	100	2	3
Xiamen	100	100	2	8
Guangzhou	100	50	2	4
Shenyang	100	50	1	2
Changsha	100	50	1	6
Liaoning	100	—	1	0
Hankou	87	93	15	15
Harbin	75	33	4	3
Beijing	72	69	11	13
Nantong	67	50	3	4
Nanjing	64	67	14	18
Qingdao	57	80	7	10
Chengdu	50	66	2	3
Jiujiang	33	100	3	1
Guiyang	—	100	0	1
Xi'an	—	66	0	3

Note: Table compiled from information in *Zhongguo zhongyao yinhang zuijin shi nian yingye gaikuang yanjiu* 1933 and *Yinhang nianjian* 1936.

As these statistics show, the number of bank offices in a city does not correlate directly to its ranking in the hierarchies of bank organizations. For example, only two of the twenty-three banks had offices in Chongqing in 1931, but both of those offices were at least branch level. Conversely, although Nanjing ranked third in number of bank offices by 1936, those offices tended to be ranked fairly low in the hierarchy. The dramatic decline by 1936 in numbers of branch-level offices for Shenyang, Liaoning, and Harbin graphically shows the impact of the Japanese occupation of Manchuria, which weakened links between cities in the northeast and the rest of China. In addition, the statistics show that banks ranked treaty ports like Guangzhou and Xiamen highly, in spite of low numbers of important banks with offices there.

Urban Systems and Bank Capital

Modern banks were not just networks of offices; they were also conglomerations of capital, and the location of a bank's general office indicated both the highest level in bank hierarchies and the primary node shareholders chose for the concentration of their capital. Individuals pooled their capital to found banks in Tianjin during two distinct periods. The first was the years 1903 to 1911, during the last decade of the Qing dynasty and as part of the so-called New Policies period. Three Chinese banks were founded with head offices in Tianjin in these years, and two of those were direct results of New Policies reforms under the Zhili governor-generalship of Yuan Shikai. After the 1911 Revolution there was a hiatus, with no new Tianjin banks until Yuan Shikai's death and the end of his regime in 1916. Prior to 1916, local banks remained small players in the Tianjin market, and seven of the eight most important Chinese banks in Tianjin were based in Beijing or Shanghai.[27]

In the second period there was a second flurry of activity, and twenty-three Tianjin banks were founded in the fifteen years between 1916 and 1932, most of those before the establishment of the Nationalist regime in 1928.[28] The complex relationship between warlords, officials, and bankers made Tianjin an attractive place to found a bank during the warlord period. On the one hand, many of the early investors in Tianjin banks were warlords and officials—like

Ni Sichong and Wang Zhilong of Jincheng Bank, interested not only in capitalizing on treaty-port prosperity, but in sheltering their money in the safety of the foreign concessions where most Tianjin banks had their offices. On the other hand, bank owners and managers saw the foreign concessions as a north China alternative to Beijing in order to minimize the demands that warlords in power might try to make on bank resources. Finally, Tianjin was a node in the personal networks of a group of men, many of whom were part of the network of official/managers involved in the reform projects of Li Hongzhang and Yuan Shikai, and who would become professional bankers in the Republic.

The native places of those who invested in Tianjin banks tell us a lot about Tianjin's emerging role in China's urban systems. Traditionally, the native place of businessmen acted to define the businesses in which they were engaged. Groups of businessmen from the same native place often made up a *bang* (clique), and regional specialization was especially prominent in native banking. Ningbo and Shanxi both were famous for their traditional bankers. In Tianjin, Jiangxi porcelain merchants and Fujian sugar traders provide two examples of regional specialization.[29] Modern banks, unlike traditional Chinese financial institutions, were joint stock corporations, and they often had many owners who did not live in the same place or have a common native place.

Non-Tianjin natives owned most of the banks with head offices in Tianjin, and many of the Tianjiners who did invest in the city did not live there.[30] Tianjin natives who actually lived in the city founded only four banks there. In the first period before 1911, Tianjin merchants had provided part of the money for the semi-official Zhicheng Bank; and the Cultivation Bank (Zhiye Bank), founded in 1911, was funded and run by the Li family, one of Tianjin's "Eight Great Families." In the second period, from 1916 to 1932, the Tianjin merchant Chen Jinding owned the Zhongguo Sicha (silk and tea) Bank, and the compradores Wei Xinchen and Du Kechen founded Yujin Bank.[31] In the period after 1916 a group of Tianjin natives who had found fame and fortune in Yuan Shikai's Beiyang Army and lived elsewhere because of their service in the military began investing in Tianjin banks. Not every Beiyang militarist who invested in banks in Tianjin was a native of Tianjin, however. The most obvious example is the military governor of Anhui Province, Ni Sichong, who was the lead investor in Jincheng Bank. In addition, even when Tianjin natives like Feng Guozhang invested in banks in Tianjin, they often did so in concert with merchants from other parts of China. In Feng Guozhong's case, he founded Continental Bank along with a group of Lianghuai salt merchants from Jiangsu (where Feng had served as military governor).[32] There was something about Tianjin that made it possible for people from various backgrounds to come together in a common business enterprise in patterns different from those used by traditional sojourning merchants. In banking, Tianjin did not function either as an arena where Tianjin natives cooperated with each other or as a node for sojourning native-place *bangs*. Instead, it served as a place where diverse groups of people, including Tianjin natives living there, Tianjin natives not living there, and non-Tianjin natives, could come together as stockholders in joint stock companies engaged in modern banking. These groups of stockholders were diverse in native place, residence, and profession and included Beiyang militarists, officials, and merchants.

To say that banks could not easily be divided into *bang* based on native place, however, is not to say that there were no patterns in the groups that came together to fund banks. The alliance of Jiangsu salt merchants and Feng Guozhang—who had been an official in Jiangsu but who was in Beijing at the time—to found Continental Bank in Tianjin is a case in point. The bank was able to capitalize (literally) on Feng Guozhang's connections to both Tianjin and Jiangsu. It was such overlapping networks, many related to government officials, that provided the capital to found banks with their home offices in Tianjin. Although the networks were complex, two primary groups can be distinguished. Already mentioned was the group related to Beiyang militarists. Less well studied (in terms of cliques and networks) was a second group of quasi-official managers—mostly from Zhejiang, Anhui, Jiangsu, and Henan—who were related to the reformist administrations of the late Qing Zhili governor-generals Li Hongzhang and Yuan Shikai. Many of the families of these official/managers had come to Tianjin to work for Li Hongzhang in the late nineteenth century, and a large number of southerners came north to work for the Bank of China and the Bank of Communications in Beijing during the first two decades of the twentieth century. Tianjin was a major node in the networks of both the Beiyang militarists and these southern official/managers, making it a preferred place to establish banks prior to the Nationalist period.

Shanghai and Tianjin were both treaty ports, but in spite of many similarities, the cities attracted capital from different groups. Like Tianjin, Shanghai's foreign concessions and active commercial economy attracted both large numbers of sojourners and many Chinese modern banks. Also like Tianjin, Shanghai was the seat of late Qing-period reforms, in some measure under the sponsorship of Li Hongzhang, and the networks involved with those reforms played an integral part in the rise of banking in Shanghai. For example, China's first modern bank, the Commercial Bank of China, was founded with a head office in Shanghai by Li Hongzhang's protégé, Sheng Xuanhuai. Other Shanghai banks founded as part of the late Qing reform movement include Zhejiang Industrial Bank, originally part of the official/merchant Zhejiang Provincial Bank; the National Commercial Bank, originally founded to fund railroad construction in Zhejiang; and Zhonghua Commercial and Savings (Shangye Chuxu) Bank, founded under Sun Yat-sen's sponsorship during his short-lived provisional government of 1912.[33] Unlike Tianjin, Shanghai was not the center of the Beiyang Army military reforms, but it was a major focus of the operations of Ningbo native banks. As a result, few militarists invested in Shanghai's banks; their capital came predominantly from Jiangnan financial, commercial, and industrial elites, especially Zhejiang native bankers.[34] Absent was the powerful presence of Beiyang militarists whose capital contributed so much to the rise of Chinese banking in Tianjin after 1916.

Investment patterns in Shanghai and Tianjin banks also varied with the political situation in China. As Shanghai became the dominant focus of bank branch networks in the late 1920s and 1930s, changes in the locations in bank general offices, the highest level of their administrative hierarchy, were more pronounced than changes in branch networks as a whole. In 1925, Shanghai had about twice as many bank headquarters as Tianjin (thirty-three and fourteen, respectively), and even Beijing, home of the state banks, hosted the headquarters of twenty-three banks. By 1934 banks headquartered in Shanghai outnumbered those in Tianjin by six to one (fifty-nine and ten, respectively), and banks with Beiping headquarters had shrunk to only two.[35] The relocation of bank general offices took place in two phases. In the first phase, after 1928, the Guomindang government moved the massive state banks, like the Bank of China and the Bank of Communications, to Shanghai, and at the same time one private Beijing bank moved to Tianjin as part of the exodus. In conjunction with these moves, another large private bank moved its general office to Tianjin from Qingdao, furthering the concentration of bank capital in Shanghai and Tianjin during the first few years of the Guomindang period. In the second phase, beginning after the Manchurian incident in 1931 and continuing through 1935, bank capital fled Tianjin to Shanghai. Not only did no major new banks establish their general offices in Tianjin after 1932, four of Tianjin's largest banks actually moved their head offices from Tianjin to Shanghai.[36] By 1935, banking capital had concentrated in Shanghai to an unprecedented degree, with Tianjin a distant second, as shown in table 4.2.

Table 4.2
Capital of China's 23 Most Important Banks by Location of General Office, 1921-1935

	1921		1928		1935	
	Capital (000's)	%	Capital (000's)	%	Capital (000's)	%
City						
Beijing	31,029	51.9%	3,000	2.8%	0	0.0%
Tianjin	10,291	17.2%	22,575	20.9%	3,791	1.7%
Shanghai	17,234	28.8%	81,184	75.3%	221,305	97.9%
Qingdao	200	0.3%	0	0.0%	0	0.0%
Chongqing	1,000	1.7%	1,000	0.9%	1,000	0.4%
Total	**59,754**	**100.0%**	**107,759**	**100.0%**	**226,096**	**100.0%**

Note: The 1921 and 1928 statistics in table 4.2 are adapted from Zhongguo yinhang, *Zhongguo zhongyao yinhang;* and the 1935 statistics (the last year for which complete statistics are available prior to the Japanese invasion) are adapted from *Yinhang nianjian 1936.*

The shift of the capital after 1927 and the growing Japanese threat after 1931 changed the way supralocal systems overlapped, and many of the advantages initially present in Tianjin disappeared. As these systems shifted south, so did Tianjin's banks, demonstrating great organizational flexibility in the face of a changing economic and political environment.

Three factors made this flexibility possible. First, the supralocal structure of the banks themselves and their large branch networks provided a large number of nodes from which to choose the location of the banks' main offices. Second, the relative dispersal of high-level urban areas in China provided a number of possible locations for the concentration of capital. Prior to the 1930s, no one city was dominant, making shifts among more or less evenly ranked cities possible. Third, like Zhou Zuomin of Jincheng Bank, who ran his Tianjin bank from Beijing before moving it to Shanghai in 1935, bank managers made up a cosmopolitan elite not tied to any one city. Rather, they circulated in the supralocal urban system, and it is to the urban identities of these cosmopolitan bankers that we must now turn.

Elites, Elite Organizations, and Bankers in Tianjin and Shanghai

My discussion of the Tianjin bankers and their Shanghai counterparts will focus on the related themes of local identity and the city's place in supralocal systems. All scholars recognize that the leading merchants in most Chinese cities were often sojourners from other provinces, but there has been significant debate over the extent to which these sojourners identified with their city of residence. William Rowe has argued that a local urban identity began to emerge in Hankou in the nineteenth century. As he states, "[I]n terms of functional participation, at least, the city's leading sojourner merchants represented themselves as fully integrated members of a Hankow [Hankou] community."[37] In contrast, based on her study of Shanghai, Bryna Goodman has argued that the continuing importance of native place has been understated by Rowe in the English language literature and by many Japanese and Chinese scholars.[38] Likewise, in her study of Shanghai modern bankers, Marie-Claire Bergère argued that native place was an important factor in both the Shanghai Bankers' Association and the development of a Zhejiang clique of financiers that stretched from Shanghai to Tianjin and Beijing.[39]

Contrary to Rowe, I argue that Tianjin's twentieth-century bankers, although urban, exhibited little or no local identity. They were a group of cosmopolitan elites with close ties to supralocal networks and a strong sense of professionalism, both of which militated against any purely local identity. Although I agree with both Bergère and Goodman on the fundamental importance of native place, I will argue against Bergère's claim regarding the primacy of Zhejiang natives (in both Tianjin and Shanghai); bankers did not organize along single native-place lines. Instead, blocs of people from different native places cooperated with each other in historically and institutionally produced cosmopolitan patterns.[40]

Just as Rowe's argument for a local Hankou identity looks primarily at merchant behavior, I will examine the behavior of bankers for clues to the extent of Tianjin bankers' identification with the city. Tianjin's bankers were stretched between forces that pulled them to look outward from Tianjin—like the supralocal structures of banks and national networks of bankers—and forces that pulled them inward—like the need to defend the local economy from excessive state extractions. Negotiations between the Tianjin Bankers' Association and warlords reveal bankers as a group engaging in practices that might conform to Rowe's definition of local functional practices, but they engaged in these practices as representatives of their supralocal banking organizations, not as locals defending their home turf. They carefully balanced local and supralocal considerations by promoting professionalism as the basis for bank management and banker solidarity, and this very balance precluded a strong local identity on the part of bankers. In addition, as individuals, their career paths, residential patterns, and lifestyles all point to a supralocal, cosmopolitan orientation.

Bankers, Bankers' Associations, and Native Place

Bankers, like the banks they worked for, had hierarchies. At the top, a general manager or president ran the affairs of the bank headquarters. For banks with general offices in Tianjin, their presidents, like Zhou Zuomin, did not necessarily live in the city. One level down, branch managers *(jingli)* ran the local branch operations and supervised a range of assistant managers and other officers who helped at the main branch or who ran the sub-branches and suboffices. The Tianjin managers of the local branches lived in the city, sometimes in exalted style.[41] Cao Yu's portrait of the bank manager Pan Yueting in his play *Sunrise* parodied the luxury of bankers. Pan Yueting is

> a massive creature swathed in silk with greying hair and ponderous movements. . . . His eyes are narrow slits and his nose like a Pekinese dog's; he has a thin drooping mustache, a large mouth, and a gold tooth that gleams ostentatiously when his lips part in a jocular smile. He is wearing a dark brown gown with otter-fur with a sleeveless satin jacket over it, hung with a gold watch-chain and an emerald pendent.[42]

This grotesque creature may have served Cao Yu's critique of urban China, but it did little to reflect reality. A large number of Tianjin's bank managers had studied in Japan or the United States, and most consciously patterned themselves after foreign businessmen. By the 1930s, many had adopted Western business suits. In addition, Cao Yu does not mention Pan Yueting's native place; for Cao, Pan's class and occupation were more important than his place of origin. If he was a typical Tianjin bank manager, however, he was most likely not a Tianjin native. Of the fifty-two managers and presidents whose native places are known, thirteen (25 percent) came from Tianjin, twelve (23 percent) came from Jiangsu, seven (13 percent) came from Zhejiang, six (12 percent) came from Liaoning, and five (10 percent) came from Anhui.[43]

At its founding in 1918, the Tianjin Bankers' Association reflected both the supralocal links among Beijing, Tianjin, and Shanghai and the great diversity in the native place of Tianjin bankers. The initial members of the Tianjin Bankers' Association included five banks with headquarters in Beijing, five with headquarters in Tianjin, and one Shanghai bank. Throughout its history, the Tianjin Bankers' Association included many banks headquartered elsewhere, and Tianjin banks never composed a majority of members.[44] When the Tianjin Bankers' Association was founded in 1918, the primacy of professional community over locality and native place was a new phenomenon among Tianjin merchant associations. Only in 1921 would sojourning and local grain merchants combine their guilds into one. Native bankers were even more parochial. Although the traditional practice separating ownership from management in native banks provided the potential for professional, rather than native place, organization, prior to 1930 only *yinhao* that were part of the Tianjin clique *(bang)* were allowed into the Tianjin Native Bankers' Association. Tianjin natives dominated the Tianjin Chamber of Commerce for much of its early history, and its leadership became only slightly more diversified during the 1920s, when non-Tianjin natives, many of them modern bankers, increased from 7 percent to 18 percent of the leadership group.[45] Banks could join the bankers' association based only on their professional identity, however, and the native place of their managers or owners was not a consideration.

In her ground-breaking work, Bergère has argued that the success of the Shanghai Bankers' Association was in part based "on the relations that modern bankers maintained with the regional associations *(bang)* and professional guilds established by the traditional bankers during the previous years."[46] This is indeed true, and probably more true for Shanghai than Tianjin, but the relationship between native place and the Shanghai Bankers' Association was not as simple as she asserts. Like the Tianjin Bankers' Association, its Shanghai counterpart needs to be understood in terms of the urban system of which Shanghai was a part and in terms of the historical patterns of cooperation among certain native place groups.

As in Tianjin, the Shanghai Bankers' Association was formed by banks with head offices in a number of cities. When founded in 1917–1918, the Shanghai Bankers' Association included three Beijing banks, one Tianjin bank, and four Shanghai banks. This group represented the close links among the three cities in the pre-1928 period and the lack of a single dominant financial center. The supralocal structures of banks linked Shanghai to the other cosmopolitan cities of China, and the power of these banks did not come from any one city alone. In fact, five banks—the Bank of China, the Bank of Communications and the Salt Bank (head offices in Beijing), the National Commercial (Zhejiang xingye) Bank (Shanghai), and Zhongfu Bank (Tianjin)—were charter members of both the Tianjin and Shanghai Bankers' Associations.[47]

In light of this cosmopolitanism, the role of native place solidarities in the Shanghai Bankers' Association needs further examination. Although Bergère claims that the Zhejiang-Jiangsu financial clique "for more than a century had controlled Shanghai (traditional) banking activities," all of the traditional bankers she lists came from Zhejiang, not Jiangsu. In fact, there had been a long connection between the Ningbo (Zhejiang) guild and the Shanghai Native Bankers' Association, but there is no evidence of a century-old clique combining Zhejiang and Jiangsu native bankers. Jiangsu sojourners did not become an important group in Shanghai business circles until the late 1870s.[48] Elsewhere, Bergère has noted that Shanghai's Zhejiang and Jiangsu bankers came from very different backgrounds. Whereas Zhejiang modern bankers were from entrepreneurial, especially native banking, families, Jiangsu modern bankers were "[b]orn into the families of minor elites in circumstances of moderate ease."[49] Her discussion of a single Zhejiang-Jiangsu clique in the Shanghai Bankers' Association ignores this important difference and places too much stress on native place as a foundation for solidarity between groups of Zhejiang and Jiangsu bankers.

Bergère asserts that "by virtue of personal and business relations, the Jiangsu modern bankers were considered to belong to the Zhejiang financial clique," and "[a]lso integrated into the Zhejiang clique were some bankers from Anhui province, such as Sun Yuanfang."[50] She implies that native place brought these bankers together, although it is not clear exactly how this happened. It is not necessary to make these Jiangsu and Anhui bankers "honorary" Zhejiang natives in order to understand the role of local solidarities in the Shanghai Bankers' Association. In Shanghai, as in Tianjin, groups of Anhui, Jiangsu, and Zhejiang elites cooperated with each other in patterns dating back to the reform organizations of the self-strengthening period. Banks and the bankers' associations of the twentieth century simply provided a new set of institutional structures for that cooperation. In addition, those patterns of cooperation stretched beyond the local arenas of particular cities, and the solidarity of the Zhejiang-Jiangsu financial clique grew from supralocal urban networks as well as local bases of power. For example, several Tianjin bankers (like Zhou Zuomin) were also members of the so-called Zhejiang-Jiangsu financial clique.[51]

Modern banking in both Tianjin and Shanghai grew from the reform movements in the late Qing period, and the networks based on those reform projects contained large numbers of elites from Zhejiang, Jiangsu, and Anhui. Bergère has observed that "[t]hrough family- and native-tie connections, Jiangsu and Anhui entrepreneurs had developed relations with the Beiyang reformers and bureaucratic capitalists of the last imperial decade and the early republican period."[52] I would extend Bergère's observation to an even earlier period, to the rise of cosmopolitan elites in Shanghai and Tianjin during the self-strengthening period of the 1870s and 1880s. Bergère raises the example of the Sun family, which founded Zhongfu Bank. Sun Duosen was related to the Beiyang clique through service to Yuan Shikai in Tianjin during the New Policies period. His father, however, was an official in Li Hongzhang's "tent" government, and Sun Duosen's mother was the daughter of Li's older brother.[53] Zhongfu Bank was a founding member of both the Shanghai and Tianjin Bankers' Associations, and the influence of the Sun family in both cities can be traced directly to the important role of Li Hongzhang in both Shanghai and Tianjin in the late nineteenth century.[54]

Founded in Beijing in the first decade of the twentieth century, the Bank of China (originally Hubu, then Da Qing, Bank) and the Bank of Communications continued the connections among Zhejiang, Jiangsu, and Anhui people. Ye Jingkui, a Zhejiang native, spent time as head of Da Qing Bank. Later he went on to run the National Industrial Bank, which was headquartered in Shanghai, and he was a founding member of both the Shanghai and Tianjin Bankers' Associations. Likewise, Sun Duosen was head of the Bank of China shortly after the 1911 Revolution. At that time he reported to Zhou Xuexi (an Anhui native who had worked for Yuan Shikai in Tianjin and whose father had worked for Li Hongzhang, and who would go on to found one of Tianjin's banks), finance minister under Yuan Shikai.[55] In fact, almost all of Tianjin's important bankers, like Zhou Zuomin, trained at one of these two banks, as did many of Shanghai's bankers: Song Hanzhang (Zhejiang), Zhang Jia'ao (Jiangsu), and Qian Yongming (Zhejiang). This common service in the supralocal organizations of the Bank of China and the Bank of Communications tied Beijing, Tianjin, and Shanghai bankers to each other. For example, the managers of the Shanghai Zhongnan Bank, the Beijing Salt Bank, and the Tianjin Jincheng and Continental Banks—the Northern Four—had all trained at either the Bank of China or the Bank of Communications.

Starting from the late 1910s, the local, urban-based organizations of the Shanghai and Tianjin Bankers' Associations—like the supralocal structures of government-sponsored reform in the late nineteenth century and the state-run banks during the first decade of the twentieth century—created a vehicle for the continued cooperation of Zhejiang, Jiangsu, and Anhui elites. In addition, foreign trained and inspired, bankers consciously adopted professionalism as a goal. A cultural ethos of professional banking emerged that went beyond traditional categories of business organization. At the same time, supralocal urban systems and elite networks came to define modern banks far more than locality or native place affiliations.[56] By the 1920s, bankers' professional ethos—combined with established patterns of cooperation among blocs of native-place associates—allowed the modern bankers of Shanghai and Tianjin to work together for financial and political reform on a national level and negotiate crises on the local level.[57] This same professionalism and cosmopolitanism defined the behavior of modern bankers.

Banker Behavior

Elite bank managers were tied into two overlapping sets of supralocal systems: the banks they worked for and the network of cosmopolitan elites. Their lifestyles amply demonstrated these supralocal ties. As employees in nationwide organizations, they often transferred from city to city as they accepted different assignments and worked their way up the corporate ladder. In addition, bankers often traveled as part of their jobs, not just from one job to another. For example, in the 1910s and 1920s, the Tianjin branch manager of the Bank of China made at least one, if not two, trips to Shanghai each year and traveled to Beijing at least once a month. As he traveled along the Beijing-Tianjin-Shanghai nexus, he met and talked with colleagues from his bank, as well as with friends from other banks and with nonbankers. Each time he took a train or a boat from one of these three cities to the other, he encountered someone he knew. When he was in Tianjin, a steady stream of colleagues and acquaintances passed through on their way between Shanghai and Beijing. His children, when they were small, went to a local school in Tianjin, but as they grew up they moved on to prep schools and colleges in Beijing, Shanghai, and even in the United States. In fact, Beijing's function as an educational center continued to link it closely to other cosmopolitan cities, even after its importance as a banking center declined.

In addition to circulating frequently among China's cosmopolitan cities, bankers also took advantage of the local cosmopolitan amenities in the cities where they lived. The Tianjin manager of the Bank of China took daily walks in parks, visited foreign book stores, went to the movies once or twice a week (sometimes with family and sometimes with other bankers), and even joined the Tianjin Rotary Club (most of whose members were Americans living in China). He enjoyed such cosmopolitan amenities at home or on the road. In Tianjin he took his daily walks in the French Concession park, while in Beijing he strolled in Zhongshan Park. In the parks, as on the trains, he regularly encountered friends and colleagues. He was part of a group of cosmopolitan elite bankers, at home within the supralocal structures of modern banks and within the cosmopolitan cities where those banks were located.[58]

Bankers' mobility, foreign education, and ability to operate within time-established patterns of cooperation among certain Zhejiang, Jiangsu, and Anhui elites all indicate a cosmopolitan and supralocal identity. For them, living and working in Tianjin, Beijing, or Shanghai (or perhaps Hankou or later Nanjing) was not a coincidence. These cities were the nodes of the urban system that supported the self-strengthening organizations of the late nineteenth century and the modern banks of the twentieth century. At the same time, the decision to live and work in one of these cities did not result from a particular local identity; the urban network itself and the cosmopolitan amenities in these cities attracted these elites. Over the course of his life, Zhou Zuomin moved from Anhui to Guangzhou and then to Japan for his education. Returning to China, his career took him from Nanjing to Beijing to Anhui, back to Beijing (where he lived while running a Tianjin bank), and then on to Shanghai. He sojourned at different nodes within a cosmopolitan urban system, not within one particular city. Interestingly, sojourning in major cities was a permanent state for Zhou Zuomin, and, to my knowledge, he never returned to his native Huai'an. It is difficult to know what psychological attachment he may have had to his native home, but his pattern of residence was indisputably urban and cosmopolitan.[59]

Nonetheless, for all their mobility, cosmopolitan bankers usually lived in only one city at a time, and sometimes in the same city for many years. They participated in many local philanthropic and social organizations, and their education, status, and access to financial resources marked them as prominent members of the local elite. Their activities in the local bankers' associations probably came closest to what Rowe calls "functional participation" in the cities where they lived. These associations were named after particular cities (e.g., the Tianjin Bankers' Association, Shanghai Bankers' Association, etc.), and their membership was composed of and defined by that city's bank offices and bankers. To test the extent to which participation in the Tianjin Bankers' Association resulted in a local identity, I will examine one of its most important activities: negotiation with warlords.

Tianjin was not just a node in a supralocal urban system; it was also a unit for the extractive activities of government and military officials. From the standpoint of the warlord in control of Zhili Province, Tianjin banking was embodied in the Tianjin Bankers' Association, and it was to that association that warlords often turned for loans to finance their regimes. Tianjin's bankers, through the bankers' association, negotiated collectively in order to increase their leverage in the face of warlord military power. Loans would then be parceled out to members based on a formula reflecting the hierarchy of banks within the association. The largest shares of the loans would be taken by the two state banks: the Bank of China and the Bank of Communications. The so-called Northern Four each would take a smaller but substantial share. The remaining portions of the loan would then be parceled out in nominal amounts to the remaining twelve or so members. Bankers readily exhibited their supralocal orientation. Once the amount of each bank's share was determined, the Tianjin branch of that bank would ask its own head office (often outside of the particular warlord's realm of power) for approval to make the loan, and head office disapproval was often used as a bargaining point to reduce warlord demands.[60]

As seen in such loans to warlord governments, the Tianjin Bankers' Association functioned in two ways. First, it provided an organizational manifestation for a "Tianjin banking community" with which warlord governments could negotiate, and second, it provided a forum in which supralocal banks could coordinate their local affairs. Thus in spite of the supralocal structures of modern banks, in the realm of state-society relations, there was indeed something termed Tianjin banking that could be called on to fund state projects. Flexible as usual, bankers worked through the Tianjin Bankers' Association to negotiate as a local civic group and also used the supralocal nature of Tianjin banks to limit government extraction. Bankers, like most people, had shifting urban identities. Depending on a given situation, they could claim either the urban arena or the supralocal urban system as their identity. The bulk of the evidence indicates, however, that their supralocal, cosmopolitan identities were never far in the background and that their primary identity was urban more than local.

Conclusion

The cosmopolitan city provided a node where supralocal networks of elites and organizations came together in the founding of modern banks. The diffuse nature of China's urban system allowed for the development of a number of banking centers, with none completely dominant before 1928. No one city could lay claim to being China's preeminent financial center, and bankers circulated freely among various cities without establishing overriding local identities with the cities in which they sojourned. Solidarities like native place, although important, served as only one basis for organization, and it was blocs of native-place groups that comprised the ranks of the so-called Zhejiang-Jiangsu financial clique. The supralocal structures of bank organization and the behavior of foreign-trained bankers, in turn, reinforced and extended the cosmopolitanism of the cities in which they operated.

In spite of similarities and close links among China's cosmopolitan cities, each one had its own local characteristics that contributed to the nature of modern banking. Shanghai was dominated by sojourning merchant elites who also played a role in the development of modern banking. Tianjin was dominated by native merchant elites who played only a limited role in the development of modern banking. In Shanghai, Zhejiang native bankers actively invested in modern banking; in contrast, Tianjin native bankers did not. Tianjin thus differed from Shanghai both in the general environment of the city, where the strong presence of native Tianjin merchants contrasted with the roles of sojourners in Shanghai, and in the kinds of networks formed by outsiders who came together in those urban environments. In both, the networks based on Qing-period official/managers from Anhui, Jiangsu, and Zhejiang were important. These official/managers combined with Beiyang militarists and Beijing officials to found banks in Tianjin, and with Zhejiang native bankers and Jiangsu industrialists to found banks in Shanghai. The state's important role in sponsoring reform organizations during the self-strengthening and New Policies periods fostered cooperation among these elites and intensified the links among cosmopolitan cities.

The state role came into play again after 1928, when the Guomindang victory reduced Beijing's importance as a financial center while increasing activity in Tianjin, Nanjing, and, especially, Shanghai. A few years later, the Japanese invasion of Manchuria again altered the balance among these cities, as capital and bankers moved to Shanghai. In the 1930s, Shanghai emerged as the dominant node in the system of cosmopolitan bankers. The nonlocal orientation of bank elites made this new configuration possible, as bankers shifted from one city to another.

My analysis here has focused on the particularity of banks and relationships to local urban arenas and supralocal urban networks in the early twentieth century. The form of my analysis, based on the contention that cities need to be understood in relation to both their local and supralocal functions, can be applied to other cases and other time periods as well. Although I disagree with his assumptions about the discreteness of administrative and economic systems, Skinner was correct when he said that "cities were at once embedded in society and essential to its overall structure."[61] The techniques of such an analysis could be applied to China's cities in other periods with fruitful results. In Tianjin, further investigation of the role of such supralocal systems as those centered on the Grand Canal or Shanxi native bankers would enhance our understanding of late imperial period cities. Likewise, Rowe's work on Hankou, which focused on urban behavior within the arena of the city, could be reassessed in light of Hankou's place in urban networks and in light of the state's role in shaping such urban networks. Like Tianjin and Shanghai, Hankou was a center of self-strengthening reforms in the late nineteenth century and a node in the network of cosmopolitan banking centers in the twentieth century.[62]

Finally, my analysis here falls short of considering the full impact of changes in urban networks and conceptions of urbanism in the 1930s. The effect of Shanghai's rise to dominance as a financial, although not political, center of urban systems and urban elite identity needs further exploration. This rise coincided with the creation of a Shanghai city government by the Guomindang in 1927, after which time Goodman begins to see "specifically urban practices which might provide a basis for the formation of Shanghai identity."[63] Likewise, Tianjin's increasing isolation under the shadow of the Japanese threat may have led bankers there to identify more closely with the city in which they lived.

In addition, the relationship—imagined and real—between cities and the countryside began to change in the

1930s, and I have no space to consider the full implications of such changes. For Cao Yu and other leftist writers, the republican period cosmopolitan city typified corruption and degeneracy. For Cao Yu in particular, bankers composed one important part of the urban elite that exploited and deceived the common people and contributed to a general decline in morals. Cao Yu saw the salvation of the city as coming from the countryside. At the end of *Sunrise,* Fang Dasheng decides not to go back to the countryside, but to stay in the city to work on urban reform. In the final scene, sunlight (the "sunrise" of the play's title) floods into Chen Bailou's sordid urban hotel room, and Fang Dasheng tells her, "If you go on living like this you'll be digging your own grave. Now listen, why not go with me after all, instead of tying yourself to these people?" Unknown to Fang Dasheng, Chen Bailou has already taken an overdose of sleeping pills. Her ties to the urban creatures, the gangster Mr. Jin, and banker Pan Yueting have condemned her.

By the mid-1930s, China's modern banking elites, those most urban and modern of city residents, began to pay more attention to rural China, but in a reversal of Cao Yu's formula, they saw the salvation of the countryside as coming from the cities. Banks had, early on, established large networks of branches in the rural hinterlands, but in the mid-1930s they began to put these networks and their resources to work to promote agricultural development. This new attention to the countryside resulted from a conscious policy of the Nationalist government and the banks themselves in the wake of spreading rural depression. For example, the 1933 savings law required 20 percent of a bank's small deposits to be loaned out in the countryside.[64] Echoing Cao Yu's viewpoint, lower-level bank employees responded quite enthusiastically to this new focus on China's countryside. Their response suggested disenchantment with city life and its regimented work styles and an idealized vision of rural society. Young bank clerks in Shanghai "embraced the new rural orientation with enthusiasm and romanticized an image of bank employees working out in the open under village trees instead of on the top floor of a multi-story office building."[65]

By the mid-1930s, at both the elite and nonelite levels, China's modern bankers realized that the future of the cosmopolitan city lay not just with the supralocal systems of similar cosmopolitan cities, but also in a new relationship between urban areas and the countryside. How that relationship might have been reshaped under the influence of banks and bankers can only be the subject of speculation, since, within a few years of these initial experiments, the Japanese invasion turned China's cosmopolitan cities into the nodes of a system of occupation and control, cutting off the tentative efforts of urban bankers to reach out to the countryside. By the end of the war, revolutionary forces had acquired a momentum that would soon sweep aside the world of elite bankers and cosmopolitan cities. Only in the last decade, perhaps, do we see the reemergence of a new type of cosmopolitanism in the cities of coastal China.

Appendix
Urban Identity and Urban Networks

Bank	Office in Tianjin[1]	Head Office in Tianjin[2]	Owner Tianjin Native[3]	Manager Tianjin Native[4]	Member Tianjin Bank Assoc[5]
Bank of China	x				x
Bank of Communications	x				x
Beiping Shangye Bank*	x				
Beiyang Baoshang Bank	x			x	x
Bianye Bank	x	x			x
Dadong Bank*	x				
Dalu Bank	x	x	x	x	x
Daosheng Bank*	x	x			
Dasheng Bank	x	x		x	x
Daye Bank*	x	x			
Dayou Bank*	x	x			
Dazhong Bank	x	x			x
Dong San Sheng Bank	x				
Donglai Bank	x			x	x
Donglu Bank	x				
Dongya Bank*	x				
Fengye Bank*	x				
Gongyi Shangye Chuxu Bank*	x				
Guohua Yinhang	x				x
Guohuo Yinhang	x				x
Hebei Minsheng Bank*	x	x			
Hong Kong Guomin Bank	x				
Houde Shangye Bank*	x				
Huabei Bank*	x	x			
Huaida Bank*	x	x			
Huaxin Bank	x	x			
Jincheng Bank	x	x	x	x	x
Juxingcheng Bank	x				x
Kenye Bank	x	x			x
Minghua Bank	x				
Rehe Xingye Bank	x				
Shanghai Shangye Chuxu Bank	x				x
Shenzhou Shiye Bank*	x	x			
Tianjin Shangye Bank*	x	x			
Tianjin Shimin Yinhang	x	x			
Tianjin Xingye Bank*	x	x			
Wuzu Shangye Yinhang	x				
Xincheng Bank*	x				
Xinhua Shangye Chuxu Bank	x				x
Yanye Bank	x			x	x

Continued on next page

Appendix—Continued
Urban Identity and Urban Networks

Bank	Office in Tianjin[1]	Head Office in Tianjin[2]	Owner Tianjin Native[3]	Manager Tianjin Native[4]	Member Tianjin Bank Assoc[5]
Yitong Yinhang*	x				
Yuda Bank*	x				
Yujin Bank	x	x	x	x	
Zhejiang Xingye Bank	x				x
Zhibian Bank	x				
Zhicheng Bank	x	x	x		
Zhili Provincial Bank	x	x		x	
Zhiye Bank	x	x	x	x	x
Zhongfu Bank	x	x			x
Zhongguo Nonggong Bank	x				x
Zhongguo Shiye Bank	x	x		x	x
Zhongguo Sicha Bank	x	x	x		
Zhongguo Tongshang Bank	x				
Zhongnan Bank	x				x
Zhongyang Bank	x				
Zhongyuan Bank	x	x			
Zhongyuan Shiye Bank	x	x			
Total	**57**	**26**	**6**	**10**	**22**

*No information available on ownership or management (18 banks).

1. Many of the banks mentioned existed, or had Tianjin offices for only a short time.
2. Head offices were sometimes moved. A bank is included here if its head office was in Tianjin any time before 1937.
3. Banks are included if one major shareholder at the time of founding was a Tianjin native. Ownership structure of many of the smaller banks is unknown, so the actual number with Tianjin owners is probably higher.
4. Based on banks, the Tianjin branch of which had a native Tianjiner as manager at least once before 1937. Information on managers was primarily, although not exclusively, obtained from the archives of the Tianjin Bankers' Association. Thus native places of managers who were not members is usually unknown. Of sixty-two managers in my database who worked in Tianjin prior to 1937, native places have been identified for fifty-two. Their native-place breakdown is as follows: Tianjin 13 (25 percent); Jiangsu 12 (23 percent); Zhejiang 7 (13 percent); Liaoning 6 (12 percent); Anhui 5 (10 percent); Hebei other than Tianjin 2 (4 percent); Sichuan 2 (4 percent); Fujian 2 (4 percent); Henan, Guangdong, and Hunan each had one (2 percent each). Some banks had Tianjin managers more than once, but were included in the table only once.
5. Based on the 1936 membership list, 129-2-1053. Prior to 1928, the Zhili (Hebei) Provincial Bank was also a member of the Tianjin Bankers' Association.

Chapter 5

Railway City and National Capital

Two Faces of the Modern in Changchun

David D. Buck

Changchun began as a small Qing administrative and commercial town on the Manchurian frontier and became transformed through two Japanese projects to construct modern cities. After a short-lived Russian endeavor, the Japanese South Manchurian Railway (SMR) produced the first modern city at Changchun. Then, following the establishment of the puppet state of Manchukuo in 1932, Changchun became the site of a high modernist national capital city, Xinjing (Japanese *Shinkyō,* or New Capital). After 1937, Japan's wars delayed Xinjing's construction, preventing the completion of many key projects. Still, the Japanese at Xinjing managed to construct the main elements of a futuristic city on par with any high modernist plans from the pre-World War II era.[1]

In its first manifestation, as a railway city, Changchun represented the inland extension of the foreign-dominated treaty-port forms that so strongly shaped modern urbanism in China. As the planned capital city for the Japanese-controlled state of Manchukuo, Xinjing offered a futuristic model for a Japanese-controlled Asia. In both instances the Japanese planned and built to the contemporary world standards of urban life. Yet, today, because of the association with Japanese imperialism, these visions have almost disappeared from the Chinese and Japanese memory of the modern.

Unlike the Chinese efforts at constructing the modern discussed in the other chapters in this volume, at Changchun the Japanese dominated planning, although the city always had a majority Han Chinese population. The Japanese exercised control first through the semiofficial SMR and then through the government of Manchukuo. Some Chinese officials and businessmen tried to match the Japanese efforts but lacked the organization and resources to compete.

The SMR settlement at Changchun was part of Japan's informal empire in northeast China (Manchuria).[2] Transformed after 1932 into Xinjing, the city was intended as the chief exhibit displaying the magnanimous and progressive character of Japan's new leadership in Asia. It showed that Asia could be modern without relying on Europeans or Americans. This model of the 1930s reflected the dominance of the Japanese Imperial Army in Manchukuo and incorporated its ideals: state planning, control of the economy, a unified and obedient public, the exclusion of political parties, and a subordinate role for private capitalism.[3] Its creators hoped the model could be transferred back to Japan to purify the political and social corruption produced by party politics and private capitalism. Gwendolyn Wright has characterized a similar mode among French colonial planners in which they saw "the *outré-mer* as a terrain for working out solutions to some of the political, social, and aesthetic problems that plagued France."[4]

In imagining Xinjing, the Japanese city planners sought to create a capital city to represent the power and modernity of Manchukuo. Their vision invites comparison with the conceptions of the early twentieth century for a British colonial capital city at New Delhi, or Walter Burley Griffin's plan for the Australian national capital of Canberra, but it goes beyond those examples because the Japanese vision of Xinjing was backed by a conception of an authoritarian, scientific, and benevolent state lacking in both the British and Australian examples. James C. Scott has labeled this phenomenon as "high modernism" and defines it as "a particularly sweeping vision of how the benefits of technical and scientific progress might be applied—usually through the state—in every field of human activity."[5] Scott finds a strong predilection in late-colonial orders, such as the Japanese in northeast China, for what he calls "high modernist" cities in which "no compromise is made with the preexisting city, the new cityscape completely supplants its predecessor." Xinjing was a truly high modernist city where the scientific, utopian plans of architects, engineers, and administrators were backed by "the unrestrained power of the modern state."[6] Louise Young, in discussing Japanese urban planning in Manchukuo, uses a similar vocabulary. She characterizes the cities of Manchukuo and especially Xinjing as "a showcase of municipal splendor, projecting the power of the colonial state as the agent of modernity" and believes the Japanese "modernist utopia rested on the foundation of the absolute power of the colonial state."[7]

As the new national capital for Manchukuo arose after 1932, its layout, architecture, and landscaping all were meant as a high modernist construction, a proof that Asia could sustain the kind of life that was coming into existence in American and European cities, which included automobiles, spacious urban housing with electric appliances, as well as bold and beautiful buildings constructed from new materials and grand ceremonial centers to embody the power of the nation-state. The creators of Xinjing drew on the knowledge of Japanese bureaucrats, planners, and architects—men who had worked in Japan's formal and informal empire in Asia as well as those who had brought modern services to cities on the Japanese home islands. Manchukuo's "National Capital" (Chinese *guodu;* Japanese *kokuto*) was Japanese in origin, reflecting the European-influenced Japanese conceptions of the modern city. Chinese, along with Manchus, Koreans, and Mongols, made up the major ethnic groups in this new multinational state. All participated in building Manchukuo, but they played minor supporting roles to the Japanese.

Changchun as Frontier Town

Before the Sino-Japanese War of 1894–1895, Changchun existed as only a small walled trading town on the great expanse of Mongol grazing lands that lay west of the Willow Palisades. On the fertile Changchun plain, crossed by the Yitong and Yinma Rivers running northward into the Sungari, Chinese immigrant farmers created nuclear villages and planted their familiar crops, sorghum, soybeans, and wheat, while they kept oxen and horses for field and transportation work.

The trading community known as Changchun borrowed its name from one of the gates in the Willow Palisades constructed in the late seventeenth century to demarcate the Mongol grasslands from the Manchu's forest and mountain homelands. In 1825, the Qing administrative offices located at the gate moved some fifty kilometers to a small trading community on the Yitong River, previously known as Broadtown (Kuanchengzi), an informal name indicating the unimportance of the place. The name "Changchun" then became used for what had been Broadtown. The Qing officials and military there tried to maintain the uneasy peace between the increasing numbers of Chinese farmers and the seminomadic Mongolian communities who had previously been the dominant inhabitants.[8]

Following the Second Opium War, the economy of Manchuria changed when Yingkou, on the Gulf of Zhili, became a treaty port in 1860. The Qing dynasty abandoned its efforts to protect its Manchurian homelands, and trade along the Liao River flourished. The effects reached all the way to Changchun, which could be reached by rafts going up the eastern branch of the Liao River, where a portage of fifty kilometers was necessary before traveling downstream along the Yitong River to Changchun and beyond into the Sungari River system. This long-distance trade, often handled by Shaanxi merchants, flourished, and specialized merchants in banking, grain milling, oil pressing, and other lines of trade established themselves at Changchun. In the summer months the trade moved by small rafts along the rivers; in the winter the frozen rivers served as thoroughfares for ox- or horse-drawn carts fitted with runners.[9]

In 1865, the threat of local banditry led Changchun's merchants to underwrite the raising of an earthen defensive wall. Changchun's population probably was no more than twenty thousand in the 1870s and 1880s.[10] By 1885 the Qing state, increasingly conscious of the need to control more firmly its frontiers against foreign incursions, raised the chief official at Changchun to the grade of second-class sub-prefect *(fumin tongpan),* but this was still a frontier title indicating that the region was not regarded as part of the inner core of the Qing empire.

In the 1880s, Changchun's townspeople added

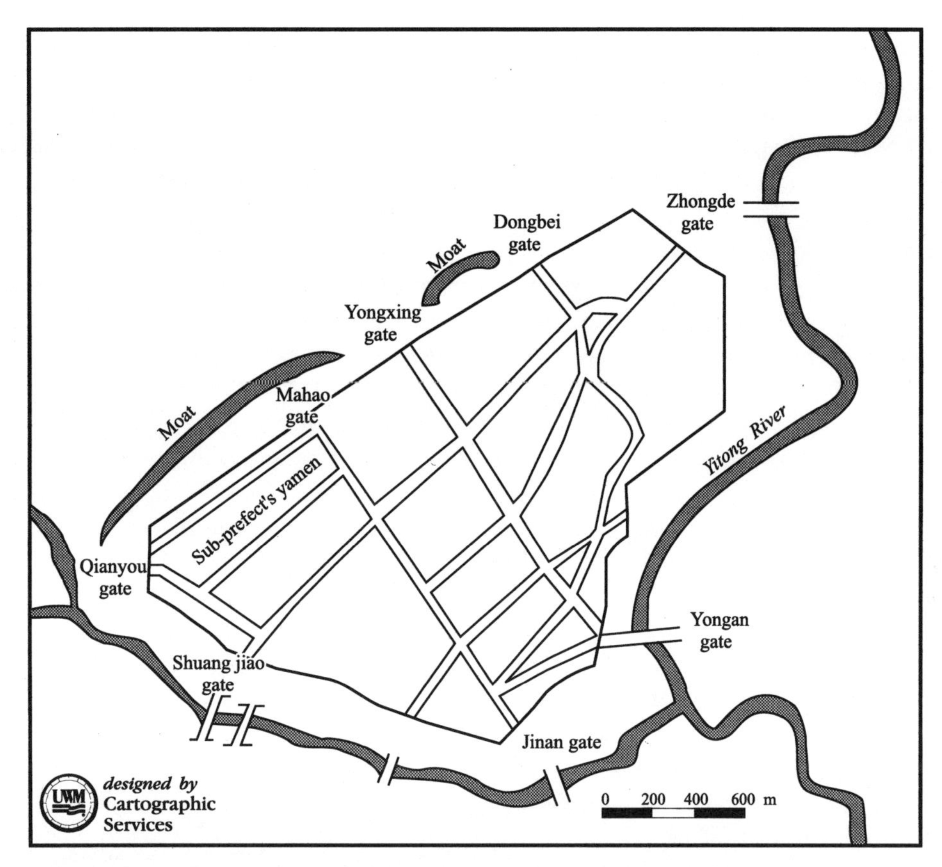

Map 5. Plan of walled city of Changchun, ca. 1900. Between 1890 and 1906 a number of Western-style buildings were constructed inside the walled city, including the Russo-Chinese Bank and French Catholic church, but their locations are unclear. After 1909, the Qing administration moved to new offices outside the walls in the newly opened Commercial District to the north. Redrawn based on a map from *Zhongguo jindai chengshi yu jianzhu* 1993, 261.

wooden planks to the mud brick walls encircling the town in an irregular pentagon shape fitting the natural topography of its location (see map 5). The main gates, such as the Exalted Virtue Gate *(chongdemen),* boasted elaborate "hat" structures reaching a height of fifteen meters. A British consul, Alexander Hosie, visited Changchun in January 1896 and found it a bustling place behind its mud walls with several kinds of handicraft manufacturing, including indigo dyeworks and felt making.[11]

The land around Changchun features long, undulating rises between which small streams flow on a seasonal or regular basis. At the site of the walled city of Changchun one of these small creeks met the Yitong River. North of the walled city ran two more such small stream beds; the one farther north, known as Second Creek (Erdaogou), became the site of the Russian railway town. The second, Big Creek (Toudaogou), closer to the old walled city, became incorporated into the Japanese SMR settlement. Later in the 1930s the Japanese planners who designed Xinjing followed the earlier example by making creek beds into parks. Thus these gullies had considerable influence on the layout of Changchun.

The first railway settlement at Changchun was Russian. The Russians began construction in 1898 of a work camp for the Russian and Chinese workers building the Chinese Eastern Railway. The Russians intended their railway settlement, which they called "Kuanchengzi,"[12] to be distinct and separate from the Chinese walled city of

Changchun. They built a station, railway shops, an employee's club, a chapel, a school, and some modest commercial buildings, along with some vernacular-style Russian homes. They kept out Chinese residents; at the same time, some Russian businesses took up offices in the walled city of Changchun. For example, the state-controlled Sino-Russian Bank (Hua-E daosheng yinhang) built a Russian-style office building inside the walled city.[13]

Linda Cooke Johnson has labeled this clear separation between Chinese and foreign communities at Shanghai a "dual city."[14] In Johnson's dual city, the foreigners dominate the waterfront (or the railway settlement in the interior), and the Chinese operate a largely separate city at a nearby location, oriented toward administrative considerations or premodern means of transportation. At Harbin, where the Russians remained in control after 1905, such a pattern did emerge, with clearly separate Russian and Chinese settlements.[15] In Changchun, both the Russian and Japanese settlements created a similar division. The SMR settlement featured many advanced urban amenities, including paved streets, electric lights, running water, and steam heat all before 1910, but it never was as segregated between Chinese and Japanese inhabitants as were Harbin and the Russian railway settlement at Changchun.

Along the SMR line the Japanese created "annexed land" *(fuzokuchi),* where they designed other towns with business considerations in mind.[16] Among Chinese cities changed by railroads, Changchun was unusual in that it had two different railway communities, one Russian and one Japanese, but both represented the new kind of settlement that appeared increasingly in China after 1895 as foreign railway companies began their penetration of China's hinterland. The railway city stands as a particular type of modern urban settlement. Especially in the Qing frontier regions that matched the climate and topography the North American Great Plains region, these railway towns resembled their North American counterparts.

Railroads and Cities in China and America

Because railroads had such a big, although delayed, impact on Chinese cities, a brief discussion is useful. In the case of Changchun, and indeed for most of China's northeast, the railroads built after 1895 had an impact comparable to that in the western parts of North America, both in the United States and Canada. In North America, the railroad began to transform cities in the 1840s, contemporaneous with the first development of treaty ports in China. In China, the impact of railroads on cities came some fifty-five years later.

Sun Yat-sen, China's great visionary leader of the early twentieth century, caught the spirit of the railroad's potential to transform China. In contrast to the existing foreign-controlled railways, Sun Yat-sen suggested huge state-owned and foreign-financed railway networks creating a tracery of iron across China equal in complexity to the North American railway system.[17] Sun Yat-sen's plans remained only dreams.[18]

Still, wherever railroads were built in China, they modified existing cities. For example, in Beijing after the Boxer Uprising, the foreigners insisted on construction of a railway station within the walled portions of the city, introducing an unmistakably modern and foreign presence into the Qing dynasty's capital city. Henri Borel, a Dutch official visiting Peking, observed:

> Thus appears Peking to me, the holy city of the Emperors, the Sons of Heaven, tarnished by the snobbery of white globe-trotters and loafers, who have forced themselves by the fuming, screeching train through its scared ramparts, which can no longer shield its virginity.[19]

Another example comes from Henan, where the Beijing to Hankou railroad was built across the North China plain, passing near the administrative town of Yancheng about 125 kilometers south of Zhengzhou. Yancheng contained a God of War *(Guandi)* temple, the county administrative office, the courts, and some new government offices. To the south, on the southern bank of the Le River, was the satellite walled port community of Lehezhen (literally, Le River Market). Because Lehezhen was closer to the railroad, it became the larger community, with more than ten thousand residents. Its streets were bustling, if dusty and unpaved, and its merchants prospered from the commercial activity associated with the railroad. Down to the present, Lehezhen overshadows Yancheng.

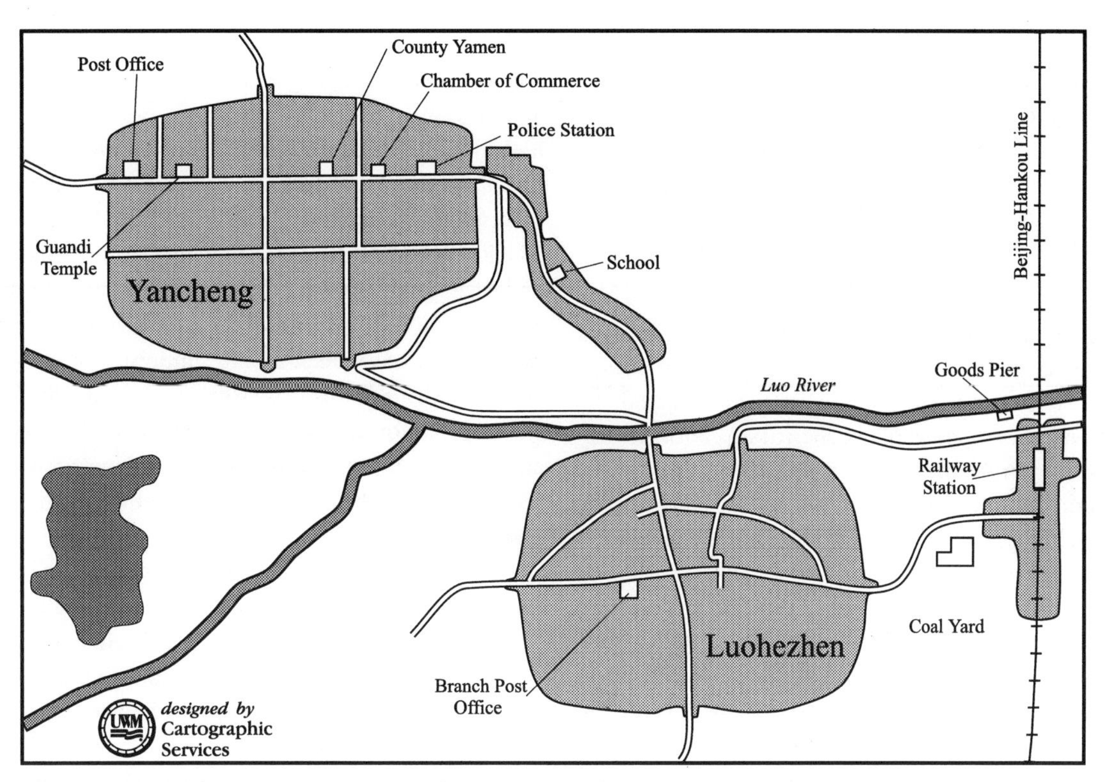

Map 6. Impact of railways on cities in North China, ca. 1915. The county-level administrative walled city of Yancheng; its commercial satellite Lehezhen, and the Beijing-Hankou Railway. Redrawn from *Shina shobetsu zenshi* (1917), vol. 4: *Henan*, 56.

Not every instance of railroad-derived change left behind such clear tracings in urban forms, but the sketch map shown here reveals neatly the pattern of change introduced by railroads in China.[20]

Within the Great Wall there are several other examples that could serve just as well, including Qingdao, Shijiazhuang, Zhengzhou, or even Kowloon (Jiulong). For example, Shijiazhuang, as its name, "stone house village," reveals, was an insignificant place on the North China plain that developed into a city only because of the railroad. Its rate of growth was rapid because it became a railway junction point where coal was moved from narrow- to standard-gauge trains.[21] Changchun, which was the transfer point between the Japanese and Russian roads, had a similar demand for porters to shift commodities and passengers between the rail lines of differing gauges. Kowloon, which lies across the harbor from Hong Kong island, became an important part of the British colony only when the 180-kilometer railroad linking it with Canton was completed in 1911. Railroads made the difference in a Chinese city's prospects for modernization.

China's northeast bears a strong resemblance geographically to the Great Plains region of the United States and Canada. The pattern of urban growth in this Chinese region after 1895 is quite similar to what occurred earlier across the Great Plains. My focus is on Changchun, but the same general situation was duplicated at Harbin, Mukden, and dozens of smaller railway towns planned and developed by the SMR along its route from 1906 through 1936.[22] John W. Reps has characterized the way in which railroads shaped urban settlement on the Great Plains as follows:

> In that portion of the Great Plains served by the Union Pacific and its rival lines to the north, virtually every important community owed its origins to a railroad townsite company. The railroads regarded

> the creation of towns and their promotion as an essential element of business enterprise. Not only did their creation afford splendid opportunities for quick profits on land sales, but their continued existence was vital in the development of passenger and freight traffic. Wherever possible, therefore, the railroad companies created their own communities.[23]

The railroad surveyors who laid out these towns preferred a simple regular grid pattern of streets, with the railway station in the central location. Important commercial and governmental buildings would be located in a business district adjacent to the railway station. Residential areas surrounded the commercial sections, with the housing usually located on higher ground where the best prevailing wind patterns kept away railroad or industrial smoke. Stockyards, mining facilities, or other local processing and industrial facilities would be located at a moderate distance from the main railway station at a site that, if possible, did not impinge too greatly on the attractiveness of the town center and residential areas.

Even more than for North American railway companies, the Russian Chinese Eastern Railway's (CER) (and later the SMR's) control was limited to its railway right-of-way and the railway towns along it. The railway and its railway towns became the chief symbols of foreign-induced change in inland China. We can see this in the urban construction endeavors undertaken by both the Russians and the Japanese in Manchuria and at Changchun.[24] Unlike the private North American railway companies, the Russian and Japanese railways were state controlled, meaning they could more efficiently and effectively impose a modern order than could private companies. These state-controlled railways functioned as semicolonial administrations focusing their attention primarily on the railway itself and the new railway settlements they built. Their new towns typically left the older walled Chinese-style settlements to continue separately.

Railway Towns in Northeast China

The two major Russian railway towns in the northeast were Harbin and Dalny (Japanese: Dairen; Chinese: Dalian). While Harbin remained a Russian-dominated city until 1932, Russia lost control over Dalny in the 1905 Russo-Japanese War. The Russian navy after 1903 had grandiose plans for Dalny, featuring a central section on high ground behind the harbor, complete with large park-like plazas and a grand boulevard derived from Baron Haussmann's reconstruction of Paris under Napoleon III.[25] The Russian plans divided Dalny into distinct zones: a port and wharf section serving the railroad; an administrative and business section north of the main station; a large and carefully laid out residential and administrative section focused on what the Russians called "Czar Nicholas Plaza" (Japanese: Ōhiroba, or Great Central Plaza), from which diagonal streets radiated outward; and a Chinese residential section south of the railroad and west of the main park (see map 7).[26]

Much of the implementation of the plan fell to the Japanese who, after 1906, made the city they called "Dairen" even more grand and impressive than the Russians had envisioned. The Japanese acquired a considerable leasehold on the Liaodong peninsula, known as the Kwantung Leased Territory (derived from the Chinese meaning "East of the Passes"), with its own Japanese administration and the Kwantung army, a special command of the Japanese Imperial Army. The Kwantung Leased Territory included both Dairen and the naval base at Port Arthur (Chinese: Lushun). Dairen served as the center for the Japanese on the Liaodong peninsula, with the headquarters of the SMR and the other key elements of Japanese expansion in the region, including, in addition to the Kwantung army, Japanese consular officials and big business conglomerates *(zaibatsu)*. Physically, elements of the Russians' plan—particularly the idea of large circular plazas cutting through the basic street grid with diagonal streets, and the construction of large parks on low ground—impressed SMR planners, who borrowed these elements when they laid out the new SMR railway settlements at Changchun and Mukden.

Kuanchengzi, the Russian Railway Town at Changchun

Since the Russians saw Changchun as a minor trading town, they did not need to lavish the kind of attention

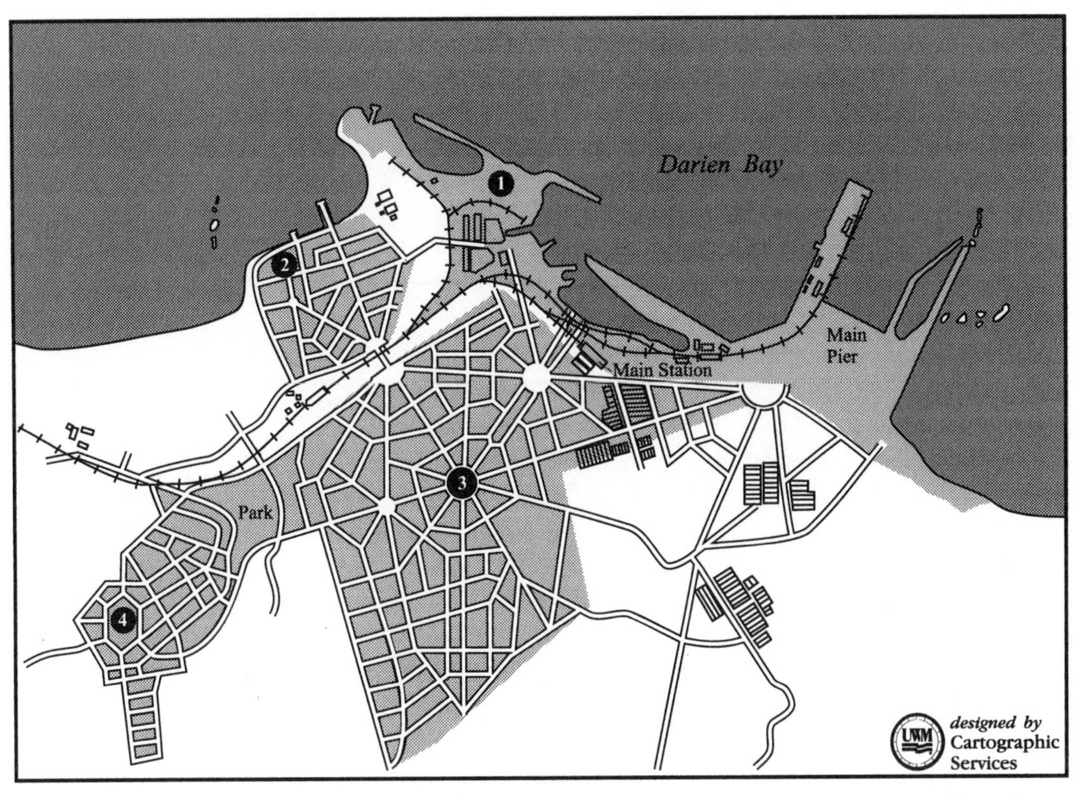

Map 7. Dairen's main functional zones: 1. Rail and port facilities. 2. Russian-built section, primarily commercial. 3. Russian-planned but largely Japanese-built section, with main offices around the Great Central Plaza (*Ōhiroba*, in Russian times known as Czar Nicholas Plaza) where the South Manchurian Railway built its headquarters and the Yamato Hotel. A large parkway leads to the main railway station near the piers. 4. Chinese district, separated by a park from the rest of the city. Redrawn from a plan dating from before 1920 in *Zhongguo jindai chengshi yu jianzhu* (1993), 236.

to its planning that they devoted to Dalny or Harbin. Changchun in the future might serve as the junction point for a railroad to the chief administrative city of Jilin, the region's most important city and the center of a growing lumber industry, located 120 kilometers east of Changchun in the mountains. The CER simply purchased about five square kilometers of land and laid out a small town in the form of a generally north-to-south rectangle on either side of the new railway line. Russian surveyors, like their North American counterparts, laid out the town streets in a grid pattern, east of the railway lines and north of Second Creek (Erdaogou). Railway yards and shops lay to the east and north (see map 8).[27]

In the summer of 1900, the anti-foreign attacks associated with the Boxers spread into Manchuria. At Changchun, groups of Boxers were composed of hastily assembled local farming youths and migrant laborers from Shandong and Zhili working on the railroad construction gangs, along with some soldiers from Qing military units. These groups attacked Russians in and around Kuanchengzi on several occasions in mid-July. The most serious attack occurred on July 15, when Boxers set fire to the new Russian railway station at Kuanchengzi, destroyed a Catholic church and missionary hospital within the walled city of Changchun, and attacked a Protestant mission chapel outside the city walls.[28] Such large-scale actions certainly must have received support from the local Qing garrisons at Nanling, although top officials in Jilin did not

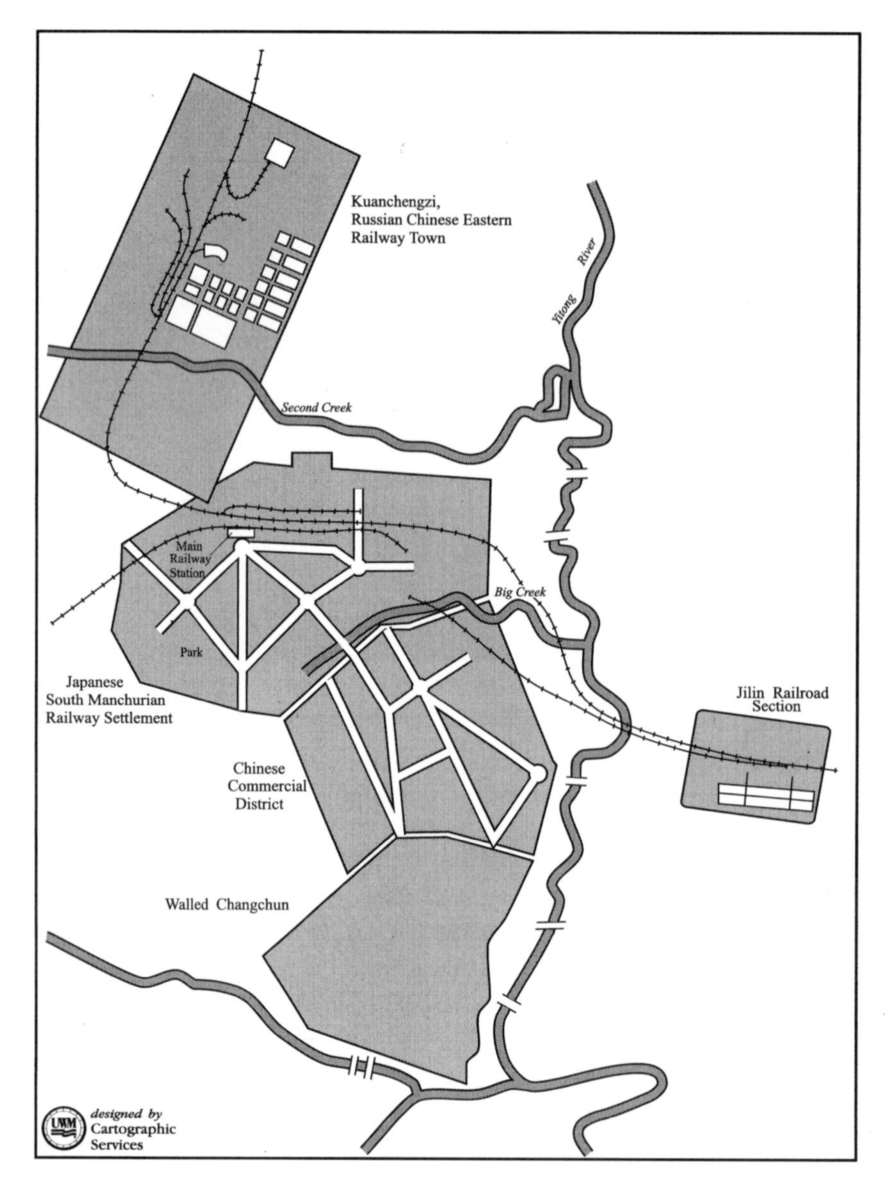

Map 8. General plan for Changchun, ca. 1912. Five major sections of Changchun under the South Manchurian Railway are shown. Based on maps of 1918, 1929, and 1931 reproduced in Koshizawa Akira (1988), 81–85.

openly endorse the Boxers. The Boxer attacks left the Russians more concerned than ever about maintaining proper distance between themselves and the Chinese, so they created a new military camp outside the western wall of Changchun in order to keep a military force between their settlement and the Chinese.

The railway linking Changchun to Dalny opened in 1902. The number of railway workers declined, but its economic impact intensified as soybean and grain exports grew following the shift to rail transportation and the price of imported goods fell as a consequence. In the Russian town most buildings were single-story brick houses, along with a few stores and shops built in simple Russian vernacular style, a chapel, and a school. The railway company's main buildings were more elaborate—the chief surviving structure was then the CER Employees Club, a two-story brick and stucco structure with a central covered portico and two wings ending in turret-like extensions. The club probably functioned as a hotel and restaurant as well as a place for worker recreation. The Russian settlement had its own fresh water supply system, which drew on wells, and an electrical generation system. It housed about three thousand inhabitants, but it was a simple and rather bleak prairie town.[29]

Acquisition of the Japanese Railway Settlement

Following Japan's victory in the Russo-Japanese War, Japan gained control over the southern half of the CER, along with a lease on territory on the Liaodong peninsula that included what they now called Dairen. Changchun became the break point between the two halves of the lines. The Japanese installed standard American gauge tracks along their portion of the railway, while the Russians maintained a wider gauge on their section. The difference in the gauges meant more costly and inefficient rail transportation, but it produced a better defensive military posture for both the Russians and the Japanese. In practical terms it meant that more Chinese porters were needed at Changchun.

Before the need to build their own settlement at Changchun was clear, the fledgling SMR, under its first president, Gotō Shimpei, purchased some land in the old walled city of Changchun through the Mitsui Trading Company, which secretly took title for the railroad. Mitsui was hoping to profit from the soybean trade, and indeed this trade proved a great source of profit in the coming years. The ease with which the new semiofficial SMR linked its interests with a private trading company is indicative of the Japanese style of these years.[30]

Once the full meaning of Russian objections to using the existing Kuanchengzi rail yards to transfer goods became clear, the SMR had to acquire much more land than the Mitsui parcel, so the SMR officials approached the Qing government about buying their own four or five square kilometer tract. The Manchu dynastic authorities, as part of the New Policies reforms *(xinzheng),* had created an urban administration form especially designed for situations such as existed at Changchun. Land designated "commercial districts" *(shangbu)* was set aside for foreign residence and business, but still under Qing dynasty control, usually on land that lay between the railway and the existing Chinese walled city. The authority within the existing Chinese walled cities did not change, but in the commercial districts Qing administration became more modern and accommodating to business and foreign residence. Such a commercial district worked well at Ji'nan in Shandong, for example, and served as a means for the Qing government to reduce German influence there.[31] At Changchun, the new administrative form served a different purpose: permitting the state-controlled SMR to purchase land they could administer themselves, with little interference from the Qing authorities.

In 1905, Qing officials declared all of the land west of the Yitong River, south of the Russian settlement and north of the walled city of Changchun, as belonging to the commercial district. They then established a uniform, low price to pay the farmers for this land, but they did not actually carry out the purchase. It was at this point that the Japanese entered the process and acquired their own parcel of land of about five square kilometers within the boundaries of the commercial district. This Japanese settlement included Big Creek (Toudaogou) and the higher ground to its north (map 8). The SMR paid the Chinese residents the price promised by the Qing dynasty, plus some additional amounts for the buildings and trees on the land. The SMR also had to settle claims from the Mongol princes who still had some residual ownership to the lands that they had long ago dealt to Chinese immigrants. Exactly what extra the Japanese paid to the farmers and the Mongol princes, and what would be called "bribes" to some Qing officials, is not known, but in any case, the SMR obtained the settlement land at bargain prices, compared to the land inside the city purchased through the Mitsui Trading Company.

The SMR administered their new land as "annexed land" *(fuzokuchi)* without any authority remaining to the Qing government. Their settlement came to have its own municipal public works and services, including police, fire, schools, and parks. Over the next few years, the Japanese at Changchun developed an interlocking administration linking the SMR, the Japanese consular authorities, and detachments of the Kwantung army together. This constituted the general pattern of Japanese presence in Manchuria from 1906 through 1932.[32]

The South Manchurian Railway and Goto Shimpei

The SMR plan for its town at Changchun borrowed from, but far surpassed, the Russians'. The plan embodied the urban planning ideas of SMR's first president, Gotō Shimpei, who played a decisive role in developing both the SMR and Japanese urban planning. Gotō (1857–1929) is a key figure in the history of Japanese colonialism, as well as a major figure in the history of twentieth-century Japanese urban planning. In these two roles, more than anyone else, he shaped the two modern faces of Changchun, both as a practical railway city and a high-modernist national capital.

Gotō was born into a samurai family in Japan's poorer Tohoku regions and received an education as a physician.[33] His official career began with military service in the Satsuma rebellion (1877). In peacetime he ran new hospitals and acquired an abiding interest in public health work. Following a period of study in Germany, Gotō became, at the age of thirty-five, chief of the public health office in the Japanese Home Ministry, where he planned fresh water supplies and sewage wastewater systems for Japan's cities. In 1895, General Kodama Gentarō selected Gotō to help in establishing public health facilities in the newly acquired colony of Taiwan. Impressed with Gotō's abilities, Kodama then appointed his protégé as civil governor of Taiwan. In Taiwan, Gotō paid special attention to public health, urban public services, street layout, and even the construction of major public buildings in Taipei. Urban planning did not exist as a separate specialty in Japan at the turn of the twentieth century, so Gotō's success in this work marked him, and the men who served under him, as Japan's specialists in this new type of administration.

Gotō's conception of urban form and design derived from European examples, drawn from his time in Germany and his voracious reading. In Taipei, which had been a melange of commercial settlements along the Danshui River before a late Qing effort at a railway modernization, Gotō expanded on the Qing plans and built a railway station facing a large square linked to a grid pattern of streets for commercial purposes, as well as imposing administrative buildings on a separate square. Underground fresh water supplies, underground sewage drainage systems, electric light, and telephone systems all featured in the city's new role as the seat of Japanese colonial administration in Taiwan.[34]

Based on his accomplishments in Taiwan, Gotō went on to a lifetime of service as one of Japan's top national leaders of the late Meiji and Taisho eras. Japan benefited greatly from his abilities to create and operate large, complex enterprises. Ramon Myers believes that the very idea of the SMR company resulted from a visit to Manchuria Gotō made in 1906 to consult with his mentor, Kodama, who was then serving as chief of the Japanese Imperial Army staff in Manchuria.[35] Kodama died before the plan was put into effect, but the Saionji Cabinet accepted the Kodama-Gotō conception of expanding on the Russian model of using a railway company with special powers, rather than some more familiar form of colonialism, to extend Japan's power into Manchuria.

The SMR was a joint government and private enterprise, capitalized at 200 million yen, with the government providing half and the rest being offered only to Japanese and Chinese investors. The initial stock offering was oversubscribed. Gotō became the SMR's first president in November 1906 and quickly assembled a team of well-qualified engineers, managers, accountants, and planners to take over the railroad from the Japanese army railway battalions that had been operating the line south of Changchun since their victories in the field during the Russo-Japanese War.[36]

The combination of private and government ownership enabled Gotō to operate the SMR with little oversight of Japanese politicians in the Diet, and he used this freedom to plan boldly and expensively the new company's operations. The SMR would derive its revenue from the transportation of goods and people throughout

Manchuria, and from the exploitation of coal, iron mines, and other natural resources of the region. Financing was obtained by selling bonds on the world market through London, where the earliest bond issues were floated in the spring of 1907.[37]

Gotō insisted that the SMR's rolling stock, yards, and facilities all were to be the most modern available. The SMR purchased American locomotives and railcars, bought the most up-to-date communication systems, and built excellent port facilities. The office buildings, residential housing, and amenities for SMR employees were of top quality. A research arm was established to provide information to the company and to its half-owner, the Japanese state. As Okamatsu Santaro put it, the SMR had "the appearance of a commercial company but really functions as an organization of the state to carry out colonial rule and colonization."[38]

Such grand conceptions and free spending became the hallmarks of Gotō's administrative style. Later, back in Japan, this caused him some political problems, but in his tenure as SMR president from 1906 to 1915, he could do almost as he wished. The SMR proceeded to build magnificent headquarters in Dairen and undertake generous construction programs at Mukden and Changchun in particular. At both locations, Gotō and his planners, in particular Katō Yonokichi, prepared designs based on the European-derived Dairen model featuring an underlying grid pattern of streets interrupted by diagonal streets passing through large, well-landscaped circular plazas, and bordered by large parks. As one would expect, there were provisions for an underground fresh water supply, sewage drainage (although not sewage treatment), and land for schools, temples, and other public uses.[39]

SMR Plan for Changchun

Katō Yonokichi, a public works specialist, designed the SMR settlements at both Changchun and Mukden under the supervision of Gotō. Katō carried out the official survey of Changchun in 1907; from 1914 until his retirement in 1923 he served as chief of SMR's Public Works Office. At Changchun, his plan covered 396 hectares of land, divided into functional zones (see map 9). In his plan, residential land constituted 15 percent, parks 9 percent; commercial and warehousing sections occupied about one-third each of the total area.[40] Katō used generous roads and broad circular plazas to shape the long-term future of Changchun. Roads took up more than twice the percentage of land as in Tokyo, or about the same as in Paris.

At Changchun, the railway line and associated warehouses and storage yards dominated the upper third of the SMR settlement; the town center, focused on the railroad station, covered the central third, and the parks and undeveloped land the lower third. The basic grid was formed by eight east-to-west streets and ten north-to-south streets, split into east and west sections by the broad main street—initially called Changchun Street (Chinese: Changchun jie) and later known as Central Avenue (Japanese: Chūō dōri; Chinese: Zhongyang jie)[41] —that ran directly south from the station.[42] The west side of Central Avenue was intended as a residential area; the east was the business district. This use of functional zoning in Manchuria preceded its use in Japan proper by more than twelve years. The first Japanese national city planning law incorporating these Western-derived approaches was passed only in 1919. Gotō was then serving as Japanese home minister and later as mayor of Tokyo. In both offices he applied the ideas he had pioneered in Taiwan and Manchuria to the improvement of Japanese cities.[43]

Katō's plan for Changchun was generous but practical. The main north-south avenue extended thirty-six meters in width flanked by sidewalks. Two diagonal streets led away from the railway station. On the eastern, commercial side, Nihonbashi Street (Nihonbashi dōri, named after a section of Tokyo) led to South Plaza (Chinese: Nanguangchang; Japanese: Minami hiroba), from where it turned southward through the Chinese-controlled commercial district *(shangbu)* and on into the north gate of the walled city. South Plaza itself had a large circular green space and roadway surrounded by two- and three-story buildings, including the Japanese state-controlled Bank of Chosen.

The chief Japanese businesses and commercial establishments of the SMR era were found in this triangular section east of Central Avenue, south of Nihonbashi Street and north of Big Creek. Within it, the best shops were found on Yoshino Street (Yoshino machi). The street was

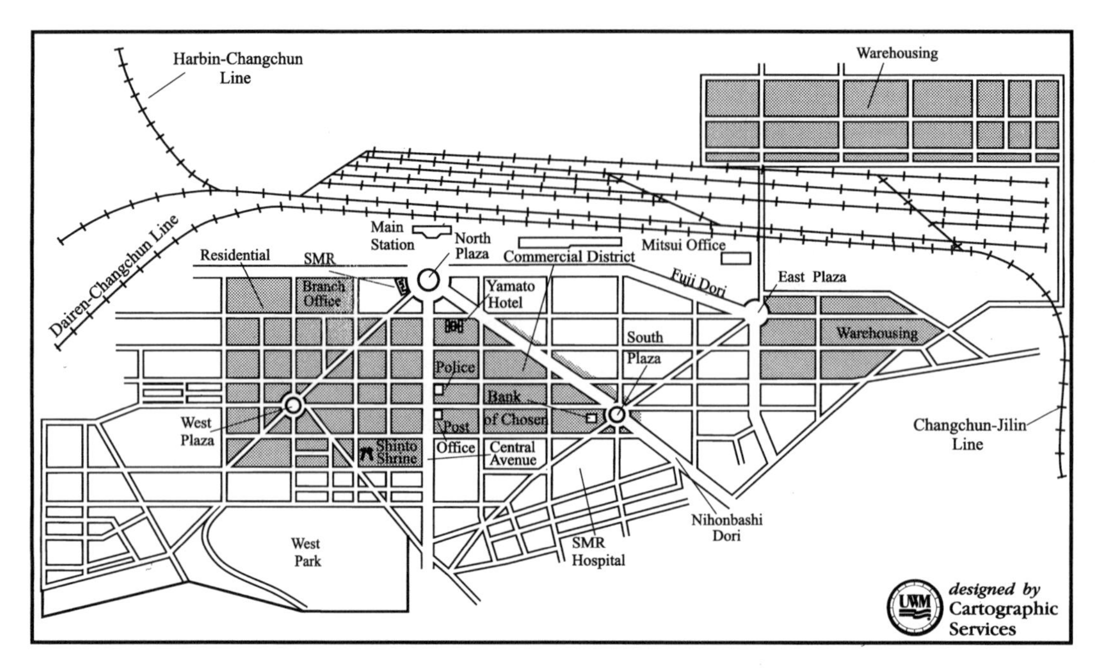

Map 9. Changchun land usage in the South Manchurian Railway settlement, ca. 1925. Map reveals the division into residential areas west of Central Avenue; location of main government offices, hotels, and banks on the plazas and avenues; the rise of restaurants, entertainment, and shopping in the streets east of Central Avenue; and the warehousing district on the far north and east sides of the settlement. Based on maps of 1918 and 1929 reproduced in Koshizawa Akira (1988), 81, 84.

eleven meters wide and could accommodate pedestrians, bicycles, and horse-drawn Russian-style carriages *(doroski)*. One block south of Yoshino Street was Celebration Street (Iwai machi), another commercial thoroughfare lined with shops. At the corner of Celebration Street and Central Avenue were the main Japanese post office and police station.[44]

At the east end of the annexed land, another circle known as East Plaza (Chinese: Dongguangchang; Japanese: Higashi hiroba) was built at the end of a road called Fuji Street (Fuji dōri), yet another thoroughfare whose original name had been changed to be more comfortable for Japanese speakers. At East Plaza began the warehouses, stockyards, stables, and carters' quarters essential to Changchun's economic functioning as a center of regional trade. Manchuria was the world's leading area of soybean production and exports in the 1920s and 1930s. Changchun became a major center in this trade and was sometimes called the "City of Beans." The Mitsui Trading Company, the leading firm in the soybean and grain trade, located its offices there (map 9). The Japanese built the streets in this section with cobblestones laid over a bed of gravel in order to support the weight of the heavily laden, wooden-wheeled carts that brought soybeans and grain into the warehouse district. A large compound belonging to the Chinese salt monopoly lay just north of Big Creek.[45] Farther east of the warehouse district, Big Creek entered the Yitong River. A bridge over the Yitong connected with the main road to the east, leading across the grasslands to the Yinma River and beyond into the upland forests and to Jilin City itself.[46]

In the early years, the SMR invested a great deal of money in the infrastructure for their railway settlement. Typically, Gotō had the SMR employ Japanese architects to design impressive and expensive buildings, including the post office (1908), the Yamato Hotel (1909), police headquarters (1910), the SMR main administration building—with steam heat and flush toilets (1910)—a large and spacious railway station (1914) (see fig. 8), schools, and a hospital. Under Gotō's express wishes all buildings were

Fig. 8. Facade of the Changchun Railway Station (built 1914). The station faced south on a large landscaped, circular plaza. Note the portico over the entrance, the large central section, and the arms with six bays of windows; also the horse-drawn *doroskis* waiting for customers. Photo from 1933, courtesy of Library of Congress.

intended to overshadow the Russian structures and to attract Japanese businessmen and residents to the community.[47]

The best residential sections from the SMR period lay to the west of Central Avenue. The housing varied in quality for different ranks of employees. The streets were somewhat narrower on this side of town; at West Plaza (Chinese: Xiguangchang; Japanese: Nishi hiroba), the water tower supplying this section occupied the center of the circle. There were schools and a large Shinto temple in this section, as well as the large public park at what was then the western end of Big Creek.

Table 5.1 shows the rising population of the SMR settlement, which was only one component of the overall population at Changchun (table 5.2). Initially, the Japanese residents outnumbered the Chinese, but by 1915, the Chinese constituted more than two-thirds of the residents in the SMR settlements. This situation continued until the founding of Manchukuo in 1932, when a new influx of Japanese established them again as the majority.

Table 5.1
Residents in the SMR Settlement at Changchun

Year	Japanese residents	Chinese residents	Total
1907	687	566	1,255
1910	2,348	1,360	3,714
1915	3,465	7,920	11,540
1920	7,749	15,856	24,087
1925	8,476	18,170	27,555
1930	10,097	23,307	35,090
1933	23,715	24,356	51,136
1935	33,281	27,272	64,025*

*Foreign nationals are included in the totals.
Source: Koshizawa Akira 1988, 81.

For administering the SMR annexed land, the railroad appointed a mayor, who was advised by a committee of prominent Japanese residents. This body was generally supportive of SMR's policies.[48] The SMR settlement actually continued in existence until 1936, four years after the establishment of Manchukuo, when it was absorbed into the administration of Xinjing.

The SMR's charter gave it the right to collect fees and charges from those residing in its communities. Expenditures on local administration throughout the SMR railway zone, however, averaged more than twice as much as the income, indicating that SMR absorbed much of the expenses of operating these communities. Akira Koshizawa points out that SMR fees for its residents at Changchun were about one-third of similar charges levied in the Kwantung Leased Territory, so Changchun was even more heavily subsidized.[49] Nevertheless, SMR continued to turn a profit for its shareholders.[50]

Other Sections of Changchun

Although the SMR district was the most dynamic part of Changchun, it was not the most populous of the city's five sections. In 1916, the 67,000 residents in the old walled section made up 60 percent of Changchun's total population (table 5.2). The numbers in the commercial district continued to increase, but its growth rate was slower than the SMR settlement. This can be explained by the better infrastructure in the SMR settlement. As the Chinese-administered commercial district grew, the old walled city of Changchun's population dipped as the numbers of its commercial outlets, businesses, and residences shifted to the Chinese-run commercial district or the Japanese-controlled SMR settlement.[51]

Table 5.2
Early Twentieth Century Population at Changchun

Section of City	1916	1928	1933
SMR District	14,000	31,000	51,000
Commercial District	30,000	44,000	56,000
Changchun Walled City	67,000	66,000	60,000
CER District/Kuangchengzi	1,600*	1,600*	5,000*
Total	**112,600**	**142,600**	**172,000**

*Kuanchengzi population for 1916 and 1928 uses a 1922 figure of 1,600; the 5,000 figure comes from 1932.
Source: Koshizawa Akira 1988, 86.

After selling part of the commercial district to SMR in 1906, the Qing officials did not begin to develop the remaining land until 1909. A reforming intendent *(daotai),* Yan Shiqing, purchased land and built three administrative offices—the intendent's own yamen, a police station, and commercial district office—all on the south side of Big Creek.[52] These new Qing administrative buildings had Western facades with stucco columns, but the interior layout remained quite traditional. Yan Shiqing's expenditures could not be considered lavish when compared with those of Gotō; nevertheless, opposition from local Chinese inhabitants to his building programs led to Yan's transfer. His replacement, Meng Xianyi, created a joint stock company in 1911 with one hundred thousand yuan of capital to help finance Chinese endeavors, and this quickly produced a host of new brick stores with semi-Western stucco facades along Main Street (Damalu) in the commercial district. Figure 1 (p. 8) shows the new businesses included the British American Tobacco Company. Still, these muddy streets of the Commercial District reveal the Qing authority's inability to spend as freely as the Japanese to pave and drain roads. As elsewhere in China, the administrative authority in Changchun continued to have a divided and overlapping character. Only in 1929 did there appear one unified administration for the Chinese sections of Changchun (commercial district, old walled city, and new Jilin railway area).[53] To the Japanese such reforms appeared as assertions of Chinese nationalism, thus further encouraging those who wanted Japan to create an independent state in Manchuria.[54]

All throughout Manchuria, Chinese traders dominated commerce outside the big cities. At Changchun, these Chinese firms congregated in the Qing-controlled commercial district, just as in Harbin the Chinese merchants operated from Fujiatian. The residential segregation between foreigners and Chinese was not quite so strict in Changchun because of the less racially tainted attitudes of the Japanese.

Surveys of Chinese business in Changchun reveal the presence of large local firms involved in the grain trade, soybeans, and distilling, as well as in local banks *(qianzhuang)* and money lending. There were also many Chinese-owned restaurants, teahouses, and stores dealing in general and special goods trades. Still, the big merchants at Changchun were Japanese *zaibatsu* (financial, industrial, and trading conglomerates). Smaller Japanese entrepreneurs were also much in evidence and prospered. Both had much better access to capital than most Chinese businessmen.[55]

A new district of Changchun, across the Yitong River and serving as the terminus for the Changchun to Jilin railroad, needs to be mentioned. The Qing retained the right to develop this line, but it fell under Japanese influence after 1909. The operating company was nominally Chinese, but its funds came from an SMR loan. Beginning in 1918, SMR assumed direct management of the line, and it was subsequently made a standard gauge and linked directly to the SMR lines at Changchun. Another community, less planned, developed around the station and yards of this railway, and subsequently this section of Changchun became a center of small industry.[56]

The Russian CER district, as its population figures suggest, languished. The relative isolation of Harbin, after trade links with the Russian homeland practically disappeared following the Bolshevik revolution, meant that the CER's trading reach extended only into the surrounding Sungari plain and not beyond into Siberia. Harbin itself remained a bustling town, but not at a level great enough to lift the fortunes of the Russian section of Changchun.[57]

The SMR, supported by its local Japanese inhabitants, formed the most consciously modernizing element in Changchun. The Japanese community kept pushing for improvements in local administration, urban amenities and public services, law and order, and regularized commercial dealings, all with the support of the SMR, the Kwantung army, and the Japanese consular service. The combined power of the Japanese private, public, and semigovernmental interests in Changchun meant that life in the city was shaped more by Japanese influences than by the Chinese, even though the Chinese did retain independent political and economic authority and were always the largest component of Changchun's population. The pattern observed at Changchun mirrors that found in Chinese treaty ports during the early twentieth century.

The development of Changchun during the era from 1906 through 1932 falls short of high modernism. The absence of a unified urban administration, the competition between Russian and Japanese state-owned railways, and the dominance of agricultural goods in Changchun's economy all reflect the modern, but lack the elements of a strong centralizing state and vision of a city as the representative of the nation-state that typify high modernism.

Changchun as a High Modern Capital City

Following Japan's military occupation of Manchuria in 1931 and the establishment of the Manchukuo state the following year, Changchun was renamed Xinjing (Japanese: Shinkyō, or New Capital). The new name announced the state's intent to remake Changchun into a grand national capital. Planners under Sano Toshikata (Riki) and others from the SMR planning bureaus were rushed into drafting a plan. At the southern end of Central Avenue they created a new Unity Plaza (Chinese: Datong guangchang; Japanese: Daidō hiroba), where key buildings of the new order were hurried into construction. By early 1933, the planners had produced a comprehensive design for the entire new city. (Map 10 presents an expanded 1940 version of the basic 1933 plan.)[58] In it, the older elements of Changchun disappear underneath a grid of broad avenues running diagonally to intersect at circular plazas. The outlines of the modern SMR settlement could be incorporated into the new high modern scheme, but the old walled city of Changchun and the commercial district were swallowed up by the scope and grandeur of Xinjing. Before 1932, Changchun's modern and more traditional sections both accommodated pedestrians and animal-drawn carts; the new city offered a vast expanse best negotiated by automobiles and buses with crosstown distances beyond the most hardy pedestrians. American geographer Norton Ginsburg captured the character of Xinjing in a 1947 description: "Wide boulevards and elm-lined streets, parks dot the city and its suburbs, large modern buildings of brick, concrete and stone rise from what was the site of soy bean farms."[59] With a special section set aside for the main Manchukuo government ministries, an airfield, a golf driving range, fancy residential suburbs on the south, and an industrial suburb to the east, Manchukuo planners cast their futurist, high modern style across the rolling plains at Changchun. This new capital was designed to reflect the vision, power,

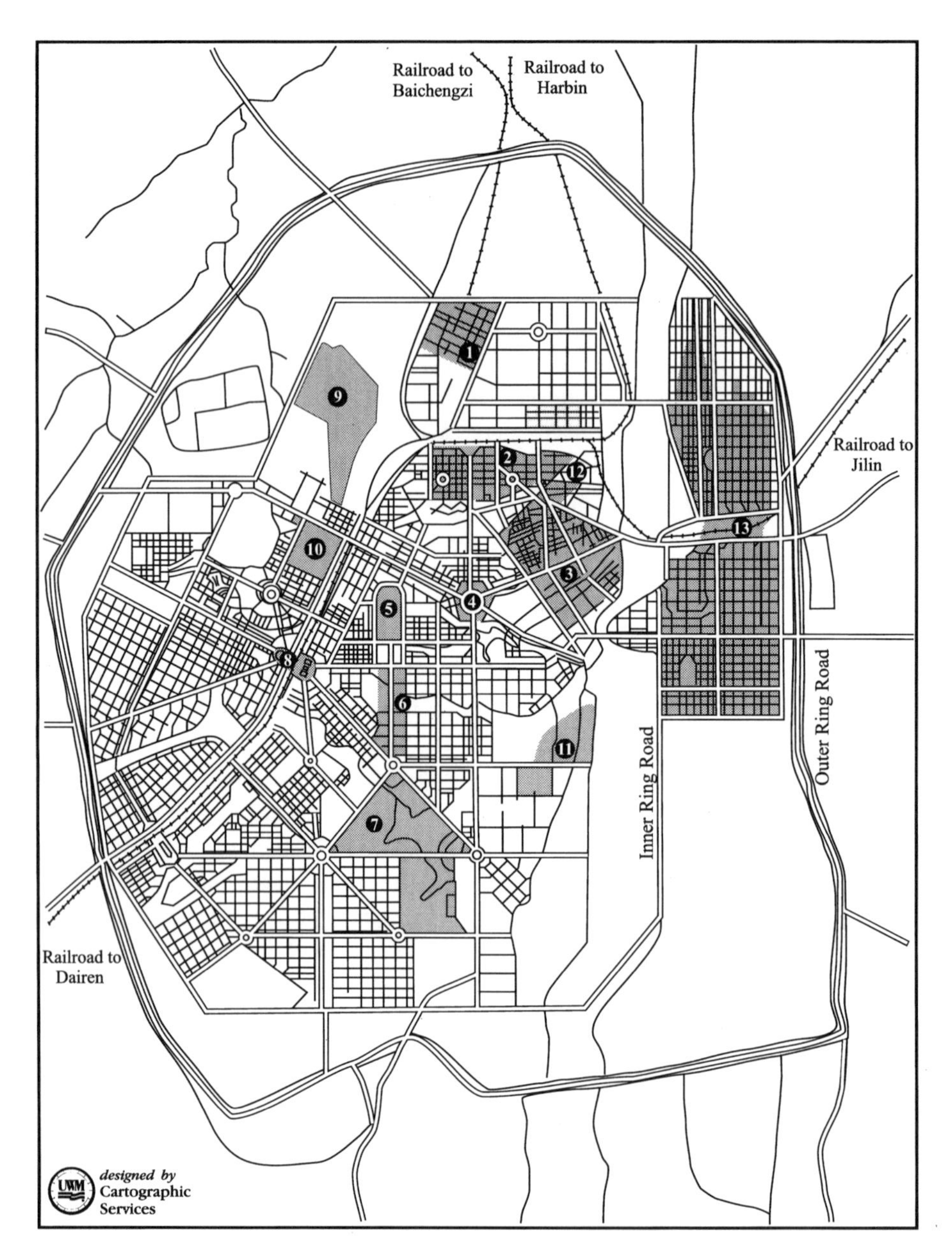

Map 10. General plan for Xinjing, ca. 1940. Main features: 1. Chinese Eastern Railway settlement. 2. South Manchurian Railway settlement. 3. Commercial District and former walled town. 4. Unity Plaza. 5. Uncompleted Imperial Palace. 6. Obeying Heaven Avenue with principal government ministries. 7. South Lake Park. 8. Planned New South Station. 9. Airfield. 10. Horse racetrack and golf driving range. 11. Nanling Sports Grounds. 12. Emperor's actual residence. 13. Industrial suburb. Many elements of this late plan were never built, in particular the imperial place (5), the New South Station (8), much of the industrial suburb (13) and the ring road, along with many of the streets in the southwestern corner of the plan. Derived from a 1933 plan of Sano Toshikata. Redrawn from *Zhongguo jindai chengshi yu jianzhu* (1993), 266.

and scientifically managed energy of the Japanese-controlled state of Manchukuo.

Manchukuo was an authoritarian version of a nation-state headed by an emperor, who implemented the Japanese military's vision of a disciplined, ordered, and intensely loyal citizenry serving the nation-state. The Kwantung army controlled the Manchu emperor, Puyi, and intended to create a state capitalist economy where soft and corrupt Japanese businessmen were stiffened by military rigor. Waves of Japanese settlers were to bring the virtues of Japanese culture to Manchuria. As a response to the ongoing world depression of the 1930s, the high modernism of Manchukuo was acceptable to many Japanese professional people who entered its service.[60] The way Manchukuo was being run had obvious transferability back to the Japanese homelands, where various military and right-wing schemes for a Showa restoration would have created a society much like what was being built in Manchukuo. Xinjing was the single most important visible manifestation of this new order.

In planning Xinjing, the Japanese drew on many sources, but three earlier twentieth century efforts offer revealing comparisons. New Delhi, the British-built capital of India, was designed and built under the architects Sir Edwin Lutyens (1869–1944) and Edward Baker between 1912 and 1931. Initially called "Imperial Delhi," the city plan emphasized the main buildings of the colonial administration by placing them at the head of a long, expansive processional boulevard. Residential and commercial areas flanked the ceremonial center and were punctuated with diagonal streets, circular plazas, and various statues and monuments radiating the glory of British colonial rule. The plan was fully high modern in that New Delhi was intended to serve as the sacellum of British rule over the Indian subcontinent, reflecting the power of Western science, art, and civilization.[61] Echoes of New Delhi are obvious in Xinjing, especially in the creation of a long ceremonial avenue flanked by the chief government ministries leading to a never-completed imperial palace (map 10, items 5 and 6). The palace was designed as a smaller, modern version of the Forbidden City at Beijing. Modern touches included garages for automobiles and a bomb shelter in the garden.[62] Xinjing was more compact than New Delhi, but it was even more an expression of high modernism in its relentlessly modern architecture and its almost complete eclipse of Changchun's short and not very distinguished history as a frontier prairie community.

The other bold high modernist city plan from the early twentieth century is Walter Burley Griffin's design for Canberra in Australia. Burley Griffin (1876–1937) won an international competition in 1907 and moved to Australia to carry out his proposals, which featured a multicentered city where government, commerce, education, residences, agriculture, and industry each had a core district built around circular plazas from which streets radiated. The largest and highest plaza was to be the location of the national legislature and capitol building. The various functional areas were arranged around a series of man-made lakes bisecting the entire city with an irregular beltway of water and green space.[63] The Australians loved the plan, but they could not stomach the cost of Burley Griffin's dream. Some parts were built, but the project languished for decades, and in 1951, T. R. Gibson, the official town planner for Canberra (then a city of only 23,500 residents), gave a sour review of what had been accomplished there when he announced, "Canberra is neither town nor country. A garden without a city; it is socially starved, wasteful and uneconomic in its layout."[64]

The contrast with what happened at Xinjing is striking. Following the style of Gotō Shimpei, the Japanese engineers and town planners presented expansive and expensive design proposals, like those for Canberra, meant to reflect the forward-looking prospects of the nation. Yet the plans for Xinjing encountered no political resistance. Construction proceeded with the greatest possible speed and the full backing of the Manchukuo government. When work began on Xinjing, it was already a city of 172,000, with a strong agricultural economic base, excellent rail transportation, and a modern city center. All during the decade of construction (1932–1942), Xinjing and its economy flourished through the steady infusion of construction money and through the generous employment provided for bureaucrats and technical specialists in the new Manchukuo government offices.[65] Xinjing was built by a state willing to pay for its high modern dreams, so it never encountered the problems that plagued Burley Griffin in Canberra.

The Japanese planners at Xinjing were also aware of the Guomindang schemes for rebuilding Nanking, described by Charles Musgrove in chapter 9 of this volume. These plans, drawn by the Capital Construction Committee after 1929, called for tearing down parts of the old city and constructing a modern administrative section along broad new streets. The Chinese used the ideas of functional zoning, and their building designs favored modern administrative blocks topped by Chinese-style roofs and adorned with Chinese decorative motifs. As Musgrove shows, while the Nanjing plans began boldly and expansively, the results were modest. At Xinjing the Japanese planned with greater boldness; rapid construction transformed these plans into dozens of great buildings. The infamous Japanese occupation of Nanjing in late 1936 ended the Guomindang efforts at city building, while the Japanese efforts at Xinjing remained in high gear for another six years. During those years, the Japanese kept revising their plans. Working in a typical high modernist style of five-year plans, the Japanese had planned Xinjing in the first five years as a city of five hundred thousand; during the second five-year period, they raised their sights to a city of one million.[66]

Planning and Building Xinjing

Akira Koshizawa has shown how the planners and architects involved at Xinjing came primarily from a coterie of bureaucrats and practitioners associated with Gotō Shimpei before his death in 1929.[67] The men can be considered part of Gotō's *gun,* or a consciously linked group whose personal and collective interests derive from association with a leader. The connections among these men extended over several decades and involved previous employment in the SMR or Japan's Home Ministry, participation in urban planning societies, work with rebuilding Tokyo after the 1923 earthquake and fire, and involvement with progressive urban places in Japan, especially Osaka, which was known in the 1930s for its efforts at modern urban development.

For many, switching from planning sections of the SMR to serving in the new state of Manchukuo was an obvious continuation in a well-established career. Still, members of the Gotō *gun* must have found the Manchukuo style more martial, more disciplined, more authoritarian than in the days when the SMR set the tone. Other factors drawing urban planners and architects to Xinjing included the relative lack of work in Japan, where the world depression halted many private projects, as well as the appeal of working on city building on a grand scale. The utopian concept of Xinjing offered architects and planners incredible opportunities, and many Japanese involved in Xinjing came out of an idealistic belief that Japan was creating a positive new order in Asia. The role of these men in Manchukuo fits closely with what James Scott conceives of as how high modernism links professionals and intellectuals to the service of the nation-state to create scientific, disciplined, and paternalistically benevolent social orders in model cities.[68]

In March 1932, immediately following the creation of Manchukuo, a new Capital Construction Bureau (Chinese: Guodu jianshezhu; Japanese: Kokuto kensetsu kyoku) was authorized. Yūki Kiyotarō took charge, and within a few months had a Japanese staff occupying the posts of chief engineer, planning section chief, and public works section chief. Mizoe Satsuki, a graduate of the University of Wisconsin who worked on the reconstruction of Tokyo and in Osaka as a city planner, headed the planning section. At the end of November, Ruan Zhenduo, a Chinese trained as a physician in Japanese medical schools in Manchuria, became the nominal bureau chief.[69]

The first project was the construction of a huge new circular plaza, over nine hundred meters in diameter at an extension of the existing SMR settlement's main north-south Central Avenue. The new thirty-six-meter wide road called Unity Avenue (Chinese: Datong dajie) was nothing more than an extension of the plaza and grid pattern of the SMR settlement, but on a grander scale (see map 11).[70] The name of the road and plaza were those of the calendar designation used by the new state of Manchukuo and echoed the title of Kang Youwei's book, *Datongshu* (1912), a call for the cosmopolitan unity of humankind. In the context of Manchukuo, however, the "unity" had a more specific meaning of joining together the Manchu,

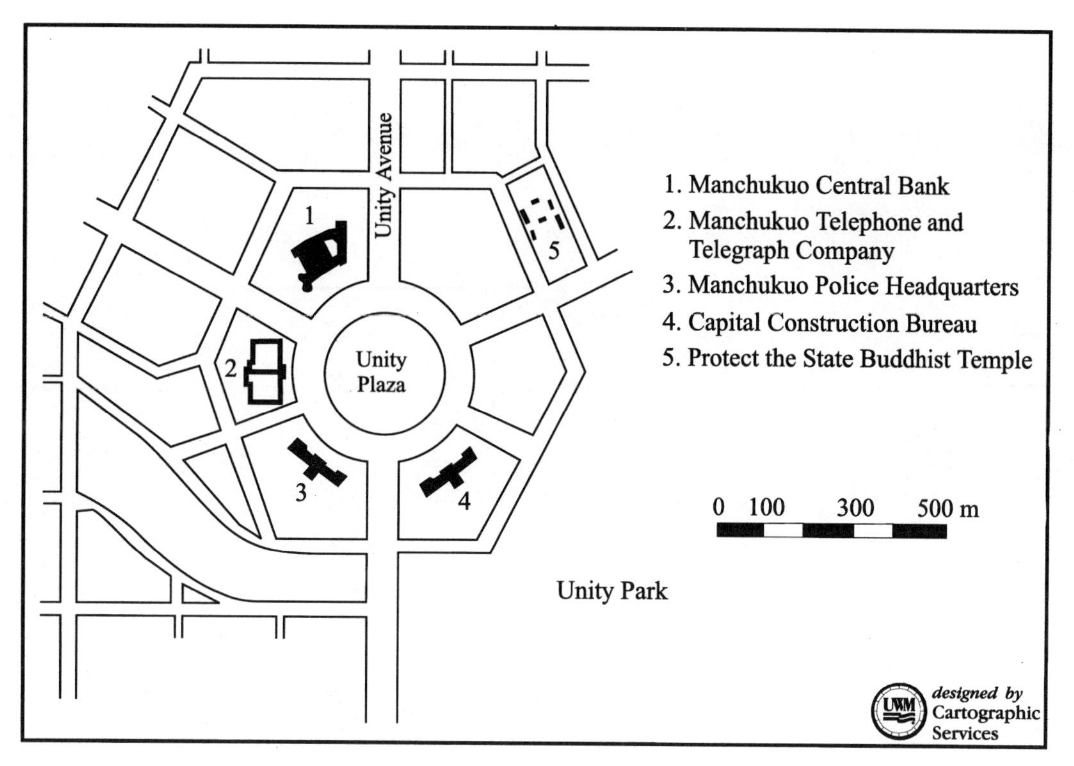

Map 11. Plan for Unity (Datong) Plaza. The plan is essentially an extension on a grand scale of the large plazas used by the Russians at Dairen and copied by the South Manchurian Railway at Mukden and Changchun. It was the first major building project at Xinjing, rushed into construction in 1932. Chief planner: Mizoe Satsuki. Based on a plan from *Zhongguo jindai chengshi yu jianzhu* 1993, 268.

Han Chinese, Mongol, Korean, and Japanese peoples.

An architectural team headed by Aiga Kensuke, who joined the Capital Construction Bureau from the SMR architectural office, worked on three new buildings, the first architectural structures of Xinjing: the Capital Construction Bureau itself, the Manchurian Telephone and Telegraph Company, and the Manchukuo Police headquarters.[71] The latter two came under the direct control of the Kwantung army and served to extend its control over the lives of ordinary residents in Xinjing.

The design and architecture of these buildings is of considerable interest. Although not on Unity Plaza, the Ministry of Justice (fig. 9) repeats the basic ground plan of the first Manchukuo building of 1932 as well as the CER Railway Club (1900), the Yamato Hotel (1909), and most of the major Manchukuo government office buildings. These buildings have a central entryway with a covered portico. The central section is larger and contains the most important offices or rooms. Two arms project outward from the center structure and end in turrets that repeat architectural elements of the central section. The buildings were low, generally two to five floors, and varied considerably in the internal floor plans concerning hallways, offices, and architectural detail. Generally, the buildings contained their own steam plants located in a structure at the back of the central section. A wall and fence combination separated the landscaped grounds from the street, while a circular drive provided for arrivals and departures by automobile. All of these buildings had large offices with good-sized windows and underground utilities. The Ministry of Justice had a typical "hat" (Japanese *tiekan*), which is generally interpreted as a militaristic or authoritarian element.[72]

These buildings used reinforced concrete and other new building methods. The Ministry of Justice had a steel

Fig. 9. Manchukuo Ministry of Justice (built 1937) at Xinjing. One of seven large government office buildings constructed along Obeying Heaven Avenue leading up to the never completed Imperial Palace. This three-story building carries an obvious "hat" in the central section with typical arms, portico entryway—all features of buildings associated with Aiga Kensuke's design preferences. This photo was taken in 1937, before landscaping was underway. Photo courtesy of Library of Congress.

framework and used a variety of Manchukuo and Japanese materials in construction: imported steel casing windows, elevators, and complex telephone switchboards. Where required, radio rooms and antennae were installed.[73] The distinctive style of these buildings will be discussed in detail later, but it should be noted that in many respects the basic features of this architecture in Xinjing is quite similar to that employed by the Guomindang at Nanjing. Both used the most up-to-date materials and employed standard international floor plans for office buildings but added elements intended to reflect the national architectural heritage.

The Role of Sano Toshikata

No single figure dominated the planning and development of Xinjing, but Sano Toshikata served as the chief advisor to the Manchukuo government on planning and architecture. Sano was part of Gotō Shimpei's *gun* and had previously been a professor at Tokyo Imperial University. He was the source of many of Gotō's city planning ideas, especially those involving the rebuilding of Tokyo. Sano also had a distinguished career as a planner in the Home Ministry, the SMR, and then Manchukuo. Working with him were several dozen associates, most members of Gotō's *gun*.

Sano's close affinity for Gotō's approach to urban planning can be seen in the solution he adopted to provide Xinjing with drinking water. The SMR settlement at Changchun had drawn its water supply from wells, but they could not supply the city of five hundred thousand, so Sano took charge of a project to create Clear Moon Reservoir (Chinese: Jingyuetan; Japanese: Jōgetsutan) southeast of Xinjing. The project began supplying water to the city in 1937 through a water filtration plant located at Nanling.[74] The underground water lines formed part of a system of underground utilities for telephone, electricity, and waste-

Fig. 10. The Full Enjoyment (Fengle) Movie Theater (1935). A fully civilian type building in *art moderne* style popular in Japan in the 1930s, employing streamlined features. It was the chief movie theater on a new street of the same name, a side street off Unity Boulevard with large restaurants, nightclubs, bars, and coffee shops, most of which had a distinctly Japanese and modern style according to their advertisements in *Sinkyō annai* (Guide to Xinjing, 1940). Redrawn from a photo in *Zhongguo jindai chengshi yu jianzhu* 1993, 278.

water drainage that Sano insisted must be part of the city plan. He and other members of the *gun* were responsible for the wide streets, extensive parks, and green spaces along Xinjing's main thoroughfares.[75] Sano's influence shows up at Xinjing in connection with his reputation as a specialist in earthquake proof design. After the great 1923 Tokyo earthquake, Sano had designed buildings that he believed safe even during big earthquakes. This led to a preference for low-rise buildings with steel frameworks. The Manchukuo-sponsored buildings followed this mode, even though there was little reason to try to implement Sano's objections to high-rise structures in the earthquake-free part of Manchuria. The central role of public health and sanitation in these projects is obvious, as is the intent to create a "garden city" environment. This all is a familiar SMR style writ even larger and more generous than in the days of Gotō.

Architectural Styles in Xinjing

The distinctive style of architecture at Xinjing is generally referred to as "Developing Asia" (*kō-A*) and is particularly associated with the many Manchukuo central government buildings constructed both around Unity Plaza and lining the broad Obeying Heaven Avenue (Chinese Xuntian dajie; Japanese Junten) that led into the uncompleted Manchukuo imperial palace grounds (map 10, items 5 and 6). The same style is found in the Kwantung army headquarters, but with a particular echo of a Japanese Tokugawa-era feudal castle in that instance. After 1945, in Japanese architectural circles there arose a criticism of these buildings and their supposedly martial "hats" as obvious and unwelcome expressions of Japanese militarism. At the time, however, Sano and his subordinates incorporated these elements in the designs of the architects working under his supervision without apparent qualms.

Still, commercial buildings at Xinjing were built in a much more restrained, clearly civilian, style. The Fengle Theater (1935) and Japanese-owned Sanzhongjing Department Store (1935) are representative of this style, which echoes the *art moderne* architecture found both in private dwellings and office buildings in Japanese cities or Japanese buildings in Shanghai.[76]

Two contemporary Western architects had some influence in the construction of Xinjing through their ideas and their students. Frank Lloyd Wright (1867–1959) lived and worked in Japan when his famous design for the Imperial Hotel was under construction. In the 1930s, one of his Japanese assistants, Endō Arata, moved to Manchukuo, where he designed the Manchurian Central Bank Club, a large compound with residences and a spacious clubhouse built in Wright's prairie style. At least five other architects worked in Xinjing with Endō and designed houses and apartments based on Wright's style.[77]

Wright produced a major utopian urban scheme in the 1930s called "Broadacres City" in which he embraced the prospect of urban sprawl. He welcomed the end of cities focused on a central business district and imaged a landscape (quite familiar in the United States after 1960) where office buildings, green space, shopping, and residences were ranged along streets traversed by automobiles. Wright felt such a city blended together the best of rural and urban life, encouraged individualism, and fostered democracy.[78] High modern in many ways, Wright remained a Midwestern American progressive and could never embrace the emphasis on the power of the nation-state, so his plans lack the emphasis on ceremonial spaces, order, and great buildings reflecting the grandeur of the state. Xinjing could never be an Asian version of Wright's "Broadacres City," but his Japanese students found they could serve the nation-state more readily than could their teacher.

The other Western figure whose influence can be seen in designing Xinjing is Le Corbusier (1887–1965), who was much more comfortable with the authoritarian aspects of high modernism than Wright.[79] Le Corbusier began in 1925 with plans for a private company to remake Paris, but realized that only governments could operate at the scale he preferred. In the 1930s, he produced plans for French colonialism in Algiers, and in the service of the Brazilian government, he made plans for the rebuilding of Rio de Janeiro. He embraced Italian fascism and was associated with the Vichy government in the early 1940s.[80] His politics were compatible with working under the direction of the Kwantung army in Xinjing.

Two young architects, Maekawa Kunio and Sakakura Junzō, came to Xinjing in 1939 after studying with Le Corbusier and produced plans for a residential area around South Lake (Chinese Nanhu; Japanese Nankai) that reflected the mixture of office buildings, apartment blocs, and individual housing favored by their teacher. Unlike most of those who designed Xinjing, the two young men went on in Japan after 1945 to become prominent architects in the new postwar style of internationalism.[81] It appears that the Japanese preference for authoritarian high modernism is largely self-generated, and that students of leading European architects easily accepted employment at Xinjing for the professional opportunity it offered, without much thought about how their teachers' values might or might not mesh with the authoritarian, high modernism of Manchukuo.

Ceremonial Spaces in Xinjing

As part of the high modernism the Japanese created in Manchukuo, there needed to be both great ceremonial spaces and activities to fill them. Photographs from the 1930s show parades down Unity Avenue celebrating the construction of the city itself. By the 1940s, public ceremonies had the purpose of marshaling support for Japan's wars in Asia. Photographs from a 1942 collection show thousands gathered in ranks for a "mass meeting to mobilize citizens of the developing Asia" (Chinese *xingya guomin;* Japanese *kō-A kokumin*) in Unity Plaza.[82] The term "developing Asia" implies that Japanese and Koreans, as well as Chinese residents of Manchukuo, all participated. The same collection shows the headquarters of the Concordia Society (Chinese: Xiehehui; Japanese: Kyōwakai), located on Concord Plaza, festooned with banners urging support for the war. The Kwantung army meant the Concordia Society to replace political parties with a single mass organization. As such, it was a means by which the high modern nation-state of Manchukuo could create an obedient population.

While the Concordia Society spoke of racial harmony and the glories of service to the nation-state, the rationing schemes in wartime Manchukuo reveal a different picture, as Japanese received preferential treatment.[83] Food rationing policies adopted in December 1941 at Xinjing show that eighteen items—including rice, wheat flour, sugar, milk products, cooking oil, matches, salt, and cotton cloth—were rationed such that the Japanese received both better quality and larger amounts of all goods.

Even though published histories from the post-1945 era are strongly anticolonial, it is difficult to know how people felt during the war.[84] Still, when we see the existence of clear favoritism toward Japanese in rationing regulations, it is hard to believe that such discrimination did not breed opposition against Japan. Hence, the high modernism reflected in the mass demonstrations held in impressive ceremonial spaces could not win true support from the Chinese majority.

Planning for a Million Inhabitants in Xinjing

Manchukuo, as one might expect of an authoritarian high modern regime, favored central planning for all phases of its development. Planning started on an ad hoc basis, but quickly shifted to that favorite tool of the domineering nation-state, the five-year plan. Xinjing was planned in two stages. Sano Toshikata and his associates carried out the first five-year plan (1932–1937), but many of them retired, entered private practice in Manchukuo, or returned to Japan after 1937. During the second stage of high modernist urban planning in Xinjing, the Japanese bureaucrats, like every Japanese, had to accept the authoritarian style of wartime Japan.[85] Thus the planners reflected more fully the intent of the autocratic military men behind the Manchukuo state.

Sekiya Tazuro took a joint appointment as mayor of Xinjing and head of the municipal planning staff.[86] In a reorganization, Xinjing was no larger managed as part of the Manchukuo national government, but became a special administrative region controlling everything at Xinjing, including the old SMR settlement. Reorganization also meant that a new, younger, and better-trained cohort of professionals appeared, but the influence of Gotō Shimpei's *gun* was still evident. Sekiya was a Tokyo Imperial University graduate with more than twenty years' experience in local administration with the SMR. Although it was wartime, Sekiya recalled that he and his staff tried to continue building Xinjing as a national capital.[87] The 1937–1942 five-year plan had six goals, including making over the streets and sanitation services in the older Chinese areas (what previously had been the walled city), constructing new housing in the southwest, and expanding sports grounds and parks in the southeastern part of the city. In typical high modern style, the old was to disappear before the irresistible force of the scientific and rational style of the new.

With the undeclared war in China, there was less funding available for construction in Xinjing; by 1942, with the demands of the Pacific War, most construction came to a halt. The planners kept spinning out their designs and altered their conception of Xinjing to accommodate an ever-larger number of residents. By 1939 it became clear that Xinjing's population would soon exceed five hundred thousand, so plans for a one-million-inhabitant Xinjing were produced. This meant adding new ring roads (never built) to the existing plans and further expanding the latticework of streets across the open plains (map 10).

Available population figures from the Manchukuo period reveal a fast-growing population in Xinjing as people came into the city to take the new jobs connected with the administration of Manchukuo and construction of Xinjing. The attraction of Xinjing for Japanese after 1935 is apparent. The war also seems to have spurred the city's population growth.

Table 5.3
Xinjing's Population

Year end	Total Population	Chinese	Japanese	Korean
1931	127,000	114,000	11,000	2,000
1933	192,000	161,000	27,000	4,000
1935	268,000	210,000	52,000	6,000
1937	335,000	263,000	65,000	7,000
1939	415,000	307,000	96,000	12,000
Mar 1940	438,000	324,000	101,000	13,000
Apr 1942	655,000	507,000	148,000	Combined w/ Japanese

Source: Koshizawa Akira 1988, 171.
Note: The Chinese remained far and away the majority population in Xinjing, with almost 90 percent in 1931, but declined to a low point of 74 percent in 1939.

In general, the second five-year plan shows a continuing balance between improvements intended for Japanese residents, other improvements of a more basic nature for Chinese residents, the continuing interest in public health, and the "garden city" ideal that mark all Japanese efforts in Changchun. These plans sought the continuation of high modernist hopes against a record of modernist improvements that goes back to 1906.

Transportation in this new city of one million drew attention for Japanese specialists, and the 1942 plans incorporated a subway. The idea that Changchun might need a subway is a fascinating reflection of the ceaselessly modernizing approach of Changchun's Japanese planners. The Xinjing planners had consultants from Osaka come to study the feasibility of such a project, but even though some materials and equipment were available, construction was delayed.[88]

Then, the wartime gasoline shortages meant that only 50 of Xinjing's 250 buses could remain in service. These few ran on charcoal gas or alcohol. With considerable ingenuity, the Xinjing city transportation planners took the equipment and supplies intended for the subway and built a streetcar system in 1941–1942 that operated with inexpensive electricity from the Fengmen Dam. That dam, completed in 1940, supplied cheap power to Xinjing. The streetcars remain in operation in the 1990s with new imported cars, while a few old Japanese streetcars are still in operation. Thus whenever possible, the Japanese continued to make Xinjing even more modern.

Conclusion

This chapter reveals a distinct Japanese style of modern urban planning and construction in China associated with Gotō Shimpei, Japan's most progressive colonial administrator. The basic elements of that approach were an emphasis on public health and sanitation, the construction of broad plazas and roads in the manner of Paris and other European capitals, the raising of impressive public buildings, and major efforts to make the city garden-like through parks, green spaces, and green belts. The plans involved functional zoning and state regulation of construction. The tradition can be seen in its earliest stages in Taiwan, and it was implemented either through a corporation such as the South Manchurian Railway or, in the case of Manchukuo, a government.

This tradition associated with Gotō and his successors was modernist and less authoritarian and dominating than the high modernist approaches used by the Kwantung army and the Manchukuo government after 1932. It proved easy for Japanese architects and planners to work either in the modernist mode of the railway city era (1901–1932) or in the high modernism period (1932–1945).

Xinjing was clearly modern, but it was also a foreign-controlled creation. How Xinjing's Chinese residents responded to Japanese domination cannot be discovered from sources from the 1932 to 1945 years, as resistance could not be voiced. As presented in historical accounts and in recollections of the Chinese residents of Xinjing, the Manchukuo period was experienced as humiliating subordination, no matter how modern Xinjing was as a city.[89]

In her study of French colonial urbanism, Gwendolyn Wright finds that, like the Japanese, the French saw their planning for cities in Indochina, Madagascar, and Morocco as experiments in the modernization of the non-European world, but for their inhabitants the cities produced strong reactions in the form of anticolonialist nationalism.[90] It is not possible here to trace this nationalist reaction in detail, but as we know from the work of Poshek Fu for Shanghai, the Chinese elite under Japanese rule responded with a combination of accommodation, passivity, and resistance. [91]

A single case from Xinjing's history can illustrate the point. Ruan Zhenduo (b. 1881), the Japanese-trained physician who became the head of the Capital Construction Bureau in late 1932, clearly was an accommodationist. In Manchukuo's service, Ruan Zhenduo rose to the post of ambassador to Japan, then served as Manchukuo's foreign minister and minister for economics.[92] As foreign minister he would have resided in a magnificent residence created by Endō Arata in the Frank Lloyd Wright style. The Soviets interred Ruan Zhenduo at the end the war and later released him before his death in Changchun, probably in the 1950s. The short biographical notice available on Ruan Zhenduo also records that his son, Ruan Shouyi, studied at the Manchukuo Army Officer's Academy at Xinjing, but in 1948 participated in underground work for the Communist Party and so became part of the new Chinese order in Changchun. Thus it seems, as one would expect, that high modernism by the Japanese produced a nationalistic, anti-imperialistic response among the young, elite Chinese living there—even among the sons of collaborators.

Under the People's Republic of China the "Developing Asia"-style buildings were given over to teaching hospitals and universities. In a particularly ironic touch, the Kwantung army headquarters became the headquarters of the Communist Party in Jilin Province. To put their stamp on Changchun, the new government located the First Automobile Works—a Russian aid project that became China's first automobile and truck factory—in the far southwest reaches of what had been a Japanese military encampment at Xinjing. The new PRC Changchun, like other Chinese cities, was becoming an industrial center. The Communist government did not destroy the SMR and Xinjing buildings or roads; instead, it renamed them, let many continue in their former roles under state socialist management, and stopped talking about the legacy of Manchukuo.

The PRC essentially left the legacy of Xinjing to sink slowly from sight and memory. *The Great Encyclopedia of China* contains a volume titled *Architecture, Parks and City Planning,* published in 1988 under the editorship of Dai Nianci. It contains no entry on Changchun, Xinjing, or Manchukuo. The entry on modern Japanese architecture refers to the influence of Western examples on the Japanese, but contains no mention of Changchun or other Japanese urban and architectural projects in China.[93] Although the roads, reservoirs, lakes, and most of the buildings still exist in Changchun and still provide their modernistic functions, their Japanese faces seem largely forgotten, almost erased from historical memory.

Chapter 6

Yang Sen in Chengdu

Urban Planning in the Interior

Kristin Stapleton

When Yang Sen rode through Chengdu's East Gate in February 1924, the residents were no doubt grateful that Sichuan's contentious militarists had transferred control of the provincial capital without a repetition of the horrendous street fighting of April and July 1917, when retreating Yunnan and Guizhou troops had terrorized the city, setting much of it ablaze.[1] In the first days of his occupation of the city, Yang Sen showed his commitment to public order by taking inspection tours through the streets and ordering his subordinates to display severed human heads—identified as those of looters—at all major intersections.[2] The warlord era had taught Chengdu's inhabitants to expect such official violence, but they could hardly have been prepared for the very different sort of devastation visited on many of their neighborhoods during the sixteen months between Yang Sen's arrival and his hasty departure, when his rivals temporarily united against him. Not since the era of the New Policies (1901–1911) had anyone been so determined to remake Chengdu, culturally as well as physically. By the summer of 1925, most of the residents of Chengdu were glad to see Yang Sen gather up his troops and his big plans for the city and leave town.

"Heian"—dark—is the adjective most often paired with "Sichuan" in commentaries on the province published in eastern Chinese periodicals during the 1920s. The story of Yang Sen's administration of Chengdu reveals that this apparent darkness was partly the effect of a sort of one-way glass that extended between the "advanced" cities of the coast and the cities of the interior. News from below the Yangzi's Three Gorges made its way fairly freely into Sichuan; Yang Sen and his assistants, like most Sichuanese leaders in the 1920s and 1930s, knew quite a lot about contemporary political and cultural movements in eastern Chinese cities and were anxious to bring these changes to Sichuan cities. But no one in the republican era looked to Sichuan for answers to the dilemmas of the day, and news that made its way down the Yangzi—that which did not have to do with warfare, opium, and harsh taxation—mostly concerned the problems stirred up as Yang Sen and others tried to refashion urban Sichuan. Sichuan natives who sojourned in the east helped consolidate the province's sorry reputation by founding numerous "reform Sichuan" societies that loudly proclaimed it a disaster area.[3] When Wu Yu, the anti-Confucian activist from Chengdu who taught at Peking University in the early 1920s, received an empty envelope in the mail from the Association of Western Sichuanese Scholars in Beijing, he remarked caustically in his diary that it "sufficiently revealed the incompetence" of the people of the Chengdu area.[4] Publicly and privately, Chengdu was pegged as hopelessly backward.

But the Chengdu that peeks from the pages of local newspapers was a more complicated place. It was a city that commemorated the death of Lenin with a mass meeting in a public park, presided over by Yang Sen's chief of police in the spring of 1924; a city where Wu Yuzhang, president of the Higher Normal School before Yang Sen's arrival, formed a socialist study association and published articles on the topic in a daily paper;[5] a city where Lu Xun's iconoclastic short story, "Diary of a Madman," became known earlier than in many eastern Chinese communities, because his admirer Wu Yu praised it in print shortly after it appeared.[6] At the same time, many in Chengdu were extremely hostile to what others called "progress" in the 1920s. Two months before the ceremony for Lenin, the Dacheng Association, a society dedicated to the study and propagation of Confucianism that counted among its members some of Chengdu's most illustrious citizens, sought and received the provincial government's promise that the city's Confucian temple would be preserved from land-hungry officials so that the society could carry out the time-honored Confucian rituals. One of the leaders of the association, Xu Zixiu, refused appointment as a teacher at Chengdu University in 1926 because, it is said, he would not serve on the same faculty as Wu Yu, who had publicly denounced his own father fifteen years previously. Wu Yu and Xu Zixiu fought and maligned each other for twenty-five years, each earning a large body of admirers and remaining fully engaged in scholarly and political life.[7]

Chengdu in the 1920s was no pluralistic seedbed for cultural innovation, nor was it perpetually isolated in the immutable grip of tradition and warlord terror. During Qing times, Chengdu had been the capital of one of the richest agricultural provinces in the empire.[8] The New Policies administrative reforms of the last ten years of the imperial era, concentrated as they were in the provincial capitals, had introduced a range of new institutions and ideas about urban planning. As the priorities of those who sought wealth and social prominence shifted from civil administration to the arts of war in the militarized early years of the Republic, many of these institutions lost their funding and languished. Nevertheless, the ideals of administrative rationalization and social order promoted in the late Qing continued to influence the thinking of older members of Chengdu's elite.

In the 1920s, new visions of urban organization and culture developing in eastern China found supporters among a younger generation of Chengdu elites, who briefly looked to Yang Sen as their champion. While in Chengdu, Yang Sen supported people who thought of themselves as progressive reformers, in touch with the currents leading China toward the future. Unfortunately for these ambitious young progressives, Yang Sen's approach to urban reform, unlike that of his late-Qing predecessors, took little account of local politics. The history of his attempt to remake Chengdu demonstrates that, even in the face of an outraged populace, a determined man at the head of an army could turn parts of a city into a monument to his "virtuous administration." Along with new streets and parks, however, Yang Sen's reforms built tremendous tension in the city—tension that was expressed in behavior that could be and was interpreted simply as cultural reaction. After Yang Sen was forced out, however, many of his initiatives were quietly sustained by a new coalition forged between some of his young advisers and older residents who had been involved in the Qing reforms. Yang Sen's career in Chengdu shows republican-era "city administration" at its most authoritarian and personal, but in its wake it is possible to see a revival of late-Qing reform ideas, recast under the influence of the social concerns of the 1920s. Ultimately, this revival led to a greater institutionalization of urban planning in Chengdu.

Yang Sen's Chengdu Labors

The city Yang Sen took over early in 1924 was not entirely new territory to him. He grew up in a village a considerable distance east of Chengdu and first lived in the provincial capital at the height of the late-Qing reforms, between 1905 and 1911.[9] In his early twenties at the time, he attended the Accelerated Officers' Training School, established in Chengdu to staff Sichuan's New Army brigades. From that vantage point he had a clear view of the first great wave of urban reform that hit Chengdu in the twentieth century.

During those years, Qing officials, in close collaboration with wealthy city residents, attempted to bring a new style of "civilization" *(wenming)* to Chengdu, inspired primarily by contemporary Tokyo. Above all, the city was to be made more orderly: among the major innovations of the New Policies era was a new police force to patrol city streets at all hours, enforcing standards of public conduct newly codified and explained to the people via a regular lecture series sponsored by the police bureau. Other attempts to bring urban life under control included a licensed quarter for prostitution, regulations requiring transparent pricing at the city's commercial arcade (a new type of public building with attached hotel and theater complex copied from Tokyo models), a new water supply system that piped river water into reservoirs in the city, and improved lighting via oil-burning street lamps and limited electrical service to government offices and upscale shops and residences.[10]

Yang Sen was serving as a low-ranking officer in Chengdu during the Railroad Protection Movement, which

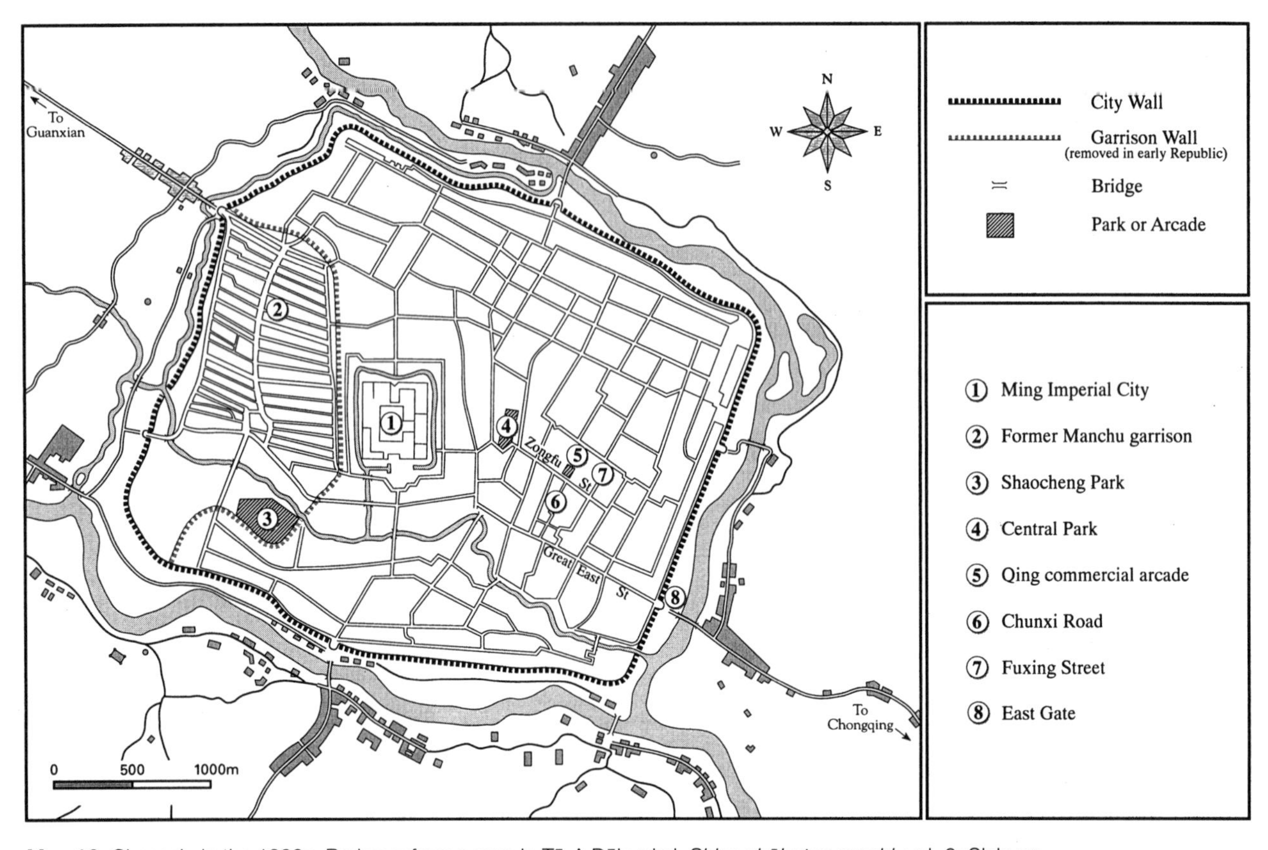

Map 12. Chengdu in the 1920s. Redrawn from a map in Tō-A Dōbunkai, *Shina shōbetsu zenshi,* vol. 6: Sichuan.

mobilized opposition to the Qing court's railway nationalization project and ultimately helped spark the 1911 Revolution. He was among the troops that restored order in the city after the revolution and the establishment of the Republic. Yang Sen then left Chengdu early in 1912 to seek his fortune in those tumultuous times, ended up on the losing side of the Second Revolution in 1913, and sought shelter in Yunnan. When Cai E's Yunnanese forces marched into Sichuan in 1916, he returned with them and very quickly became a dominant figure in a crowded field of Sichuan militarists who divided and contested control of the province. Between 1916 and 1924, he visited Chengdu periodically to attend military conferences at which Sichuan's generals fruitlessly attempted to negotiate a lasting peace and recruited aides and junior officers from among the city's educated youth.

Yang Sen had already established a name for himself as an urban innovator during his occupation of Luzhou, a small city on the Yangzi west of Chongqing. There, he had assembled a group of energetic young assistants, many of them graduates of Peking University, who helped him develop a new vision of himself as an urban reformer, destined to create new cities for Sichuan. With this image of himself, Yang Sen arrived in Chengdu ready to act.

One of Yang Sen's first gestures in Chengdu, however, was entirely in keeping with the city's political traditions: he presided over the opening of Chengdu's annual flower festival. Although the flower festival was said to have been part of Chengdu's civic culture since the Tang dynasty, it had taken on new political significance in the late Qing, when provincial officials began calling it the Sichuan Commercial and Industrial-Promotion Exposition (Sichuan shangye quangonghui) and required all counties to display agricultural and industrial products. In a concerted attempt to encourage development of industries in Sichuan, prizes were awarded in many categories, with the highest reserved for practical new machinery or reproductions of foreign machines.[11] In 1920, the exposition, which had declined following the revolution, was revived with much fanfare, as May Fourth activists promoted economic nationalism and boycotted Japanese goods.[12] In the 1920s, successful expositions were a mark of good administration for Sichuan's militarists. As a young military student in Chengdu, Yang Sen undoubtedly attended the late-Qing industrial expositions. The two he presided over in 1924 and 1925 could not rival their predecessors as province-wide events, given the political fragmentation of Sichuan. Still, the 1925 fair attracted exhibits from 40 to 50 of the province's 144 counties.[13]

As the 1924 fair wound down, Yang Sen gave a major financial boost to a more novel event: a citywide campaign to promote literacy. The Chengdu branch of the National Association for the Advancement of Mass Education (Zhonghua pingmin jiaoyu cujinhui) began its work in the spring of 1924, with a budget of some seven thousand yuan, three thousand of which came from Yang Sen and the city government office *(shizheng gongsuo)* supervised by Yang's elementary school classmate, Wang Zuanxu. Well-known educational leaders in the city led twelve teams that vowed to recruit one thousand volunteers to hold night classes for Chengdu's tens of thousands of shop clerks and laborers, using the "Thousand Character" textbooks published by James Yen's national movement. In September Yang Sen attended a meeting of the association and congratulated it for setting up 297 teaching stations where 10,267 students were learning to read. Citing a *Shenbao* article that pointed out the ephemeral quality of much literacy training, the general encouraged the association to maintain its enthusiasm and carry on.[14]

Although he encouraged the mass literacy movement, one of Yang Sen's true loves was physical exercise and its promotion among the citizenry. To this end, he added a large swath of land to Chengdu's Shaocheng Park and turned it into a public exercise ground. Like the flower festival, Shaocheng Park was invested with much political symbolism. In Qing times it had been part of the Manchu garrison on the west side of town, called the Shaocheng, that occupied a fifth of the territory inside Chengdu's walls. When stipends of Manchu bannermen were cut in the last years of the dynasty, the Manchu general attempted to secure new income for his impoverished community. One project was the public park at the southeastern edge of the garrison, close to the central city axis. The park proved hugely popular and quickly became the focal point of Chengdu civic culture. In 1913, an obelisk was erected there to Chengdu martyrs who had died in the Railroad Protection struggle two years before, and many public ceremonies and demonstrations were held beneath it.[15] Before Yang Sen built a running track, however, the only daily users of the park were patrons of the many teahouses and restaurants with which it was jammed. In the spring of 1925, Yang Sen presided over a province-wide athletic meet—the first, he claimed, since the late Qing.[16] He urged all Chengdu's residents to exercise regularly.[17]

Another addition to Shaocheng Park made during Yang Sen's administration was the Popular Education Institute (Tongsu jiaoyuguan). The director, Lu Zuofu, had set up a similar institution in Luzhou when Yang Sen occupied that town. Lu Zuofu and his staff designed a museum with exhibits on natural history, history, agriculture, industry, sanitation, education, and military technology. There were also a zoo, a library, a concert hall, and classrooms.[18] The institute hosted performances by school groups of new-style plays, to "reform Chengdu's traditional customs."[19]

Yang Sen himself took up residence within the Shaocheng, in the former headquarters of the Manchu general. By establishing himself in the former Manchu quarter, Yang Sen advanced a process that had been occurring since the fall of the Qing, when wealthy Han residents of Chengdu rushed to buy property from the desperately poor and worried bannermen. By 1924, the Manchu garrison area had become the home of the city's military and political elites. Most of Sichuan's militarists maintained Western-style mansions there and courteously refrained from damaging the estates of their rivals, after driving them out of town.[20]

The development of the southern end of the Shaocheng into an elite quarter made it an obvious target for Yang Sen's most dramatic—and disruptive—plan for remaking Chengdu. The area between his office-residence and Shaocheng Park was to be the site of one of Chengdu's first macadamized streets. Yang Sen's street-widening and paving project, launched within weeks of his arrival and continued right up to the time he departed, is what he is most remembered for in Chengdu today. A team of engineers from the city government office drew up a list of the city's streets, divided them into several grades, and designated a required width for each, allowing space for sidewalks. The group decided to begin where the most widening was required: along Great East Street, Chengdu's most important commercial district, which stretched all the way from the middle of town to the East Gate, through which most traffic to Chongqing and the rest of eastern Sichuan passed. Plans were published in the newspapers, and street headmen with responsibility for the affected neighborhoods were put in charge of raising money for the new streets from owners and tenants of all the adjacent properties.[21] The results were quite dramatic, as seen in before (fig. 11) and after (fig. 12) photographs of Fuxing Street, a street near the late-Qing commercial arcade.

Fig. 11. Fuxing Street before widening. This photograph and its companion (Fig. 12) were published together in the 1928 Chengdu Yearbook *(Chengdushi shizheng nianjian)* to illustrate the success of the city government's road building project.

Fig. 12. Fuxing Street after widening. Photo from *Chengdushi shizheng nianjian.*

In addition to paving old streets, Yang Sen built a new one—Chunxi Road—that he hoped would become the symbol of his administration of Chengdu. The road was constructed on the site of the Qing provincial judge's yamen, a sprawling compound that extended between Great East Street and the commercial arcade built at the end of the Qing. Bordered as it was by the two busiest commercial centers in the city, the old judicial yamen was an obvious choice for the model modern street that Yang Sen wanted to build. In January 1925, the new road was completed and a commemorative plaque installed. Yang Sen invited an elderly scholar to choose a name for the new road, and he chose "Chunxi" (Spring-brilliance), an allusion to a verse in chapter 20 of the *Daodejing* that speaks of the pleasures of the common people.[22] The opening of Chunxi Road marked the beginning of a new era in Chengdu's transportation history; it was the first street along which rickshaws were able to pass. Several dozen were operating in the city before Yang Sen left, and soon they outnumbered the old-style sedan chairs that had hitherto been the primary means of transportation for those who chose, and could afford, not to walk.[23]

In addition to his cultural and construction projects, Yang Sen brought a third type of innovation to Chengdu: a political style that might be characterized as authoritarian populism. He tried to craft for himself an image as a direct, plain-speaking, simple man, who appeared in the public park in shirtsleeves and opened his office every day for two hours to any visitors who desired to meet with him. He reopened a public lecture hall from the early years of the Republic and gave the ceremonial first lecture standing on a table in front of a huge crowd. A local newspaper reported that, because he wore simple street clothes and a straw hat when he entered the hall, those in attendance failed to recognize him, and no one stood up. His speech on that occasion explained that he had revived the public lectures because he desired to ascertain the thoughts of the people and address them directly as he carried out his administrative plans.[24]

This emphasis on accessibility and folksiness was paired, however, with a decidedly disciplinarian manner, which he developed well before coming to Chengdu in the mid-1920s. As ruler of Luzhou in the early 1920s, Yang Sen received boys from a local elementary school into his office one day and gave them candy and little copper plaques engraved with the characters for "Will not marry a girl with bound feet." He insisted that they immediately pin the plaques to their uniforms.[25] During a Luzhou athletic meet, he rounded up more than one hundred female spectators who had bound feet and ordered a youth corps to drive them to his office. There, he lectured them and ordered them to take off the binding strips, which he burned.[26] In Chengdu, he nailed signs to lampposts and walls, with a series of instructions for appropriate behavior based on his own cultural reform program. "Yang Sen says: By wearing short clothes, you not only save cloth but also promote martial spirit!" is one example. In a recent biography of Yang Sen published in Chengdu, local historians assert that these instructions were not regarded by the general merely as helpful suggestions—they claim he instructed teams of inspectors to shear off the bottoms of men's long robes and beat any man found in a public place without a shirt.[27] A contemporary observer noted that all city residents were forced by the police to donate money and ordered to appear at the tree-planting site for the Arbor Day ceremony at which Yang Sen presided, although only several dozen ordinary citizens actually joined the students, who were forced to go.[28] Yang Sen himself boasted of taking a whip to gamblers he spotted while riding by Shaocheng Park. When police ignored his orders to clear the streets of residents' pigs, he recalled that he beat the police chief in front of a crowd, despite the man's cries that "he should not be struck, since he was a *xiucai*" (imperial degree holder).[29]

The Sources of Yang-Senism

Although his memoirs—written on Taiwan when he was ninety—imply otherwise, Yang Sen's program for Chengdu did not spring fully grown from his own head. His policies, which he tended to unite under the term "city administration" *(shizheng)*, combined strands of several discrete currents of the times. With his ersatz populist style and his enthusiasm for novel schemes that could be presented as "civilized," Yang Sen attracted to him many enthusiasts of various social movements. The director of the memorial ceremony held upon his death in 1977 observed that Wu Yuzhang and other Communists had even held out hope of convincing Yang Sen to become "China's Lenin"[30]—which helps explain why two months after Yang Sen arrived in Chengdu, a thousand people were permitted to gather in Shaocheng Park to honor the deceased Soviet leader.

Yang Sen's choice of the term "city administration" to encompass his reform program reflects its growing currency in republican Chinese cities in the early 1920s, after the establishment of an office for city administration in Beijing in 1914 and the promulgation by the Beiyang government in 1919 of national regulations for city organization.[31] Sun Yat-sen's son, Sun Fo, designed a rival city organizational plan for Guangzhou, headquarters of the Nationalist movement, in 1921 (see chapter 2 in this volume). The example set by the Beijing and Guangzhou city governments was quickly followed by political leaders in other cities. Looking back in 1928, at the height of what might be called the city administration movement, one observer noted that "over the past ten years the cities and towns of every province have been affected by the current of the times and have begun some sort of construction. . . . City government offices in each region have sprung up like bamboo shoots after a rain."[32]

New governmental institutions were not the only sign of a burst of interest in city administration. Chinese who had been attracted to the field of urban planning and related subjects while studying abroad returned to China in the early 1920s and set up academic programs at colleges in Beijing and Shanghai. Articles on city administration appeared in many different publications in the 1920s, including the Beijing and Guangzhou city government gazettes, which provided readers with accounts of urban administration in other countries, in addition to reports on work in their own cities.

In the early 1920s, Sichuan was wooed by both "national" governments—the Beiyang government of the north and the Nationalist government of the south—and undoubtedly received government publications from both capitals. It would seem Chengdu's officials placed great importance on at least nominal adherence to central regulations. In 1921, Liu Xiang, then the supreme power in Chengdu, opened a new, Beijing-style city government office *(shizheng gongsuo)* in the city. As in Beijing, one of the first projects the office undertook was laying plans for a central park, plans Yang Sen inherited. A road-widening project was also in the works under Liu Xiang, but little was accomplished except for a ring road outside a length of the city wall, which was quickly destroyed by heavy carts. To fund the park and road projects, the city government instituted a popular monthly "city administration public benefit" lottery *(shizheng gongyijuan)*. Most of the proceeds of the lottery went to military use, but Yang Sen later used it to fund some of his projects.[33]

Other, more robust examples of city administration were occasionally cited in the city's newspapers. In 1922, a Chengdu newspaper reporter traveled to Nanchong, in eastern Sichuan near Yang Sen's old home, to investigate the urban reform undertaken by Zhang Lan, Yang Sen's childhood teacher. Zhang Lan had recently returned to his hometown from a sojourn in Beijing, bringing with him new concepts in city administration and planning. The reporter found Nanchong to be orderly, with newspaper reading rooms, a library, a dye factory, and an educational society. Although Nanchong could not compete with Nantong, the Jiangsu base of industrialist Zhang Jian, he explained, in terms of development, it surpassed any city in Sichuan. However, he added, if one were to talk of city administration, it "simply cannot be counted as that."[34] What did this reporter mean by "city administration"? What was lacking in Nanchong? His article supplies a list of goals that could not be accomplished due to a shortage of funds: knocking down the city wall and building roads around the city, constructing a "model street" in the city center, and refurbishing the markets. All are public construction projects.[35]

Many of the men who advised Yang Sen during his administration of Luzhou, Chongqing, and then Chengdu shared this infrastructure-oriented view of the most pressing tasks facing city governments. The emphasis on public construction can be traced in large part to the influence of the National Road-Building Association of China (*Zhonghua quanguo daolu jianshe xiehui*). This association was founded in Shanghai in 1921 and may have served originally as a sort of employment agency for civil engineers.[36] By the mid-1920s it claimed more than eighty thousand members and supported both scholarship and advocacy in public construction, transportation, and urban planning.[37] In 1928 and 1930, the association published two huge volumes—*The Complete Book of City Administration (Shizheng quanshu)* and *The Complete Book of Roads (Daolu quanshu)*—that encapsulated its members' expertise and plans for the development of China's cities. [38]

The association's approach to city administration, as revealed in the volume on that subject, emphasized the construction of roads within and around the city and between cities. A comprehensive network of finely engineered roads was most definitely an early twentieth century hallmark of modern urbanism. In pointing out the "backward" state of the early Greek city-states, the standard American text on ancient history in the years after World War I cited their "narrow, wandering streets, which we should call alleys," along with their "dingy sun-dried brick houses" to create a visual image of listless antiquity.[39] In Europe, Le Corbusier criticized the "corridor streets" of the cities of the past, clogged with city people and commerce, and urged that they be replaced by "an abstract gridded green plane dedicated to the movement of cars, while buildings . . . and pedestrians are lifted from the ground."[40] On the other hand, bridge and road building had long been considered ideal philanthropic activities for Chinese elite interested in displaying their virtue. As Qin Shao points out in her study of Nantong, the expression "build bridges and repair roads" *(xiuqiao bulu)* came to be a common metaphor for accomplishing a good deed with long-lasting effects.[41] In addition to the new and old symbolic attractions of road-building projects, the economic benefits attendant on such projects were touted by no less an authority than Sun Yatsen, in his *Fundamentals of National Reconstruction*. The relationship between improved transportation and local prosperity was quite clear in eastern China, where the road-building activities of such men as Zhang Jian had strongly influenced the fortunes of towns in the Yangzi delta.[42]

The National Road-Building Association did not confine its urban-reform advocacy strictly to roads. Wu Shan, the Sichuanese executive director of the association, argued in the city administration volume that human capital for the cities of the future could best be developed in Soviet-style model nurseries, run by specialists trained in scientific child rearing.[43] Other articles cited the health advantages of the "garden city" model of urban planning developed in England and the importance to the human spirit of the beautification of cities. While the ideas and proposals encompassed in the association's vision of city administration are quite rich, the experts represented in *The Complete Book of City Administration* have relatively little to say on the topics of urban social welfare and popular participation in city government. To them, city administration seems to have been primarily a matter of training specialists to design, build, and properly manage the physical infrastructure of the modern city.

The city administration advocates of the early 1920s may have been technocrats, but they were also enthusiasts. Dong Xiujia, who had studied urban economics at the University of Michigan and city administration at the University of California, celebrated the rise of the city as China's best hope for the future. In what was very likely a conscious rebuttal of traditional Confucian and contemporary Chinese romantic views on the moral superiority of simple country living, Dong Xiujia argued that city culture was a progressive culture of cooperation, which could reform the selfish and isolationist culture of China's rural areas. City people were forced by proximity to accommodate each other, and successful city administration promoted human harmony. Humanity would be elevated by urbanization, if it could develop a proper understanding of city administration.[44]

Chengdu first learned of the National Road-Building Association from Chen Weixin, a friend of Wu Shan, in the spring of 1924. Chen Weixin, a native of Chengdu, had been trained as a YMCA organizer in Shanghai. During World War I, he joined James Yen's YMCA mission among the Chinese laborers in France. After the war, back in Shanghai, he became involved in the National Road-Building Association and helped set up branches in Henan and Wuchang. In 1923, he returned to Chengdu as the Commercial Press' agent and a missionary of urban reform. Because of his experience with the YMCA, however, his understanding of the proper goals of urban administrators differed somewhat from that of his colleagues in the association.[45]

In Chengdu, Chen Weixin threw himself into many projects. He organized a Chengdu branch of the association, which worked with Yang Sen on his various projects. He was also on the board of directors of the Mass Education Movement. In the spring of 1924, Chen Weixin's name appeared in Chengdu newspapers more frequently than any other local personage, excepting Yang Sen and Wang Zuanxu, director of the city government office.

In April 1924 and then again in May, Chen Weixin published long articles setting out what he saw as the most urgent tasks facing Chengdu's administrators. In the first, he listed eight priorities:

1. Recover the public streets from encroaching shops and houses
2. Fix the city's sewer system
3. Construct new tree-lined streets, with benches along them
4. Open new public toilets with attendants to collect fees and provide toilet paper (women's toilets were to be free, however, since only poor women would use them)
5. Establish official farmers' markets to get stalls out of intersections and raise revenue
6. Turn temple grounds into small public parks throughout the city so children are not obliged to play in the streets
7. Encourage public lectures so that the people will understand the intentions of the government
8. Set up a rickshaw company with two thousand to three thousand rickshaws.[46]

In this conception of city administration, the influence of the National Road-Building Association is quite apparent, although Chengdu residents who remembered the New Policies reforms would not have considered any of these proposals novel. Over the next year and a half, Yang Sen and his administrators implemented all of them, to some extent.

Chen Weixin's next series of city administration suggestions, published in May, shifted the emphasis from construction to other types of reform. It began with a call for wider participation in city affairs:

> As to the nation, whose nation is it? Of course it is the Chinese people's nation. What about city administration? It is the city administration of the residents of Chengdu. If we want to reform the country, it cannot be done by a small group of government officials. If city administration is bad and we want to renew it, how can two or three people in power achieve that?

The eight tasks Chen Weixin pointed to in the May article are as follows:

1. Regulation of prostitution
2. Regulation of the poor people employed in funerals and other public events
3. Reorganization and regulation of the sedan chair business
4. Institutionalization of beggars
5. Prohibition of the impressment of laborers
6. Prohibition of opium dens
7. Development of a "garden city"
8. Reopening the city gates (several had been closed in early 1924, due to nearby fighting).

If these eight problems were solved, Chen Weixin argued, the people of Chengdu would be imbued with a new, energetic spirit, which would save them from the fate of such people as the Koreans, whose weakness led them to become subjects of a foreign power.[47]

In this new list it is still possible to see influences from the city administration movement—the call for the creation of a "garden city" and the concern for transportation and communication implied in his eighth point on the city gates. The links made between urban reform, civic participation, and national strength also feature in the arguments of the National Road-Building Association. But Chen Weixin's vision contains a concern with social conditions in the city, such as the prevalence of opium smoking and prostitution, which owes much more to his YMCA background than to the city administration experts. Shirley Garrett's summary of the philosophy of the Chinese YMCA seems almost a restatement of Chen Weixin's ideas on urban priorities: "If large numbers of people could learn to read, if laborers would stop gambling and brush their teeth, if beggars could be trained to useful occupations, if people as a whole could hear lectures on the importance of health and good citizenship, China might yet pull itself up by its bootstraps."[48]

Yang Sen was also concerned with infusing Chengdu's citizens with a new, energetic spirit. One of the city's Moslem residents recalled that when Yang Sen, out of curiosity, visited a mosque during a prayer service, he was so impressed with the orderliness and gravity of the worshippers that he exclaimed, "A people like this could never be defeated!"[49] But, like Chiang Kai-shek with his New Life Movement a decade later, Yang Sen believed that a new spirit of discipline and energy could be achieved in Chengdu entirely through personal physical cultivation and clean living on the part of the masses, who would be rigorously and severely guided in their efforts by dedicated political leaders such as himself.[50] He had little interest in religious, social, or economic issues. One missionary resident in Chengdu reported that Yang Sen's grasp of social conditions in the city seemed very superficial:

> Governor Yang was at our home one evening and I asked him if the government had any information or any department investigating industry from the human standpoint. He said there were fourteen factories in Chungking [Chongqing] employing in all several thousand women, but he knew nothing of Chengtu [Chengdu]. He switched on to a short dissertation on wet nurses and their lucrative opportunities.[51]

Yang Sen's justification of his road-building campaign did not even touch on economic development. His speech at the first meeting of the Chengdu branch of the National Road-Building Association included this statement:

> Warfare has been going on in Sichuan for many

> years and the people have suffered much. It is all due to the poor state of our roads. If we can complete the roads quickly, then we can concentrate the armies and transport military supplies very conveniently. War won't continue long after that.

After the roads are built, he concluded, rival general Liu Xiang and he would not fall into any more misunderstandings, which were entirely due to the difficulties of communicating with each other.[52]

Although the influence on Yang Sen of Chen Weixin and the National Road-Building Associations' plans was great, parts of his reform program are attributable to the predilections of his Luzhou advisers. Most important of these was Lu Zuofu, who attained fame later as the founder of the Minsheng Shipping Company. Lu Zuofu was powerfully influenced by the events and ideas associated with the May Fourth movement. At the time of the May Fourth incident in 1919, he was an editor and reporter for an upstart newspaper in Chengdu that had been sympathetic to the nationalistic student protests. Its Beijing correspondent, Wang Guangqi, telegraphed reports on the Beijing demonstrations and helped found the Young China Study Society. Lu Zuofu and his newspaper colleagues, Sun Shaojing and Li Jieren, set up a Chengdu branch of the society. The Popular Education Institute he helped build in Chengdu reflects Lu Zuofu's commitment to the Young China Study Society's reform program, particularly the call for a more broadly based educational system.[53] Sun Shaojing, on the other hand, became one of the leaders of the "road-association" brand of city administration after he returned to Chengdu from study in Japan and Germany. He served as manager of Chengdu's city government office from 1924 until his assassination in 1927 and was instrumental in carrying forward Yang Sen's policies after the general's abrupt departure.

The most striking characteristic of Yang Sen's administration of Chengdu, his political style coupling a superficial populism with a harsh disciplinarianism, is a fit subject for psychoanalysis, were such a thing possible posthumously. Some elements of his background that may have fed into it include his early exposure to intensely emotional Gelaohui ritual,[54] with its emphasis on loyalty, righteousness, and the use of violence in the name of those principles; his military training, which he loved for its physical challenges; his rapid rise to prominence, caused by and cause for his extraordinary self-confidence; and the flood of revolutionary ideas that entered Sichuan in no orderly way throughout the early republican era.

Yang Sen in the Eyes of Urban Elites

As is clear by now, parts of Yang Sen's urban development and reform agenda had strong advocates in Chengdu before he arrived. Despite the lackluster record of the city government office between 1921 and 1924, proposals for "city administration" initiatives appeared with some regularity in the local papers throughout those years. A few days after Yang Sen established himself in the city, six people placed an appeal in a local paper identifying city administration as the "foundation of civil government, which all countries with the rule of law try energetically to establish." They complimented Yang Sen on what he had accomplished in Luzhou and asked that he make it a top priority to investigate the budgets of previous Chengdu city administrators to discover how they had diverted funds from the city development lottery to military and other uses, and to prevent any such practices in the future.[55]

The courtship was a two-sided affair. Yang Sen's philosophy for managing young Sichuanese who had received advanced educations abroad or in Beijing and Shanghai was to invite them to join his administration or often, if they were female, his household.[56] One of the very few holdouts among this group of "new people" in Chengdu was the writer Li Jieren, who antagonized his fellow returned students by refusing to attend the banquets Yang Sen lavished on their group and openly criticizing them as political opportunists *(zhengke)*.[57]

Also absent from Yang Sen's banquet table, although not by choice, were Chengdu's more traditional elite. The most prominent of these, a group of Qing degree holders known as the Five Elders and Seven Sages *(wulao qixian)*, had long considered themselves mediators between the people of the city and their various overlords. Many of Sichuan's first generation of republican-era militarists had studied in schools run by the Elders and Sages. They usually felt a strong obligation to seek the advice of their revered teachers on matters of civil administration and found such advice difficult to ignore entirely.[58] The key figure in this regard was Xu Zixiu, who led a contingent of military students to study in Japan in 1905 and was director of the provincial higher normal school in the last years of the Qing. Xu Zixiu maintained a teacher-pupil relationship with an extraordinary group of Sichuan's most prominent political and military leaders in the years after 1911. These included, among many other less well known figures, the first military governor, Yin Changheng; Dai Jitao, Nationalist Party theorist and drafter of Sichuan's 1922 provincial constitution; Wu Yuzhang, one of Sichuan's first Communist activists and later president of People's University; and Zhang Qun, head of Chengdu's police department in 1918 and mayor of Shanghai and governor of Sichuan in the Nationalist period.[59]

The Elders and Sages were by no means ideologically opposed to all of Yang Sen's urban reform agenda. Most of them had been quite supportive of Chengdu's New Policies reforms in the late Qing, which had also emphasized public construction and the value of discipline and productivity. As the standard bearers for "Confucian values" in the city, they did not support Yang Sen's encouragement of coeducation in the public schools. Rather than openly fight it, however, they chose to concentrate on running their own school, attached to the Dacheng Association.[60] Xu Zixiu's response to the growing prestige and significance of the military, which began in earnest in Chengdu around the time Yang Sen arrived in the city for officer training in 1905, was to compile a collection of accounts of valorous and virtuous military heroes in Chinese history.[61] Whether or not he read Xu Zixiu's book, Yang Sen clearly did not model himself on Confucian warriors of the past, however, and neither did he appeal explicitly to any Chinese tradition in his speeches to the residents of Chengdu. The YMCA leader Chen Weixin often cited the Chinese classics in his calls to action; nothing of the sort may be found in Yang Sen's speeches and writings.

While Yang Sen's fascination with "newness" and lack of respect for the classical tradition may have rankled Xu Zixiu, who held up Yan Xishan as a model of the modern-day Confucian warrior-administrator, what infuriated the Elders and Sages most during Yang's administration was the disrespect with which he treated them as unofficial, but widely acknowledged, spokesmen for the people of Chengdu. Their open confrontation with Yang Sen occurred after the road-widening plan had been issued and the worried merchants along Great East Street calculated that many were likely to lose more than half of the area of their shops to the new road and sidewalks. The merchants petitioned to reduce the planned width of the road, and when their appeals were ignored, they approached the Elders and Sages to present their case to Yang Sen. According to one of Yang Sen's military attachés, Yang received them politely, and while pointing out to them the advantages of improved transportation and sanitation that the wider streets would bring, he secretly instructed his aides to order soldiers to proceed at full speed with the destruction of property in the planned roadbed. When the Elders and Sages left their meeting with Yang Sen, they discovered that what they had hoped to prevent had already largely occurred.[62] Shortly afterward, adding to the insult, Yang Sen is said to have issued a proclamation stating that further objections to the road-building project would be considered obstructions to urban progress and dealt with severely.[63]

Once Yang Sen had humiliated Chengdu's most prestigious city fathers, the merchant community seems to have swallowed its losses quietly. Harry Franck, an American adventurer passing through the city, assessed its mood as one of deep outrage, although he observed that Yang Sen

> showed no more outward sign of resentment at their dislike than the merchants and shopkeepers, sitting among the scanty remainders of their marts and homes, did of the dejection and anger underneath their placid pale-yellow faces, though every one knew they would "get" the reforming governor at the first opportunity.[64]

Chengdu's merchants had no powerful organization to lead a challenge to the general. Although there had been a chamber of commerce in the city since late Qing times, it had always been very weak compared to those of the industrial cities of eastern China.[65] Its president in the first years of the Republic was a publisher who had close ties to the Elders and Sages. He used his connections to the literati elite and the visibility of his business to try to moderate militarists' demands on the merchant community. When he was assassinated in 1917 while campaigning against harsh levies on salt merchants, the chamber lost its only strong leader.[66]

Sichuan's militarists, including Yang Sen, had sources of income outside of Chengdu, which rendered them relatively free from the necessity to compromise with the city's merchants.[67] Instead, they tried to coopt the more affluent merchants, some of whom were willing to abandon merchant solidarity in exchange for the opportunities that collaboration with militarists could bring. Yang Sen worked most closely with an entrepreneurial transplant from Shanghai, Yu Fenggang, who had come to Chengdu in 1916 as accountant for the local branch of the Commercial Press. Yu Fenggang used his financial talents for the benefit of a series of Chengdu militarists, building up, in the meantime, enough personal capital to allow him to leave the Commercial Press and open several jewelry stores in the center of town. One of the stores was close to the commercial arcade, next to a pharmacy owned by a translator employed in the French consulate-general. The plans for the construction of Chunxi Road called for the leveling of the pharmacy, which put Yang Sen in a diplomatic bind. Yu Fenggang earned his gratitude by offering the site of his jewelry store as an alternative route. In exchange, Yang Sen gave him the right to buy as much of the new street-front property as he wanted. Yu Fenggang, who envisioned Chunxi Road as Chengdu's equivalent to Shanghai's Nanjing Road, bought most of it and, over the next ten years, earned a fortune as Chunxi Road did indeed become Chengdu's premier location for upscale consumer items and entertainment.[68]

Yu Fenggang became head of the chamber of commerce in 1925, and subsequent efforts to oust him succeeded only in dividing merchants into warring factions.[69] A letter to the editor published in a local newspaper in 1927 recommended changing the entire structure of the chamber, arguing that, as things stood, it was so expensive to buy the votes required to become head of it that merchants who did so were practically forced to oppress their weaker colleagues and conspire with the militarists.[70]

Maintaining Public Order in the Face of Unpopular Urban Reform

Beyond the elite community, Yang Sen's programs could be quite disruptive. Although the destruction of buildings for the widening of Great East Street and other existing commercial areas affected primarily wealthier merchants, peddlers who worked the streets were shooed away during and after construction. The Chunxi Road site had been occupied by hundreds of squatter families after the 1911 Revolution; all were forced to move before their houses were flattened, with no compensation. But no public demonstrations seem to have accompanied the destruction. By 1924, Chengdu's students and educators were fully capable of mounting mass demonstrations to protest cuts in educational funding or imperialistic pressure on China,[71] but organized public protests by neighborhood groups over municipal issues such as street widening or public services did not occur. This was due partly to the severity and violence of Yang Sen's rule and partly to the fact that Chengdu's neighborhoods were, themselves, quite orderly places.

The disturbed state of the countryside had helped push the population of Chengdu from some 350,000 in the late Qing to well over 400,000 in 1924.[72] Unlike the huge population increase during the years of war with Japan after 1937, Chengdu's new residents in the 1920s seem not to have strained substantially the cohesion of the city's neighborhoods. In 1926, Western missionaries in the city published a guide to polite conduct in Chengdu in which they advised that the proper response to "the calls of the inevitable small boy" in the street, when they are particularly offensive, is to send one's Chinese teacher to the neighborhood in question to see the "local elder":

> He will see the street official, relate the circumstances, and ask to have the children in that neighborhood exhorted to behave themselves, which means that several families of parents will hear of the matter: and in all probability there will be no more rudeness on that street for a year or two.[73]

The "street official" referred to here is probably the *jiezheng*, or street headman, a position created in the late

Qing in an attempt to graft aspects of Chengdu's traditional *baojia* "mutual surveillance" system to the new professional police force formed in the city in 1903. In the last decade of Qing rule, these street headmen had played a decidedly subordinate role relative to the powerful police organization. After the 1911 Revolution, however, the police lost their provincial funding, and the institution began to crumble. Street militia were formed for neighborhood self-protection, and the street headmen took on greater responsibility for local affairs.[74]

The collapse of Qing authority also made possible the rapid growth of the Society of Brothers and Elders, or Gelaohui, a loosely integrated network of semisecret fraternal lodges. Gelaohui lodges were declared illegal during the Republic, but a large percentage of the men in Chengdu joined them anyway. Many of the street headmen and militia leaders, as well as the police, were thought to have been members of various lodges in Chengdu, and the leaders of these lodges regulated markets and kept order in their sectors of the city.[75]

Yang Sen was quite familiar with the Gelaohui. As a boy he had been awestruck at the sight of a Gelaohui ceremony to which his father had taken him.[76] He was coy, however, about discussing his own participation in the network of "Gowned Brothers" *(paoge),* as lodge members called themselves. Still, there seems little doubt that he knew very well who was influential among the Chengdu lodges and did what he could to coopt them as he had the wealthy merchant Yu Fenggang. It is not surprising, in this light, that the two items on Chen Weixin's reformist agenda that Yang Sen did absolutely nothing about were prostitution and opium dens, two sources of income for lodge leaders.[77]

With street headmen and Gelaohui leaders effectively regulating public conduct, Yang Sen did not have to fear the development of spontaneous resistance to his plans within the city's neighborhoods. Even had it occurred, there is no doubt that Yang Sen, whose commitment to his own vision of Chengdu's development was so powerful that he dared to humiliate the Elders and Sages publicly, would have had few scruples about suppressing the protests of the common people. According to a Western observer, Yang Sen's soldiers were among the least disciplined in the province,[78] adding insecurity about the arbitrary actions of soldiers to the certainty of suppression of any acts of protest. It was not an environment that welcomed public acts of resistance.

Resistance via Ridicule: Liu Shiliang's "Reactionary" Wit

Despite the vigilance with which Yang Sen and his fellow militarists surveyed their territories for potential rebellion, in Chengdu Yang quickly became a target of widespread ridicule in the teahouses and bathhouses frequented by the male multitudes. Evidence for this comes first from Yang Sen's own speeches, during which he often remarked on the rumors flying around the city, as if he were proud of having befuddled and affronted the ignorant masses. In September 1924, he told the Mass Education Association that their efforts were being hampered by rumors that the real reason for gathering together uneducated people was to make it easier for his military to conscript laborers, or collect exorbitant fees, or pick out the pretty women.[79] After calling for free and open criticism of his urban reform projects in a speech at the model public lecture hall, he went on to attack those who had circulated malicious stories about him: that he could not bear to see long hair coiled on women's heads, and therefore cut it off with scissors, or that he had seen some female students eating snacks at a peddler stand during the Flower Festival and had called them over and smacked them in their faces.[80] Older residents of Chengdu interviewed in 1991 shared a number of wild and unverifiable stories about Yang Sen's conduct in 1924. These included the time when, to promote exercise among women, Yang Sen ordered one of his wives to swim in the river, and threw her in when she hesitated, and the time when he had soldiers beat to death a student from the higher normal school who had become involved romantically with a fellow student, another one of Yang Sen's wives, whom Yang also killed. In a collection of essays memorializing her deceased father, Yang Sen's daughter, Wanyun, bewailed the fact that throughout his life her father was suspected by many of having more wives than he could count and being unable to recognize his own children.[81] Chengdu residents, forced to bear Yang Sen's heavy-handed ways and destructive public works projects, got back at him by making fun of him.

Of all Yang Sen's Chengdu critics, the most witty and audacious was Liu Shiliang, who grew up in Sichuan's salt-well district and came to Chengdu shortly after 1911 as a representative of salt merchants. He quickly became a good friend of the publisher who headed the city's chamber of commerce and set up his own business, a bathhouse, in the center of town. He was fond of satirical verses and composed a couplet every year on the anniversary of the founding of the Republic, pointing out by means of puns and other devices the huge gap between republican ideals and militarist reality. He displayed these on the pillars of a prominent office building in the neighborhood of his bathhouse.[82] He wrote a particularly bitter couplet on the occasion of the assassination of his friend, the head of the chamber of commerce, that implicated a leading militarist in the man's death.[83]

In 1924, new sanitary regulations promulgated by Wang Zuanxu's city government office required Chengdu's bathhouses to substitute porcelain tubs for wooden ones. Liu Shiliang, who could not afford to upgrade his equipment, closed his bathhouse and opened a teahouse. At the same time, many of his merchant friends lost their shops to the Chunxi Road construction. All of the upheaval prompted Liu Shiliang to write a couplet that became the epitaph of Yang Sen's career in Chengdu:

> *The road has already been leveled, when will the Duli [Yang Sen's title] roll?*
> *The people's homes have been torn down, we hope the General will drive soon.*

The verse's superficially congratulatory message was a thin cover for the underlying hostility and scorn. The cleverness of the couplet lies in its pun on the character for "roll" *(gun),* which could refer either to the technical process of compressing a road surface with a stone roller or to the colloquial expression *"gundan"*—roll away like an egg or, in other words, get the hell out of here.[84] Liu Shiliang's couplet was immediately popular in Chengdu and attached itself so tenaciously to Yang Sen that the director of his memorial ceremony in 1977 chose it as the title of his memorial essay, regarding it as a fitting tribute to Yang Sen's steadfastness against those who would stand in the way of progress and economic development.[85] During the rest of Yang Sen's stay in Chengdu, Liu Shiliang lay low, protected, according to his biographer, by some of the Five Elders and Seven Sages, who found in his somewhat coarse wit a useful tool in their feud with the general.

Many of the rumors that surrounded Yang Sen concerned issues of proper conduct between men and women and acceptable behavior and dress for people of both sexes, but especially women. Given the nature of Yang Sen's own household, this is not surprising. Yang Sen's family would have been an oddity in any city in China, at any period of its history. His collection of well-educated, short-haired, fashionably dressed wives appeared frequently in public, sometimes on bicycles.[86] A sarcastic observer quoted them greeting the participants in a convention of Christian missionaries in January 1925 with hearty cries of "Ham is really greasy!" (*huo tui you duo,* or "how do you do"). It was widely believed that the provincial higher normal school had only agreed to take on female students in the fall of 1924 because one of Yang Sen's wives wanted to attend.[87]

It is difficult to assess the extent to which the ridicule heaped on Yang Sen's unusual family hampered his efforts to reform what he considered Chengdu's indolent and frivolous culture and backward cityscape. His military defeat in the summer of 1925 ended his Chengdu experiment too soon to judge whether he could have won over the populace to his program of construction and cultural change. In his sixteen months in Chengdu, Yang Sen did not achieve his vision of a "New Sichuan." Even at the height of his efforts in 1925, a member of the Chengdu elite wrote a letter to a friend in Beijing that declared the "eight beautiful sights" of the city—"visible everywhere in the streets"—to be *qiuba* (slang for soldiers), thieves, opium, food and drink peddlers, toilets, vagrants, bound feet, and coffin shops.[88]

Yang Sen's authoritarian style undoubtedly helped foster a cynical view of city administration and planning among a large sector of Chengdu society. By trying to force his ideas down the throats of the people, Yang Sen stirred up tremendous resentment. Unable to protest in any other way, Chengdu's people responded with scorn and laughter, interpreted by Yang Sen and his supporters as a stubborn rejection of modern ways. Yang Sen turned Liu Shiliang into a popular hero, enabling the latter to enjoy a successful career as a satirical poet and magazine publisher. By the time Chiang Kai-shek introduced the New Life Movement to Chengdu in the mid-1930s, Liu Shiliang had had a decade of practice poking fun at such attempts at "cultural renewal," and he did not hesitate once more to display his skills.[89]

But at the same time, Yang Sen did encourage those in the city who wanted to introduce some of the new planning ideas becoming popular along the coast. Many of his city administration initiatives were carried on by his successors, less flamboyantly but, perhaps because of that, more successfully. In 1928, the city government noted with pride that shopkeepers along one street had actually requested to have their street widened before it was scheduled to be.[90]

The city government yearbook in which officials celebrated this fact makes it clear that the post-Yang Sen city administration had done what it could to involve the more conservative city elites in its work. A preface by Deng Xihou, one of the militarists who helped defeat Yang Sen, cites precedents for city government in the Classics, ending with the statement, "We do not look to the aliens of the four directions for our models; our Chengdu long ago had a city head, and we are reviving this abandoned administrative position" *(Xue buzai siyi; wu Chengdu jiu you shizhang, wu xiu feiguan yi).*[91] Each of the subsequent sections of the book begins with a title page inscribed by one of the Five Elders and Seven Sages. Photographs of Fuxing Street in the yearbook (figs. 11 and 12) indicate that Yang Sen's demands for men to stop wearing long gowns had no lasting effect.

From 1927 to 1932, city officials in Chengdu took steps to give the institutions of the city government more visibility and prestige than they had enjoyed in Yang Sen's time, when the general had taken such a prominent personal role in city affairs. A weekly city government gazette was launched in July 1927. It reported on the regular meetings of city officials, with detailed accounts of deliberations over such issues as regulation of public toilets and rickshaws and how to increase popular awareness of the work of city administration. One suggestion they adopted was to have city workers engaged in street repair wear uniforms identifying them as city workers, as they had seen done in Shanghai.[92] The weekly gazette also published letters from citizens with recommendations for civic improvement, including advice on such matters as how to keep the trees that had recently been planted along the roadsides alive.[93] The grander schemes of the city government of the late 1920s, including a plan to build a comprehensive water system for the city, had to be shelved for lack of funds.[94] Nevertheless, in addition to keeping alive the memory of the New Policies institutions as they had been in their prime, the city government office served as a conduit for information about the new Nationalist government's urban policies. City government publications helped introduce the rhetoric of the Nationalist Party to Chengdu and tried to make it seem relevant to a city far from the center of the revolution. "If the plans the Premier [Sun Yat-sen] set out in his *Fundamentals of National Reconstruction* are followed and a system of railroads links the Northwest and Southwest, Chengdu's future prominence will be no less than that of Moscow, Berlin, or Chicago," one writer enthused.[95]

Yang Sen's interest in the city administration movement arose because he sought an arena in which to demonstrate his talents as a modern man of action. By 1924, advocates of city planning and development had articulated an alluring vision that made well-regulated cities the key to a powerful Chinese nation. Their city boosterism, with its emphasis on public construction, could easily be extended to cities where industrial development was not yet apparent. Far beyond the city experts' own bases in Shanghai and other coastal cities, their enthusiasm for paved streets and parks and planned development in general caught the imaginations of people, like Yang Sen and his young colleagues, who wanted to be doing great things. For older residents of Chengdu, on the other hand, elements of the city administration movement recalled the New Policies reform programs of their own youth. Once the impetuous and authoritarian Yang Sen was out of the way, Chengdu's more traditional elites joined hands with the city experts Yang had hired. Together, they ensured that new concepts of proper city planning and administration continued to have an important place in the local political discourse, long after the most ardent early supporter of "city administration" in Chengdu fled the city.

Part II
Tradition and Modernity

Chapter 7

Tourism and Spatial Change in Hangzhou, 1911–1927

Liping Wang

For most visitors today, Hangzhou evokes sentimental feelings of a romantic past, where elegant temples, fine pagodas, and carved bridges frame the delicate landscape of rolling hills and are mirrored in the placid water of West Lake. Benefiting from this abundance of classic beauty, Hangzhou enjoys a status that many other cities are trying to establish for themselves—an ideal place for tourism. Like so many other popular tourist destinations in the world, Hangzhou's attraction rests upon a combination of the seeming purity of its natural beauty and its presumed timelessness. It seems natural to speak about Hangzhou in terms of its historicity, since records about the city begin from about 200 B.C., and it served as the capital of the Southern Song (1127–1279). In the tourist guidebooks of the republican period, every "must see" site in Hangzhou was said to have a history of at least one millennium. Books that were published after 1949 understandably eulogized the People's Republic of China's effort to preserve the antiquities of Hangzhou. Crossing these recent political eras, the basic message remains consistent: Hangzhou's identity lies in the city's supposedly unaltered spatial arrangement, in which the city seems always to have turned its face in the direction of West Lake.

But when we look at the period before 1911, this image of an ancient Hangzhou, which seemed to exist because of West Lake, is cast into doubt. Yu Dafu, the writer who gained his middle school education in Hangzhou, remembered the city at the turn of this century very differently. The "downtown" area where he often went for fun was called the City-God Hill (Chenghuang shan), which is a hill in the southern part of the city, far away from West Lake.[1] On City-God Hill Yu Dafu often went to buy books, sip tea, savor tasty snacks, and enjoy the hustle and bustle of the city. Yu Dafu's description of the center of Hangzhou city life sounds similar to the one found in *The Scholars (Rulin waishi),* an early Qing novel. In the novel, a poor scholar visited Hangzhou and found his friend, who was a fortune-teller, at City-God Hill. It was a place crowded with temples, where the eating, tea drinking, buying and selling of books, and various kinds of fortune telling all made for a lively scene.[2]

This Qing portrait of Hangzhou certainly does not bear much resemblance to our contemporary image of the city that centers around the picturesque and history-laden West Lake. What happened in between the two pictures is a process entailing a reorganization of the urban hierarchy in Jiangnan, which found expression in Hangzhou's spatial arrangement. Starting in the mid-nineteenth century, imperialist aggression, foreign trade, and domestic rebellion contributed to the rapid ascendance of Shanghai in this region and the decline of some of the older urban centers. Hangzhou's role as a center of handicrafts and commerce was lost to the industrialized metropolis of Shanghai. In the 1910s, however, Hangzhou sprang from the ashes as one of the most famous tourist destinations in China, and its role as a "culture garden" continues to this day. This chapter examines the creation of modern Hangzhou and the tourist trade that has enveloped the city in an aura of "tradition." In particular, I will focus on the spatial transformation of the city in the early twentieth century that allowed the modern-day tourist vision to develop.[3]

Looking at spatial transformation within cities like Hangzhou during the early republican period can help us to understand the changes that brought China into the modern era. Hangzhou's altered cityscape reveals important changes in the social and cultural relationships between the city and its surrounding countryside, as well as between the city and its metropolitan neighbor, Shanghai. As China itself was being transformed, Hangzhou had to reposition itself to provide new services in order to replace those that were rapidly moving elsewhere. This chapter is about the process whereby changes in Hangzhou's physical layout both reflected and influenced this repositioning, ultimately resulting in the emergence of a new kind of tourism. Faced with a modern regional arrangement that severely constrained the possibility for further development, Hangzhou discovered that what it had to rely upon was precisely its "antiquity." Given that much of this antiquity was not as ancient as claimed, these spaces in Hangzhou also illustrate how "tradition" and "modernity" do not form a linear history, but were instead constructed, or "invented," simultaneously.

Spatial Layout and City Life in Qing Hangzhou

Hangzhou during the Qing was one of the top cities for handicraft production and commerce in the empire. Due to its strategic position at the southern terminus of the Grand Canal, Hangzhou was an important commercial nodal point that connected Jiangnan and the mountainous southeast China.[4] The city's central role in silk production made it the location of one of the three imperial Bureaus of Silk Weaving.[5] Yet Hangzhou's economic importance was only part of the story. As the popular saying went, "There is paradise above, and there are Suzhou and Hangzhou below" *(Shang you tiantang, xia you Su Hang).* Hangzhou's image of a "paradise on earth" was also closely related to the city's role as a major center of elite culture and popular religious activity.

Long before the modern era, travel and sight-seeing had been part of a distinctive literati way of life, and travel writing was an important genre of elite cultural production.[6] Hangzhou had a special role in this elite cultural tradition because of its proximity to West Lake. The refined landscape of the lake area just outside the city was canonized by a host of poet-officials, among them two saints of poetry, Bo Juyi (772–846) and Su Shi (1037–1101).[7] Literature from the Tang (618–907) and Song (960–1279) periods created a reputation for West Lake, placing it among the most culturally significant sites that any well-educated member of the elite would be obligated to visit and appreciate. In fact, sight-seeing around West Lake was such an important element in cultural politics that in the seventeenth and eighteenth century the Qing emperors Kangxi (r. 1661–1722) and Qianlong (r. 1736–1795) both patronized it for the purpose of coopting the Han Chinese elite in Jiangnan. During their visits to Hangzhou, Kangxi and Qianlong blessed many scenic wonders with their calligraphy. Traveling palaces were built for them on Lone Mountain (Gu shan), which had one of the choicest views of West Lake.[8]

However, at the same time that West Lake was important to Hangzhou's spatial position, it was also separated from the city by a tall and thick wall. The city wall was eleven and half miles in length, thirty feet high, and thirty-five feet wide on top. This city wall effectively blocked the view of West Lake from most parts of the city. By closing off the line of sight, the wall imposed a clear boundary on the urban space, turning the city into a closed space vis-à-vis the surrounding scenery. Furthermore, these walls were used to control movement between the city and its surroundings. City dwellers' access to the lake was limited to the three city gates opening westward during daytime: the Qiantang Gate (Qiantang men), the Yongjin Gate (Yongjin men), and the Qingbo Gate (Qingbo men) (see map 13). The constraining effect of the city wall was very much highlighted during the turmoil of the mid-nineteenth century. When Hangzhou was attacked by Taiping rebels in 1861, the residents were trapped in the besieged city for over three months. Cut off completely from outside aid, about six hundred thousand people starved to death or committed suicide.[9]

The spatial layout of Qing Hangzhou was also shaped by conditions that were unique to the Qing dynasty. The city contained a second closed space. A sizable area in the west part of the city between the Qiantang Gate and the Yongjin Gate was surrounded by another wall that was about three miles in circumference. This was the banner garrison *(qiying),* one of the larger garrisons in the Qing empire.[10] The construction of this garrison dated to 1648, in the wake of the Manchu conquest of Jiangnan and the southeast coastal areas. Tenacious Ming loyalist resistance in these areas made the Manchu conquest a prolonged and particularly bloody process. It was in this con-

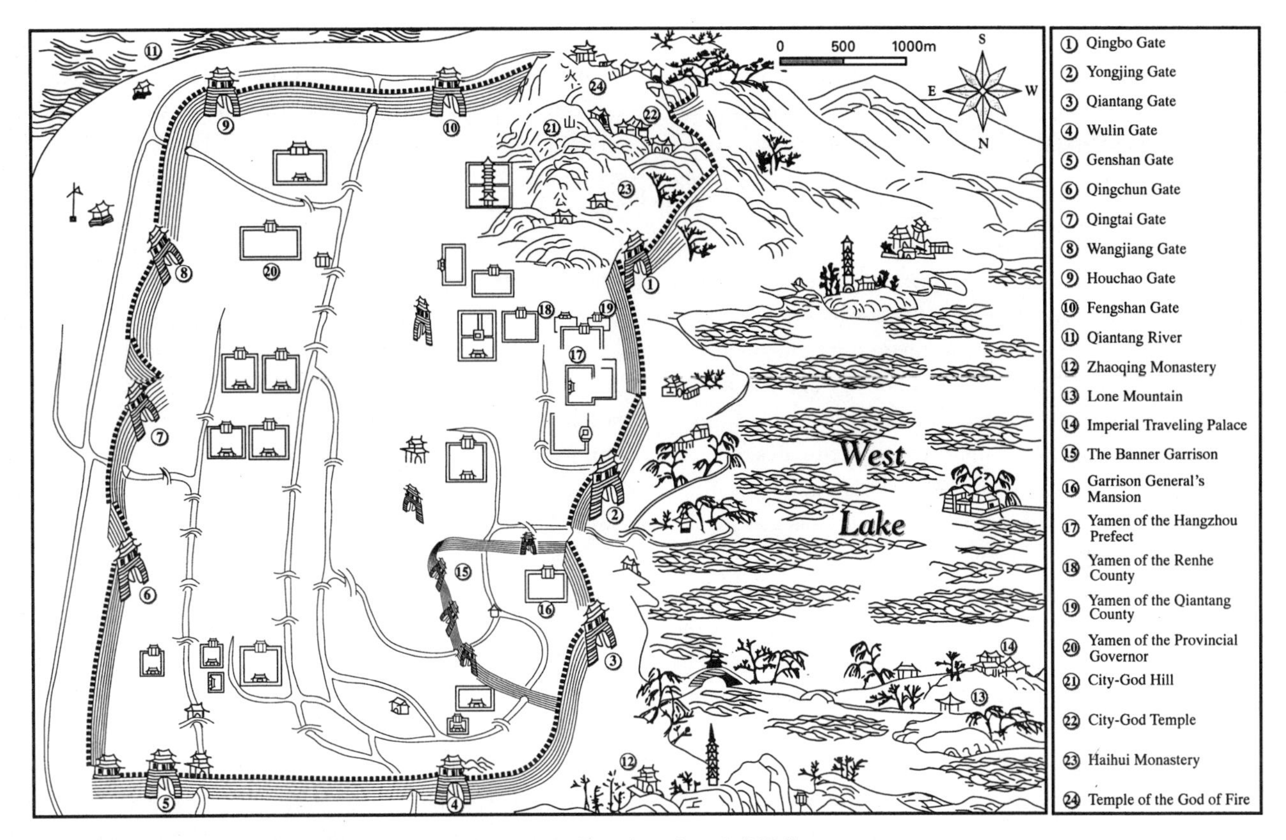

Map 13. Hangzhou during the Qing dynasty. Redrawn from Tong Longfu, ed. (1993).

text that the Qing court emphasized the strategic importance of Hangzhou: "This is a crucial location [which connects] river and sea. In order to secure order, a large military force must be stationed [in the city]."[11] Clearly intending the garrison to be a symbol of Manchu conquest, the victors encircled about 7,000 *mu* of land in the densely populated center of Hangzhou. The construction of this garrison subsequently caused a serious dislocation of local people and a severe housing shortage. All the previous residents of the enclosed area—about ten thousand families—were driven from their homes. Not only were the former property owners denied compensation for their loss, but for the next two decades they had to pay taxes on the land now occupied by bannermen.[12]

The garrison, with a stone wall over twenty feet high and six gates, took the shape of a city within a city and imposed further spatial restrictions on access to West Lake from Hangzhou itself. One of the city gates opening to the lake, the Qiantang Gate, was incorporated as one of the garrison gates. If people wanted to reach West Lake through that gate, they had to pass through the garrison, where the bannermen guards would routinely search passing sedan chairs. In order to avoid harassment, most people would reach the lake through the other two gates, Yongjin or Qingbo.[13]

Both the city wall and the banner garrison imposed physical barriers that effectively separated Hangzhou and West Lake into two spatially distinct units. As a result, sight-seeing on West Lake was largely considered an activity that took place outside the city and was not the focus of Hangzhou's city life. In fact, the most important social space within the city was quite a distance from West Lake. The American council Fredrick D. Cloud, writing about Hangzhou in the early 1900s, identified Main Street

(Dajie) as the center of Hangzhou commercial activities. This street, about four miles in length, formed a key north-south axis in the city. Commercial space along the street was so valuable that the flagstone pavement had narrowed to five feet in many places as wooden buildings and shops encroached upon it from both sides.[14] The southern stretch of the street, especially the section near City-God Hill, was the most crowded commercial quarter. There, shops spread out from this thoroughfare onto the nearby side streets. The city's best scissors shops, cosmetic stores, medicine shops, dry-food stores, bookshops, and fortune-tellers were located there. Hangzhou's famous teahouses, wine shops, and restaurants also were concentrated in this area.[15]

The story of a medicine shop, Huqingyu tang, owned by the powerful native banker Hu Guangyong (1823–1885), reveals the high commercial value of the City-God Hill area. Hu Guangyong acted as General Zuo Zongtang's financier during the campaigns to suppress the Taipings and thus gained imperial favor. By the 1870s Hu Guangyong was at the height of his wealth and power, and he decided to engage in the Hangzhou medicine trade, which had long been very competitive. He considered the location of the new shop to be one of the key factors in determining its competitiveness and picked a location on a street that led up to City-God Hill. In 1878, a magnificent two-story business compound was built there. Hu Guangyong's success was instant. The new medicine shop surpassed all others of its kind in Hangzhou in volume of business and soon became one of the largest medicine shops in China.[16]

At first glance, the reason behind Hu Guangyong's choice appears simple: the area around City-God Hill was the city's commercial center. But why had this particular area developed as a commercial center? Part of the answer is found in the close relationship between urban space and religious activities in Hangzhou. The hills, originally named Wu Hills (Wushan), gained the popular name City-God Hill during the Qing because at that time all the city-gods in Hangzhou were enshrined there.[17] In addition to the city-god temples, there were some thirty Buddhist and Daoist temples on the hills. Haihui Monastery (Haihui si) was believed to be the "natal home" *(niangjia)* of a famous Guanyin statue in a West Lake-area monastery, Upper Tianzhu Monastery (Shang Tianzhu si). The bodhisattva was often evoked to protect Hangzhou from calamities, and Haihui Monastery had always hosted the Guanyin statue that was brought into the city for worship. The Daoist deities that were enshrined on the City-God Hill fell roughly into two groups. The first included Guandi, who was worshipped as a god of wealth, and the God of Letters (Wenchang). These deities, together with the city-gods, were favored by the imperial government and could be found in most Chinese cities. Meanwhile, City-God Hill hosted a second group of deities that were particularly important to Hangzhou people. Among them were the God of Fire (Huode) and the God of Water (Shuishen) because the city, crowded with wooden buildings, was extremely susceptible to destruction by fire. Atop the hill was a temple that enshrined the God of Medicine (Shennong) in which the guild of medicine trades held yearly meetings and made sacrifices.[18]

The Qing state played an active role in making City-God Hill a space of religious symbols and rituals. Many deities were on the official worship list, thus regular offerings and ritual ceremonies were dedicated to them. Temple buildings and statues were sometimes repaired or rebuilt at government expense. Official patronage was crucial to the revival of this area in the decades after the Taiping Rebellion, as Hangzhou had suffered great destruction during the Taiping occupation. At that time almost all the buildings on City-God Hill had been burned to ashes. In the rebellion's aftermath, the City-God Hill temples were gradually rebuilt with financial support from high officials and donations from wealthy families. In fact, all of the above-mentioned temples on City-God Hill were rebuilt during the 1870s and the 1890s with official encouragement.[19]

The concentration of temples on City-God Hill made it central to many annual religious festivals and related entertainment. Large crowds of festival participants patronized the shops and made the place a bustling commercial area. "Have you been up to City-God Hill?" became the typical greeting among Hangzhou residents during the New Year holiday.[20] At New Year's time there were at least two celebrations that made City-God Hill worth visiting. First was the Lichun Festival, celebrating the beginning of the spring season. In Hangzhou the ritual was customarily called "The God of Soil goes to [City-God] Hill *(Taisui shangshan).*" On this occasion, the Hangzhou prefect and the magistrates of the two counties (Qiantang and Renhe) under which Hangzhou City was administrated went to the eastern suburb to welcome the spirits of spring. Dressed in ceremonial robes, riding in open sedan chairs, and accompanied by their staffs, the officials escorted the statues of the God of Soil and a paper ox into the city, symbolizing spring and a good harvest. When the parade entered the city, people filled the streets to shower grain on the paper ox. The statues were carried to City-God Hill and put in the temple for the God of Soil. A long procession was arranged with various kinds of lantern displays, performances, music bands, and burning incense. Shortly after this came the second celebration, the Lantern Festival, when all the dragon lanterns in Hangzhou City and its suburbs were taken to the Dragon King Temple (Longshen miao) on City-God Hill. The eyes of the dragons had to be painted at the temple, a ritual that marked the beginning of the festival.[21]

Although city people participated in such public activities at City-God Hill, the content of these activities was not distinctively urban. The festivals' timing and the type of gods honored, such as the God of Spring and the God of Soil, were closely related to the agricultural cycle.[22] The officials' activity in the Lichun Festival thus reminds us of one very important function of the Chinese imperial state: consciously basing itself on agriculture, the state played a significant role in fostering connections between urban and rural areas. One of the important duties of city-based officials was to offer sacrifices to gods on key dates in the calendar issued by the emperor—rituals that were thought to bring a good harvest to the countryside. City life in Hangzhou during the Qing was punctuated by this calendar, which was closely related to the agricultural cycle, and city dwellers shared many religious celebrations with people in the surrounding rural areas.

The close connection between Hangzhou and its rural hinterland lay also in its unique role as the destination of annual pilgrimages undertaken largely by peasants from Jiangnan. In other words, Hangzhou had the image of a "paradise on earth" partly because of its importance in popular religious beliefs in Jiangnan. Hangzhou was a holy city with hundreds of temples and shrines located inside and in its vicinity. The above-mentioned Guanyin statue in Upper Tanzhu Monastery and the provincial city-god on City-God Hill were popularly thought to have especially great efficacy and miraculous origins.[23]

Every spring, as many as one hundred thousand pilgrims traveled to Hangzhou.[24] Most were peasants from Hangzhou, Jiaxing, and Huzhou Prefectures in northern Zhejiang; some came from Suzhou, Songjiang, and Changshu, the prefectures in southern Jiangsu.[25] Moreover, many of the pilgrims were rural women. The peasants traveled on boats adorned with special yellow flags inscribed with the term "pilgrimage to the mountains to burn incense" *(chaoshan jinxiang),* and most boats anchored at the canal bank outside the northern city wall. From there the men and women would either go westward to arrive at the large Buddhist monasteries near West Lake, especially the "Indian Temples" (Tianzhu si), or they would enter Hangzhou City and walk along Main Street to the temples on City-God Hill. They had to spend days in Hangzhou to complete incense burning at all the important temples, but they did not lodge in hotels. Some had special connections with certain monasteries and stayed there; others simply slept on their boats.[26] The purpose of these spring pilgrimages and prayers to the gods was to secure a good harvest in farming and especially in silkworm raising. Ever since the Ming dynasty, sericulture had become an indispensable part of the peasant household economy in the Lake Tai area, especially in the three prefectures of northern Zhejiang. Silkworm raising was much more than a simple production process making use of rural women's labor; in Jiangnan it had given rise to a distinctive culture with elaborate rituals. The spring pilgrimages to Hangzhou were an integral part of this culture.[27]

The annual pilgrimage demonstrates that Qing Hangzhou was closely connected to its rural hinterland. The pilgrimages had a great impact on the urban economy. The needs of these pilgrims, the timing of their trips, and the volume of trade they generated in Hangzhou were very important in shaping handicraft production and urban commercial life. The items pilgrims required for religious purposes, such as candles, incense, and especially tin foil paper for making spirit money, constituted a major part of the city's handicraft business. More important, pilgrimages were also shopping trips for peasants. Local people observed that most pilgrims were well-off peasants who carried large quantities of cash and spent it generously.[28] The commercial aspect of the spring pilgrimage was so important that the entire event was popularly called "incense trade" *(xiangshi).* A popular saying held that for retailers, "three months in the winter depended on one month in the spring."[29] Commerce in Hangzhou was so dependent on the pilgrimage trade that it had a seasonal and festival character. Moreover, women's participation in the pilgrimages left its imprint on the typical shopping list: cosmetic powder, scissors, silk thread, and fans were some of Hangzhou's best-known products.

One crucial reason that City-God Hill existed as the center of commerce was that it was a holy site inside the city. Famous shops in the area used various strategies to attract peasants. For example, Hu Guangyong not only built his medicine shop right on the path leading from Main Street up to City-God Hill, he also held his grand opening during the pilgrimage season of 1878. On opening day Hu Guangyong put on his first-rank official robe to serve his pilgrim customers, and on one occasion he personally exchanged the medicine with which a peasant buyer was unhappy.[30] Meanwhile, Hangzhou's best cosmetic store, Kongfengchun, promoted its product through exploiting peasant belief that auspicious words would bring luck in silkworm raising. The store advertised its powder with the slogan: "Buy one chunk of the fragrant powder, get the best harvest for your silkworms."[31]

The 1911 Revolution and the Spatial Transformation in Hangzhou

From the mid-nineteenth century, Hangzhou was adversely affected by factors that eventually resulted in a rearrangement of the hierarchy of urban centers in the Jiangnan area. First, Hangzhou was deprived of its strategic importance in the old commercial network, of which the Grand Canal was the main north-south artery. When the Taiping rebels occupied Jiangnan in 1853, they blocked transportation along the Grand Canal. The Qing court and merchants responded to this by developing sea shipments through Shanghai instead. Second, fighting between the Taiping and Qing armies accelerated Hangzhou's declining fortune. In the early 1860s, rebels destroyed the city, and its population was reduced from about one million to less than two hundred thousand. Significantly, Hangzhou's decline coincided with the rise of Shanghai. Benefiting from precisely the two factors that damaged Hangzhou's prosperity and from the stimulus of foreign trade, Shanghai rapidly developed from a market town to a metropolis.

Hangzhou was "opened up" after the Sino-Japanese War of 1894–1895, but it never flourished as a treaty port. Unlike the foreign concessions in its more prominent neighbor, Shanghai, the Japanese Concession in the suburbs of Hangzhou failed to become a new center of modern industry and commerce; instead, it merely became a den for gambling and prostitution.[32] Influenced by the Qing court's reformist New Policies, some wealthy Zhejiang merchants invested in a few modern industrial enterprises in Hangzhou. In 1896, a cotton mill and a silk reeling factory were built in its northern suburb.[33] For the most part, however, these factories never became a prominent feature of the city. As it entered the twentieth century, Hangzhou was a stagnant, marginalized city, struggling to reposition itself in a drastically changed world. Not only was Hangzhou's role as an economic and cultural center taken over by Shanghai, but the city itself also became increasingly dependent upon that Westernized metropolis.

Modernity came to Hangzhou most dramatically with a new mode of transportation connecting the city to Shanghai: the Shanghai-Hangzhou railroad, completed in 1909. The struggle to protect Chinese control of this railway had the immediate political effect of feeding the growing anti-Qing sentiment in Zhejiang. The coming of the train also had a long-term social impact, putting Hangzhou within easy reach of Shanghai. The tracks shortened travel between the two cities from a three-day journey by junk to a three and a half-hour trip by train. The drastically reduced "distance" between the two cities meant an increasing flow of people between them. Modern transportation worked to subject Hangzhou more and more to the direct influence of Shanghai, and it provided the necessary condition for Hangzhou to become a convenient playground for middle-class tourists from Shanghai.

Two years after the railway linked Hangzhou to Shanghai, the 1911 Revolution provided another crucial moment in Hangzhou's search for a modern identity. In the city, the 1911 Revolution was essentially a coup d'état. The conspirators were mostly military officers of Qing New Army units stationed in the suburbs, and in early November Hangzhou was taken over by these New Army units. The coup lasted less than two days, as there was no serious resistance from the banner garrison. The bannermen gave up their weapons after a peace agreement was negotiated and signed by a garrison representative and the revolutionaries.[34] Despite the easy transfer of power, developments that occurred afterward force us to conclude that 1911 had a truly revolutionary impact on the city.

The existence of a banner garrison inside Hangzhou meant that the anti-Manchu revolution would be especially relevant to the city's subsequent spatial transformation. The revolutionaries took the Manchu and Mongol bannermen inside the garrison as their main target in the military conspiracy. Having taken the city, the revolutionaries declared the "liberation" of the garrison area and the elimination of this symbol of Manchu rule. The revolutionary government quickly confiscated the garrison land, and all bannermen and their families were expelled from their homes.[35] Through such violent political action, the new republican authority in Hangzhou was able to put a huge space under its control. The manner in which the new government exploited this rare opportunity determined important aspects of Hangzhou's future. In accord with the spirit of the time and the emphasis on promoting commerce and industry, the new provincial government decided that "except for the land that is reserved for streets and for public uses, the rest of the land will be sold to people for building a commercial quarter."[36] In fact, "New Business District" (Xin shichang) became the new name for the former bannerman garrison.

The man responsible for this decision was Zhu Fucheng (1873–1948), head of the Provincial Department of Civil Administration from 1912 to 1913. Zhu Fucheng participated in the 1911 revolutionary conspiracy in Hangzhou as a Tong Meng Hui representative. He was fervently anti-Manchu and had schemed to murder several bannerman leaders in the garrison after their surrender. It is hardly a surprise, then, that he used his power to erase all traces of the garrison. Zhu Fucheng's life prior to the 1911 Revolution is also representative of the new republican elite that embraced modernist ideas through Western-style education and experience abroad. Zhu Fucheng was a native of the neighboring county, Jiaxing, and was one of the radical youth who turned his back on classical education and went to study in Japan in the 1890s. While in Tokyo, he studied law and politics. In 1905, Zhu Fucheng joined the Tong Meng Hui and returned to his hometown in Jiaxing, where he spent some years doing business and managing new-style schools. He became an important figure in late Qing provincial politics after he was elected a standing member of the provincial assembly.[37] Zhu Fucheng's personal experience in the newly modernized Tokyo, his interest in law and order, public education, and commerce all seemed to have informed his design for the New Business District.

The creation of the New Business District meant more than constructing a new commercial center. The planning triggered a spatial transformation in the city by opening the closed urban space. The section of the city wall from Qiantang Gate to Yongjin Gate was torn down with the rest of the garrison. A Lakeshore Boulevard (Hubin lu) took over the space on which the wall once stood.[38] With the physical barrier having been removed, West Lake was incorporated into the city. The lake was thus transformed from a suburban scene into an integral part of Hangzhou's cityscape. The magnitude of this change was not lost on the locals and is perhaps best described by their own saying: "West Lake moved into the city"[39] (see map 14).

The actual work of topographic surveying, road design, and selling the land was entrusted to a planning office headed by Ruan Xingyi, who came from a prominent Hangzhou family and had studied in Japan. He returned to Hangzhou after graduation from a Japanese school of rail-

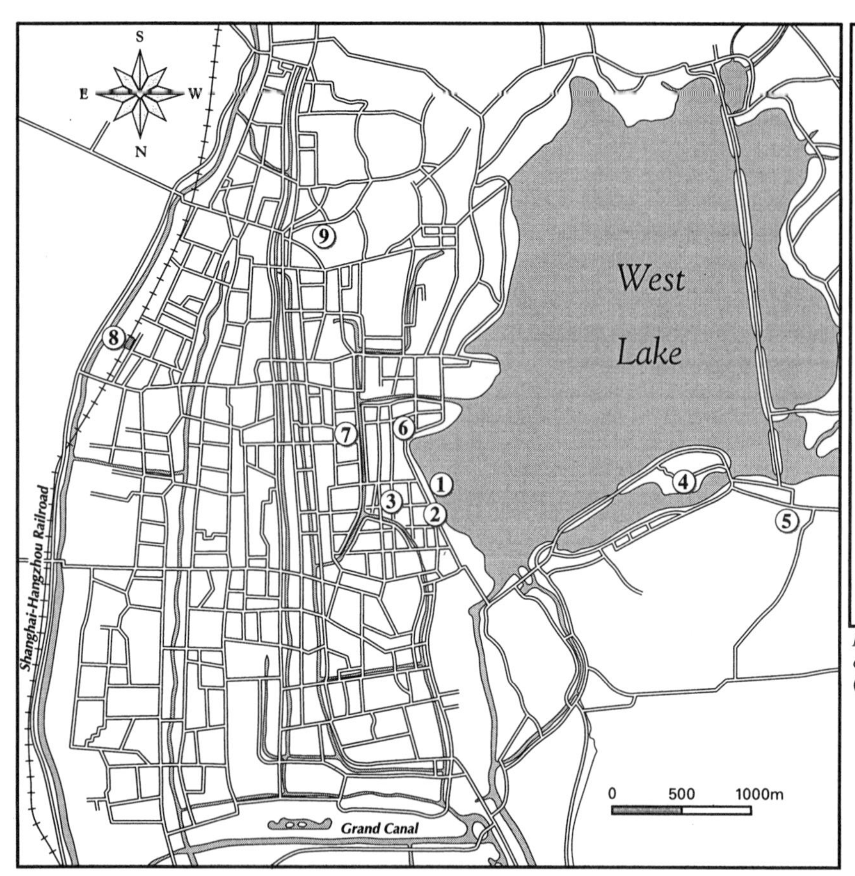

① Lakeshore Parks (Hubin gongyuan)

② Lakeshore Boulevard (Hubin lu)

③ New Business District (Xin shichang)

④ Lone Mountain (Gu shan)

⑤ Shrine of Yue Fei (Yuefen)

⑥ Provincial Governor's Mansion (Dujun fu)

⑦ Hangxian County Government (Hangxian gongshu)

⑧ Hangzhou Railway Station (Hangzhou cheng zhan)

⑨ City-God Hill (Chenghuang shan)

Note: this map is oriented South so that a comparison can be made between it and the other map of Hangzhou (gazetteer-style map) which also appears in this chapter.

Map 14. Hangzhou in the 1920s. Redrawn from a map in Yu Shouzhen, Ge Suicheng, Zhou Baidi, eds., *Quanguo duhui shangbu luxing zhinan* (1926).

road management and was hired as an engineer on the Shanghai-Hangzhou railway project.[40] Ruan Xingyi's group began planning the New Business District in 1913. The first step was road construction in the district. Working with the idea of creating a new commercial center as if it were built upon an empty space, the road design completely ignored the streets that had existed in the garrison. The New Business District was given the kind of rational grid system that is typically found in modern planning for new cities. The streets were all leveled and "as straight as arrows," because the plan was not to be compromised by any preexisting building. With most of the streets intersecting one another at ninety-degree angles, the entire district looked "like a chess board."[41] Each of the four main streets was 19.2 meters wide and had sidewalks 3.2 meters wide. There were twenty-three secondary streets, each 9.6 meters in width, plus 1.92 meters for sidewalks[42] (see fig. 13).

In addition to the orderliness intended by such rationally designed streets, the plan of the New Business District required another necessary component of the modern urban landscape: parks. The design of the parks demonstrated the planners' tremendous emphasis on connecting the future commercial quarter with scenic West Lake and made it a crucial element of the New Business District. A chain of five garden-size parks *(hubin gongyuan)* occupied the lakeshore next to Lakeshore Boulevard. In the parks, a stone embankment protected the lakeshore, and railings made of stone and iron were set up for decoration. Lawns, plants, and benches invited sightseers. Moreover, docks that were built between the parks enhanced the link be-

Fig. 13. A main street in the New Business District in the 1920s. Note the contrast between the Western-style buildings and the men walking in traditional long gowns. Photo courtesy of Library of Congress.

tween the New Business District and West Lake. The docks had stone steps descending to the waterfront, providing easy access to tour boats on the lake.[43] Not only was the visual barrier between city and lake removed with the razing of the banner garrison, but the facilities at the New Business District now made it the starting point for tours on the lake itself.

Although the New Business District had the potential to serve sight-seeing, there is ample evidence that Zhu Fucheng and his colleagues intended it to be Hangzhou's civic center. Important public institutions, such as an athletic field, a library, an exhibition hall for promoting native products, were all located in this district. At the southern end of Lakeshore Boulevard, the Provincial Public Athletic Field (Zhejiang shengli gongzhong tiyu chang) and the public library *(tongshu tushu guan)* were built next to each other.[44] The sports field was a particularly important public space because it allowed mass gatherings that were more often political in nature. A slot at the intersection of the two main streets, Yingzi and Yanling Boulevards, was reserved for the Exhibition Hall for Zhejiang Products (Zhejiang shangpin chenlie guan), although actual construction of the hall was delayed until 1918. Once again, Ruan Xingyi was called upon to design it, and he traveled to Japan to study public buildings before he drew the blue prints. The finished exhibition hall was a compound of four two-story buildings, three of which were organized into a department store for domestic products while another exhibited Zhejiang's native products.[45] The provincial military governor's mansion, home to the most powerful government organ in the province, was also located in the New Business District.[46]

Except for the land used for streets and public buildings, all land in the New Business District was publicly advertised for sale, and the money was used to fund road construction in this area. An official announcement in 1913 declared that any individual with Chinese citizenship was entitled to bid for the land. An Office of Government Property (Guanchan chu) was in charge of dividing the land into two hundred lots and stipulated that the minimum land purchase would be one lot. The office ranked these lots in categories and assigned different prices for each according to their commercial value. First-class lots were located along Lakeshore Boulevard or at intersections of main streets and were sold at the highest price—1,500 yuan per *mu.* Land along the main streets and at intersections of smaller streets fell in the next price category—1,000 yuan per *mu.* Lots along the smaller streets or by canals ranked third at 600 yuan per *mu.* Last, lots neither close to the lake nor to any street were given the lowest price of 300 yuan per *mu.*[47]

Although the entire plan treated the former garrison as an empty space, the land was actually crowded with temples, shrines, arches, gardens, and yamen buildings, all of which had been built after the Taiping Rebellion. To clear out the area, the government resolved to tear down the old buildings and sell the bamboo and timber taken from them. The government also used tax regulations to speed up the realization of the planned New Business District, urging bidders to start construction work immediately after they purchased the land. If a landowner failed to do so within a year, the government would raise his property tax.[48] Therefore, the creation of this modern commercial center was based on an effort to erase completely the architectural remains that preserved memories of the former garrison as a historical space. As property owners were given strong incentive to fill the New Business District with new buildings, the rapid change left few physical remnants to inspire nostalgic feelings. In the early 1920s, a man returning from Shanghai found that this area had nothing he recognized from the old banner garrison. All he found were some broken bricks from the garrison wall, and they were used to build a stove in a wine shop.[49]

By the early 1920s, all the land in the New Business District had been sold. But even before that, the district had emerged as the new "downtown" of Hangzhou. The centrality of the New Business District is suggested by the continuous rise in its land values, and real estate in the district was priced the highest in Hangzhou. By 1926, land prices in the New Business District were generally eight to nine times higher than the original sales prices; sometimes they were more than ten times higher.[50] But this district was important in the city not because it functioned as the civic center the planners had initially envisioned, nor as a commercial center that focused on serving local people. In fact, the type of businesses that dominated the New Business District relied primarily on patrons from *outside* local communities.

As West Lake was incorporated into the city, a new type of visitor started to appear on the scene: tourists from other cities, a large number coming from Shanghai. The tourists of the early twentieth century belonged to a new urban middle class that was on the rise in China. The period from the beginning of World War I to the mid-1920s has been recognized as the golden age of Chinese industrial growth. Rapid development in industry, commerce, and Western-style education created a bourgeois class in coastal cities. Shanghai was at the center of this Western-inspired modernizing process, and it was during this period that its middle class became socially and culturally the most influential group in this metropolis.[51] It is not a coincidence that the tourist business developed in Hangzhou just as the new middle class was forming in its neighboring city, Shanghai.

Inventing a New Tourist Tradition

The popularity of sight-seeing in Hangzhou among the Shanghai middle class was tied to a fundamental change in the notion of time in urban China after the 1911 Revolution. The republican government replaced the lunar calendar with the Gregorian calendar and made great efforts to enforce the use of the Western-style calendar, even going so far as to abolish all festivals in the lunar calendar. Although people still held on to a few festivals, such as the Chinese New Year, the new calendar gradually became the measure of time by which people in major cities lived their lives. With the introduction of a weekly schedule came a clear differentiation between working hours and leisure time. While the work pace became more hectic in modern cities like Shanghai, middle-class people also learned through their Western-style education that they needed to fill weekends and holidays with leisure activities. An indication of how quickly and enthusiastically the middle class embraced the new schedule can be seen in their subscriptions to *Saturday (Libailiu)* as one of the most popular leisure-time periodicals in Shanghai.[52]

The desire to spend leisure time traveling was particularly acute in Shanghai, because living space was extremely crowded and the city had little space for public parks. The writer Mao Dun once tried to probe into the psychological reasons of Shanghai middle-class residents' need to "get out," even if only to the overly crowded parks in the city. He reasoned that white-collar workers in foreign trade companies and their educated wives felt they would be betraying their beliefs in a progressive modern life if they stayed in their tiny apartments for the weekend, where their children could only play hide and seek under the dining table.[53]

Another factor that facilitated the emergence of tourism was the development of modern transportation. As mentioned above, the Shanghai-Hangzhou railway was of crucial importance in making Hangzhou easily accessible from Shanghai. Furthermore, it was also in the railway company's own interest to encourage tourism. Unable to compete with the low-cost shipment of cargo on the lower Yangzi region's many rivers and canals, the railway company pursued passenger transportation as its main source of profit. In the 1910s, over 70 percent of the railway company's annual income came from passenger transportation; only slightly over 20 percent came from cargo shipments.[54] The company printed its own guidebook for sight-seeing in Hangzhou and offered low fares for weekend round trips between Shanghai and Hangzhou. Not only were tourist groups given discount prices, but after the mid-1920s the railway company arranged "tourist trains" each spring and fall to capitalize on tourist business.[55]

Business in Hangzhou responded quickly to the arrival of Shanghai tourists. After 1911, Hangzhou experienced constant growth in the number of hotels, restaurants, photography shops, teahouses, and theaters. Before 1911, there had been only fifteen hotels in Hangzhou; by 1927, the number had reached ninety-one—a six-fold increase.[56] Quantitative growth was only one aspect of this particular kind of commercialization. The location of many of the new businesses reveals a close connection between commercial development and the spatial transformation of Hangzhou under the new city planning. These service businesses tended to concentrate in the New Business District. One guidebook printed in 1916 listed eight hotels, seven teahouses, nine restaurants, and one theater in the area.[57] A tourist who visited Hangzhou in 1917 observed that the main street in the New Business District, Yanling Boulevard (Yanling lu), had few businesses besides hotels, teahouses, bookshops, and restaurants.[58]

The service businesses used carefully designed strategies to cater to the needs of the middle-class sightseers. One of the common marketing strategies was to juxtapose modernity and tradition and to suggest that they could offer the best of both worlds. Hotel advertisements promised the pleasure and beauty of classical landscape with modern comforts. One hotel in the New Business District boasted that "our hotel faces West Lake and it is a great three-story mansion. The hotel has an elegant and clean environment with fresh air. The rent is low for rooms of large or small sizes. Our service is comprehensive and our cuisine exquisite. We have prepared tour boats, rattan sedan chairs, and cars and rickshaws for rent. If you stay at our hotel while visiting the famous historical scenery on West Lake, you will definitely be satisfied"[59] (see fig. 14).

The modern comforts provided by service businesses also helped to sell tradition, as that was the heart of Hangzhou's attraction. Publishers in Shanghai and Hangzhou printed dozens of guidebooks, as well as stories of famous historical figures related to Hangzhou and collections of literati travel writings. This body of tourist literature presents Hangzhou as a contrast to Shanghai: whereas Shanghai was the symbol of modernity, Hangzhou was the embodiment of "tradition." In the guidebooks, the refined West Lake landscape and many scenic sites were

Fig. 14. The juxtaposition of tradition and modernity. A Western-style building sandwiched between a traditional-style bridge and the garden "Curved Courtyard with Lotus Flowers in Wind" (Quyuan fenghe on Hangzhou's West Lake). Photo courtesy of Library of Congress.

traced back to their "origins" many centuries earlier—especially the thirteenth century, when Hangzhou was the imperial capital of the Southern Song dynasty. A good example is a lyrical list of ten beautiful views *(xihu shijing),* which were recommended by most guidebooks as "must see" sites because they were established in the thirteenth century. Rarely was any physical alteration of the views mentioned, let alone their destruction and subsequent reconstruction. In fact, these views had disappeared at the end of the Southern Song. Although they were reinvented by local officials in the early eighteenth century for the pleasure of the touring Qing emperors, the successor sites were destroyed again by the Taipings in the mid-nineteenth century and were only partially recovered after the rebellion.

The image of West Lake as an unchanging beauty was not only created on paper; scenes were physically created according to historical records so they would match the tourists' expectations of antiquity. The local government's role in inventing a new tourist tradition is particularly worth noting. In a city where there was little industry, local officials found that the best way to maintain an adequate tax base was to promote tourism. Thus the provincial governors Yang Shande and Lu Yongxiang sponsored a project to "repair" the Southern Song loyalist general Yue Fei's tomb (Yuefen). What this project actually accomplished was the total transformation of a simple tomb with one small sacrificial hall into a large courtyard with tall walls and several halls in the palace style.[60] Ironically, this imposing structure actually seemed better suited to the deified general, who was given the rank of prince in Southern Song, and remains to this day one of the most frequently visited sites around West Lake.

Building upon a similar fascination with the past, Hangzhou restaurants offered "traditional" dishes to attract tourists. It seemed only natural that a tour on a beautiful lake should involve sampling local fish dishes. One delicacy was fresh-water fish cooked in sweet and sour sauce *(cuyu),* with the origin of recipe traced back to the Southern Song. With such a long history from the glorious past, this dish became the most famous "Hangzhou dish." But in reality, the recipe was created after the Taiping Rebellion by a restaurant owner from Shaoxing.[61]

These inventions reaching back to the past served to create a feeling that little had changed in the ways of sight-seeing on West Lake and that modern tourists were emulating what the elegant literati had done centuries before. The major sight-seeing points promoted by guidebooks and created by the government were mostly the remains of elite culture. Perhaps more important, these sites were designed not only as views to be seen, but as points where the act of seeing was to take place. The emphasis on the act of viewing had been a distinct element in the old literati way of appreciating West Lake. But literati sight-seeing was not merely a momentary action performed by the eyes, as the proper appreciation of a scene could be accomplished only through a recognition of its poetic, cultural precedents and through the contribution of one's own poetic commentary. Thus sight-seeing in imperial times was simultaneously a participation in and a reproduction of literati culture. What happened in the republican period was not a revitalization of the literati aesthetic taste, because the new tourist trade was not developed to encourage intellectual input from the sightseers. Instead, it invented traditional culture for *display.* The gaze of literati was replaced by the gaze of tourists, who came only as consumers of culture. In the end, the objectification of West Lake, making the place a "thing" to be seen, was simultaneously traditional and modern.

The celebration of the literati aesthetic taste was only one aspect of an entire process of inventing tourist culture. Another aspect was the gradual disappearance of many of the older popular customs of Hangzhou city life. In contrast to the planned enrichment of the New Business District, City-God Hill lost the official patronage it enjoyed during the Qing. After the 1911 Revolution, the new Zhejiang government no longer performed the religious ceremonies that had been so central to the routines of Qing officials. The Lantern Festival was prohibited as part of the government's effort to enforce the Western calendar. The Dragon King Temple lay in ruins, and its building materials were stolen by soldiers.[62] The old commercial and entertainment quarter near City-God Hill declined alongside the old popular culture so crucial to it. All but one of the teahouses on the hill went out of business, as did most of the wine shops and restaurants.[63]

The decline of the old commercial center at City-God Hill also indicated the widening gap between urban and rural areas in the republican period. City people had adopted a schedule in accordance with the Western calendar, but in the countryside, peasants continued to live by the lunar calendar. While Hangzhou business increasingly focused on tourists from Shanghai who spent their leisure time around West Lake, the peasant pilgrims who continued to come to Hangzhou worshipped their gods in the deteriorating temple buildings of City-God Hill.

Conclusion

Hangzhou's story raises larger issues in both modern Chinese history and historiography. One point concerns our evaluation of the 1911 Revolution. Many people, after witnessing the political chaos that followed the revolution, found themselves greatly disappointed in its results. Indeed, there has been a debate on whether the 1911 Revolution can be considered a revolution at all. While it surely did not bring a stable parliamentary government to China, the revolution nonetheless changed city life in Hangzhou permanently. Just as the destruction of city boundaries had been crucial for creating a new kind of social space during the French Revolution,[64] the 1911 Revolution should be reevaluated in terms of its impact on society, especially in urban areas. It is highly suggestive that this urban-based revolution in Hangzhou turned a symbol of Manchu military conquest into a commercial quarter. It is especially worth noting the speed with which the spatial change followed in the wake of political change. The present-day spatial arrangement of Hangzhou was determined in just a few months immediately following the 1911 Revolution.

Recent studies of the early period of the republican era have shown that despite the political chaos and military strife, this was a rather innovative period.[65] What the Hangzhou story can add here is another kind of innovation: the phenomenon of cultural creation in the name of tradition. The changes that took place in Hangzhou in the early republican period amounted to what Eric Hobsbawm and his colleagues have called "the invention of tradition." In that city, "responses to novel situations" took the form of "reference to old situations."[66] A new tourist culture was created around scenic West Lake by celebrating and reinventing the sophisticated lifestyle and aesthetic tastes of the departed literati. Sight-seeing without any practical purpose was itself the purpose. West Lake was thus objectified and made into a "thing" to be seen. The essence of this invention of tradition was the commercialization of space. The city was repacked with all kinds of new modern comforts to sell its supposed antiquity. This rather smooth juxtaposition of "modernity" and "tradition" in Hangzhou was accomplished in part by suppressing truly distinctive local and popular cultural traditions. Old customs and religious ceremonies, many of them central to peasant culture, were either downplayed or eliminated. Whereas the new tourism was geared to attract middle-class people from Shanghai, the pilgrims were no longer the concern of the new urban elite of the Republic who viewed popular belief as superstition. This dual process of inventing and forgetting tradition was manifested in the concrete forms of the city's spatial arrangement.[67]

The development of Hangzhou's modern tourism in connection with the rise of Shanghai also points to China's multiple paths to modernity. In recent years Shanghai has been the focus of many Chinese urban studies.[68] This metropolis has been held up as a window on changes in China since the mid-nineteenth century. But the social and cultural significance of Shanghai in a regional context and an examined comparison of its fortune to the decline of older cities such as Hangzhou have yet to be addressed. The Hangzhou business world's vision of its customers underscored the need for a close relationship among the cities in the lower Yangzi area—especially Hangzhou's relationship with industrialized Shanghai.

Shanghai, the jewel of imperialism and colonialism in China, rose to become the center of modern industry and culture at the expense of older cities in the Jiangnan area. Hangzhou was one of the "losers." As the Qing military garrison has shown, Hangzhou was not at all a "culture garden" before the rise of Shanghai; it was a regional center with great strategic and economic importance. However, it was bypassed by the mainstream of modernization in the twentieth century. The promotion of a prosperous tourist industry must be understood as the strategy of an old urban center that lost its previous economic power and needed to find a new role in the drastically changed regional arrangement. The new tourist business that was developed in Hangzhou signified an unbalanced relationship between the two cities—an imbalance that was an effect of imperialism and industrialization. The industrialized metropolis had a decisive impact on nearby secondary cities. After all, tourism is a business of leisure. The industrialized center created a class of people who needed leisure time and had the money to enjoy it. Places like modern Hangzhou presuppose the existence of places like Shanghai.

Chapter 8

Defining Beiping

Urban Reconstruction and National Identity, 1928–1936

Madeleine Yue Dong

The year 1928 marked a watershed in Beijing's history; some even compared its impact on the city to the shock of the Boxer Uprising in 1900.[1] The city was seriously challenged by the central administration's move to Nanjing after the establishment of the national government. Having monopolized the position of capital city without interruption for centuries, Beijing had grown used to all the privilege that dynastic-capital status brought it. With the city's well-being symbolizing the legitimacy of imperial rule and national power, the government and residents of Beijing had long taken for granted appropriating national wealth for local use, so much so that the city had hardly developed a self-sustaining economy. Losing its status as capital had more than symbolic meaning; it posed a sobering threat to the city's livelihood and future prospect.

Beijing, heavily immersed in a "capital mentality," was forced in the post-1928 years to break away from its previous mode of existence. In the midst of brewing international and national crises, those years also became a time when serious and systematic thinking about the future of the city took place, a time when Beijing took decisive steps to redefine its nature and image. It was "the beginning of government-sponsored city planning in Beijing."[2] Proposals and plans were drawn, some of which materialized; ideals of urban planning were tested against the challenging reality. This imagining of Beiping (as the city was called from 1928 to 1949) as a noncapital city, especially the "Plan for Beiping as a Tourist District" sponsored by the Beiping municipal government, forms the focus of this chapter. Beiping's experiences during those years reveal much about the ways in which urban spaces were contemplated in relation to state politics, ideals of urban planning, and concerns with Chinese cultural identity.

From Beijing to Beiping

As the armies of the Northern Expedition marched victoriously toward Beijing, a debate boiled between Nationalists and Beijing residents on the future location of the central government. Northerners proposed keeping the capital in Beijing, arguing that Nanjing was too close to Shanghai, the symbol and center of Western power in China. As the site where many past states had been extinguished, Nanjing had a history associated with a decadent and extravagant lifestyle. In contrast, Beijing had been the capital city of the Yuan, Ming, and Qing, all powerful and prosperous dynasties. Southerners insisted that Nanjing was the capital city chosen by Sun Yat-sen, and the National Father's will could not be disobeyed. Moreover, since Beijing had been the capital of the imperial state, it was portrayed as a lair of an outmoded Qing official lifestyle.[3] These were, of course, all secondary factors. The location of the capital was essentially determined by concrete military and political concerns. Nanjing was chosen as the new capital because Chiang Kai-shek's power base was in the south. On June 28, 1928, the Nanjing government declared that the city's name, Beijing (northern capital), be changed to Beiping (northern peace) Special Municipality (Beiping tebie shi), which was changed again in 1931 to Beiping City (Beiping shi).

During the eight years from 1928 to 1936, Beiping experienced devastating chaos as well as rising hopes. In 1928, the city was regarded as an "unlucky" place to live, and many left Beiping without a backward glance. But in early 1930, many Beiping residents cheered possible "signs of revival" as a capital city again as Chiang Kai-shek's alliance with the warlord Yan Xishan broke down and Beiping became a center of anti-Chiang forces. [4] The new Beiping government, led by Yan Xishan, declared its independence from the Nanjing central government, passed new laws, and collected its own taxes. In early May, Yan Xishan called an "enlarged meeting of the Nationalist Party's Central Executive Committee," and a new Beiping-based national government *(guomin zhengfu)* was organized. Yan Xishan was "elected" president; but he would not enjoy his new position for long. To fight the forces Chiang Kai-shek dispatched, Yan Xishan went to the front at Shijiazhuang on the very night of his inauguration. Chiang Kai-shek convinced the warlord leader from the northeast, Zhang Xueliang, to fight against Yan Xishan, and on September 22, Zhang's army occupied Beiping; the Nationalist government recovered control of the city.[5]

Beiping's dream of revival collapsed as quickly as Yan Xishan's short-lived government. Nonetheless, even after the Nationalists regained control, the city witnessed the return of many things that the Northern Expedition had tried to eliminate:

> [A]ll the slogans [put up by the armies of the Northern Expedition] were taken down, the blue paint [on the surface of buildings] faded, riding jacket (*magua,* a kind of short jacket worn by men in the Qing) again became the required attire for clerks. The titles of *Daren* and *Laoye* (master) have made their way back, as have Qing-style greeting rituals and funeral ceremonies.[6]

The domestic chaos represented by these rapid political swings was amplified by Japanese aggression from the north. In 1931, the Japanese armies occupied the northeast and quickly approached the Great Wall north of Beiping. Air-raid shelters were dug at Huairentang in the center of the city, where the highest political figures resided. Despite the threat of the Japanese to the north, the return of some eminent scholars created a strong sense of Beiping as the cultural center of the nation and boosted the city's morale. This lasted until 1933, when the Chinese army was defeated at Yuguan and Beiping was again seriously threatened. The Tanggu Agreement signed on May 30 stopped the Japanese army north of the Great Wall. With the growing Japanese threat, however, the national government shipped much of the Palace Museum's art collection and archives to Nanjing in 1934, raising fears that the national government was incapable of protecting the city. The people of Beiping descended into a troubled sense of insecurity.[7] In 1935, the He-Umezu Agreement was signed, establishing the Japanese-supported "North China Autonomous Zone," in which Beiping was included. The two sides compromised again, since neither the Japanese nor Chiang Kai-shek was ready for full-scale warfare. The temporary compromise between China and Japan lasted until July 7, 1937, when the Japanese resumed aggression against China, starting a war that would last until 1945.

Many had expected that the transfer of the capital to Nanjing would turn Beiping into a stagnant backwater. But events took a surprising turn. During all the turmoil of the 1930s, Beiping witnessed impressive achievements in urban construction. In June 1933, Yuan Liang, a graduate of Waseda University in Japan who had served as the police chief of Shanghai,[8] was appointed the city's mayor. He held the position for about two years before resigning in 1935, refusing to collaborate with the Japanese. The years under Yuan Liang were considered the best for the city's reconstruction since the early years of the Republic, when Zhu Qiqian led the restoration projects of Beijing. A contemporary writer commented in 1936, "Viewed from a high location, Beiping shines gloriously in gold, appearing more orderly than in the imperial period. Even though the national crises are deep, we cannot afford slowing down the efforts of sustaining the old capital."[9]

How could Beiping be sustained when it was no longer the capital city? What could Beiping be if not the capital city? This was the first problem the new Beiping municipal government had to deal with, and its plan for Beiping's development provided some answers to the question.

Planning Beiping

There was no illusion about Beiping's condition in 1928. The city was weak in both industry and transportation. According to Zhang Youxin, a major contributor to the semiofficial journal, *Review of City Administration,* the city had only about seven thousand industrial workers, and only one in eight of its families was involved in business. A large portion of the population was unemployed. Zhang Youxin observed that some of the world's old capital cities sustained themselves as ports or centers of transportation despite their loss of political centrality. But this option was not open for Beiping. Although it was the terminus of the Beiping-Hankou, Beiping-Suiyuan, Beiping-Mukden (Fengtian), and Beiping-Pukou (Nanjing) railways, the real transit point for these railways was Fengtai, outside of the city itself. One way out of the dilemma, Zhang Youxin argued, was to develop transportation to "end Beiping's geographic isolation." His solution was elaborate: extend the Zhangjiakou-Kulun railway to connect with the Siberian railway, and expand the Beiping-Suiyuan line into Xinjiang. With these two railroads extended, Beiping would attract more European visitors and businessmen. Zhang Youxin also envisioned a central station built in Beiping's southwest corner for transit between the Beiping-Hankou, Beiping-Suiyuan, and Beiping-Pukou lines. But even Zhang Youxin himself was aware that this plan was well beyond Beiping's control and capacity.[10]

There were even more urgent problems in addition to the long-term ones. When Beijing was the capital, forty million yuan of the central government's spending flowed in every year, not including spending by visiting officials. After the political center moved to Nanjing, Beijing's economy deteriorated sharply.[11] The Beiping municipal government acknowledged that

> After the recovery of Beiping [in the wake of the Northern Expedition], the whole city was celebrating, and the residents were excited. But the capital unexpectedly moved to the south, the ministries were abolished, and the city became desolate. In addition, rich households left Beiping, leading to decreased wealth in the city. Beiping's finance is in crises and it is extremely difficult to maintain its previous condition. The bandit warlords had also exhausted the city's wealth.[12]

Facing these difficult conditions and no longer able to rely on the central government's financial support, Beiping had to reconsider its raison d'être.

A "Proposal for Beiping's Construction" was circulated among departments in the Beiping municipal government in 1929, half a year after its formation. This proposal set up "the fundamental principles for Beiping's construction in order to maintain its permanent prosperity after the capital moved away."[13] The proposal suggested seven long-term goals for Beiping's development: to build the city into a center of "national tradition" *(guo gu),* "scholarship and arts" *(xueshu, meishu, yishu),* and as "an expression of Oriental culture" *(dongfang wenhua biaoxian),* an industrial center in the inland, a center for tourism and national defense.

Achieving these goals required a new definition of the city. One of the issues discussed at the first meeting of the Beiping municipal government in August 1928 was the determination of the city's new boundaries. When Beijing was the capital city, it was the center of an entire district, which included twenty counties, called Shuntian fu (Shuntian Prefect) in the Qing, and Jingzhao (capital district) from 1911 to 1928. During both the Qing and the early Republic, the offices of Shuntian fu and Daxing and Wanping Counties were all located in Beijing. As a result, there was no clear division between urban and rural in the administration system, and Beijing heavily relied on supplies from adjoining rural districts. In 1928, the headquarters of Hebei Province moved to Beiping and took over the twenty counties; meanwhile, the two county seats of Daxing and Wanping moved out of Beiping. In 1931, the headquarters of Hebei Province transferred to Tianjin but still maintained control of the twenty counties. What Beiping faced in 1928 was shrinking territory and resources: for the first time in history, Beiping was purely a city with a small suburb, without control of its surrounding agricultural regions.

To make the best out of a devastating situation, four principles were set forth in a proposal of the Beiping municipal government: convenience for administration and the transportation system, geographic coherence, and potential for the city's future development. The new proposal, although unsuccessful in the end, demonstrated that the city's desire to include all the resources was crucial for Beiping's future development as a modern metropolis within the city's boundaries.

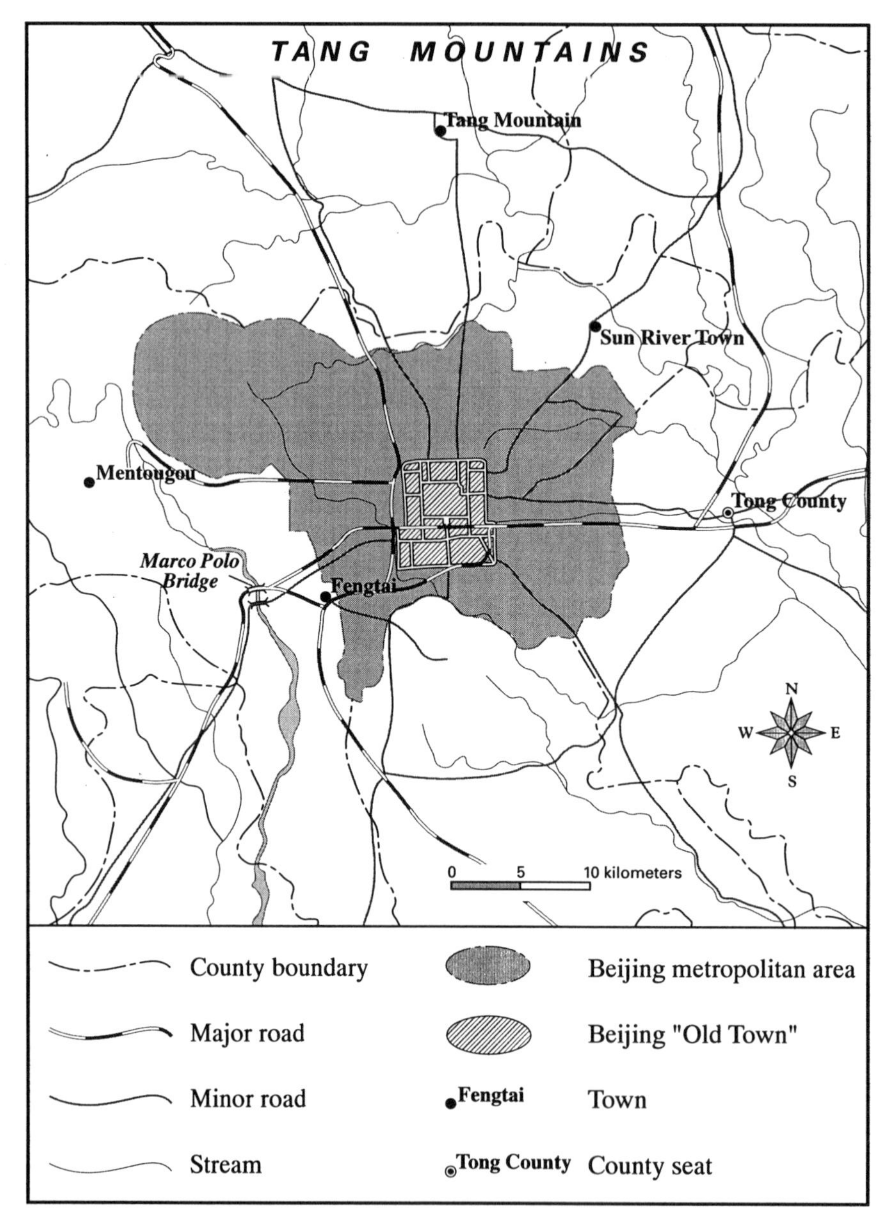

Map 15. Beiping municipal area in the 1930s. Based on a map in Hou Renzhi, ed., *Beijing lishi ditu ji* (1988).

In order to ensure the water supply for Beiping, the planners desired to expand the eastern boundary of the city to a line from Sunhe zhen (Sun River Town) in the northeast to Maju qiao (Maju Bridge) in the southeast. The plan also suggested the annexation of Tong County, where the power plant supplying Beiping's trolley system was located. Also included in the new boundaries was Mentougou, the terminus of Beiping-Mentougou railway and Beiping's most important coal supplier. It was annexed with the reasoning that "it should be beneficial to the city's income when we reform the mines and develop industry in the future." Beiping also recognized the value of a transport hub. Marco Polo Bridge (Lugou qiao), being a key point on the Beijing-Hankou railway, also became part of Beiping. Fengtai, a key point on the Beiping-Mukden (Fengtian), Beiping-Suiyuan, and Beiping-Hankou railways, was included in Beiping's new boundaries as well. In the north, the Tang Mountains, connected to Beiping by two bus routes, were targeted for annexation. With their warm springs and resort palaces, it was argued, the Tang Mountains formed a unit with the gardens and forests in the west and were an important resource for the city's tourist industry, as well as for the well-being of the city's residents:

> Today progress in urban planning is most importantly expressed in the idea of "garden city" so that people can escape the dust and noise and fulfill their own development. The northwest suburbs host many mountains and hills, continuing into the Tang Mountains. The view is beautiful and charming. It is a large area of highlands for Beiping. We should use this area to contribute to the "garden city." Either inheriting the old sites or constructing new areas can be easily achieved.[14]

The Yongding River and some farmland in the Nanyuan area were included in the proposal to supply the city's need for vegetables and food.[15]

The desire for Beiping to become a self-sustaining metropolitan unit and the vision for its future demands as a modern city were clearly expressed in the revision of the city's boundaries. The city's annexations naturally provoked protest from Hebei Province. In a November 1928 open letter to the central government, the Beiping municipal government, and several newspapers, the provincial government of Hebei argued that, unlike during the imperial period, when consolidating imperial interests was the single purpose determining the capital city's boundaries, a modern city's boundaries should benefit people's livelihoods. The letter expressed the concern that after the towns and villages close to Beiping, which were very often the most prosperous ones in their respective counties, were ripped away, the portions that were left would not be able to form functional counties. Neither would there be enough resources to run schools, control rivers, and conduct other projects for public interests. It was argued that what was proper for the city would not necessarily be best for the villages.[16]

Beiping was defeated in the battle to expand its boundaries. Nevertheless, the principles on which the revision of the city's boundaries was proposed prevailed in deciding the new direction for post-1928 Beiping.

Even though recognized as the long-term goal for the city, developing industry and transportation could not help solve Beiping's immediate financial problems. Some leaders saw education as the solution to Beiping's financial difficulties. It was commonly held among contemporary analysts that one of Beiping's strengths was its large number of modern educational institutions. Highly regarded institutions such as Peking University, Qinghua University, and Yanjing University were recognized as the best in higher education, second only to going abroad. The tuition and expenses were low, and facilities were superior to any others in China.[17] It was hoped that with its tradition of scholarship,

> Beiping will not die. Not only will it survive, but the nation depends on it to pump life into other places. No one can deny that the renaissance of Chinese culture in recent years originated from the gathering of scholars in Beijing in the early years of the Republic. Since then, and with the opportunity given by the May Fourth movement, the atmosphere came alive. The . . . dull air was thus broken, and all the reforms in recent years were made possible.[18]

The revenue generated from education, however, was insufficient to sustain the city. Other options had to be found. Lacking resources in industry and commerce, the only asset Beiping had was the city itself. Beiping's dream to become a modern city would be realized by turning itself into a commodity, capitalizing on the city's imperial past.

Early Republican Models

The new Beiping municipal government took charge of a city that had already undergone fundamental transformation in the years following the downfall of the Qing during 1911 to 1928. Beijing's imperial past was a material reality that all political powers in the Republic had to deal with, as asset or burden. The previous governments' experiences in reconstructing the city provided the new power holders both models and lessons. Despite being rattled by the disruptive comings and goings of warlords in the seventeen years between 1911 and 1928, Beijing's municipal authorities maintained remarkable control and were able gradually to effect the city's modernization amid the cataclysms of civil war. As the centuries-old imperial spatial order was no longer deemed appropriate for the new Republic, the government made consistent efforts to transform the city. A new spatial order began to take the place of the old. Mobility took priority over stability as the principle dominating city planning. Republican political ideals—popular participation, promotion of commerce and industry—replaced barricaded spatial hierarchies and ethnic segregation in determining the pattern of neighborhoods. The building of a mass transit system changed the spatial scale and pattern of everyday activities for city residents, enabling them to make longer trips in the city and disappear in anonymity in crowds beyond their immediate neighborhoods.[19]

Fig. 15. A muddy street in the southern part of Beijing, ca. 1880. The original caption on this photo contrasts the mud of the rainy season to the "clouds of dust that prevail during the dry weather." The shop on the left sells tea leaves; on the right an inn welcomes "officials from all provinces." Photo courtesy of Library of Congress.

Fig. 16. Newly widened and paved street in Beijing, early Republic. Note rickshaws in the central section, horse carts in lane to right. Photo courtesy of Library of Congress.

The republican period witnessed great achievement in road construction. In 1912, when the Republic was established, there was no asphalt or concrete road in Beijing; only about 33.87 miles were built with macadam. The city was famous for its "three feet of dust without wind and streets full of mud with a little rain." In 1949, the length of roads built with asphalt, concrete, and macadam was 158.73 miles, a five-fold increase during the Republic. The construction of new roads in the suburbs started in 1917; their total length reached 247.6 miles, and at least one-third of it was built with asphalt, concrete, or macadam. New lights were added to major streets, making it much easier to walk along the streets at night.[20]

Despite the great transformations Beijing experienced, the imperial past lingered on in the city, staying most visible in Beijing's newly designated public spaces, which were highlights in the transformation of Beijing's built environment, as Mingzheng Shi demonstrates in his work.[21] Under closer examination, spaces designed for public use represented a diverse range of social and cultural implications and consequences, demonstrating a complex relationship of the city to its past. Three examples of public spaces—the Central Park, the Citizens' Park, and the revolutionary monuments—can best illustrate the range of spatial changes in Beijing.

During the early republican period, most of Beijing's public parks were transfigured from what had been forbidden spaces, such as imperial gardens, ceremonial sites, and the Forbidden City itself. The Qing's Altar of Earth and Grain became Central Park at the initiation of Zhu Qiqian. When the Qing empress dowager, Longyu, died in March 1913, Zhu Qiqian, then the minister of transportation, was responsible for public order outside of Tiananmen. It was then that he first noticed that the Altar of Earth and Grain was becoming extremely desolate, with the guards raising pigs and grazing sheep. When Zhu Qiqian became minister of internal affairs of the national government in October 1913, the Qing imperial household had already turned over the altar to the republican government, and Zhu formally suggested changing it into a public park. In order to save money for the financially strapped Ministry of Internal Affairs, he suggested that a committee, composed of citizens donating more than fifty yuan or institutions donating more than five hundred, be organized to develop the park. By the spring of 1914 Zhu Qiqian had collected over forty thousand yuan.[22]

The park opened on October 10, 1914, the National Day of the Republic. At the time, "the park was mostly empty ground, there was not much garden scenery to see. . . . There were no ponds, no hills, no pavilions," only ceremonial halls, some temples, and ancient trees. Despite the desolate condition of the park, a large number of visitors came that day, "the men all dressed in long robes and 'riding jackets,' the women mostly in Manchu hair-style and dress." The opening of the park served as an opportunity for people to satisfy their curiosity and appetite for a small taste of imperial life.[23]

Educational facilities, playgrounds for exercise, an exhibition on hygiene sponsored by the Department of Internal Affairs, and an exhibition of goods produced in "model prisons" run by the Department of Law were later added to the park, but they were not its real attractions. Rather, the visitors to the park remembered the atmosphere of leisure and relaxation they enjoyed there.[24] Qi Rushan, the famous playwright of Beijing operas who lived in Beijing for decades during the republican period, recalled that Central Park had a sizable income from entrance tickets and taxes on the restaurants and teahouses there, and the money was used to improve the park, building pavilions, and ponds. The places that attracted the largest number of visitors were commercial establishments. Visitors of varying status and social groups all found their own spots in the park. The "fashionable" liked to gather in the restaurants Bushixin and Chunming guan because they could enjoy various Western and Chinese foods there. "These places were always filled with customers, especially on Sundays. There was a time when prostitutes also came here to attract customers. These places were nicknamed 'fly paper' since they attracted such a large number of people." The "bureaucrats and gentry members" usually went to Laijin Rain Pavilion; artists preferred the small island. People with little money would go to the riverbank in the north. The picture Qi Rushan drew of Central Park was one of great flexibility in this space; the park had some-

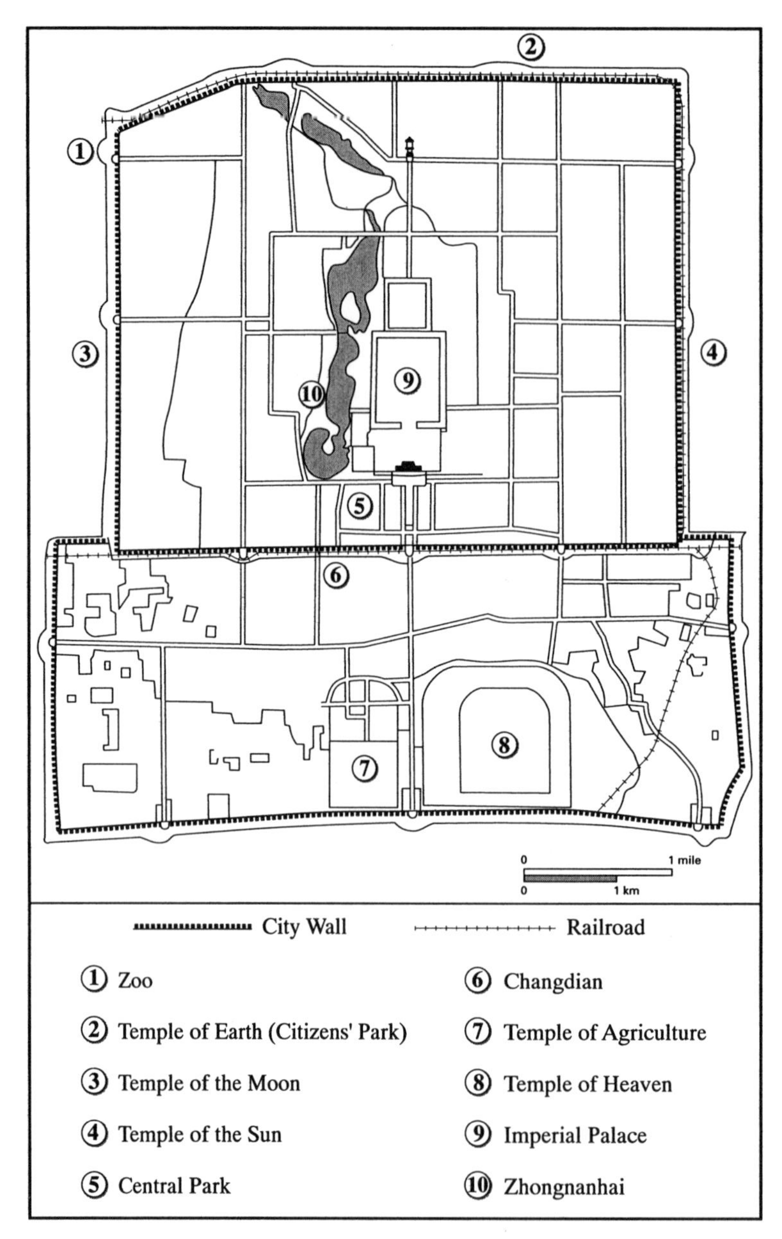

Map 16. Beijing/Beiping walled city during the republican era. Based on a map in Xi Wuyi and Deng Yibing, *Beijing Tongshi,* vol. 9 (1994).

thing for everyone.[25] In the words of the writer Shi Tuo, in Central Park "among the college students were prostitutes; in the middle of prostitutes were merchants; mixed among the merchants were concubines; and next to them were gentlemen, and professors . . . a long row in a confusing mixture."[26]

Unlike Central Park, which provided a cosmopolitan style of leisure for the city's relatively well-off residents, Jingzhao Park (Capital Park) was dedicated to the education of ordinary people. In 1925, the Shuntian prefect Xue Dubi instigated the transformation of the Altar of Earth

(Di tan) into a public park and personally oversaw its reconstruction; upon its completion, he wrote a lengthy essay. In 1928, its name was changed to Shimin gongyuan (Citizens' Park).[27] When explaining his motivation for opening the park, Xue Dubi expressed concerns for citizens' well-being and education; the spatial transformation of Beijing was to serve both ends.

> All cities in the civilized countries of the world have complete infrastructures for public transportation, hygiene and other urban facilities. Much attention is paid to citizens' morality, intelligence and health (*deyu, zhiyu, tiyu,* the Chinese equivalent of spirit, mind, and body). Public parks are such facilities. Beijing is the best place in the country, but facilities and institutions of civilization have not been developed. I feel deeply sorry when I think of it. The Altar of Earth outside the Anding Gate . . . can serve naturally as a park. The fundamental principles for equipping this park are two: first, to promote public health; second, to develop culture. Also embodied in the opening of the park is the wish to preserve historical sites and develop tourism. . . . [W]e shall try to integrate education and public entertainment.[28]

But entertainment and the preservation of historical sites were not the focus in practice. The new Capital Park resembled a three-dimensional billboard proclaiming the government's hope to train citizens through a new ordering of space. The north part of the park was called "World Garden" (Shijie yuan), in which a world map was constructed with rocks standing for mountains, grass for water, and flowers for national boundaries. Each country's capital city, important commercial centers, railways, and trade routes were clearly labeled. "Once one enters this garden, the general picture of the world becomes very clear," proudly claimed Xue Dubi. In "China," the provincial capitals, famous mountains, and the Yangzi, Yellow, and Pearl Rivers were highlighted, as were all the treaty ports and land China had lost in treaties. A wooden board, accompanied by couplets about "remembering the national shame," was posted on the edge of the garden, detailing China's territory, population, products, and history.

Three pavilions—Jiaojia (Instructing agriculture), Youqiu (Enjoyment of autumn harvest), and Gonghe (Republic)—provided space for visitors to rest and recreate, but, more important, to be educated. The Republic Pavilion was a pentagon, each side painted with a different color representing the Han, Manchu, Hui, Mongol, and Tibetan nationalities officially comprising the Republic. The Yellow Emperor, Nurhaci (founder of the Qing dynasty), Genghis Khan, Muhammad, and Zongkaba were chosen to represent each nationality, and their portraits adorned the walls, implying "five races, one family." Pictures adapted from Chinese and foreign patriotic stories were painted on wooden boards. The park was strewn with mottoes preaching moral principles: diligence, concentration and perseverance, self-reflection, critical thinking, healthy living, and public mindedness. People were encouraged to buy national products, support education, oppose foot binding, advocate filial piety, abide by the laws, and help each other. They were expected to be modest, tolerant, honest, progressive, and patriotic. Walkways were bedecked with illustrated biographies of "great men," including Emperor Wudi of the Han, Confucius, Peter the Great, the Meiji emperor, George Washington, Horatio Nelson, Napoleon Bonaparte, Abraham Lincoln, and Christopher Columbus.

The south section of the park contained a playground with sports facilities for visitors to "improve their health." Xue Dubi argued that "people living in the north suburb of Beijing have a low level of education and never pay attention to their health. This park can help them improve their character and widen their knowledge. Children living here can have a place for sports so that they will not engage in unhealthy activities." Courts for tennis, basketball, and soccer were provided, as were running tracks, a swimming pool, and swings. The national flag fluttered on a pole. A slogan at the entrance proclaimed: "Promote militancy; encourage national spirit; advocate popular education; re-shape national souls." The south wall was inscribed with the Darwinian motto: "Victory goes to the strong, Defeat to the weak" to encourage the "spirit of competition and bravery." Xue Dubi explained his choice of mottoes:

> We should know that the survival of the nation depends on people's strength, and the people's strength depends on the spirit of bravery and competition.

> Our country developed the earliest [in the world], but we have not progressed in the past thousand years due to stagnation and low morale. It is painful to witness the weakening of the people, the invasion of powerful countries, and the decline of our nation. To promote sports activities and encourage people's morale should be our fundamental principle.[29]

Also in this area, a lecture platform for educational speeches and two public libraries were built on a former Qing ceremonial ground to "promote education through public entertainment."

But the glowing optimism of Xue Dubi's essay was never realized. Despite these efforts, Capital Park never succeeded in attracting a large number of visitors. Located outside Anding Gate in Beijing's northeast corner, it was too far from most of the city's residents. Warlord troops were often stationed there, and they damaged and looted the facility.[30] Probably just as important was that the atmosphere of Capital Park, in contrast to the sense of leisure in Central Park, was made depressingly heavy by the inscribed didactic messages found throughout.

Revolutionary Monuments

In addition to the experiences of the early republican years, the Beiping municipal government had lessons to learn from the national government's first attempts to replace Beijing's image of imperial monumentality with one that was "revolutionary." When the army of the Northern Expedition reached Beijing in 1928, it was utterly dissatisfied with the city. This disdain was reflected in the Nationalists' treatment of the city. As one observer noted:

> When the army of the Northern Expedition had just arrived in Beiping, they treated those in the old government as captives. They wanted to wipe out everything. Not only were Manchu women's hairstyles banned and temple fairs no longer allowed to follow the Chinese calendar, but even [the Manchu style] riding jackets were banned. Blue and white slogans were to cover the sky and earth. Some people even suggested painting a layer of blue on the yellow tiles of the palace roof.[31]

To the revolutionaries, even Xue Dubi's Capital Park did not go far enough in indoctrinating the people. "Beiping was the capital of past dynasties, people's knowledge is very limited. There is hardly any revolutionary architecture."[32] The meaning of "revolutionary architecture" was never clearly defined, but one way proposed by the Nationalists to correct the city's problems was to build monuments for the martyrs of the revolution, to set up role models for the northern people, and "to glorify the feats of the revolution in order to eliminate feudal relics."[33]

The Nationalist government was in part riding a wave of national monument construction surging in many nations in the years after World War I. George Mosse remarks in his study of Germany that "[n]ational monuments and public festivals together provided the myths and symbols that comprised a national liturgy appropriate for national self-representation."[34] China was no exception. Political events and figures were memorialized in metal and stone, new names and meanings were given to old structures, and history was erased from and rewritten into space.

Beijing had its revolutionary emblems before the Northern Expedition arrived. The northern warlord leader Feng Yuxiang had ordered two statues to be erected in Central Park in 1922 for his comrades Wang Jinming and Shi Congyun, who had died in the 1911 Revolution. But when Feng Yuxiang was forced out of Beijing in 1925, Wang Huaiqing, who had led the army that fought and killed Wang Jinming and Shi Congyun, became the chief commander of the Beijing garrison. In November 1926, Feng Yuxiang suffered further defeats, and Wang Huaiqing ordered the two statues pulled down and sold to an antique shop as scrap metal.[35]

The period immediately following the Nationalists' arrival in 1928 witnessed the construction of a few monuments, expressing the Nationalist government's aspiration to inscribe its own history permanently in space. Their construction of monuments, however, hardly ever met with local support. Only after lengthy and difficult negotiations with the railroad company was a monument commemorating the martyrs of the 1911 Revolution built at the Nankou Train Station in 1929. In the same year, a branch of the National Revolutionary Army asked permission from the Beiping municipal government to build a monument to the revolution and a cemetery for its unknown soldiers who died in the Northern Expedition. The army wished to erect these outside the north gate of the Summer Palace, and the city government agreed. The representatives of the Summer Palace, however, were extremely resistant to the proposal, although they eventually gave in.

The monuments were rarely built with the kind of enthusiasm that was supposed to accompany the construction of "revolutionary architecture." At Dai Jitao's behest in 1928, the Beiping municipal government decided to build a monument and statue of Peng Jiazhen, a Sichuan native who died in Beijing when trying to assassinate Yuan Shikai. Sun Yat-sen had bestowed on Peng Jiazhen the title of "General" and promised to build a grave and monument for him, which remained unrealized until 1928. Its design imitated a Buddhist pagoda, with eight corners and eight round pillars. The white stone used for imperial palaces was to top off the monument, with Peng Jiazhen's picture and biography inscribed. The coffin was to be of Sichuan cedar priced at two thousand yuan. Two thousand copies of Peng Jiazhen's writings and a biography were to be printed and distributed. His monument was to be located at the zoo, and a memorial hall for him was also planned for North Lake Park. Most of these plans existed only on paper, because neither the Beiping municipal government nor the Hebei provincial government, which jointly ran the project, was willing to take financial responsibility.

While the monument was being designed, Peng Jiazhen's father and wife traveled to Beiping to ask for financial assistance from the Nationalist government. Peng Jiazhen's brother lobbied the government to complete the monument. Neither the monument nor the memorial hall was built until 1930, when Peng Jiazhen's relatives, having sat vigil in Beiping all this time, could wait no longer. They pooled together some money themselves, purchased some private houses at Laoqianggen in an ordinary neighborhood, repaired them, and built a private temple for Peng Jiazhen. They were charged fifty-eight yuan in real estate taxes, for which they petitioned the Department of Public Works for an exemption.[36] In 1931, Peng Jiazhen's coffin was finally moved into a government-built grave.[37]

Although purposely erected to challenge the lingering spatial and visual traces of Beijing's imperial past, the revolutionary monuments hardly stirred a ripple in China's foremost city of imperial monumentality. Donald J. Olsen precisely pins down the key elements that would make a national monument successful:

> A monument is intended to call forth fear or wonder in the observer: to remind him of the antiquity of the dynasty, the power of the regime, the wealth of the community, the truth of its ideology, or of some event—a military victory or successful revolution—that demonstrated such wealth, power or truth. To succeed in its aims, a monument needs to jolt the individual out of his mundane concerns—catching the 5:37, remembering to renew a driver's license, buying postage stamps—to remind him that life involves more than such concerns, and that he is fortunate to be a citizen of such a splendid metropolis, a subject of such a benevolent ruler, and adherent of the one true faith. Any evidence of restraint, understatement, or, worst of all, parsimony, will subvert its intention. It should aspire to the sublime and evoke sensations of awe, not of affectionate familiarity, and certainly not of amused condescension.[38]

Almost all these elements were missing in the Nationalists' enterprise of monument construction. On the contrary, the construction of revolutionary monuments in Beiping was characterized by a lack of enthusiasm, delays in construction, and negligence upon completion. They were not visited by Beiping's residents nor by tourists to the city, and they hardly ever appeared in literature about Beiping.

All three projects—Central Park, Capital Park, and the revolutionary monuments—were connected in some way to Beijing's imperial past: either utilizing it for new purposes, covering it over with a new face, or directly challenging it. Be they successes or failures, all of them were designed for the residents of the city, regardless of the differences in their intended functions. They also embodied the principles of urban construction in pre-1928 Beijing, which was characterized by an eagerness to catch up with other capital cities in the world and to transform the city's spatial order for the training of citizens for the new Republic. In the first year of the Republic, the newspaper *Da ziyou bao* (Great liberty news) stated that "a nation's capital city must have three crucial conditions: convenient transportation, wide and clean streets, grand and ordered buildings. Paris in France, New York in America, Berlin in Germany, London in Britain are such examples."[39] In 1916, the issues that most concerned the city government were distributing water among the city's residents and commercial and industrial needs; constructing a sewage system and cleaning the accumulated garbage; improving streets and constructing new roads to make transportation more convenient in the city; building a trolley system that could connect the entire city; and establishing parks and museums.[40]

The flexible and experimental nature of dealing with the city's imperial past before 1928 would disappear in the 1930s, replaced by more standardized practices aimed at shaping Beiping into a modern showcase of Chinese tradition. This was clearly reflected in the 1930s interpretation of what enabled Zhu Qiqian to succeed with the opening of Central Park, which was chosen as the model for the development of 1930s Beiping. Different from the sense of flexibility and mobility created by commercial establishments vividly conveyed in the accounts of Qi Rushan and Shi Tuo, the new interpretation emphasized that Zhu Qiqian avoided imposing anything out of place on the original harmonious architectural style.[41] Authenticity of tradition became the key term in the new era.

A New Orientation: Tourist Beiping

Yuan Liang, Beiping's new mayor in 1933, was determined to make the city into a "modernized metropolis of the world,"[42] which was to be achieved through his "Plan for the Beiping Tourist District." This plan was among the most aggressive programs for city development adopted by the municipal government since 1911. Highly acclaimed and praised, it distinguished itself from previous governmental efforts to reconstruct the city: instead of erasing imperial sites or modifying them for new purposes, they were to be preserved as emblems of Beiping and Chinese culture.

Released from the pressure to figure among the world capitals, the rethinking about the city under Yuan Liang's leadership was characterized by a clear and conscious effort to define Beiping as a city of Chinese traditional culture. The new municipal government criticized its predecessor for behavior such as "mindlessly tearing down the walls of the Forbidden City and the walls surrounding the Altar of Agriculture." The new government made it simple and clear: Beiping was to be a modern city of tradition.[43] Contemporary discussions of Beiping's condition concluded that its strongest attraction was its historical sites. Its position as a "cultural center" was also evinced by its heritage of architecture, historical documents, and libraries against which no other city could compete. They were deemed to impart "a feeling of history" and "the spirit of an ancient country" and were regarded as merits with which the city could bring glory and pride to the nation. Many believed that foreigners had very positive impressions of Beiping and hoped that the income of tourism and education could combine to produce a fair sum.[44] These discussions revealed a new kind of attitude toward the past and an ideological commitment to certain spatial practices that departed sharply from the radicalism of the May Fourth Movement.

This new confidence in and demand for "tradition" was put into practice under the leadership of Yuan Liang. In 1934, the Beiping municipal government prepared an official master plan for modern Beiping—a plan to transform the city into a "tourist district." The plan was based on the belief that Beiping represented "the quintessence of the whole country." It proudly claimed that Beiping's palaces, gardens, and ancient temples "are not only the ultimate display of East Asian civilization, but also great achievements of the world." In a letter the city government sent to the semiofficial *Review of City Administration,* the goal of the project was explained:

> Beiping was a capital city for hundreds of years. The palaces are grand, the streets wide, the gardens large. People from Europe and America are all amazed by the beauty of oriental culture, and praise it as unprecedented. Since the capital moved to the south, there has been crisis after crisis. Many buildings are falling down, not to mention the necessary facilities to host tourists. Considering this situation, the Municipal Government put together this

> project which includes plans for palaces, gardens, temples and other famous sites, naming it "The Plan for Beiping Tourist District." We expect to develop this old capital into a great city. We will preserve the famous sites to develop international tourism. On the one hand we can make the city prosperous, on the other hand we can change Chinese and foreigners' impressions [of China], inspire morale and evoke new life [in the city].[45]

The planners expected that the development of tourism in Beiping could also strengthen Beiping as a locale of national defense against the Japanese encroachment, because "to attract foreign tourists to visit our country is really the only strategy to propagate Chinese national culture and to increase international understanding." If we consider the lack of other feasible strategies to attract the concerns of the international community about the Japanese invasion and the Chinese public concern for national defense, this argument, seemingly farfetched, could very well have been convincing to the Nanjing regime. The planners believed that promoting industry was the goal for which the government and people should strive, but it was not as rapid a solution as drawing foreign money and sympathy by attracting foreigners to come visit. Beiping envied France, which profited enormously from tourism, and fixed its sights on the pocketbooks of the Americans, who were quoted as spending over sixty million dollars on travel abroad. It was calculated that if one-tenth of that money could be spent in China, it would yield sizable revenues.[46]

The plan diagnosed problems in the listless tourist business and proposed solutions. The project first provided a perfect opportunity for the Beiping municipal government to claim control over a larger area of the city. All the historical sites in Beiping's vicinity, including the Great Wall, were encompassed in the plan, and the municipal government demanded rights to these sites. The plan argued that the central government's control over these sites hindered the development of tourism because there was scant collaboration among the different government branches; neither was there a unified standard for the preservation of the sites. The Beiping municipal government's plan involved repairing historic buildings and laying roads to make sites accessible; asphalt roads were to replace dirt and macadam. The list for repair included the arrow and corner towers of the city walls and all the previous imperial structures. Former imperial gardens were to be better tended; the city walls and gates that had been torn down were to be repaired.

Advertisement constituted another crucial part of the plan. A network of advertising bureaus and travel agents was considered necessary not only to make "the magnificence of Chinese civilization" known to foreign tourists, but also to defeat "false propaganda" that represented China "as a disorderly country where people dare not come." In emulation of Japan, a tourist bureau would be in charge of travel arrangements, translation, and the shopping needs of the tourists. Starting capital was pegged at 200 million yuan—70 million to be paid by the municipal government, 70 million by local merchants, and 60 million by the railways connected to Beiping.[47] The city would print guidebooks in English, French, and Japanese and distribute them to every country that had an embassy in China.[48]

Although modern infrastructure was deemed mandatory for tourism, the real attraction would be "Chinese tradition." The planners argued that although Beiping boasted some Western-style hotels, "there were no Chinese-style hotels with good facilities to satisfy foreigners' curiosity." Yuan Liang was perturbed that most tourists, both foreign and Chinese, stayed at Western-style hotels, and his ambition was to change Zhongnanhai (the present site of the government and party leadership of the People's Republic of China) into an ideal tourist hotel, "modern" and "Chinese" at the same time. An imperial garden converted into the residence of the president of the Republic and then into a park in 1928, Zhongnanhai contained over eight hundred rooms, pavilions, lakes, and hills, "the arrangement and structure of which all have great Oriental charm." In the summer tourists could swim and row boats; in winter they could skate. Dancing and dining halls were to be built and sanitary facilities and telephones installed. Four names were proposed: The Old Capital, Oriental Garden, Zhongnanhai (to remind people of past emperors), and Imperial Palace Hotel. The expectation was that it would "deserve the name of an ideal Oriental garden hotel."

Chinese tradition would also be the draw of tourist entertainment. A large Beijing Opera theater catering to foreign tourists would be built. "When there are foreign tour groups in Beiping, famous performers should act in the theater so that the beauty of Oriental music and drama can be propagated, and the foreigners can understand the real essence of Chinese drama." The theater could also serve as a site for adult education of city residents. It had to suit foreign and Chinese audiences, with a stage for drama, old and new, as well as movies.

A year after this proposal was drawn up, the Nanjing government set up a Committee for Preserving Historical Sites in the Old Capital (Gudu wenwu zhengli weiyuanhui) and officially promoted Beiping as a tourist city open to foreign visitors. Yuan Liang was in charge of implementing the projects, and the committee included several architects who had studied abroad. Also involved in the program was the Society for Chinese Architecture (Zhongguo yingzao xueshe), an academic association studying traditional Chinese architecture that had been organized by Zhu Qiqian and architectural historian Liang Sicheng. Under the organization of the committee and the counsel of the experts, the edifices of the imperial court were repaired, as were altars and temples, with an eye to preserving architectural "authenticity." The rule of preservation was to extend the life of the structures rather than make them look totally new. Anything from the original structure that could be preserved would be repaired and reused. New materials should be left recognizable as new if they were absolutely needed. In the preservation of decorative arches *(pailou),* concrete and steel were used to reinforce and widen their bases so they would not block traffic, while the tops of the arches were left untouched.

The imperial building method was mythicized during the preservation process, both confirming that the 1930s was a modern time distant from the imperial past and enabling the rhetoric of authenticity. The Altar of Heaven was the most representative preservation project. Rebuilt in 1890 after being struck by lightning, it had been only partially repaired since. The roof leaked and the paint was peeling, leaving the wood structure unprotected. The city government realized that these problems required some expertise to handle, so it hunted down a man known as "Zhao of the glazed tile kiln" (Liuliyao Zhao), who was eager to work on the project. Zhao noted, however, that some key minerals were now unavailable, making the luster of the past tiles unattainable and perhaps affecting their colors. He insisted that red glazes from Germany and green glazes produced in China were the most durable and could last for hundreds of years without fading, but both were difficult to get. Noting the difficulty in obtaining "ancient" *(gu dai)* tiles, the government decided to use tiles from the Old Summer Palace (the Yuanming Yuan), which were stored at Qinghua University. These tiles had been taken from structures less than thirty years old, but they were nonetheless referred to as "ancient architecture" *(gudai jianzhu).*[49] The rebuilding process and the architectural techniques of the Qing were further mythicized by the fact that all the workers who had participated in the rebuilding of the altar at the end of the dynasty were reported to have died. Qing records noted only how many rooms were built and how much material used, but mentioned nothing on the process of construction or detailing techniques. The government sent people to visit old carpenter workshops and found an "old man with white hair" who said that his grandfather had supervised the construction in the Qing, but he never produced the mysterious blueprint. Hence the original plan to repair only parts of the Altar of Heaven to protect the original "noble quality" proved to be too difficult in practice. The committee decided to have the entire structure repainted.[50]

As with many other cities in the world, Beijing's spatial transformation and search for an aesthetic style created cultural capital for the construction of a nation-state. Eric Hobsbawm has incisively described such practices in the Western context as "inventions of tradition." When testing the experiences of Beijing with this concept, some important distinctions become visible. In the Qing, the Altar of Heaven had been a living part of the state organism, representing both a cosmological and political order. The state represented divine power, which was conveyed spatially and visually through architecture and planning in the Altar of Heaven. State power would diminish without the altar. In the Republic, the state's power was expressed not by worshipping at the altar, but by officiating at the funeral of the system the altar represented. As Hobsbawm remarks, "Tradition shows weakness when it is justified pragmatically. . . . Conversely, objects or practices are liberated for full symbolic and ritual use when no longer fettered by practical use."[51] Traditions can be invented only when practical use value disappears. To preserve the altar for its "matchless beauty and solemnity" rather than as a place for official ceremonies was in this sense an invention of tradition. Unlike Hobsbawm's examples, however, in the republican period these historic sites were not used as places of active ritual to indoctrinate the city's residents. Instead, the ideological tutelage was directed primarily at tourists and foreigners. The altar no longer represented a living system. Its value was solely imbedded in its representation of the past; even pieces of new tile would totally destroy its former power, although, ironically, German glazes were acceptable simply because they had been used in the imperial times.

To create an "authentically" traditional image of the city for the tourists required a unified version of Beiping's history. The plan criticized the tour guides for being mostly unqualified "translator-tour guides" retained by foreign-owned hotels who had no knowledge of Chinese history. "Not only is the goal of propagating our country's civilization not achieved, but [they convey] many things humiliating to our country . . . damaging our country's position in the world." A contemporary commentator confirmed this criticism: "I have seen western tourists at the Altar of Heaven and the Great Ancestral Temple who needed to ask their tour guide everything. But the tour guide had no knowledge of ancient rituals and institutions and just tossed out whatever they could come up with to tell them. No insult to the nation is worse than this."[52] To rectify the situation, a standard history of Beiping, *A Record of Cultural Treasures of the Old Capital (Jiudu wenwu lue),* was compiled and published by the municipal government. In the preface, Yuan Liang wrote,

> A nation must be built upon a foundation, which is its national character. If water is not deep, it will not have enough power to carry a large ship; if wind is not strong, it does not have enough power to keep big wings aloft. . . . The Chinese nation is the oldest. Our ancestors left a long, glorious history. Beijing is where the Yellow Emperor set up [the first] nation. . . . Beijing is the representation of our nation's great spirit.[53]

The book differed from ordinary guides in that it contained nothing but historical sites with relatively detailed narratives accompanied by pictures. Nonetheless, some still believed that the city's history was being popularized or vulgarized. One critic complained that the descriptions were too "superficial."[54]

The "tourist district" project was halted as the Japanese approached the city in 1937. Yuan Liang, however, did succeed in fortifying Beiping's image as the urban representation of traditional Chinese culture. The city's oldness became an asset, not merely a sign of being decrepit and out-of-date. Yuan Liang was not only highly praised in China for "adopting scientific methods to preserve historical architecture" and for his "courage in taking responsibility,"[55] he also received an award from King Leopold II of Belgium for his achievements in preserving Chinese civilization.[56]

Beiping and 1930s' Cultural Debate

With Beiping's new orientation toward foreign tourism, the city construction programs of the early 1930s stressed preservation of historical sites. This orientation was not an isolated whim, and Yuan Liang's attempt was much more than an effort to gain foreign tourist dollars. Rather, when situated in the 1930s' debate on the future of Chinese culture, the Beiping projects became part of a national concern as to how modern China should be imagined. City planning and construction served as an important base on which the new image of China could be projected, and historical architecture provided a material anchor for the new search for cultural confidence.

The 1930s debate started with Hu Shi and Chen Xujing's insistence that China take the road of Westernization. In 1929, Hu Shi, one of the most eminent leaders in the New Culture Movement, published an article in *The China Christian Year Book,* elaborating his opinions on "cultural conflicts." He argued that China's problem was how to adjust to the conflict between cultures. He observed that total refusal of Westernization had proved futile. As a consequence, most people favored "modernization with choices," which meant that some aspects of modern civilization could be accepted as necessary evils, but that Chinese civilization should be preserved at all cost. Hu Shi argued that such an attitude amounted to saying "China must change but definitely should not change." In his writings, the half-hearted reformers included not only Chinese, but Westerners as well. To Hu Shi's dismay, there was opposition whenever any changes occurred. For instance, American tourists complained that the streetcar system in Beijing spoiled the city's atmosphere. Foreigners affirmed that China should "maintain her traditional values, and only [adopt] those things that satisfy the urgent needs of reality." As a result, Hu Shi argued, traditional values remained intact, and protecting "national essence" had become a top priority. In Hu Shi's opinion, China's old civilization belonged to the past; it could not help China solve the problems of poverty, disease, ignorance, and political corruption. He suggested that China follow the example of Japan, establishing at least minimum subsistence with the help of modern technology and industry. If there was anything that could be said to have "authentic Chinese characteristics," it would grow in a soil of health, wealth, and leisure produced by scientific and industrial progresses.[57]

Chen Xujing, an American-trained professor in Guangzhou, followed Hu Shi in advocating "total Westernization" in 1933 and 1934. He refuted the argument that even Westerners wished to protect Eastern culture, arguing that

> It is the Westerners' business if they want to advocate Eastern culture; but it is the responsibility of people of the East to Westernize. In fact, Westerners' attitudes toward the study of Eastern culture is the same as their attitude toward African aboriginal culture. Are they trying to advocate African culture when they study it?[58]

But Chen Xujing's insights into the Orientalist nature of Western study of Chinese culture did not convince people of his goal of total Westernization. Hu Shi and Chen Xujing's ideas met with more opposition than support. A national debate intensified with a manifesto, "The Construction of a China-based Culture," written by ten professors in 1935. They argued that China and the real Chinese were disappearing from the world. In order to maintain Chinese characteristics, it was necessary to begin a China-based cultural construction. They discarded the idea of going back to the past, as well as the path of following the West's example. Demanding that people pay attention to China's particular temporal and spatial conditions, they proposed the slogan that China should "have a self understanding, but also learn about the world; have the courage to open the door, but also the determination not to blindly follow anyone." Although they put together no explicit proposal, they claimed that "the construction of China-based culture is a reflection of national confidence."[59]

When the vice director of the Nationalist Party's Propaganda Department, Ye Qing, joined the debate, he labeled total Westernization the "cultural colonialization of China," and Hu Shi "an international scholar produced by the material and spiritual pillars of European and American imperialism." Ye Qing argued that China should strive for cultural independence, which was a symbol of the awakening of the Chinese nation. Reflecting a significant politicization of this academic debate, Ye Qing held the position that Westernization was "the culture of traitors."[60]

That Yuan Liang's project, consciously or unconsciously, echoed and materialized the "China-based cultural construction" was best illustrated by Qinghua University professor Zhang Xiruo's discussion of Beijing's architecture. In his comments on the issue of national culture, Zhang Xiruo gave an example of what definitely should not be Westernized: Chinese palace-style architecture. He argued that the best palace and imperial ceremonial architecture could "make anyone who had a little sense of beauty fall to his knees" *(bai dao)* because it perfectly integrated the principles of beauty and solemnity. In his view, the Altar of Heaven and the Hall of Great Harmony in the Forbidden City were two indisputable examples. He related an anecdote to prove his point: a friend of his had felt that China had nothing that could compete with other cultures and thus always felt inferior when talking to foreigners. Once, he took a Western guest to the Hall of Great Harmony. As soon as he entered the outer gate of the hall, he felt a sense of great pride, feeling that he was equal to, even better than, his guest. Zhang Xiruo fully agreed with his friend and further argued that among all the palace architecture he had seen in the world, he saw nothing worth "one percent, or one thousandth, of the artistic value of those in Beiping. The vulgarity of London, clumsiness of Berlin, repetition of Paris and Versailles, tediousness of Rome, what can be a match for Beiping?" Whether the palaces were practically useful or not was not something that concerned him. He cared only about "beauty," which was something he believed Chinese architecture manifested much more of than Western architecture.[61]

Zhang Xiruo was not alone in his confidence in Beijing's imperial architecture. A researcher on urban land use, Wei Shudong, expressed a similar opinion:

> Chinese architecture, Chinese culture, Chinese society—Beijing stands in the world as a representative of them all. We do not need to discuss the Chinese people's admiration and feeling toward Beijing. Even for foreigners who come to China, visiting Beijing is always the most pleasant experience. There is no other city to match its grandeur and greatness.[62]

Except for Chinese architecture, the advocates of "China-based cultural construction" failed to present other concrete examples of what should be preserved and serve as the foundation of a new Chinese cultural identity. Yuan Liang's plan, aimed at overwhelming the hearts of foreign tourists through Chinese imperial architecture, realized their ideas. In this sense, the 1930s redefinition of Beiping was a material example of the efforts to institute a new understanding of Chinese history different from the May Fourth iconoclasm.

Conclusion

Post-1928 Beiping distinguished itself from the previous seventeen years in important ways. In the first years of the Republic, most construction projects in Beijing involved toppling walls and liberating sealed spaces, as if the city's space itself was imprisoned and the walls were shackles. As modern China's republican capital, it was imperative for Beijing to shed the cumbersome remains of its past and to don that weave of metal rails and asphalt arteries distinguishing a thriving, industrialized city. An important motivation behind the transformation was the creation of a new spatial order that would train imperial subjects to become republican citizens. Yet despite the modernization efforts, the city still wore its disheveled imperial robes. The past could not simply be discarded; it would not die in a single moment of rebellion as the May Fourth ideologues might have hoped. It lived on and occupied space; it simply needed to be cleaned up. The modernization projects and the resilience of the city's past formed a dynamic consanguinity.

Among all the modernization efforts, it was Zhu Qiqian's project of Central Park that was the most successful. What enabled Zhu Qiqian to succeed was his skillful utilization of the imperial spaces. Central Park thrived on a fusion of several factors: the natural beauty provided by the remaining imperial space, the new attraction of a cosmopolitan style of leisure for the city's better-off residents, and the sense of flexibility in the park created by commercial activities.

The pre-1928 years were a time of experiments and struggles; the construction projects during these years did not culminate in a standard aesthetic style for the city. After the unification of the nation and the establishment of a stronger national government, the post-1928 years witnessed an obvious desire to shape the city with a set of fixed criteria and practices. Defining and representing an "authentic past" became both possible and desirable. The spatial transformation of Beiping shifted from a dialogue between the government and the intended new citizens to one between the Chinese national state and foreign tourists. The Beiping municipal government led the way in historical preservation, clearly defining Beiping as a city of tradition, a center of Chinese culture. Interestingly, however, assertion of Chinese tradition in Beiping occurred when it was no longer the capital city. The city could not rely solely on political status to sustain itself, but had to transform itself into a modern, self-sustaining metropolitan unit.

Although oriented toward different directions, the pre- and post-1928 history of Beijing/Beiping represented two sides of the same coin. The Chinese nation-state needed to establish itself as modern, and at the same time secure the "distinct Chineseness" of the new nation. To live on in continuity with the imperial past would imply "stagnation" and thus humiliation; yet not being able to claim a past would indicate a lack of "civilization." In order for the new state to thrive in the present, this "Chineseness" had to be distanced from the imperial past and had to assure itself that the past was dead. The solution was to preserve the past as history irrelevant to the present while asserting the sole right over its interpretation. Rather than replacing the past through full-scale modernization of the entire city, as had been vaguely contemplated in the early Republic, the focus of the 1930s was to frame the past, repair it, and preserve it.

Remains of imperial Beijing survived throughout the republican period—not as a system as they had been before, but as fragments; not as a consistent narrative, but often in material forms scattered in daily life. Yuan Liang's plan for Beijing represented an attempt to create a new unified, consistent narrative of the city's history told from the perspective of an ambitious nation-state. In this attempt to create a hegemony, the political message was inscribed on imperial spaces, and a material reality held its own resiliency and allowed different interpretations. Peter Demetz, when commenting on Walter Benjamin's theories of materialist hermeneutics and the power of "things," argues that "the failure of the systematic thinker constitutes the true triumph of the master of hermeneutics who, in 'reading' the things of the world as if they were sacred texts, suddenly decodes the overwhelming forces of human history."[63] While it is perhaps difficult to argue that Yuan Liang's plan to develop tourism empowered ordinary Beiping residents at the time, it did play an important role in preventing the spatial erasure of the city's history. The monuments on which the cultural preservation projects of the 1930s focused are the same ones that define the history and pride of today's Beijing, and the Altar of Heaven has been one of the favorite public parks for ordinary Beijing residents—people who continue to use these spaces in their own creative ways.

Chapter 9

Building a Dream

Constructing a National Capital in Nanjing, 1927–1937

Charles D. Musgrove

The Conception of a Dream

Sixteen years before the Guomindang stripped Beijing of its capital status, Sun Yat-sen, the party's founder, had advocated the construction of a "model capital" at Nanjing.[1] In 1912, Sun Yat-sen argued that new Nanjing would become an exemplar for the modern China to come, combining modern technology and materials with the best of Chinese architecture and aesthetics. In its modernity, the capital would be clean and efficient, offering the latest in technological conveniences. It would represent "the nation in its forthcoming glorious rejuvenation."[2] Meanwhile, the new capital of China would hearken back to the "time of her greatest past glory," instilling patriotism in the hearts of all Chinese people. It would represent the New China, proud of its past while taking control of its future. The capital would adhere to an international standard set by modern nations before it, but modified to the specific conditions of China. To one *China Press* writer at the time, the plan read "like a mind picture—a dream."[3]

Sun Yat-sen's dream called for tremendous economic growth and prosperity. Thus the nation needed a capital that could grow as abundance increased the burdens of administration. Too many old, inefficient buildings and obstructionist conservatives crowded the streets of Beijing for the old capital to meet this need. Beijing, Sun Yat-sen argued, was stagnant. Nanjing, on the other hand, offered a fresh environment that was centrally located and "accessible by river, sea, and by rail." Nanjing was also less developed, providing room for city planning to manage the anticipated economic expansion. Sun Yat-sen and his followers hoped to build this capital out of Nanjing's lowlands, just as early American patriots erected Washington, D.C., from the marshes of Virginia.[4]

Sun Yat-sen did not live to see his vision realized. The expectation during his brief tenure as provisional president in 1912 turned to frustration during the warlord era. Two years after his death in 1925, however, the Guomindang (GMD) was in the midst of its Northern Expedition. Revolutionary zeal was at a peak, and optimism was widespread. In many cities in China, this optimism took the form of ambitious municipal-improvement projects, as seen in this volume and in studies of Shanghai.[5] In 1928, the right GMD, led by Chiang Kai-shek, eager to utilize this national enthusiasm for its own benefit, sponsored the creation of a plan to transform Nanjing into the model capital that Sun Yat-sen had always wanted.

In this chapter I explore the construction of a capital city in republican-era Nanjing as it moved from its initial conception through the planning stages into actual building. I focus on the attempt to build an area devoted to the national administration, the central administrative zone. With this zone, the GMD hoped to mark Nanjing as the central city in China, unlike peripheral cities of China's past such as Hangzhou and Beijing, and unlike monuments to foreign imperialism such as Shanghai. By looking at how a national capital was envisioned in its ideal state, and how this capital was actually constructed with limited financial resources, we can study the priorities of the GMD-led government. What did the national government feel was most important in its early efforts to forge a nation, both ideologically and materially? I also hope to come to a better understanding of republican-era conceptions of modernity. What did it mean to create a "modern" nation or transcend a "traditional" one? What new forces were at work, and how were they represented spatially in street plans and government buildings? I also look at how space was manipulated in an attempt to "naturalize" a seemingly new system of power relationships.

Planning the Dream

Nanjing occupies a peculiar position on China's historical terrain as a site of both conservatism and change. Its occupants have often felt that the city represents a bastion of timeless Chinese values. Lying at a strategic crossroads along a north-south overland route and an east-west riverine route on the Yangzi, it is a city with relatively easy access to much of China. Due to this centrality and its distance from the northern and western frontier, Nanjing was seen as an ideal place to preserve Chinese culture when invaders overwhelmed the north. During the Northern and Southern dynasties period (317–589), the Toba and other horse-riding "barbarians" controlled the north, while Nanjing served as the capital in the south, preserving "Chineseness" for future generations. This cultural and strategic centrality convinced the Ming dynasty founder, Zhu Yuanzhang, to build his imperial capital in Nanjing after driving off the Mongol rulers of the Yuan.[6] Meanwhile, Nanjing has also been a site of ambitious attempts at transformation. The utopian Heavenly Kingdom of Great Peace (the Taiping) established its capital from 1853 to 1864 in the city, and Sun Yat-sen inaugurated the Republic of China there in 1912. In 1927, when this cultural heritage and the legitimizing power of Sun Yat-sen's prescribed wishes meshed with Chiang Kai-shek's political and military needs, the right GMD established Nanjing as the capital of a soon-to-be-reunited China on April 28, 1927.[7]

The city was in rough shape. It had never fully recovered from the near total destruction by the Qing forces' extermination of the Taiping in 1864. Prior to 1927, about 370,000 inhabitants occupied only two sections on opposite sides of the vast area within the Ming walls.[8] The region between the southern commercial quarter near the Qinhuai River and the shipping center on the north side of the city facing the Yangzi was occupied by little more than ruins and an occasional farm. No street lights, sewers, or running water eased the lives of Nanjing's inhabitants; and before 1927 there was no municipal government.[9] These rough conditions made Nanjing all the more appealing, since the city was seen as a place where modern facilities and infrastructure could grow into the empty space.[10] Construction on empty lots would be less expensive than replacing extant buildings.

To oversee the planning and construction of the model capital, the GMD-led national government established the Capital Construction Committee (Shoudu jianshe weiyuanhui) in January 1929.[11] Chiang Kai-shek himself was chairman of the standing committee, which also boasted Sun Fo, the son of the "founding father" and mayor of Guangzhou; Song Ziwen (T. V. Soong), the minister of finance; Kong Xiangxi (H. H. K'ung), the minister of industry and commerce; and Zhao Daiwen, a high-ranking official in the Ministry of Internal Affairs.[12] With these and other GMD politicians overseeing the process, the construction of the model capital was clearly deemed an important task.

Yet the bulk of the actual planning would be handled by a subcommittee called the National Capital Planning Office (Guodu sheji jishu zhuanyuan banshichu), which had actually been at work on the project since November 1928.[13] Lin Yimin, an engineer trained at Harvard University, headed the committee, which included Zhe Yue, chief of the engineering staff, and Huang Yuyu, the "principal architectural assistant." Four prominent members of the board were Americans. Guiding the planning of the city were Ernest P. Goodrich, consulting engineer, and H. K. Murphy, chief architect.[14] The pair had experience in this work, as they had collaborated with Sun Fo to create a plan to renovate Guangzhou in 1927.[15] Assisting them were Col. Irving C. Moller and Theodore T. McCrosky, as well as "a group of Chinese engineers."[16]

Several reasons explain this strong American presence on the committee. Even when the model capital was but a dream of Sun Yat-sen, Nanjing was being conceptualized as the new Washington, D.C.[17] To emulate an American city, the GMD would need American advisors. Also, supported by scholarships under the Boxer Indemnity Fund, many Chinese architects, as well as other members of the construction committee, had received their professional training in the United States during the previous two decades.[18] Finally, since the GMD leaders wanted to obtain foreign funding for their vision, the plans would need to meet with foreign approval. To prove that their project was safe for

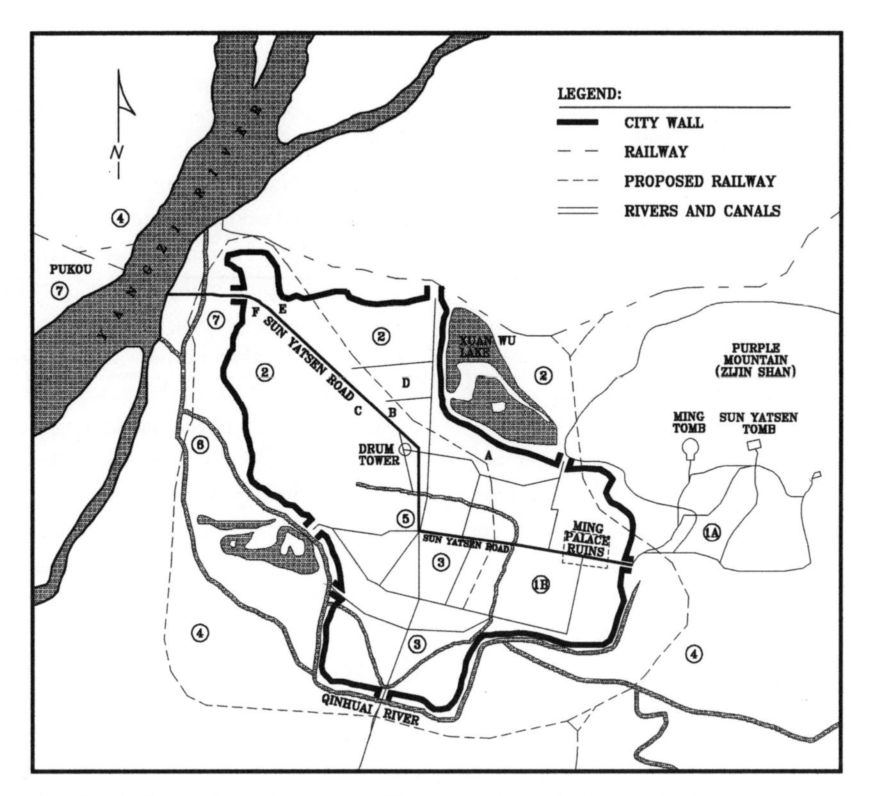

Map 17. Nanjing as the national capital. Numbers indicate Nanjing's main zones: 1a. Central Administrative Zone, original site; 1b. Central Administrative Zone, second site; 2. Residential districts; 3. Business district; 4. Airfields; 5. Banking district; 6. Industrial zone; 7. Port districts. Letters indicate the location of buildings mentioned in this chapter: A. Examination Yuan; B. Ministry of Foreign Affairs; C. Supreme Court; D. Jiangsu Provincial Assembly; E. Ministry of Railways; F. Ministry of Communications. Redrawn from maps in *Shoudu jianshe* 1928 and *Shoudu jihua* 1929.

Western investment, they needed strong ties to respected Western advisors.[19]

Using the newsletter *Capital Construction (Shoudu jianshe)* to publicize and discuss issues surrounding the process, the Planning Office chairman, Lin Yimin, initiated the dialogue with a reminder of the current political situation. With the "completion of unification" and the "beginning of political tutelage" under the GMD, the planning of the nation's capital could finally begin.[20] As a planner employed by the national government, Lin Yimin felt the need to emphasize that GMD leadership would bring prosperity and international respect for the people of China. A later issue of the newsletter explored the role of the GMD even further. "Our party is China's only revolutionary party," insisted one writer in "How to build the capital under the direction of the party."[21] "It is the only party which can break the control of the feudal parties and the only party which represents the whole nation of China"—thus making it the only power that could direct the construction of a capital for all of China. At the time, the issue was not uncontested. While these writers espoused a belief in a "revolutionary" future for China, it was to be carefully controlled and led by the GMD. Furthermore, at a time when major figures such as Wang Jingwei and Hu Hanmin still challenged Chiang Kai-shek for ultimate authority, the right GMD wanted to stress national unity, a precondition for educating a modern people.

Many articles in the newsletter emphasized public responsibility. For example, Mayor Liu Jiwen reminded his audience that "all the people of the nation should pool their ideas and make concerted efforts to complete successfully the grand plans for the capital city."[22] Another writer insisted that "the great capital is the political center of the whole nation. It must have large-scale construction first in order to be a model for the whole nation, to be emulated by all." To encourage people from all over China to contribute, the writer suggested that bond sales be guaranteed by each provincial government. He insisted optimistically that "since people of the whole nation have a responsibility to construct the capital we can predict that they will purchase these bonds enthusiastically."[23] Committee members were worried that too much of the burden of construction would fall on the residents of Nanjing.[24] Although the government firmly controlled only two provinces, Zhejiang and Jiangsu, these nominal leaders of the "entire country" sought to make the construction of the capital a truly "national" project.

There was no indication that "public responsibility" meant anything more than financial support. In this silence we see the kind of contradictory outlook that would plague the GMD throughout the Nanjing Decade. The party and the intellectuals associated with it faced the question, "How is a modern public created?" GMD leaders evidently did not think very highly of the democratic potential of the people of China in the 1920s and 1930s. Political tutelage was necessary to teach the people to be proper, modern citizens before they could be allowed any political responsibility. This condescending attitude could be traced back even to Sun Yat-sen, who said in 1920: "China's enslavement has already been effected for several thousand years. Thus, in republican China, although it is nine years old, the common people still do not know how to be their own masters. Today, we have no other choice, we must use forceful methods to make them into their own masters."[25] Reflecting this idea, the planning process faced a fundamental contradiction: how does one meet the needs of political tutelage while creating spaces for the use of a future citizenry, which would behave as responsible political participants, disciplined in the exercise of their freedom?[26]

In addition to calling for national responsibility, the construction committee also outlined the needs of a modern capital city. Foreign models greatly influenced conceptions of this new space. Washington, D.C., London, Berlin, Paris, and New York were all held up as cities that could teach Nanjing planners valuable lessons.[27] The committee focused on two Western capitals that represented different styles of grand-scale city planning. Washington, D.C., was a capital built from an "idealistic" plan. "If we could build a new capital city from nothing, then we could act from the ideal and follow a perfect and beautiful plan, like North America's Washington." The committee calculated, however, that because Nanjing was already a fairly well established city, it would be necessary to follow a second model. Paris provided an example of "realistic" capital planning. "For Nanjing, we must carefully consider the situation and proceed step by step, as in Paris."[28]

The city planners saw an international standard that a modern capital city had to meet, and they hoped to make Nanjing fit respectably within this standard. China wanted to enter the modern world, and to do so it would have to join in the "international ceremonial rivalry," underway since the late nineteenth century.[29] New capital city designs and even completely new capital cities had been appearing all over the globe: Paris (1850s and 1860s), Vienna (late 1850s), Tokyo (1880s), Washington, D.C. (1901), London (1906–1913), New Delhi (1911), Canberra (1913), Ankara (1927).[30] Some of the characteristics that these cities shared were wide, rationally ordered streets to accommodate automobile traffic and increase fresh air and sunlight; drainage systems to keep the streets from flooding; electricity to power the buildings; plentiful parks for recreation; and efficient land-use zones for industry, commerce, residence, and administration. The Capital Construction Committee believed Nanjing had to develop these elements of order and efficiency to meet the international criteria for capital cities.[31]

Yet the committee was not content merely to imitate Western cities. One member wrote, "We should learn from Europe and America, but more importantly, we should learn from their mistakes."[32] The committee wanted Nanjing to be "more grand and prosperous than any other famous capital city in the world."[33] To accomplish this, Lin

Yimin instructed planners to remember the significant contributions of Chinese architecture. After all, he said, "planning for our capital is quite different from the theories of Europe and America." Besides, he reminded them, Chinese architecture and urban planning enjoyed a heritage reaching back to the time when "Greece and Rome first became strong and prosperous."[34]

Thus the committee instructed planners to make spatial and aesthetic references to China's own history, where ostensibly ever since the Zhou dynasty, architecture and urban planning were closely tied to a unifying (largely Confucian) cosmology of legitimation for the imperial-bureaucratic system. This cosmological system placed the emperor at the center of "all under heaven" and ordered his subjects into well-defined spaces around him. Although the particular spatial manifestations of that cosmology changed over time, the arrangement at any given moment took on an air of timelessness, as varying forms of monumentality imbued the spaces of daily life with a sense of lasting imperial power. "Tradition" was reinvented again and again to create a sense of continuous authority, as architectural conventions served ruling versions of dynastic power relationships. Although social conditions of power changed, symmetry, balance, axiality, strict north-south orientations, grid-style streets, city sections "zoned" for commerce and residence, large buildings (not necessarily tall, by Western standards) with impressive, curved roofs, regularized internal spaces (based on the symbolic numerical multiplication of the unit of space, the *jian*), and city walls all became consistent symbols of imperial authority.[35] As such, these were appropriate sites for the many rituals, from the imperial to the commonplace, that were performed in them and that naturalized the Confucian power arrangement.[36] Ultimately, it was up to the designers, and the GMD officials who would approve their plans, to determine what aspects of this spatial heritage were appropriate to a modern capital and the conditions of modern nationalism.

The committee called for a central administrative zone that would combine elements from both the modern world and Chinese tradition. Occasionally, the designers recognized some of the characteristics of Chinese cities that paralleled those of a modern city. For example, Lin Yimin pointed out that most streets in Nanjing (built in the early Ming) were originally quite broad, but that shop owners had encroached upon them. Furthermore, the streets were "not without any order." Thus the city streets had only to be "remodeled" to make them "wide and straight."[37] Still, most agreed that major work had to be done for Nanjing to fit the international model of respectability.

The newsletter's discussion of GMD political tutelage, public responsibility, international standards, and Chinese legacies was for the benefit of those architects who would participate in an open competition, announced by Mayor Liu Jiwen in September 1929, to design the new capital. In setting the parameters of the contest, the committee asked participants to design the central administrative zone and place it in an undeveloped region on the southeast side of the city.[38] This region consisted of roughly nine square kilometers at the southern foot of Purple Mountain (Zijin shan), just outside the city walls (see map 17). The southern face of the mountain was already significant, as it was the site of the Ming dynasty tombs and the newly erected Sun Yat-sen mausoleum. In addition to such historical significance, the planning office argued that the only efficient way to develop the large area needed for an ideal governmental center was to build it on undeveloped land, as it would not incur the financial and political costs of clearing out a large swath of businesses and residences. (While there was still plenty of open space within the city walls, the only site auspicious enough for the administrative zone, south of the Ming Palace area, was designated to become a commercial center.) Finally, the "dignity of Purple Mountain" made it the "most suitable place in terms of outward appearances," offering a pleasing view as well as strategic security in the event of a military attack.[39]

The choice of the south face of Purple Mountain indicates that the planners wanted to attach the national government to two important cultural symbols. "Expel the Qing! Restore the Ming!" had been a common rallying cry for unhappy patriots prior to the Revolution of 1911. Even for revolutionaries who loathed an imperial form of government, the Ming represented a native Chinese power that successfully repelled foreign invaders and reestablished

Han sovereignty. More important to the GMD, locating the government center under the large monument to Sun Yat-sen would provide a constant visual link to the party's founding father. Sun Yat-sen was immensely popular, and these planners hoped to cultivate emotional ties to his legacy in order to reinforce the party's political legitimacy.[40] In short, the committee wanted a site that referred to China's glorious indigenous past while bearing the promise of a modern, visionary future.

In addition to the spatial link on Purple Mountain, the committee indicated that the designs themselves should be inspired by the legacy of Sun Yat-sen. "The basic ideal should come from the essence of Sun Yat-sen's Three Principles of the People." The Three Principles, used like some mystical formula, implied that the plans for the government zone should be "practical, beautiful, grand and solemn." The area should not only be a place "where the central government can use its power," but it should also "promote cultural life in urban society." Using the Three Principles as a model, Nanjing would be "the source of energy for the whole nation and a role model for the whole world."[41] The nebulous use of Sun Yat-sen as a national symbol helped disguise the divisions that still plagued the country and the GMD. Sun Yat-sen, in all his vagueness, made an ideal unifying symbol around which to build a new national myth.[42] Everyone could agree that Sun Yat-sen, who never wielded nationwide power himself, had been the selfless leader of China's revolution. Furthermore, he had personally founded the GMD and bequeathed to it his mantle of revolutionary leadership. However, the "ideology" of this practical-minded revolutionary, whose thought seemed to transform before different audiences, was hard to pin down to any consistent vision, making it a useful, if somewhat problematic, unifying tool.

Continuing in its instructions, the committee explained that the administrative sector should be divided into two parts. The first was the political center where the People's Congress would face a large open square graced with a statue of Sun Yat-sen. A prominent aspect of this political center would be the GMD central headquarters. "The central headquarters should be a great hall . . . because after the revolution is over and the constitution is in place, whether or not the GMD still exists, its accomplishment will be considered a great historical achievement." People far into the future would flock to see its old headquarters. The second part would be the cultural center, located near the public square. There they hoped to have a national fine arts museum, a national library, a temple to Chinese sages, and a historical museum, as "all of these would glorify the Chinese nation's culture." Thus the committee envisioned a space that served not only as the administrative nerve center of the country, but as the cultural core as well. This centralization would place the GMD as the dominant element, uniting all under its gaze.[43]

The central theme of this discourse was how the capital could create the kind of unity necessary to modernize China. National, political, and ideological unity would all have to be realized to bring China into the modern age. A well-designed capital city would help create this unity by invoking a proud indigenous past and the revolutionary vision of the party's selfless founder, who hoped to see a strong China enter the community of modern nations. But such appeals alone could not achieve modernization. GMD-led political tutelage would be needed as well and was reflected in the central place occupied by the party headquarters in conceptions of the new capital city.

Contest "Winners" and the Capital City Plan

Nine firms submitted plans to the contest. Details and drawings from four of these appeared in the newsletter's November 1929 issue. Each design featured an underlying grid, in which a rational pattern of streets allowed for an efficient flow of traffic. In addition, long diagonal streets formed axes interrupting the rectilinear grid. These axes served two main purposes for the modern city planner. First, they created an efficient artery for traffic connecting two important points within the city. Second, a large diagonal street cutting across the grid architecturally emphasized the elements on the ends of the diagonals. Each of the plans also featured a large, open mall, much like the mall between Washington D.C.'s Capitol Building and the Washington Monument or that between the Arc d' Triomphe and the Obelisk in Paris. To city planners, the mall served as another, more grandiose, symbolic accent for the elements at the ends.

These broad boulevards and malls would create grand vistas to emphasize monumental government structures. In the administrative sector, the viewer's perspective would always be drawn toward the government. This use of perspective differed from Chinese imperial conventions, which required more than just vision to create monumentality. For example, in Qing Beijing, one was forced to traverse a series of architectural mini-climaxes, such as gates, parks, and halls. In the words of Andrew Boyd, "The whole length of the axis is never revealed at once; it does not present a vista but a succession of varied spaces in a related sequence, each one blocked but visibly leading to a further stage."[44] The feeling of monumentality in the imperial spatial layout is achieved by moving through the scene, not just viewing it. Both kinds of monumentality are designed to impress upon the subject the power of the state, but one invites participation in ritual-like involvement; the other merely commands attention as the focus of public view.

One design explicitly referred to a traditional arrangement, using a series of yamen-style building groups with large open courtyards arranged in front of a larger building cluster. The entire area resembled a huge yamen. The larger building group occupying the position of power at the northern end would be the GMD central headquarters. This design was praised for its economy, but not for its layout. The direct imitation of the imperial, self-enclosed style did not represent the break from the past that the GMD wanted people to associate with the modern state. Another entry was praised for using the "magnificent form" of Chinese-style architecture along with modern steel and cement building materials. Yet it was criticized for not utilizing the "Western scientific method" to increase the efficiency of traffic and air circulation.[45] Chinese characteristics were important, but the modern capital required more than just traditional elements.

The design that earned the most praise, the work of Chinese architects Huang Yuyu (an engineer in the city planning office) and Zhu Shenkang, also contained elements of modern efficiency and symbolism in the layout of its streets (see map 18). But the judges especially praised

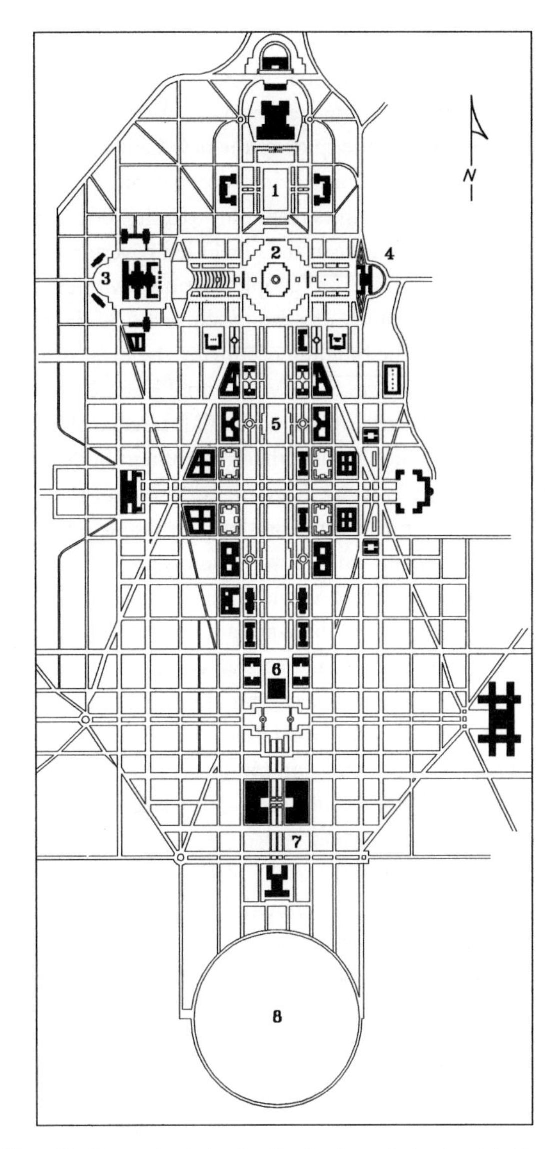

Map 18. Top-ranked plan for Nanjing's central administrative zone. Plan from 1928. In the northernmost section of the plan is the Central Party Headquarters area (1). South of the headquarters is the main square with a fountain at its center (2). To the west of the square is the national government building (3) and to the east of the chairman's official residence (4). The various Yuan and ministries face the mall extending south of the main square, with the Executive Yuan at the southern end (6). Further south, the massive war and navy departments face each other (7), with the ministry of aviation to the south. The circle at the bottom of the plan is the proposed airport (8) to service the national government. Redrawn from plans in *Shoudu jianshe* (November 1928).

the patriotic flavor of the building designs. "[The plan] follows the Chinese ancient style in that all the buildings project a feeling of magnificence and enchantment." The layout also reflected the spirit of the new China. "The arrangement is very systematic, in order to express freedom and equality in the Chinese republic." To the judges, the plans evoked confidence in the GMD-led government, which would "represent" a "people's nation," with the "appearance of the stability of a mountain rock."[46] The pride of this plan, and the building occupying the most prominent position in it, was the GMD central headquarters. The party building was to crown a hill located at the foot of Purple Mountain, "while other government buildings would be grouped further down on both sides of the valley."[47] In addition to occupying the most visible point of the entire area (from which it was also easiest to oversee the people), the headquarters would sit at the head of an expansive mall, occupying the same position that the Capitol Building does in Nanjing's American counterpart. Meanwhile, the arrangement of lesser buildings in front of the headquarters appears to form a massive marble gateway leading to the headquarters on top of the hill. Overall, the judges felt the design's grand-scale architecture would "bring patriotic feeling and impress the foreigners."[48]

Unfortunately, none of the plans submitted for the contest were deemed good enough to win the top prizes, with the best two designs garnering only third-place prizes.[49] Generally speaking, the Capital Construction Committee found that "many of the designs are good," but none of them "fit completely with the rules."[50] They were too costly. Providing figures that ranged from fifteen to twenty million yuan, they far overshot the targeted six million yuan. The best design was the most expensive, requiring more than twenty million yuan for the first stage of construction alone. Another reason the committee rejected the designs was that several members felt Purple Mountain was not appropriate for the central administrative zone after all. One foreign adviser wrote in October 1929 that the Purple Mountain site was "unrealistic," since it would be too expensive to build on the slope.[51] Another member of the committee's advisory board, Hong Lanyou, was more outspoken in his criticism of the National Capital Planning Office's efforts. He felt that the designers had taken too much from Western models. "When we build our capital," he wrote, "we must not take England or Germany as models. . . . We also cannot take the capitals of other countries to be our blue print and make our capital imitate them." Blindly following Western models was incompatible with the Chinese spirit. "The construction of our capital cannot be forced to be like that of other countries; just like the Chinese national characteristics cannot be forced to be like any other nation in the world."[52] Thus modernization in GMD China would not simply be a matter of imitating Western leaders.

The National Capital Planning Office continued its work, undaunted by the failure of the contest, and on December 31, 1929, it published the *Capital City Plan (Shoudu jihua)*. This plan for the whole of Nanjing utilized the latest in modern city-planning theory by dividing the city into distinct zones. For its administrative zone, the planning office utilized one of the top-ranked drawings "as a reference," even though the construction committee had rejected it. The city planning office defended its placement of the central administrative zone on Purple Mountain, saying that the space within the city walls would be needed for the expansion of commercial and residential areas. Furthermore, Purple Mountain still provided the most authoritative spatial position in the city: "The important public buildings in other countries are placed in the most focused location to let normal citizens see them from afar and have respectful feelings about them."[53] Only a site on Purple Mountain would meet this international standard.

In addition to the government district, Nanjing would feature clearly defined business districts, residential areas, industrial zones, suburban residential areas, and a financial district.[54] While zoning ordinances are common in many communities in today's developed world, in 1929, zoning was a relatively new concept. Of course, Chinese city planners had separated their important cities into "zones" for thousands of years. For example, Chang'an, the Tang capital, had separate areas for government, markets, craftsmen's residences, and common residences.[55] While designers of the 1920s and 1930s did not entirely ignore this history of Chinese city planning, in the general planning discourse in China, foreign thinkers such as Le Corbusier and G. E. Haussmann earned the most praise for "modern" city planning, especially for their respective emphases on efficient use of space and aesthetic beauty of plan.[56] One reason for the oversight may have been that traditional imperial city planning was more limited in scope, emphasizing the use of districts to control the movements of the population, while modern city planning was supposed to make living in the city more efficient for the circulation of commerce and the increased functional differentiation of life in industrial society. Directly referring to the imperial form of control was probably seen as going against the spirit of the "people's capital." Of course, modern zoning is also a form of control over the environment and the activities of the population, but most architects did not emphasize this point.[57] They preferred to use terms more palatable to the modern audience (e.g., efficiency and rational order). The Chinese planners did not discuss the control issue at all in the newsletter.

Michel Foucault has provided one answer to why such means of control may have been hidden from the publics affected in the West. According to recent scholarship informed by Foucault, the unstated goal of modern-era architecture, city planning, and zones has been to create a naturalized discipline within the subject. This modern discipline, in order to work from within, requires that the elements of particular social processes be broken down into their separate functions and then reassembled into more productive (or more efficient) combinations (hence the "zones"). City planning and architecture, with their rational, classic, standardized forms, work together to create a new environment for the modern subject. In part, through the power of the *habitus* of external structures, which "enframe" the lives of the people in the ordered spaces of buildings and cityscapes, the hierarchies of new power relations become internalized. By presenting themselves as merely neutral containers of space, modern structures reinforce newly created social hierarchies by making them a seemingly natural (and thus forgettable) part of everyday life. When this order and the place assigned to the individual become accepted as natural and timeless, the modern subject is born.[58] The GMD planners wanted to use space to create a new Chinese citizen, to reshape the way people lived, and to create a new sense of responsibility to the nation. There was also a need to strengthen the ability of the state to encourage the growth of the modern economy and, by extension, rationalize the movements of the people who were involved in it. These ideas already seemed natural to planners who wanted to modernize the country. Despite the fact that planners knew they were trying to influence the lives of the Chinese people, perhaps they did not think in terms of "control," since that implied something more artificial and contrived than the natural human progression of modernity they believed they were trying to achieve.

The published plan also described the architectural style of the government buildings themselves, providing illustrations of what this style should resemble. The buildings depicted had overtly Chinese characteristics, the most obvious being the upturned roofs on each structure and the dual-roofed central towers. The model for the GMD headquarters was particularly impressive. With a large circular structure in the center and curved roofs, it resembled the Temple of Heaven in Beijing. By employing such measures of association with a sacred past, the planners intended to appeal to the GMD's own sense that its role in the building of the country was paramount; and they hoped to use such structures to make that sentiment take root among the people as well. The other drawings provided stylistic models for government buildings, suggesting their appearance and relative grandeur rather than giving a concrete plan of design. Each of these drawings reflected similar associations with imperial-era structures. One key departure from the past, however, was the use of concrete, steel, and stone in their construction, to replace the ephemeral wooden materials of dynastic buildings. The overall architectural style was to consist of "a modification of the classic Chinese style." The architects borrowed the "stateliness and splendour" of imperial palaces and temples while using "modern materials and modern methods" to "meet every need of an up-to-date government office."[59]

For the planners who advocated this combination of new and old, the results were to be revolutionary in the field of Chinese architecture. Mixed in with the Chinese roofs and towers, there were elements informed both by Chinese conventions of symmetry and an international standard of classical architecture. For example, the windows on the buildings were to be arranged in a standardized manner and interspersed with a row of stone columns, the veritable symbol of European (and colonial) neoclassical style. These columns would be accentuated at the entrances of three buildings and replaced by a grand archway in the fourth. Columns and symmetry were also a standard symbol of imperial order in Chinese architecture. The fact that these aspects of form could suggest a neoclassical order as well as provide links to the Chinese past must have made them doubly useful, appealing to domestic as well as international audiences.

The plans presented for the city, the administrative sector, and the buildings that would comprise it resembled designs created for the "City Beautiful" movement, which was in international vogue from the 1890s to the early 1910s (when many Chinese architects were studying in the United States). The City Beautiful formula consisted of scientific city planning to create conditions for peak efficiency in production and circulation, the generous application of open spaces (such as wide boulevards, malls, and parks) and grand vistas for recreation and education, as well as the aesthetics of Beaux Arts informed neoclassical buildings and monuments. Thus conventions of absolutism and despotism were adapted to modern, seemingly atemporal use to create a sense of timeless "values" in an era when social change occurred at a dizzying pace.[60] Chinese city planners were certainly influenced by these ideas. This spatial order, along with the installation of the latest technological advances in communications, hygiene, and transportation, is what planners meant by "learning from new western science to satisfy the needs of modern life."[61]

The influence of American design principles does not mean that Chinese designers were simply aping their American mentors. The nature of their task precluded such an attitude. China, unlike European nations or the United States, needed more than neoclassical stability. The leaders of the country agreed that the nation's revolutionary process had only just begun. China had spent over "three thousand years" in a condition of atemporal "stagnation." The spaces for the new government had to evoke a sense that the nation was moving forward, that after ninety years of humiliation, it had finally taken control of its own future. Meanwhile, the party hoped that by creating a sense of national community through spatial references to a common past, China could avoid the class-based divisiveness plaguing the rest of the modern world. This required the invention of a uniquely Chinese "neoclassical" tradition. In the end, China wanted to surpass the world in its modernity through the blending of the "best of the East and West."

While the GMD wanted to create an efficient national collective in order to achieve modernization as quickly as possible, it did not think the people responsible enough for self-government. The people needed political tutelage, under which they would learn how to modernize the nation and act in its own best interests. In these circumstances, the City Beautiful was an appropriate model, creating spaces for efficient production and trade while providing symbolic national dignity through the use of open spaces, grand vistas, and monumental architecture.[62] This display of national dignity, in the plans for China's capital, did not invite the participation of the nation's citizens. Instead, these designs informed the viewer that the GMD government was both powerful and capable of leading tutelage.

Building the Dream

By December 1929, months of work had gone into the planning of the administrative center; however, the central leadership of the GMD dismissed the effort. Shortly after the publication of the National Capital Planning Office's intentions for the administrative sector, the state council decided to place the government sector closer to the more developed sections of the city, where it could take advantage of existing, sparse infrastructure.[63] The council relocated the sector to a site near the Ming Palace, just inside the city walls to the west of the construction committee's site. Financial considerations were paramount in this decision. The national government had trouble raising the funds it needed for its high military expenses and numerous infrastructure projects. From 1929 to 1937, the national government operated at a deficit. Increased taxa-

Fig. 17. The Ministry of Railways. This building group, with its massive curved roofs topping concrete walls, large glass windows, and painted columns, reflects the ideal depiction of a "modern" and "Chinese" building called for in the capital city plan. Note also the wide, open field in the foreground. Photo from Su Gin-Djih (1964), pl. 134.

tion could not supply the funds necessary, since the people were already being "squeezed" rather heavily.[64] The GMD faced the daunting task of building a nation without the benefit of political unity or adequate funds. The GMD had to make some tough prioritizing decisions. What was vital? What could wait until later?

The administrative sector officially entered the stage of construction when ground was broken for the Ministry of Railways on September 10, 1929. Designed by a Chinese architect trained in the United States, the building had a large curved roof atop a modern concrete facade, which featured large, regularly spaced windows to allow fresh air to circulate through the interior and to give the exterior a feeling of openness. With roof curves, pseudocolumns, and fenestrations associated with traditional Chinese architecture, and modern construction materials, the Ministry of Railways resembled the ideal ministry building suggested in the *Capital City Plan* (see fig. 17). The building group, consisting of a general administration building, the minister's residence, and staff residences, was completed in May 1930, at a cost of $969,380.[65]

That the Ministry of Railways was the first building constructed might surprise us in light of the overwhelming emphasis placed on the GMD headquarters in the original plans. The party was apparently content to continue operating from its temporary home in the Jiangsu Provincial Assembly, so the government preferred to use its limited resources to build structures that would bring a quick return on its investment. Railroads were seen as the key to industrial modernization and prosperity. Sun Yat-sen felt so strongly about the issue that he had drawn up plans for more than one million miles of railways to be built in a span of ten years![66] The Nationalist government of the early 1930s understood the symbolic and practical importance of railroads and set to work "acting on Dr. Sun's injunction." With planned railways requiring more than $57 million in public bonds and foreign loans, it was critical to convince financiers that China's railways were a good investment. One way to accomplish this goal was to invite prospective investors to meet the minister of railways in the classy surroundings of a new, modern building.[67]

A desire for improved modern infrastructure also explains the construction of the Ministry of Communications, which was designed by a Russian architect.[68] Work began in July 1930 but was not completed until 1934—an unusually long period of time to erect one building group.[69] Two events, a serious flood in Nanjing in 1931 and the Shanghai undeclared war with Japan in 1932, interrupted the timetable and exemplified how GMD troubles were exacerbated by external forces. The facade of the Ministry of Communications also reflected the modified Chinese classicism of the ideal plan, although it was not an exact copy of the Ministry of Railways. The ground-floor facade consisted of a series of arches for windows and doors, which had precedent in Chinese convention. Many drum and bell towers (both traditional forms of communication—one to warn, one to mark time) had two small arches on either side of a larger one. In the Ministry of Communications, this convention was utilized as a reference, but in a repetitive manner that denoted the changed nature of communication technology (see fig. 18).

Not all new buildings in the Nanjing Decade were constructed "from scratch." Economic reality forced the GMD to refurbish existing structures as well. The party decided to transform a temple into the Examination Yuan, a site for the selection of the modern bureaucracy. The

Fig. 18. The Ministry of Communications. "East and West Meet in a Building—And All is in Harmony." So states the caption for this photo of the Ministry of Communications as it appeared in *National Geographic Magazine* 73(2) (February 1938): 214.

Wumiao Temple, dedicated to gods of martial vigor, was built by the Qing in 1868 on the site of a temple to Confucius, which itself dated back to the Tang dynasty (739 A.D.).[70] To modify the site for modern use, the GMD rebuilt the main tower in May 1931 and added four buildings to the three temple halls that still existed. In all, the structures that made up this group cost $600,000 to "repair."[71]

While prospective bureaucrats took the civil service examination in one former temple hall and personal archives were stored in another, the Examination Yuan still served as a site dedicated to the martial deities Guandi and Yue Fei. The tablets and images previously housed in the main hall were moved to another section of the complex, where a shrine was preserved. The door to this shrine featured a wooden tablet, engraved by the head of the Examination Yuan, reminding people to be respectful.[72] The GMD felt that the patriotism of these heroes served an important function in the new nation. The selfless loyalty of these model figures exemplified a healthy tradition that should be preserved and encouraged within the bureaucracy that would be created at the new site.

The construction of the Ministry of Foreign Affairs, completed in 1933, provided another interpretation of the modified Chinese architectural style called for in the ideal plan. Extra attention given to it at the time provides an opportunity to explore in more detail what this style entailed, both for the people who viewed it from the outside and for those who worked within. Designed by Zhao Shen, an architect trained at the University of Pennsylvania,[73] the building was considered an architectural success. To one writer, "[t]his building is a successful attempt to combine the exquisite details of the Chinese classical architecture with the simple mass and lines of modern architecture, doing away boldly with the sloping roof"[74] (see fig. 19). Shortly after its completion, the trade journal *Zhongguo jianzhu* (Chinese architecture) published the floor plans.[75]

The exterior plan revealed imperial-era influences on the overall orientation of the buildings. While not exact, the orientation did follow a roughly north-south axis, with the entrance of the main building facing south. This orientation was no accident. The writer for *Zhongguo jianzhu* commented that despite the fact that Nanjing's main ar-

Fig. 19. The Ministry of Foreign Affairs. This building was praised for boldly eliminating the curving roof while still retaining a "Chinese" spirit. Some considered it the high point of the Chinese architectural "renaissance" in Nanjing. From *National Geographic Magazine* 73(2) (February 1938): 217.

tery, Sun Yat-sen Road (Zhongshan lu), lay west of the site, a westward-facing building would be "unsuitable in the winter and summer seasons." So the building "faces the direction of the Drum Tower" (a couple blocks to the south) instead.[76] In traditional Chinese architecture, entrances to all important buildings faced the auspicious southern direction. When someone met with an important figure, he faced north, while the host faced south. The entrance of the main building of the Ministry of Foreign Affairs faced south, while the entrance to the official residence faced north. In terms of traditional conventions, those who stayed at the official residence, where the minister himself resided and entertained guests, were in a politically inferior position to the ministry itself, and to the government it represented.

The overall arrangement of the site showed significant variation from traditional forms. Despite the symmetrical design, which was consistent with imperial convention, the fronts of the main buildings faced each other across a circular drive, while the main entrances to the compound did likewise on the east and west sides. In other words, the site was arranged around a radial axis, common in Western design, but unheard of in the government buildings of imperial China. A pragmatic concern for the ease of vehicular traffic was offered as the reason for this decision.[77] The garden design also showed Western influence. Two gardens flanking the main building to the east and west were patterned after Cartesian designs, like the ones at Versailles. Their orthogonal paths were based on a single-point perspective, whereas Chinese gardens of the imperial era were asymmetrical, with winding, overlapping paths and a multiplicity of views. The Ministry of Foreign Affairs gardens emphasized rationalism, revealing an aesthetic of public space that differed from the private gardens of Chinese convention. A garden should be pleasing to the eye, but time should not be wasted with useless meandering.

The external layout and the facade of the Ministry of Foreign Affairs were designed to create a break from the past. Whereas a strict set of principles governed the construction of the imperial building and tied the functions of government to a whole cosmological system designed to place the emperor (and his representatives) at the center of "all under heaven," the republican-era building would be laid out according to principles of rationalism and efficiency of movement. Even when the layout followed traditional precedents, designers used pragmatic terms to explain the continuity. No longer dependent on "stagnant" conventions of imperial design, republican-era architects and GMD state builders were intent on expressing China's modernity with the use of alternative, Western models.

Yet to construct a modern nation-state, the continuity of history was necessary to create a sense of national progress. For this end, the designers turned to aesthetics. While the exterior facade of the main building was an example of the "simple mass and lines of modern architecture" the planners sought, the architects used ornament to show that its essence was still Chinese. Without the dramatic upturned roof, the designers relied on more subtle indications such as brackets protruding from the port cochère and along the bottom of the roofline. Traditionally, such brackets were structural members that supported the sloping roof. The brackets were also integrated with the cosmology of the structure, which mirrored the cosmology of the state and society. The roof served as a symbol of heaven; the platform floor was the earth, and the beam construction, its prominent external feature being the bracket system, linked the two, just as the Son of Heaven and his government linked man and the forces above.[78] In the Ministry of Foreign Affairs the ornamental bracket was divorced from its traditional cosmological significance, but it acquired new meaning as a sign of continuity with China's past, which itself was to be transformed into a symbol of power for the modern nation-state. Perhaps by giving the bracket a prominent aesthetic role in this building, the designer was also signifying that it was the "link," that is, the state, and not heaven, which was the prime force in modern China.

By disposing of the monumental roof, the designer also added greater emphasis to the plentiful, large windows. Internalized reinforced concrete columns made these windows possible by eliminating the structural stress on the walls. Not only were more light and fresh air allowed into the building, but the entire external appearance gained a feeling of lightness and thinness. The windows also indicate an architectural shift in the relationship between inside (the government) and outside (the governed). The imperial government building complex had no windows facing the outside, and all attention was directed to its center. With one-story buildings arranged around a courtyard directing one to a central building, the yamen was an inward-looking, centered space. In the Ministry of Foreign Affairs, the windows served as a new link between the state and the people.

Moving to the interior layout of the building, the most striking example of a break from Chinese tradition was in the rooms and corridors. In all, there were about one hundred rooms in the Ministry of Foreign Affairs, and each of these rooms was assigned a discrete function. From the boiler room, to the passport office, to the minister's office, to the sex-specific bathrooms, each room was labeled in the blueprints to serve a distinct purpose in the bureaucratic machine. Functional differentiation itself was not a new feature in republican-era government buildings, but the degree of spatial specialization was significantly increased. These functions were increasingly separated as well. Instead of being marked off by screen-like panels and joined directly to adjacent rooms, as in an imperial building, each room in the ministry was enclosed by walls. These rooms were then each connected to a functionally separated, double-loaded corridor outside. The bureaucrat would know his proper place in the government machine by the room that enclosed his workspace. When he needed to interact with the other parts, he could go directly to the appropriate office, without having to witness any extraneous institutional interconnections. While one could sense the totality of the system with all of those office signs compacted under one efficient roof, there was no need to see exactly how the totality operated.

Meanwhile, the working spaces of service personnel (such as cooks, janitors, etc.) were kept out of sight, relegated to the rear, lower levels of the building. In fact, service workers used the back door to enter the building, instead of the main entrance designated for "official" personnel. Official spaces were also arranged hierarchically. Prime corner locations were allocated to important individuals, such as the minister and department directors. The separation of workers, common bureaucrats, and important individuals was not a new practice, either. What distinguishes this layout from a traditional one is that these hierarchically arranged spaces were enclosed in the same building, creating a new kind of unity in the division of labor, one "scientifically" based on efficiency and (for the higher officials) comfort rather than traditional cosmological power arrangements.

One aesthetic feature of the interior prominently displayed in *Zhongguo jianzhu* was the coiffured ceiling. According to imperial-era dictates, only the most important buildings could utilize these elaborately carved and painted ceilings. The one in the entrance hall of the Ministry of Foreign Affairs was supported by four massive vermilion pillars. In the guest hall the coiffured ceiling was augmented by large hanging lanterns and a grand double-door crowned by a carved wooden lintel. These elaborate ornaments were not mere attachments; they provided a necessary link to a powerful past. In the context of the modern building, they were separated from cosmology and could, therefore, serve as symbols of power in an age of modern progress. This blending of progress and tradition into a new Chinese space, free from a seemingly superstitious past and the domination of foreign powers, is what Chinese planners hoped for when they called for "the best of East and West." At the same time, they expected the subject that occupied the space would be infected with the rationalism and efficiency of the arrangement, that in the regulated, segmented, and specialized spaces a new social being would emerge: the modern citizen, whose role in the national machine would be dictated by his working environment.

The diversity of styles and methods in constructing each of these yuan and ministry buildings highlights the variety of motives and priorities of the GMD government itself. Yet one significant architectural element was used in each of them: the outer wall. In the imperial era, walls were used to set government structures apart from the rest of the city. In republican China, this convention was utilized again. Although never discussed in the capital city plans, pictures from the 1930s confirm that these buildings were walled off, setting them physically apart from their surroundings. (For one striking example of this physical barrier, see the photograph of the Supreme Court, built in 1933, in fig. 20.)[79] Furthermore, the massive, multistory government buildings rose above the walls to become more visible to pedestrians on the opposite side. The new government buildings were monuments to a new kind of state, but the citizen was not invited to participate, only to view.

In sum, the "revolution" in Chinese architecture was an attempt to utilize space to create a new form of rational discipline both within the government and for the people in general. The use of permanent concrete and steel, along with the simplicity and "sincerity" of modern standardized forms, created a style of "neutral" aesthetics that was labeled "international" and represented an ethic of efficient administration and production. This space of republi-

Fig. 20. The Supreme Court. *National Geographic* states simply that this building is "Western, even to the awnings and lampposts." The archway, however, is "carrying out an old tradition that a building, public or private, must be enclosed by a low wall to be dignified." From *National Geographic Magazine* 73(2) (February 1938): 202.

can, modern discipline resonated with previous forms of ritualized imperial spaces in that it emphasized the hierarchical relationship between the government and the governed. What may not have been fully developed in the new spaces, however, was a meaningful ritual that would make the sense of mutual responsibility clear for both parties. The GMD was clearly in the process of developing such a national ritual,[80] but its effectiveness needs to be examined more closely before any conclusions can be made. (After all, space, as opposed to place, does not exist without meanings ascribed by human movement, or as Michel de Certeau has put it, *"space is practiced place."*)[81] Yet the frames themselves reveal contradictions between exclusionary elements and those that hint at an openness to future participation by the disciplined citizen. A monumental, classical facade with large windows greeted persons on the street, and a wall kept them away. Meanwhile, the architectural tradition embodied in these buildings ensured that residents recognized three important messages from the GMD. First, by using conventions of China's past, the party asserted that it was not "selling out" to the foreigners. Second, the party claimed to represent the will of the entire nation (not just a single class), which stemmed from a common past that all Chinese people shared. Finally, the party wanted to show its power.

Awakened by Nightmares

As the 1930s progressed, the GMD's attentions were diverted to their struggles with the Communists and with the Japanese. Money grew tighter as the world faced an unprecedented economic depression, which caught up with China at the end of 1931. Factionalism within the party intensified. From an administrative standpoint, corruption and poor decision making were taking their toll on an already strained treasury.[82] As a result, the administrative zone was put on what would become a permanent hold. Many government buildings were never completed. The most prominent structure in the *Capital City Plan* of 1930 that was never built was the GMD central headquarters. That this ostentatious structure was not a high priority in the actual construction process shows that the party had some sense of the need for restraint in representing its own power. The GMD Central Committee must have been fairly content to remain in the former Jiangsu Provincial Assembly building, a relatively auspicious home itself. After all, it was the site from which the birth of the Republic of China was announced in January 1912, and the place where Sun Yat-sen was inaugurated as the first president.[83] Other prominent government organs that remained in their "temporary" homes included the national government, the Legislative Yuan, the Nanjing municipal government, and many others.[84] One writer in 1937 complained about the lack of "suitable" modern structures, as the typical government department was forced to use a "tumble down old building, with cramped office space for the staff."[85]

In addition to abandoning plans for new buildings, the construction committee relinquished hope of creating a central administrative zone. Most government organs remained in their "temporary" structures, and the new buildings were built at the most cost-effective locations. Thus government bureaus were scattered about the city. The government provided official justification for the abandonment of the zone along Sun Yat-sen Road (Zhongshan lu) by saying that the area would better serve as a residential zone. "Upon finding that the steady growth of the population of the city necessitated more and more living quarters, that part of Chungshan Road covering 2,500 mow was reserved as a residential section."[86] In the face of these executive decisions, all that the construction committee could do was shrug its collective shoulders and say, "Time may yet demonstrate the wisdom of permitting government buildings to remain scattered."[87]

Although the GMD abandoned much of its capital plan, a few structures were built in the 1930s, including the Ministry of Railways, the Examination Yuan, the Ministry of Foreign Affairs, and the Ministry of Communications. Railroads and communications were symbols of modernity that also served economic and strategic purposes, making them central to the GMD's modernizing mission. The GMD felt that these important ministries required modern facilities. The party leadership also realized that it needed massive amounts of capital to undertake basic infrastructure projects. These buildings would not only serve as modern centers of bureaucracy, but also as trophies to impress prospective investors and foreign diplomats. The GMD figured that by spending a few hundred thousand dollars, they could increase the amount of investment in the country by millions.

As the buildings were completed, they received a warm public reception, at least from the clients themselves. In a 1937 report on the progress of Nanjing's development, the director of public works praised the "new styles of architecture" and said that "many of the public buildings are really gorgeous."[88] The new buildings also impressed foreigners. The "beautiful" Ministry of Railways especially impressed one group of expatriates, the Nanjing Woman's [sic] Club. They particularly liked the Chinese aspects of the building, "the massive roofs of temple tiles and stone pillars of Chinese red." They also praised the modern qualities of the buildings. "These buildings, and those of the Railway Administration, are an architectural addition to Nanking and are excellent examples of the adaptation of Chinese architecture to modern needs and uses."[89]

But not all observers, especially after the Nanjing Decade was over, felt that the "model capital" was such a success. The leftist writer Guo Moruo's memoirs of a visit to Nanjing in 1945 were not kind: "There are many vast, open spaces and desolate areas, in the midst of which lie mostly low and ugly houses." In this context, he felt that these combined "Chinese/Western" buildings were quite jolting. Out of the desolation and low buildings, "suddenly there emerge some enormously colossal, Chinese-Western combined palatial-style buildings. These Chinese-Western palaces are all government buildings." Guo Moruo did not approve of how the GMD architects portrayed China's architectural tradition. "It is as if 10 generations have been reduced to one hour in this place." He also did not enjoy the combined style, feeling that the structures were not in proper harmony. Because these combined-style buildings were placed on "overly broad" boulevards, these "would-be palaces" actually resembled an "emerging thicket of grass." Finally, Guo Moruo felt these buildings were dominated by even larger, purely foreign, buildings. "Occasionally, there are huge foreign-style buildings . . . making the palaces seem like they are bowing to the foreign buildings."[90] In addition to Guo Moruo's criticism, a later architect described these buildings as "not remarkable,"[91] and another derided them as "flat" and "without context."[92]

The GMD constructed a capital without a center. In terms of the spaces that enframed the lives of its inhabitants, Nanjing had monumental pretensions, but the lack of coherence in siting and the clear discontinuity between the government buildings and their dingy surroundings belied the order and rationalism of the new spaces. The grand vistas hardly represented the spirit of a state in touch with the needs of its citizens. Instead, they became monuments to the disparity between modernist intentions and social reality. It seems unlikely that in this total scene, the discipline represented in such structures was hidden, and it is even less likely that such discipline became internalized as a naturalized loyalty to the GMD state. Perhaps, if the buildings had been grouped together so that a person was absorbed into the monumental orderliness of a rationally designed central administrative zone, temporarily forgetting the poverty just beyond the enclosed view, the effect might have been more powerful. But Nanjing, the capital, lacked this clear center; it lacked a *capitol,* which could serve as a ceremonial center of the modern state.[93]

Conclusion

What can be said about the priorities of the GMD in its efforts to forge a new national capital? The GMD publicly stated that it wanted to remake the capital city because it needed new facilities to govern effectively a modern Chinese state. Underneath these explicit intentions lay the implied desire to impress upon the people of China that the party was the best (and only) vehicle to bring the country into the modern age. Buildings constructed with sturdy, modern materials and equipped with modern features would be a good start, as long as these structures did not neglect the aesthetics of traditional Chinese architecture. Furthermore, the GMD would need to raise a large amount of capital in order to bring the Chinese infrastructure up-to-date. To do so, they required modern facilities for entertaining both foreign and domestic financiers. Such structures helped reassure the prospective investor that China was indeed a country with a bright, low-risk future. From the decisions that the GMD made in selecting which buildings would be built, we can see what their highest priorities were. By choosing to erect buildings that were generally tied to infrastructure and foreign affairs, the GMD confirmed the implied goal of raising capital, especially foreign funds.

To help create a modern nation under the tutelage of the party, the GMD relied upon architects and urban planners to construct an environment conducive to the needs of a modern nation, while simultaneously creating a space that would legitimate its rule for an audience both at home and abroad. These goals required a new spatial arrangement that emphasized rational order and efficiency through modern methods of production and administration. They also entailed the creation of new symbols for the community of the nation, and spaces for a new set of rituals. All would be required to create the modern citizen, a new social being; but for the GMD, this newly disciplined social being could only be realized with the passage of time and the strict guidance of the self-proclaimed revolutionary party. These attempts to transform Chinese society comprised the "modernist project," with its communication facilities, transportation networks, public utilities projects, social welfare programs, public health works, financial establishments, police patrols, government bureaus, urban planning, and building construction.

This chapter has dealt with only a small aspect of the modernist project, but one that was essential to the creation of the new, disciplined individual: the attempt to construct government spaces that would internalize and naturalize the new power relations between the Chinese citizen and GMD authority. The tools for this planned spatial transformation included City Beautiful-informed urban design and Beaux Arts-inspired neoclassical forms, as well as the grandeur of China's own architectural past. This combination was supposed to revolutionize Chinese space by utilizing modern, permanent materials and the latest in international design techniques combined with creative, nondeterministic references to traditional Chinese aesthetics and style. The GMD and its planners wanted to frame the lives of the people in rationalism, efficiency, and order by enclosing them in an international-style capital—but this capital would outdo all the others because it was more dignified, more *Chinese.* Ultimately, they intended to create a monumental space, which would awe the viewer (whether foreign or domestic) with the dignity of the Chinese nation and the power of the modern GMD state. It was to be modern, without mirroring Shanghai's Bund, and Chinese, without mimicking the Forbidden City.

The creators of self-proclaimed "revolutionary" Chinese architecture were fortunate in that many of the underlying values of a modern, orderly, disciplined nation-state could be readily found in the conventions of imperial-era architecture. GMD planners recognized that underneath the detritus of generations of gradual encroachment lay wide, rational, grid-like streets. They realized that premodern buildings were standardized and orderly in their construction, even if some were dedicated to superstitious and feudal practices. There was an order to Confucian life, and there was a discipline in the lives of the people who participated in the rituals of that life. Unfortunately, that order was based on an older, cyclical way of life and unfit for the needs of efficient production in a modern world. Confucian discipline had lost its legitimacy, and members of the GMD felt it was up to them to reweave the pattern of Chinese life to form a new discipline and reunite the fractured populace with a common cause: to modernize and preserve the nation and its culture. To do so, however, would require all the powers and intrusiveness of a modern state apparatus to teach the people how to be collectively responsible for themselves.

Looking at the plans presented and the buildings constructed reveals certain contradictions in this effort. Large windows and links to a "common," rational architectural heritage were supposed to create a sense of a state open to public view and sharing in the common mission of modernizing the national collective. However, the proposed grand vistas and the monumental edifices that greet one with a guarded gate may create a kind of coerced discipline. These frames do not invite participation or a feeling of self-responsibility from the citizen on the outside looking in. Thus removed, the large windows seem more conducive to the government watching over the people than vice versa. Confucian discipline, and its spaces, had given people roles, or names, which implied a two-way form of hierarchical responsibility between patron and client. Little mutual responsibility was implied in either the frame of idealized Nanjing or in its actual 1937 configuration. The lives of the people were framed by overt references to state power and the new hierarchical relationship between state and people.

What remains unanswered is how the GMD conceived each of these government buildings as spaces for the creation of a national ritual. After all, space—even Foucault-style disciplinary space of the modern nation in all its orderly rationalism—is nothing without performance: ritual actions make those spaces meaningful to the people who live and work in and around them. This chapter has shown some of the contradictions within the frames, or structures, of the modernist effort to construct discipline, but such contradictions do not mean that modern discipline could not be realized if properly naturalized. In this chapter I have also shown how construction with limited resources led to a significant gap between idealized visions and concrete realities, which damaged the GMD's ability to create the kind of total scene conducive to naturalizing discipline. Yet even if the plan had been followed precisely, building a rationally designed city does not mean that the resulting space necessarily succeeds in fulfilling the planners' intentions. Modern discipline might have existed in republican China, but if so, it was probably very fragile indeed. To judge the success of the buildings built, or of the new model capital in Nanjing, requires more investigation of the relationships between space and ritual, and between government intentions and the ways these spaces were actually used.

Part III
City and Nation

Chapter 10

Wuhan's Search for Identity in the Republican Period

Stephen R. MacKinnon

"Wuhan is the birthplace of the Republic of China, the high point of the revolutionary northern expedition (of 1927), and now the center of the Chinese nation's war of resistance. These three eras of the 1911 Revolution, northern expedition, and War of Resistance have become great milestones in the renaissance or rebirth of the Chinese nation."

Zhou Enlai, October 10, 1938, Wuhan

The republican history of the tri-city complex of Wuhan illustrates well the tension between the themes of modernity and national identity that frame this volume. Although the tri-city was largely unplanned as a whole, it included an economic center in the bustling port of Hankou, which pursued economic and cultural modernity through commerce and became a railroad terminus early in the century. Across the Yangzi River, Wuchang, while clinging to the urban morphology of the traditional administrative capital, led in the search for national identity. Thrice—in 1911–1912, 1927, and 1938—Wuchang succeeded in thrusting Wuhan to the center stage of national politics. The tension between the crass, commercial modernity of Hankou and the bombastic political posturing of Wuchang gave twentieth-century Wuhan a split personality that is still evident architecturally today. Caught in the middle was the smaller third city, the down-to-earth industrial center of Hanyang.

Thus the tri-city urban sprawl that made up republican Wuhan was just as amorphous and difficult to define as contemporary greater Los Angeles. Spatially and administratively, it had no center: no unified police force, school system, waterworks, fire department, or city administration. Yet culturally and geopolitically, by the 1920s Wuhan had a self-conscious identity and a pushy sense of itself as the politically unruly but strategically important and economically booming urban complex straddling the Yangzi at its junction with the Han River. Politically, Wuhan had been important since the 1911 Revolution toppled the Qing dynasty. In 1938, the United Front defense of Wuhan cost a million Chinese and Japanese lives. Still, not until 1957, when new bridges were built to stitch together the three cities of Hankou, Hanyang, and Wuchang, did Wuhan become the integrated municipality it is today.

Like other inland cities of the republican era, Wuhan operated in the shadow of Shanghai, dependent commercially for capital and trade, which brought modernization to banking, infrastructure, and education. But its citizenry seemed little concerned with drawing comparisons to Shanghai. As often noted at the time, the Wuhan/Shanghai relationship resembled that of Chicago and New York. By the late 1920s the boomtown growth of the tri-city gave its press license to boast self-confidently about Wuhan's identity as inland China's most modern city. In part, this may have been because Wuhan effectively publicized itself to itself through an energetic local press that rivaled Tianjin and Shanghai in size.[1] But there was also Wuhan's place in the revolutionary tradition of republican China.

Three times during the first four decades of the twentieth century, Wuhan was at the center of Chinese politics. Wuchang had been the site of the October 10, 1911, uprising, sparking a revolution that toppled the Qing dynasty and led to the establishment of the Republic. With the completion of the Guomindang's Northern Expedition in 1927, Wuhan briefly became the capital of the new republican government under the left wing of the Guomindang. In both 1911 and 1927, Wuhan embodied the spirit of the Chinese republican revolution in its most liberal democratic anti-imperialist form. Indeed, Wuhan's pretensions as a revolutionary capital seemed to frighten the revolution's own leaders. Uncomfortable with the behavior of self-proclaimed revolutionaries in Wuchang, Sun Yat-sen in 1911 declared Nanjing his provisional capital, and again during the summer of 1927, Chiang Kai-shek jettisoned the leftist Wuhan government in favor of a more conservative regime in Nanjing. Wuhan's last opportunity as the romantic alternative capital of republican China came in 1938. For ten months the tri-city metropolis again assumed center stage as the wartime seat of a new coalition government after the Japanese had taken Shanghai and Nanjing and before Chiang Kai-shek retreated to Chongqing.

Another distinguishing feature of Wuhan's modern history was the cycles of physical destruction and reconstruction the metropolis experienced and its inhabitants came to expect. The Wuhan area had been repeatedly laid to waste by war since the middle of the nineteenth century. Hankou was destroyed or dismantled over four time periods: thrice razed and seized by Taiping rebels in 1850s, burned to the ground by Qing troops in 1911, badly damaged by war in 1927–1928, and pummeled by Japanese bombing raids in 1938. Wuchang was spared until the 1920s and 1930s, when the city's new commercial and industrial districts were badly damaged: first by rioting warlord troops in 192l, then by rampaging Guangxi units in 1927–1928, and finally by the destruction of 1938–1939. Hanyang suffered similarly as a war zone in 1911, 1927–1928, and 1938–1939. Yet out of the ashes of war, or perhaps because of them, the Wuhan cities quickly rebuilt and reemerged more confident, prosperous, and romantically optimistic about becoming the alternative "progressive" capital of republican China and the most "modern" of China's interior cities.

Wuhan in the Early Twentieth Century

Wuhan's cycles of renewal and destruction were well established in the nineteenth century. Linked only by ferry crossings over hundreds of yards of treacherous river, each of the three cities of Wuchang, Hanyang, and Hankou had a distinct identity and history. Together they formed what William Rowe called a "regional metropolis," dominating the economic and political life of the central Yangzi for well over a millennium.[2]

Since at least the Han dynasty, Wuchang was strategically important because of its location at the Yangzi's juncture with its most important tributary, the Han River. Wuchang was not only the capital of Hubei Province, but since the Ming period its scholar-officials oversaw the entire Huguang region (Hubei and Hunan). The Huguang governor-general was arguably the third most important provincial official in the empire (the first being the Zhihli governor-general with oversight over the region around Beijing). Wuchang was an intellectual and educational center where student candidates prepared for and took the civil service examinations. Laid out as an administrative city on the southern bank of the Yangzi, its towering walls projected political power. By function and design, Wuchang fit the traditional Chinese urban model in which the role of commerce was secondary.

Across from Wuchang, at the northwest juncture of the Han and Yangzi Rivers, lay Hanyang. Although also walled, through the nineteenth century it was a much smaller, sleepy county seat. During the Qing period Hanyang's sister city, Hankou, to the northeast across the Han, became the commercial hub of central China. At the time that Hankou was razed by Taiping troops in the 1850s, it was larger than Wuchang (over half a million residents sprawled along the banks of the Han and Yangzi). In 1862, the ruins of Hankou were declared a treaty port, enhancing its potential as the exchange center of domestic and foreign trade in raw goods and finished products for the central Yangzi region. Large and unruly, Hankou's social and economic life was almost purely commercial. It stood as a city on the periphery of the administrative orbit and jurisdiction of neighboring Hanyang. In terms of Chinese urban history, Hankou's crass commercial nature made it unorthodox. Twice, in 1855 and 1911, Wuchang officials refused to commit troops to Hankou's defense, and the city was burned to the ground as a result. But like their European counterparts, Hankou's burghers turned devastation of their city into an opportunity for growth and renewal. After its destruction by Taiping rebels, Hankou bounced back in a few decades. By the 1890s the tri-city region's population was again over a million, with the majority split between Hankou and Wuchang.

During the first decade of the twentieth century, as a

major beneficiary of the New Policy reforms, the tri-cities prospered, and their integration as a single metropolis began.[3] The catalyst was the sweeping self-strengthening reforms that Governor-General Zhang Zhidong initiated in 1893, with the establishment of the Wuchang Textile Bureau. These reforms included the creation of a large steel and munitions complex at Hanyang. There was a jump in domestic and foreign trade after the rapid expansion of steamship activity at Hankou. The foreign concession area quickly filled out, with newly established German, Russian, French, and Japanese zones bustling after 1895 (chiefly because the Treaty of Shimonoseki granted foreigners the right to open factories in the treaty ports). Customs receipts indicate a tripling of foreign trade between 1890 and 1910, to 135 million taels a year.[4] The boom in the foreign concession areas stimulated local trade. Reinforcing the strategic importance of Hankou in domestic commodity trade was the completion in 1905 of China's first north-south railway, the Beijing-Hankou line. Along the lines that David Buck has argued in chapter 5 of this volume, there is no doubt that the new railway led to further industrialization of the Wuhan economy. Obviously the existing heavy industry at Hanyang benefited. Light industry, textile factories in particular, began to appear in Wuchang along with the city's first commercial zone.

With all this activity and new wealth, the nouveau riche of Hankou, led by the tea, silk, tung oil, and hide merchants, drew up big plans for expansion of infrastructure and construction of new buildings, banking centers, and hospitals in the Hankou metropolitan area. Two large structures had major symbolic significance. The first was the Chinese-managed Huashang racetrack in Hankou, built in 1906 to rival the British track in their concession area. The second was the completion in 1909 of a six-story Western-style water tower near the Bund in Hankou that dominated the landscape for miles around. The key figures in these and other projects included scions of old well-established merchant-gentry families like Cai Fuqing, as well as pushy new traders like Liu Xinsheng, the Christian hide merchant and former comprador turned real estate magnate.[5] Led by such men, the gentry and merchants of Wuhan began to plan the financing and construction of a southern extension to the Beijing-Hankou railway, to run from Wuchang to Canton.

Then, on October 10, 1911, fighting broke out in the Wuhan area between Qing and mutinying republican rebel forces. Wuchang remained relatively unscathed, but before a cease-fire was negotiated, Hanyang became a war zone, and in late October Hankou was burned to the ground by Qing troops advancing down the railway from the north. Hankou burned for four days and nights, and the only large structures left standing outside the concessions were the racetrack and the water tower. Yet within a few months, as an endorsement of the new Republic of China, the chamber of commerce and merchant associations of Hankou, led by the Cai clan and Liu Xinsheng, began raising money for an ambitious reconstruction effort.

Local economic and architectural histories make it clear that Wuhan experienced a golden age of growth and prosperity between 1912 and 1927. Fed by an international environment that benefited Chinese business interests during World War I, expansion continued into the 1920s, with the commercial economy of Wuhan, like that of Shanghai, reaching new highs. Sophisticated, large-scale processing and manufacturing facilities for overseas markets were on the rise. The enterprises at Hanyang that Zhang Zhidong started—like the Hanyeping Iron and Steel Works, brick factory, and wire and nail factory, as well as the ceramic tile works at Wuchang—moved from official supervision *(guandu shangban)* to merchant control. Steam-powered manufacturing processes (in cotton textile mills, wheat flour mills, rice mills, cigarette factories, tea-processing plants, oil presses, and cotton-packing plants) became widespread after 1911. A measure of Wuhan's competitiveness was its ousting of foreign yarn and cloth from the middle Yangzi market. In 1915, there were over 300 privately owned cotton-weaving mills in Wuhan, which collectively employed nearly 12,000 workers.[6] By the late 1920s scholars noted 13,017 manufacturing and commercial establishments in the Wuhan area, of which 236 were said to be mechanized. Included were six cotton mills (five Chinese owned, one Japanese), which together employed over 20,000 workers.[7] In terms of heavy industry, by 1922 the new Yangzi Ironworks at Hanyang was the largest opera-

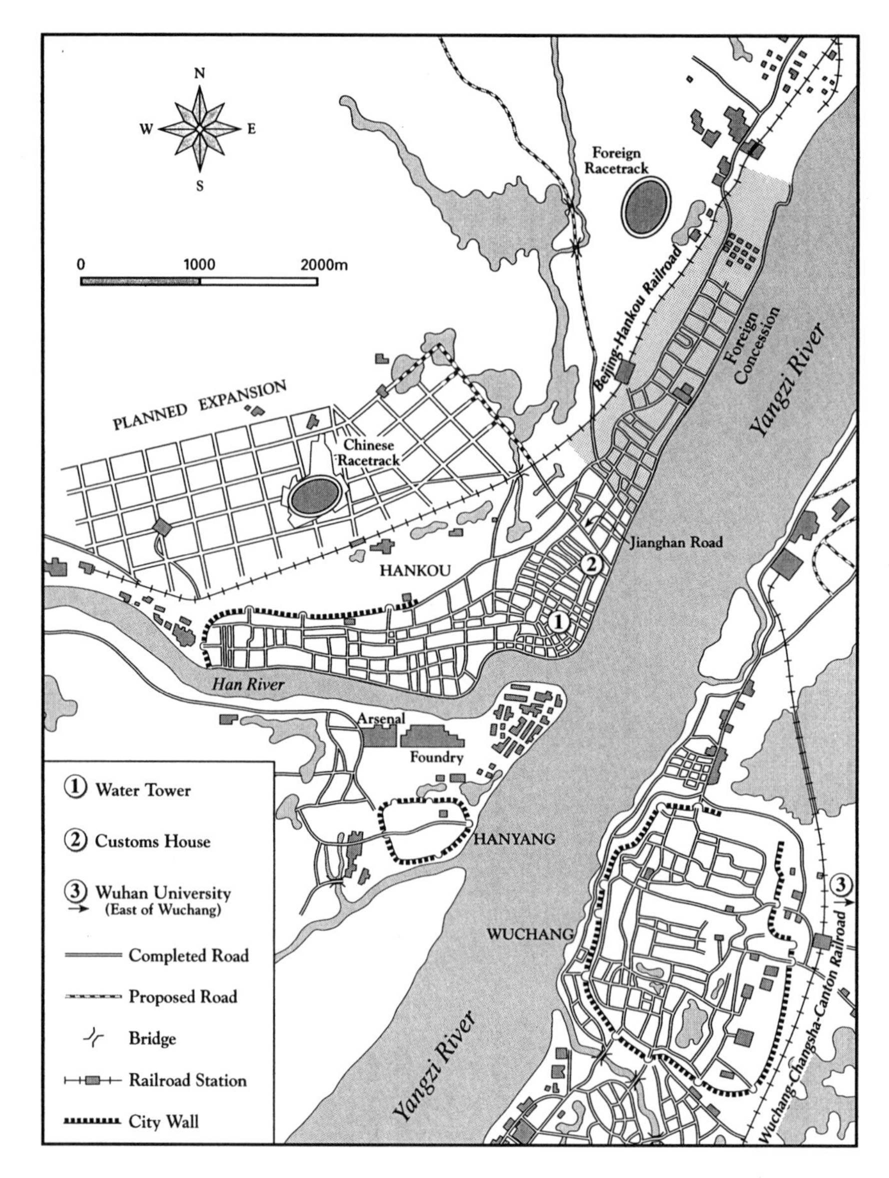

Map 19. Wuhan tri-cities, ca. 1927. Based on a map in Su Yun-feng (1981), Pi Mingxiu (1993), and *Shina shōbetsu zenshi: Hubei.*

tion of its kind in central China outside of Shanghai. Finally, Hankou had become a major financial center, with its stock market and banking sector important enough by the 1920s to influence Shanghai and Tianjin. In 1924, a lead article in the important Shanghai journal *Dongfang zazhi* featured Wuhan as a tri-city complex in the midst of a strong merchant-driven effort to modernize its economic and civic life as quickly as possible.[8]

Although a building boom was underway, there was little coordinated effort at overall urban or architectural planning—given the lack of municipal institutions. Instead, growth had concentrated power, money, and ambition in the hands of Hankou businessmen Liu Xinsheng and Cai Fuqing, and they in turn worked hard to boost the tri-cities' architectural profile. Hankou in particular acquired a new look when a string of striking new buildings went up in the 1920s in the heart of the old commercial district. Streets were redrawn, thoroughfares widened, and plans laid out for a new gridded district west of the railway. The heart of the city became the New Market complex on Jianghan Road separating the Chinese city from the concession area. Indeed, most of the major buildings of republican Hankou, Wuchang, and Hanyang were built during the golden age from 1912 to 1927. Foreign architects and consultants were brought in from Shanghai. Most of the more dramatic buildings, such as the New Market, the Power and Light Company, Nanyang Towers, and the new Hankou Philanthropic Society (Cishanhui), had foreign architects and a decidedly Western look.

Wuchang saw less dramatic change until 1918, when the completion of the Wuchang-Changsha railway line forced the dismantling of the eastern wall and the reshaping of the downtown area by expansion of the business district to the east. The process was aided by the fighting in the city, which lasted for over a year after the mutiny of warlord Wang Zhanyuan's troops in June 192l. Wuchang for the first time experienced serious war damage, and thus the opportunity to rebuild and reshape the city around the new railway terminus. Moreover, by the early 1920s the north-south railway connections were forcing economic integration so that on the surface, at least, Wuhan as a whole acquired a modern, industrializing facade that could be compared with Tianjin and even Shanghai.[9] In the foreign press Wuhan was being called "the Chicago of China."[10]

In January 1927, after the Guomindang's Northern Expedition reached the Yangzi valley, Wuhan resurfaced politically as the capital of the national government. Wang Jingwei and others on the left of the Guomindang dominated this new government at Wuhan. For the first time, albeit briefly, an integrated municipal government for Wuhan as a whole was established, with a full panoply of municipal departments. The new regime had a strong anti-imperialist thrust and built popular support on Wuhan's well-organized labor and student movements. Its most notable success was the recovery of Chinese sovereignty over the British Concession zone.[11] But merchant support from Hankou for the new government was weak. More important, in the spring of 1927, Chiang Kai-shek and then Wang Jingwei moved to the right, first against the Communists in Shanghai and Canton, and then in the fall against the government at Wuhan itself. By the end of 1927, the second Wuhan moment in national politics was over. Wuhan's unified municipal government was dismantled, and the tri-cities fell under the control of Guangxi warlords. In the process, fighting damaged parts of Wuchang, Hankou, and Hanyang. Although few of the leaders of the 1927 revolutionary government were Hubei natives, the repression of the local press and student and labor communities was severe. Thus Wuhan's second experience on the center stage of republican politics ended badly for Wuhanese, be they rich or poor. Although the physical damage to the tri-cities in 1927 was not as severe as during the 1911 Revolution, the atmosphere changed. Gone was the self-confident golden age from 1912 to 1927, when a bold merchant leadership pushed their city into the modern age.[12]

From late 1929 to December 1937, Wuhan was under the relatively tight control of two rival Guomindang factions within Chiang Kai-shek's government. Municipal government reverted to the semidivided administrations of the past, with Hankou administered under the province as a special administrative zone, Hanyang as a county seat, and Wuchang as the provincial capital.[13] To a degree, the internal rivalries of the Guomindang, coupled with its heavy-handed tactics, stifled the economy.[14] Most new government initiatives, including revenue collection for infrastructure projects, were stymied.[15] But more fundamental to the slowdown and stagnation of the Wuhan economy during the 1930s were changes in economic conditions. By 1932, a combination of factors, including two years of devastating floods, environmental degradation, poor provincial leadership, global economic crisis, and protectionist trade policies, produced deep depression in the countryside around Wuhan.[16]

In the 1930s, the urban economy of the tri-cities stagnated but did not crash because of its strategic position as the commodity trade and industrial processing center for the entire middle Yangzi region. But the metropolitan area was affected. Hundreds of thousands of desperately poor peasants flooded into the tri-city complex, living in shantytowns along its outskirts. Total population of the tri-cities exceeded two million (with two-thirds in Hankou). In a pattern similar to Shanghai and other large cities, social control was largely exercised through a gangster king with triad origins named Yang Qingshan, who had cut lucrative deals with Nationalist officials in Wuchang, notably Gen. He Chengjun, the governor of Hubei Province.[17]

The strongest economic sector was foreign trade. By the mid-1930s, during high water periods, foreign freighters of eight to ten thousand tons berthed at Hankou, thus circumventing transshipment of their cargoes at Shanghai. And with trade came missionaries in greater numbers. By the 1930s, the YMCA and YWCA were well entrenched as social service providers in Hankou. Still, the foreign presence could be overemphasized. Hankou's foreign population never exceeded four thousand, of whom half were Japanese. To most of Shanghai's "Old China Hands," Hankou was considered too dangerously nationalist and crassly commercial.[18]

Except for the construction of new foreign bank headquarters and a city park in Hankou, relatively little in the way of impressive new buildings went up in the business districts of Wuchang or Hankou during the 1930s. Architecturally speaking, the big event was the construction of Wuhan University, which was built from scratch on a hilly suburban site overlooking Wuchang to the west and Donghu Lake to the north. Its impressive campus layout and imposing "Chinese renaissance" structures remain one of the few lasting monuments from the Nationalist era that Wuhan residents still admire. Carefully planned at the national level by a blue-ribbon commission headed by the famous mathematician Li Ziguang and constructed by a team of Chinese architects led by the American F. H. Kales, the resulting complex combined Chinese and Western architectural and landscaping styles[19] (see fig. 21).

Intended as a constructive response to the student turmoil of the 1920s, Wuhan University combined architecture with politics, the modernist project with the search for national identity. Wuchang had been a center of educational reform since the time of Zhang Zhidong. Before 1927 three universities in Wuchang served the Wuhan tri-city complex: Sun Yat-sen (formerly Wuchang University and public), Zhonghua (private), and Huazhong (Christian). All three had thrived because of strong support from local elites and a feeder system of over thirty middle schools. Student participation in the political arena began in earnest around organizing a response to the May 4, 1919, demonstrations in Beijing. The student uprisings of 1926 and 1927 helped to bring to power in Wuhan the insurgent republican government of the Guomindang left. In the "White terror" that followed, students became a major target. By 1928–1929, Sun Yat-sen and Zhonghua Universities were closed, university administrators and professors arrested, and dozens of students shot. With faculty carefully selected from its defunct predecessors, Wuhan University was established by the Nationalists in the early 1930s as a flagship institution under firm central government leadership that would serve by example to counter, control, and rechannel student activism.[20]

Thus by the mid-1930s, Wuhan was under relatively tight Guomindang control and out of the national political spotlight. The city was flooded with refugees from the deep depression gripping the countryside. General He Chengjun's chief enforcer of law and order, gangster king Yang Qingshan, operated a large network of thugs running rackets and intelligence operations out of hundreds of teahouses. Communists were major targets. In 1930, there were hundreds of executions. On one day in mid-August, for example, nineteen alleged Communists were officially executed in front of the Jianghan Customs House in Hankou.[21] Yang Qingshan, illiterate and a product of the local secret society underworld, was nevertheless well connected and widely feared. In 1934, when Yang Qingshan's mother died, General He Chengjun attended the funeral and Chiang Kai-shek sent his condolences. Probably the atmosphere became most threatening and uncertain for the tri-city's elites in 1936, with the mysterious assassination of the political study clique's Yang Yongtai, General He Chengjun's chief rival in provincial government affairs. The repressive mood was reflected also in Wuhan's historically lively press, which seemed more intimidated than usual and suffering from close government scrutiny.[22]

Fig. 21. Wuhan University, ca. 1935. Photo shows classroom and administration buildings in the monumental Chinese Renaissance style. Courtesy of Library of Congress.

Wuhan in 1938

Wuhan's return to the political center stage during China's War of Resistance was sudden. The war refocused civic energies and resulted in greater social integration of the tri-cities. Compared to the events of 1911 and 1927, the defense of Wuhan in 1938 was a greater turning point in the history of the city per se.

For ten months, from January to October 1938, Wuhan was the staging and logistics base for defense of the central Yangzi region and for massive counterattacks by two million Chinese troops engaged against the onslaught of Japanese armored units advancing from the north and east. To the Chinese commanders, the populace of Wuhan, and even foreign observers, the outcome was not a foregone conclusion. The city itself was not under siege until the very end. Initially the Chinese victories were impressive: these included the major victory of the war at Taierzhuang in southern Shandong in March–April 1938, which made national heroes of the Guangxi generals Li Zongren and Bai Chongxi, who were independent regional commanders only loosely tied to the Nationalist camp. The defeat of the Japanese at Taierzhuang and the devastating effects of blowing up the Yellow River dikes by Chiang Kai-shek in northern Henan Province in June successfully delayed the Japanese advance for a number of months. But these successes also misled the defenders of Wuhan into the romantic notion that the city could be saved: that high morale and massive numbers could offset the overwhelming firepower and discipline of the Japanese Imperial Army.

In the midst of an atmosphere of carnage, heroics, and false hope, Wuhan blossomed. For a rare moment in

Chinese history, a unity forged through the toleration of political diversity became more important than the politics of control. The full-scale war declared in July 1937 between China and Japan had forced the Communists and Guomindang to suspend the civil war that had raged since 1927 and join in a united-front government of resistance to the Japanese. Thus at Wuhan in 1938, Communist cadres led by Wang Ming and Zhou Enlai arrived from Yan'an to join Chiang Kai-shek's Nationalists in the new government.

Given previous hostilities, it was an uneasy coalition in which there was open competition for political support between the Guomindang and Communists and toleration for Communist dissenters like Chen Duxiu, Zhang Guotao, and the Trotskyist left. At Wuhan in 1938, more than in any Chinese capital before or since, there was public debate and political experimentation, the flowering of a free press, and an unleashing of enormous creative energies in the arts, especially drama and music. Culturally and politically, the uniquely liberal and cosmopolitan atmosphere of Shanghai was transported to Wuhan and reshaped to serve the war effort. The comparisons with Madrid in the Chinese and foreign press helped to attract an international radical chic set of writers like W. H. Auden and Christopher Isherwood and idealists like Dr. Norman Belthune, who came directly from the Spanish Civil War along with one of the best war reporters of his generation, Jack Belden. Fresh from a big film on the Spanish Civil War, European filmmaker Joris Ivens, with funds raised by Archibald MacLeish, Dos Passos, and Ernest Hemingway, came to Wuhan with the Spanish Civil War's most famous photographer, Robert Capa, to record the valiant defense of this Asian outpost against fascism.[23]

The other comparison that loomed large in many Chinese minds was with the revolutionary events and idealism of 1927. The continuities between 1927 and 1938 were real, embodied in people who played a role in the governments of both eras. The Communist leader Dong Biwu, a Wuhan native and immensely popular, was the one figure who participated in all three of Wuhan's "political" periods—1911, 1927, and 1938. Beginning as a student activist in 1911, by 1927 he was in charge of security for Wuchang, and in 1938 was made interior minister in charge of social programs for the military government. The leftist writer and May Fourth intellectual Guo Moruo, who had been head of propaganda for the 1927 government, returned in 1938 as the official in charge of culture. General Ye Ting, a garrison commander in 1927, became the commander in 1938 of the reorganized Communist-dominated New 4th Army. Wang Jingwei and Chen Gongpo had played major swing roles in the politics of 1927 and would later defect to form a Japanese puppet government—but in 1938, they held a variety of high government posts. Zhang Guotao and Chen Duxiu, who were leading Communist figures at Wuhan in 1927, played the roles of leading political dissidents in 1938. It was not surprising, then, that in the October l0, 1938, speech quoted at the beginning of this chapter, Zhou Enlai, the highest-ranking Communist in the united-front government, explicitly linked the Wuhans of 1911, 1927, and 1938.

The extraordinarily open political atmosphere of Wuhan in 1938 was possible because Chiang Kai-shek was not really in control of his own capital. The military struggle with the Japanese dominated politics, culture, and society. The presence of regional militarists like Li Zongren and Bai Chongxi, who were lead commanders in the field and heroes of the victory at Taierzhuang, neutralized Guomindang authoritarianism. The formerly powerful General He Chengjun and his gangster enforcer, Yang Qingshan, were overpowered by the new political order. Although the general kept his position in Wuchang as governor of Hubei Province, his authority to police Wuhan was lost to the coalition of generals in charge of defending the capital and the large body of troops stationed in and around the metropolis. The few assassinations and arrests that did occur in 1938 were limited to Chinese suspected of collaborating with the Japanese.[24]

The dilution of the repressive power of the state and the new spirit of unity against the Japanese gave the Wuhan press a surprisingly free hand. In productivity and variety, the Chinese press blossomed as never before. China's major publishers and editors from Shanghai, Tianjin, and elsewhere converged upon the city. The number of dailies shot from three to fourteen in three months, the number of weeklies from twenty to thirty, and journals from thirty to over two hundred within ten months.[25] Factions within the major parties and smaller parties like the National Socialists or Chinese Youth brought out new publications representing their views. Censorship, which had been severely enforced locally under General He Chengjun before November 1937, was broken by the united front and the generals' support of a free press. Erratic attempts by Dong Xianguang and others in the Ministry of Propaganda to impose restrictions proved largely ineffective. No editors or publishers were arrested or assassinated during the defense of Wuhan.[26]

The impact of refugees from Shanghai was probably clearest in the cultural sphere, especially drama and music, but influences ran in both directions. Wuhan became more cosmopolitan overnight, and Shanghai's artists more attentive to rural concerns. Urbane treaty-port cultural forms from Shanghai were reshaped to appeal more broadly to the illiterate soldier and rural partisans who gathered in Wuhan. Dramatists like Tian Han and Hong Shen went to the front and worked closely with the Guangxi generals Li Zongren and Bai Chongxi in the creation of a new kind of guerrilla theater. At the same time, the Beijing author Lao She, who was allied to another militarist, Feng Yuxiang, wrote five plays about the war from Wuhan. From his official position as a kind of wartime minister of culture, the Communist scholar and poet Guo Moruo promoted toleration for the views of the left in the arts in general. Songwriters like the Shanghai Christian YMCA worker Liu Liangmo organized choral singing of patriotic songs, often in celebration of the victory at Taierzhuang.[27]

China's cultural center of gravity had moved inland from the coastal cities, especially Shanghai, and this was new. Wuhan had not experienced the same kind of cultural transplant in 1911 or 1927. A new sense of unity and patriotism was engendered among intellectuals living now under much more straitened personal circumstances. For the first time, most rallied behind the Chiang Kai-shek-led united front. Criticism of the government was muted. This meant, of course, that the kind of intellectual independence figures like Ba Jin and Lu Xun had exercised earlier was voluntarily sacrificed to the war effort.[28]

After 1945, Shanghai never fully recovered culturally or economically from the wartime exodus of intellectuals and technically trained professionals. In this sense the massive evacuation of talent in 1937–1938 to Wuhan and beyond was a turning point. In 1938, writers like Mao Dun, Xiao Jun, Ba Jin, Xia Yan, Hu Feng, and Ye Qing converged on Wuhan and founded new publications. Zou Taofen restarted his Shenghuo (Life) publications in Hankou, as did Zhang Jiluan, the publisher of the independent Tianjin newspaper, *Dagong bao.* After the fall of Wuhan, China's cultural elite scattered to Chongqing, Hong Kong, Kunming, Yan'an, Singapore, and beyond, becoming increasingly dispirited and less unified. Hong Shen, for example, attempted a much-publicized suicide in Chongqing in 1941. Xiao Hong died under mysterious circumstances in Hong Kong; the same could be said of Yu Dafu's demise in Singapore. Zou Taofen fled first to Hong Kong and then to the Communist bases in south China, where he became ill and died in 1944. Fan Changjiang, of *Dagong bao,* who was probably China's best-known war correspondent at the time, found his work heavily censored after 1941.

The Wuhan flowering of 1938 was made possible in part by the successful evacuation of large quantities of printing equipment from Shanghai. The *Dagong bao* and Zou Taofen's publishing empire were particularly effective in getting equipment to Wuhan. The military also paid close attention to propaganda. The major military paper was the *Saotang bao,* whose equipment was brought to Wuhan by the Guangxi generals Li Zongren and Bai Chongxi.[29]

As we have seen, the commercial economy of Wuhan had been based on transshipment of commodities and processed goods in and out of the port at Hankou. The war had shut down most of this trade, putting the great commodity merchants and textile magnates of Hankou out of business. What was required and achieved within a matter of months was the conversion of the Wuhan economy to a war footing, with an emphasis on industrial production. There is no question that the Wuhan business community contributed to the war production effort, but the addition of machinery, capital, and expertise from Shanghai and elsewhere made the real difference. Ultimately, six hundred factories are said to have been moved inland (with over four hundred resuming operations in Wuhan and/or later in Chongqing). By the spring of 1938, about 170 factories from the Shanghai area had reached Wuhan and were operational; most were privately owned and had made the move without much government help. Along with the machinery came skilled labor—including large numbers of engineers and technicians. It is estimated that over forty thousand skilled workers fled inland during the war, and most of them passed through Wuhan in 1938.[30]

Wartime production in Wuhan peaked just as heavy bombing raids by Japanese planes began in March 1938. By August Wuhan had lost over 12 percent of its industrial capacity to bombing, and clearly the situation was only going to get worse. In addition, there was now the threat of a Japanese siege, which might cut off escape to the west. Moreover, the government's earlier lack of evacuation preparations during the battle of Shanghai had aided the enemy economically and hurt Chinese ability to arm and feed its army. Thus by the fall of 1938, a major effort was made at Wuhan to redeploy and/or destroy Wuhan's industrial base in order to prevent it from falling into Japanese hands. The geologist Weng Wenhao was head of the National Defense Planning Commission, with ministerial rank. His Industrial and Mining Adjustment Administration (Gongkuang tiaozheng chu) began dismantling and removing most of Hanyang's aging state-run steelworks, as well as the nearby arsenal and munitions factories. Throughout the summer, state or municipally run enterprises, including water and energy generating plants, were relocated. The expense and organizational efforts were considerable. By autumn the private sector had followed suit, with a massive relocation of textile, cigarette, and food-processing businesses to the interior. All told, more than 108,000 tons of equipment were transported out of Wuhan; at the state's expense, over 10,000 workers were moved as well. In addition to the relocation of 13 large heavy industrial plants, about 250 major light industrial units were removed. By October about 57 percent of the productive capacity of the metropolis had been moved farther inland. This meant that by the time the Japanese took Wuhan in late October, over 70 percent of the city's industrial capacity was either destroyed or relocated. By war's end, two-thirds of all of Wuhan's structures, including homes, shops, schools, and factories, had been destroyed, and the city would not recover from these blows until well after 1950. Wuhan's population in 1953 was still hundreds of thousands below the 1938 figure.[31]

A concerted effort was also made to destroy equipment that might be of military use to the Japanese, like the tracks and equipment of the Beijing-Hankou railway. These efforts sometimes were misguided and overzealous, with disastrous results. In early October 1938, Changsha, a major city and capital of Hunan Province 150 miles by rail to the south, was torched prematurely, destroying the lives and property of its citizens and in effect aiding the enemy.[32]

At the same time that the war produced such a rapid rise and fall in industrial capacity, the flood of civilian refugees and wounded soldiers overwhelmed existing services. The resulting chaos was so great that it seemed to level class and regional differences among the burgeoning refugee population. In Hankou, locals were outnumbered by newcomers two to one.

The refugee communities of Wuhan during its ten months as the de facto capital represented a remarkable cross section of Chinese society. Although children made up a large number of refugees, the age and gender distribution was wide indeed. Whole families were on the move. Peasants were the most difficult to track as refugees, but were also the most numerous. Small-time business and crafts persons represented a relatively high proportion of the visible refugee population in Wuhan—and as already suggested, the number of educated "intellectuals" was extraordinarily high.

In January 1938, the newly reconstituted press of Wuhan began to point with alarm to the massive refugee crisis gripping the tri-cities—a crisis that threatened to undermine the defense of the city and destroy public health. At the very least, the basic needs of children for food and shelter needed to be met. Although at any one time, inside and outside of Wuhan in 1938, no more than a quarter of the refugee population received some kind of help, governmental and private efforts were impressive and unprecedented. By mid-June 1938, shelters were being provided for over 63,000 refugees. Over half were in shelters run by the central government's National Relief Committee or by the local governments of Wuchang-Hankou-Hanyang.[33]

In terms of public health, malaria epidemics were especially serious among refugees, cutting a devastating swath through both the civilian and military populations of Wuhan. Women and children were particularly vulnerable. In response, the most extensive pre-1949 effort in crisis management in Chinese public health history was launched from Wuhan. Led by Harvard-trained Dr. J. Heng Liu, the cream of China's medical establishment from Beijing and Shanghai descended on the tri-cities in an effort to organize and deliver health care to civilians and soldiers alike. In the early 1930s, Dr. Liu had headed the Peking Union Medical College before becoming minister of health in 1933. He was joined in Wuhan by Dr. Robert K. Lin (Lin Kesheng), an Oxford-trained overseas Chinese, who reorganized the Chinese Red Cross at its headquarters in Wuhan around a new mission of penetrating the countryside. In a short time, public health and sanitation in the city improved. Vaccination and public health centers were set up all over the city. Existing hospitals were nationalized and put on a war footing. Where the failure lay was in the surrounding countryside and in the treatment of wounded soldiers, most of whom received little or no care. Still, Wuhan represented a turning point in the history of Chinese public health and an important new beginning.[34]

Geographically, the three cities that made up Wuhan adopted distinct identities related to their roles in the war effort. Wuhan still had no central municipal government. Wuchang housed the central government offices, Guomindang party headquarters, and General Chen Cheng's military headquarters. Leading Nationalist politicians operated out of the old provincial government buildings in central Wuchang, some of which dated back to Zhang Zhidong and the late Qing. The Guomindang held its Extraordinary Party Congress in early April 1938 in the new gymnasium on the Wuhan University campus. Hanyang turned into a munitions center for the war effort, with its factories humming until its dismantlement began during the summer.

Hankou became the logistical and transport entrepôt for the defense of central China. It was also the cultural and media center, and its former concession area was the place where non-Guomindang groups and publications were located. The Wuhan headquarters of Guangxi generals Bai Chongxi and Li Zongren and of Feng Yuxiang were in Hankou. It was in Hankou's largest commercial theater (*haida xiyuan*) that the first meeting of the People's Political Council was held for ten days beginning July 6, 1938. Nearby, in a modest two-story building of a former concession area, was the headquarters of the Yangzi Bureau of the Communist Party, led by Wang Ming and Zhou Enlai.

Railway terminals at Wuchang and Hankou, as well as the ferries crossing the Yangzi between the two cities, were major targets for Japanese bombers. Braving bombs with the refugees on the ferries were students ferrying back and forth from Wuchang to participate in events on the Hankou side. Students were probably the most mobile part of the Wuhan populace, and the energy and mobilization efforts of youth did much to bind the different parts of Wuhan together politically into an integrated unit dedicated to the war effort and to redefining national identity.

In 1937 and 1938, some sixty-two colleges and universities moved inland, with many passing through Wuhan. As in 1927 and 1911, students and youth in general were the shock troops of the mass mobilization efforts that energized the tri-cities in 1938. They were enlisted by the tens of thousands as volunteers to help solve the social crisis in the city and surrounding countryside. Moreover, student involvement was important in the long run because their wartime experiences unified and shaped the outlook of the generation that would run mainland China and Taiwan after 1949.[35]

Politically speaking, such a large refugee student body was seen either as an asset or a powder keg. Youth mobilization was as sensitive politically in 1938 as it was in 1927 or 1911. Beginning in December 1937 and running to October 1938, there were twelve major organizational meetings in Wuhan involving thousands of students and accompanied by massive rallies staged formally to commemorate such dates as May 4 or July 7. But more ad hoc demonstrations took place frequently on the streets of Wuhan, usually as spontaneous celebrations of such events as the victory at Taierzhuang or the downing of Japanese planes. To meet this challenge, competing political groups, as well as the major military commanders, created their own auxiliary youth organizations.

In their rhetoric at mass meetings, organizers put the defense of Wuhan into a global context in order to give an international dimension to China's new wartime identity. For example, one of the largest student rallies was held at Wuhan University in June 1938 to receive a world peace delegation of international students. In welcoming speeches, Communist Wang Ming and Nationalist commander Chen Cheng played up the Wuhan-Madrid connection in a unified and carefully orchestrated effort to capture the imagination and energy of youth, as well as the eye of the foreign press.[36]

Conclusion

Today, the memory of Wuhan in 1938 has survived as a reminder of alternative paths not chosen in modern Chinese history. After its fall to the Japanese in late October, the Wuhan model, or "spirit," lived on, surviving in the national imagination as an alternative to the more socially and politically repressive capitals that Chongqing, Yan'an, Nanjing, Beijing, or Taibei became. The Wuhan spirit, a term that is wistfully evoked today, signified the kind of open, patriotic political culture a modern Chinese capital ought to project—and did, for ten brief months in 1938.[37]

Thus in the evolution of Wuhan as a single urban complex there were clear continuities and breaks from the patterns of the nineteenth century. Trade and industrialization as engines of economic growth continued unabated at a breathtaking pace over the entire period. Socially and culturally, the business community became increasingly dominant, especially during the golden age between 1912 and 1927. It was also business elites—not the state—who encouraged increasing integration of tri-city communities. The exception was 1927, when politics forced a premature integration under a single municipal government. Links between Wuchang and Hankou in particular became stronger, with each becoming less distinct in character, especially after both had railway terminals by 1918.

The 1930s reversed these trends, and the state assumed greater importance. The undermining of the business leadership of Wuhan began in the early 1930s under Governor He Chengjun. The process culminated in 1938, when national political and military figures, led by General Chen Cheng, pushed for the integration of the tri-cities in order to meet wartime exigencies. After 1938, the loss of business leadership was accelerated by the Japanese occupation authorities and the destruction of most enterprises. Between 1945 and 1949, the business community and local economy had no time to recover, leaving Wuhan to be stitched together in its present form by Stalinist planning, bridge building, and a strong emphasis on heavy industry in the 1950s under Marshal Li Xiannian. It was under the latter that local governments of Hankou, Hanyang, and Wuchang were finally combined and communications linked, with Wuhan becoming a single, functioning municipality for the first time in 1949.

The relationship between republican Wuhan and Shanghai has been likened to that of Chicago with New York. In trade and business there was real dependency, but there seems to have been little civic inferiority complex. Wuhan's vibrant local press and revolutionary traditions conveyed a sense of self-importance; there was also the issue of the foreign influence that Shanghai symbolized. Economically and culturally, Wuhan's foreign concessions were an important stimulant to local trade, especially after 1896. Cultural influence is hard to measure, but in architecture at least, foreign influences dominated the building boom of 1912–1927. Visually, Wuhan wanted to look like Shanghai; yet the foreign community in Wuhan was never large. The revolutionary uprisings of 1911 and 1927 were in part directed against imperialism, and the latter resulted in the partial recovery of the concession areas. Moreover, by the 1930s Wuhan industrialists and traders had beaten back foreign interests in the competition to control domestic markets from cigarettes to textiles.

In a sense, the 1938 wartime experience of Wuhan represented the culmination of all these trends. As in 1927, there was partial expropriation of foreign properties (in this case Japanese-owned enterprises). More important, in 1938, the foreign press and diplomats were present as observers and targets of united-front propaganda. They were not seen as a threat to Chinese sovereignty, but as witnesses to the resistance to Japan. More than in 1911 or 1927, Wuhan in 1938 was in the international spotlight as the capital of a courageous Chinese people who, like the citizens of Madrid, were locked in a life-and-death struggle against the evil forces of fascism.

More important, Wuhan in 1938 was again at the center of the effort to redefine national identity. Obviously, wartime concerns with mobilization and patriotic propaganda dwarfed the Hankou business community's earlier civic concerns with modernity. But as I have argued, this wartime redefinition of national identity was certainly informed by such institutional modernist concerns as public health, expansion of mass media, international image, social welfare relief work, and industrialization. The wartime situation seemed to resolve the contradiction between modernity and the search for national identity, the two themes that Hankou and Wuchang had represented separately earlier in the century.

Chapter 11

The City as Nation

Creating a Wartime Capital in Chongqing

Lee McIsaac

The national government's announcement in the fall of 1937 that Chongqing would serve as one of its alternate capitals during the War of Resistance against Japan drew that city almost overnight from the margins of China's national politics and culture toward its center. Throughout most of the republican era, Sichuan had remained largely independent of central government control. After coming to power in 1927, the Guomindang government used a variety of measures to increase its own power and influence there, but these were mostly ignored by the local militarists who controlled the province through a garrison system. It was not until the mid-1930s, when Communist troops moved through the province, that the central government found an opportunity to send its own troops into Sichuan, weakening the power of the militarists and thereby enabling the central authorities to gain a foothold in the province and to begin integrating it into the national political structure. Despite these advances, on the eve of war in 1937, the national government's position in Sichuan remained tenuous. Moreover, many of the militarists who still controlled the province and owned much of its land were less than enthusiastic about the central government's intrusion into territory they continued to regard as their own.[1]

During the war years, municipal officials appointed by the national government and social reformers worked to extend the central government's influence and power in Chongqing (and Sichuan more generally) by modernizing and nationalizing the new wartime capital. Streets were renamed and widened, monuments and other new buildings were constructed, new forms of transportation were introduced, and a modern industrial base was established. An image of the city as a symbol of the nation was projected. Many of these activities, of course, resembled those carried out by urban reformers and officials in other cities in China. In Chongqing, however, they were a crucial but largely overlooked part of the national government's overall strategy for strengthening its own weak position in Chongqing in particular and Sichuan in general.[2] Moreover, in much the same way that urban design in the French colonies of Morocco, Indochina, and Madagascar served to reinforce perceptions of the legitimacy and power of France back home, as Gwendolyn Wright has demonstrated, the Guomindang government's efforts to modernize Chongqing helped to strengthen its own legitimacy and power in the eyes of many Chinese and of the foreign powers.[3]

Chongqing was in many ways an unlikely site for a national capital. In addition to its relative autonomy from central control in the years before the war, as a physical space it was not suited to the wide avenues and grid-like street patterns associated with past national capitals in China.[4] Located on a narrow promontory at the confluence of the Yangzi and Jialing Rivers, Chongqing has often been called the "Mountain Town" (Shancheng) because of the extreme hilliness of its terrain. At the eastern tip of the peninsula, the old city wall encircled an area measuring less than one-half mile wide at its widest point and just under two miles long. This relatively small space sits atop steep cliffs that rise up from the water's edge to an area of uneven terrain reaching an average height of 230 feet above the river level. The land beyond the western gate of the city contains some flat areas but also many hills, some of which rise even higher than those within the old city walls. Fuxingguan, the highest point, towers 370 feet above the water.[5]

Chongqing's geography also made expansion difficult as its population nearly tripled during the war, with thousands of refugees following the national government from war areas in central and eastern China.[6] Swiftly flowing rivers on three sides of the city not only prevented the

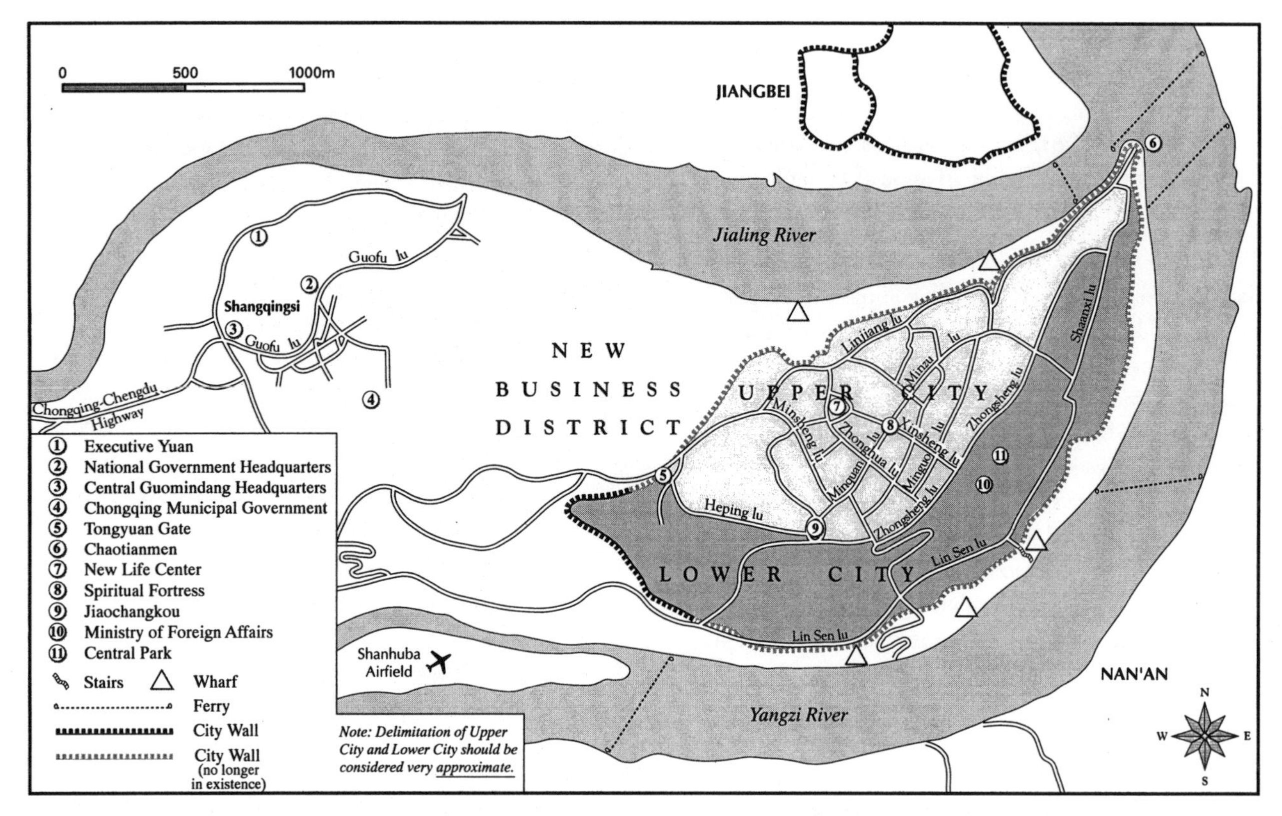

Map 20. Major streets and landmarks of Chongqing. Based on a 1943 U.S. Army map titled "Map of Chungking City" in the Yale University Library, and Spencer (1939).

pattern of extramural expansion that has long characterized the growth of Chinese cities, but also made it difficult to integrate fully Jiangbei and Nan'an, the satellite communities that had developed on the banks of the Jialing and Yangzi Rivers opposite the main part of the city. In a central area of approximately 2.5 square miles in and immediately to the west of the old city, 261,000 people lived and worked in 1937. With a population density of 104,400 people per square mile, Chongqing on the eve of the war must have been one of the world's most crowded cities.[7]

In addition to these drawbacks, the poverty and backwardness that overwhelmed foreign visitors and "downriver" sojourners, as refugees from central and eastern China often called themselves, detracted from the image of modernity the Guomindang wished its capital cities to project. Dilapidated and flimsily constructed buildings tumbled down steep cliffs, ubiquitous piles of garbage and open ditches of sewage clogged its narrow lanes, chickens and dogs ranged freely, and an emaciated and diseased populace apparently relied on hard manual labor, begging, or prostitution to stay alive. In fact, to many downriver refugees, most of Chongqing did not even look like a city, much less a national capital. Even though Shanghai was at that time China's most modern city, it was the standard by which Chongqing was frequently judged. Wu Jisheng, a wartime refugee who returned to Shanghai after only one year in Chongqing, provided a typical comparison in his description of the view from the riverfront, where most arriving visitors caught their first glimpse of the city:

> From along the river's edge Chongqing appears extremely dilapidated. Your eyes can't take it all in. All you can see, high and low along the riverbank, is a very steep and lofty mountain town with row after row of tumbledown inadequate old wooden rooms

> and grass shacks *(maopeng),* leaning over and all askew. When new arrivals see this they wonder how Chongqing, the [largest] city in southwest China, can have fallen into such a state. When you compare it to the wharf areas of Hong Kong and Shanghai, the gap is really too huge.

Wu Jisheng hastened to add that a delightful modern enclave existed at the top of the hill, complete with "paved roads, solid buildings that were four and five stories high, big mansions, cinemas, theatres, coffee houses, western eateries, shiny cars and buses and neon lights—all the things one expects to find in a city," and "as different from the riverfront as heaven is from earth."[8]

Despite these shortcomings, Chongqing was chosen as the wartime capital for strategic reasons, not because it corresponded with Chinese notions of capital cities. The city's inland location and the high mountains that separated Sichuan from the rest of China protected it from land attacks by Japanese armies. Moisture rising from the Sichuan plain created dense fog, which hid the city from enemy air raids for much of the year. Its hilly geography and rocky foundation made it a natural spot for the construction of air-raid shelters. Finally, Chongqing was connected by rivers to the abundance of goods and raw materials produced in Sichuan, making it virtually self-sufficient.

Chongqing was intended to serve only as a wartime site for the national government, not as a permanent national capital. The national government had no way of knowing in 1937 when, or even if, it would return to Nanjing, but the uncertainty of the nation's future could not be given concrete expression in the form of a new national capital without fatally jeopardizing the legitimacy of the Guomindang regime as the government of all China. Thus, following the announcement that government offices would be transferred to Chongqing, the city was redesignated a "temporary capital" *(xingdu)* to be directly administered by the central government. Even after September 1940, when Chongqing was renamed the permanent "alternate capital" *(peidu)* (as Nanjing itself, or Jinling as it was then known, had been during the Southern Song dynasty), its status continued to be secondary to that of the national capital *(shoudu),* which remained in Nanjing.

Although the national government did not aim to create a copy in Chongqing of the capital it had left behind in Nanjing, there were some striking similarities in its vision for both cities. In both Nanjing and Chongqing, the national government sought to create cities that were both modern and nationalistic; and in both cities these reforms were calculated to impress foreign investors and governments in the hope that they would provide support for Guomindang projects. However, despite similarities in the rhetoric of modernization and nationalism, the meanings ascribed to these terms were quite different in each city. Whereas in Nanjing modernity was closely identified with modern technology, infrastructure, and materials, in Chongqing it took on meanings more closely associated with (an idealized view of) the urban culture of the coastal treaty ports, especially Shanghai. Whereas in Nanjing the architecture of government buildings was used to project state power, in Chongqing the city as a living community and the supposedly shared experiences of its inhabitants became the basis for projecting a different view of national power, one based on the strength of a unified population to resist foreign aggression.

During the war years, popular literature and government propaganda depicted Chongqing as a microcosm of a richly diverse nation. Yet even as wartime literature celebrated this diversity and painted an idealized portrait of harmonious relations between the various groups it encompassed, it divided Chongqing's wartime population into two unequal and opposing groups: "downriver" refugees from cities and provinces outside of Sichuan, who were depicted as the exclusive representatives of "modernized" cities such as Shanghai; and "native" Sichuanese, who were customarily portrayed as representatives of the backwardness and isolation of China's interior. These two groups were seen as organically related and important components of the nation Chongqing represented. But at the same time, images of them were juxtaposed in Chongqing and in the wartime literature about the city in such a way that they reinforced perceptions among downriver refugees of their exclusive claim to represent modernity as well as their own centrality to the nation and their dominant position within it, while native was subordinated and marginalized.

Defining "native" Chongqing as a poor and backwards "other" was crucial to this process.

A "nightmare of mud, bamboo, and brick"

Even before the war brought first-hand confirmation to downriver refugees, Chongqing had acquired a reputation within China and abroad as one of China's poorest and dirtiest cities. Few Chinese from coastal provinces actually ventured as far inland as Chongqing, but those who did were almost universally overwhelmed by its poverty and dirt. Summing up his impressions after visiting Chongqing in the mid-1930s, Xue Shaoming wrote: "Lots of prostitutes, lots of singing girls, and lots of beggars—these are my overwhelming impressions of the Heavenly Storehouse of Chongqing after this short visit."[9]

Foreigners who visited Chongqing before the war were appalled by the chaos and squalor they saw there. Even from a distance across the Yangzi River, where many travelers got their first view of the city, its decrepit appearance overwhelmed visitors. George C. Basil, an American medical doctor who lived and worked in Chongqing during the early 1930s, described his first impressions of his new home as the ship carrying him to Chongqing from Shanghai approached the dock:

> Built high on tier after tier of a rocky peninsula formed by the meeting of the Yangtze and the Kialing . . . the city presented, from the lowest strata of huts perched on bamboo stilts above the mud to the highest spot on its ancient gray stone wall, a dilapidated, down-at-the heel appearance. The swift, muddy current between us and the shore was alive with dirty houseboats and sampans, whose unkempt, ragged crews, competing for the steamer's business patronage, worked feverishly—jostling, shouting, screeching like a mob of scarecrows abruptly come to infuriated life.[10]

Impressions of Chongqing did not improve as travelers entered the city. Like many other foreign visitors, H. G. W. Woodhead, editor of *The China Yearbook,* was struck by the city's filth:

> The city, which competent observers rank among the dirtiest in China, is situated on a promontory on the left bank of the Yangtsze. . . . There are no proper landing places on the water-front. One has to make one's way ashore as best one can, sometimes clambering over half a dozen junks to reach the garbage-strewn foreshore. The approach to all the gates from the river is up long flights of steps, some mere indentations in the rubbish heaps, some roughly carved out of the rock, and some well and truly laid, but one and all dripping with slime from the endless procession of water carriers.[11]

Descriptions of Chongqing's foul dirt similarly dominate wartime descriptions of it. Recording her first impressions as she entered the city after her boat docked, Han Suyin wrote:

> We were carried up through a cleft in the precipice between close-crowding hovels. Semi-liquid black filth drained along open ditches on either side of the road. Huge dump heaps spread down the cliff; dogs and beggar children dug in the refuse.[12]

The presence of open sewage and garbage on Chongqing's streets, as well as the enormous rodent population, alarmed downriver refugees, who understood both to provide ideal breeding grounds for disease. The refuse that lined Chongqing's narrow lanes was removed only when rainfall, which could be torrential during the rainy season, carried it down the steep streets and alleys and into the rivers. Grace Service, who lived in Chongqing during the 1920s, pointed out that such a "system" had some beneficial aspects, explaining that she had heard some doctors claim the city was actually "better off for sanitation than most Chinese cities . . . [because] heavy rain (of which there is plenty) flushes away all the refuse and sewage."[13] But wartime refugees were convinced that there was a link between the "foul ditches of filthy, stagnant water" and the high rate of disease and epidemics in Chongqing.[14]

Chongqing's rats were legendary—for their numbers, size, and boldness. Wu Jisheng recalled:

> The rats in the Mountain Town are gigantic. Large ones are the size of cats. Moreover, they are extremely fierce and cruel. They are always gnashing their teeth and smacking their chops ready to go have a taste of anything, no matter what it is. . . . Sometimes they

> gnaw and chew at things they cannot eat, like wooden chairs and cupboards, and leave them covered with marks. They run wildly everywhere not only at night, but also during the day, and are not in the least afraid of people. They move around in packs and jump out from the roofbeams in groups.[15]

Local newspapers fueled public concern about the dangers of Chongqing's rats by frequently pointing out the important role they played in spreading disease and by even providing detailed discussions of various methods of annihilating rodents.[16]

Wartime refugees were also struck by the poverty of Chongqing's local populace. In describing the city's inhabitants, writers invariably focused on a relatively narrow group of occupations, thereby conveying the impression that native population was comprised solely of beggars, prostitutes, opium addicts, and coolies. The many local industrialists, journalists, teachers, and store and office clerks who lived and worked in Chongqing were almost entirely absent from wartime descriptions of its "natives." Outsiders were particularly impressed by the city's beggars, not only because of their large numbers and the size of the groups they traveled in, but also because of their persistence. One visitor reported that beggars would follow wealthy people (often, the writer noted, those who came from outside of Sichuan) for up to one *li*, running in front of them to block their way and kowtowing "noisily" before them.[17] Wartime residents joked that Chongqing's beggars were so persistent that they would even chase after passengers in rickshaws.[18]

The frail and disease-ridden bodies of the native inhabitants of Chongqing provided downriver refugees with further evidence of the destitution that to them characterized the city. In a 1938 study of the health of 5,031 students in Chongqing, it was discovered that only 96 were "completely healthy." The others suffered from one or more of twenty-one different diseases, including unspecified eye diseases (41.14 percent) and tooth problems (31.62 percent), swollen tonsils (26.61 percent), swollen lymph glands (14.47 percent), malnutrition (20.25 percent), and anemia (12.05 percent).[19] Chongqing's coolies, whose labor provided most of the transport that moved goods and people around the hilly city, were universally described as emaciated and even deformed by their hard labor. One journalist wrote that the shoulders of the sedan-chair bearers looked as if they had been "warped into great lumps from the carrying poles, and [their] legs looked foreshortened and squashed with all their muscles, from being pressed downward."[20] The popular belief that these people were all addicted to opium was expressed by Jiang Yuanying in 1937: "The coolies who carry sedan chairs are all of sallow complexion and wear black clothes. I suspect that they live on opium rather than rice."[21]

Nothing seems to have symbolized the poverty and backwardness of Chongqing's population to wartime refugees as much as the sight of large numbers of dead bodies on its streets. During the damp, chilly winter season, hundreds of impoverished people died on the streets every month from hunger and cold.[22] In the first two months of 1935, a particularly bad year because of a severe drought, the police department reported that 2,870 people starved or froze to death on Chongqing's streets. In February and March of that year, 3,800 people met the same fate.[23] Two years later, even in the relatively temperate months of spring and fall, the streets still seemed to contain a large number of people who had died from starvation or illness. For example, in October 1937, normally not a cold month, 604 dead bodies were picked up by the police; the following April, the corpses included 562 adults and 19 children.[24]

Dead bodies were not unique to Chongqing's streets, but in other cities they do not seem to have elicited the horror and disgust that they did in Chongqing. Esther Tappert Mortensen, an American missionary who had lived in Nanjing for years before going in 1937 to teach English at Chongqing University, wrote in a letter home, "Never until I came to Szechuan had I seen dead bodies along the roadside of people who had actually starved to death. This is a province which has not yet been touched by the war."[25] Chinese refugees who encountered dead bodies on the street were appalled not only by the sight, but also by the indifference of the local police to whom they reported their findings. Most disturbing of all was the fact that so many of the dead were infants and young children.[26]

Chongqing was viewed by downriver refugees not

only as poor, but also as extremely "backward." This backwardness was apparent to them in the styles of clothing worn by locals, the types of entertainment available, modes of transportation, architecture, and in attitudes toward work. For example, when downriver refugees migrated to Chongqing, they found it necessary to bring hairdressers with them from Shanghai, because they believed local hairdressers did not know how to do the fashionable cuts and permanents popular in Shanghai. While many downriver refugees found the simple blue *qipao* favored by Chongqing's women and the plain gray Sun Yat-sen uniform worn by some men to be merely uninteresting, they were repulsed by the Sichuanese laborers' practice of wrapping a white cloth turban-style around their heads. This custom had been adopted for practical reasons, but to refugees from outside of Sichuan it was "offensive," because white was suggestive of death, and to wear it on the head was associated with mourning.[27]

Chongqing's transportation and infrastructure seemed primitive to refugees. The absence of wide roads or vehicular traffic in the city was as much a result of its hilly terrain as of its relatively late start in the "modernist project" that had been underway in other cities since the late Qing. In most areas the lanes and alleys were too narrow for cars, buses, or streetcars. The stairways that provided the only route between the waterfront where ferries docked and the upper levels of the city, which were the destination of the city's well-heeled residents, precluded the use of any wheeled vehicles at all. On these routes those who did not wish to walk up or down as many as seven hundred stone steps had no choice but to be carried in sedan chairs, an experience many found especially unnerving. By the late 1930s Chongqing had limited bus service, but most of the people who could afford hired transportation found rickshaws or sedan chairs to be faster and more efficient.[28] Limited ferry service, which provided passage across the rivers, was not enough to meet the needs of the city's expanded population, especially during air-raid warnings, when there was a mad dash out of the main part of the city toward the opposite banks. Sampans provided most transport from the main city to the opposite banks, but the service was irregular, chaotic, and somewhat dangerous.

Reliance on these older forms of transport seemed hopelessly backward to refugees who came from cities where modern streetcars had already replaced rickshaws as the desirable mode of public transportation. In Shanghai, one downriver refugee explained, rickshaws were such an uncomfortable and unappealing mode of transportation that the city's rickshaw pullers were always eager for fares. Thus in Shanghai the typical conversation between pullers and customers went something like this:

"To the Bund!"
"That's thirty cents."
"Twenty cents."
"All right."

In Chongqing, however, this downriver refugee found that passengers enjoyed no bargaining advantage with rickshaw pullers, who regularly overcharged passengers. Consequently, the typical conversation between customers and pullers went as follows:

"To Tongyuan Gate!"
"You want to go there?"
"How much is it?"
"The fare is calculated according to distance."[29]

Chongqing's distinctive architecture provided downriver refugees with further evidence of its poverty and backwardness. Like so many aspects of the city, its architecture was at least partially a result of its geography. In the slums nestled in the precipitous cliff areas along the rivers, buildings were constructed along narrow, steep passageways by using the cliffs for support. Known to locals as "hanging foot houses" *(diaojiaolou),* these structures were made of bamboo and wood and either rose up from the narrow lanes or fell away below them with the assistance of heavy bamboo poles used to prop them against the cliff. Extra stories (usually one or two) were added wherever possible by either expanding up or down the cliff, and additions were often built onto one or more sides. The effect was, as one journalist put it, "a shabby-looking cliff on which houses were propped with every sort of wooden beam, strut, or stilt, sticking out from the rocky wall at any possible angle that would balance."[30]

Below the cliffs the land along the river shore provided living space for the city's laboring poor. During the winter months, when river levels dropped as much as one hundred feet, Chongqing's poorest residents extended their living and working space out onto the seasonally dry land of the riverbed. As the river receded, usually in September or October, they used bamboo matting to build makeshift shack communities along the beach, where they lived until melting snow in the mountains of Tibet and heavy summer rains caused the river levels to rise again. By spring each year the riverfront was "covered with shanties, shops, opium dens, wood and coal stoves."[31] When the rivers rose, sometimes as much as forty-eight feet in as many hours, this temporary city was hastily dismantled and its residents ran, often with the rising water literally at their heels, up to dry ground in the city proper.

In the eyes of cosmopolitan refugees, even Chongqing's teahouses and newest movie theaters were emblematic of the new capital's backwardness. By 1938, a number of modern cinemas had opened there, but the films they showed had played in Shanghai and Hankou theaters several years earlier. Nor were wealthy refugees impressed with the city's many teahouses. Scattered throughout the lanes and alleys of the city, these establishments were not like the "elegant" Guangdong-style teahouses found in Shanghai and Hong Kong. Most were simple rooms lit by kerosene lamps and furnished with low tables and chairs that faced out onto the street, and they were patronized by the city's workers, who went there in the evenings to drink tea and listen to storytellers.[32]

For some refugees, the gap between Chongqing and the "modern" city of Shanghai went beyond physical appearances to the mentality of each city's inhabitants. Downriver refugees were struck by the apathy of Chongqing's natives, especially toward work. For these refugees, the signs hung by Chongqing's restaurateurs to announce that they were open for business were proof of their indifference toward work. In a busy, modern city like Shanghai, one writer explained, such signs were not necessary, because businesses always remained open from dawn until late in the evening. But in Chongqing, if a shopkeeper had something to do on any given day, or felt he had already done enough business that day, he simply closed the shop. The author found this indifference to work distinctly antimodern.[33]

While the view that Chongqing's native population was comprised only of poverty-stricken laborers who eked out a living in appallingly miserable conditions was exaggerated, the bulk of the population was in fact extremely poor. By the mid-1930s a significant proportion of the people living there were refugees from poor rural areas in eastern and northern Sichuan who had been driven to the city by exorbitant taxation and the devastation wrought in their home districts by warlord armies. A series of natural disasters, including a serious drought in 1935, further exacerbated the desperate situation in rural Sichuan and contributed to the growing number of poverty-stricken refugees who filled Chongqing's streets during the 1930s. A study undertaken by the police department and published in January 1937 counted 71,458 "rather poor" *(cipin)* or "very poor" *(jipin)* adults and 27,176 poor or very poor children in a total population of about 400,000.[34] During the war years the city continued to be flooded with poor refugees from rural areas in Sichuan, drawn there by the prospect of finding work in its expanded service, transport, and industrial sectors.

Chongqing was not, however, entirely a city of paupers; it was also home to a number of wealthy militarists, merchants, and entrepreneurs. Many of these people or their children had been educated in China's top universities in Shanghai and Beijing or abroad. They owned extensive properties in the city and throughout the surrounding countryside, lived in spacious mansions, and shopped for goods imported from Shanghai and abroad in the new department stores that had opened in the decade before the war. Some played tennis and socialized with the tiny foreign community of missionaries, diplomats, and businessmen who lived in Chongqing and across the Yangzi River at Nan'an during the years before the war. They had established commercial, industrial, and mining enterprises, some of which were extremely successful. Lu Zuofu, the founder of the famous Minsheng Shipping Company, which had successfully beat out foreign competition and controlled shipping on the upper Yangzi River by 1930, was only the most successful and well known of Chongqing's local entrepreneurs. Others, such as Kang

Xinru, had accumulated considerable wealth through banking and investment in commercial and industrial enterprises in and around Chongqing. Although this elite represented only a small fraction of Chongqing's overall population, their presence in the city was hardly invisible or insignificant. Yet these people and their families are almost entirely absent from descriptions of wartime Chongqing. Instead, wartime literature about Chongqing invariably portrayed the city's "native" population as poor and backward. Wealth and modernity were associated, at least in the minds of foreigners and downriver refugees, with wartime refugees from cities in eastern and central China. As the municipal government, which was dominated after July 1938 by downriver refugees appointed by the national government, embarked on a program of modernization in Chongqing during the early years of the war, these impressions were strengthened.

"Shanghai Imperialists"

During the war municipal officials drew up a number of regulations and launched programs aimed at modernizing Chongqing's appearance, sanitation, and services. Streets were widened and given new names, new and modern buildings were constructed, regular ferry service was introduced, and efforts were made to establish a modern industrial base. These objectives were ambitious, but actual reforms focused primarily on the relatively small area of higher ground running along the ridge on the northwestern side of the peninsula, known as the Upper City (Shangcheng). The "native" working-class districts along the waterfront and steep cliffs of the Lower City were left untouched.

Shanghai—or rather the modernity that city represented to downriver refugees in Chongqing—was the implicit model for the efforts of municipal officials and social reformers to transform their wartime base into a "modern" city. One wonders why Shanghai, rather than another national capital such as Nanjing or even Beijing, served as a model for Chongqing. In addition to the political and psychological difficulties the Guomindang would have faced in attempting to recreate a national capital, the answer seems to lie in Shanghai's status as China's most modern city. The modernity it represented provided a set of cultural values and practices that the national government sought to appropriate and use as a basis for legitimating its own dominance in an area of the country in which it had previously had minimal influence.

In their efforts to transform Chongqing, municipal officials barely acknowledged the work of local military and business elites who had promoted an energetic program of modernization beginning in the mid-1920s under the leadership of Liu Xiang, the militarist who controlled Chongqing from 1926 until his death in early 1938. These efforts were, of course, part of the wave of urban reform that had swept through China's cities during the republican era. Although this "modernist project" began relatively late in Chongqing compared to such cities as Canton and Tianjin, it was no less ambitious in its objectives.

The first task undertaken in the mid-1920s by these early modernizers was the dismantling of the large cemetery that lay just outside Tongyuan Gate to the west of the city wall, thereby permitting expansion of the city in that direction. A New Business District (Xin shichang) was built in its place, and shops and businesses located just inside the wall were encouraged, with limited success, to move there.[35] Also outside the main part of the city, a small steel mill, a cement factory, an arsenal, and a couple of machine shops were established. Coal mines were opened up along the northern shore of the Jialing River to provide fuel for this emerging modern industrial sector.

Inside the old city walls, narrow lanes were widened so they could support modern vehicular traffic in the Upper City. The new streets, which ranged from forty to sixty feet in width, were lined by curbs, sidewalks, and four- and five-story buildings of "the best modern architectural design."[36] Wheeled vehicles were also introduced, beginning with rickshaws in 1927 and expanding to include private automobiles and sporadic public bus service by 1933. Efforts to bring electricity, regular telephone service, and modern plumbing to Chongqing enjoyed only partial success. A new modern plant purchased from Germany provided electricity to limited sections of the city, making it possible for stores and offices along the newly constructed main roads to advertise their products in neon and to light their interiors with electric lights. A few water mains were installed during the mid-1930s, but the solid rock on which the city was built made the work difficult and expensive, and progress was slow. The few pipes that had been completed were destroyed in the first air raids of the war. Plans were also drawn up to improve docking facilities and build a bridge that would span the Jialing River, but work was not even begun on the bridge until after the war. These early efforts to modernize Chongqing were confined largely to the Upper City and did result in a "new look" there that was noted by a number of foreign observers. But beyond this tiny modern enclave, the rest of the city remained largely untouched.

Although the success of Liu Xiang and his associates in modernizing Chongqing was limited and did not bring about a complete transformation of the city, it is important to remember, as Robert Kapp has pointed out, that they started almost from scratch.[37] Most important, by opening up the way for expansion westward from the walled city and establishing even a limited urban infrastructure in the Upper City, the modernizing reforms undertaken in Chongqing during the decade before the war established a solid base upon which the wartime modernization programs were built.

Before the national government could launch any reforms in Chongqing, it was necessary to gain control of the municipal government. This was done during the second half of 1938, as Japanese armies advanced upon Wuhan and the final transfer of most central government offices to Chongqing took place. Jiang Zhideng, a native of Zhejiang and graduate of Beijing and Berlin Universities, was appointed mayor by the Guomindang and took up his duties on July 25. Under his direction the municipal government was reorganized, and powerful bureaus such as the Department of Municipal Taxes were either reorganized under new names or restaffed. Key positions were filled with downriver refugees appointed by the Guomindang. These changes were completed by the end of the year, and the new appointees formally took up their posts on the first day of 1939.[38] Sichuanese accounted for less than half of the officials in the new municipal administration, which was structurally and numerically dominated by refugees from central and eastern China.[39] The irony of this (quasi-colonial) administration was noted by Theodore White, who observed that Wu Guozhen (K. C. Wu), a native of Hubei and former mayor of Hankou who had been educated at Princeton and was mayor of Chongqing from 1939–1942, spoke English but could not understand the local Chongqing dialect.[40] Local elites, shut out of most formal positions in the newly organized municipal government, were given positions on the Temporary Assembly (Linshi canyi hui), headed by Kang Xinru. This body had no formal power within the municipal government, but the informal power it wielded in Chongqing is suggested by the regularity with which the mayor met with it and sought its cooperation in municipal reforms and governance.

During the war municipal officials drew up at least two relatively comprehensive plans for the modernization of Chongqing's infrastructure and economy. If fully implemented, these ambitious plans would truly have transformed Chongqing by creating a modern urban infrastructure and providing a basis for the reconstruction of its economy along industrial rather than commercial lines. However, for a number of reasons, most of these plans remained on paper until the end of the war.[41] First, regular air raids during the summer months of 1938–1941 destroyed large sections of the city and provided a strong disincentive to the creation of any infrastructure that would almost certainly become a target for enemy bombs.[42] After the outbreak of the Pacific War in late 1941, when the air raids ceased, more substantial construction projects were undertaken; however, in the midst of war, public funds for projects that did not directly contribute to the war effort were limited. Second, after 1941, the Guomindang government, confident that Japan would eventually be defeated and that the capital would be moved back to Nanjing, lost interest in expending limited resources on a city that was now clearly only a temporary haven.[43] Finally, Guomindang officials may have been reluctant to finance and implement plans that would play into the hands of, or in any way bolster the position of, local elites long interested in modernizing Chongqing for their own purposes.[44]

Examination of the actual modernizing reforms undertaken by municipal officials indicates that their primary concern was to create a city that was sufficiently modern to establish the authority and legitimacy of the national government and to impress the foreign governments to whom it looked for aid. Consequently, "window-dressing" projects that aimed to create a sense of the cleanliness, order, and prosperity associated with modernity in the eyes of wartime refugees and foreign visitors received a high profile.

Improving Chongqing's appearance *(shirong)* was one of the top objectives of reform-minded officials. In November 1938, shortly after the final move from Wuhan to Chongqing, the first of several campaigns was launched to give the city a face-lift by removing all signs of poverty and backwardness from its streets. Beggars, prostitutes, and vagrants *(youmin)* were rounded up and shipped out of town, ostensibly to shelters, training centers, and factories.[45] An ambitious series of laws was passed that prohibited not only begging, prostitution, gambling, and vagrancy, but also the offensive local practice of wrapping white cloths around the head and walking in bare feet on the main roads.[46]

Cleanup efforts in this and other campaigns also focused periodically on eliminating the shack settlements where Chongqing's poorest residents lived. During the war years these settlements ceased to be confined to the riverfront and spread throughout the city. As in other Chinese cities, Chongqing's reformers considered these structures unsightly, and city officials claimed (probably with justification) that they increased the danger of fires spreading during air raids. But despite periodic campaigns to have them removed, these shacks represented the only type of shelter available to the city's growing population of poor immigrants. Moreover, they were a practical means of establishing temporary shelter in a city where housing was regularly destroyed in air raids. As a result, their numbers actually increased during the war.

Efforts to improve Chongqing's appearance also aimed to discipline its population by eliminating "chaos" and creating "order." Several laws were passed that aimed to establish an orderly traffic pattern on the streets and to keep pedestrians confined to the sidewalks. Peddlers and vendors were prohibited from spreading out mats to display their wares along the edges of city streets, restaurants from placing stoves in doorways or displaying food and drink on the street.[47] Given Chongqing's extreme crowding, many of these objectives seemed unrealistic. Indeed, the frequency with which these activities were reported suggests that the prohibitions generally were not successful. Beggars, peddlers, prostitutes, sewage, and garbage continued to clog Chongqing's lanes and alleys and to elicit the disgust of downriver refugees throughout the war years.

Efforts to improve hygiene and sanitation in the city were closely related to the campaigns to improve the city's appearance. To tackle the problems of sanitation, a Municipal Bureau of Sanitation (Weisheng ju) was established in November 1938 with an annual operating budget of (a rather paltry) four thousand yuan. Directed by the former head of Nanjing's Bureau of Sanitation, its first objective was to decrease the city's rodent population, and a rat-catching movement was immediately launched. Rat-killing teams were organized, traps were manufactured and sold by the bureau itself, and propaganda materials were distributed to inform the population of the dangers rats posed to public health. Residents were offered two fen for each dead rat turned in at a central collection station.[48] The bounty on dead rats was later discontinued when it was discovered that people were breeding rats in order to collect the money.[49]

The Municipal Bureau of Sanitation also targeted the garbage and sewage that lined Chongqing's narrow lanes and alleys and piled up on its docks. Enlisting the assistance of the Municipal Police Department, the bureau planned to take some positive measures such as setting up garbage cans and increasing the number of street cleaners. But it relied more on the city's *baojia* heads by making them responsible for seeing that each household in their district cleared sewage from the ditches near its own living space. In addition, laws were passed that "strictly" forbade garbage dumping and urinating in the streets.[50]

The New Life Movement was also involved in efforts to improve public sanitation by sponsoring cleanup competitions. In these competitions inspectors were sent into the streets to check on hygiene in markets, restaurants, food stalls, bus stations, docks, and private residences. The cleanest places were rewarded with banners identifying them as "good households" *(hao jiating),* while the dirtiest were censured and shamed by posting banners identifying them as "households that should improve" *(ying gailiang jiating).*[51]

Like the efforts to improve Chongqing's appearance, these campaigns ultimately did little to clean up the city's streets, as they did not seriously address the fundamental need for an urban infrastructure for disposing of garbage and sewage. No concrete measures were taken to create alternative means of garbage disposal or a sewer system. In a reference to the old and well-known joke about Chongqing's "three plenties" (prostitutes, singing girls, and beggars), *Xin Shubao* reported in 1941 that Chongqing had a "new three plenties" *(xin sanduo):* opium addicts, rats, and excrement and garbage.[52]

Municipal officials did bring more substantial changes to Chongqing's streets during the war as well. In 1938, the municipal government established a survey and planning team that spent the next year and a half surveying Chongqing's roads and drawing up plans for their improvement.[53] The reforms that followed ultimately played a crucial role in altering the spatial layout of the city. Within the city, the widening of narrow lanes continued during the war years. As in the prewar street-widening program, this process involved destroying the existing homes and buildings that lined narrow lanes in designated sections of the city. Air raids between 1939 and 1941, as well as frequent fires, helped city officials overcome substantial local resistance to these plans by providing much of the preliminary demolition work. By the end of the war the Upper City had a well-established network of paved roads, which have remained the major transport arteries in Chongqing into the 1990s.

Existing streets were also "modernized" by having their names changed. Street names typically reflecting either their location within the city or their function were declared to be "feudal."[54] Moreover, as a result of Chongqing's topography, many streets were short, and even on longer streets the names changed frequently within one area—a situation that was confusing to downriver refugees.[55] Consequently, many street names were changed during the first year of the war. On the renamed streets, words such as "lane" *(xiang)* and "street" *(jie)* were discarded in favor of the more modern-sounding "road" *(lu)*[56] (see map 20). And, as will be seen below, the new names emphasized the political values of the national government.

A road system was constructed outside Tongyuan Gate that linked the main part of the city with the university and residential and industrial districts emerging in the areas of Shapingba and Ciqikou to the west.[57] The creation of these roads, together with the movement of the population outside of the old city to avoid air-raid destruction, greatly contributed to the development of these areas. After the devastating air raids of early May 1939, the municipal government encouraged people and businesses to move out beyond the city center to the outlying areas, where they would be safe from future attacks. A number of government offices and factories moved as well, and some of the most strategically important were buried in caves dug in the hillsides around the city. By 1943, Greater Chongqing had expanded to include ten well-defined districts; these included a docking and warehouse district and a commercial and banking district located within the old part of the city. Immediately to the west of the old Tongyuan Gate was the administrative district, site of the Guomindang party and national government offices. Farther west was the industrial district in the area around Xiaolongkan, a residential district, a cultural district at Shapingba, and a recreational area in the vicinity of scenic Geleshan. Agriculture was scattered throughout the western districts. A "shack district" was located along the riverbanks in the old city.[58]

The improved system of roads in the Upper City made it possible to upgrade public transport. The tiny bus company that had been established by local elites in 1933 was gradually expanded during the war years. In September 1940, Chongqing had forty-one public buses, of which only sixteen were actually in operation. These vehicles operated along four routes covering a total of nearly ninety kilometers. By the end of 1944, ninety-three buses operated along eighteen routes covering nearly 150 kilometers of road.[59]

In response to the city's swelling population and the increased demand for regular transportation between the main city and the new factories and homes in Jiangbei and Nan'an, the Chongqing Ferry Company was formed in

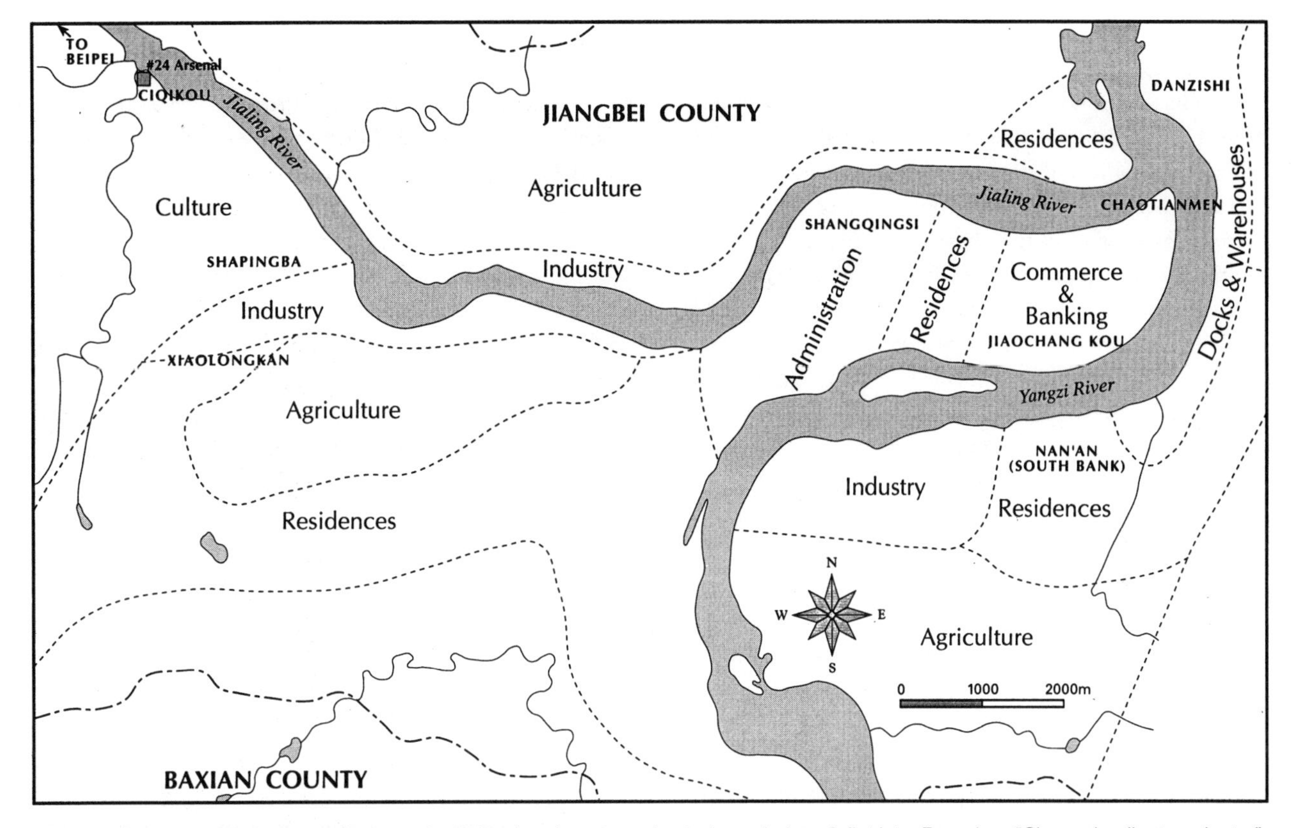

Map 21. Chongqing and surrounding area in 1943, showing approximate boundaries of districts. Based on "Chongqing jiaotong luetu," published in the PRC by Chengdu ditu chubanshe.

early 1938 with capital from the state and private entrepreneurs. By July of that year it had leased and purchased six steamers that operated along four routes connecting various docks on both sides of both rivers.[60] Although the ferry company continued to operate throughout the war years, further large-scale expansion was impractical in view of the damage the company's equipment suffered in air raids.

Modern industrial production was viewed as essential to the Guomindang's war effort and as an important aspect of modernity. Because Chongqing in 1937 lacked factories capable of sustaining the level of production needed for China's wartime effort, as well as the ability to manufacture quickly the machinery and tools required by new factories, thousands of tons of equipment, raw materials, and skilled workers were transferred there during the early years of the war. By the middle of 1940, over two hundred factories had been transferred to Chongqing from industrial centers in central and eastern China, including textile mills, arsenals, machine works, steel plants, and publishing houses.[61] These factories and workers comprised the core of Chongqing's modern industrial sector during the war years but did not entirely supplant the factories established before the war.

Despite the ambitious range of modernizing projects undertaken by municipal officials during the war, the scope of their efforts was limited. No attempt was made to improve the riverfront slums or the docks that had served as the primary focal point of activity before the war years. Not only were these areas completely ignored by reformers, they were actually marginalized by a modernizing process that shifted the city center away from them toward the modern enclave that had been created in the Upper City. The government's encouragement of the growth of new districts outside the main part of the city and the location of "modern" industry in them further contributed to this process.

The Guomindang's neglect of the old city must have been at least in part a pragmatic response to the impossibility of transforming it. The narrow and steep areas of the riverside cliffs were physically unsuited to building a city that reflected a vision of modernity based on wide avenues and multistoried concrete buildings. But beyond these practical considerations, reforms undertaken by refugee municipal officials and reformers during the war were superficial because their objective was not fundamentally to transform the city through modernizing reforms. Rather, the purpose of the reforms was to establish the supremacy of the notion of modernity in Chongqing, to assert the Guomindang government's right to define its characteristics and its own exclusive claim to it, and to strengthen the association between itself and modernity in the public (and foreign) mind. As one observer shrewdly noted, this superficial approach to modernization reflected the national government's limited commitment to creating anything more than a facade of modernity for the purpose of impressing foreign visitors.[62]

Whether or not the process of marginalizing backwardness and poverty in Chongqing and confining association of it to certain areas of the city was intentional, it ultimately served the national government's political purposes by strengthening the separation of modernity and backwardness in the public mind. Moreover, the poverty and backwardness of the riverfront slums served to enhance the modernity of the Upper City and the newly created districts west of the city. Wartime accounts of journeys into Chongqing typically describe a sense of despair and horror provoked by the visitor's initial view of the working-class districts along the shore. These reactions sharply contrast with the delight and relief experienced as the traveler reached the modern district at the top of the hill. In these areas a clear Guomindang and "downriver" presence had been established by 1940, which helped to strengthen the association of the party and the national government with the new and "modern" Chongqing. At the same time, "native" Sichuanese continued to be associated with the sections of the city that remained poor and "locked in tradition."

Nationalizing Chongqing

In addition to these modernizing reforms, the Guomindang also worked during the war years to transform Chongqing into a capital city that conveyed a sense of national identity and power. This was done in two ways: first through the creation and construction of national images and symbols in Chongqing, and second through the construction of an image of Chongqing itself as a national symbol. By projecting a series of national images associated exclusively with Chongqing, the Guomindang government succeeded not only in making the city a fitting representative of the wartime spirit of the nation, but also in promoting its own vision of the nation through the city.

As in Wuhan, the construction of government buildings did not figure prominently in the national government's plans for creating a national wartime capital in Chongqing. The area known as Shangqingsi, located in the New Business District to the west of the old city gate, was designated as an administration zone for the national government. By 1939, several government buildings had been constructed in this area, and other offices had been relocated in existing structures. Wu Jisheng, one of the few people who bothered to describe this area, found the Central Party Headquarters and the Executive Yuan to be the most magnificent *(jia)* of the newly constructed Guomindang buildings, with luxuriant and well-spaced trees and flowers that reminded him of Chaofeng Park in Shanghai. Next in magnificence, in his view, was the Examination Yuan. However, he found the Ministry of the Interior to be a real disappointment. Located on a busy street, it was fronted by a large gate that had been finished with a coat of cement, "probably because the designers were not familiar with the architectural system *(jianzhu zhidu)* of government buildings. When people first see it, they almost mistake it for an inn or bathhouse." The Department of Education was established nearby in the Eastern Sichuan Normal School. Although surrounded by pleasant gardens, it seemed small and cramped to Wu Jisheng. Recalling the former capital and the architecture of the Ministries of Communications and Railways, he sighed and lamented that the new buildings simply could not compare with the wealth and elegance expressed by the buildings in Nanjing.[63]

A number of factors contributed to the national government's decision not to construct grand and impressive government offices like the ones left behind in Nanjing. In addition to the pragmatic concern that government buildings would be a natural and likely target for air raids, the necessity of treating Chongqing as a temporary refuge for a government in exile, rather than as a new and substitute capital city, must have been uppermost in the minds of the wartime capital's planners. Even if the national government had believed it would never return to Nanjing, it could not construct buildings that would reflect such pessimism about its future. Thus by the temporary and unsatisfactory nature of its office buildings in Chongqing, the Guomindang government hoped to assure citizens and foreign governments that its stay in Chongqing would be temporary.

Within the city, the government worked to create a national presence by overlaying the bustling and modernized downtown area around Duyou Street (Duyoujie) with national symbols. In addition to redesignating these streets as *"lu,"* as discussed above, new and modern names were given to streets in this area that reflected the national orientation and political values of the Guomindang government. Thus the stretch of road formerly known as Immortals Assembling Bridge, Small Roof Beam Street, Dragon King Temple, and Administering Peace Temple became Nationality Road (Minzu lu). Miscellaneous Goods Market and Arsenal Warehouse Street became part of People's Livelihood Road (Minsheng lu). Capital Post Street (Duyoujie) became People's Rights Road (Minquan lu). Other new street names were Peace Road (Heping lu), New Life Road (Xinsheng lu), City Residents Road (Shimin lu), and Lin Sen Road, named after the titular president of the Republic. The new names created a great deal of confusion because local residents never bothered to learn them and because rickshaw pullers were unable to find addresses using the new street names. Nevertheless, the overtly political vocabulary of the new names provides one of the clearest indications of the political agenda underlying the national government's modernizing efforts. Most of the names remained on city maps after the war and are still used today.

The construction of monuments did not figure prominently in the central government's efforts to create a national presence in Chongqing. Its one attempt to build a national monument was, by its own admission, a complete failure. The monument, officially called the Spiritual Fortress (Jingshen baolei), was placed in the busiest downtown district at the junction of Duyou and Shizi Streets to commemorate the fifteenth anniversary of Sun Yat-sen's death on March 12, 1940. A three-tiered structure made of wood and coated with cement, its base had eight sides, on each of which was written one of the following characters: loyalty *(zhong)*, filial piety *(xiao)*, sincerity *(xin)*, righteousness *(yi)*, unity *(he)*, tranquillity *(ping)*, benevolence *(ren)*, and love *(ai)*. The second and third levels of the structure were also covered with slogans representing a similar mixture of Guomindang political values with Confucian and Christian virtues. In order to prevent it from becoming a target in air raids, the outside of the monument was painted black, making it an exceptionally forbidding structure.[64]

One might expect that a national monument such as this, situated in a large and centrally located square, would be used by the Guomindang for the regularly staged patriotic rallies and parades commemorating important national events and leaders, but most of these activities were actually held at the New Life Center in nearby Fuzichi. On the first anniversary of the monument and the second anniversary of the Spiritual Mobilization Movement (Jingshen zong dongyuan), the celebratory activities were moved from Fuzichi to the Spiritual Fortress to accommodate the expected crowd of over one thousand people[65]—but it does not seem to have been a first choice.

Inhabitants of Chongqing never expressed much interest in the monument, perhaps because of its intimidating physical appearance. Lin Yutang, one of the Guomindang's chief propagandists for audiences in the United States, described it as "a concrete pole that resembles a magnified chopstick," and found it "hideous as a name and as a piece of architecture."[66] As it turned out, the monument did not last long. Because it was built of wood, it quickly decayed, and when it finally collapsed, the debris was simply cleared away. The space it had occupied was planted with grass, and a flagpole flying the national flag was put in its place.[67]

It is doubtful that any monument the Guomindang might have constructed would have captured the popular imagination both within the city and abroad as effectively as Chongqing did itself. Since most wartime visitors arrived by river steamer or ferry, they caught their first view of the wartime capital from the rivers below, where they could see it as a discrete and complete entity. The descriptions they wrote testify to the powerful impact its physical appearance had on visitors. In contrast to the poverty and backwardness that overwhelmed visitors after they had entered Chongqing, the city as a whole was viewed by many wartime refugees and foreign journalists as a monument to the strength and endurance of the Chinese people. Its fortress-like appearance played an important role in creating this impression. The high rocky peninsula on which it stood suggested strength and invincibility, while the swiftly flowing rivers and currents surrounding it on three sides brought to mind the turmoil that engulfed the nation.

The wartime experience of Chongqing's inhabitants also played a role in constructing an image of the city as a monument to national strength. The perseverance and invincibility suggested by its physical appearance was reinforced by its perceived indestructibility in the face of the thousands of air raids that occurred during the summer months of 1939 to 1941, when the fog usually covering the city was burned off by the hot sun. During these raids Japanese bombs destroyed lives, buildings, homes, factories, and roads throughout the city, but many observed that the rocky foundation on which the city was built remained unaffected. To them, the indestructibility of the city's foundation represented the indestructibility of the essential "spirit" of the Chinese people. As Adet Lin put it in 1940, "Men may be killed, but Chungking itself will go on forever."[68] These sentiments were somewhat poetically expressed by the journalist Ke Mao immediately following a particularly devastating air raid on May 25, 1939:

> Chongqing, this ill-starred Mountain Town, having been greatly stirred and agitated is leaping up. Roar! everlasting Mountain Town. Let the Yangzi and Jialing Rivers fiercely clamor! Chongqing has not been destroyed. No matter how ruthless you Japanese fascists of ten thousand evils are, you can never extinguish our will to resolutely struggle! . . . This undying Mountain Town which now embraces thousands upon ten thousands of people, is supporting a strong and everlasting heart![69]

Newspaper and journal articles written during the war portrayed Chongqing not only as a site of great suffering and destruction, but also as the site on which national rejuvenation *(minzu fuxing)* would occur. The power of the city to inspire this attitude struck one writer when he visited Chongqing for the second time in 1943: "If you stand at Fuxingguan . . . the Mountain City rises abruptly, carried by the two rivers. This foundation *(genju di)* for national rejuvenation is really stirring!"[70] Another writer, perhaps inspired by the fires that frequently followed air raids, saw Chongqing as a great furnace in which a new spirit of the people was forged: "I believe the alternate capital is the most profound and powerful furnace *(ronglu)* for summoning [our] spirit *(jingshen)*. As people emerge one by one and in groups from this furnace, the rejuvenation of their spirits is revealed."[71]

During the war, then, the city of Chongqing itself came to represent a vision of national strength that was derived from its "resistance" to foreign aggression and the almost superhuman endurance of its population. The unity of the city's diverse population was an essential component of this vision, and wartime literature made much of Chongqing's power to draw together the variegated elements that made up the Chinese nation and to recast them as a new and powerful whole.

Chongqing: Microcosm of the Nation

To many observers, wartime Chongqing seemed to be a microcosm of the nation, a multicultural city where refugees, factories, and businesses gathered from all over China. On its crowded docks and streets, government workers, wealthy urbanites, industrialists, intellectuals, and factory workers from war areas in central and eastern China rubbed shoulders with the thousands of poor peasants who had migrated from poverty-stricken rural areas in eastern and northern Sichuan to seek work in the rapidly expanding city. China's diversity was always on display on the streets of wartime Chongqing. It was audible in the range of dialects spoken, and visible in the variety of fashions, hairstyles, shops, and businesses from all over China that had moved there during the war. It could even be tasted in the restaurants that served up dishes representing China's various ethnic and regional cuisines. Descriptions of the city celebrated this diversity and helped to create an image of Chongqing as representative of the Chinese nation in more than a strictly political sense. As Lin Yutang wrote:

> As you wander along [the main streets of the city], you suddenly discover the famous shop names you knew elsewhere in China; the silver and silk shops of Shanghai, the scissors shop of Hangchow and the old medicine shop of Peiping, all transplanted. So are the newspaper offices of Shanghai and of Hong Kong, not in their former grandeur, but all bearing the familiar names. You find the Tasanyuan and Kuanshengyuan Cantonese restaurants of Shanghai, reopened here, and in fact as you start looking for restaurants, you find there are more Shanghai and Canton restaurants than restaurants of Szechuen. . . . And you walk into a sweetmeat shop and find exactly what you would find in a Shanghai *Taohsiangchun,* cakes and pastry, lichee, *kweiyuan,* sugared plums, dates and Foochow shredded meat and Yunnan ham and sesame candies and "ox-hide gum." And you find that the Commercial Press, Ltd., and Chung Hwa and Kaiming and World Book Companies have all moved here, holding on and waiting to go down the river after the war is over. In a word, you find all the different cities telescoped into Chungking, and you wonder no longer that Chungking is jammed.[72]

Other writers saw the range of clothing styles worn by the people who crowded on Chongqing's busy downtown streets as further evidence of the city's and the nation's diversity. "On the main roads one sees fashionable modern young ladies *(shimao modeng nulang),* whose numbers are as great as those on the streets of prosperous and flourishing cities like Nanjing and Shanghai. But emaciated coolies are also equally numerous. Impeccably dressed ordinary people *(pingmin)* are a rare sight. Looking around, these glaring differences seem out of proportion."[73]

In descriptions of Chongqing's diverse wartime population, whether expressed in occupational, subethnic, or class terms, tensions between the various groups were rarely acknowledged and never emphasized. Instead, the various social groups on display on downtown Chongqing's busy streets were portrayed as mingling together in a sort of pleasantly disordered chaos that was somehow fundamentally harmonious. All were depicted as essential components of a greater whole represented by the Chinese nation—but they were not all equal. Even as images of variety and mingling dominate descriptions of Chongqing's wartime population, an underlying division into the unequal and fundamentally incompatible categories of "native" and "downriver" was also articulated. On the most basic level these terms referred to differences in geographic origins. The term "native" *(bendi ren)* has been used throughout China to refer to the native population of any given locality. But in wartime Chongqing, "native" was regularly used to refer not only to the relatively small proportion of the population claiming to be natives of the city, but also to immigrants from other parts of Sichuan. Chongqing's "native" population therefore consisted of both natives and immigrants. Nevertheless, their common identity as Sichuanese, as well as certain similarities in dialect, food preferences, and culture, which distinguished them from immigrants from other regions of China, may help to explain why they were all grouped together as "natives." "Downriver people" *(xiajiang ren)* were an even more heterogeneous group. The term "downriver" *(xiajiang)* has been used in China since at least the Han dynasty to refer to the region around the lower reaches of the Yangzi River, especially Jiangsu and Anhui Provinces.[74] Downriver people were natives of those areas. But in wartime Chongqing, natives of areas as far away from the Yangzi River as Beijing were reportedly called "downriver people" by local Sichuanese.[75] Because the term was used to describe people of such varying local origins, "downriver people" was understood by many refugees to refer to all immigrants who came from provinces other than Sichuan.[76]

Fig. 22. Downtown Chongqing during the War of Resistance.

In other words, many refugees from eastern and central China understood the term to be essentially a synonym for "outside province people" *(waishengren)*—a term used throughout China to refer to visitors who were natives of other provinces.

The exact geographical boundaries encompassed by "downriver" and "native" are ultimately not what gave these terms significance in wartime Chongqing. Although each referred to geography, their meanings were derived from what that geography represented to wartime refugees from central and eastern China. In the minds of these people, "downriver" was associated with the industrialization, Westernization, and modernity of China's prosperous treaty ports, especially Shanghai, while "native" connoted the backwardness and poverty of Chongqing in particular and the interior provinces of China in general. By reducing Chongqing's (and by extension, China's) extraordinarily complex population into these two groups and suggesting that together they represented the entire nation, wartime discourse on Chongqing helped to establish a dichotomous relationship between the "modernizing and westernizing" coast—represented by the "downriver" refugees from cities such as Shanghai—and the "backwards" and "antimodern" interior—represented by prewar Chongqing.

In the wartime literature on Chongqing, the relationship between these two groups was hierarchically ordered. The poverty and backwardness of "native" Chongqing was acknowledged and accepted as an integral part of the nation in the vision of a modern, nationalistic city projected by municipal reformers. At the same time, however, it was clearly subordinated to the modernized urban culture of "downriver" cities and the national government that represented it in Chongqing. By juxtaposing images of backwardness and modernity in the wartime capital, the national government and downriver refugees succeeded in strengthening the association of the interior in general and Chongqing in particular with the former and themselves with the latter. And by asserting the hierarchical but organic relationship of these two aspects of China, the Guomindang defined a vision of the Chinese nation that confirmed its own dominant position. In this way the Guomindang government and the downriver refugees who followed it to Chongqing claimed for themselves a dominant position in Chongqing society and, by extension, in the nation it represented.

The hierarchical relationship between these components of the Chinese nation—and the political groups they represented—was neatly reflected in the spatial reconstruction of Chongqing that took place during the war. Before the war, the city's center had been located along the docks and riverfront, where the commerce that was its lifeline took place. The modernization process begun by the city's local elites before the war and continued by the national government and downriver reformers during the war shifted the center to the higher ground of the Upper City, where the modernized "downtown" area, new offices of the national government, parks, public squares, and monuments dominated the landscape and projected the power of modernity. The moving force behind all this was the national government that brought modernity and represented China.

By the early 1940s, downriver refugees and foreigners who visited Chongqing credited the national government with its modernization, despite the important role of local elites in the modernization process. The national government's success in establishing a link between itself and Chongqing's wartime modernization was accomplished not so much through the thoroughness of its modernizing reforms (which, as this chapter has shown, were rather superficial and incomplete) as it was through its success in defining "native" Chongqing as backward and using images of that backwardness to enhance the limited modernization that took place during the war years. And by subordinating and marginalizing that native "other" in the spatial layout of the city as well as in wartime discourse on Chongqing, the national government also succeeded in projecting itself as the dominant power in the Chinese nation.

Chapter 12

Locating Old Shanghai

Having Fits about Where It Fits

Jeffrey N. Wasserstrom

It is no simple matter for a Shanghai specialist to respond to the collection of historical snapshots of different Chinese cities provided in the preceding chapters. One reason it is so difficult, ironically, is that the snapshots in question fit together so well. When taken as a whole, they give the reader a compelling vision of a coherent urban landscape—a vision that puts in effective relief many of the basic features of Chinese cities (as places) and Chinese city life (as a genre of experience) during the republican era. The problem this creates for someone who works on Shanghai has to do with issues of comparability and typicality. The celebrated and notorious city by the muddy Huangpu River—or more precisely the treaty-port era incarnation of it that is now often referred to as "Jiu Shanghai" (in Chinese language texts) and "Old Shanghai" (in English language ones)—was never an average or ordinary place.[1] Where, in a work devoted to drawing attention to common strands and teasing out overlapping themes in the urban experience, is there room for a discussion of a metropolis so anomalous that one of the best-known guidebooks of the 1930s referred to it simply as "Shanghai the Incomparable"?[2]

This is the question that is addressed in the pages that follow, albeit in a variety of divergent ways, in a chapter that looks at a series of interrelated topics—all of which are linked in some ways to problems of comparability and uniqueness. This chapter takes the form of a set of fragments; it does not strive to construct a linear argument. This admittedly unusual structure seems appropriate, however, not just because we are dealing here with an unusual city, but also because one of the chapter's main arguments is that Old Shanghai itself is best apprehended as a collection of pieces, not as an urban whole.

An Introduction to Shanghai Exceptionalism

It may help at the outset simply to describe some of the main things that made Old Shanghai unusual and indeed in some sense unique as a physical place and human community. But where should such an account begin? One can start with matters of urban development and note that between the 1890s and the outbreak of World War II, Old Shanghai grew faster, geographically and demographically, than any other Chinese city. Or one can point to the unusually wide array of occupational groups found in a city that had republican China's largest concentration of industrial laborers, sex workers, shopkeepers, Chinese novelists, foreign journalists, filmmakers, rickshaw pullers, night-soil transporters, sailors, actresses, and who knows how many other types of urban employees. Or one can note that the tripartite administrative division of the city into the International Settlement, the French Concession, and a Chinese municipality—a division that started to evolve when the port was formally opened to foreign trade in 1843 and assumed its final form some two decades later—was not precisely like that found in any other metropolis. Or one can focus first on the fact that the precise mixture of ethnic and national groups within Old Shanghai was not replicated elsewhere.[3]

These last two points require a bit of elaboration, since there were quite a few treaty ports established between the 1840s and the 1910s, and each of these was subdivided in some fashion and contained a diverse population. Nevertheless, several factors made Old Shanghai stand out from the other coastal cities forcibly opened to international trade. This is true even of Tianjin and Canton, two treaty ports examined in detail elsewhere in this volume (see chapters 2, 3, and 4) and the two with which one could claim Old Shanghai had the most in common.

One thing that made the metropolis by the Huangpu unusual, even among treaty ports, was that the main enclaves of most other coastal cities were run by individuals who had to answer directly to a single foreign power. By contrast, Old Shanghai's most economically dynamic foreign-run section was, appropriately enough, named the "International Settlement," and it was governed by a locally elected body, the Shanghai Municipal Council (SMC), that was unusually cosmopolitan. Unlike the more straightforwardly colonialist French Concession, whose top official was appointed by Paris, the SMC had a great deal of autonomy and was never made up exclusively of people from a single national group. Even though it was often described (sometimes with good reason) as an organization dominated by and serving the interests of the Anglo-American residents of the city known as "Shanghailanders," the SMC typically had at least one—and not infrequently more than one—member belonging to a different segment of the local population.

In addition, by the 1930s, no other Chinese city had large blocks of new immigrants, sojourners, and second-generation settlers with ties to such a wide array of different places. Many of the local Chinese, or "Shanghairen" (who throughout the republican era made up the great majority of residents within each of the city's three main administrative districts), came from the two neighboring provinces of Jiangsu and Zhejiang. Most of China's other regions were represented within the local demographic kaleidoscope as well, however, in some cases by good-sized communities. One result of this diversity was that native-place societies, or "tongxianghui," played key roles in the city's social life. Another related phenomenon was that, far from seeing themselves only as undifferentiated Shanghairen, many local Chinese drew clear lines of distinction, which took on the force of ethnic divisions, based on place of origin. For example, immigrants with ties to northern Jiangsu, known as Subeiren, were looked down upon by many other groups in much the same way as those dubbed "Oakies" in dustbowl-era California were.[4]

Old Shanghai's residents also included a mixture of different sorts of foreigners. More than fifty different nationalities were represented in the city by the 1930s, and by then the Shanghailanders (clustered in the International Settlement) and the urban center's Francophone residents (mostly based in the French Concession) were far outnumbered by white Russian refugees and Japanese sojourners and settlers.[5] Old Shanghai's non-Chinese diversity was reflected in the proliferation of foreign associations and clubs that (like the Chinese native-place societies) were founded in part to provide a sense of belonging and a network of connections to newcomers. Such diversity was also reflected in the local publishing scene. At least one, and in some cases several, Shanghai-based daily newspapers served readers of English, French, German, Yiddish, Russian, and Japanese.

The city's hybridity had an impact on things that went far beyond formal governance and demographics. One famous case in point is architecture. Some of the best-known civic landmarks were the Western-style buildings of the International Settlement's waterfront Bund, which looked as though they would have been equally at home in 1920s Chicago, and the tree-lined Parisian-style boulevards of the French Concession, which was the more southerly of the two foreign enclaves. There were many storefronts in the Chinese-run sections of the metropolis, which included the old walled city to the south of the French Concession and assorted districts to the west and north of both enclaves, that looked much like those found in any of the Jiangsu or Zhejiang urban centers of the Lower Yangzi region. The same was true of many of the temples found in the oldest section of the city—the walled area sometimes called the "Native City" by foreigners of the treaty-port era, and described to me in 1996 as Shanghai's old "Chinatown" by a wisecracking local tour guide. Many edifices in all parts of the metropolis, meanwhile, combined imported and domestic features.[6]

Two of the many other forms of cultural hybridity that could be mentioned relate to food and entertainment. Heading westward from the International Settlement section of the Bund, moving along the border of that enclave and the French Concession, then heading either south into the older walled section of the Chinese municipality or north into one of its newer sections, the intrepid diner could, in the course of an hour's promenade, pass by restaurants serving dishes from more than a dozen foreign lands, as well as ones that catered to the tastes of those reared on at least as many regionally distinctive Chinese

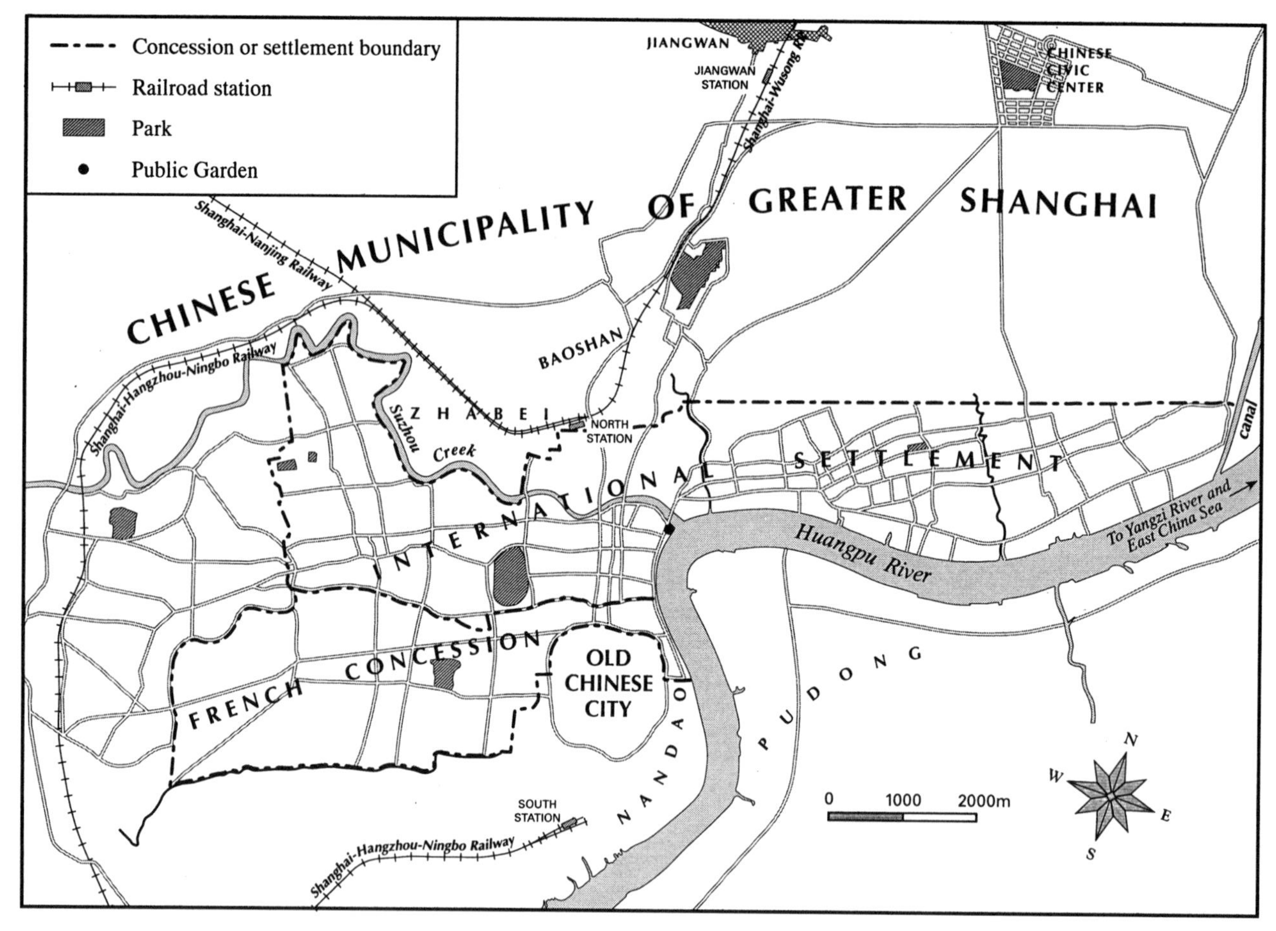

Map 22. Old Shanghai, ca. 1930s. Based on a map in William Crane Johnstone, Jr., *The Shanghai Problem* (1937).

cuisines. If the same person were more interested in music than food, the choices would be almost as varied, with everything from the sounds of Western jazz to those of several very different sorts of Chinese opera to any one of a number of mixed genres being offered up in theaters and nightclubs along the same route.

Old Shanghai's Exceptionalism as a Symbol

The preceding sketch of material, social, and cultural anomalies gives some idea of the enormity of the problem facing anyone seeking to put in comparative context the complex and unusual urban center that stood to the west of the Huangpu, but the issues need to be magnified still further by taking into account Old Shanghai's special role as an object of representation and analysis. One needs to consider not just Old Shanghai's life as a historical city, which came into being in the aftermath of one international military conflagration (the Opium War) and disappeared during the course of another (World War II), but also its afterlife as an imagined and remembered place that continues to generate an enormous amount of often passionate commentary. It matters as well that this commentary has taken an unusually wide array of forms, being created by everyone from purveyors of popular culture to academics, and that many contributors to this activity seem convinced that Old Shanghai is best represented as a veritable paradise on earth, a terrestrial equivalent to the netherworld, a spot where elements of heaven and hell coexisted in curious juxtaposition, or as a symbol of all the glories and terrors of cosmopolitan modernity.[7] In comparing this treaty port, in other words, one needs to pay attention not just to the physical place that once occupied ground now encompassed within the urban center sometimes known as "New Shanghai," but also to the various Old Shanghais less closely linked to geography that are continually being revisited and conjured up in academic departments, film studios, museums, and so forth.

It is worth noting, lest the preceding paragraph appear too fanciful for a scholarly volume, that it is virtually impossible to separate cleanly discussion of the special status of Old Shanghai as a concrete entity and as a represented object—and that this same situation also exists for a handful of other historical and contemporary cities that have proved capable of inspiring comparable sorts of utopian and dystopian reveries. Consider, for example, urban theorist Michael Sorkin's comments about contemporary Los Angeles, which he dubs "the most mediated town in America" and calls a place that has become "nearly unviewable save through the fictive scrim of its mythologizers." If we substitute "in China" for the last two words in the first phrase, we have statements that work well as descriptions of the treaty port by the Huangpu.[8]

It is also worth noting that it is in part due to the same constellation of features that once made the city so unusual that the mystique of a remembered (or rather reimagined) Old Shanghai has remained so strong. If the city of history had not been so special as a physical and social place, it is doubtful it would continue to fascinate everyone from Hollywood filmmakers (Steven Spielberg set not just *Empire of the Sun* but also part of *Indiana Jones and the Temple of Doom* in the treaty port) to Hong Kong scriptwriters (the authors of the first movie starring Bruce Lee, *Jingwumen,* or *The Chinese Connection,* cast the martial arts hero in a story set by the Huangpu in 1908) to European novelists (J. G. Ballard being perhaps the most famous, but by no means the only, case in point). Just as in the 1920s–1940s, when the city inspired a slew of novels and feature films that ranged from the enduring (the movie *Shanghai Express,* starring Marlene Dietrich, and *Shanghai Hotel* by Vicki Baum) to the immediately forgettable (the movie *Charlie Chan in Shanghai* and works of fiction such as *The Shanghai Bund Murders* by a now obscure author), its name and best-known streets and buildings continue to appear in a surprising range of popular culture creations (from director Zhang Yimou's much-praised *Shanghai Triad* to the widely panned Madonna star-vehicle, *Shanghai Surprise*).

It is also fair to say that at least some of the same factors alluded to above have contributed to the recent flourishing of Shanghai studies within the academy. There is more to the story of the rise of this international academic subfield, but surely the special features of the old treaty port need to be factored into the tale. Old Shanghai's peculiarities are one reason that so many academic works about it are now being brought out by publishing houses based in cities such as London, New York, Hong Kong, Paris, and Tokyo. In addition, while politics and civic pride always play a role in the generation of works of urban local history within the People's Republic of China (PRC), the special features of Old Shanghai need to be taken into account as well when trying to explain the unusually large number of scholarly works on the treaty-port period of the city's past that are currently being produced within New Shanghai.[9]

The Hong Kong of Its Day?

One way to begin thinking through the problem of Old Shanghai exceptionalism and the to-compare-or-not-to-compare dilemma it poses is to draw analogies across the 1949 watershed with another anomalous Asian trading center: Hong Kong. Thanks to the myriad ways that Old Shanghai stands out among republican-era cities as unusual, the issues confronting a specialist in that city's past reflecting on the preceding chapters are not unlike those that until 1997 confronted Hong Kong specialists attending conferences focusing on urban centers of the PRC. This is an attractive way to conceptualize the issue, since other sorts of connections between Old Shanghai and the former Crown Colony have so often been highlighted by commentators—hardly a surprising thing given the number of Western and Chinese businessmen who relocated from the banks of the Huangpu to the Hong Kong waterfront in the 1940s and 1950s.[10]

There are differences to be reckoned with in the two cases, of course. Old Shanghai was a "semicolonial" city, or at least not a fully colonial one in the way that pre-handover Hong Kong was. In addition, the two cities have in the past—and still do—occupy distinctive niches in the Chinese and international imaginations. And it is the case as well that, unlike Hong Kong of any period, Old Shanghai had a section in which French, as opposed to either English or any form of Chinese, was the official language.

Nevertheless, the two cities of history share enough key features to make it natural to think about placing them in the same category. When it comes to urban development, for example, Old Shanghai was much like Hong Kong of the 1950s–1980s, in the sense of being detached from in some ways but connected in others to general mainland patterns. The two places were also similar in that each had parts more closely linked to other parts of China (the so-called native city of Old Shanghai and the New Territories, respectively) and parts more free-floating in national terms (the International Settlement and the French Concession, in the one case, Kowloon and Hong Kong island, in the other).[11]

One can also claim with justification that each place served a comparable metonymic role, or rather pair of metonymic roles, in the period in question. The names of each metropolis could be, and sometimes were, used to stand for a much larger whole—that is, to invoke a chain of associations that made the city represent something much bigger than an urban center. The curious thing is that, in each case, within China and outside of it, the force of the metonymic use of the place-name was very different.

More specifically, to many Westerners of the first decades of this century, the very term "Shanghai" was an evocative metonym for all of "China," or indeed a mysterious "East" that included all of Asia. One indication of this is that New York restaurants that wanted to conjure up images of the mysterious Orient in the 1930s would often do so simply by inserting the word "Shanghai" into the name of the establishment, even if the food it showcased was Cantonese. Similarly, from the 1950s until the early 1990s, when Westerners heard the word "Hong Kong," this was often enough to set off a chain of associations that when taken together made up an image of China or of an Eastern world with an even larger compass.

In both cases, however, the term in question sometimes served a contrasting but equally powerful and equally metonymic role within China. To say "Shanghai" in China of the 1930s or "Hong Kong" in the PRC before 1997 was to conjure up images, at least in some minds, of the products and customs and attractions and terrors of a larger whole—but the West, not the East. It is important to note, however, that competing with both of these metonymic notions was an image of first Old Shanghai and later Hong Kong as a place that was in some fundamental way so cosmopolitan that it was part of neither the East nor the West. The magical allure of or threat posed by each place, in some minds, was linked to the fact that they were spots where two worlds long kept apart intermingled in enticing or disturbing ways.[12]

These remarks on Old Shanghai and Hong Kong suggest that, just as we have come to expect specialists working on the latter city to decide whether to emphasize or play down the things that make it similar to or different from other Chinese urban centers, so, too, do historians of Old Shanghai have to wrestle with comparable dilemmas. For example, just as Hong Kong specialists once had to choose whether or not to stress the unusual way the Crown Colony was governed, specialists working on Old Shanghai have to make an analogous decision about how to handle the unique tripartite system of administration within the treaty port by the Huangpu. This point needs to be stressed because although, as already demonstrated, there is certainly a case to be made for highlighting the unusual features of Old Shanghai's system of governance, there is also a case to be made for deemphasizing the anomalousness of its three-cities-in-one composite character. The specific dilemma posed by the complex nature of the treaty port's administrative setup is worth a bit of consideration on its own terms, so central is it to the theme of this chapter.

Old Shanghai as a Fragmented Entity

The first thing to note about the administrative division alluded to above is that it made Old Shanghai at least a "triple city" (and it was actually more cities than that), so the phrase "dual city," used by Linda Johnson in a recent book, will not take us far enough.[13] Johnson's term has some validity for the two decades immediately preceding the formal establishment of the International Settlement in 1863, and to be fair this is the period to which she suggests it be applied. One could also use it, perhaps, to describe Hong Kong from the 1950s until 1997, since—at least where some political and juridical matters were concerned—Kowloon and Hong Kong Island, on the one hand, and the New Territories sections, on the other, were distinctive.[14] For Old Shanghai from 1863 on, however, to speak of two-way divisions, between a foreign city and a Chinese one, just will not do. There are quite a few different cities to be reckoned with in this period, not just a pair.

The second thing to note about the three-way division is that it laid the basis for competing visions of the city's place within China and indeed the larger world. Most notably, it provided a vantage point from which some residents could question the very Chineseness of Old Shanghai, so that groups of foreigners could think of "their" city as a piece of France surrounded by China (taking very seriously the "Paris of the East" nickname for the city that has endured to this day) or as a modern-day equivalent to the autonomous European trading metropolises of an earlier epoch (as was true of the Shanghailander merchants fond of comparing the port to Venice in the days of mercantile city-states).[15] Other sobriquets for the treaty port that equated it with foreign urban centers (it was called the "New York of the West," for example, as well as the "Paris of the East") reinforced the hold of this sort of imagery of the city as a non-Asian entity. So, too, did works of popular culture (including Hollywood movies) that made it seem that all there was to Old Shanghai was the Bund, with its Western-style buildings and its Public Garden, which was clearly designed with an eye toward making displaced Britons feel at home.

There is no question that the three-way split in the city's administration made the metropolis a much more fragmented one than any large inland urban center (such as Chongqing or Chengdu). In the details, it also made Old Shanghai different from other treaty ports, since as noted above none was subdivided in quite the same manner. And the distinctiveness of the urban center's division had a wide range of implications, some of which have little to do with civic administration or the imagining of Old Shanghai's relationship to China. The cities-within-a-city structure of the metropolis helps explain, for example, why Old Shanghai was such an attractive spot for gangsters and also those involved in radical politics. In both cases, when the police force of a given section of the city became too interested in one's activities, it was easy to shift one's base of operations to another district, especially as cooperation between the law enforcement agencies of the different parts of the metropolis was often strained by political tensions and logistical complications.[16]

If one focuses on the direct or indirect impact of the administrative peculiarities of Old Shanghai, in short, it is easy to end up treating the metropolis as a whole as a strange and sui generis creation. This is especially true if one focuses on the International Settlement, which had something much closer to full self-governing status than did virtually any other foreign enclave. This degree of autonomy is significant, in part, because it helps to explain how a distinctive mindset and tradition of civic pride, which was celebrated by some Shanghailanders but also criticized by some local Westerners (as well as many Shanghairen and outsiders), developed among the Anglo-American elite within this section of the city. It is part of the reason that some Shanghailanders tried for decades to pretend that their metropolis was not one where the majority of residents were Chinese, and who also attempted to downplay the size of the white Russian and Japanese segments of the city's foreign population, which, as noted above, were from the 1920s onward very significant indeed.

On the other hand, however, if one breaks the metropolis into its three parts and looks at each separately, one can find important and illuminating parallels between each of these sections and other Chinese cities that had sections administered in similar ways. There were a couple of other treaty ports with cosmopolitan enclaves not so very different from the International Settlement, except of course in size and influence (Gulangyu in Xiamen, for example). There were several coastal cities with French concessions.

Most important of all, Old Shanghai's Chinese municipality had much in common with not just the Chinese-run parts of other divided coastal cities, but also with some inland urban centers. This calls attention to just one type of choice—albeit a particularly important one—that has to be made by anyone trying to come to terms with the exceptional characteristics of Old Shanghai. When one is looking at issues of governance, as well as at many other things, one has to decide: should one look for comparability or just emphasize uniqueness?

Another example of this kind of choice, which relates to issues that have already been raised, has to do with Old Shanghai's reputation and hold on the popular imagination. On the one hand, it is certainly true that no other East Asian city of the day was quite so famous and infamous. It is also true that no other metropolis in the region was so frequently said to be a place best compared not to other Chinese cities of the day, but to far-off, historical, mythical, or decidedly otherworldly places, such as El Dorado and heaven itself (according to boosters) or Sodom and hell (according to detractors).[17] One could also claim, with justification, that no other Chinese city had as much power as a double-facing metonym for the pleasures and dangers of a radically different and exoticized other.

But as unusual as all this certainly was, parallels of a sort can still be teased out, if one tries, between Old Shanghai's reputation and that of other places seen to represent (admittedly to a lesser degree) either China (in Western minds) or cosmopolitan modernity (in Chinese ones). For starters, Old Shanghai was not the only Chinese city to be called the "Paris of the East"; Harbin was sometimes dubbed that as well (as was Budapest and some other spots scattered around the world). In addition, the word "Canton" was sometimes used in the West much as the term "Shanghai" was—that is, inserted into the names of products or businesses just to add an exotic touch. In short, even when it comes to reputation, one must choose whether to treat Old Shanghai exceptionalism as a matter of difference in kind or merely degree—as of course must the Hong Kong specialists dealing with the pre-1997 period, whose predicament has been described above.

Most generally, one must decide at each step along the way in trying to locate Old Shanghai in the urban landscape of the day whether or not actively to seek out common ground—connections, overlaps, or shared experiences—that might link its history to that of some or all other Chinese urban centers. And even if one chooses to try to compare this supposedly "incomparable" place, there are still further choices to be made. For example, it is possible to argue that the best strategy for the comparatist is to concentrate on the treaty port's ties to other cities of the lower Yangzi region, such Suzhou and Hangzhou (which, after the 1840s, it displaced as the region's dominant commercial center) and Ningbo (from which many members of its business elite hailed).

A regional focus of this sort is particularly attractive because it helps place the treaty port into a long-term historical perspective. Lower Yangzi networks not only played a key role in shaping life in Old Shanghai, but they have continued to shape the urban experiences of residents of New Shanghai. More than this, they were of great importance in the city's pre–Opium War incarnation as a bustling market town of some two hundred thousand people—an incarnation that might best be called "Ur-Shanghai" (not a happy choice, but the adjective "old" has been spoken for already).[18]

There are, however, at least two compelling alternatives to this regional approach, and each is worth some attention. The first involves insisting that Old Shanghai needs to be seen as part of a comprehensive social landscape made up of all Chinese urban centers. Looking backward from the Civil War era (1945–1949)—that part of the republican era during which all of Shanghai was, for the first time in over a century, brought under the control of a single Chinese government—this approach seems particularly attractive. It is also implicitly called for in some recent works by Chinese authors that present treaty-port fragmentation as merely a temporary divergence in very long-term urban processes—that is, which highlight the continuities that link Ur-Shanghai to New Shanghai via Old Shanghai.[19]

An alternate strategy involves focusing on similarities between Old Shanghai and other entrepôts. There are, moreover, two possible variations on this theme. In one, the metropolis by the Huangpu is treated as an example of a politically fragmented treaty port. In the other variation, the administrative peculiarities of such cities are less important than the economic ones, and Shanghai is simply classified as a "coastal city," which shares key features not only with treaty ports, but also with some trading centers that were fully colonized or did not contain any enclaves. Here again, as in the regional approach, an advantage is the ability to move easily between Ur-Shanghai, Old Shanghai, and New Shanghai.[20]

Old Shanghai and Beyond

Decisions relating to whether Old Shanghai should be compared to other Chinese cities—and if so, which ones—would have to be made by a specialist in the history of that metropolis in any case, but the specific way that this volume evolved gives an additional twist to the consideration. As noted in the preface, most of the chapters began as papers presented at a workshop devoted to moving "Beyond Shanghai" in Chinese urban studies. That gathering was convened, in part, to generate debate over the proper place of Shanghai studies within the modern China field. In light of this, it seems that the most useful role for a Shanghai specialist to play in a volume such as this may be to help readers think through, in something approaching a systematic fashion, the various ways to come to terms with the issue of exceptionalism. The preceding prefatory comments have been offered up with this in mind. The rest of this chapter follows up on some of the cues provided above but moves on to wrestle with the topic in a somewhat more straightforward, although still admittedly idiosyncratic, way.

In a nutshell, what I do below is analyze the pros and cons of following five specific comparative strategies. In doing so, I try to draw attention to the main advantages and disadvantages, both to Chinese urban studies and to Shanghai studies, of each approach. The chapter argues that all five strategies for comparison have something to be said for them. It concludes, however, that the one with the most to offer is the fifth one taken up—an approach based on the idea that we need to break away from any lingering sense of Old Shanghai as a single entity. In order to do justice to the complexity of any large city's past, it is important to recognize and come to terms explicitly with the multiple ways the metropolis was configured and imagined. A concern with multiplicity is particularly important when dealing with an urban center as fragmented as Old Shanghai. In such a setting, any comparison that focuses on the notion that "Shanghai" was like "X" is bound to be flawed, if for no other reason than that it fails to specify which of several possible Shanghais is being compared.

One final prefatory note is in order, before describing the various approaches and then making a plea for the fifth one. This note has to do with chronology and in a sense helps set the stage for the arguments to come concerning multiple Shanghais. The point worth stressing at the outset is that, when it comes to issues of comparability and typicality, not all incarnations of Shanghai are equally ambiguous or problematic; it was during the treaty-port era that the metropolis was most unlike other Chinese cities.

This is not to say that Ur-Shanghai (which was made up of the old walled city and the villages linked to it most closely) had no distinctive features—it had them, just as all urban centers do. For instance, simply due to its location near the sea, it was more prone than most Chinese cities to predations by pirates, and this affected everything from local architecture to civil governance. Ur-Shanghai was also more closely tied to networks of transnational trade than most Chinese urban centers of the day, thanks to the role it played as a transshipment point for good circulating between cities located up the Yangzi River and trading ports in Southeast Asia. Nevertheless, this incarnation of Shanghai was in many ways a fairly ordinary midsize Chinese city. It was, for example, one of several such lower Jiangnan urban centers known as a "Little Suzhou" or a "Little Hangzhou," as a sign of their inferiority to the cities of the region then seen for good reason as the most exceptional in the area.

Similarly, New Shanghai is definitely quite unusual in some specific ways but not nearly as atypical overall as was Old Shanghai. One special characteristic of New Shanghai is obvious—its size. Until Chongqing's rapid expansion and demographic explosion, it was without question the most populous city in the PRC. Now one has to choose whether to give its Sichuan competitor this title (the official population of the Chongqing metropolitan area is larger, but included in this figure are many residents of outlying agricultural communities) or defend Shanghai's claim to it (the number of people living in unambiguously urban parts of this city remains far greater, and its central districts continue to be more densely populated).[21]

In addition, special features of the city's history have, periodically, helped New Shanghai stand out within the PRC. For example, its traditional role as a center of radicalism and labor activism was reprised during the Cultural Revolution, when the city became a center of militancy. Then, in more recent years, its traditional role as a center of international commerce and symbol of modernity has been invoked in various ways. It now plays a special role in Beijing's drive to transform the PRC into a land of "Socialism with Chinese Characteristics." It is also no accident that the Pudong (East of the river) part of the city (which is now incorporated into New Shanghai to an extent that would have seemed unimaginable to many residents of Old Shanghai) was chosen as the site for the Pearl Tower—one of the tallest buildings in the world and a source of both local and national pride.

In many regards, however, Shanghai's recent history has been fairly similar to that of a few other big metropolitan centers. This was certainly true from the 1950s through the early 1990s, when the reglobalization of the city began and New Shanghai may have started off on a distinctive developmental path. It remains true even today, at least where noneconomic issues are concerned. For example, the cultural and political relationship between the metropolis and the nation as a whole is much like that of a couple of other very large Chinese cities, and this kind of statement could not have been made about Old Shanghai.

One implication of all this is that if, as is argued here, it is important to keep in the forefront of our minds the existence of multiple Old Shanghais, it is also important to remember that more than just nomenclature separates historical incarnations of the city from one another. So strong is the tendency to see urban history as urban biography (as though stages in the history of a metropolis were like stages in the development of the same person) that it is easy to lose track of the disjunctures that can be far more dramatic than those typically experienced in a human lifetime (which suggests that some changing incarnations of cities are better anthropomorphized as a series of progeny). This said, it is time to survey the basic paths that can be followed when attempting to come to terms with Shanghai's exceptionalism.

Five Roads to Comparison

The first strategy I have in mind builds on what can be described as a moderate reading of the "Shanghai is not China" axiom. In this reading, the saying is meant to focus our attention on the potential for distortion that comes in when analysts treat the port city by the Huangpu as in any way representative. It sees a danger, in other words, in people coming to think of Old Shanghai's past as illustrative of republican China's urban experience as a whole. A fear that this has been happening already or could easily happen soon is a very real one—if for no other reason than because of the momentum generated by the rapid growth of Shanghai studies as an academic subfield. One reason the "Beyond Shanghai" conference was organized was as a kind of corrective measure to or preemptive strike against this sort of distortion. So much of what was being published about republican-era cities was focusing on this one unusual place that the organizers worried it was becoming easy to forget that there were other, more typical, urban centers in existence.

The second approach to the treaty port's exceptionalism involves a stronger reading of the "Shanghai is not China" phrase. This one suggests that what is most likely to be misunderstood when the two entities are confused is the city (Old Shanghai), not the country (China). Proponents of this view insist that Old Shanghai was not really a part of China at all, but rather a misplaced piece of the West. This way of thinking is not represented much in scholarly writings today, but is important to take seriously nevertheless because it made its mark on many texts produced by influential residents of the treaty port and thus reveals an important part of one local mindset. The prevalence of the extreme reading of the "Shanghai is not China" axiom, in documents produced during the treaty-port era, is reflective of the pervasiveness among Shanghailanders (and some Shanghairen as well) of the notion that the "real" city was composed only of the International Settlement, or at most that enclave and the French Concession.

The third approach to the treaty port's exceptionalism can be called (with a nod to the title of a justly acclaimed essay by Marie-Claire Bergère) the "Shanghai as the Other China" vision. Bergère argues (and many have followed her lead) that Shanghai was not a completely anomalous place. Instead, it was one of a series of exceptional Chinese cities that, between them, offered up a road not taken for political and urban development.[22]

Had the "Beyond Shanghai" conference been organized with elaborating this view as its main goal, one could imagine all of the papers dealing with coastal cities that were forcibly opened to international trade in the aftermath of the Opium War. One could also imagine more attention being paid to the emergence of the kind of elite that Brett Sheehan describes in chapter 4. Chinese businessmen and perhaps intellectuals as well, who identified themselves less as residents of a particular city than as people immersed in a certain type of cosmopolitan urban milieu, would have been discussed at greater length in the chapters.

A fourth approach to Shanghai exceptionalism can be described as an eclectic or agnostic one. Here, the issue of comparability is ignored, or at least placed to the side, while specific similarities or links between Old Shanghai and other Chinese cities are examined from time to time in an ad hoc fashion. In this sort of approach, connections between the treaty port and other urban centers are stressed whenever it seems natural or unavoidable to do so, given what was going on or being said in those other Chinese cities. No firm decision is made about Old Shanghai's status by proponents of this strategy, who simply embrace a pragmatic stance of seeing what emerges while exploring other issues.

This, it seems to me, is what most of the contributors to the "Beyond Shanghai" conference have done. Many make passing reference to Shanghai. Usually such comments are made, however, with an eye simply toward explicating a feature of another city's past. Sometimes Old Shanghai is mentioned as having experienced a related transformation, sometimes as containing a related sort of social group, and sometimes simply because residents of a different city defined their experiences as being either similar to or different from those of Shanghairen.

The fifth sort of approach to Shanghai exceptionalism is an ambiguous one that will be spelled out at the end of this chapter. It stresses the need to think in terms of multiple spatial and symbolic Old Shanghais, as well as the need to distinguish between all of these and the temporally distinct Ur-Shanghais and New Shanghais that preceded and followed them. In a sense, this is just a variation on the eclectic approach. What makes it different is that it demands a more explicit reckoning with the fact that, when scattershot attempts are made to compare and contrast other places with "Shanghai," there is always a risk the author will distort the situation by looking at only one of several possible Shanghais that might be relevant, while writing as though it were the only city that stood by the banks of the Huangpu.

Thinking seriously about Shanghai's multiplicity also highlights the potential value of spending more energy drawing different sorts of comparisons than those typically made by urban historians working on China. A good deal of useful searching for similarities and differences can be done among the various Shanghais that coexisted or succeeded and followed one another, as well as among the different sorts of cities experienced by Shanghailanders as opposed to Shanghairen, by Westerners who lived in separate parts of the metropolis, by Shanghairen belonging to contrasting social classes, and so on.

Having given these bare bones synopses of the five approaches, it is time to look at each of them in more detail. The rest of this chapter does just this, beginning with a section devoted to the two variations on the "Shanghai is not China" axiom, then moving on to a section that pairs the "Other China" and "Eclectic" visions of the city's exceptionalism, and finally concluding with a brief for the multiple Shanghais idea, which is presented less as a rejection than a modification and critical synthesis of the other approaches.

Shanghai Is Not China: The Moderate Reading

There is much to be said for this approach, but in the end it does not provide a fully satisfying method for handling Old Shanghai's exceptionalism. It is best seen as offering a useful corrective measure, a way of slowing a potentially dangerous bandwagon effect within Chinese studies. There is a big difference, however, between saying an approach has value as a corrective measure and embracing it as a methodology.

What, then, are the advantages and limitations of this strategy? Before this question can be addressed, another needs to be asked: is there justification for fearing that a Shanghai-centered discourse on Chinese cities has been emerging or could easily emerge in the future? The answer is yes—and I say this as someone who is not apologetic about his own decision to continue working on Old Shanghai, a place I still find fascinating for its own sake and an ideal locale to look at when exploring certain kinds of theoretical questions. I also say this, however, as someone who has often been frustrated by the disparity that exists between the amount of work being done on this one city and the amount being done on other Chinese urban centers.

One way to gauge this disparity is to focus, for the moment, just on scholars working in English. Even a quick glance at recent issues of British, American, and Australian Chinese studies journals or at programs for the annual meetings of organizations such as the Association for Asian Studies (AAS) shows just how disproportionate an amount of high-profile work is being done on Old Shanghai. What is striking, and should be a bit worrisome—even to Shanghai specialists—is that the treaty port has not just become the most studied of republican-era cities, but it has been getting more scrutiny than any three or four other Chinese urban centers of the time combined.

This is, it should be noted, a relatively recent phenomenon. Until the 1980s, although there was a lively local history industry within Shanghai itself, the number of academic panels and conferences devoted to the city's past that had taken place outside of the PRC could be counted on the fingers of one hand.[23] It was also the case just a couple of decades ago that, in an average year, one was likely to find no more than two or three papers dealing with Old Shanghai on the programs of the annual meetings of organizations such as AAS and its various European and Australian counterparts. It was somewhat unusual in those days as well if more than a couple of serious scholarly articles or books on Old Shanghai were published in any given year in languages other than Chinese.

Now, however, Shanghai studies has gone from being a locally based cottage industry to a major international subfield that plays a significant role in the Chinese studies communities of North America, Australia, and Europe, as well as China and Japan. There are several major Asian studies centers located outside the PRC where one can find not just one but several scholars with an abiding interest in the history of the treaty port by the Huangpu. It has become commonplace, moreover, to find Shanghai specialists from a variety of countries gathering together periodically in all sorts of academic gatherings. Not surprisingly, there is sometimes a fair amount of grumbling among China specialists (usually good-natured, although sometimes with an edge to it) about the unhealthy influence that the "Haipai" (Shanghai group) or "Shanghai Mafia" (a derogatory and self-explanatory term) is exerting over Chinese studies.

To illustrate the kinds of changes that have taken place since the early 1980s, one need only look at the publications on the city that appeared in English in 1995 alone. At least four academic books on the city were published in the United States and Britain, and in the same twelve-month period the *China Quarterly* (one of England's leading Asia journals), the *Journal of Asian Studies* (the most prominent official AAS periodical), *Republican China* (a respected forum for the presentation of more specialized research), and *Chinese Studies in History* (a journal usually devoted primarily to translations of articles originally published in the PRC and Taiwan) all ran symposia devoted to Shanghai. A variety of individual articles on the city's past appeared in major journals in 1995 as well; it was also a year during which, in the United States alone, at least four graduate students filed dissertations that focused on Old Shanghai.[24] The year of 1995—which also saw the publication of one of the best books in Japanese to date on the history of the city as well as a few very good pieces on the city in French and German and a host of publications in Chinese—may ultimately prove to have been a peak year for the development of Shanghai studies. Nonetheless, if the fascination with the city that has grown so dramatically since the early 1980s is starting to abate, it is doing so very slowly indeed.[25]

It is not necessary to see any nefarious design in the flourishing of Shanghai studies just described, nor is there any reason to present the loosely configured group of China specialists involved as having a single agenda. The emergence of Shanghai studies is due mainly to a mixture of relatively benign factors. For one, there are simply a great many attractive things about studying the place, including a diverse array of archival materials (ranging from police files to consular reports to oral histories), some of which need to be consulted in China but others of which are available elsewhere (some in such intrinsically interesting settings as London and Paris). In addition, the Shanghai Academy of Social Sciences has been more energetic than some comparable institutions within China at exploring various forms of international cooperation.

Other factors need to be taken into account as well, including some unusual characteristics of the types of documents with which the specialist in Old Shanghai's history can work. For example, at least where native speakers of English are concerned, it is certainly relevant that many of the documents relating to the treaty port take very accessible forms. Not only is the weekly newspaper *The North China Herald* written in English, for instance, but it also presents an unusually comprehensive—albeit in many ways biased—record of local affairs. In addition, for many years of its history, it comes with a very nicely done semi-annual index.

Yet another appeal of Shanghai studies today is the simple fact that those who choose to specialize in the history of this city now have many informed colleagues with whom to converse and argue. Bandwagon effects of this sort are by no means inconsequential. They become especially important when (and this does have to be noted where Shanghai studies are concerned) some of the leading figures involved in an emerging field are prominent scholars based at leading institutions, and hence are individuals unusually well positioned to secure funding for conferences and workshops and less formal types of gatherings.

However one explains the rise of Shanghai studies, one must acknowledge that it has become a force to be reckoned with in the China field, that this has created problems for our understanding of the urban experience of the republican era, and that it has even become a problem where our knowledge of this treaty port itself is concerned. As a result, it is both good for the field of Chinese studies and good for Shanghai studies that a volume such as this one has been created. Steps need to be taken to encourage scholars to work on other cities, not only to enrich our picture of the variability of Chinese urban development, but also to place in clearer perspective recent findings about Old Shanghai.

Why is the relative dearth of studies of other cities something for Shanghai specialists to worry about? Examples from my own work may help illustrate this point. When trying in the late 1980s to analyze Shanghai student activism of the republican period, I frequently found myself wishing that scholars interested in the same kinds of questions that intrigued me had written about Nanjing and Beijing. Not only would it have been useful to be able to compare and contrast patterns of protest in the different cities, so as better to tease out what was and was not distinctive about Shanghai students, but it would have helped me explore the interconnections between events in the various urban centers. For instance, the arrival of protesters from Beijing played a key role in the development of Shanghai's May Fourth movement in 1919, and some later local struggles of the 1930s peaked with mass expeditions of educated youths to Nanjing on group petition drives, during which they joined demonstrations organized by their counterparts in the city that were already underway. As it was, these kinds of connections often remained fascinating but difficult to unravel.[26]

I also found it vexing, when attempting to write in a general way about the social and cultural setting of the metropolis, that it was often impossible to get a quick sense of whether something a Shanghai specialist was working on was distinctive to that city or typical of the Chinese urban milieu. For example, one subject that intrigued me, and that was definitely relevant for student activism, was the key role Shanghai native-place organizations played as building blocks for political mobilization drives. There was useful Shanghai-based work then underway on this subject, by Bryna Goodman, from which I could draw.[27] However, because her project dealt only very peripherally with comparative issues, and because no comparably rich studies of native-place ties were being done by scholars focusing on other cities, it was very difficult to get a sense of whether the parts played by such organizations in Shanghai student movements were typical or atypical. There was reason to think that native-place societies might be particularly important in Old Shanghai, due to the rapidity with which immigrants had increased the size of the local population, but it was difficult to verify or qualify this assumption until work on other cities of various sorts had been done.

The preceding comments are offered merely to suggest that there are good reasons for Shanghai specialists, as well as those who work on other cities, to be sympathetic to efforts to shift the focus of scholarly attention toward urban centers far from the Huangpu. It is not just possible, but perhaps even sensible, for specialists in the history of the most celebrated and notorious of Chinese treaty ports to welcome events such as the "Beyond Shanghai" conference as corrective measures. This said, more harm than good is likely to come if the theme of moving urban studies "Beyond Shanghai" is allowed to have too much of a bandwagon effect of its own.

The reason for this is simple: the imagined and tangible relationships between Old Shanghai and other Chinese urban centers are too important to be glossed over or ignored. The metropolis was one that had economic as well as political links to many other coastal and inland cities; it was one that was looked to for inspiration or in horror by reformers and urban planners around the country (as some of the contributors to this volume have noted); and it was one against which many Chinese urbanites defined their own identities (most notably, perhaps, the Jingpai, or "Capital School," of Beijing depended for its own sense of self-definition on a vision of the Haipai ideals and mores they rejected). In moving Old Shanghai out of its central position in scholarly discourse, we need to make sure not to throw out the baby with the bathwater.

What this means is that, just as there is a danger of letting Shanghai studies dominate Chinese urban studies, there is a risk of overcompensating by peripheralizing it completely. This would be unfortunate for many reasons, including the fact that it would lead people working on other cities to miss out on being able to make selective use of what is unarguably the most sophisticated literature at present on any one Chinese city.

To take just one example from the present volume, consider Lee McIsaac's impressive discussion of the differing senses of local identity associated with temporary sojourners in and long-term residents of the Chongqing area (see chapter 11). As illuminating as this section of her chapter was, it could perhaps have been made still richer by drawing on the studies of comparable divergences within Shanghai populations. There are parallels to be noted, for example, between the splits within the Chongqing population, as McIsaac describes them, and divisions in Old Shanghai between immigrants from Subei and those from other parts of China that Emily Honig has detailed.[28] PRC scholar Zhang Jishun's work on campus activism in Old Shanghai, which stresses the differing psychological orientations of college-educated youths raised in the treaty port and *waidi* (outsider) students, might also have been relevant here.[29]

These comments on McIsaac's excellent discussion of civic fragmentation are offered simply to underscore a general point—namely, that we need to find a way to move beyond treating Old Shanghai as a metonym for republican China, but without sacrificing our ability to see it as part of that country. Scholars studying different parts of the urban landscape also need to find ways to engage with each other, without running the risk of having the voices of those working on other cities drowned out by the noisy subfield of Shanghai studies.

Shanghai Is Not China: The Extreme Version

What, then, of the more extreme reading of the old axiom? How seriously should we take the notion that the treaty port by the Huangpu is best thought of as a wayward bulwark of "Western civilization" (as some Shanghailanders liked to put it), which just happened to be located to the east of the Urals or on the wrong side of the Pacific? It is tempting to dismiss this idea out of hand: first, because, for understandable reasons, it is anathema to nationalist historians within the PRC in general and civic boosters based in New Shanghai in particular; and second, because it has been attacked recently by Western scholars who stress, among other things, the tendency of proponents of this sort of approach to dismiss incorrectly pre–Opium War Shanghai as a mere "fishing village," when it was actually a bustling city. The image of the treaty port as a completely non-Chinese metropolis also glosses over the role that Shanghairen played in the economic and political developments that took place on the banks of the Huangpu after 1843. Should we thus simply dismiss the idea of Old Shanghai as a wayward piece of the West as nothing more than the Orientalist product of ethnocentric mythmaking by self-important Shanghailanders? Before taking up this question, it is worth surveying the varied forms through which this particular approach to Old Shanghai, which now seems so anachronistic and offensive, was once expressed.

The notion that Old Shanghai was not a Chinese city was articulated, in more and less explicit ways, in a host of different treaty-port era documents. The authors of such texts were usually Shanghailanders or other Westerners. It is important to note, however, that there were foreigners of the day, including some Shanghailanders, who criticized the idea as presumptuous and parochial. There were also some Shanghairen who identified themselves so closely with the non-Chinese aspects of the metropolis that they were ready to embrace the notion. Among the most vocal promoters of visions of a non-Chinese Old Shanghai were the British publishers of the *North China Herald*, and it has been claimed by some that American Shanghailanders were less prone to think in these terms. It is true that certain periodicals closely tied to the U.S. contingent within the International Settlement, such as *China Weekly Review*, were openly critical of the mindset in question, but there were definitely some Americans in the enclave who embraced versions of the extreme "Shanghai is not China" argument. The best-known contemporary Western critics of the argument, meanwhile, included both American writers such as Edgar Snow (who lampooned the city's foreign business elite for pretending that the Chinese mainland was a vast hinterland put near Shanghai simply for trading purposes) and British ones such as Arthur Ransome (whose scathing treatment of the "Shanghai Mind" in the *Manchester Guardian* is the most frequently cited work ever produced to focus on the prejudices of Shanghailanders).[30]

The documents that articulated the extreme form of the "Shanghai is not China" idea ranged from popular histories of the city to speeches at civic ceremonies to guidebooks written for locals and travelers.[31] One can even see the influence of this notion in the form taken by maps produced within and for the use of the foreign community. The maps often claimed to be depictions of "Shanghai" as a whole, but were in fact only representations of the foreign enclaves. The Chinese municipality was quite literally in some cases either effaced (parts of it presented as blank spots devoid of roads and places of interest) or marginalized (pushed off toward or over the edge of the page).[32] The same kind of effacement and marginalization shaped discussions of specific features of local life: for example, when articles with headings such as "Shanghai's Architecture" or "Shanghai Ladies" appeared in local periodicals such as the *North China Herald* and the *Shanghai Evening Post and Mercury*, the accompanying text would often deal exclusively with Western buildings or people. It was taken for granted by the writers in question (and presumably this conceit was shared by some readers) that the only "Shanghai" worthy of attention was a foreign one.

One occasion during which the extreme form of the "Shanghai is not China" idea was put forth with particular force took place in 1893, when a festival was held to mark the passage of half a century since the city was opened to international trade and the first enclave established. Throughout this daylong celebration of the "Shanghai Jubilee," the notion that the city's name and the foreign sections of the metropolis were synonymous was taken for granted. So, too, was the centrality of the Western minority in the urban center's population. When the Jubilee Oration was delivered, for example, foreigners were allowed to stand near the stage, but Shanghairen and Chinese visitors were kept at a distance, beyond a cordoned-off area. In addition, "Shanghai" is used continually as shorthand for the city's enclave areas throughout the commemorative albums produced in honor of the occasion by the publishers of the *North China Herald* and the *Shanghai Mercury*.

These two works, although nodding occasionally toward the contributions Chinese had made to Shanghai's rapid post-1843 development and mentioning from time to time that a place known as Shanghai did exist before Westerners arrived, are filled with references to the city as a "republic dropped down on an alien empire," a far-flung outpost of "Western civilization," and so forth. They also stress that the current city has little real relation to anything that stood by the Huangpu in an earlier epoch, presenting the growth of the treaty port as a wondrous thing, as something that came from nowhere and grew "as by enchantment" on what had previously been an unpromising piece of swampland near a fishing village. Needless to say, throughout these volumes, when the recent history of "Shanghai" is recounted, only things that took place within the International Settlement or (less frequently) the French Concession tend to be discussed in detail.[33]

There is no question that this kind of view of Old Shanghai distorts important aspects of the city's past. Ur-Shanghai was much more than a mere fishing village surrounded by a "wilderness of marshes" (as Shanghailanders sometimes put it). Shanghairen played important roles in the development of the International Settlement and French Concession, and took the lead in transforming the parts of Old Shanghai that lay beyond these enclaves; and the city as a whole was much more than the sum of its two foreign-run parts. Nevertheless, taking seriously the prevalence of the extreme form of the "Shanghai is not China" axiom has a certain usefulness as a corrective measure, just as was true of the moderate version. In this case, however, what it helps to counteract is a teleological tendency that crops up within virtually all national histories—namely, that of assuming that every piece of land currently considered part of a nation has always been part of that imagined community, or, if temporarily detached from it, that it was somehow predestined to be reintegrated into it.

The point here is simple: we should not take for granted that what was left of the enclaves of Old Shanghai would eventually be transformed into parts of a PRC, and we should also not be too quick to dismiss completely the notion that something was created virtually from nothing in some parts of the treaty port. The contributors to the Jubilee volumes overstate the case, to be sure, but it is true that many of the buildings of the International Settlement stood on reclaimed land—land that may have been part of China before the arrival of the Westerners but was not a part that contained permanent residents. More important, there was no reason to think in 1893 that fifty years later, in the midst of World War II, control over that enclave would be formally ceded by the Allies to the Chinese authorities. Far from it, during the 1893 celebrations, some Shanghailanders looked forward to 1943 as the year when the local foreign community might gather together to celebrate a Second Jubilee, marking the passage of the first hundred years in the history of their "little republic" surrounded by Asia. Both before and after the first Jubilee, some Shanghailanders also dreamed of strengthening the autonomy the International Settlement already had and extending the territorial authority exercised by the enclave's governing body—by convincing the Chinese officials in the capital and the consular officials of the relevant foreign countries that Shanghai should be made a free city, over which a refashioned SMC would be given full control.

Free-city proposals were never accepted and put into practice, but that they were floated from time to time is worth remembering. In discussing Old Shanghai, in other words, it is important to keep in mind that some people living there (including influential shapers or articulators of Shanghailander opinion) viewed themselves as residing in an urban center that had never been and might well never be part of China. It is also important to keep in mind that, to some of these same people, attachment to their city took precedence at times over loyalty to the nation from which they or their parents had come. In a sense, then, there were Shanghailanders who traveled at least part way down the path toward being China's equivalents of the Afrikaners of South Africa—that is, in due time they might have come to think of themselves as white Asians. All this may seem odd and even objectionable when viewed from a contemporary standpoint, due not just to knowledge of the wrongs done in the name of imperialism but also to knowledge of how the Shanghai story turned out from 1943 on, but it is a mistake to overlook the phenomenon.

This said, in the end, the same conclusion needs to

be drawn concerning both versions of the "Shanghai is not China" approach to comparison. Each is useful as a corrective measure, but neither is satisfactory as an overall methodology—because to embrace either one is to leave out too much that needs to be included.

The "Other China" Approach

The third strategy for comparison requires a good deal less special introduction, as its strengths should by this point be clear. There are obvious reasons to place Old Shanghai in the special category of Chinese treaty port. There is, however, a danger here again of missing out on things worthy of discussion and mistaking a major part of the city for the metropolis as a whole.

For example, if the city is compared only to other treaty ports, many important phenomena of the republican era that were based in or primarily affected the Chinese municipality (where the majority of local residents lived) are likely to be misinterpreted or only partially understood. The urban reform and development schemes with which the local representatives of the Nationalist regime experimented during the Nanjing Decade (1927–1937) are a significant case in point. When these authorities took control of Shanghai's Chinese municipality, brought to power by the successful Third Worker's Uprising of 1927, they embarked on an ambitious campaign to remake that part of the metropolis—a campaign that Christian Henriot has analyzed skillfully in a recent study. As Henriot notes, their grand plan (which was never carried out completely, in large part simply because the Japanese invasions of the 1930s made urban survival a more pressing concern than urban renewal) included everything from the building of a completely new civic center north of the International Settlement to shifting the Huangpu's trajectory.[34]

To understand fully the meaning of this campaign, the treaty port context must be taken into account. The disparity between the more modern architecture and more sophisticated infrastructure of the foreign enclaves as opposed to that of the Chinese municipality had long been a source of concern to Shanghairen, in much the same way that similar contrasts vexed native residents of other coastal cities. The existence of the enclaves, as urban forms that could serve as models for Chinese development schemes and also trigger a form of competitive nationalism to fuel such projects, is crucial to keep in mind when considering efforts to refashion parts of Old Shanghai.

Nonetheless, as earlier chapters show, in terms of the form it took and the motivations behind it, the campaign launched in the Chinese municipality of Shanghai had a good deal in common with efforts undertaken in some cities that were *not* treaty ports. The symbolic use of references to Sun Yat-sen's plans to transform China's economic infrastructures, which Kristin Stapleton describes nicely in her discussion of Chengdu (see chapter 6), had Shanghai parallels. So, too, at a more general level, did the search for hybrid styles of architectural representation to suit a new time, which Charles Musgrove analyzes well with regard to Nanjing (see chapter 9).

It is also worth noting that focusing on Old Shanghai's treaty-port nature may blind us to some interesting parallels to be drawn between the Nationalist reforms and those that have been launched in recent decades. New Shanghai is no treaty port, but the urban renewal efforts launched by Chinese Communist authorities, which have included the dramatic buildup of Pudong, have often contained within them interesting echoes of the past. Like their Nationalist predecessors, they, too, have been fond of citing Sun Yat-sen's proposals when trying to legitimate grandiose restructurings of the city. Again like their Nationalist predecessors, they, too, have tried to reorient radically the physical and political geography of the city by building a new central district to compete with the Western Bund area—this time directly across the river from it as opposed to up to the north. Even the renaming of the city by the Communist Party's representatives has a Nationalist precursor, as the phrase "New Shanghai" was used by local Chinese officials in the late 1920s and 1930s. In contrast to the current regime, however, the Nationalists were much less successful in carrying out their dreams of remaking Shanghai. The Western Bund remained the dominant hub of activity in Old Shanghai throughout the republican era, and it was only after the Communists gained control of the entire city that its center was shifted. The first shift took place in the 1950s, when the area west of the Bund that was once the foreign racetrack and is now People's Park was constituted as the ritual center of the metropolis. Arguably, a second shift of sorts has taken place in the 1990s, with the buildup of Pudong changing the Huangpu River from a waterway that marked the eastern edge of Shanghai proper to one that now stands firmly at the city's center.

In general, then, to focus on Old Shanghai's role in the "other China" of coastal hybridity is to run the risk of overlooking the importance of the Chinese municipality, underestimating that district's similarities with non–treaty port urban centers and missing out on opportunities to compare between time periods. This kind of approach can also lead us to overstate the extent to which the cosmopolitanism of the enclaves affected even those who lived within their borders. Just as there were Shanghailanders who only rarely ate Chinese food or interacted with Chinese who were not their employees, there were many Shanghairen in the enclaves who had little contact with foreigners or imported ideas.

Eclecticism and Multiplicity

These last two approaches to the comparison issue are so close that they can be discussed together, and they can be seen as drawing in some way on all of the strategies discussed above. The key difference between them, which makes an explicit engagement with multiple Shanghais preferable to an ad hoc method of drawing connections and looking for similarities and contrasts, has to do with the now familiar problem of mistaking a part for a whole. In a nutshell, this hydra-like danger, which seems to sprout a new head as soon as one has cut off an old one, all too easily shows up yet again when an eclectic approach to comparison is taken.

Consider, for example, the way references to Shanghai, which seem straightforward enough on first glance but turn out to be somewhat problematic in its reduction of multiplicity to singularity, is worked into Liping Wang's excellent discussion of Hangzhou (see chapter 7). Wang's analysis of the role of the tourist industry in Hangzhou sensibly underscores the importance of the Zhejiang city's proximity to Old Shanghai. So many of the tourists who came to Hangzhou were Shanghairen that to overlook the connections between the two places would have been foolish.

The problem comes simply in the phrasing Wang uses to describe the phenomenon as tied to the emergence of *Shanghai's* middle class. It makes sense to say, as she does, that "a new urban middle class" was forming in the metropolis by the Huangpu early in this century, and that the same thing was happening in other treaty ports. It is not accurate, however, to move from there to speaking of this new group as *the* Shanghai middle class. Old Shanghai had at least two quite different sorts of middle classes (however that tricky word is defined), one of which was foreign and the other Chinese. Hangzhou was an important destination for some middle-class Shanghailanders in search of recreation, to be sure, but it was not one that was as significant to this group as a whole as it was to Shanghairen of the sort Wang has in mind.

The preceding may seem a picky point, but it is a useful way of illustrating that the danger of using phrases such as "Shanghai" (to refer only to parts of the city) and "residents of Shanghai" (to refer to only some types of people living there) can cut both ways. They can serve to marginalize or efface the experiences of foreigners as well as Chinese. Even simple acts (such as recreational jaunts) could and did mean very different things to different sorts of local residents, depending in part on whether they were part of one or another Old Shanghai. For example, an English language guidebook from the 1930s includes in its section on excursions to Hangzhou a discussion of a stop along the way that is seldom mentioned in comparable Chinese works. This stop is the tomb of Frederick Townsend Ward, an American adventurer who led troops against the Taipings in the 1860s. The text claims that "many Chinese" took part in the annual pilgrimages to this site promoted by a group of "American war veterans in Shanghai," but even if this rather suspect assertion is true, one imagines that the significance of this particular trip did not mean the same thing to Shanghailanders as it did to Shanghairen, and that it probably meant different things to British as opposed to American members of the former group as well.[35]

Turning to another aspect of urban life discussed in this volume, public parks of the sort examined by

Madeleine Yue Dong in her discussion of Beijing (see chapter 8), we find another example of an instance in which an eclectic approach to comparing and contrasting can lead analysts to fall into the familiar trap of mistaking the enclaves for the city as a whole. One thing that is sometimes said to have made Shanghai different from Beijing, for example, is that the treaty ports' parks, unlike those of the northern capital, were off-limits to all Chinese. Shanghai's recreation grounds have a special status in much Chinese nationalist mythology as symbols of imperialist humiliation, due to the oft-repeated but not quite accurate claim that signs banning "dogs and Chinese" from entering these parks once stood by their entrances. Robert Bickers and I have demonstrated elsewhere the reasons that the story of any such notice is better treated as urban myth than historical fact, as well as the justification for Chinese outrage at the very real existence of exclusionary policies that made certain Shanghai parks off-limits to all native residents other than servants until 1928.[36] My point here, however, is somewhat different. I am interested simply in arguing that is it very problematic to refer to "Shanghai's parks" as having been governed by a common set of exclusionary rules.

First, the only parts of the city where parks had any rules limiting access by Chinese residents were the French Concession and the International Settlement. There were never rules banning any particular group of people from using recreation grounds in the Chinese municipality. Moving to an even greater level of detail, it is not even quite right, once one gets to the republican era, to contrast in sharp terms the rules governing the parks of Old Shanghai's enclaves and the Beijing ones described in chapter 8. The problem here is that there was a good deal of variation in the exclusionary policies that existed by then, even within the foreign-run areas of the city. Up until 1928, most Chinese (other than servants attending to foreigners) were indeed denied access to the Public Garden, which stood along the Bund of the International Settlement and was Old Shanghai's oldest and best-known park. As early as the 1890s, however, at least one park located in the International Settlement was open to all Chinese who wanted to use it: the "Chinese Park," established in part to defuse the first public outcry over the Public Garden's exclusionary policies, which took the form of letters of complaint from elite Shanghairen in the 1880s. Within the French Concession, meanwhile, exclusionary rules similar to those in force for the Public Garden existed for some recreation grounds, but were slightly different in the case of others.

Once again, it may seem as though I have seized on a very picky point. It remains an important distinction that up until the late 1920s, Old Shanghai had parks from which most Chinese were excluded and Beijing did not. It is also true that exclusionary rules such as those associated with the Public Garden were not only objectionable in and of themselves, but also symbolic of many of the less-savory general features of the treaty-port system. Nevertheless, it is important to keep straight that not all of the Old Shanghais with which we need to be mindful contained spaces reserved for the use of foreigners, and that even in the enclaves, not all public areas were restricted in the same fashion. Here, yet again, we need to specify which particular Shanghai (defined in terms of physical boundaries, cultural differences, or some combination of the two) we are using as a referent.

By this point, many direct and indirect illustrations have been offered of the value of approaching Old Shanghai as a collection of fragments rather than as a coherent whole. We have seen how various fragments can be compared to good effect to different sorts of places, and have been alerted to the danger of mistakenly presenting things that are actually just individual pieces of the urban puzzle as being much more than that—indeed the whole metropolis. We have arrived at a new axiomatic statement of sorts—"There was no Shanghai, just many Shanghais"—that could be substituted, perhaps, for the old "Shanghai is not China" one. We have not looked, however, at the question of how exactly a comparative approach based on this idea can be put into practice.

The prospect of trying to answer this query is a daunting one that would require another chapter of equal length to do it justice. A very short answer can and should be offered, nonetheless, that involves once again breaking down into moderate and extreme forms an axiom relating to Old Shanghai.

The less extreme way of moving forward with the idea that "There was no Shanghai, just many Shanghais" is easy enough to describe. All that is involved is making the kinds of comparative forays described in each of the preceding sections—looking at times for ways that the metropolis by the Huangpu was most similar to cities outside of China, at times for ways it was most like other treaty ports, at times in an eclectic fashion for ways it was similar to and different from all sorts of Chinese urban centers—but clarifying at key moments the nature of the particular Old Shanghai that is serving as a referent for the comparison. All that takes this beyond the sort of eclecticism described above is a self-conscious concern with providing reminders to readers that one is aware that it is fragments that are being compared, not wholes.

This moderate approach would, I think, mark a useful step forward, but it is worth pondering where one might be led if more radical readings of the axiom were taken as starting points. For example, taking the multiplicity of Shanghais seriously could be seen as an invitation to draw more comparisons that reach beyond China and that focus on similarities and differences between this metropolis and others that were unusually fragmented or have names (as is the case with New York and Los Angeles) routinely used to stand for physical entities and social units of widely varying shapes and forms.

At times this might mean simply creating variations on interpretive strategies that have already been tried. Ever since the first nostalgic sojourners from Britain began writing about their new identity as Shanghailanders, for instance, people have been comparing Old Shanghai to London, a city whose recreation grounds served as a model for the Public Garden and whose civic celebrations provided inspiration for the 1893 Shanghai Jubilee. Taking seriously Old Shanghai's multiplicity raises new questions about this sort of comparison, by reminding us that it was only part of the city that was patterned after London. But it also presents us with new types of opportunities for drawing analogies between the urban centers associated with the Thames and with the Huangpu. After all, as the urban theorist Ruth Glass argues, one of the things that makes London special is that its name can be used to signify so many distinctively different entities. She writes that while "all large cities have multiple patterns of differentiation," this is more pronounced in some urban centers than in others. Glass continues that "in London such multiplicity has been particularly marked; for there have long been many different Londons for different purposes, and as seen from different points of view."[37]

Even sticking within the Chinese mainland, a radical reading of the multiplicity idea can present us with a provocative challenge: finding ways of making sense of Old Shanghai as a whole by getting a better handle on how its parts fit together. To take seriously the existence of many Old Shanghais is to open the possibility that some decompartmentalizing of discussions of the city is in order. This is important because, while Shanghai specialists have been willing enough to focus on the implications of the administrative subdivisions within the metropolis, we have tended to be less ready to think creatively about all the ways that different social and cultural Shanghais might be compared and contrasted.

Once issues of multiplicity are brought to the foreground, for example, the logic of asking how the roles Chinese native-place societies played in the social worlds of Shanghairen were similar to and different from those played by national clubs in the worlds of Shanghailanders and other foreigners becomes obvious. It begins to seem surprising, in fact, that specialists have tended to analyze the two types of organizations in isolation from one another. A similar point could be made about hierarchies within the Chinese and foreign communities; the position of Subeiren in the former was comparable in some ways to that of white Russians in the latter, but again, studies of the two groups have rarely paid attention to the potential value of exploring this analogy.

What all this suggests is that there are good reasons for many different kinds of China specialists to explore new strategies for moving "Beyond Shanghai," in an effort both to complicate and clarify our understanding of Chinese cities and city life. In doing so, we may need not only to find new ways to move out from the Huangpu, but also to look for new pieces of the Shanghai puzzle and explore new ways to rearrange the fragments we already have.

Chapter 13

New Chinese Cities

David Strand

In the early twentieth century, Chinese variously described the modern city, epitomized by Paris, Chicago, and Tokyo, as "contemporary," "foreign," "developed," "urbanized," "civilized," "modern" (literally, new-style), "hygienic" (as discussed by Ruth Rogaski in chapter 3), or simply "new." A 1924 article about the lower Yangzi River city of Nanjing, describing the city four years before the planners profiled by Charles Musgrove arrived (see chapter 9), depicted a place caught in "a time of transition between old and new":

> In historical and geographical terms, Nanjing was the cultural, political and military center of southeast China. Everyone knows that. . . . But now what is left of [past glories] lies in ruins. The walls of this once great and powerful city and its surroundings raise people's sense of expectation. The spirit of the age is a progressive one. The Nanjing of the past may be called "Old Nanjing" while the Nanjing we look to now is a great tree come back to life, bursting with vitality as it develops. We may call it the "New Nanjing." Still, success in smashing old habits and reforming the [urban] environment is not something that can be won with a single blow.[1]

In fact, the city detailed in the report that followed seemed to conform more to the old than the new. True, there were new institutions like modern hospitals, schools, libraries, and a municipal government that daily touted the "New Nanjing," new technologies like telephones, the telegraph, and electric lights, and new customs like team sports, newspaper reading, and tourism by motor car. But in the absence of modern plumbing, most well or river water available locally to residents was unsafe or harsh tasting, delivered by price-gouging carriers or available as boiled water *(kaishui)* from neighborhood teashops. Muddy Yangzi River water was treated with chemicals and brought into the city by rail to be sold at a premium. A waterworks had been founded but remained unbuilt because of a lack of capital. Most ordinary housing was described as constructed in a "slovenly," impermanent fashion, with "hovels built low to the ground" lining the roads—a reaction closely resembling the negative comments made by foreigners on 1860s Canton, noted by Michael Tsin in chapter 2. Cheap vernacular architecture struck modern observers as unsafe, unsanitary, and ugly rather than cost-effective and simply constructed. Customs relating to marriage, funerals, and the lunar New Year were characteristic of China's "interior" and required—or so it seemed to the modern-minded author—extravagant outlays on incense and other festival expenses. As Lee McIsaac explains in her discussion of Chongqing (see chapter 11), critical judgments against the backwardness of the interior tended to be blanket in scope, including not only the charge of "superstition," but a host of other bad habits, bad health, and general ignorance of civilized—that is, coastal and downriver—standards. Police exhortations in Nanjing to be more careful about where garbage and other waste were deposited had not changed residents' actual behavior. And yet the author Zhu Dingzhang had no doubts that, given its geographical advantages and with the addition of more rail connections, Nanjing would one day become China's New York, just as others presumed Beijing would become the country's Paris and that industrial Wuxi would rival Pittsburgh. Confidence in the power of the new and contempt for customs that needed to be "smashed" made New Nanjing as vivid to Zhu Dingzhang as Old Nanjing, where most residents still lived.

The labels "new" and "old" were fighting words. Kristin Stapleton (see chapter 6) points out that Chengdu reformer Yang Sen, although a warlord rather than an intellectual or professionally trained planner or engineer, was enamored of nearly everything new. Madeleine Yue Dong (see chapter 8) highlights the rise in Beijing and other cities in 1931 of "Destroyers of the Modern" teams that attacked anyone wearing new-style, Western clothing. As one essayist in 1920 observed:

> Everyone knows that the two words "new" and "old" are opposites and therefore everything under the sun has [one or the other] hanging out as shop-signs; everyone is always criticizing or utilizing them. Writers and reporters make them into doctrines; politicians and militarists write them on their banners.[2]

The idea of the new city carried the same promise—and provocation—as the New Policies of the post-Boxer reforms, the "new citizen" proposed by Liang Qichao, the "new movements" of the more recent May Fourth era, and the New Life Movement of the 1930s (which, ironically, encouraged attacks on modern dress). Institutions like Nanjing's modern police force and the idea that modern Chinese needed to cultivate themselves by exercising their bodies or visiting museums were outgrowths of these earlier and continuing commitments to a new China. Of course, with the exception of a few instant cities like Hong Kong, Qingdao, or the Changchun described by David Buck (see chapter 5), everything new about Chinese urban life, from tap water to chambers of commerce, was built within or alongside the old cities that were the latest expression of China's long-standing urban tradition.[3] Even Shanghai abutted and enclosed the old, walled city of pre–treaty port days. These older cities were sophisticated and flexible in the way they treated property, financed interregional trade, mounted enterprises of all sorts, and managed public affairs.[4] As a result, certain enduring urban institutions and practices—markets, bureaucracies, book publishing, business associations (as guilds), charities, and criminal organizations—could never be entirely new in China and might easily find places in Chinese cities recut and reordered to a modern mold. In some cases the old, in the form of temples and guildhalls, would be given new meaning or functions as stops on tourist itineraries or sites of political meetings. Old walls and ruins were often obstacles to development because they blocked the passage of rail lines or inhibited the expansion of commerce—but they also reminded Chinese of the greatness they were capable of and raised the "sense of expectation" of reformers even as they attacked things the old city had bequeathed. The fact that Nanjing had more extensive city walls than most European capitals was a point of pride for Zhu Dingzhang, just as the beauty of Beijing's palaces could be cited by intellectuals to counter the technical and theoretical superiority enjoyed by Western architects and planners.

Newness meant coming to grips with unprecedented technologies and institutions, from electric lights to popular elections. These novelties might be shocking in intensity, like the garish glow of nighttime Shanghai, or superficial or fleeting in application, like the fading role of municipal elections in republican politics. In some cases the "shop-sign" of newness was frankly presented as merely a new name for the old way of doing things. In sorting out its history of name changes, representatives of the Suzhou fresh pork trade explained:

> In examining our trade's guild [we note that it] was founded in Daoguang 25 [1845] as the "Three Righteousness Guild." Afterwards, during the Tongzhi reign [1862–1875] the name was changed to the "Carefully Attend to Business Guild," which continued [unaltered] into the Republic—because any change would be the same as our former system—until reorganization in 1930 [on orders from the Nationalist government] as the "Wu County United Fresh Pork Association." However, although "guild" and "association" are different titles, the meaning is the same: to put right practices injurious to our trade.[5]

These pork butchers from Suzhou may have protested too much on behalf of continuity of practice behind changing names. Government-induced name changes sometimes included significant reorganization of guilds to make them more democratic in procedure and transparent in operations.[6] The panorama of such signs along streets and avenues advertised the new Chinese city as coming attraction and work in process. Meanwhile, the ability of established interests to restrict change to the outer realm of names and titles irritated reformers who wanted deeper levels of compliance and real institutional transformation. Many of the chapters in this volume suggest the double-edged nature of symbolic structures, name changes, advertising, and propaganda campaigns. New signs mark old structures and habits for reform and demolition. They signal the direction change is supposed to take. But if, after a period of time, old structures and social practices remain intact and the banners, slogans, and blueprints fade or are forgotten, the leverage the new has against the old is lost, or worse, is remembered as a sign of powerlessness and incoherence.

The proportions of the new, old, pseudo-new, and renewed—the new imbued with older habits, values, and interests—varied from city to city and neighborhood to neighborhood. Coastal cities like Shanghai and Canton boasted whole modern districts and quarters. Parts of Tianjin, as Rogaski observes, took on the concentrated, chock-a-block appearance of a treaty port "world-as-exhibition." Provincial cities were characterized by the spot development of an exhibition hall here and a paved road there that often, however, added up to impressive ensembles of modern institutions. Wartime investment and construction brought Chongqing a "tiny modern enclave" in the Upper City section of the town. Most provincial capitals had complements of public utilities, factories, modern educational institutions, and hospitals.[7] Smaller towns might have cigarette advertisements painted on walls and the odd store selling foreign goods or Shanghai newspapers. As befit an urban world in transition, what a city was in some essential sense really depended on where one looked, at whom, and for how long. Just as 1924 Nanjing, from a certain, carefully chosen angle, could look modern and Western, Shanghai "away from Nanjing Road" could appear old and Chinese.[8]

Picturing Modernity

Another word for "modern" or "new" in early twentieth century China was "Shanghai." No Chinese city with progressive or modern aspirations or institutions could ever really escape the influence of Shanghai, even when those charged with developing a new Nanjing or Canton consciously sought their own, alternative model. Observers saw Nanjing Road wherever modern stores lined up along paved and widened streets. This was true of Chengdu, where militarist Yang Sen's Chunxi Road, with its "well-ordered and bustling" appearance, "strangely resembled Shanghai's Nanjing Road," and of even more remote Lanzhou, with silk, cloth, and foreign goods stores "by and large patterned on Shanghai department stores."[9] Similarly, as Tsin points out, the Canton Bund was regarded by visitors as a "replica" of Nanjing Road. These pictures of development, found in magazines and advertisements or carried in the minds of travelers, illustrated and underlined what was written or spoken about topics such as urban planning, new forms of architecture, or modern transportation. Images also assumed concrete form in large numbers of demonstration projects inspired by what had already taken place on the coast. In this way, the "world-as-exhibition" on display in cities like Tianjin moved inland along waterways and rail lines.

Of course, the picture cities offered to journalists, tourists, other visitors and residents on any given day might vary considerably. Because of the relative safety city walls still afforded, urban centers periodically filled, as they had in past eras of turmoil, with rural refugees fleeing war and natural disaster.[10] The severed heads Yang Sen left hanging on the streets of Chengdu certainly rivaled in impact other demonstration projects he sponsored and suggested how atavism and modernism might inhabit the same urban space. Dead bodies on the streets of wartime Chongqing disturbed refugees hoping to find something better at the end of their westward trek than a "capital" city seemingly indifferent to the sight of the unattended corpses of Chinese citizens. Such jarring and perplexing juxtapositions of old and new and the "well-ordered" and the chaotic encouraged the quest for a new urban order characteristic of cities that both functioned efficiently and looked, smelled, and sounded right.

Confucian ideas of order had in the past stimulated urban reform. In the 1870s in Hankou, merchant Fan Chengyun cleaned up a derelict cemetery after commenting that "when the heavy rains come and drainage is stopped up, the bones of the dead become mired in water and excrement. It is worse than throwing corpses into a ditch."[11] Such scenes violated conventions of decorum and ritual propriety, and Fan Chengyun responded thoughtfully but viscerally. Bad smells and disturbing scenes run through critical writing on the republican Chinese city. Excrement, which once had its accepted place in cities never very far from an agricultural society that valued human waste as fertilizer, now became a sign of disease and uncivilized life.[12] In urban theory and commentary advanced in China in the 1920s, notions of visual, aural, and olfactory order assumed new proportions as an "urban aesthetic" *(dushimei)* mandating cities with properly ordered streets, modern public architecture (the list might include city hall, public lecture rooms, schools, libraries, and theaters), planned markets and commercial centers, parks and leisure areas, tree-lined avenues, and a commitment to "harmonizing the sights and sounds" of city life.[13] Garden City plans had particular appeal as means of beautifying a gritty metropolis like Shanghai, annexing picturesque suburban tourist enclaves to metropolitan Beiping, adding an avant-garde edge to the social reforms in Chengdu described by Stapleton, taking advantage of the smaller scale of inland cities like Lanzhou to steal a march on the treaty ports, and including green space in a planned city like Japanese Changchun.[14]

As Rogaski shows for Tianjin in her discussion of the emergence of "hygienic modernity" as a new standard for city life, and as other chapters document as well, aesthetic concerns were joined to fears that disordered cities produce disease and potentially fatal contamination. Instead of restoring decayed urban spaces to conditions dictated by past standards, reformers imagined cities in which the disordered past and present were removed in favor of a new model of order, progress, and cleanliness. In some cases aesthetic concerns signified superficiality rather than a real commitment to change. McIsaac notes how Nationalist worries about "appearances" led to a quick clearing of beggars and prostitutes from the streets of Chongqing but left the underlying causes of poverty and social distress untouched. Other reformers and planners demanded change in depth: new sanitation systems and other expensive infrastructure projects as well as campaigns to change the behavior of residents in order to complete the picture of a city without beggars or noxious waste implied.

Because of its size, location, and peculiar foreign pattern of settlement and control, Shanghai could be pictured or modeled but never be exactly replicated. Nor could Shanghai achieve unquestioned dominance of other cities. No city in China held a position of primacy as Paris did in France or Tokyo in Japan. For a time, Beijing and Shanghai split functions as political and economic centers, but the political decline of Beijing in the 1910s and 1920s was not effectively exploited by Shanghai. The mixed Chinese and foreign nature of Shanghai prevented it from becoming either China's Paris—a fusion of administrative and economic power—or China's Calcutta—headquarters of unchallenged colonial rule. The claims of rival treaty ports like Canton and Tianjin (the "ultimate treaty port" in Rogaski's words) and the many smaller cities and towns left as a legacy of imperial administration and long-standing regional economic development also played roles in limiting Shanghai's influence. As Brett Sheehan's account of the banking industry demonstrates (see chapter 4), powerful groups like China's financial elite were mobile and flexible enough to avoid association with any one city like Shanghai. The profits and protection that issued from intercity and "supralocal" interactions militated against relying on one center alone. In addition, smaller provincial and prefectural capitals had their own walls and sense of prestige and centrality. While Shanghai dominated imports and exports, as much as 80 percent of China's national product was still produced and marketed outside Shanghai.[15] No city needed to fear being wholly engulfed by Shanghai's economic power, especially if it appropriated Shanghai-style development for its own purposes.

Given the controversy attending the role of foreign power in Shanghai and the bad habits and evil practices attributed to the city, some cities took pride in the fact that they were *not* Shanghai. The growth of Lanzhou as a rear-area supply and transport center in the late 1930s and 1940s emboldened reformers there to claim the superiority of unspoiled, more reasonably scaled cities of the interior compared to "orphaned" and "poisoned" Shanghai.[16] Even when Shanghai's superior qualities were recognized outside the coast, motivations in bringing Shanghai into the local picture might be more complex than promoting Shanghai's interests. As McIsaac observes, the Nationalist regime relied on public awareness of Shanghai standards to keep Chongqing in its place as a backwater. Despite its upriver location and daunting physical challenges as a "mountain city" of steep inclines, Chongqing, like many other provincial cities, had demonstrated a potential for development in a series of modest modernization projects since the 1920s. But none of this provincial effort added up to much in the eyes of downriver refugees and officials who hoped to return soon to the coast. When the Nationalists planted their propaganda banner of New China in Chongqing, they found in Old Chongqing perversely convenient, local color for their national efforts.

A Chinese urban perspective emerged not from Shanghai alone but from a range of cities drawn together rhetorically and also by actual improvements in communications. People, goods, and ideas moved ever more quickly even as war and other disasters periodically disrupted communications and reextended distances measured by the length of time it took to move from point to point. When distances shrank, they often did so dramatically. Liping Wang notes that the Hangzhou-Shanghai journey dropped from two days by boat to three and one-half hours by train (see chapter 7). And it was not simply a matter of fewer hours or days in transit but the medium of travel itself that made the difference. The bankers studied by Sheehan seem to have been as at home on the train as at any other place where they transacted their business. Their urban—but not exclusively Shanghai or Tianjin—identity reflected the intercity pattern of their professional lives. The circuits made by these new professionals inscribed their identities as Chinese banker, reporter, and engineer within a new, unified country as surely as nationalist movements, national armies, or a standardized currency did.

Individual cities took on new dimensions or housed new components, but urban China as a system of modular units and connecting elements was also new. Urban China in composition was greater than the sum of Shanghai, Nanjing, Canton, and a host of other cities and towns, great and small. The material basis of this system is still a matter of debate. Geographer Clifton Pannell argues that China did not have a "truly national urban system" in the first half of the century.[17] But the urban China planned and presumed by local and national elites and their followers and consumers strained at these material limitations. For example, China's interurban rail system encompassed both the track and trains currently running and a much larger expanse of lines planned but yet to be laid. National leader Sun Yat-sen was famous for his grand visions of railway development. But the local applications of such plans were also conventionally included in newspaper and gazetteer articles on cities like Nanjing or Lanzhou, predicated on the hope that what had been projected and surveyed would eventually be completed.

Partly as result, the objective facts of urban change were not always a reliable guide to how or why a city was seen or imagined in a particular way. The context of modernity could be broadly cultural and conditioned by forces like tourism and commerce, or more narrowly drawn to fit the agendas of parties, regimes, and other political agents seeking to use cities to build a base of support or make a rhetorical point. Issues of primacy and importance could be contested. In 1924, a month after Zhu Dingzhang pronounced Nanjing to be "bursting with vitality," a more skeptical visitor who "drifted in" found a rather different city: "Nanjing is a very strange place. Everyone calls it the cultural hub of the southeast, to the point that municipal government, democratic rule . . . even warlords are made models. Those who come from the interior to study it crowd in and fill the streets."[18] But this reporter found little to cheer about in a city where militarists were praised as "benevolent" for not shooting students, intellectuals uncritically "worshiped" American-style, Christian education, the only women with short hair were nonnatives and female students were of the "Miss and wife-style," and the factory-poor economy invited comparison with European cities prior to the eighteenth century. Out of such disagreements over whether or not a city was progressive or backward emerged the notion of the city as model to be emulated or criticized. Nanjing's claims to larger significance as a city were helped along by the Nationalist commitment to make it the country's capital. But, reflecting the unsettled nature of urban China, such claims did not go unchallenged. A city like Wuhan, as Stephen MacKinnon points out (see chapter 10), might lack physical coherence in the absence of a yet-to-be-built bridge over the Yangzi River, and fail to achieve preeminence over Shanghai in areas like industrial production. But it had historical credentials as a revolutionary site that could be parlayed into a self-image among some sojourners and residents as a "liberal democratic and anti-imperialist capital of new China." Wuhan's brief experience in 1938 as home to the Nationalist regime in flight, Chongqing's role as wartime capital, and Changchun's status as "New Capital" of Japan's Manchukuo showed how quickly a new, paramount position could be won and lost. Loyang, Xi'an, Guangzhou, and Yan'an also had their moments of glory or infamy in that regard as putative center of regime or counterregime.[19] Meanwhile, as Dong indicates, facing the loss of Beijing's status as capital, Beiping municipal leaders, like their counterparts in Hangzhou, sought to recast the city as cultural and tourist center. Particular Chinese cities had long been endowed with reputations for beauty, or trouble, or riches. Now urban leaders aggressively pursued image as a form of symbolic capital convertible, they hoped, to tourist dollars, private investment, budgetary assistance, and national importance in politics and culture.

Critics and Boosters

One reason journalists, urban planners, and others could see, on the basis of very little evidence, new cities in the midst of the old—or a national capital in a provincial town—was that they looked at urban China through the lens of national and international urbanism. Many reformers on the inside of the Chinese urban system, like the Japanese planners discussed by Buck, saw their cities from the outside, often worrying out loud about what foreigners would think about the pace and nature of progress toward internationally accepted standards. As Stapleton notes, when late Qing reformers imagined making Chengdu a "civilized" city, their model was Tokyo, even as they built avenues that looked like Shanghai's. In some instances the audience for reform and renewal projects might be more foreign than Chinese. Planning documents of the kind cited by Dong and Rogaski tended to place Chinese urban life in the context of "all cities in the civilized world" and demanded the introduction of the "civilized living" available abroad. International standards put pressure on Chinese to add what seemed essential to modern life. If you were to have a modern capital or city or town, you needed a certain ensemble of devices like streetcars, a waterworks, and public parks. These strongly felt needs made the Chinese city a consumer of new products and systems not so different from the West Lake tourist described by Wang who was instructed by new guidebooks to carry a watch, a telescope, and (if possible) a camera on his or her excursion. Excursions into the future of Chinese urbanism likewise demanded preparation and the proper equipment. As it happened, the relative weakness of democratic institutions meant that planners had the luxury of paying more attention to non-Chinese and nonlocal constituencies. Nanjing needed purer water because the people would benefit (although not necessarily the water carriers and teashops), the waterworks would make money (if it could persuade clients to pay their bills), reformers could check that item off their list (if they stayed in the city long enough to see the project through), and foreigners would grant the imprimatur of modern city (unless the project failed to meet French, American, British, or Japanese standards).

As the presence of these several constituencies for urban reform suggests, cities are rarely designed and maintained just for themselves and their own residents. Nanjing was being rebuilt, as Musgrove shows, not mainly for the people of Nanjing, but for a regime that claimed to represent the whole Chinese people before a global audience. Yang Sen was free to reform Chengdu in part because he had revenue sources outside the city and could ignore complaints from moneyed and propertied groups about some of his projects, like street widening. Changchun was first of all a Japanese imperial beachhead, secondarily a home for expatriate Japanese, and, much lower on a list of priorities, a city for Chinese residents. Authorities in wartime Chongqing favored the needs of downriver newcomers over longtime, and long-suffering, natives. At the same time, the city as combination of abstract longing for progress and specific constructions of mortar, brick, and cement naturally attracted the attention of those in closest proximity. One beneficiary of this urban optic, who mediated between larger systems and the particulars of urban life, was the city booster who strove to create the new Nanjing, Canton, or Chengdu on the site of the old.

The pattern of modern urban diffusion that resulted was complicated and not simply a matter of ordered descent down the urban hierarchy or out from coastal Shanghai. A vision or model glimpsed or studied in Beijing or Shanghai could skip rather wildly out to a remote or otherwise unlikely community because such a place was the reformer's hometown. Qin Shao's recent study of the lower Yangzi town of Nantong demonstrates how the "world-as-exhibition" effect could be felt anywhere sufficient leadership and resources could be mustered.[20] With the guidance of hometown native Zhang Jian, the small city of Nantong acquired an impressive array of integrated, modern institutions ranging from factories and banks to a library and movie company. Patterns of urban reform were shaped by personal networks and connections that made the flow of ideas and resources idiosyncratic. In other cases, huge, often brutal, forces moved entire populations and governments from city to city, as happened in the great wartime westward migration. As MacKinnon shows for Wuhan, the influx in 1938 of printing machinery and Shanghai artists and intellectuals in flight, as well as international attention as the "Madrid" of China, suddenly supercharged the political and intellectual atmosphere of the city. Cities were not simply levels in an administrative hierarchy or nodes of exchange in regional or national markets, but points on a succession of overlays cut and applied by itinerant regimes, political exiles, or reformers returning home. Even when brute power was applied in systematic fashion, as in the creation of a Japanese imperial city on the site of Chinese Changchun, the pattern of global influences led not only to the expected construction of a great central plaza, but also to the surprising addition of houses and apartments in the style of Frank Lloyd Wright.

In the 1930s, the Communists made their famous extra-urban "long march," which avoided major cities and the modern armies based there. Later in the same decade the Nationalists made an urban long march by boat, rail, foot, and airplane as they retreated from river town to river town until they reached Chongqing. In the 1920s, political Beijing in the person of members of defunct parliaments, clerks, and other politicos had taken the train south, while political Canton as cadres and soldiers fought its way north. Transregional and transurban movements carried radical Cantonese printers north to Beijing, reformist officials to China's far west, leftist intellectuals to Wuhan, and educators to Kunming. As Sheehan shows for bankers as a new professional group, some city residents managed highly complicated lives that were both fixed to particular places, like a bank headquarters or branch, and, at the same time, also in transit through "supralocal urban systems" that sent cash, favors, contracts, and the bankers themselves moving as fast as telegraph, post, and train could carry them. Capital and the professionals who managed China's money could "march" too, when political and military circumstances dictated. While not a completed urban system in a geographer's sense of the term, the network of urban places involved in these transfers was dynamic by dint of its very derangement and unpredictability: urban China as part catch-basin for volatile elements ranging from famine refugees to reformers and investors, and part centrifuge separating and fostering local variations and models.

While reformers like Zhu Dingzhang may have imagined their cities and projects in arborescent terms as growing trees with deep roots, a solid trunk, and an umbrella-like presence, their genesis often had more in common with rhizome-like actions that wander far afield, suffer breaks, and reestablish themselves in more favorable soil.[21] Provincialism benefited from these decentered and multicentered developments and became progressive in ways that transcended any notion of simply copying the metropolitan center. In a period without such a center, this systemic capacity helped sustain the modernization of cities. As Tsin notes, traditional Chinese urbanism had always been more relaxed about how or whether provincial capitals followed norms of planning set in the capital. "Provincial" might have meant less grand, but still walled and centered and, by definition, more flexible in adapting urban form to local practice. As the builders of the modern city sought both a fullness of resources to tap and room to build in, the provinces exerted an attractive power and offered spaces to exploit and fill. As Stapleton shows for the case of Chengdu, provincial reputations for backwardness sometimes concealed significant interest in urban reform and renewal. As MacKinnon observes, successors to late Qing reformers in 1920s Hankou such as merchants Liu Xinsheng and Cai Fuqing played key roles in rebuilding their city as a modern business center.

Depending on the kind of connections local or provincial boosters had with colleagues and compatriots in other cities, provincial or local development could connect to higher and broader realms of commerce, planning, and consciousness. As Sheehan's study of bankers suggests, one current in this expansion was a cosmopolitan flare for bringing people, wealth, and power together to invest financial, cultural, and political assets in projects that spanned two or several cities. The preeminent "Tianjin Banker," Zhou Zuomin, hailed from Jiangsu and lived in Beijing. So positioned, he could think and act locally or nationally (or internationally) as circumstances required. The construction of city-based banking empires proceeded both by sinking roots in local bases and retaining the suppleness and flexibility associated with networks and informal connections. Networking of this kind, a characteristic feature of Chinese urbanism, could give localism a cosmopolitan face and turn a banker into a politician.

While many local boosters were private entrepreneurs, limits on the spread of industrialism meant construction associated with new cities would usually be carried out by public officials (although often with private money). Tsin's chapter shows how a combination of zeal for comprehensive, future-oriented planning and an appreciation of the potential power represented by a new ordering of urban space and function energized the careers of public administrators like Canton's Sun Fo. The governmental or administrative new city, staffed by a new class of idealistic or opportunistic officials, was often easier to begin developing than industrial cities funded by large amounts of private capital. Where development was not possible on any significant scale, officials made up for a lack of construction with regulatory zeal, attempting to force small but symbolic changes, from wooden to porcelain tubs in bathhouses (Chengdu) or from dirty to clean and paved streets (practically everywhere). This is one reason the migration of industrial China to the interior during the war, with the cooperation of the government, was important as a forced spring of industrial development for the interior. While many of these firms and industries moved back to the coast after 1945, industrialism and government planning had been fatefully joined in the context of urban development. The roots of state socialism as a pervasive and accepted strategy after 1949 may be found in the more uniform application of state-sponsored urban development in the republican period.

The move toward state-directed and public management of the city was hardly universal or invariably effective. For one thing, contentious and convoluted political conditions tended to exhaust government reformers. The disordered nature of state power in treaty ports like Tianjin or Shanghai during this period made private solutions to public problems often quite feasible, partly because private capital was available for enterprises like water delivery and partly because demand for public services was highly individuated and skewed toward those who could afford to pay. Such privatization schemes stirred some opposition. That differential delivery of public services did not provoke greater resistance and outrage was not only a measure of governmental decay, but also a sign of the weakness of urban communities. In fact, under these circumstances, the kind of stable political order provided by Japanese occupation and puppet forces after the initial wave of fighting, massacre, and disorder permitted relatively steady urban development.[22] As Buck's discussion of Changchun shows, the imposition of this kind of external order could also sponsor utopian projects of impressive scope.

The Particulars of Material Culture

Privatization is less surprising as an option in contexts where market and commercial arrangements already shape individual and collective actions. In China, strong commercial traditions made the market a widespread alternative to reliance on the state or acceptance of subsistence agriculture.[23] Chinese traditions of luxury consumption and connoisseurship made the possession of certain things like rocks from Lake Tai or a ceramic pillow from a particular kiln a matter of desire and pride.[24] In his study of Ming dynasty elite material culture, Craig Clunas is careful to draw a distinction between the highly developed patterns of elite consumption he finds for the lower, urbanized Yangzi region and the "consumer society" of the future.[25] That future was beginning to arrive in Chinese cities of the early twentieth century. In some cases the products—like toothbrushes and cigarettes—were entirely new. In others, like health tonics with claims of Western provenance and contents filled with Chinese herbal medicine, the novelty was in the advertising and the mentalities that supported scientific claims for familiar products.[26]

In certain cases, as in the remodeling of gardens and palace precincts to form Beijing's Central Park, a broader desire to partake in late imperial elite culture was the mainspring behind a hybrid of teahouses, promenades, and entertainments. As Dong indicates, the first visitors to Central Park in 1914 were keen to walk where the Son of Heaven had strolled. Elite (not just Western or folk) styles of leisure were thus made available to a wider audience of consumers who now were able to sip tea in elegant gardens and gaze at objects and scenes once reserved for emperors and those who could afford to share in literati culture. Connoisseurship broadened to consumerism. Wang shows how a similar, even more comprehensive, conversion took place as Hangzhou became a modern tourist site. Showcasing the "ancient" scenic wonders of West Lake, this new Hangzhou emerged in reaction to nearby Shanghai's unassailable industrial modernity and its market for Hangzhou as a cultural commodity. If the nature of what was to be acquired changed radically both in terms of type of products and the size of the market, the practice of confirming cultural values through material possessions and purchased experiences was not without precedent. Hangzhou's retrograde-sounding claim that "we have everything but we don't produce anything" signaled a forward and outward-looking attentiveness to national and international markets even as the city returned to a partly fictionalized past. In the context of decentered development and pervasive commercialization, the particulars of urban life that really mattered were less likely to be monuments or government regulations than commodities or commodified experience. Commerce as a pervasive force both separated urban Chinese on the basis of class and unified population in the pursuit of commodities as simple but elusive as drinkable water and as subtle, and equally elusive, as a whole new way of life.

The impact of new institutions was heightened by the placement and architectural style of the buildings that housed factories, chambers of commerce, department stores, and libraries. Building on the outskirts of the city, along newly developed waterfronts, or in areas flattened or emptied by war or revolution, publishing houses, public utilities, and government buildings took on monumental significance. Some cities, like the Hankou described in MacKinnon's chapter, were accustomed to cycles of "destruction and renewal" that made rethinking patterns of urban development—as a prelude to rebuilding in the aftermath of flood or fire—a natural turn. Following a practical logic, new construction often flowed into areas where preexisting interests suddenly weakened or disappeared. An outstanding example mentioned in Wang's chapter on Hangzhou and Stapleton's on Chengdu was the Manchu garrison districts that became the sites of new development. In these cases, urban renewal meant Manchu removal. In Hangzhou, not only was the old banner area cleared for new construction, but the wall separating the city from West Lake was taken down. As Wang notes, this combination of destruction and construction opened up new vistas and new sites for development for Hangzhou as a tourist city. An early example of urban renewal in Chongqing exploited an old cemetery outside a city gate. As Rogaski indicates in her chapter on Tianjin, the city waterworks was located at a site that had undergone progressive decay from elegant mansion to foreign troop barracks, making what had been built up and privileged an empty space free for new construction. In Musgrove's chapter we find Nanjing's relative emptiness as a vast, walled city housing a shrunken, post-imperial mix of ruin and settlement stimulating planners who saw a blank canvas for their architectural drawings and few established interests to challenge their monumental projects. Perhaps the blankest canvas of all emerged from the kind of railway development Buck discusses, where the geometry of rail systems permitted picking new points to become cities that then suddenly unfold from train stations. Of course, in the case of Changchun, what seemed empty to Japanese planners progressively filled with Chinese resentment at the taking of national territory—in the Chinese case, an act of geographic imagination that transcended urban and rural distinctions.

Resistance and Progress

Cities also resisted change. They were not infinitely plastic under the prod and push of planners, developers, and regulators, partly because the pressure was often weaker than the original conception called for, but also because of the inertial force of existing property rights and other mentalities and customs. Resistance was rooted in various forces: habits of doing without government, suspicions that projects were flawed or fraudulent, and wariness about costs.[27] No matter how much reformers talked about or demanded a new society or a new citizenry, wishing could not make it immediately so, and the small things planners were able to do could only change the margins of people's lives. There were always fewer citizens than residents and less "society" than people. But as Tsin's account of the rise of new thinking about Chinese cities as integral administrative and social entities underlines, it is also remarkable how few citizens were necessary to justify modern politics and how little society was needed to provoke social policy. In the case of Tianjin, the idea of public health and a health interest presumed for all residents encouraged the Bureau of Hygiene discussed by Rogaski to close polluting factories even in the face of strenuous resistance.

As Tsin shows for Canton, municipal reformers were actively engaged in creating a new society of residents whose social needs and problems would be addressed by a proliferating set of government service organizations. In some cases gestures were revealing of things to come. Giving a piece of toilet paper to poor women in Chengdu or passport savings to Feng Yuxiang's troops suggests a horizon later reached by Mao's big state and Deng's big market economy. Beijing Legation Quarter buildings breaking imperial bans against any structure higher than the throne room at the center of the Forbidden City likewise signaled impending change long before the full weight of new cityscapes and Sino-foreign hybrids emerged to dominate the city. Such changes also could provoke a modern defense of traditional aesthetic values, as Dong discusses in her account of Beijing as planned "cultural city." Signs of change might appear in the details of dress or personal style or conversation: the distinctive haircut of a modern woman or her distinctive opinions. Modernity and novelty were in this sense portable. "Modern women from the south" might appear at a temple festival in the remote northwest. Yang Sen's many wives (old) in short hair (new) and on bicycles (new) circulated through Chengdu around more stolid signs of an enduring past.

Urban Hybrids

Binary conceptions of new and old, while highlighting the real power of both modernity and tradition, also mask widespread collaboration and accommodation. A paved road was new in the kind of traffic it could bear and the speed it made possible. But the path it ran along and many of the vehicles that continued to use it had been familiar for centuries. A chamber of commerce was new in its ability to aggregate business interests to higher levels and promote new economic and political ideas. As a 1909 Shanghai chamber of commerce manifesto declared in advocating an all-China business association: "When merchant and merchant come together the result is a chamber of commerce. . . . [I]f chamber and chamber unite and form a Grand Chamber, the degree of its effectiveness will increase one hundred-fold."[28] But the enterprises, trades, and guilds that composed the chambers and the patterns of elite interaction were built solidly on a foundation of provincial and local ties and late imperial fortunes and business practices. This was not a matter of new technologies and institutions being dynamic and the old being stagnant. Existing networks and organizations had a large capacity for what Bryna Goodman, in her study of Shanghai provincial associations, has termed "expansiveness."[29] Goodman describes how the introduction and dissemination of crucial imports like print lithography in Shanghai hinged on the entrepreneurial and investment capacities of rival groups of Ningbo and Cantonese sojourners. Such examples show how the "prospects of new technological implants depended on their successful grafting onto specific native-place networks."[30] When new things grew it was often because they had harnessed or simply boarded an older and still dynamic vehicle. As the undercapitalized waterworks in Nanjing in the early 1920s suggests, the new often was as problematical as the old. Influence on the part of new systems was often purchased at the cost of accommodation, as was the case in the expansion of the Tianjin waterworks, which both laid pipe to neighborhood hydrants and employed manual laborers and contracted with water shops to carry and sell the water to customers. Hybrids that mixed modern technologies and organizations with existing commercial networks and patterns of employment often were stronger than unadapted, "purer" institutions.

Place and Time

Newly designed or reformed Chinese cities, like post-1928 Nanjing, were meant to reshape urban forms and human behavior to conform to national and international agendas. Ironically, one of the most powerful examples of this kind of intentional urbanism was Changchun's designation as the "New Capital" of Japanese Manchukuo, a city built to deny Chinese national claims and consolidate Japan's national empire on the Chinese mainland. As Buck notes, citing a recent book by James Scott, this kind of willful, visionary, and often reckless project typifies the global phenomenon of "high modernism" in which state power seeks to transform in both stark and subtle ways physical and human landscapes. The specific use of urban planning to accomplish larger collective goals involves what James Holston has termed "developmental inversion": reversing the notion of the city as the product of existing social forces by building cities that instead change society by shocking residents out of older habits and conventions.[31] Certainly this was what the planners and reformers Dong identifies hoped to accomplish on a smaller scale with the construction of new parks in Beijing. But it was also the case that citizenship might take hold in improvised settings like Tiananmen "square" rather than in parks designed for the purpose of civic education.[32] A broad front of public expansiveness in urban life made it possible and necessary for more people to appear in public as students, shoppers, tourists, and commuters. This diffuse "publicness" in turn provided the context for more focused moments like Tiananmen demonstrations.

Certain sites within cities, like private gardens opened for public events, parks and squares, public libraries, movie theaters, and train stations, held strategic importance beyond their size and physical prominence because they connected the here and now of city life to larger events of the past, future, and present, and to more distant places in China and abroad. One might go to a Beijing teahouse or a Hangzhou temple in a mood of nostalgia and step back into the Qing or Tang.[33] Or one could step into the future in a lecture hall or YMCA reading room. Urban residents could also experience a new, spatially expanded present shared by compatriots throughout China by joining a parade or demonstration that was nationwide in scope. The May Thirtieth Movement of 1925 spread from its point of origin and the shootings of Chinese by foreign-led police in Shanghai to six hundred cities and towns in China over a period of hours, days, and weeks.[34] During moments like these, the news from Shanghai or Beijing or Canton unified the nation through the telegraphic and newspaper-carrying circuitry of interurban communication. These largely urban-based developments were part of a more general nineteenth- and twentieth-century "tendency to bring places together in space at a single time" through the media of modern communications.[35] While it still took weeks or months to bring news to remote parts of China, much of urban China was now separated only by the minutes it took to send and receive a telegram or the hours it took for trains bearing newspapers and travelers to reach nearby cities. The process of unification could highlight differences but also lead to a greater and overarching homogeneity as what happened in different parts of the country was imagined as happening in and to "China." A propaganda poster used in central China during the Nationalist's Northern Expedition of 1926–1928 showed a drawing of bombs bursting over the walls of the distant upper Yangzi River town of Wan County, along with the caption: "The British [gunboats] killed 2,200 of our compatriots with their cannon blasts in Wan County locality. The Beijing government has not only said nothing. It still colludes with the British. How can the Northern Expedition not overthrow this traitorous regime?!"[36] Any place—

either central or remote—could now stand for the larger question of Chinese sovereignty and represent the connection between local affairs and the new, militant China. Perhaps this is why, in part, the building of national monuments in places as diverse as Chongqing and Beijing failed. A new, politically charged consciousness of China as a place embattled in time made the roll of place-names—largely cities and urban sites—and associated dates of triumphs and atrocities sufficient to serve the same commemorative purpose.

Not everyone was pleased with the results of these expanded and tightened interconnections. An editorialist in Beijing in 1924 lamented:

> China's boundaries are vast, communications organs are incomplete, and trade back and forth is extremely inconvenient. However, socially there often develops a kind of phenomenon in which in a moment something will spread from place A to place B. And then, in the blink of an eye, it spreads over the whole country, almost like a kind of plague. . . . For example, Beijing often has student upheavals and then the provinces respond like an echo. School A attacks its president and School B assaults its teachers and then the whole body of teachers and students is accusing each other and fighting for power.[37]

Nationalists in China, anticipating Benedict Anderson's more recent insights into the role of mass communications in imagining the nation-state, understood the relationship between nation-spanning institutions, networks and movements, and nationalism as a shared emotion. In this vein the writer He Luzhi argued:

> In an incompletely evolved social organization [like republican China], one part of society is destroyed and the other parts don't feel it, like China losing four provinces in the northeast and many officials and people still undisturbed. This is because our social evolution has not reached the stage of national social organization. . . . In a modern, organized nation, there are elections so that people participate in politics, a free press to disseminate accurate news, various kinds of associations to combine the feelings of a part of the people [into a whole], and the means of communication necessary so that the life of the whole nation is more and more intimately connected.[38]

The northeast provinces, or Wan County, or any other place served the purpose of national mobilization as long as the connections were there to spread the news and propaganda. The Beijing editorialist's "plague" syndrome made such associations and interactions possible and formed the essence of He Luzhi's "living body" and healthy "nervous system."[39] Mechanical and organic images of the nation intermingled as Chinese worked out the meaning and implications of overlapping and interconnected new selves, new cities, and a new nation. For example, Yang Sen's drive in Chengdu to foster physically fit and spiritually sound citizens revealed a powerful faith in health as a necessary property of individuals, communities, and the nation that also could be expressed in clean streets, sanitary sewers, immunizations, and physical education programs.

This new, more productive, and healthier nation was as "incompletely evolved" as China's new cities. But municipal governments—elected or not—chambers of commerce and student federations, local and national newspapers and magazines, and the infrastructure of rail connection, all-weather roads, and telegraph lines based in cities were helping to spur the kind of feelings and ideas nationalists wanted to advance. As Tsin points out, a key difference between older and newer forms of Chinese urbanism was the intentionally integrative and homogenizing nature of the latter. Twentieth-century Chinese cities modeled and distributed a kind of national integration that rural dwellers eventually received as rusticated propaganda themes and methods originally developed in the cities.[40]

Ironically, self-promotion by cities of their distinctive qualities as models and martyrs ultimately worked to reduce differences among cities and underline their common modernity and Chineseness. This interplay between city space and local, national, and global histories could make something as elusive and abstract as the "nation" suddenly visible in a city square among protesters and also could erase long-standing local memories of what was once real and vivid. As Wang shows, near-complete erasure was the fate of once-thriving City-God Hill in Hangzhou as the rise of West Lake reoriented the city away from past commercial and religious connections to the surrounding countryside. A city could also be overtaken by events and transformed into player on a larger national and global stage—and so, for those seized by the historic significance of Nationalist China's stand against the Japanese on a world stage, Wuhan for a few weeks ceased being China's Chicago and became instead an Asian Madrid. A Chongqing crowded with refugees from all over China and under bombardment from the Japanese could serve as a "microcosm of the nation." The image of a "mountain city" rising up from the turbulent Yangzi River under attack by enemy warplanes made that part of urban China represent the entire country as a beleaguered but unvanquished citadel. As many urbanites were well aware, urban China was not the entire country—but cities were well placed and well equipped to exercise a national imagination. How powerful that exercise was depended on circumstances and the resources invested. In Chongqing, an unwillingness to spend heavily on infrastructure and government buildings left nationalism deployed in shop-sign format as a medley of national symbols of dubious persuasiveness. On a smaller scale, Beijing's Jingzhao Park, with its maps of the world, biographies of great men, and facilities for physical and moral uplift, likewise failed to mount a convincing display of symbols and standards. However, even these incomplete gestures suggested the dimensions of future cities and regimes that were better able to make the pattern of urban life a template for a new society and polity.

The relationship between the city and the nation was accordingly complex. Chinese advocates for the city declared that in the evolutionary scheme of things, "cities are the foundation of the nation,"[41] but cities also benefited from national disorders as safe havens for the flight of people and capital. They could play Venice to the Byzantium-like hulk of decayed and disordered China. Cities were big enough to generate resources necessary for significant projects but smaller than regions, or the nation itself, and therefore excused from the challenge of defending borders or doing something about the rural crisis beyond offering poor shelter to desperate villagers in the suburban shantytowns described by MacKinnon. But cities as parts of a larger urban system were also harmed by the disorders associated with war and revolution. Urban autonomy benefited from the weakness of central governments, but since certain urban needs required the stalemate-breaking intervention of central authorities, low levels of government capacity at higher levels created obstacles to problem solving. Perhaps the true completion of China's urban potential required a powerful state as much as or more than rail lines or garden cities alone.

The Rural beyond the Urban and the Global beyond the National

Studies of the significance of the city and the urban experience in China confront the fact that Chinese history this century was made in large part by rural revolution and on a stage that was merely one of many in an enveloping global drama. More recent developments at the end of the twentieth century have restored the place of urban life at the center of things and reinforced and widened the influence of foreign countries and foreign cities. One might even argue that the Maoist regime, for all of its pro-village and anti-city rhetoric, was fundamentally urban after all.[42] The earlier, republican city lacked the power by itself to sustain and complete a nationwide revolution or to stop one from erupting in the country's interior. Nor could urban China effectively protect the country except by offering regimes, movements, enterprises, institutions, and individuals an escape route into the interior and bases for development. What can be said, however, is that cities at several levels and in many places were powerful enough to reset the terms of debate so that "rural" came to mean the near or total absence of urbanism and "urban modernity" came to mean the presence of materials and practices culled or inserted from a global modernity. More subtle interconnections, like those apparent in the annual pilgrimage of peasants to City-God Hill in Hangzhou, faded as cities faced each other as familiar competitors and the village as alien ground. New relationships, like those Sheehan finds promoted by bankers willing to provide aid to agriculture and rural development, presumed a widening gulf between modernizing cities and a backward countryside, a divide to match an equally vexing gap between Western standards and Chinese realities. Part of the appeal of Maoism had to do with its capacity to make something new, revolutionary, and world-shaking out of the customs and conditions found in the interior, rural expanses of China. This revamping of rural images and institutions to meet an urban standard of dynamism and progress suggests that the mediating power of urban life had spread far beyond city walls or all-weather roads. The chapters in this volume demonstrate both the diversity of the twentieth-century Chinese urban experience and the central role those experiences played in forging the tools and firing the imaginations of modern Chinese.

Notes

Chapter 1. Modernity and Nation in the Chinese City

1. In the voluminous literature on nationalism, the most important studies for our purposes are Benedict Anderson, *Imagined Communities: Reflections on the Origins and Spread of Nationalism* (London, 1991); Ernest Gellner, *Nations and Nationalism* (Ithaca, 1983); Partha Catterjee, *Nationalist Thought and the Colonial World* (Minneapolis, 1993); and E. J. Hobsbawm, *Nations and Nationalism Since 1780: Programme, Myth and Reality* (Cambridge, 1990).

2. Clifford Geertz, *The Interpretation of Cultures* (New York, 1973), 258.

3. John A. Agnew, *Place and Politics: The Geographical Mediation of State and Society* (Boston, 1987), ix.

4. Marshall Berman, "Why modernism still matters," in Scott Lasch and Jonathan Friedman, *Modernity and Identity* (Oxford, 1992), 35–36. See also Berman 1982.

5. Steinhardt 1990; G. William Skinner, "Urban Development in Imperial China," in Skinner 1977; Arthur Wright 1977; Chang 1977.

6. du Halde (1735), cited in Fernand Braudel, *Capitalism and Material Life, 1400–1800,* trans. Miriam Kochan (London, 1967), 394.

7. Murphey 1953 and 1974; Zhang Yingjin 1996. For a narrative diplomatic and economic history of all of the treaty ports and concessions, see Zhang Hongxiang 1993; for urban histories of the five southern treaty ports, see Zhang Zhongli, ed., *Dongnan yanhai chengshi yu Zhongguo jindaihua* (The southeast coastal cities and China's modernization) (Shanghai, 1996).

8. MacPherson 1987; Martin 1996; Wakeman 1995a, 25–34; Coble 1980, 12, 32–36.

9. Johnson 1995, 320–346.

10. Schinz 1989, 171, cf. 139.

11. Steinhardt 1990; G. William Skinner, "Urban Social Structure in Ch'ing China," in Skinner 1997; Arthur Wright 1977; Chang 1977; Sit 1995, 7–81.

12. Dray-Novey 1993.

13. Helmer 1985, 30–31, 39; Vale 1992, 30.

14. Geertz 1973, 258.

15. Zhang Yingjin 1996, 61–113.

16. Vale 1992. Vale notes and studies other examples, including such failures as Dodoma in Tanzania, which could not overcome the centrality of Dar es Salam.

17. Finnane 1994.

18. Pa Chin (Ba Jin), *Family* (Prospect Heights, Ill., 1972); Mao Dun, *Rainbow,* trans. Madeleine Zelin (Berkeley, 1972).

19. Holston 1989, 17–18.

20. Gaubatz 1996, 91–92, 96.

21. Schinz 1989, 24–28, 126–131, 148–154, 272–279, 282–288, 291–297, 348–350.

22. Finnane 1994, 1154, 1164; and McIsaac, chap. 11, in this volume.

23. In the 1980s, first twenty-four, then a total of sixty-two, cities were so designated (Schinz 1989, 41–42).

24. Albert Feuerwerker, "Economic Trends, 1912–49," *The Cambridge History of China,* vol. 12: *Republican China 1912–1949,* Part I, ed. John K. Fairbank (Cambridge, 1983), 43.

25. Schinz 1989, 118–119.

26. Gaubatz 1996.

27. Joshua Goldstein, "Theatrical Imagi-nations: Beijing Opera and China's Cultural Crisis, 1900–1937" (Ph.D. dissertation, University of California–San Diego, 1999).

28. "Chronological Autobiography of K'ang Yu-wei," trans. in *K'ang Yu-wei: A Biography and a Symposium,* ed. Jung-pang Lo (Tucson: University of Arizona Press, 1967), 36.

29. Ravetz 1986, 15; MacPherson 1987, 40–42.

30. Jordan 1995.

31. Ibid., 185.

32. Cody 1996; MacPherson 1990.

33. Henriot 1993, 111–114.

34. James A. Cook, "Bridges to Modernity: Xiamen, Overseas Chinese and Southeast Coastal Modernization, 1843–1937" (Ph.D. dissertation, University of California–San Diego, 1998), chap. 6.

35. Mumford 1961, 410. On the 1912 destruction of Shanghai's walls and the laying of "Republic Road," see MacPherson 1990, 47.

36. Strand 1989, esp. 23–26; Lu Hanchao forthcoming, chap. 2.

37. See MacPherson 1987 for pioneering public health efforts in the Shanghai foreign concessions.

38. Strand 1989, 65.

39. Storch 1976.

40. Wakeman 1995a, 212; see also Wakeman 1995b, 19–20.

41. Shi 1993; Stapleton, chap. 6, in this volume.

42. Henriot 1993, 175–184; MacPherson 1990; see also Schinz 1989, 172, 178–179, 189–190.

43. Jordan 1995, 227–245.

44. Henriot 1993, 130–155, 175–184.

45. Ibid., 173–175; Tsin and Rogaski, chaps. 2 and 3, respectively, in this volume.

46. In addition to Dong, chap. 8, in this volume, see Shi 1998, 219–254.

47. Zhang Zhongli 1996, 577–578.

48. Zhang Yingjin 1996, 9–10; cf. Berman 1982, 183, 198, on St. Petersburg; and David Nasaw, "Cities of Light, Landscapes of Pleasure," in David Ward and Oliver Zunz, *The Landscape of Modernity: Essays on New York City, 1900–1940* (New York: Russell Sage, 1992), 273–286.

49. Skinner, "Urban Social Structure in Ch'ing China, in Skinner 1997, 547–548; Chang 1977, 99; Schipper 1977.

50. Skinner, "Urban Social Structure in Ch'ing China," 527–528; Johnson 1995, 96–121; Antonia Finnane, "Yangzhou: A Central Place in the Qing," in Johnson 1993, 132–133.

51. A recent book proclaims, "Nanjing Road reflects greater Shanghai. Greater Shanghai reflects modern China" (Cheng Tongyi, *Kaibu—Zhongguo Nanjing lu 150 nian* [Open Port—150 years of China's Nanjing Road] [Beijing, 1996], 3).

52. Mumford 1961, 368–370, 429; Sennet 1994, 22–23, 257–258.

53. Daniel Lerner, *The Passing of Traditional Society: Modernizing the Middle East* (New York, 1958), 27–28, 400.

54. See Yeh 1992.

55. F. W. Mote has stated the case most forcefully. See Mote 1977, 102–104, and the qualified endorsement in G. William Skinner, "Urban and Rural in Chinese Society," in Skinner 1977, 267–269.

56. Rowe 1993a, 13–15.

57. Mann 1984 documents the Chinese consensus of an "urban separateness."

58. Zhang Yingjin 1996, 3–20; Lu Hanchao forthcoming, "Introduction," chaps. 5–6.

59. Liping Wang is responsible for many of these ideas, in her dissertation (Liping Wang 1997) and in conversation. See also Yeh 1995 and 1997, 382, 384, 393.

60. Honig 1986, 154–155, 159–164, 170.

61. Marshall Berman, "Why Modernism Still Matters," 42.

62. Pa Chin 1972, 131.

63. Shi Xiaochuan, *Tianjin zhinan* (Guide to Tianjin), vol. 2 (n.p., 1911), 45–51.

64. Lu Xun, "Shanghai Girls" (August 12, 1933), in Lu Xun, *Selected Works,* vol. 3, trans. Yang Xianyi and Gladys Yang (Beijing, 1959), 332–333 (translation slightly altered).

65. G. William Skinner, "Cities and the Hierarchy of Local Systems," in Skinner 1977, 275–352.

66. Murphey 1953, 166.

67. Zhang Zhongli 1996, 21, 622–623; Cheng Tongyi 1996, 106.

68. Pa Chin 1972, 329.

69. *Tianjin zhinan* (Guidebook to Tianjin), vol. 1, no author (n.p., 1921), 4.

70. Schinz 1989, 294.

71. Finnane 1994, 1154.

72. MacPherson 1990, 49.

73. Vale 1992, 42.

74. Cited in Carol Willis, "Form Follows Finance: The Empire State Building," in Ward and Zunz 1992, 162.

75. Vale 1992, 273.

76. Ibid., 94; Cody 1996, 357, where he refers to "architectural nostalgia."

77. Wang Liping 1996.

78. Andrew D. Morris, *Cultivating the National Body: A History of Physical Culture in Republican China* (Ph.D. dissertation, University of California–San Diego, 1998), 367–385.

79. Goldstein 1999.

Part I: The Modernist City
Chapter 2. Canton Remapped

1. It may be instructive here, following Michel de Certeau, to draw a distinction between "place" and "space." Place, to de Certeau, is "an instantaneous configuration of positions," while space "is composed of intersections of mobile elements." As he puts it, "*space is a practiced place.* Thus the street geometrically defined by urban planning is transformed into a space by walkers [italics original]" (de Certeau 1984, 117). From this perspective, what we call spatial ordering and regulation here is not just the arrangement of the location and distribution of things. It is, rather, the constitutive part of an *active* process through which specific forms of "space" are produced to facilitate the exercise of power. In a similar vein, Piper Rae Gaubatz, in her study of frontier cities in China, reminds us that cities are "cultural artifacts" and that "cities and their shapers are at once agents of and the results of social and cultural processes" (Gaubatz 1996, 8).

2. Ozouf 1988, 126.

3. Dasgupta 1995, 145. Also Matthew H. Edney, *Mapping an Empire: The Geographical Construction of British India, 1765–1843* (Chicago, 1997).

4. Arthur Wright 1977, 45.

5. Imperial structures, for instance, were the only ones allowed to be higher than one story in late imperial Beijing. See Dray-Novey 1993, 890.

6. Chang 1977, 88.

7. Liang Sicheng 1981, 205.

8. See Foucault 1991, 87-104.

9. Wakeman 1995a, 46.

10. For some useful discussions of the various aspects of modernity, see Hall et al. 1996; Touraine 1995; Lefevre 1995; and Osborne 1995.

11. Arendt 1958, 38–49.

12. Schwartz 1993, 222.

13. See Harvey 1990, 66.

14. Ibid., 16.

15. Kerr 1891, 2–3.

16. Turner 1894, 23–24.

17. Chang 1977, 99; Mote 1973, 38.

18. Such a phenomenon was of course not unique to China. In Tokugawa Japan, for instance, "the physical boundaries of Edo varied according to which ideation of Edo one advocated." See Katō 1994, 42.

19. *Panyuxian xuzhi* (1931), 9: 11a. The figure I have come across for the "population" of late Qing Canton is 96,614 households *(hu),* taken from a survey conducted in 1909 (Qiu Jie 1983, 364). Using Gilbert Rozman's estimate (Rozman 1982, 60–66) of a mean household size of 6.09 in large urban centers of Qing China, the number of Canton residents should then be around 600,000.

20. Mote 1977, 116.

21. Mote 1973, 54. Commenting on several studies of Jiangnan cities, William Rowe argues that there was the evolution of "an autonomous urban culture" in late imperial China. He suggests, for example, that the cities' elites and administrators were preoccupied with distinctly urban problems. The fact that the elites were concerned with the problems of their living environment and were willing to provide organized solutions was not surprising, but whether that can be interpreted as evidence of a general urban consciousness, it seems to me, remains a debatable question. See Rowe 1993a, 13.

22. Kerr 1891, 1.

23. Xu Junming et al. 1984, 16–18; Turner 1894, 32.

24. Kerr 1891, 13. Also Turner 1894, 34.

25. Deng Yusheng 1910, 2: 1a–1b.

26. Foucault 1991, 100.

27. The compound *jingji,* like many other terms such as *shehui,* had long been used in classical Chinese texts. Their meaning then, however, was quite different from that of their modern usage. *Shehui,* for instance, usually denoted little more than a kind of "communal gathering." *Jingji,* on the other hand, was usually associated with the notion of *jingshi jimin,* that is, the administration of the realm. In most cases, these

Chinese compounds were endowed with new meanings as a result of their appropriation by Meiji Japanese intellectuals, who used them to denote Western concepts such as "society" or "economy." They were then reincorporated into the Chinese language. It is perhaps superfluous to point out that the exercise of a new form of governmental power was tied to the articulation of such new discursive terms. For a useful collection of such "returned loan words" from Japan, see Lydia Liu 1995, Appendix D.

28. Sun Fo 1919, 1.

29. Ibid., 8.

30. Harvey 1990, 249.

31. Sun Fo 1919, 13–14.

32. As F. W. Mote observes, "China's cities have no town halls, hence no town squares; there were no civic activities, no circuses and no parades, hence no need for great public spaces. . . . [N]o promenades or parks were a social necessity" (Mote 1973, 59). In his work on gardens in the Ming period, Craig Clunas suggests that historians might consider privately owned gardens in the urban areas as a kind of "public space" in view of their openness to outsiders. While Clunas has demonstrated that those gardens in the Ming were often more accessible than we have hitherto been led to believe, he seems to have overstated the case in construing them as "public space," given the fact that access to them was at the discretion of their owners. See Craig Clunas, Fruitful Sites: Garden Culture in Ming Dynasty China (Durham, 1996), 95–97, 102. Temples and markets, on the other hand, served as sites for public gathering only for specific purposes.

33. Sun Fo 1919, 15–17.

34. Frank Dikötter (1995, 2) reminds us that "[f]or the modernizing elites in republican China, individual sexual desire had to be disciplined and evil habits eliminated, and couples were to regulate their sexual behavior strictly to help bring about the revival of the nation."

35. Lee, 1936, 14–15.

36. Wang Jingyu, ed. 1957, 626–629.

37. *Guangzhou zhinan* 1934, 455; Lee 1936, 62.

38. *Guangzhoushi dianli gongsi ershi nianlai zhi gaikuang* 1929, 5–9; *Guangzhou zhinan* 1934, 456; Lee 1936, 51. The change in the denomination of the currency from tael to yuan was a result of the Qing government's decision to circulate paper notes from about 1908 onward.

39. See MacPherson, ed. 1998, 33–89.

40. Chen Xingwu 1986, 124–125, 135. For an interesting discussion of the effects of "set pricing" on the retail trade, see Perrot 1994, 59–60.

41. See Miller 1981. Mitchell (1991, 11–12) relates a telling tale of two Egyptian visitors who got lost in a store in Paris in the nineteenth century.

42. Cited in *Shanghai Yongan gongsi de chansheng, fazhan he gaizao* 1981, 6.

43. For more on Sincere, see Wellington Chan 1998, 66–89.

44. Xiao Fanbo 1981, 127–129, 131–134.

45. Ni Xiying 1936, 33.

46. Xiao Fanbo 1981, 129; Chen Xingwu 1986, 132.

47. Ni Xiying 1936, 33–34.

48. Miller 1981, 169.

49. The old "Guangxi clique" was headed by the ex-bandit Lu Rongting, whose henchmen Chen Bingkun and Mo Rongxin successively held the post of "military governor" *(dujun)* of Guangdong from 1917 to 1920. This group should be distinguished from the more reform-minded new "Guangxi clique" of Li Zongren and Bai Chongxi, who were active in the politics of the Guomindang era from the 1920s to the 1940s. See Lary 1974.

50. Yang Yongtai went on to become the governor of Guangdong under the Guangxi clique until he was replaced upon Chen Jiongming's return to Canton in October of 1920.

51. The movement grew out of a demonstration in Beijing on May 4, 1919, where students and others protested the terms of the Versailles Treaty, which recognized the Japanese claim to the rights previously held by Germany in the Chinese province of Shandong.

52. See "Guangzhoushi yan'ge shilue," in *Guangzhoushi shizheng baogao huikan* 1924, 69.

53. Lee 1936, 13.

54. The effort to "modernize" a city through redesigning and renovating its physical layout has been associated with the name of Baron Georges Haussmann, who, during his tenure as the prefect of Seine (1853–1870), was responsible for reshaping a large part of Paris. See Jordan 1995.

55. In his article on the influence of American planning in republican China, Jeffrey Cody suggests that through the adoption of "the American system of condemnation and assessment," many landowners in Canton, despite their initial resistance, were then not only compensated promptly but were able to make handsome profits because of rising land values. See Cody 1996, 344. Cody, however, might have been too optimistic in his evaluation. Even a quick reading of the records reveals that conflicts between residents and the government in Canton in subsequent years were still often centered around issues of adequate compensation for forced relocation, loss of properties and trade, etc.

56. "Canton Intelligence Report: December quarter, 1921," Public Record Office, London, FO 228/3276, 393.

57. *Guangzhoushi shizhengfu tongji nianjian* 1929, 257.

58. *Guangzhoushi shizheng baogao huikan* 1924, 345–347, 351–357.

59. Enclosure dated March 16, 1922, in "Alston to Curzon, 1922/3/24," Public Record Office, London, FO 405/236/219 [F 1597/84/10], 845. Chen Jiongming, of course, has long been treated as a pariah in orthodox Chinese history due to his "rebellion" against Sun Yat-sen in 1922. Writings on him thus tend to be fiercely partisan. To make matters worse, few of his own writings, with the notable exception of *Zhongguo tongyi chuyi,* seem to be extant. See Duan Yunzhang et al. 1989.

60. According to Cody, Sun Fo persuaded Chen Jiongming to transform the municipal council, and "to alter the hierarchical arrangement of appointees being beholden to a patron by granting the city a charter." See Cody 1996, 343.

61. "Guangzhoushi zanxing tiaoli," reprinted in Huang Yanpei 1921, 5–6, 10–12.

62. Reprinted in Huang Yanpei 1921, 17–21.

63. Xiao Fanbo 1981, 127; Chen Xingwu 1986, 132. Both stores were located on Hui'ai zhonglu (now Zhongshan wulu). The *Hui'ai shangdian,* however, did not last long, as it was closed by the early 1930s.

64. For a description of how each street in West Gate was characterized by a specific trade, see Ni Xiying 1936, 41–43. There were, of course, some newer and larger stores in West Gate, particularly along Shibafu (Eighteenth Ward). But in general, the entire area had a rather "old-fashioned" air to it. Indeed, the West Gate area still possesses a somewhat distinct ambiance even today.

65. Ni Xiying 1936, 39.

66. See *Guangzhoushi caizhengju renli shouche chezhan jiamubiao* 1927.

67. One of the projects for the municipal government was the construction of a bridge across the Pearl River. That did not, however, materialize until the 1930s. It is perhaps instructive to compare such trends in early republican Canton with Mote's comments on Chinese cities prior to the

twentieth century. "There were no zones of uniform land use in Chinese cities," he writes, "and no evident concentric rings or other zone patterns of land values. Only small cities, incapable of supporting a proliferation of commercial activities, had one 'main street,' or 'city center.'" Mote 1973, 59.

68. *Guangzhoushi shizhengfu tongji nianjian* 1929, 446, 454.

69. "Guangzhoushi zanxing tiaoli," reprinted in Huang Yanpei 1921, 3.

70. Thongchai 1994, 56.

71. "Guangzhoushi zanxing tiaoli," reprinted in Huang Yanpei 1921, 4.

72. Huang Yanpei 1921, 23–24. The six bureaus were Finance, Public Security, Health, Public Works, Public Utilities, and Education.

73. "Ni hejian xingzheng gongshu zhongshu banfa," reprinted in Huang Yanpei 1921, 47–48.

74. Huang Yanpei 1921, 45–46. Yet as late as 1929, the new building had yet to be constructed. An official report then stated that the lack of a *shizheng heshu* had rendered the administrative and supervisory tasks of the government rather difficult, and that its construction was an extremely urgent matter. *Guangzhoushi shizhengfu tongji nianjian* 1929, 454.

75. Huang Yanpei 1921, 49.

76. *Guangzhoushi shizheng baogao huikan* 1924, 220.

77. The figure for London is cited in Dray-Novey 1993, 905. According to Dray-Novey, the ratio of policemen to residents in nineteenth-century Beijing could be as high as one to thirty, which, if true, would surely make it by far the most heavily policed city in the world at that time.

78. "Guangzhoushi zanxing tiaoli," reprinted in Huang Yanpei 1921, 8. The twelve wards were apparently changed to forty later, as a proposal was made to reduce the number to thirty in 1929. See *Guangzhoushi shizhengfu tongji nianjian* 1929, 461.

79. Storch 1976.

80. "Guangzhoushi zanxing tiaoli," reprinted in Huang Yanpei 1921, 8. Also Lai Zehan 1984, 93.

81. "Guangzhoushi zanxing tiaoli," reprinted in Huang Yanpei 1921, 9.

82. *Guangzhoushi shizhengfu tongji nianjian* 1929, 459.

83. Lai Zehan 1984, 94.

84. Mitchell 1991, xi.

85. Foucault 1991, 102.

Chapter 3. Hygienic Modernity in Tianjin

1. The introduction of Western concepts of public health into a treaty port has been chronicled in Kerrie Macpherson's ground-breaking work on Shanghai, albeit with an exclusive focus on the activities of Western doctors and administrators in the Anglo-American Settlement. Macpherson 1987.

2. On sanitation measures in Roman urban planning, see Robinson 1992, 111–129; Harry Evans 1994.

3. Foucault 1980, 175. The connection between the nation, the urban environment, and public health in eighteenth- and nineteenth-century Europe is explored in William Coleman 1982.

4. On Paris, see Jordan 1995. For England's sanitary renaissance, see Wohl 1983. New York's hygienic transformation is chronicled in Duffy 1968. On the importance of boundaries in urban hygiene, see Sennet 1994, 222–237.

5. Since the late 1980s a large body of literature has traced this connection between empire and "imperial medicine." Some noteworthy examples include MacLeod and Lewis, eds. 1988; Arnold, ed. 1988; Vaughn 1991; Harrison 1994.

6. This link between European civilization and hygiene was embodied in the bacteriologist Robert Koch's scathing criticism of Hamburg's municipal authorities during the 1892 cholera epidemic. A national hero famous for his discovery of the tuberculosis bacterium, Koch had been sent by the German government to cities in the Middle East and Asia in search of other deadly bacteria. He returned convinced that a municipal administration's ability to keep a city clean and to control epidemics was what distinguished the "enlightened" Western city from the "degraded" Eastern metropolis. During a tour of Hamburg's rat-infested dock neighborhoods, Koch reportedly remarked to his entourage in a grave voice, "Gentlemen, I forget that I am in Europe," a comment that was widely reported in the German press. See Richard Evans 1987, 312–313.

7. Cooper and Stoler, eds. 1997; Rabinow 1989; Gwendolyn Wright 1991; Yeoh 1996. For discussion of the phrase "laboratory of modernity," see Stoler 1995, 13–26.

8. For a summary of the construction of germ theory in the nineteenth century, see Tomes 1997 and 1998. Also see Geison 1995 and Latour 1988. On debates between "sanitarians" and proponents of germ theory, see Duffy 1990. On local resistance to public health policies in a Western context, see Leavitt 1982.

9. Arnold 1994, Yeoh 1996. For a recent discussion on the mediation of medical knowledge around the globe, see John Harley Warner and Nancy Tomes, "Introduction to Special Issue on Rethinking the Reception of the Germ Theory of Disease: Comparative Perspectives," *Journal of the History of Medicine and Allied Sciences* 52(1) (Winter 1997): 7–16.

10. On medical facilities in late imperial China, see Leung 1987. On the recycling of waste, see Yoshinobu Shiba, "Ningbo and Its Hinterland," in Skinner, ed. 1977, 391–439. For drainage, see Shi 1993.

11. Fan Bin, "Jinmen xiaoling," in *Zili lianzhu ji,* ed. Hua Dingyuan (1819; reprint, Tianjin: Tianjin guji chuban she, 1986), 106.

12. Benedict 1996, 108.

13. For example, see Xie Xue'an, "Zhongguo gudai dui jibing chuanranxing de renshi" (Ancient Chinese knowledge of the contagious nature of disease), *Zhonghua yishi zazhi* 13(4) (1983): 193–198.

14. Andrews 1997.

15. Latour 1988, 20.

16. For a brief discussion of Chinese ideas of pathogenesis in turn-of-the-century Singapore, see Yeoh 1996, 117. For Western doctors' contempt for such theories in Shanghai, see Macpherson 1987, 62–63.

17. I use this term in contrast to Sun Yat-sen's formulation of China as a "hypo-colony." Sun Yat-sen claimed that since China was "semi-colonial" (partially colonized by many different powers), it was more poorly managed and had more difficulty developing indigenous nationalism than "true" colonies such as Korea or Vietnam. Borrowing the term *ci* (hypo) from chemistry, Sun described China's status as that of a *ci zhimindi*, a "hypo-colony." Sun Yat-sen, *Guofu quanji* (Taibei: Chung-yang wen-wu kung-ying she, 1961), vol. 1, *san-min zhu-yi* lecture 2:19. The ironic implication of Sun Yat-sen's statement is that China would have been better off colonized by only one foreign nation, a conclusion at odds with my understanding of the complexities of Tianjin's political and cultural circumstances at the turn of the century.

18. Germany's move to acquire a foothold in Tianjin foreshadowed its seizure of Qingdao in 1897. Japan laid claim to Tianjin land after its victory in the Sino-Japanese War. See *Tianjin zujie dang'an xuanbian* 1992, 161–166.

19. Lai Xinxia, ed. 1987, chart between pages 196 and 197.

20. Mitchell 1991, 12.

21. For photographs of Tianjin's foreign architecture in the 1920s, see Rasmussen 1925, passim; see also *Jindai Tianjin tuzhi* 1992.

22. For conflicts between nations, see Rasmussen 1925, 114. On the Tianjin provisional government, see Rasmussen 1925; Mori Etsuko 1988; and Bernstein 1988.

23. From 1901 to 1927, Tianjin's population grew from less than three hundred thousand to well over one million. By 1927, nine out of ten residents in the foreign settlements were Chinese. Li Jingneng 1990; Luo Shuwei et al, eds. 1993, 455–457.

24. For similar concerns in Shanghai, see Bickers and Wasserstrom 1995.

25. The overlap between public health administration and issues of Chinese sovereignty has also been noted by Benedict 1996, 151–153; and Goodman 1995, 158–175.

26. Johnston 1995, 167–178.

27. Tsuzuki 1904.

28. The passage reads: "[T]raipsing and trailing about with other things, riding along with them on the same wave—this is the basic rule of guarding life *(wei sheng)*, this and nothing more." See Burton Watson, trans., *The Complete Works of Chuang tzu* (New York, 1968), 253.

29. Johnston 1995, 179. According to Johnston, the original word Nagayo was trying to translate was *Gesundheitspflege*, literally, "health care." Commentary by Ban Tadayasu on Nagayo's autobiography states that the original word was *Hygiene*. See Ban Tadayasu, *Tekiju to Nagayo Sensai: Eiseiga to Shoko shishi* (Osaka: Sōgensha, 1987), 151–157

30. Johnston 1995, 174.

31. Ibid., 179.

32. Ban Tadayasu 1987, 156.

33. For the official's poem, see Zhang Tao (1884) 1986, 124–125. Details of Li Hongzhang's views on British public health measures can be found in Tianjin Consulate to Peking Embassy, June 19, 1894, PRO, FO 674/60, 45. For details on the Hong Kong plague, see Benedict 1995, 131–149; and Elizabeth Sinn, *Power and Charity: The Early History of Tung Wah Hospital, Hong Kong* (Hong Kong: Oxford University Press, 1989), 158–169.

34. Benedict 1996, 110–128; Katz 1995.

35. *Zhibao*, October 5, 1895, 3. On Japan's difficulties with epidemic disease in Taiwan, see Paul Katz, "Germs of Disaster: The Impact of Epidemics on Japanese Military Campaigns in Taiwan, 1874–1895," *Annales de demographie historique* 1996: 195–220.

36. On the Japanese lobbying for the bureau, see Mori Etsuko 1988, 316. The following discussion on the TPG Bureau Sanitaire's activities is drawn from *Dutong yamen huiyi jiyao* (Minutes of the meetings of the Tianjin provisional government). Chinese translation of the original French manuscript, Tianjin Academy of Social Sciences.

37. Mori Etsuko 1988, 315.

38. The medical inspection of native prostitutes was one of the thornier moral issues of imperial rule. See Antoinette Burton, *Burdens of History: British Feminists, Indian Women, and Imperial Culture, 1865–1915* (Chapel Hill: University of North Carolina Press, 1994), particularly chap. 5. On the debate between British administrators over the establishment of a lock hospital in 1870s Shanghai, see Macpherson 1987, 213–258.

39. On the Ningbo cemetery riots in Shanghai, see Goodman 1995, 158–175.

40. Zhu Renxun, *Wenjian lu*, GX 26/11/9 (December 30, 1900), GX 26/11/17 (January 7, 1901).

41. Liu Mengyang, "Tianjin quanfei bianluan jishi" (Record of Tianjin during the Boxer debacle), in *Yihetuan* (The Boxers), Zhongguo shixue hui ed., vol. 2 (Beijing: Zhongguo jindaishi ziliao congkan, 1951), 49.

42. Yan Renzong, ed. 1990, 130.

43. Police maintained order at the train station by whipping those who got out of line. See Hua Xuelan 1936, 1–17.

44. Ding Zilang, preface to *Shuo yi*, reprinted in *Zhuyuan conghua* 10 1924, 113–116.

45. Ding Zilang had considerable impact on Tianjin's medical and political circles through his frequent pieces published in numerous turn-of-the-century Tianjin publications, including *Dagong bao, Shang bao, Minxing bao,* and *Aiguo bao.* He also founded the Tianjin Medical Research Association (Tianjin yiyao yanjiu hui) and was affiliated with the Tianjin *baihua* (vernacular) movement.

46. Mori Etsuko 1988, 320–324.

47. Located in the French Concession, the Beiyang Medical School was founded in 1881 by the London Missionary Society, with the support of the Beiyang "viceroy," Li Hongzhang. In the first years of the school, students were recruited from among the Cantonese and Fujianese youths who had been sent to the United States to study in the first Qing overseas education mission. In 1888, the Qing took over the administration of the school from the British missionaries and affiliated with the more secular doctors of the French Concession. The school is now remembered as the first Chinese government school of Western medicine. Rogaski 1996, 114–131. On Qu Yongqiu, see *Tianjin jindai renwu lu* (Biographical dictionary of modern Tianjin) (Tianjin, 1987), 261.

48. Gan Houci, ed. (1907) 1966, 25: 1826.

49. Tianjin Weisheng Bureau to the Tianjin Chamber of Commerce, GX 32/2/4 (February 24, 1906), in *Tianjin shanghui dang'an huibian* 1989, vol. 2, 2275.

50. Ibid., 2276.

51. *Dagong bao,* February 9, 1907. My thanks to Man-bun Kwan for bringing this citation to my attention.

52. This desire was particularly keen during the early years of the concession. In the eyes of European observers and Japanese authorities alike, the first Japanese settlers in Tianjin were of a poorer class, ignorant of both personal and public hygiene. *Tenshin kyoryū mindan ni—jū shū nen kinenshi* 1930, 543.

53. On the impact of Japanese education, see Reynolds 1993. On the marketing of Japanese medicines in China, see Sherman Cochran, "Marketing Medicine and Advertising Dreams in China, 1900–1950," in *Becoming Chinese: Passages to Modernity and Beyond, 1900–1950,* ed. Yeh Wen-hsin (Berkeley: University of California Press, forthcoming).

54. For an overview of Japanese Eisei Bureau functions, see *Tenshin kyoryu mindan ni—jū shū nen kinenshi* 1930.

55. On the Manchurian plague crisis of 1911, see Carl Nathan, *Plague Prevention and Politics in Manchuria, 1910–1931* (Cambridge: Harvard University, East Asian Research Center, 1967); Wu Lien-teh, *Plague Fighter: The Autobiography of a Modern Chinese Physician* (Cambridge: Heffer and Sons, 1959); and Benedict 1996, 155–163.

56. On radical plague prevention measures in the Shanghai International Settlement and the resulting Chinese riots, see Goodman 1995, 154–155.

57. *Tenshin kyoryū mindan ni—jū shū nen kinenshi* 1930, 559.

58. *Tenshin kyoryū mindan jimu hōkokushu, eiseibu* 1911.

59. On Japan's medical efforts in the colonies, see Wataru Iijima, "On Japanese Imperial Medicine: A Case Study in Colonial Taiwan (1895–1945)"; and Kohei Wakimura, "Disease and Public Health under Colonial Rule: India and Taiwan," papers delivered to the Society for the Social History of Medicine conference "Medicine and the Colonies," Oxford, July 19–21, 1996. See also Lo Ming-cheng, "Taming the Colonial Body: Placing Taiwan within the Japanese Medical Empire," paper presented at the Association for Asian Studies Annual Meeting, Honolulu, 1996.

60. On the city "moving underground" through sewers and water systems, see Mumford 1961. On the establishment of waterworks in Shanghai, see Macpherson 1987, 83–122; for Beijing, see Shi 1993.

61. *Tenshin kyoryū mindan nijū shū nen kinenshi* 1930, 511.

62. Ibid., 294.

63. Li Shaobi and Ni Pujun 1982, 37.

64. On the *weisheng* of fitted sleeves, see Yan Renzong, ed. 1990, 130; on Western pants, see Susan Brownell, *Training the Body for China: Sports in the Moral Order of the People's Republic* (Chicago, 1995). Frequent admonitions against the wearing of high heels can be found in Tianjin's *Weisheng zazhi* (Magazine of modern hygiene, 1929–1930).

65. Campbell 1995.

66. The northwest section of Tianjin's old city, a predominantly Muslim neighborhood, received such a *bu weisheng* rating in a Tianjin tourist guidebook from 1923.

Chapter 4. Urban Identity and Urban Networks in Cosmopolitan Cities: Banks and Bankers in Tianjin, 1900–1937

The research for this article, in part, was made possible by a grant from the Committee for Scholarly Communication with China.

1. A modern bank was distinguished by having one or more of the following characteristics: it was called a bank, or *yinhang*, in Chinese; it was a joint stock corporation; it was a large organization with capital investment at least several times greater than the largest native banks; it used foreign management and accounting methods; it had a branch system under centralized management; it made loans based on collateral; it adopted distinct architectural styles, usually foreign, that identified the institution as uniquely a bank. "Native bank" is a catchall English term used to translate a variety of Chinese terms, including *qianzhuang, piaohao, yinhao, lufang,* and *qianpu.* In spite of its imprecision, I follow convention in using "native bank" to refer to these institutions as a whole.

2. Unless otherwise indicated, I have relied on the A. C. Barnes translation in Tsao (Cao) Yu 1978. Quotes here are from 51, 103–104. Where I refer to the Chinese text, I use Cao Yu 1978. In the above passage I follow Joseph S. M. Lau (1970, 31n) in translating Xiao Dongxi as "Little Creature."

3. Yeh 1995, 113. On the importance of the Shanghai Bankers' Association, see also Bergère 1992, 15. On the Beijing Bankers' Association, see Strand 1989, 113–116. On the Tianjin Bankers' Association, see Sheehan 1997.

4. Lau 1970, 34, 35.

5. Ibid., 35, n. 4.

6. The similarity of the Chinese term for city to the word for city in ancient hieroglyphic script of the Mediterranean is striking. "In the earliest hieroglyphic script the ideogram meaning 'city' is a cross enclosed in a circle. The cross represents the convergence of routes bringing in men, merchandise and ideas: the circle is the moat or wall which physically binds the citizens together, emphasizing their distinctiveness." Pahl 1968a, 3.

7. deVries 1984, 10. DeVries discusses the problems understanding early modern European cities that have arisen by focusing only on behavioral urbanism and not on urbanization as a larger process.

8. deVries 1984, 253.

9. Banks and bankers also played key roles in the relationship of urban centers like Tianjin to their rural hinterlands, but space does not permit treatment of that topic here. For an excellent treatment of Tianjin's place in its own regional trading system, see Kwan 1996, 181–193. The 1937 invasion and occupation of coastal China by the Japanese, and the ongoing inland war, changed the dynamics of China's urban systems as well as the economic and regulatory environment for banks in Tianjin, and so this discussion will focus on the prewar period. Bergère 1992 was the first to describe Chinese bankers as "cosmopolitan."

10. On the relatively decentralized nature of China's urban system in the late imperial period, see Rozman 1973, 277.

11. Pahl 1968b, 273 and passim.

12. Information on Jincheng and biographical information on Zhou Zuomin are found in Boorman and Howard, eds. 1967–1971, 427–429; Xu Youchun, ed. 1991, 517; *Tianjin renwu lu* 1987, 253; Ji Xiaocun and Yang Guzhi, "Zhou Zuomin yu Jincheng yinhang" (Zhou Zuomin and Jincheng Bank), *Tianjin wenshi ziliao* 13 (1981): 100–134; and interviews with three former Jincheng employees in Tianjin in 1994 and 1995. See also the unflattering portrait of him as a backstage manipulator and wheeler-dealer in Strand 1989, 102–116.

13. All figures on Jincheng Bank shareholders are from *Jincheng yinhang shiliao* 1983, 18–33.

14. Stockholdings were actually quite diversified, with shareholders of fifty thousand yuan or more (thirty-three people) accounting for only half the seven million yuan total in 1927.

15. A license to print money from the Chinese government was a rare and valuable commodity. The Shanghai-based China and Southsea Bank was owned by a Fujian native who had made a fortune in Indonesia and who used his special overseas status to obtain permission to issue currency. Its president was a Jiangsu native named Hu Bijiang. On Hu Bijiang and the China and Southsea Bank, see Yang Guzhi and Tan Zaitang, "Zhongnan yinhang gaishu" (A brief account of the China and Southsea Bank), *Tianjin wenshi ziliao* 13 (1981): 159–175; and Liu Xiaobai, "Qiaoshang Zhongnan yinhang" (The Overseas Chinese China and Southsea Bank), in *Jiu Shanghai de jinrong jie,* ed. Shanghai wenshi ziliao (Shanghai: Renmin 1988), 172–179.

16. Ji Xiaocun and Yang Guzhi 1981, 125.

17. Skinner's application of central place theory to China began with his seminal series of articles on "Marketing and Social Structure in Rural China," 1964–1965. His analysis was refined and extended in his articles in Skinner, ed. 1977. At about the same time, he applied his findings to regional specializations in Skinner 1976. Quotes are from Skinner, ed. 1977, 220; and 1976, 334.

18. Tianjin was the seat of the Changlu salt gabelle and the location of the first Shanxi *piaohao,* which was established in the city by a sojourning Shanxi merchant in the late 1700s to finance the long-distance trade with Sichuan. On Tianjin's salt merchants, see Kwan 1990. On early trade networks and Tianjin, see Xiaobo Zhang 1995. On Shanxi *piaohao* in Tianjin, see Shen Danian et. al., *Tianjin jinrong jianshi* (A brief history of Tianjin finance) (Tianjin, 1988), 4.

19. Actually, the first banks with branches in Tianjin were foreign banks, but I am concerned here mostly with the development of a domestic industry. In addition, I do not consider joint foreign-Chinese-owned banks. On the early Tongshang Bank, see Chen Zehao, "Zhongguo tongshang yinhang shimo" (The Commercial Bank of China from start to finish), in *Jiu Shanghai de jinrong jie* 1988, 194, 195.

20. Yuen-sang Leung, "The Shanghai-Tientsin Connection: Li Hung-chang's Political Control over Shanghai," in *Li Hung-chang and China's Early Modernization,* ed. Samuel C. Chu and Kwang-Ching Liu (Armonk, N.Y.: M. E. Sharp, 1994), 108–118.

21. Kong Xiangxian, *Da Qing yinhang hangshi* (A history of the Da Qing Bank) (Nanjing: Nanjing University, 1991), 110.

22. For the ranking of international banking centers in 1905, see Howard Curtis Reed, *The Preeminence of International Financial Centers* (New York: Praeger, 1981), 131.

23. New bank office openings did not cease entirely in Tianjin after 1934, although new activity was very limited. At least two new offices were opened in 1934 and 1935, *Tianjin tongzhi: jinrong zhi* 1995, 19. Changes in foreign bank activities in China presaged the changes in the relationship between Chinese cities and domestic banks. By 1925 Shanghai had grown to be the third most important international banking center in the world, ahead of fifth-place Hong Kong and ninth-place Tianjin. After 1925, Tianjin dropped out of the top ten, although Shanghai managed to appear among the top ten on and off through at least 1935. Reed 1981, 133, 134.

24. *Quanguo yinhang nianjian* 1936, A16, A17. On the establishment of banks in Tianjin, see Sheehan 1997; Luo Shuwei, ed., *Jindai Tianjin chengshi shi* (An urban history of modern Tianjin) (Beijing: Zhongguo Shehui Kexue, 1993), 392–406; *Tianjin tongzhi: jinrong zhi* 1995, 14–19, 101–159; and Shen Danian et al. 1988, 28–39. Information on banks with branches in Tianjin is summarized in the appendix.

25. Bank headquarters were usually called *zonghang* or *zong banshichu;* branches *fenhang;* sub-branches *zhihang;* and suboffices *banshichu.*

26. My definition of the most important banks in China follows that of my sources: those banks that by 1931 were large enough to have a branch in Shanghai and that branch was important enough to join the Shanghai Bankers' Association. Although this is a Shanghai-centered definition, reflecting the fact that Shanghai was the center of financial publishing, it does have the ring of truth. Any bank that had more than just local or regional interests would want a branch in Shanghai, and only those banks with financial or political clout would have been allowed to join the Shanghai Bankers' Association. These 23 banks had more than 64 percent of all the capital of China's 154 banks in 1935. In all statistics, I have excluded Hong Kong, Singapore, and Philippine banks in order to understand supralocal systems in a domestic context. Note that some banks had more than one office in a given city, so the total number of bank offices in a city was usually greater than the number of banks with at least one office there.

27. For banks with head offices in Tianjin, see the applications to join the Tianjin Bankers' Association, Tianjin yinhang gong hui (Tianjin Bankers' Association) Archives, 129-2-1625; *Quanguo yinhang nianjian* 1935 and 1936. In 1917, the eight most important banks in Tianjin included the two state banks, the Bank of China and the Bank of Communications, and a Shanghai bank, the National Commercial (Zhejiang xingye) Bank. The only local bank included in the eight was the Zhili Provincial Bank, an organ of the provincial government. The remaining four included three banks with headquarters in Beijing and one from Shandong. See "Tianjin zhi jinrong tan" (A discussion of finance in Tianjin), *Dongfang zazhi* 14(4) (April 1917): 154. Some of the banks founded during the warlord period would join the ranks of the most important banks in the local market, but it was never an exclusively local club.

28. One bank, the Hebei Minsheng Bank, was actually founded with a main office in Tianjin in 1932, but it closed almost as soon as it opened due to lack of capital. *Quanguo yinhang nianjian* 1934, A8.

29. Skinner 1976 points out that regional specializations were not limited to businessmen, although that is the focus of my treatment here. On Ningbo bankers, see Susan Mann, "Finance in Ningpo: The Ch'ien Chuang, 1750–1880," in *Economic Organization in Chinese Society,* ed. W. E. Willmott (Stanford: Stanford University Press, 1972), 47–77; and Mann, "The Ningpo Bang and Financial Power at Shanghai," in *The Chinese City Between Two Worlds,* ed. Mark Elvin and G. William Skinner (Stanford: Stanford University Press, 1974), 73–96. On Shanxi bankers, see Zhang Guohui, *Wan Qing qianzhuang he piaohao yanjiu* (Research on *qianzhuang* and *piaohao* in the late Qing period) (Beijing: Zhonghua Shuju, 1989). On native place and specialization in Tianjin, see Xiaobo Zhang 1995, chap. 4. The notion of regional *bang* in Chinese business is the subject of the recent book edited by Zhang Haipeng and Zhang Haiying 1993, which includes chapters on both the Shanxi *bang* and the Ningbo *bang.*

30. Statistics on the shareholders and directors of banks founded in Tianjin indicate 28 percent were from Tianjin or Hebei, 23 percent from Jiangsu, 21 percent from Zhejiang, and 15 percent from Anhui, with the balance made up of people from Guangdong, Jiangxi, Fengtian, and Shandong. My discussion of shareholders of Tianjin banks is based on Sheehan 1996; and the appendix.

31. Several very small banks had their main offices in Tianjin and may have had Tianjin natives as shareholders. Their small size and limited scope of operations limits both the available information on them and their relevance for discussion here.

32. Tianjin natives who were militarists and who invested in Tianjin banks include Feng Guozhang (Continental Bank), Xu Shichang (Jincheng Bank), Meng Enyuan (Dazhong Bank), Li Chun (Continental Bank), and Tian Zhongyu (Jincheng Bank). In addition, there were merchants who made money supplying the Beiyang army, such as Wang Zhilong (Jincheng Bank, Dasheng Bank, and Bianye Bank) and Pan Yaoting (Jincheng Bank and Dasheng Bank). Of all these investors, only Feng Guozhang (Continental Bank) and Wang Zhilong (Jincheng Bank) were significant shareholders at the time the banks were founded, and Wang Zhilong was not the primary investor in Jincheng.

33. *Zhongguo jinrong shi* 1993, 179, 180. On Zhonghua Shangye Chuxu Bank, see *Zhongguo zhongyao yinhang zuijin shi nian yingye qaikuang yanjiu* 1933, 124.

34. This was true of the first Chinese modern bank, the Commercial Bank of China (Tongshang), and also the early Ningbo Commercial and Saving (Siming) Bank (founded by Ningbo native bankers) and the so-called "Southern Three Banks," Shanghai Commercial and Savings Bank (Shanghai shangye chuxu), National Commercial Bank, and Zhejiang Industrial (Shiye) Bank, with their head offices in Shanghai. *Zhongguo jinrong shi* 1993, 172–176, 179–183, 215–219.

35. Shen Danian et al. 1988, 35; and *Quanguo yinhang nianjian* 1934, A5. Some of Shen Danian's dates for the movement of banks disagree with the primary sources, and I have relied on the latter where possible.

36. One Tianjin bank, Zhongfu, actually moved to Shanghai in 1930, before the Manchurian incident. The National Industrial Bank of China (Zhongguo Shiye) and Donglai Bank moved their head offices from Tianjin to Shanghai in 1932. The Salt Bank (which had just moved from Beiping to Tianjin in 1928), Jincheng Bank, and Dazhong Bank (not

considered one of Tianjin's largest) all moved in 1935. *Quanguo yinhang nianjian* 1934, A7; 1935, A5, B93. The 1935 *Quanguo yinhang nianjian* states that the National Industrial Bank moved to Shanghai in 1930 (A5), but the bank's own account of its history (B93) says 1932, and I accept the latter date.

37. Rowe 1984, 247–248. See also Rowe 1989.

38. Bryna Goodman also notes the importance of native-place links that transcended Shanghai's borders. Goodman 1995, 32, n. 44, and 44–46.

39. Bergère 1992, 15–34, passim.

40. Thus I go one step further than Goodman, who allows only for the strategic inclusion of nonnatives. Goodman 1995, 35–36.

41. For example, the manager of the Tianjin branch of the Bank of China lived at the center of the bank's compound, described as follows: "Leading straight from the gates to the center of the landscaped compound was a long footpath that ended at the steps of a large, two-story Western-style building, which was the residence of the branch manager. Flanking the manager's residence, two to a side, were four more two-story buildings for the four associate managers, reduced in size to reflect the occupants' comparative status." Yeh 1995, 109.

42. Tsao (Cao) Yu 1978, 27.

43. The number of people from Tianjin may actually be somewhat higher; I have identified native places for fifty-two of the sixty-two managers. It is possible that there are native Tianjin people among the ten whose native place I do not know. See the appendix. The relatively large number of Liaoning people worked as managers at two banks—Bianye and Dongsansheng—sponsored by the Fengtian warlord Zhang Zuolin.

44. Banks joined the Tianjin Bankers' Association as institutions, not bankers as individuals. Tianjin yinhang gonghui (Tianjin Bankers' Association) Archives, 129-2-1612. Founding members of the association were the Bank of China, the Bank of Communications, the Commercial Guarantee Bank of Zhili (Beiyang baoshang), Xinhua Trust and Savings Bank, the Salt Bank (head offices in Beijing), Zhili Provincial Bank, Zhongfu Bank, Zhibian Bank, Jincheng Bank, the Cultivation Bank (Zhiye) Bank (head offices in Tianjin), and the National Commercial Bank (Shanghai). At the time of its founding, one bank, the Salt Bank (a Beijing bank), was appointed manager and two were appointed assistant manager of the association—the Bank of Communications (a Beijing Bank) and Zhongfu Bank (a Tianjin bank).

45. Under the practice of "separation of ownership and management," owners and managers of *yinhao* were sometimes of different native places. This diversity did not lead to organization along professional lines, however. The *bang* to which a given native bank belonged was determined by the native place of its manager, not its owner. For example, the warlord Wang Zhanyuan (a Shandong native) owned two *yinhao* in Tianjin, one of which was part of the Tianjin *bang* and one of which was part of the Shenji County *bang*. Yang Guzhi, Tan Zaitang, and Zhang Zhangxiang, "Tianjin qianye shilue" (A brief history of Tianjin's native bank business), *Tianjin wenshi ziliao* 20 (1985): 105, 112. On the persistence of native place as a principle of organization in the chamber of commerce, see Xiaobo Zhang 1995, 285–287. Yang Guzhi, Tan Zaitaing, and Zhang Zhangxiang 1985, 112, say the integration of the Native Bankers' Association came in 1928, but 1930 is more likely, because it was in the early 1930s that the Nationalist government encouraged the reorganization of trade associations. See Xiaobo Zhang 1995, 184–206, 296, 311.

46. Bergère 1992, 16.

47. Ibid.

48. Mann 1974, 78; and Goodman 1995, 37. On the late rise of Jiangsu sojourners in Shanghai, see Goodman 1995, 121, n. 2.

49. Bergère 1986, 148. Contrast this to the picture of Shanghai mill owners, mostly from Jiangsu, who came from the merchant, not the literati, sector. Marie-Claire Bergère, Noel Castelino, Christian Henriot, and Pui-yin Ho, "Essai di Prosopographie des Elites Shanghaiennes à L'époque Republicaine, 1911-1949," *Annales*, no. 4 (July–August 1985): 905, 906.

50. Bergère 1992, 17, 18.

51. Zhou Zuomin was a Jiangsu native, but from Jiangbei, not Jiangnan—an important distinction in the creation of ethnicity in twentieth-century Shanghai. See Honig 1992.

52. Bergère 1992, 18.

53. Sheehan 1996, 7.

54. For a picture of the networks based on Li Hongzhang, see Folsom 1968.

55. On Ye Jingkui's time at Da Qing Bank, see Kong Xiangxian 1991, 118–122. On the relationships of Zhou Xuexi and Sun Duosen, see Sheehan 1996.

56. On the cultural and professional standards of banking in republican China, see Bergère 1992, 19; and Yeh 1995, 106–107. "Upton Close" (pseud. for J. W. Hall), "Closeups of China's Money Josses," *China Review* 2(4) (April 1922): 200, noted that Chinese bankers were "endeavoring to force business methods, for the sake of profit as well as altruism, upon the Ministry of Finance."

57. For the reform activities of bankers on the national level, see Bergère 1992, 26–33.

58. The description in these paragraphs is based on a close reading of Bian Baimei's diary. Bian Baimei was branch manager of the Tianjin branch of the Bank of China and chairman of the Tianjin Bankers' Association for much of the republican period.

59. In fact, to my knowledge, none of the Tianjin bankers I have studied ever returned to their native places as adults.

60. Yanye yinhang, Tianjin fenhang (Tianjin branch of the Salt Bank) Archives, 213–299; Sheehan 1997, chap. 4.

61. Skinner 1977, 346. There is no space here to attempt a comprehensive critique of Skinner, merely to suggest my doubts about "natural" economic systems. His approach grows from Christaller's central place theory, which argued from a very specific, and unique, urban structure in medieval Bavaria (Christaller's home), which in fact was intimately linked to state structures. Vance 1990, 99–100.

62. Wakeman (1993, 108) has criticized Rowe for ignoring the supralocal connections of Hankou merchants.

63. Goodman 1995, 27.

64. *Quanguo yinhang nianjian* 1935, 46. On the relationship between the financial crisis of the mid-1930s and Shanghai bankers, see Yeh 1995, 115, 116; and Bian Baimei's diary, October 10, 1932, when his superior asked Bian to investigate the village self-government in Ding County.

65. Yeh 1995, 117.

Chapter 5. Railway City and National Capital: The Two Faces of the Modern in Changchun

I wish to thank a number of people for research assistance and comments on earlier drafts: Andrew Buck, Jeff Cody, Hou Ming, Kerrie MacPherson, Yukari Pak, Bill Sewell, Paul Sprague, Kristin Stapleton, David Tucker, Xie Hong, and Yu Li. Donna Schenstrom and Jarret Livesey of the University of Wisconsin-Milwaukee cartographic laboratory prepared the maps; Ingrid Ebner redrew the views of the

Fengle movie theater from a photograph too poor for reproduction.

1. This chapter draws extensively on the research and writings of Koshizawa Akira, a historian of Japanese urbanism and architecture who since the mid-1970s has studied the cities created by both the South Manchurian Railroad and state of Manchukuo. His most relevant works are listed in the bibliography and cited frequently in these notes. Without his research I would never have discerned the linkages among the Japanese bureaucrats, planners, and architects described here.

2. Duus et al., eds. 1989, xxiv–xxix.

3. Louise Young 1996, 71–96.

4. Gwendolyn Wright 1991, 3.

5. Scott 1998, 90.

6. Ibid., 90, 104.

7. Louise Young 1998, 250.

8. Yang Yulian 1991, 389–391; *Changchun shizhi: shangye zhi* 1995, 9–15; Dong Yuying 1987, 68–73.

9. Colquhuon 1900, 220–225.

10. This figure is only an estimate based on the size of the walled area. Several other sources suggest a much higher figure in excess of 65,000, but this seems unreasonable to me given the post-1900 size of Changchun, when the economy and immigration both flourished.

11. Hosie 1904, 22.

12. The name Kuanchengzi (Broadtown) after 1900 refers to the Chinese Eastern Railway settlement, while Changchun meant the mud walled town on the banks of the Yitong River.

13. Li Weiwei 1993, 248.

14. Johnson 1995, 322–346.

15. On Harbin, see Koshizawa Akira 1988; Wolff 1991; Clausen and Thøgerson, eds. 1995.

16. Myers 1989, 109–110.

17. Julie Lee Wei et al. 1994, xxxi–xxxii, 12–13, 33–34, 104–105.

18. Cyril Pearl, *Morrison of Peking* (Sydney, 1967), 263–264.

19. Borel 1912, 35.

20. *Shina shōbetsu zenshi,* vol. 8: *Henan,* 1917, 55–59.

21. *Shina shōbetsu zenshi,* vol. 18: *Zhili,* 1917, 267–270.

22. Koshizawa Akira 1982, 44–45.

23. Reps 1979, 547.

24. Myers 1989, 100–132.

25. Wolff 1991, 120–128.

26. Yang Zhaoyuan et al. 1993, 226–228; for a contemporary description of planning at Dairen, see Hokuto Ryosei 1921, 38–40.

27. Li Weiwei 1993, 247–248.

28. Liao Yizhong et al., eds. 1981, 273–276.

29. Koshizawa Akira 1988, 36–38.

30. Account of land acquisition summarized from ibid., 46–50.

31. Buck 1978, 50–53.

32. Duus 1989, xxiv–xxix.

33. This account of Gotō's life is based on Kitaoka Shin'ichi 1988.

34. Takeyoshi Yosaburo 1907, 309–310.

35. Myers 1989, 101.

36. Ibid., 104–105.

37. Ibid., 105–106.

38. As paraphrased by ibid., 118–119.

39. Koshizawa Akira 1988, 61–66.

40. Ibid., summarized from Koshizawa Akira 1988, 51.

41. Most street names have both a Chinese and Japanese pronunciation. I have assumed that in the SMR settlement, Japanese pronunciations dominated, but it is not always clear.

42. Koshizawa Akira 1988, 77–78.

43. Kitaoka Shin'ichi 1988, 64–72.

44. Koshizawa Akira 1988, 54–58.

45. For reference to Changchun as "City of Beans" see SMR General Directorate of Railways, *Along Manchurian Railways* (Dairen, n.d. [ca. 1937]), 18. The major anomaly in the new capital city of Xinjing was the location of Henry Puyi's residence on the grounds of this former salt storage yard. Puyi moved into these grounds in 1932 and kept his residence there until 1945. The location was hardly desirable in that it was close to the railyards and a bustling, rather noisome market that occupied Big Creek. Puyi resisted relocation to the more imposing imperial palace grounds that the Manchukuo authorities planned but never finished for him at the head of a grand street lined by government ministries. Instead, he stayed at the former salt yards, where the Japanese had erected an imposing modern residence in 1939. See *Weiman huanggong jianshe* (Architecture of the Manchukuo Imperial Palace) (Changchun, 1985).

46. Koshizawa Akira 1988, 56–61.

47. Ibid., 78.

48. *Mantetsu fuzokuchi keiei enkaku zenshi* 1939, 245–247.

49. Koshizawa Akira 1988, 42–43.

50. On the profitability of the SMR, see Myers 1989, 109–115.

51. Li Weiwei 1993, 250.

52. *Changchun shizhi: shangye zhi* 1995, 18–25.

53. Koshizawa Akira 1988, 82–86.

54. *Shinkyō annai* 1940, 51–52.

55. *Uchimi Shigeo* 1937, 49–50; *Manchuria Year Book* (Tokyo, 1931), 147–148; *Manchuria: A Survey of Its Economic Development* 1932, 59–60.

56. *Changchun shizhi: shangye zhi* 1995, 25–29.

57. I. A. Mihailoff, ed., *North Manchuria and the Chinese Eastern Railway* 1924 (Harbin, 1924), 21–26.

58. "Rapid Expansion of Hsinking," *Manchuria* 1(5) (September 1, 1936): 165–167; Koshizawa Akira 1988, 110–120; Nishizawa Yasuhiko 1995, 379–381.

59. Ginsburg 1947, 293.

60. Louise Young 1998, 241–268.

61. Vale 1992, 88–97. For New Delhi, see also Anthony D. King, *Colonial Urban Development: Culture, Social Power and Environment* (London, 1976); and Robert G. Irving, *Indian Summer: Lutyen, Baker and Imperial Delhi* (New Haven, Conn., 1981).

62. Li Weiwei 1993, 271.

63. Fishman 1977, 122–134.

64. Birrell 1964, 118.

65. Nishikawa Yasuhiko 1995, 407–414.

66. Koshizawa Akira 1988, 155–157. Japanese planners also would have known of the plan to rebuild Shanghai. This highly visionary modernistic effort never was carried out. See MacPherson 1990.

67. Ibid., 10, 51–59.

68. Scott 1998, 66; Louise Young 1998, 282–291.

69. Ruan Zhenduo, "Kokutō daishinkyō to toshi keikaku" (Urban planning and the national capital Xinjing), *Toshi* (Cities) special issue (1934): 77–88; also Koshizawa Akira 1998, 110–112; Nishikawa Yasuhiko 1995, 407–414.

70. Koshizawa Akira 1988, 120–130.

71. Ibid., 125–130; Nishikawa Yasuhiko 1995, 450.

72. Koshizawa Akira 1988, 183, 187–188.

73. Li Weiwei 1993, 253.

74. Koshizawa Akira 1988, 134–139, 188–189.

75. Ibid., 134–139; Nishikawa Yasuhiko 1995, 417–432.

76. Koshizawa Akira 1988, 140–142.

77. Ibid., 197–200; Kostka 1966, 5–6.

78. Fishman 1977, 122–134.

79. Koshizawa Akira 1988, 164–168; Scott 1998, 103–118.

80. Fishman 1977, 235–242.

81. Arthur Drexler, *The Architecture of Japan* (New York, 1955).

82. *Kokuto Shinkyō* (The National Capital "New Capital") (Shinkyō, 1942), photographs before section 1.

83. *Changchun shizhi: shangye zhi* 1995, 28–29.

84. Jiang Niandong et al., *Wei Manzhouguo shi* (History of the puppet state of Manchukuo) (Changchun, 1980).

85. Nishikawa Yasuhiko 1995, 417–429.

86. Koshizawa Akira 1988, 155–157, 164–168.

87. Ibid., 153.

88. Ibid., 169–171.

89. There are multivolume collections, such as Wang Jizhong, ed., *Dongbei lunxian shisinianshi yanjiu* (Research on the northeast's fourteen-year occupation) (Shengyang, 1991), filled with articles recounting the military, political, and economic exploitation of the region and local resistance.

90. Gwendolyn Wright 1991, 301–313.

91. Poshek Fu 1993.

92. Gao Pikun 1988, 127–128.

93. Dai Nianci, ed. 1988.

Chapter 6. Yang Sen in Chengdu: Urban Planning in the Interior

1. For a chronology of republican Sichuan's complicated military history, see Zhou Kaiqing 1972a and 1974; and Kapp 1973.

2. A dramatic account of Yang Sen's arrival in Chengdu is found in "Shengcheng bimen wuri ji" (Record of five days when the provincial capital gates were closed), *Guomin gongbao* 12 (February 1924).

3. Some of these groups published periodicals. An example is *Xin Sichuan* (New Sichuan), published in Nanjing by the propaganda department of the Comrades' Association of Nationalist Party Sichuanese Sojourning in the Capital (Zhongguo Guomindang Sichuan lujing tongzhihui). This publication is replete with detailed accounts of the brutality and treacherousness of all Sichuanese power holders.

4. Wu Yu 1986, entry for January 18, 1925, vol. 2, 232.

5. *Guomin gongbao,* May 3, 1924.

6. Fan Puzhai, "Wu Youling xiansheng shilue" (Brief account of Mr. Wu Youling), in *Wu Yu ji* (Wu Yu's Collected Works), ed. Zhao Qing and Zheng Cheng (Chengdu, 1985), 486.

7. The disputes between Wu Yu and Xu Zixiu may be followed in the two volumes of Wu Yu's diary. Xu Zixiu's side of the story is harder to unearth, although his memory is still revered by many older people in Chengdu. Most published biographies of Xu Zixiu omit mention of his battles with Chengdu's famous May Fourth hero. A manuscript by Tao Liangsheng on Chengdu's "Five Elders and Seven Sages " does explicitly defend Xu Zixiu, claiming that his deep and implacable disgust for Wu Yu formed because the latter did not merely publicly criticize his elderly father in 1910, but beat him bloody as well.

8. On Sichuan's modern socioeconomic history, see Wang Di 1993 and Adshead 1984.

9. For biographical details, see Ma Xuanwei and Xiao Bo 1989; and "Yang Sen xiansheng fangwen jilu."

10. The history of the New Policies reforms in Chengdu is treated in my "Civilizing Chengdu: Chinese Urban Reform, 1895–1937" (Stapleton forthcoming). Tokyo's development in the Meiji era is discussed in Westney 1987 and in Seidensticker 1983.

11. *Sichuan Chengdu disanci shangye quangonghui diaochabiao* (Investigative report on the Third Commercial and Industrial-Promotion Exposition in Chengdu, Sichuan) (Chengdu, 1908).

12. *Guomin gongbao,* January 1 and February 28, 1920.

13. Shu Xincheng 1934, 223.

14. *Guomin gongbao,* April 14, May 2, and September 16, 1924; *The West China Missionary News* 26(9) (October 1924): 31–32.

15. Gu Yuanzhong, "Chengdu gongyuan shihua" (History of Chengdu's public parks), *Sichuan wenwu* 2 (1989): 73–75.

16. Han Lei, "Jindai tiyu zai Chengdu de chuqi chuanbo" (The early period in the spread of modern physical education to Chengdu), *Chengduzhi tongxun* 5 (1985): 32.

17. Ma Xuanwei and Xiao Bo 1989, 41.

18. Lu Guoji, *Wode fuqin Lu Zuofu* (My father Lu Zuofu) (Chongqing, 1984), 47–52.

19. *Minshi ribao,* October 17, 1924.

20. Xu Xiaohui, "Guanyu Chengdu 'Mancheng' de huiyi diandi" (Snippets of a memoir of Chengdu's Manchu city), *Sichuan wenshi ziliao xuanji,* no. 10 (1964): 38–40.

21. Both *Guomin gongbao* and *Minshi ribao* reported extensively on the plans for the road-building campaign in April and May 1924.

22. Jiang Mengbi, "Chengdu Chunxi Lu de youlai he fazhan" (The origin and development of Chengdu's Chunxi Road), *Dongcheng* (Chengdu's East City district) *wenshi ziliao* 1 (1990): 3–4.

23. Wu Yu, teaching in Beijing, learned about the new rickshaws in Chengdu from a friend's letter. See Wu Yu 1986, entry for January 15, 1925, vol. 2, 232. A rickshaw company had been formed in Chengdu as early as 1898, but that effort and another launched shortly before the 1911 Revolution failed very quickly.

24. *Guomin gongbao,* April 15 and 16, 1924.

25. Luo Cairong, "'Wang jiangjun zaori <kaiche>': Jinian Yang Sen jiangjun" ("Hoping the general starts his car soon": In memory of General Yang Sen), in *Yang Sen jiangjun jinian ji* 1979, 436.

26. "Yang Sen xiansheng fangwen jilu," interview 6.

27. Ma Xuanwei and Xiao Bo 1989, 41. A list of "Yang Sen says:" proclamations may also be found on this page. See also Yang Sen, "Jiushi yiwang" (Recalling the past at age 90), in *Yang Sen jiangjun jinian ji* 1979, 107.

28. Shu Xincheng 1934, 220.

29. "Yang Sen xiansheng fangwen jilu," interview 8.

30. Luo Cairong, in *Yang Sen jiangjun jinian ji* 1979, 439.

31. This institution and its activities are described in Mingzheng Shi 1993.

32. Lu Danlin, "Xu" (Preface), in *Shizheng quanshu* 1928.

33. This summary of the record of accomplishments of Chengdu's new-style city managers was published in *Guomin gongbao* on November 18, 1923, well before Yang Sen arrived in the city. The work of the city government office is also described in an article in *Minshi ribao* from July 9, 1922.

34. *Minshi ribao,* July 19, 1922.

35. Zhang Jian's Nantong, which was an important model of urban administration for older conservative elites in the late 1910s and early 1920s, is described in Shao 1994.

36. On the influence of American engineers and planners in establishing these professions in republican China, see Cody 1996.

37. *Guomin gongbao,* March 1, 1924.

38. Both of these volumes were edited by Lu Danlin and published in Shanghai by the National Road-Building Association.

39. James Henry Breasted, *Ancient Times: A History of the Early World,* 2d ed. (Boston, 1935), 352. This statement is echoed in an American observer's comment on changes in Chinese cities in the 1930s: "Wide streets take the place of narrow, ill-smelling crooked alleys. . . . All the mechanical gadgets of our civilization have been taken over and put to work . . . the Chinese are able successfully to function as a modern corporate society." Frank B. Lenz, "Take a Look at China," in *Brooklyn Central* (New York: YMCA, n.d.), cited in Garrett 1974, 213.

40. Agrest 1996, 58–59.

41. Shao 1994, 161–162.

42. Ibid., 55–62.

43. On Wu Shan, see the brief biography by Lu Danlin, chief editor of the *Complete Book of City Administration.* According to this account, Wu Shan was trained in law and administration in Japan in the early republican era and then joined Sun Yat-sen's staff in Guangzhou. Although he had no expertise in engineering or public works, he was recruited by C. T. Wang (Wang Zhengting), Chinese founder of the National Road-Building Association and leader of the Chinese YMCA, to replace the foreigners directing the association in 1921. In 1928–1929, he oversaw road construction in Henan and areas of the northwest and was criticized for destroying historic structures when he had a road built through the Hangu Pass. Lu Danlin, "Wu Shan de shengping" (The life of Wu Shan), *Sichuan wenxian* 59 (1967): 11.

44. Dong Xiujia 1927, 1–4. For a survey and analysis of a range of ideas about cities among Chinese of this era that gives prominence to antagonistic views, see Mann 1984, 86–107.

45. My knowledge of the career of Chen Weixin is based on his speeches, recorded in the *Guomin gongbao,* and interviews with Ren Zili, former director of the Chengdu YMCA, in Chengdu in 1991.

46. *Guomin gongbao,* April 2–10, 1924.

47. *Guomin gongbao,* May 25, 1924.

48. Garrett 1974, 231–232.

49. Ma Yanhu, "Yiju hua" (One sentence), *Chengdushi Yisilanjiao xiehui hexun* 9 (July 1989): 40.

50. Yang Sen's emphasis on clean living could be selective. Opium addiction among Chengdu residents, which probably contributed substantially to his income, was not something he brought up in his public lectures.

51. "Women Who Work," *The West China Missionary News* 27(5) (May 1925): 7–13.

52. *Guomin gongbao,* March 3, 1924.

53. The Chengdu city government yearbook from 1928 (the only one published in the republican era) cites the May Fourth movement as the inspiration for many patriotic demonstrations, but states that the only way to establish real national strength is to spread literacy, to make citizens out of the masses of people. *Chengdushi shizheng nianjian* 1928, 357.

54. "Yang Sen xiansheng fangwen jilu," interview 2.

55. *Guomin gongbao,* February 14, 1924.

56. Ma Xuanwei and Xiao Bo cite, for example, the case of Hu Lanjia, a teacher from Luzhou with leftist leanings. When Yang Sen's fourth wife was sent to invite her to join the family, she replied that the daughters of prominent leaders of the Gelaohui did not become people's concubines. Ma Xuanwei and Xiao Bo 1989, 35.

57. Shu Xincheng 1934, 149–153. Li Jieren studied literature in France and, like Sun Shaojing, returned to Chengdu in 1924. Unlike Sun Shaojing, however, he kept out of all city administration projects until he became vice mayor of Chengdu in the 1950s. In the late 1920s, he edited newspapers and help set up a paper factory south of Chengdu. In the 1930s, he worked in some of Lu Zuofu's enterprises.

58. The Elders and Sages were Chengdu's version of what David Strand has called Beijing's "thin line of long-gowned gentlemen" who "emerged to preserve social peace" during military upheavals. Strand 1989, 198.

59. Tao Liangsheng, who attended Xu Zixiu's Dacheng school.

60. On the Dacheng Association, see the *Dachenghui conglu.*

61. *Dachenghui conglu* 3 (July 1923).

62. Wang Liankui, "Zhuisui Huigong wushiba nian" (Fifty-eight years of following Yang Sen), in *Yang Sen jiangjun jinian ji* 1979, 441. See also Ma Xuanwei and Xiao Bo 1989, 38–39.

63. Jiang Mengbi 1990, 2.

64. Franck 1925, 547. Franck spent a month in Chengdu and met with Yang Sen several times.

65. For a general survey of Chinese chambers of commerce in this period, see Yu Heping 1993. A detailed examination of one chamber may be found in Strand 1989, chap. 5.

66. Shao Ying, "Chubanjia Fan Kongzhou" (The publisher Fan Kongzhou), *Chengdu zhi tongxun* 10 (1986): 55–59.

67. Sichuan's industry was still primarily small-scale. The money that supported Sichuan's armies came primarily from the land tax, often levied years in advance, taxes on the salt produced in the Ziliujing area, sales of opium, and control over shipping on the Yangzi and commerce in Chongqing. See Kapp 1973, 40–43; and Zhou Kaiqing 1972b.

68. Jiang Mengbi 1990, 2–7.

69. Tang Juecong, "Wang Jianming yu Chengdu shanghui" [Wang Jianming and the Chengdu chamber of commerce], *Jinjiang wenshi ziliao* 1 (1991): 135–144.

70. Letter from Ye Maoru, *Minshi ribao,* March 17, 1927. Ye Maoru recommended that a committee structure be adopted with twenty or thirty representatives, each selected by groups of two or three guilds. He cited Sun Yat-sen as the proponent of this sort of arrangement.

71. Such activities in Chengdu are the focus of Ba Jin's autobiographical novel, *Family.*

72. *Chengdushi shizheng nianjian* 1928.

73. "Chinese Forms of Politeness," *The West China Missionary News*

28(3) (March 1926): 33.

74. In 1923, the City Government Office drew up regulations that set out guidelines for what it hoped would be a cooperative relationship between street headmen and the city officials. *Chengdushi shizheng nianjian* 1928, 5.

75. I discuss the history of Chengdu's police and street headmen in detail in chapter 3 of Stapleton forthcoming. I discuss the Gelaohui in Stapleton 1996, 23–64.

76. "Yang Sen xiansheng fangwen jilu," interview 2.

77. On the involvement of Chengdu Gelaohui lodges with commerce in opium, see Shao Yun, "Chengdu 'paoge' shilue" (A rough history of Chengdu's "Gowned Brothers"), *Chengdu zhi tongxun* 16 (1988): 61. Their involvement in prostitution in Chengdu is not discussed in any published accounts, but seems likely. Organized gambling was another major source of income for lodges, according to Shao Yun. Yang Sen's attacks on gambling seem to have been limited to that done in public.

78. U.S. Archives, Chongqing consular correspondence, letter from John R. Muir to U.S. consul-general in Chongqing, May 22, 1924.

79. *Guomin gongbao,* September 16, 1924.

80. *Guomin gongbao,* April 16, 1924.

81. Yang Wanyun, "Daonian fuqin" (In memory of my father), in *Yang Sen jiangjun jinian ji* 1979, 421. Yang Sen was close to all of his twenty-eight children, she emphatically declared, noting that the children were the offspring of eight wives. Like Yang Sen himself, however, she avoided the question of exactly how many wives he had had in his life.

82. The life of Liu Shiliang is described in Zhong Maoxuan 1984. Many of Liu Shiliang's verses may be found in Lin Kongyi, ed. 1982.

83. Zhong Maoxuan 1984, 33–34.

84. Ibid., 89.

85. Luo Cairong, in *Yang Sen jiangjun jinian ji* 1979.

86. Lu Guoji 1984, 35; Franck 1925, 558.

87. Shu Xincheng 1934, 194, 131–132.

88. Wu Yu 1986, entry for February 8, 1925, vol. 2: 240.

89. Lin Kongyi, ed. 1982, 106.

90. *Chengdushi shizheng nianjian* 1928, 7.

91. Ibid., 5. The use of the name "Chengdu" in this text may have seemed grating to the aesthetic sensibilities of the Elders and Sages, since the city was usually referred to as "Furongcheng" (Hibiscus City) or the poetic abbreviation "Rong" in writings in classical Chinese.

92. *Chengdushi shizheng zhoukan* (Chengdu city government weekly) 4 (August 6, 1927). Even in Yang Sen's time, the desirability of openness in administration was recognized by some. Several of Yang Sen's advisers, including Sun Shaojing and Lu Zuofu, joined with newspaper reporters to form a "Friday Inspection Team" (Xingqiwu canguantuan) that announced its intention to make regular visits to governmental and nongovernmental institutions and report on what it saw, while making suggestions for improvement. *Guomin gongbao,* April 27, 1924.

93. *Chengdushi shizheng zhoukan* 1 (July 16, 1927).

94. An essay on Chengdu's need for a water supply system urged the city to learn from the failures of the waterworks of Tianjin, Beijing, and Guangzhou and set out regulations for a committee that would oversee preparations, but a new system was not set up until 1946. *Chengdushi shizheng zhoukan* 4 (August 6, 1927).

95. Zhou Zhongsheng, "Chengdushi zhi jianglai" (Chengdu's future), *Chengdushi shizheng zhoukan* 6 (August 20, 1927).

Part II: Tradition and Modernity
Chapter 7. Tourism and Spatial Change in Hangzhou, 1911–1927

1. Yu Dafu 1982, vol. 3, 402–403.

2. Wu Jingzi 1986, 138–139.

3. The concept of space has been receiving much attention lately, as scholars in a wide range of disciplines have begun to recognize the complex and intimate relationship between people and the social space they inhabit. Social space connects the abstract spaces of history, culture, economics, geography, and politics, and it also ties them together conceptually to the concreteness of buildings, roads, parks, and walls. Thus changes in the layout of physical locations not only indicate, but also are part of, changes in the larger social space. In fact, Lefevre would even go so far as to say that revolutionary social change could not occur without a simultaneous change in the space of society. Lefevre 1991; Harvey 1985.

4. Fu Chonglan 1985, 98–101, 109–115.

5. Fan Jinmin and Jin Wen 1993, 138–187.

6. Strassberg 1994, 25–27.

7. Su Shi's contribution to the traditional image of Hangzhou was especially significant. For Su Shi's life, see Egan 1994.

8. Liping Wang 1997, 63–82.

9. Ding Bing, ed. (1896) 1972.

10. For the Qing banner garrison system, see Kaye Soon Im 1993.

11. Zhang Dachang 1972, 474. For the Qing conquest of Jiangnan area, see Wakeman 1985; Crossley 1990, 58–62. During the Three Feudatories rebellion in the seventeenth century, the Hangzhou garrison was the focal point for transferring troops from the north and west to the southeast coastal area.

12. Ding Bing (1896) 1990, vol. 8, 430–431; Zhong Yulong 1983, 188–189.

13. Ruan Yicheng 1974, 36; Jianshe weiyuanhui diaocha Zhejiang jingji suo (1932) 1971, vol. 1, 157.

14. Cloud (1906) 1971, 13–14.

15. Zhou Feng, ed. 1990, 173, 211; Gong Jiajun and Li Rong (1922) 1974, 1510–1513; Zhong Yulong 1983, 208.

16. Huqingyu tang zhiyao chang, Zhongguo minzhu jianguo hui Hangzhoushi weiyuanhui, and Hangzhoushi gongshangye lianhehui 1990, no. 14, 171.

17. For the importance of the cult of the city-god in popular religion during the late imperial period and its connection to the local administrative institutions, see Hamashima 1992, 13–49.

18. Gong Jiajun and Li Rong (1922) 1974, 358.

19. Ibid., no. 76, 1530.

20. Zhong Yulong 1983, 310.

21. Fan Zushu (1928) 1989, 1–3.

22. Xiao Bing 1992, 687–701.

23. Yu Chun-fang 1992, 1–38; Chen Jingzhong and Mo Shi (1881) 1974, no. 11, 6843.

24. Bird 1948, 22.

25. Regarding pilgrimage in Ming and Qing periods, see Naquin and Yu 1992. The annual pilgrimage to Hangzhou originated from the cult of Guanyin in Jiangnan and dated back to the Southern Song period. Yu Chun-fang 1994, 334–335.

26. Zhong Yulong 1983, 316–318.

27. Broadwin 1993.
28. Fan Zushu (1928) 1989, 9.
29. Zhong Yulong 1983, 317. Zhou Feng, ed. 1990, 523.
30. Zhou Feng, ed. 1990, 138–139.
31. Lou Jixin 1990, no. 14, 93.
32. Zhou Feng, ed. 1992, 58–65.
33. Yan Qiang 1990, no. 14, 264–265.
34. Schoppa 1982, 145–149; Xu Heyong, Zheng Yunshan, and Zhao Shipei 1983, 260–261.
35. When the livelihoods of thousands of homeless bannermen became too much of a social problem to be ignored, the new government agreed to build a poor house of two hundred rooms for them at a corner near the former garrison area. Huang Yuanxiu 1981, 521–522; Ruan Yicheng 1974, 39–40. Many bannerman in Hangzhou experienced hardship during the republican period, and in the early 1930s many of them worked as food vendors on the streets. Jianshe weiyuanhui diaocha Zhejiang jingji suo (1932) 1971, 930–931.
36. "Toupiao Qiying dimu zhe zhuyi," *Zhejiang ribao* (November 7, 1913).
37. Zhejiang sheng sheke yanjiusuo, ed. 1984, 54–55.
38. The government limited itself to tearing down the walls and barracks of the garrison; the rest of the city wall remained until after 1949.
39. Zhong Yulong 1983, 191.
40. Ruan Yicheng 1974, 77.
41. Ibid., 40.
42. Zhou Feng, ed. 1992, 241.
43. Chi Changyao, ed. 1985, 22; Ruan Yicheng 1974, 40.
44. Xu Ke 1923, 159–160.
45. Ruan Yicheng 1974, 76–77.
46. Xu Ke 1923, 150.
47. "Toupiao Qiying dimu zhe zhuyi" (November 7, 1913).
48. Ibid.
49. Rou Bing 1924, 2.
50. Shiyebu guoji maoyiju, ed. 1933, 14–15.
51. Liu Huiwu, ed. 1987, 2; Luo Suwen 1991.
52. Luo Suwen 1991, 167.
53. Mao Dun 1986, vol. 11, 152.
54. Hu Ning Hu Hang Yong liang lu bianchake 1918, 8.
55. Zhongguo Luxingshe 1963, 5.
56. Jianshe weiyuanhui diaocha Zhejiang jingji suo (1932) 1971, no. 2, 785–786.
57. Fuji tushushe 1916, 1.
58. Fang Shaozhu (n.d), 3.
59. Shi Keshi 1934, advertisement.
60. Zhou Shoujuan, ed. 1929, 56–60.
61. Lin Zhengqiu and Shen Guanzhong 1993, 2–3.
62. Fan Zushu (1928) 1989, 3.
63. Ibid.
64. Ozouf 1988.
65. Strand 1989.
66. Hobsbawm and Ranger, eds. 1992, 1.
67. I am currently working on a book on urban space and the social transformation of Hangzhou, which will explore more fully the idea of the contemporaneity of modernity and tradition.
68. Wakeman and Yeh, eds. 1992; Johnson 1995.

Chapter 8. Defining Beiping: Urban Reconstruction and National Identity, 1928–1936

Abbreviations

JSH: Jingdu shizheng gongsuo, ed. 1919. *Jingdu shizheng huilan.* Beijing.

BGD/J: Beipingshi Gongwuju dang'an (Beiping Public Works Department Archives). Beijing Municipal Archives.

1. Zhu An 1936a, 107–108.
2. Xi Wuyi and Deng Yibing 1995, 160.
3. Ibid., 42.
4. Zhu An 1936c, 362.
5. Xi Wuyi and Deng Yibing 1995, 45–47.
6. Zhu An 1936a, 108.
7. Zhu An 1936b, 282.
8. On Yuan Liang in Shanghai, see Wakeman 1995a, 52–54.
9. Zhu An 1936c, 362.
10. Zhang Youxin 1934, 5–8.
11. Huang Zixian 1934, 9–14.
12. BGD/J1/4/1.
13. Ibid.
14. BGD/J1/7/6.
15. Ibid.
16. Ibid.
17. "Zhuang Ke" (pseud.) 1934, 2–3.
18. Zhu An 1936b, 282.
19. Dong Yue 1996.
20. Xi Wuyi and Deng Yibing 1995, 170–171.
21. Shi 1998.
22. *JSH,* 189–191.
23. Jianming 1996, 23–25.
24. *JSH,* 183–184.
25. Qi Rushan 1964, vol. 7, 4–5.
26. Shi Tuo (1935) 1997, 256.
27. Wu Tingxie, ed. 1990, 508, 535, 536, 544.
28. Xue Dubi 1925 (unpaginated).
29. BGD/ J17/398, J17/734.
30. Zhu An 1936a, 108.
31. BGD/J17/351.
32. Ibid.
33. Mosse 1975, 127.
34. *Beiyang huabao* (November 13, 1926): 2.
35. BGD/ J17/351, J17/354, J17/353, J17/352.
36. Beijing kaogu dui, ed. 1962, 80.
37. Olsen 1986, 9.
38. *Da ziyou bao* (November 14, 1912): 7.
39. BGD/J17/57.
40. Zhu An 1936c, 363.

41. Yuan Liang 1935, 17.

42. BGD/J1/4/1.

43. "Zhuang Ke" (pseud.) 1934, 2–3.

44. *Shizheng pinglun* 2(11) (November 1, 1934): 13.

45. Beipingshi zhengfu, eds. 1934, 1.

46. Ibid, 2–29.

47. Huang Zixian 1934, 9–14.

48. Wang Shiren and Zhang Fuhe 1993, 21–22.

49. *Shizheng pinglun* 3(14) (February 16, 1935): 11–25.

50. Hobsbawm and Ranger, eds. 1992, 4.

51. Zhu An 1936a, 108.

52. *"Jiudu wenwu lue* xu*"* (Preface to *Historical Relics of the Old Capital*), in Beipingshi zhengfu mishu chu, ed. 1935.

53. Zhu An 1936a, 108.

54. Zhu An 1936c, 362–363.

55. *Shizheng pinglun* 3(14) (July 16, 1935): 25.

56. Hu Shi, "Wenhua chongtu lun" (Cultural conflict) (1929), in Luo Rongqu, ed. 1990, 361–369.

57. Chen Xujing, "Quanpan xihua de liyou" (Reasons for total Westernization) (1934), in Luo Rongqu, ed. 1990, 376–391.

58. Wang Xinming, "Zhongguo benwei de wenhua jianshe" (Construction of a China-based culture) (1935), in Luo Rongqu, ed. 1990, 399–403, 475–478.

59. Ye Qing, "Quanpan xihua? Zhimindi hua?" (Total Westernization? Colonization?) (1935), in Luo Rongqu, ed. 1990, 555–557.

60. Zhang Xiruo, "Quanpan xihua yu Zhongguo benwei" (Total Westernization and China-based cultural construction) (1935), in Luo Rongqu, ed. 1990, 447–460.

61. Wei Shudong (1934) 1977, 40403.

62. Peter Demetz, "Introduction," in Walter Benjamin 1978, xvi.

Chapter 9. Building a Dream: Constructing a National Capital in Nanjing, 1927–1937

Abbreviations

USDS: U.S. Department of State. *Records of the Department of State Relating to the Internal Affairs of China, 1910–1929*

SDJS: Shoudu Jianshe

Thanks go to my mentors at University of California–San Diego: Paul G. Pickowicz, Joseph W. Esherick, and Dorothy Ko, who have each exceeded their normal responsibilities in guiding me through the research, writing, and editing of this chapter. I would also like to thank others who have taken exceptional time in assisting me along the way: Joce Lin, Liping Wang, Saul Thomas, and Anya Bernstein. Their criticism and encouragement have greatly influenced the nature of this chapter, although in the end I am responsible for its content.

1. The selection of the capital in republican-era China was always a contentious issue, which often broke down along regional lines. For more on the political feuds in 1912 between Yuan Shikai in the north and the revolutionaries in the south, see Ernest Young 1968, 435–439. For more on the debate that erupted when the GMD took Beijing in 1928, see Coleman 1984, 11–13.

2. *China Press* clipping in Nanjing consulate report to Knox, January 22, 1912, USDS 893/1088, M329, roll 9.

3. Ibid.

4. Ibid.

5. Henriot 1993; MacPherson 1990.

6. Mote 1977.

7. Wilbur 1983, 91–94, 105–107, 112–113.

8. Coleman 1984, 19. Nanking Woman's Club 1933, 16–17.

9. The Nanjing municipal administration was inaugurated under the GMD on April 24, 1927, with Liu Jiwen appointed as the first mayor. Wang Shou-fang, "Municipal Administration," in Ma Chao-chun, ed., *Nanking's Development,* 1937, 33. Running water was available in parts of the city beginning April 1, 1933 (T. C. Chow, "The Nanking Waterworks," ibid., 55). A sewage system entered the planning stages in 1933 and by 1937 consisted of 7,847 meters (Sung Hsi-shang, "Construction Activities," ibid., 40–42). See also Coleman 1984, 33.

10. Nanjing consulate to Knox, January 22, 1912, USDS 893/1088, M329, roll 9.

11. Coleman 1984, 68.

12. See *huiyi* (meeting) sections of *SDJS,* October 1928–July 1930. Chiang Kai-shek did not attend meetings regularly, so Kong Xiangxi usually acted as chairman.

13. In the organizational meeting of the Capital Construction Committee on June 22, 1929, the National Capital Planning Office was placed under its direct authority. *SDJS* 1 (October 1929): *huiyi,* 2.

14. Tyau, ed. 1930, 380.

15. Cody 1996, 352–353. Murphy's first architectural projects in China were U.S.-connected colleges: Yale-in-China in 1913 and Jinling Woman's College in Nanjing. Cody 1989.

16. Tyau, ed. 1930, 380.

17. A report by the southern revolutionaries described their intentions for the new capital. A copy of this report is included in a Nanjing consul to Knox, January 22, 1912, USDS 893/1088, M329, roll 9.

18. From 1921 to 1928, at least nineteen of these overseas students returned from the United States. Most of them had studied at the University of Pennsylvania, but others went to Cornell, Michigan, MIT, etc. A handful of architects returned from France and Japan. See Su 1964, 133–134.

19. For more on the influence of American architects and engineers in China, see Cody 1996, 339–377.

20. Lin Yimin 1929, *lunzhu,* 3.

21. Hong Lanyou 1929, *lunzhu,* 21.

22. Liu Jiwen 1929, *lunzhu,* 2.

23. Hong Lanyou, "Jianshe shoudu zhi jingfei wenti" (On the question of funding capital construction), *SDJS* 1 (October 1929): *lunzhu,* 20, 22.

24. The Nationalist government, for the most part, refused financial assistance to municipal administration—even to Shanghai, its important revenue generator. Henriot 1993, 148.

25. "Zai Shanghai Zhongguo Guomindang benbu huiyi de yanshuo" (Speech at the headquarters of the Guomindang, Shanghai), November 9, 1920, in Sun Zhongshan (Sun Yat-sen) 1985, vol. 5, 401.

26. My idea of discipline is informed by Foucault. See Foucault 1970, 1977; Burchell et al., eds. 1991.

27. Lin Yimin 1929, 3.

28. Lu Yanzhi 1929, *jihua,* 20.

29. The phrase is Fujitani's (1996, 73), referring to a description in Cannadine 1992.

30. Vale 1992; Tafuri and Dal Co 1976, chap. 3; Manieri-Elia 1983; Irving 1981; Fujitani 1996; Fischer 1984.

31. Lin Yimin 1929, 3–20, mentions all of these elements.

32. Lu Yanzhi 1929, 20.

33. Liu Jiwen 1929, 1.

34. Lin Yimin 1929, 3.

35. On the conventions of this relatively "timeless" imperial spatial order, see Boyd 1962; Lawrence Liu 1989; Mote 1977; Arthur Wright 1977; and Sen-Dou Chang, "The Morphology of Walled Capitals," in Skinner, ed. 1977. For a particularly illustrative example of how the transition from the Zhou feudal system of "first among equals" to the imperial system of the Qin and Han created vastly different conceptions of monumentality, see Wu Hung 1995.

36. On the cosmological spaces of everyday life, see Bray 1997; on domestic architecture, see Knapp 1989; on the naturalizing power of Confucian ritual, see Zito 1993.

37. Lin Yimin 1929, 12.

38. "Ni xuanze Zijin shan nanli wei zhongyang zhengzhi quyu an" (Draft to select the southern face of Purple Mountain as the central administrative zone), *SDJS* 1 (October 1929): *gongdu,* 29.

39. Shu Bade, "Duiyu ni xuanze Zijin shan nanli wei zhongyang zhengzhi quyu an zhi yijian shu—qi san" [Opinions on the selection of the southern face of Purple Mountain as the central administrative zone—number three], *SDJS* 1 (October 1929): *gongdu,* 39–41.

40. Wang Liping 1996.

41. Lu Yanzhi 1929, 20.

42. For more on Sun Yat-sen as a national symbol, see Wang Liping 1996.

43. Lu Yanzhi 1929, 23–24. Compare to Albert Speer's vision for German National Socialist monuments. Speer 1970, 55–56.

44. Boyd 1962, 73.

45. Zhu Baochu's comments on design number 7, in *SDJS* 2 (November 1929): *jihua,* 6.

46. "Shoudu zhongyang zhengzhi qu dang xuan tu'an shuoming shu" (Explanation of the selected plans for the central administrative zone), *SDJS* 2 (November 1929): *jihua,* 1.

47. Tyau, ed. 1930, 384.

48. *SDJS* 2 (November 1929): *jihua,* 1.

49. This could conceivably have been a crude ruse on the part of the committee to save money, since a third-place design would only earn 1,000 yuan, as opposed to the 1,500 and 2,000 yuan for second- and first-place works, respectively. "Pingxuan zhongyang zhengzhi qu yingzheng tu'an bing chengqing guofu he bo ci xiang jiangjin an" (Proposal to select the plans for the central political district through public appraisal and a request for the National government to deliberate and allocate award money), *SDJS* 2 (November 1929): *gongdu,* 7.

50. "Shoudu zhongyang zhengzhi qu dang xuan tu'an shuoming shu," *SDJS* 2 (November 1929): 1.

51. Shu Bade, "Shoudu jianshe ji jiaotong jihua shu" (Capital construction and traffic planning), *SDJS* 1 (October 1929): *jihua,* 19.

52. Hong Lanyou 1929, 20–22.

53. Sun Mou, Xia Quanshou, Shen Zuwei, "Shencha shoudu daolu xitong jihua zhi yijian shu—qi si" (Opinions on the investigation of the capital city road system plan—number four), *SDJS* 2 (November 1929): *jihua,* 42–43.

54. Nanking Woman's Club 1933, 12.

55. Arthur Wright 1977, 55–60; Boyd 1962, chap. 3.

56. Shang Qixu 1935.

57. On city planning in the West, see Hugo-Brunt 1972. On the disciplining potential of the spaces designed, see Gosling and Maitland 1984. On spatial control in Qing, Beijing, see Dray-Novey 1993.

58. In addition to the works by Foucault cited above, see Bourdieu 1990 on *habitus.* For a Foucault-informed analysis of city planning in the United States, see Boyer 1983. On colonial Egypt, see Mitchell 1991. On the modernist design of Brasília and evidence that modernist intentions are not always realized, see Holston 1989.

59. Sun Mou, Xia Quanshou, Shen Zuwei 1929, 42–43.

60. Manieri-Elia 1983; Boyer 1983; Girouard 1985.

61. "Shoudu zhongyang zhengzhi qu dang xuan tu'an shuoming shu," *SDJS* 2 (November 1929): 6.

62. Girouard 1985, 355.

63. Tyau, ed. 1930, 384.

64. Eastman 1974, 14, 185–186, 231.

65. The building was designed by Robert Fan (Fan Wenzhao), an architect with a bachelor's degree from St. John's and a master's degree from the University of Pennsylvania. Su 1964, 133, 137. "Shoudu weida jianzhu wu" 1937, 83–84. Fan Wenzhao had also worked for Sun Fo in Guangzhou, assisting in overseeing the construction of the Sun Yat-sen Memorial Hall. Cody 1996, 354.

66. Sun Yat-sen 1953.

67. Tyau, ed. 1930, 244. It is probably no coincidence that the Overseas Chinese Reception Hall was built a couple of blocks away from this building group.

68. Eigner 1938, 214.

69. "Shoudu weida jianzhu wu" 1937, 84–85.

70. Chen Jimin, ed. 1991, 48–50.

71. "Shoudu weida jianzhu wu" 1937, 84. During the Japanese occupation, the Examination Yuan housed Wang Jingwei's puppet government, an interesting choice of a less modernist structure. Wang Nengwei et al., eds. 1993, 55.

72. "Nanjing shi guan yue miao diaocha biao," June 22, 1935, Neizheng bu Archives, *chun fang* 12, *juan* 528, Second Historical Archives, Nanjing. I would like to thank Rebecca Nedostup for this archival information. See Nedostup forthcoming for more on how temples were converted to public use in this period.

73. Su 1964, 133, 137. Zhao Shen was a successful architect in China. He not only designed a number of buildings in Shanghai, Nanjing, and New York, but he had also won a contest (similar to the one for Nanjing) to design the Civic Center in Shanghai in 1930. MacPherson 1990, 52.

74. "Famous Buildings in Nanking" in Ma Chao-chun, *Nanking's Development,* 49–50.

75. "Shoudu guomin zhengfu waijiao bu ban'gong dalou ji guanshe" 1935, 4–16.

76. Ibid., 4.

77. Ibid.

78. Laurence Liu 1989, 35.

79. Space does not allow me to detail the construction of this building in this chapter. For more, see Musgrove, dissertation on architecture and urban planning in Nanjing, 1927–1937, University of California–San Diego, forthcoming. See also Chen Jimin, ed. 1991, 139–142.

80. Recent scholarship has just begun to explore the GMD efforts to create a national ritual. See Esherick and Wasserstrom 1994, 51–53; Wang Liping 1996; Nedostup forthcoming. For comparative discussion,

see Kertzer 1988.

81. de Certeau 1984, 117.

82. Eastman 1974, 185–186; Eastman 1991.

83. Jiang Yongcai and Di Shuzi, eds. 1991, 48.

84. Nanking Woman's Club 1933, 18.

85. Lee 1937, 133.

86. Chow Hsiang, "Land Adminstration," in Ma Chao-chun, *Nanking's Development,* 100.

87. Lee 1937, 134.

88. Sung Hsi-shang, "Construction Activities," in Ma Chao-chun, *Nanking's Development,* 36.

89. Nanking Woman's Club 1933, 18.

90. Guo Moruo n.d., 3.

91. Su 1964, 244.

92. Laurence Liu 1989, 273.

93. On capitol and capital, see Vale 1992, chap. 1.

Part III: City and Nation
Chapter 10. Wuhan's Search for Identity in the Republican Period

Research for this chapter was supported by a grant from the Pacific Cultural Foundation.

Abbreviations

WHWS: Wuhan wenshi ziliao

HBWS: Hubei wenshi ziliao

WHKZSL: Wuhan kangzhan shiliao xuanbian

WHKZSY Liu Jizeng et al.: Wuhan kangzhan shiyao

1. Liu Wangling 1991.

2. Rowe 1984 and 1989.

3. Good general studies focused on the local economy are Esherick 1976; Su Yun-feng 1981; Rowe 1993b; and Pi Mingxiu 1993.

4. Chang Ke-ming, "A Study of the Import and Export Trade of Hankow," *Chinese Social and Political Science Review* 20(2) (July 1936): 293–294.

5. Yang Bingde, ed. 1993, 145–148; Pi Mingxiu and Yang Pulin, eds. 1990, 375–435; *Jianghan wenshi ziliao* 1988, no. 2: 135–146. On Cai and Liu, see Rowe 1984, 50–51, 66, 395; *WHWS* 1985, no. 2: 130–137; *WHWS* 1988, no. 4: 148–153; Pi Mingxiu 1993, 301–305.

6. Su Yun-feng 1981, 82.

7. "Wuhan Industries after the Flood," *Chinese Economic Journal* 11(2) (August 1932): 83–100; "Wuhan Commerce after the 1931 Flood," *Chinese Economic Journal* 11(2): 201–212; and "Industries of Hankou," *Chinese Economic Journal and Bulletin* 19(2) (August 1936): 124–143; Pi Mingxiu 1985, 174–175; *WHWS* 1990, nos. 3, 4: 115–119. For a comprehensive overview of Wuhan's development, 1912–1938, see Pi Mingxiu 1993, 271–447.

8. "Wuhan sanzhen zhi xianzai ji qi jianglai" [The three Wuhan cities and their future], *Dongfang zazhi* 21, no. 5 (10 March 1924): 62–86.

9. Yang Bingde, ed. 1993 145–148; Pi Mingxiu and Yang Pulin, eds. 1990, 375–435.

10. Walter Weyl, "The Chicago of China," *Harper's* 18 (October 1918): 716–724.

11. *Hankou Jiujiang shouhui yingzujie ziliao xuanbian* (Historical materials on the recovery of the British Concessions at Hankou and Jiujiang) (Wuhan, 1982); Pi Mingxiu 1993, 307–331.

12. On the 1927 Wuhan government, see *Liu Jizeng et al.* 1986; Wilbur 1983; and the classic work by Isaacs (1938) 1972.

13. Pi Mingxiu and Yang Pulin, eds. 1990, 321–333; Pi Mingxiu 1993, 349–356.

14. Wuhan became a battleground in Guomindang bureaucratic politics between the "political study" and "C.C." cliques. Eventually a ruthless Wuhan area native and C.C. clique supporter, Gen. He Chengjun, prevailed, delivering the coup de grace with the 1936 assassination on the streets of Wuhan of the highest political study clique official, Yang Yongtai. See *WHWS* 1985, no. 1: 126–142; and 1990, nos. 3, 4: 237–239.

15. *WHWS* 1985, no. 2: 16–36.

16. Rowe 1993b argues this point.

17. *WHWS* 1982, no. 9: 85–112.

18. Abend 1944, 173–174.

19. Yang Bingde, ed. 1993, 156–157, 186–189; *Wuhan daxue xiaoshi* 1993, 102–132.

20. Pi Mingxiu 1985, 280–285.

21. *Jianghan wenshi ziliao* 1988, no. 2: 14–15.

22. Cao Ji'ou, 109–125; *WHWS* 1985, no. 1: 68–71; *WHWS* 1982, no. 9: 99.

23. See W. H. Auden and Christopher Isherwood, *Journey to a War* (New York, 1939), a journal in verse and prose about their mid-1938 trip to Wuhan and the war zone. The Ivens film became "400 Million" and was not released until the Pacific War period. See also Richard Whelan, *Robert Capa* (New York, 1985).

24. *WHKZSL* 1985, 242–244.

25. Yuan Jicheng 1987, 26. I have argued elsewhere that the flowering of the national press at Wuhan in 1938 was a critical step in the history of the Chinese press and in the reformulation of a national wartime identity. See Stephen R. MacKinnon, "Toward a History of the Chinese Press in the Republican Period," *Modern China* 23(1) (January 1997): 3–32.

26. *WHKZSY* 1985, 190–204, 362–366; *WHKZSL* 1985, 166–171, 259–262; *WHWS* 1985, no.1: 68–71.

27. Hung 1994.

28. For a penetrating analysis of the negative impact of the war on Chinese culture, see Feng Chongyi, *Kangzhan shiqi de zhongguo wenhua* (Chinese culture during the Sino-Japanese War) (Guilin, 1995); and in English, Edward Gunn,"Literature and Art of the War Period," in *China's Bitter Victory: The War with Japan, 1937–45,* ed. James Hsiung and Steven I. Levine (Armonk, N.Y., 1992), 235–274. Zou Taofen's political odyssey during this period involved such a sacrifice of autonomy.

29. Liang Jialu 1984, 360–399.

30. *WHKZSL* 1985, 249–258; *HBWS* 1985, no. 2: 170–185; *WHKZSY* 1985, 17–22, 377–380; *Kangzhan shiqi neiqian xinan de gongshang qiye* 1989.

31. Yang Bingde, ed. 1993, 157; *WHKZSL* 1985, 249–257; Pi Mingxiu and Yang Pulin, eds. 1990, 334–339; Pi Mingxiu 1993, 658–671.

32. *WHKZSY* 1985, 394–396.

33. Sun Yankui,"Kangzhan chuqi Wuhan nanmin jiuji zouyi" (Wuhan refugee relief work at the beginning of the War of Resistance), *Jianghan luntan* 6 (1996): 43–48.

34. J. Heng Liu papers, manuscript division, Butler Library, Columbia University. For prewar background and an excellent bibliography, see Ka-che Yip, *Health and National Reconstruction in Nationalist China: The Development of Modern Health Services, 1928–1937* (Ann Arbor, Mich., 1996).

35. *WHKZSY* 1985, 185–190. Combined enrollment during wartime in colleges and universities rose from thirty thousand in 1938 to seventy thousand by 1945.

36. Huang Jianli, "The Formation of the Guomindang Youth Corps: An Analysis of Its Original Objectives," *East Asian History* 5 (June 1993): 133–148; *WHKZSY* 1985, 175, 181, 213–215, 266, 292–293, 366–369; *WHKZSL* 1985, 147–150.

37. The classic celebration of the Wuhan spirit is Guo Moruo's poetic tribute, *Hongboqu*. It was first published just after the war and then reprinted a number of times; see also Mao Dun's memoirs for a 1970s invocation of the Wuhan ideal. Interviews with Zhou Libo, Ge Baochuan, Mao Dun in 1978; with Ding ling, Zhou Yang, Qian Junrui in 1980; and with Hu Sheng and Hu Qiuyuan in 1992. From local histories, *HBWS* 1987, no. 2: 117–139 is typical. See also introduction to *Wuhan kangzhan shi* 1995.

Chapter 11. The City as Nation: Creating a Wartime Capital in Chongqing

Abbreviations

SWRB: Shangwu ribao

XMB: Xin Minbao

XSB: Xin Shubao

1. Kapp 1973, 62–86, 99–120.

2. Other aspects of this strategy included removing large numbers of provincial military forces out of Sichuan to front lines where, ill-equipped and poorly prepared, they suffered heavy losses; placing Guomindang appointees in political and administrative positions; establishing relationships with leading members of the powerful gang known locally as the Robed Brothers (Paoge); and working to undermine local militarists and entrepreneurs. See Ibid., 136–138; and Tang Shaowu et. al., "Jiefang qian Chongqing de Paoge" (The Robed Brothers of Chongqing before liberation), *Chongqing wenshi ziliao* 31 (1989): 164–171.

3. On the relationship between French colonial urban design and politics, see Wright 1991.

4. On imperial Chinese capitals, see Steinhardt 1990, 1–28.

5. Chen Ershou 1943, 116.

6. For statistics of Chongqing's wartime population, see He Yaozu 1945, 19. Because of the large number of refugees, obtaining accurate population figures for wartime Chongqing presented even more of a challenge than usual for census takers. The actual number of people in 1945 was probably much higher than the figure of just over one million reported by the police department.

7. Chen Ershou 1943, 128.

8. Wu Jisheng (1939) 1978, 15.

9. Xue Shaoming (1937) 1986, 134.

10. Basil 1940, 18–19.

11. Woodhead 1931, 49.

12. "Han Suyin" (pseud.) 1942, 208–209.

13. Service, ed. 1989, 252.

14. *XSB*, September 9, 1940.

15. Wu Jisheng (1939) 1978, 120–121.

16. See, for example, the three-part series on Chongqing's rats in *XMB*, January 6, 1939–January 8, 1939.

17. Xue Shaoming (1937) 1986, 134.

18. Interview with He Hongjun, November 13, 1992.

19. Lu Sihong 1939, 182. No information about the grade level of the students in this survey is given by Lu Sihong.

20. Hahn 1944, 114.

21. Jiang Yuanying 1937, 73–75.

22. *Sichuan yuebao* 10(3) (March 1937): 278.

23. Chongqing shi difangzhi bianzuan weiyuanhui zongbianji shi 1989, 150–151. With the available data, it is not possible to know how much the figures overlap.

24. *Sichuan yuebao* 11(5) (November 1937): 187–188; and *Sichuan yuebao* 12(5, 6) (May–June 1938): 273. The publication of such statistics ended after the Guomindang government moved to Chongqing.

25. Esther Tappert Mortensen to family, October 26, 1937, Record Group 21, folder 4, no. 57. China Records Project, Day Missions Library, Yale Divinity School, New Haven, Conn. Mortensen's comment may reveal more about differences between the urban structure of Chongqing and China's coastal treaty ports than it does about the level of poverty in Chongqing. Roadside corpses were, of course, not unique to Chongqing. Wakeman (1995a, 84), citing a Western source, notes that during the 1920s police in Shanghai "annually disposed of about twenty thousand corpses decomposing in the streets and alleys of Shanghai." Perhaps Chongqing's social and geographic structure provided fewer opportunities to shield elite residents from urban poverty. Or perhaps Shanghailanders looked down on Chongqing's poverty as Westerners looked at Shanghai.

26. "Ke Fei" (pseud.) 1938, 369–370.

27. Lu Sihong 1939, 156.

28. Interview with He Hongjun, November 13, 1992.

29. Xia Yan 1943, 62. In an attempt to cut down on rickshaw pullers' overcharging of passengers, especially during air-raid alarms, the municipal government regularly set fares according to distance. As this imaginary conversation suggests, these efforts had little impact on rickshaw fares.

30. Hahn 1944, 113.

31. Little 1888, 241.

32. Wu Jisheng (1939) 1978, 124–125.

33. Xia Yan 1943, 62.

34. *Sichuan yuebao* 10(1) (January 1937): 224–225.

35. Kapp 1974, 150.

36. Spencer 1939, 52–53.

37. Kapp 1974, 152.

38. Lu Sihong 1939, 3.

39. See Chen Jianming 1991, 546, 548. According to Chen Jianming, only 446 of the 1,038 employees in Chongqing's municipal government in October 1939 were from Sichuan. Most of them worked in the Police Bureau (Jingcha ju), where they numbered 310 among a total of 623 employees. Eighty of the remaining Sichuanese in the municipal government worked in the Treasury Bureau (Caizheng ju).

40. Theodore White 1978, 83.

41. Chen Jianming 1991, 560–564.

42. Electric streetlights provide a good example of this problem. By 1939 more than 2,500 electric streetlights had been installed along Chongqing's main thoroughfares in the New and Old Cities, as well as in outlying satellite towns. But as streets and these lights suffered heavy damage during air raids, no sooner were repairs completed than they were destroyed again. In the devastating air raids of August 19–20, 1940, alone, more than half the city's streetlights were destroyed. See Hu Daoxiu 1991, 481.

43. The lack of interest in developing Chongqing after 1941 is suggested

by the disbanding of the Committee for Planning the Reconstruction of the Alternate Capital late that year, and the subsequent failure to implement any of its recommendations until after the war. Zhou Yong 1991, 283–284.

44. Throughout the war years, local elites in Chongqing and the chamber of commerce were a persistent voice for more substantive modernization. A full discussion of their role is beyond the scope of this chapter. Studies of Chongqing's wartime modernization emphasize the role of the Guomindang government to the exclusion of these important local figures, but scattered glimpses of their modernizing activities may be found in local wartime newspapers, articles in *Chongqing gongshang shiliao,* memoirs published in *Chongqing wenshi ziliao,* and biographies found in *Chongqing mingren cidian.*

45. However, in at least the one case mentioned above, some of the beggars who were removed from Chongqing's streets in 1938 were sent off to the army as conscripts.

46. *SWRB,* November 28, 1938.

47. See ibid. for a full list of the regulations aimed at improving the city's appearance.

48. *XMB,* December 7, 1939.

49. Forman 1948, 160.

50. *SWRB,* November 28, 1938.

51. *XSB,* March 2, 1941.

52. Ibid.

53. Hu Daoxiu 1991, 473.

54. *XMB,* December 7, 1938.

55. Lu Sihong 1939, 33.

56. Streets in Shanghai were all called *"lu"* at this time.

57. Hu Daoxiu 1991, 473–474.

58. Chen Ershou 1943, 134–136.

59. Hu Daoxiu 1991, 496–498.

60. Chongqing Municipal Archives comp. 1990, 117.

61. The exact number of factories that were transferred to Chongqing during the war is difficult to determine with certainty. For varying estimates, see Lin Jiyong, *Lin Jiyong Xiansheng fangwenji* (Reminiscenses of Mr. Lin Jiyong) (Taipei, 1983); also Eastman et al. 1991, 130–131.

62. See, for example, Peck 1950, 412–430 and passim.

63. Wu Jisheng (1939) 1978, 14–15.

64. Zhou Yonglin 1991, 63

65. See, for example, *XSB,* March 12, 1941.

66. Lin Yutang 1944, 36.

67. The exact date on which the remains of the Spiritual Fortress were cleared away and the flagpole erected are uncertain, but it seems to have occurred during the war. In 1947, the monument was reconstructed and renamed "Victory Monument" to celebrate the end of the war. After 1949, it was renamed "Liberation Monument" (Jiefang bei). It still stands at the center of the commercial district in the central section of downtown Chongqing.

68. Adet et al. (1941) 1975, 240.

69. Mao Ke, "Busi de shancheng" (Everlasting Mountain Town), *Qunzhong* 3(4) (June 11,1939): 143.

70. Wang Yinnong 1943, 47.

71. Lou Zikuang 1943, 43.

72. Lin Yutang 1944, 37.

73. Jiang Yuanying 1937, 75.

74. According to the *Ciyuan Cidian* (1990, 0053), it refers to the lower reaches of the Yangzi River below Jiangling County in Hubei.

75. See, for example, Han Suyin 1942, 206; also Zhang Henshui 1946, 12. Despite the perception that "downriver" was a local Sichuanese term, it actually seems to have been used most frequently by immigrants from central and eastern China to refer to themselves with pride.

76. Lu Sihong 1939, 37.

Chapter 12. Locating Old Shanghai: Having Fits about Where It Fits

1. Two of the best general introductions to Old Shanghai are Liu 1985 and Takahashi Kōsuke and Furuya Tadao, eds. 1995. In English, Murphey 1953 is still useful, as is Howe, ed. 1981. For good samplings of recent scholarship, see Wakeman and Yeh, eds. 1992; Zhang Zhongli et al., eds. 1990; and Yeung and Sung, eds. 1996, which, despite its title, contains a good deal of discussion of pre-1949 phenomena. The arguments in this chapter were first developed in talks I gave at Columbia University, the Nordic Institute of Asian Studies, the School of Oriental and African Studies, University of California–San Diego, University of California–Santa Barbara, University of California–Berkeley, and Indiana University, and in a think piece I did for the Chinese urban studies newsletter, *Wall and Market.* I am particularly grateful to the audiences at those presentations for comments that helped me refine my thinking about Shanghai comparisons, as well as to the editors of *Wall and Market* for the same reason. Others whose criticisms, suggestions, or encouragement have been particularly beneficial include Robert Bickers, Soren Clausen, Paul Cohen, Michael Curtin, Joe Esherick, Harriet Evans, Susan Glosser, Mike Grossberg, Anne Haila, Barbara Mittler, Liz Perry, Mark Selden, Steve Smith, Kristin Stapleton, and the students who have taken my courses on Old Shanghai and on comparative urban history.

2. *All about Shanghai: A Standard Guidebook* 1983 [1934–1935], 44.

3. Many of these distinctive characteristics are dealt with in the encyclopedic Shanghai yanjiu zhongxin and Shanghai renmin chubanshe, eds. 1991. See also Tang Zhenchang, ed. 1993 and Tang Zhenchang 1994. On specific points made above, many important recent works could be cited, ranging from Hershatter 1997 (on sex workers) to Clifford 1991 (on governance).

4. On *tongxianghui,* see Goodman 1995, as well as various contributors to Wakeman and Yeh, eds. 1992 and to Perry and Wasserstrom, eds. 1993–1994.

5. According to Goto-Shibata 1995, 5–6, there were 18,902 Japanese living in Shanghai by 1925, and by 1931 there were some 20,000, making up 70 percent of the foreign population. For an excellent introduction to the tremendous diversity found within the foreign community in Shanghai that looks at distinctions related to class and gender as well as national origin, see Bickers 1998.

6. A good popular work that deals with architectural variation, along with many other topics, is Pan 1982; ample visual evidence is provided in Tang Zhenchang, ed. 1993 (probably the best pictorial history of the city) and Takahashi Kōsuke and Furuya Tadao, eds. 1995.

7. The city's ability to inspire utopian and dystopian visions is clear in many popular works published during the treaty-port era; for academic discussion of the phenomenon, see Wakeman and Yeh, eds. 1992, 1–14; MacPherson 1996; and Wasserstrom 1996.

8. For further discussion of Sorkin's comments, in particular, and the parallels between Shanghai and Los Angeles, in general, see Wasserstrom 1996.

9. For an insightful general introduction to the way that cities have been studied by historians in the PRC, see Clausen and Thøgersen, eds. 1995.

10. Clifford 1991 begins with the comment: "Seventy years ago, Shanghai occupied a position very much like that of Hong Kong today," xi; many of the Hong Kong-based contributors to Yeung and Sung, eds. 1996 also draw parallels between the two urban centers.

11. These themes are handled well in Evans and Tam, eds. 1997.

12. For a good deconstruction of the East-meets-West image of Hong Kong, see the "Introduction" to Evans and Tam, eds. 1997, 1–21.

13. Johnson 1995.

14. For an intriguing case study that draws attention to the gendered implications of such divisions, see Seline Ching Chan 1997.

15. On city-state imagery, see MacPherson 1987. See also, for an impressive discussion of Western understandings (and distortions) of Old Shanghai's history, Bickers 1993.

16. See Wakeman 1995a; Martin 1996; Perry 1993; and Wasserstrom 1991.

17. Examples of this sort of imagery are sprinkled through many of the Chinese and Western language guidebooks cited in works such as Bickers and Wasserstrom 1995; Wasserstrom 1996; Ye Shaoqing 1992; and Hershatter 1997. For some additional relevant sources, see Wakeman 1995b.

18. The most significant effort to date to root Shanghai history in a comparative lower Yangzi context is Johnson, ed. 1993.

19. See, for example, the claim in Shanghai Municipal Tourism Administration and Hong Kong China Tourism Press, eds. 1995 that the building of a bridge connecting Pudong and western Shanghai was the fulfillment of a dream Shanghai people had cherished for seven hundred years—no matter that for most of that period Pudong was looked down upon as a backwater area with which most of those living in Puxi wanted little to do.

20. Interestingly, this approach also facilitates comparison between Shanghai and at least one Taiwan city, Taizhong. Shanghai and Taizhong are two of the thirteen urban centers that get a chapter to themselves in a recent work on coastal cities: Yeung and Hu, eds. 1992; curiously, Hong Kong is not given its own chapter in that collection. Hong Kong is included, however, in an important recent chapter by White and Cheng 1993 that uses a similar classificatory technique.

21. Useful recent statistics on Shanghai's overall population and population density can be found in Fung et al. 1992. See also the map in this same work, 136, which illustrates very nicely just how much bigger Old Shanghai was than Ur-Shanghai and how much larger still New Shanghai has become since 1949.

22. Bergère 1979.

23. For an overview of the development of Shanghai studies within China up to the 1990s, see Tang Zhenchang 1994, 180–197. Discussion and translation of sample works on specific subjects are provided in Perry and Wasserstrom, eds. 1993–1994 and Stranahan, ed. 1994–1995.

24. Sample publications include Wakeman 1995a and 1995b; Goodman 1995; Johnson 1995; Gota-Shibata 1995; Yeh 1995; and Bickers and Wasserstrom 1995.

25. Hershatter 1997 is one of the more noteworthy.

26. For my piecemeal efforts to untangle connections of this sort, see Wasserstrom 1991.

27. Goodman 1995.

28. Honig 1992.

29. Zhang Jishun 1993–1994, 71–77.

30. For discussion of differences of opinion within the Shanghai foreign community and relevant citations, see Clifford 1990; Huskey 1987; and Bickers and Wasserstrom 1995.

31. Two key examples of the popular history genre are Clark 1921 and Lanning and Couling 1921.

32. This point has been made by Catherine Vance Yeh as well, in a fascinating unpublished paper delivered at the 1996 annual meetings of the Association for Asian Studies. One of the most frequently reproduced Shanghailander maps is in Pott 1928. I should note that, while in typical fashion it presents the Native City as an essentially blank space, it does list a few points of interest—but these turn out to be missionary establishments and other places with clear links to the foreign community

33. *North-China Daily News* 1893 and *Shanghai Mercury* 1893 are the commemorative albums with which I have worked. Three scholarly studies that refer to the Jubilee are Ye Shaoqing 1992; MacPherson 1987; and Bickers and Wasserstrom 1995.

34. Henriot 1993; see also MacPherson 1996.

35. *All About Shanghai: A Standard Guidebook* 1983 [1934–35], 135.

36. For more on local parks, the rules governing their use, and confusions surrounding the issue, see Bickers and Wasserstrom 1995.

37. Glass 1989, 154 and passim.

Chapter 13. New Chinese Cities

1. Zhu Dingzhang 1924, 76.

2. Wang Shuigong 1920, 80. Wang Shuigong argues for recognizing the value and place of both in the unfolding of history.

3. See Barth 1975.

4. The classic statement of late imperial urban capacity in these areas is found in Rowe 1984 and 1989. For a summary and discussion of work on this question by Rowe and others, see Strand 1995a.

5. Quoted in Yu Heping 1993, 171–172.

6. For assessments of the significance of such reorganizations that stress the novelty of what was taking place, see ibid., 158–172; Goodman 1991, 83; and Wu Zhezheng 1988, 88.

7. Lang 1946, 78.

8. Lu Hanchao 1994 shows the limits of modern Shanghai weighed against the daily life of most residents.

9. Fang Wenpei, "Sichuan kaocha ji" (An investigation of Sichuan), *Fangzhi yuekan* (Gazetteer monthly) 6(7) (July 1, 1933): 3; and Ren Mei'e, "Lanzhou fujin dizhi yanjiu" (An investigation of the topography of Lanzhou and vicinity), *Fangzhi yuekan* 8(45) (April 1, 1935): 7.

10. A description of Nanjing in 1926 opens conventionally by noting the city's key importance "politically, militarily and commercially" and then notes the growing presence of rural folk begging on the city streets after fleeing drought and war. Bian Nofu, "Nanjing gaikuang" (A survey of Nanjing), *Xiangdao zhoubao* (The weekly guide) 153 (May 15, 1926): 1467.

11. Rowe 1989, 118.

12. For an interesting discussion of the broader issues involved in the social history of human excrement, see Andrew Morris, "'Fight for Fertilizer!': Excrement, Public Health, and Mobilization in New China," *Journal of Unconventional History* (May 1995).

13. Gu Yaqiu 1931, 49, 50.

14. Dong Xiujia 1925; and *Gansu minguo ribao* (July 1, 1941): 1.

15. Cheng Guangyu 1953, 24; and Mann 1984, 83.

16. See editorials championing Lanzhou and critical of Shanghai in Lanzhou's *Gansu minguo ribao* (July 1, 1941), (July 3, 1941): 5; and (April 8, 1942): 3. Lanzhou "boosterism" is discussed in Strand 1995b.

17. Pannell 1981, 98.

18. "Nanjing tongxin" (Nanjing communique), *Xiangdao zhoubao* 60 (March 26, 1924): 482.

19. For a discussion and inventory of China's many capitals during the first half of the century, see Liu Jingkun and Fu Bing, "Minguo shiqi de shoudu, peidu yu xingdu" (Capitals, secondary capitals, and administrative capitals during the republican era), *Minguo dang'an,* no. 1 (1994): 114–117.

20. Shao 1994.

21. See Mayfair Mei-hui Yang's discussion of arborescent and rhizome-like tendencies in Chinese culture and society. Yang, *Gifts, Favors and Banquets: The Art of Social Relationships in China* (Ithaca, N.Y., 1994), 307–308.

22. Zhou Junqi 1994, 107.

23. Hill Gates, *China's Motor: A Thousand Years of Petty Capitalism* (Ithaca, N.Y., 1996). Gates argues that Chinese history, at least since the Song, involves competition between rival strategies: one a "tributary" approach keyed to the state and state-centric hierarchies, and the other a choice to turn resources, including self and family members, into commodities. For a summary and comment on the evidence for long-term waves of commercial development, see William T. Rowe, "Approaches to Modern Chinese Social History," in *Reliving the Past: The Worlds of Social History,* ed. Olivier Zunz (Chapel Hill, N.C., 1985), 270–283.

24. Clunas 1991, 41, 60.

25. Ibid., 172–173.

26. Cochran 1995.

27. For an interesting discussion of the sources of resistance to urban development, see Dong Xiujia 1936.

28. Yu Heping 1993, 104.

29. Goodman 1995, especially chap. 5.

30. Ibid., 138.

31. Holston 1989, 87–89.

32. During the republican period the area outside Tiananmen had not yet been redesigned as a formal square. This formalization of what students and townspeople had become accustomed to using as a protest site took place in the 1950s.

33. A very interesting recent study that complements points made on this issue by Dong is Timothy B. Weston, "Intellectuals in a Fading Capital: Living and Writing in Republican Beijing," a paper presented to a panel on "The City and Its People," Association of Asian Studies, 1997 meeting.

34. Ren Jianshu and Zhang Quan 1985, 240.

35. Susan R. Brooker-Gross, "The Changing Concept of Place in the News," in *Geography, the Media and Popular Culture,* ed. Jacquelin Burgess and John R. Gold (New York, 1985), 72.

36. "Northern Expedition poster," Library of Congress file 8535, LC-USZ62-62487.

37. *Yishi bao* (Social welfare) June 29, 1924, 7. Quoted and discussed in Strand 1995a, 419–420.

38. He Luzhi, *Guojia zhuyi gailun* (An outline of nationalism) (Shanghai: Zhongguo renwen yanjiusuo, 1948), 12.

39. Ibid., 5. He Luzhi argues that the nation, properly understood, is not a machine but a body capable of feeling, thinking, and acting as one.

40. For the urban origins of rural popular culture and propaganda, see Hung 1994, 3–4.

41. Lin Yungai 1919, 1.

42. See, for example, Kate Xiao Zhou's argument that even before the Deng reforms, the Communist regime had become deeply alienated from the countryside. Zhou, *How Farmers Changed China: Power of the People* (Boulder, Colo., 1996), 243–244.

Glossary

Well-known personal and place names are omitted from this glossary.

Aiga Kensuke　相賀兼介
Anding men　安定門
baidao　拜倒
banshichu　辦事處
baojia　保甲
Baojing ke　保淨科
baowei　保衛
Beiping shi　北平市
Beiping tebie shi　北平特別市
Beiping zhengzhi fenhui　北平政治分會
Beiyang fangyi chu　北洋防疫處
bendi ren　本地人
Bōekika　防疫科
buerjia　不二價
Bushixin　卜士馨
Cai Fuqing　蔡輔卿
canshihui　參事會
celiang　測量
Changdi　長堤
chaoshan jinxiang　朝山進香
Chen Xujing　陳序經
Chenghuang shan　城隍山
chengshi　城市
chong　蟲
Chongde men　崇德門
Chunming guan　春明館
chunshu shiwu xingzhi　純屬事務性質
Chunxi　春熙
Chūō dōri　中央通り
ci zhimindi　次殖民地
cipin　次貧
cishanhui　慈善會
cuyu　醋魚
Dajie　大街
Damalu　大馬路
Daodejing　道德經
daotai　道台
daren　大人
datong　大同
Daxin　大新
Daxing　大興
deyu, zhiyu, tiyu　德育智育體育
Di tan　地壇
diaocha　調查
diaojiaolou　掉腳樓
Ding Ziliang　丁子良
Dong Xianguang　董顯光
Dongfang wenhua biaoxian　東方文化表現
dongshi　董事
doucheng　豆城
Duan men　端門
duchong　毒蟲
duli　獨立
dushi guihua lun　都市規畫論
dushi mei　都市美
eisei　衛生
Eiseibu　衛生部
Endō Arata　遠藤新
Erdaogou　二道溝
Fan Bin　樊彬
fangbiansuo　方便所
Fengle　豐樂
fengqi jishu xishang yiyi　風氣既殊習尙亦異
fenhang　分行
Fuji-dōri　富士通り
Fukushima Yasumasa　福島安正
fumin tongpan　扶民通判
fuzokuchi　附屬地
ganhua　感化
Gelaohui　哥老會
genju di　根據地
gongbi hua　工筆畫
gongde　公德

Gonghe 共和
Gongkuang tiaozhengchu 工礦調整處
Gotō Shimpei 後藤新平
Gu shan 孤山
guanchan chu 官產處
Guandi 關帝
guangchang 廣場
Guanyin 觀音
Gudu wenwu zhengli weiyuanhui 故都文物整理委員會
gundan 滾蛋
Guo Le 郭樂
Guodu sheji jishu zhuanyuan banshichu 國都設計技術專員辦事處
Guomin zhengfu 國民政府
Guowuyuan 國務院
Haida xiyuan 海大戲院
Haihui si 海會寺
Haipai 海派
hao jiating 好家庭
He Chengjun 何成濬
heian 黑暗
Heping gongyuan 和平公園
Heping lu 和平路
hiroba 廣場
Hojōka 保淨科
Hong Lanyou 洪蘭友
Hong Shen 洪深
Hu Guangyong 胡光庸
Hua Xuelan 華學蘭
Hua-E daosheng yinhang 華俄道勝銀行
Huairentang 懷仁堂
Huang Fu 黃郛
Huang Yuyu 黃玉瑜
huangcheng 皇城
huaxue 化學
Hubin gongyuan 湖濱公園
Hubin lu 湖濱路
Huode 火德
huotui you duo 火腿油多
Huqingyu tang 胡慶余堂
Iwai-machi 祝町
jia 佳
jian 間
jianzhu zhidu 建築制度
jiaojia 教稼
jie 街
jie 界
Jiefang bei 解放碑
Jieyuan 芥園
jiezheng 街正
jingli 經理
Jingpai 京派
jingshen 精神
Jingshen baolei 精神堡壘
jingshen zong dongyuan 精神總動員
jingshi jimin 經世濟民
Jingyuetan 淨月潭
Jingzhao 京兆
Jingzhao gongyuan 京兆公園
jipin 極貧
Jiu Shanghai 舊上海
Jiudu wenwu lue 舊都文物略
Jiushantang 九善堂
kaishui 開水
Katō Yonokichi 加藤与之吉
kejizhe 客籍者
Kō-A 興亞
Kō-A kokumin dōin taikai 興亞國民動員大會
Kodama Gentarō 見玉源太郎
Kong Xiangxi 孔祥熙
Kongfengchun 孔鳳春
Koshizawa Akira 越沢明
Kuanchengzi 寬城子
Kulun 庫侖
Kyōwa hiroba 協和廣場
Kyōwakai 協和會
Laijin yu xuan 來今雨軒
Laocheng 老城
Laoqianggen 老墻根
laoye 老爺
Li Siguang 李四光
Libailiu 禮拜六
Lichun 立春

Lin Kesheng 林可勝
Lin Yimin 林逸民
Linshi canyi hui 臨時參議會
Liu Jiwen 劉紀文
Liu Xinsheng 劉歆生
Liuliyao Zhao 琉璃窯趙
Longshen miao 龍神廟
Longyu 隆裕
lu 路
Lu Yongxiang 盧永祥
lufang 爐房
Lugou qiao 蘆溝橋
Luohezhen 漯河鎮
Ma Yingbiao 馬應彪
Maekawa Kunio 前川國男
magua 馬褂
Maju qiao 馬駒橋
Manshū seinen renmei 滿洲青年連盟
meishu 美術
Meng Xianyi 孟憲彝
Mentougou 門頭溝
Minsheng lu 民生路
minzhi 民治
minzu fuxing 民族復興
Minzu lu 民族路
Mizoe Satsuki 溝江五月
Nanhu 南湖
Nanling 南嶺
Nanyuan 南苑
niangjia 娘家
Nihonbashi-dōri 日本橋通り
nong 農
ōhiroba 大廣場
pailou 牌樓
paoge 袍哥
peidu 陪都
Peng Jiazhen 彭家珍
piaohao 票號
pingmin 平民
qianpu 錢鋪
Qiantang men 錢塘門
qianzhuang 錢莊
Qingbo men 清波門
Qinhuai he 秦淮河
qipao 旗袍
qiuba 丘八
qiying 旗營
Qu Yongqiu 屈永秋
qunzhong 群眾
Renhe 仁和
Ri pai 日派
ronglu 熔爐
Ruan Shouyi 阮守一
Ruan Xingyi 阮性宜
Ruan Zhenduo 阮振鐸
Sakakura Junzō 坂倉準三
San dadian 三大殿
Sanmin zhuyi 三民主義
Sano Toshikata (Riki) 佐野利器
Sanzhongjing 三中井
Sekiya Tazuro 関屋悌藏
Shancheng 山城
Shang Tianzhu si 上天竺寺
shang you tiantang, xia you Su Hang 上有天堂，下有蘇杭
shangbu 商埠
shangcheng 上城
shanshi 善士
shehui 社會
shehui guojia 社會國家
Sheji tan 社稷壇
Shengxun 聖訓
Shennong 神農
shi 市
Shi Congyun 施從云
Shi Tuo 師陀
shihui 市會
Shijie yuan 世界園
shimao modeng nulang 時髦摩登女郎
Shimin lu 市民路
shirong 市容
shizheng 市政
shizheng gongsuo 市政公所
shizheng gongyijuan 市政公益卷

Shizheng heshu 市政合署
shouding 瘦丁
shoudu 首都
Shoudu jianshe weiyuanhui 首都建設委員會
Shuangmendi 雙門底
shuidian 水店
Shuishen 水神
Shuntian dajie 順天大街
Sichuan shangye quangonghui 四川商業勸工會
Subeiren 蘇北人
Sunhe zhen 孫河鎮
Taimiao 太廟
taisui shangshan 太歲上山
teikan 帝冠
Tianjin fangyi baowei yiyuan 天津防疫保衛醫院
Tianzhu 天竺
Tongsu jiaoyuguan 通俗教育館
Tongsu tushuguan 通俗圖書館
tongxianghui 同鄉會
Toudaogou 頭道溝
Tsuzuki Jinnosuke 都筑甚之助
tubaozi 土包子
Tudigong 土地公
tuoli 脫離
waishengren 外省人
Wang Huaiqing 王懷慶
Wang Jinming 王金明
wangdao 王道
Wanping 宛平
weisheng 衛生
weisheng ju 衛生局
weiyuan 委員
Wenbing pai 瘟病派
Wenchang 文昌
Wenhua dian 文華殿
wenming 文明
wenyi 瘟疫
Wu men 午門
wulao qixian 五老七賢
Wumiao 武廟
Wushan 吳山
Wuying dian 武英殿
Xiacheng 下城
xiajiang ren 下江人
xiang 巷
xiangshi 香市
Xianshi [Sincere] 先施
Xiao Dongxi 小東西
xiaoshimin 小市民
Xiguan 西關
Xihu shijing 西湖十景
xin sanduo 新三多
Xin shichang 新市場
Xincheng 新城
xingdu 行都
Xingqiwu canguantuan 星期五參觀團
xingzheng weiyuanhui 行政委員會
Xinjing 新京
Xinsheng lu 新生路
xinzheng 新政
xiucai 秀才
xiuqiao bulu 修橋補路
xue buzai siyi; wu Chengdu jiu you shizhang wu xiu feiguan yi 學不在四夷; 吾成都舊有市長吾修廢官矣
Xue Dubi 薛篤弼
xueshu 學術
Yan Shiqing 顏世清
Yang Qingshan 楊慶山
Yang Shande 楊善得
yanghuo 洋貨
Yanling lu 延齡路
Ye Qing 葉青
Ye Ting 葉挺
yi tongji de xingshi biaolie 以統計的形式表列
ying gailiang jiating 應改良家庭
yinhang 銀行
yinhao 銀號
Yinma 銀馬
yiqi 疫氣
yishu 藝術
Yitong 伊通
Yongan 永安
Yongding he 永定河
Yongjin men 涌金門

Yoshino-machi 吉野町
youmin 游民
Youqiu 有秋
Yuan Liang 袁良
Yuanming Yuan 圓明園
Yuefen 岳墳
Yuguan 榆關
Yūki Kiyotarō 結城清太郎
Zhang Youxin 張又新
Zhao Daiwen 趙戴文
Zhao Shen 趙深
Zhejiang shangpin chenlie guan 浙江商品陳列館
Zhejiang shengli gongzhong tiyu chang 浙江省立公眾體育場
zhengke 政客
zhihang 支行
Zhongguo yingzao xueshe 中國營造學社
Zhonghua pingmin jiaoyu cujinhui 中華平民教育促進會
Zhongnanhai 中南海
Zhongshan gongyuan 中山公園
Zhongshan lu 中山路
zhongshu 中樞
Zhongyang gongyuan 中央公園
Zhu Fucheng 諸輔成
Zhu Qiqian 朱啓鈐
Zhu Shenkang 朱神康
zhuangding 壯丁
Zijin shan 紫金山
zilai shui 自來水
zong banshichu 總辦事處
zonghang 總行

Bibliography

Titles mentioned only one or two times in the notes of a single chapter are given a full reference in the notes. All other titles are listed below.

Abend, Hallet. 1944. *Treaty Ports.* New York.

Adshead, S. A. M. 1984. *Province and Politics in Late Imperial China: Vice-regal Government in Szechwan, 1898–1911.* London.

Agrest, Diana. 1996. "The Return of the Repressed: Nature." In *The Sex of Architecture,* ed. Diana Agrest, Patricia Conway, and Leslie Kanes Weisman, 49–68. New York.

All about Shanghai: A Standard Guidebook. [1934–1935] 1983. Hong Kong. Reprint with a new introduction by H. J. Letheridge of a 1930s handbook titled *All about Shanghai and Environs.*

Andrews, Bridie. 1997. "Tuberculosis and the Assimilation of Germ Theory in China, 1895–1937." *Journal of the History of Medicine and Allied Sciences* 52 (1) (January): 114–157.

Arendt, Hannah. 1958. *The Human Condition.* Chicago.

Arnold, David, ed. 1988. *Imperial Medicine and Indigenous Societies.* Manchester.

———. 1993. *Colonizing the Body: State Medicine and Epidemic Disease in Nineteenth-century India.* Berkeley.

Barth, Gunther. 1975. *Instant Cities: Urbanization and the Rise of San Francisco and Denver.* New York.

Basil, George Chester. 1940. *Test Tubes and Dragon Scales.* Chicago.

Beijing kaogu dui 北京考古隊 (Archaeological Team of Beijing), ed. 1962. *Beijing mingsheng guji* 北京名勝古跡 (Places of historic interest and scenic beauty in Beijing). Beijing.

Beipingshi Gongwuju dang'an北平市工務局檔案 (Beiping Public Works Department Archives.) BGD/J

Beipingshi zhengfu 北平市政府, ed. 1934. *Beiping youlan qu jianshe jihua* 北平遊覽區建設計劃 (Plan for constructing Beiping tourist district). Beiping.

Beipingshi zhengfu mishu chu 北平市政府秘書處, ed. 1935. *Jiudu wenwu lue* 舊都文物略 (Historical articles in the old capital). Beiping.

Beiyang huabao 北洋畫報.

Benedict, Carol. 1996. *Bubonic Plague in Nineteenth-century China.* Stanford.

Benjamin, Walter. 1978. *Reflections: Essays, Aphorisms, Autobiographical Writings.* Trans. Edmund Jephcott. New York.

Bergère, Marie-Claire. 1979. "Shanghai ou 'l'autre Chine,' 1919–1949." *Annales ESC* 5 (September–October): 1039–1068; English trans. in Howe, ed., 1981, 1–34.

———. 1986. *The Golden Age of the Chinese Bourgeoisie, 1911–1937.* Trans. Janet Lloyd. Cambridge.

———. 1992. "The Shanghai Bankers' Association, 1915–1927: Modernization and the Institutionalization of Local Solidarities." In *Shanghai Sojourners,* ed. Frederic Wakeman, Jr. and Wen-hsin Yeh. Berkeley.

Berman, Marshall. 1982. *All That Is Solid Melts into Air.* New York.

Bernstein, Lewis. 1988. "A History of Tientsin in Early Modern Times, 1800–1910." Ph.D. dissertation, University of Kansas.

Bian Baimei 卞白眉. Diary. Manuscript.

Bickers, Robert. 1993. "History, Legend, and Treaty Port Ideology, 1925–1931." In *Ritual and Diplomacy: The Macartney Mission to China, 1792–1794,* ed. Robert Bickers, 81–92. London.

———. 1998. "Shanghailanders: The Formation and Identity of the British Settler Community in Shanghai, 1843–1937." *Past and Present* 159 (February): 161–211.

Bickers, Robert, and Jeffrey Wasserstrom. 1995. "Shanghai's 'Dogs and Chinese Not Admitted' Sign." *China Quarterly* 142 (June): 444–466.

Bird, George. 1948. *Hangchow Holidays: Where to Go and What to See.* Shanghai.

Birrell, James. 1964. *Walter Burley Griffin.* Melbourne.

Boorman, Howard L., and Richard C. Howard, eds. 1967–1971. *Biographical Dictionary of Republican China.* New York.

Borel, Henri. 1912. *The New China: A Traveller's Impressions.* Trans. C. Thieme. New York.

Bourdieu, Pierre. 1990. *The Logic of Practice.* Trans. Richard Nice. Stanford.

Boyd, Andrew. 1962. *Chinese Architecture and Town Planning: 1500* B.C.–A.D. *1911.* Chicago.

Boyer, M. Christine. 1983. *Dreaming the Rational City: The Myth of American City Planning.* Cambridge, Mass.

Bray, Francesca. 1997. *Technology and Gender: Fabrics of Power in Late Imperial China.* Berkeley.

Broadwin, Julie. 1993. "Raising Silkworms: Women and Rituals of Early 20th Century Jiangnan." Seminar paper, University of California–San Diego.

Buck, David D. 1978. *Urban Change in China: Politics and Development in Tsinan, Shantung, 1890–1949.* Madison, Wis.

Burchell, Graham, et al., eds. 1991. *The Foucault Effect: Studies in Governmentality.* Chicago.

Cai Ji'ou 蔡寄鷗. 1943. *Wuhan xinwen shi* 武漢新聞史 (History of Wuhan journalism). Wuchang.

Campbell, Cameron. 1995. "Chinese Mortality Transitions: The Case of Beijing, 1700–1990." Ph.D. dissertation, University of Pennsylvania.

Cannadine, David. 1992. "The Context, Performance and Meaning of Ritual: The British Monarchy and the 'Invention of Tradition,' c. 1820–1977." In Hobsbawm and Ranger, eds., 101–164.

Cao Yu 曹禺. 1978. *Cao Yu xuanji* 曹禺選集 (Collected works of Cao Yu). Beijing.

Chan, Seline Ching. 1997. "Negotiating Tradition: Customary Succession in the New Territories of Hong Kong." In Evans and Tam, eds., 151–173.

Chan, Wellington K. K. 1998. "Personal Styles, Cultural Values, and Management: The Sincere and Wing On Companies in Shanghai and Hong Kong, 1900–1941." In MacPherson, ed., 66–89.

Chang, Sen-Dou. 1977. "The Morphology of Walled Capitals." In Skinner, ed., 75–100.

Changchun shizhi: Shangye zhi 長春市志商業志 (Gazetteer of Changchun: Industry). 1995. Changchun.

Chen Ershou 陳爾壽. 1943. "Chongqing dushi dili" 重慶都市地理 (The urban geography of Chongqing). *Dili xuebao* 地理學報 (Geography review) 10: 114–138.

Chen Huimin 陳惠民 and Lou Jixin 婁繼心. 1990. "Fangyuhe nanbeihuo shangdian" 方裕和南北貨商店 (The Fangyuhe dry food store). In *Hangzhou lao zihao (Hangzhou wenshi ziliao di shisi ji)* 杭州老字號 (杭州文史資料第十四輯) (Old shops of Hangzhou), ed. Zhengxie Hangzhoushi weiyuanhui wenshi ziliao weiyuanhui 政協杭州市委員會文史資料委員會, 90–96. Hangzhou.

Chen Jianming 陳建明. 1991. "Chengshi xingzheng guanli" 城市行政管理 (Municipal administration). In Wei Yingtao 隗瀛濤, ed., 517–602.

———, ed. 1991. *Jinling zhanggu* 金陵掌故 (In search of old Nanjing). Nanjing.

Chen Jimin 陳濟民, ed. 1992. 國民官府 *Guomin guanfu* (National offical buildings), Nanjing.

Chen Jingzhong 陳景鍾 and Mo Shi 莫拭. (1881) 1974. Qingbo san zhi 清波三志 (Three accounts of the Qingbo Gate area). In *Wulin zhanggu congbian* 武林掌故叢編, ed. Ding Bing 丁丙, 6817–6924. Taibei (reprint).

Chen Xingwu 陳醒吾 . 1986. "Ma Yingbiao yu Xianshi gongsi" 馬應彪與先施公司 (Ma Yingbiao and the Sincere Company). *Guangzhou wenshi ziliao* 廣州文史

資料 (Source materials on the history and culture of Guangzhou) 36: 124–135.

Cheng Guangyu 程光裕. 1953. *Zhongguo dushi* 中國都市 (Chinese cities). Taibei.

Chengdushi shizheng nianjian 成都市市政年鑒 (Yearbook of Chengdu city government). 1928. Chengdu.

Chengdushi shizheng zhoukan 成都市市政周刊 (Chengdu city government weekly). 1927–1928. Chengdu.

Chengdushi shizheng gongbao 成都市市政公報 (Chengdu city government gazette). 1928– .

Chi Changyao 池長堯, ed. 1985. *Xihu jiuzong* 西湖舊蹤 (A pictorial album of West Lake in the old days). Hangzhou.

The Chinese Times. 1886–1889. Tianjin.

Chongqing consular correspondence. U.S. National Archives.

Chongqingshi difangzhi bianzuan weiyuanhui zongbianji shi 重慶市地方誌編纂委員會總編輯室 (General editorial office of the editorial committee for the Chongqing local gazetteer), ed. 1989. *Chongqing dashi ji* 重慶大事記 (Chronology of important events in Chongqing). Chongqing

Chongqing Municipal Archives, comp. 1990. Chongqingshi dang'anguan jianming zhinan 重慶市檔案館簡明指南 (A concise guide to the Chongqing municipal archives). Chongqing.

Ciucci, Giorgio, et al. 1983. *The American City: From the Civil War to the New Deal.* Trans. Barbara Luigia La Penta. Cambridge, Mass.

Ciyuan Cidian 詞源詞典 (Dictionary of word origins). 1990. Beijing.

Clark, J. D. 1921. *A Short History of Shanghai.* Shanghai.

Clausen, Søren and Stig Thøgersen, eds. 1995. *The Making of a Chinese City: History and Historiography in Harbin.* Armonk, N.Y.

Clifford, Nicholas R. 1990. "A Revolution is Not a Tea Party: The Shanghai Mind(s) Reconsidered." *Pacific Historical Review* 59 (November): 501–526.

———. 1991. *Spoilt Children of Empire: Westerners in Shanghai and the Chinese Revolution of the 1920s.* Hanover, N.H.

Cloud, Frederick Douglas. (1906) 1971. *Hangchow, the "City of Heaven": With a Brief Historical Sketch of Soochow.* Taibei (reprint).

Clunas, Craig. 1991. *Superfluous Things: Material Culture and Social Status in Early Modern China.* Urbana, Ill.

Coble, Parks. 1980. *The Shanghai Capitalists and the Nationalist Government, 1927–1937.* Cambridge, Mass.

Cochran, Sherman. 1995. "Marketing Medicine and Advertising Dreams in China, 1900–1950." Paper presented to a conference on "Becoming Chinese," Center for Chinese Studies, University of California–Berkeley, June 2–4.

Cody, Jeffrey W. 1989. "Henry K. Murphy, An American Architect in China, 1914–1935." Ph.D. dissertation, Cornell University.

———. 1996. "American Planning in Republican China, 1911–1937." *Planning Perspectives* (October) 11 (4): 339–377.

Coleman, Maryruth. 1984. "Municipal Politics in Nationalist China: Nanjing, 1927–1937." Ph.D. dissertation, Harvard University.

Coleman, William. 1982. *Death Is a Social Disease: Public Health and Political Economy in Early Industrial France.* Madison, Wis.

Colquhoun, Archibald. 1900. *The "Overland" to China.* London.

Cooper, Frederick, and Ann Laura Stoler, eds. 1997. *Tensions of Empire: Colonial Cultures in a Bourgeois World.* Berkeley.

Corbin, Alain. 1986. *The Foul and the Fragrant: Odor and the French Social Imagination.* Cambridge, Mass.

Crossley, Pamela K. 1990. *Orphan Warriors: Three Manchu Generations and the End of the Qing World.* Princeton.

Da ziyou bao 大自由報 (Great liberty news). Beijing.

Dachenghui conglu 大成會叢錄 (Dacheng Association recorder). 1922–1925. Chengdu.

Dagong bao. 大公報 (L'Impartial). 1902–1938. Tianjin.

Dai Chuanxian 戴傳賢 [Dai Jitao]. 1919. "Geming! Hegu? Weihe?" 革命! 何故? 爲何? (Revolution! Why? For what?). *Jianshe* 建設 1 (3): 1–31.

Dai Nianci 戴念慈, ed. 1988. *Jianzhu, yuanlin, chengshi guihua* 建築, 園林, 城市規劃 (Architecture, parks, and city planning). *Zhongguo dabaike quanshu* 中國大百科全書 (Great encyclopedia of China). Beijing.

Dasgupta, Keya. 1995. "A City Away from Home: The Mapping of Calcutta." In *Texts of Power*, ed. Partha Chatterjee, 145–166. Minneapolis.

De Certeau, Michel. 1984. *The Practice of Everyday Life.* Translated by Steven Rendall. Berkeley.

Deng Yusheng 鄧雨生. 1910. *Quanyue shehui shilu chubian* 全粵社會實錄初編 (A draft record of Guangdong society). Guangzhou.

DeVries, Jan. 1984. *European Urbanization, 1500–1800.* London.

Dikötter, Frank. 1995. *Sex, Culture and Modernity in China: Medical Science and the Construction of Sexual Identities in the Early Republican Period.* Honolulu.

Ding Bing 丁丙, ed. (1896) 1972. *Gengxin qi Hang lu* 庚辛泣杭錄 (Mourning for Hangzhou in the years 1860 and 1861). Taibei (reprint).

———. (1896) 1990. *Wulin fangxiang zhi* 武林坊巷志 (Gazetteer of streets and wards in Hangzhou). Reprint. Hangzhou.

Dong Biwu nianpu 董必武年譜 (Chronological biography of Dong Biwu). 1991. Beijing.

Dong Xiujia 董修甲. 1925. Tianyuan xinshi yu woguo shizheng 田園新市與我國市政 (Garden cities and municipal government in China). *Dongfang zazhi* 東方雜誌 22 (11) (10 June).

________. 1927. *Shizhengxue gangyao* 市政學綱要 (Outline of the study of city administration). Shanghai.

________. 1936. *Guomin jingji jianshe zhi tujing* 國民經濟建設之途徑 (Avenues of national economic reconstruction). Shanghai.

Dong Yue. 1996. "Memories of the Present: Vicissitudes of Transition in Republican Beijing, 1911–1937." Ph.D. dissertation, University of California–San Diego.

Dong Yuying 董玉英. 1987. "Qingdai Liaohe hangyun matou" 清代遼河航運碼頭 (Shipping ports on the Liao River in the Qing period). *Shixue jikan* 史學集刊 (Collected papers on historical science) (February): 68–73.

Dray-Novey, Alison. 1993. "Spatial Order and Police in Imperial Beijing." *Journal of Asian Studies* 52 (4) (November): 885–992.

Duan Yunzhang 段雲章, et al. 1989. *Chen Jiongming de yisheng* 陳炯明的一生 (The life of Chen Jiongming). Zhengzhou, Henan.

Duffy, John. 1968. *A History of Public Health in New York City, 1625–1866.* New York.

———. 1990. *The Sanitarians: A History of American Public Health.* Urbana, Ill.

Duus, Peter. 1989. "Japan's Informal Empire in China, 1895–1937: An Overview." In Duus, Myers, and Peattie, eds., xi–xxix.

Duus, Peter, Ramon H. Myers, and Mark R. Peattie, eds. 1989. *The Japanese Informal Empire in China, 1895–1937.* Princeton.

———. 1996. *The Japanese Wartime Empire, 1931–1945.* Princeton.

Eastman, Lloyd E. 1974. *The Abortive Revolution: China under Nationalist Rule, 1927–1937.* Cambridge, Mass.

Eastman, Lloyd E., et al. 1991. *The Nationalist Era in China, 1927–1949.* Cambridge.

Egan, Ronald C. 1994. *Word, Image, and Deed: The Life of Su Shi.* Cambridge, Mass.

Eigner, Julius. 1938. "The Rise and Fall of Nanjing." *National Geographic Magazine* 73 (2) (February): 189–234.

Elvin, Mark, and G. William Skinner, eds. 1974. *The Chinese City between Two Worlds.* Stanford.

Esherick, Joseph W. 1976. *Reform and Revolution in China: The 1911 Revolution in Hunan and Hubei.* Berkeley.

Esherick, Joseph W., and Jeffrey N. Wasserstrom. 1994. "Acting Out Democracy: Political Theater in Modern China." In *Popular Protest and Political Culture in Modern China*, 2d. ed. Ed. Jeffrey N. Wasserstrom and Elizabeth J. Perry, 28–66. Boulder, Colo.

Evans, Grant, and Maria Tam, eds. 1997. *Hong Kong: The Anthropology of a Chinese Metropolis.* Surrey.

Evans, Harry. 1994. *Water Distribution in Ancient Rome: The Evidence of Frotinus.* Ann Arbor, Mich.

Evans, Richard. 1987. *Death in Hamburg: Society and Politics in the Cholera Years, 1830–1910.* Oxford.

Fan Jinmin 範金民 and Jin Wen 金文. 1993. *Jiangnan sichou shi yanjiu* 江南絲綢史研究 (Studies of the history of Jiangnan silk production). Beijing.

Fan Zushu 範祖述. (1928) 1989. *Hang su yifeng* 杭俗遺風 (Memories of old customs in Hangzhou). Shanghai (reprint).

Fang Shaozhu 方紹翥. n.d. "Luxing Hangxian Xihu ji" 旅行杭縣西湖記 (Records of touring West Lake in Hang County). In *Xin youji huikan* 新游記匯刊 vol. 25: 1–25. Shanghai.

Finnane, Antonia. 1994. "A Place in the Nation: Yangzhou and the *Idle Talk* Controversy of 1934." *Journal of Asian Studies* 53 (4) (November): 1150–1174.

Fischer, K. F. 1984. *Canberra: Myths and Models: Forces at Work in the Foundation of the Australian Capital.* Hamburg.

Fishman, Robert. 1977. *Urban Utopias in the Twentieth Century: Ebenezer Howard, Frank Lloyd Wright, and Le Corbusier.* Cambridge, Mass.

Folsom, Kenneth E. 1968. *Friends, Guests and Colleagues: The Mu-fu System in the Late Ch'ing Period.* Berkeley.

Forman, Harrison. 1948. *Changing China: A Factual Account of China as It Is and as It Was.* New York.

Foucault, Michel. 1970. *The Order of Things: An Archaeology of the Human Sciences.* New York.

——— 1977. *Discipline and Punish: The Birth of the Prison.* Trans. Alan Sheridan. New York.

——— 1980. "The Politics of Health in the Eighteenth Century." In *Power/Knowledge: Selected Interviews and Other Writings, 1972–1977,* ed. Colin Gordon. Brighton.

———. (1970) 1991. "Governmentality." Trans. Pasquale Pasquino. In *The Foucault Effect,* ed. Graham Burchell, Colin Gordon, and Peter Miller, 87–104. Chicago.

Franck, Harry A. 1925. *Roving through Southern China.* New York.

Fu Chonglan 傅崇蘭. 1985. *Zhongguo yunhe chengshi fazhan shi* 中國運河城市發展史 (A history of cities along the Grand Canal). Chengdu.

Fu, Poshek. 1993. *Passivity, Resistance, and Collaboration: Intellectual Choices in Occupied Shanghai.* Stanford.

Fuji toshosha 富士圖書社. 1916. *Kōshū shinan* 杭州指南 (Guide to Hangzhou). Hangzhou.

Fujitani, T. 1996. *Splendid Monarchy: Power and Pageantry in Modern Japan.* Berkeley.

Fung, Kai-iu, et al. 1992. "Shanghai: China's World City." in Yeung and Hu, eds., 124–152.

Gan Houci 甘厚慈, ed. (1907) 1966. *Beiyang gongdu leizuan* 北洋公牘類纂(Classified collection of public documents of the commissioner of trade for the northern ports). Taibei (reprint).

Gansu minguo ribao 甘肅民國日報 (Gansu republican daily).

Gao Pikun 高丕琨, ed. 1988. *Weiman renwu* 僞滿人物 (Manchukuo personalities). Changchun.

Garrett, Shirley S. 1974. "The Chambers of Commerce and the YMCA." In Elvin and Skinner, eds., 213–238.

Gaubatz, Piper Rae. 1996. *Beyond the Great Wall: Urban Form and Transformation on the Chinese Frontiers.* Stanford.

Geison, Gerald L. 1995. *The Private Science of Louis Pasteur.* Princeton.

Ginsburg, Norton S. 1947. "Ch'ang-ch'un." *Economic Geography* 23 (October): 290–307.

Girouard, Mark. 1985. *Cities and People: A Social and Architectural History.* New Haven, Conn.

Glass, Ruth. 1989. *Clichés of Urban Doom and Other Essays.* Oxford.

Gong Jiajun 龔嘉雋 and Li Rong 李蓉. (1922) 1974. *Hangzhou fu zhi* 杭州府志 (Gazetteer of Hangzhou Prefecture). Taibei (reprint).

Goodman, Bryna. 1992. "New Culture, Old Habits: Native-Place Organization and the May Fourth Movement." In Wakeman and Yeh, eds., 76–107.

———. 1995. *Native Place, City, and Nation: Regional Networks and Identities in Shanghai, 1853–1937.* Berkeley.

Gosling, David, and Barry Maitland. 1984. *Concepts of Urban Design.* London.

Goto-Shibata, Harumi. 1995. *Japan and Britain in Shanghai, 1925–31.* London.

Goubert, Jean-Pierre. 1986. *The Conquest of Water: The Advent of Health in the Industrial Age.* Trans. Andrew Wilson. Princeton.

Great Britain, Foreign Office. Archives. Public Record Office, London.

Gu Yaqiu 顧亞秋. 1931. "Jianzhu sheji yu dushimei zhi guanxi" 建築設計與都市美之關係 (The relationship between architectural design and urban aesthetics). *Dongfang zazhi* 東方雜誌 28 (5) (March10).

Guangrentang 廣仁堂 (Hall for Spreading Benevolence). Record group 130. Tianjin Municipal Archives.

Guangzhou zhinan 廣州指南 (A guide to Canton). 1934. Guangzhou.

Guangzhoushi caizhengju renli shouche chezhan jiamubiao 廣州市財政局人力手車車站價目表 (The Bureau of Finance's table of stops and fares for rickshaws in Canton). 1927. Guangzhou.

Guangzhoushi dianli gongsi ershi nianlai zhi gaikuang 廣州市電力公司二十年來之概況 (The Canton Electricity Company in the last twenty years). 1929. Guangzhou.

Guangzhoushi shizheng baogao huikan 廣州市市政報告匯刊 (A collection of reports of the Canton municipal government). 1924. Guangzhou.

Guangzhoushi shizhengfu tongji nianjian 廣州市市政府統計年鑒 (The statistical yearbook of the Canton municipal government). 1929. Guangzhou.

Guo Moruo 郭沫若. n.d. *Nanjing yinxiang* 南京印象 (Impressions of Nanjing). Litong chubanshe.

Guomin gongbao 國民公報 (Citizen's gazette). 1912–1936. Chengdu.

Hahn, Emily. 1944. *China to Me.* Boston.

Hall, Stuart, David Held, Don Hubert, and Kenneth Thompson, eds. 1996. *Modernity: An Introduction to Modern Societies.* Oxford.

Hamashima, Atsutoshi. 1992. "The City-God Temples (*ch'eng huang-miao*) of Chiangnan in the Ming and the Ch'ing Dynasties." In *Memoirs of the Research Department of the Toyo Bunko* 5 (Spring): 13–49.

"Han Suyin" (pseud.). 1942. *Destination Chungking.* Boston.

Harrison, Mark. 1994. *Public Health in British India: Anglo-Indian Preventive Medicine, 1859–1914.* Cambridge.

Harvey, David. 1985. *Consciousness and the Urban Experience: Studies in the History and Theory of Capitalist Urbanization.* Baltimore.

———. 1990. *The Condition of Postmodernity: An Enquiry into the Origins of Cultural Change.* Cambridge, Mass.

He Yaozu 賀耀組. 1945. *Chongqing yaolan* 重慶要覽 (Important facts about Chongqing). Chongqing.

Helmer, Stephen D. 1985. *Hitler's Berlin: The Speer Plans for Reshaping the Central City.* Ann Arbor, Mich.

Henriot, Christian. 1993. *Shanghai, 1927–1937: Municipal Power, Locality, and Modernization.* Berkeley.

Hershatter, Gail. 1986. *The Workers of Tianjin, 1900–1949.* Stanford.

——— 1997. *Dangerous Pleasures: Prostitution and Modernity in Twentieth-Century Shanghai.* Berkeley.

Hobsbawm, Eric, and Terence Ranger, eds. 1992. *The Invention of Tradition.* Cambridge.

"Hokuto Ryosei" 北斗老星 (pseud.). 1921. "Manshu toshi keikaku gaikan" 滿洲都市計画概觀 (An overview of urban planning in Manchuria). *Toshi kōron* 都市公論 (Urban journal) 4 (11) (November): 38–40.

Holston, James. 1989. *The Modernist City: An Anthropological Critique of Brasilia.* Chicago.

Hong Lanyou 洪蘭友. 1929. "Zenyang jianshe dang zhi xia de shoudu" 怎樣建設黨治下的首都 (How to build the capital under the rule of the party). *Shoudu jianshe* 2 (November): *lunzhu*, 20–23.

Honig, Emily. 1986. *Sisters and Strangers: Women in the Shanghai Cotton Mills, 1919–1949.* Stanford.

———. 1992. *Creating Chinese Ethnicity: Subei People in Shanghai, 1850–1980.* New Haven, Conn.

Hosie, Alexander. 1904. *Manchuria: Its People, Resources and Recent History.* London.

Howe, Christopher, ed. 1981. *Shanghai: Revolution and Development in an Asian Metropolis.* Cambridge.

Hu Daoxiu 胡道修. 1991. "Chengshi jichu sheshi yu shizheng jianshe" 城市基礎設施與市政建設 (The construction of urban infrastructure and municipal administration). In Wei Yingtao, ed., 459–516.

Hu Ning Hu Hang Yong lianglu bianchake 滬寧滬杭甬兩路編查科. 1918. *Hu Ning Hu Hang Yong tielu luxing zhinan* 滬寧滬杭甬鐵路旅行指南 (A guide to travel on the Shanghai-Nanjing and Shanghai-Hangzhou-Ningbo railroads). Shanghai.

Hua Xuelan 華學蘭. 1936. *Xinchou riji* 辛丑日記 (1901 diary). Shanghai.

Huang Yanpei 黄炎培. 1921. *Yisui zhi Guangzhoushi* 一歲之廣州市 (Canton at one year old). Shanghai.

Huang Yuanxiu 黄元秀. 1981. "Xinhai Zhejiang guangfu huiyilu" 辛亥浙江光復回憶錄 (Memoir of the 1911 Revolution in Zhejiang). In *Xinhai geming Zhejiang shiliao xuanji* 辛亥革命浙江史料選輯 (Selected historical materials on the 1911 Revolution in Zhejiang), ed. Zhejiang xinhai geming shi yanjiuhui and Zhejiang tushuguan 浙江辛亥革命史研究會浙江圖書館, 516–525. Hangzhou.

Huang Zixian 黄子先. 1934. "Fanrong Pingshi zhi wo jian" 繁榮平市之我見 (My opinions about reviving Beiping). *Shizheng pinglun* 1 (June): 9–14.

Hubei wenshi ziliao 湖北文史資料 (Materials on the history and culture of Hubei). 1985–1990.

Hugo-Brunt, Michael. 1972. *The History of City Planning: A Survey.* Montreal.

Hung, Chang-tai. 1994. *War and Popular Culture: Resistance in Modern China, 1937–1945.* Berkeley.

Huqingyu tang zhiyao chang 胡慶余堂制葯廠, Zhongguo minzhu jianguo hui Hangzhoushi weiyuanhui 中國民主建國會杭州市委員會, and Hangzhoushi gongshangye lianhehui 杭州市工商業聯合會. 1990. "Huqingyu tang zhiyao chang" 胡慶余堂制葯廠 (The Huqingyu tang medicine factory). In *Hangzhou laozihao (Hangzhou wenshi ziliao di shisi ji)* 杭州老字號 (杭州文史資料第十四輯) (Old shops of Hangzhou), 165–190. Hangzhou.

Huskey, James. 1987. "The Cosmopolitan Connection." *Diplomatic History* 11 (3) (Summer): 227–242.

Im Kaye Soon 任桂淳. 1993. *Qingchao baqi zhufang xingshuaishi* 清朝八旗駐防興衰史 (The rise and decline of the eight banner garrisons in the Qing period). Beijing.

Imperial Maritime Customs. 1882–1931. *Decennial Reports (1882–1931).* 5 vols. Shanghai.

Irving, Robert Grant. 1981. *Indian Summer: Lutyens, Baker, and Imperial Delhi.* New Haven, Conn.

Isaacs, Harold. (1938) 1972. *The Tragedy of the Chinese Revolution.* Stanford.

Ji'an zilaishui youxian gongsi 濟安自來水有限公司 (Tientsin Native City Waterworks Company, Ltd.). Tianjin Municipal Archives, Tianjin.

Jiang Yongcai 蔣永才 and Di Shuzhi 狄樹之, eds. 1991. *Nanjing zhi zui* 南京之最 (The most of Nanjing). Nanjing.

Jiang Yuanying 蔣沅瑛. 1937. "Kangzhan zhong de Chongqing" 抗戰中的重慶 (Chongqing in the midst of the War of Resistance). *Wenyi yuekan—zhanshi tekan* 文藝月刊—戰時特刊 (Literature and arts monthly review—special wartime edition) 4 (November 21): 73–75.

Jiang Zhongzheng 蔣中正 (Chiang Kai-shek), ed. 1929. *Shoudu jihua* 首都計劃 (Capital city plans). Nanjing.

Jianghan wenshi ziliao 江漢文史資料 (Materials on the history and culture of Jianghan). 1988. Wuhan.

Jianming 建明. 1996. "Zhongyang gongyuan kaifang ji" 中央公園開放記 (The opening of the Central Park). *Jinghua guji xunzong* 京華古跡尋蹤 (The search for historical sites in Beijing), 23–26. Beijing.

Jianshe weiyuanhui diaocha Zhejiang jingji suo 建設委員會調查浙江經濟所. (1932) 1971. *Hangzhoushi jingji diaocha* 杭州市經濟調查 (Economic survey of Hangzhou). Taibei (reprint).

Jincheng yinhang shiliao 金城銀行史料 (Historical materials on Jincheng Bank). 1983. Ed. Zhongguo renmin yinhang Shanghai shi fenhang jinrong yanjiu shi 中國人民銀行上海市分行金 融研究室 (Finance research office of the Shanghai branch of the People's Bank of China). Shanghai.

Jindai Tianjin tuzhi 近代天津圖志 (Illustrated history of modern Tianjin). 1992. Ed. Tianjin lishi bowuguan 天津歷史博物館 (Tianjin Historical Museum) et al. Tianjin.

Jingdu shizheng gongsuo 京都市政公所 (Beijing municipal council), ed. 1919. *Jingdu shizheng huilan* 京都市政匯覽 (Review of administration of the Capital City). Beijing.

Jingshi jingcha gongbao 京師警察公報 (Reports of the Beijing Police Department).

Johnson, Linda Cooke, ed. 1993. *Cities of Jiangnan in Late Imperial China.* Albany, N.Y.

———. 1995. *Shanghai: From Market Town to Treaty Port, 1074–1858.* Stanford.

Johnston, William. 1955. *The Modern Epidemic: A History of Tuberculosis in Japan.* Cambridge, Mass.

Jordan, David P. 1995. *Transforming Paris: The Life and Labors of Baron Haussmann.* New York.

Kangzhan shiqi neiqian xinan de gongshang qiye 抗戰時期內遷西南的工商企業 (Evacuation of business and industry to the southwest during the anti-Japanese War). 1989. Kunming.

Kapp, Robert A. 1973. *Szechwan and the Chinese Republic: Provincial Militarism and Central Power, 1911–1938.* New Haven, Conn.

——— 1974. "Chungking as a Center of Warlord Power." In Elvin and Skinner, eds., 143–170.

Katō, Takashi. 1994. "Governing Edo." In McClain, Merriman, and Ugawa, eds., 41–67.

Katz, Paul R. 1995. *Demon Hordes and Burning Boats: The Cult of Marshal Wen in Late Imperial Chekiang.* Albany, N.Y.

"Ke Fei" 克非(pseud.). 1938. "Sishu yu yingshi" 死鼠與嬰尸 (Dead rats and infants). *Wenyi yuekan—zhanshi tekan* 文藝月刊——戰時特刊 (Literature and arts monthly review—special wartime edition) 2 (4) (October): 369–337.

Kerr, J. G. 1891. *The Canton Guide.* 5th ed. Hong Kong.

Kertzer, David I. 1988. *Ritual, Politics and Power.* New Haven, Conn.

King, Anthony D. 1976. *Colonial Urban Development: Culture, Social Power and Environment.* London.

Kitaoka Shin'ichi 北岡眞一. 1988. *Gotō Shimpei* 後藤新平. Tokyo.

Knapp, Ronald G. 1989. *China's Vernacular Architecture: House Form and Culture.* Honolulu.

Koshizawa Akira. 越沢明. 1978. *Shokuminchi Manshū no toshi keikaku* 殖民地滿洲の都市計画 (City planning in colonial Manchuria). Tokyo.

———. 1982. "L'urbanisme en Mandchourie." *Urbi* 6 (1) (March): 78–81.

———. 1988. *Manshūkoku no shuto keikaku: Tokyo no genzai to mirai o tou* 滿洲國の首都計画: 東京の現在

と未來を問う (The planning of Manchukuo capital city: An inquiry into Tokyo's present and future). Tokyo.

———. 1989. *Harubin no toshi keikaku, 1898–1945* 哈爾濱の都市計画, 1898–1945 (City planning in Harbin, 1898–1945). Tokyo.

Kostka, Robert. 1966. "Frank Lloyd Wright in Japan." *The Prairie School Review* 3 (3) (September): 5–12.

Kwan, Man Bun. 1990. "The Merchant World of Tianjin: Society and Economy of a Chinese City." Ph.D. dissertation, Stanford University.

———. 1996. "Mapping the Hinterland: Treaty Ports and Regional Analysis in Modern China." In *Remapping China: Fissures in Historical Terrain,* ed. Gail Hershatter et al. Stanford.

Lai Xinxia 來新夏, ed. 1987. *Tianjin jindaishi* 天津近代史 (Modern Tianjin history). Tianjin.

Lai Zehan 賴澤涵. 1984. "Sun Ke yu Guangzhoushi de jindaihua" 孫科與廣州市的近代化 (Sun Fo [Sun Ke] and the modernization of Canton). In *Zhongguo xiandaishi lunji* 中國現代史論集 (Essays on contemporary Chinese history), vol. 7, ed. Zhang Yufa 張玉法et al., 83–102. Taibei.

Lang, Olga. 1946. *Chinese Family and Society.* New Haven, Conn.

Lanning, George, and Samuel Couling. 1921. *The History of Shanghai: Part I.* Shanghai.

Lary, Diana. 1974. *Region and Nation: The Kwangsi Clique in Chinese Politics, 1925–1937.* Cambridge.

Latour, Bruno. 1988. *The Pasteurization of France.* Trans. Alan Sheridan and John Law. Cambridge, Mass.

Lau, Joseph S. M. 1970. *Ts'ao Yü, The Reluctant Disciple of Chekhov and O'Neill: A Study in Literary Influence.* Hong Kong.

Leavitt, Judith Walzer. 1982. *The Healthiest City: Milwaukee and the Politics of Health Reform.* Princeton.

Lee, Edward Bing-Shuey. 1936. *Modern Canton.* Shanghai.

———. 1937. "Nanking—Yesterday and Today." In *Nanking's Development, 1927–1937,* ed. Ma Chao-chun. Nanjing.

Lefebvre, Henri. 1991. *The Production of Space.* Trans. Donald Nicholson-Smith. Oxford.

———. 1995. *Introduction to Modernity.* Trans. John Moore. London.

Leung, Angela. 1987. "Organized Medicine in Ming-Qing China: State and Private Medical Institutions in the Lower Yangzi Region." *Late Imperial China* 8 (1) (June): 134–166.

Li Jingneng 李競能, ed. 1990. *Tianjin renkoushi* 天津人口史 (Population history of Tianjin). Tianjin.

Li Shaobi 李紹必 and Ni Pujun 霓普均. 1982. "Tianjin zilaishui shiye jianshi" 天津自來水事業簡史 (A brief history of water supply in Tianjin). *Tianjin wenshi ziliao xuanji* 21: 27–53.

Li Weiwei 李偉偉. 1993. "Yuan wei Manchouguo 'Guodu' Changchun" 原僞滿洲國 "國都" 長春(Changchun, 'National Capital' of the puppet-state of Manchukuo). *Zhongguo jindai chengshi yu jianzhu,* 247–279. Beijing.

Liang Jialu 梁家祿. 1984. *Zhongguo xinwenye shi* 中國新聞業史 (Business history of the Chinese press). Nanning.

Liang Sicheng 梁思成. 1981. *Zhongguo jianzhushi* 中國建築史 (A history of Chinese architecture). Taibei (reprint).

Liao Yizhong 廖一中, Li Dezheng 李德征, and Zhang Xuanru 張旋如, eds. 1981. *Yihetuan yundong shi* 義和團運動史 (A history of the Boxer Movement). Beijing.

Lin Kongyi 林孔翼, ed. 1982. *Chengdu zhuzhici* 成都竹枝詞 (Chengdu bamboo-branch poetry). Chengdu.

Lin Yimin 林逸民. 1929. "Dushi jihua yu Nanjing" 都市計劃與南京 (City planning and Nanjing). *Shoudu jianshe* 1 (October): sect. 1: 3–23.

Lin Yungai 林雲陔 . 1919. "Oumei shizhi gailun: dushi yu wenming zhi guanxi" 歐美市制概論: 都市與文明之關係 (An introduction to urban government in Europe and America: The relationship between cities and civilization). *Jianshe* 1: 2.

Lin Yutang. 1944. *Vigil of a Nation.* New York.

Lin Zhengqiu 林正秋 and Shen Guanzhong 沈貫忠. 1993. *Zhongguo Hangzhou Louwailou* 中國杭州樓外樓 (The Louwailou Restaurant in Hangzhou, China). Hangzhou.

Lin, Adet, Ador Lin, and Meimei Lin. (1941) 1975. *Dawn over Chungking.* New York (reprint).

Little, Archibald J. 1888. *Through the Yang-tse Gorges.* London.

Liu Huiwu 劉惠吾, ed. 1985. *Shanghai jindaishi* 上海近代史 (A modern history of Shanghai). Shanghai.

Liu Jiwen 劉紀文. 1929. "Shoudu jianshe yu Nanjing shizheng" 首都建設與南京市政 (Capital city construction and Nanjing city government). *Shoudu jianshe* 1 (October): sect. 1: 1–2.

Liu Jizeng 劉繼增, Mao Lei 毛磊, and Yuan Jicheng 袁繼成. 1985. *Wuhan kangzhan shiyao* 武漢抗戰史要. (Important points in the history of Wuhan during the Anti-Japanese War). Wuhan.

———. 1986. *Wuhan guomin zhengfu shi* 武漢國民政府史 (History of the Wuhan national government). Wuhan.

Liu, Laurence G. 1989. *Chinese Architecture.* New York.

Liu, Lydia H. 1995. *Translingual Practice: Literature, National Culture, and Translated Modernity—China, 1900–1937.* Stanford.

Liu Wangling 劉望齡. 1991. *Heixue, jingu: Xinhai geming hou Hubei baokan shishi changbian* 黑血, 金鼓: 辛亥革命後湖北報刊史事長編 (Dark blood, golden drum: Extensive history of the Hubei press after the 1911 revolution). Wuhan.

Lou Jixin 婁繼心. 1990. " Kongfengchun huazhuangpin chang" 孔鳳春化妝品廠 (The Kongfengchun cosmetics factory). In *Hangzhou laozihao (Hangzhou wenshi ziliao di shisi ji)* 杭州老字號 (杭州文史資料第十四輯) (Old shops of Hangzhou), 54–61. Hangzhou.

Lou Zikuang 婁子匡. 1943. "Peidu xing" 陪都行 (Travels in the alternate capital). *Wenxun* 文訊 (Literary news) 4 (2, 3) (March): 43–62.

Lu Hanchao. 1994. "Away from Nanking Road: Small Stores and Neighborhood Life in Modern Shanghai." *Journal of Asian Studies* 53 (4) (November): 93–122.

———. Forthcoming. *Beyond the Neon Lights: Everyday Shanghai in the Early Twentieth-Century.* Berkeley.

Lu Sihong 陸思紅. 1939. *Xin Chongqing* 新重慶 (The new Chongqing). Kunming.

Lu Yanzhi 呂彥直. 1929. "Guihua shoudu dushi qu tu'an dagang cao'an" 規劃首都都市區圖案大綱草案 (Draft of the general outline design for the capital city plan). *Shoudu jianshe* 1 (October): *jihua*, 19–28.

Luo Rongqu 羅榮渠, ed. 1990. *Cong xihua dao xiandaihua* 從西化到現代化 (From Westernization to modernization). Beijing.

Luo Shuwei 羅澍偉 et al., eds. 1993. *Jindai Tianjin chengshi shi* 近代天津城市史(The modern history of Tianjin). Beijing.

Luo Suwen 羅蘇文 . 1991. *Da Shanghai shikumen: xunchang renjia* 大上海石庫門: 尋常人家(Shikumen housing in greater Shanghai: The ordinary families). Shanghai.

Ma Chaojun 馬超俊 (Ma Chao-chun), ed. 1937. *Shi nian lai zhi Nanjing* 十年來之南京 (Nanjing's last ten years). Nanjing.

Ma Chao-chun (Ma Chaojun), ed. 1937. *Nanking's Development*: 1927–1937. Nanjing.

Ma Xuanwei 馬宣偉 and Xiao Bo 肖波. 1989. *Yang Sen* 楊森. Chengdu.

MacLeod, Roy, and Milton Lewis, eds. 1988. *Disease, Medicine, and Empire: Perspectives on Western Medicine and the Experience of European Expansion.* London.

MacPherson, Kerrie L. 1987. *A Wilderness of Marshes: The Origins of Public Health in Shanghai, 1843–1893.* Hong Kong.

———. 1990. "Designing China's Urban Future: The Greater Shanghai Plan, 1927–1937." *Planning Perspectives* 5, 1 (January): 39–62.

———. 1996. "The Shanghai Model in Historical Perspective." In Yeung and Sung, eds., 493–528.

———, ed. 1998. *Asian Department Stores.* Honolulu.

Manchuria: A Semi-Monthly Review. 1936–1942. Dairen.

Manchuria: A Survey of Its Economic Development. (1932) 1980. Supervised by Baron Y. Sakatani, revised by Grover Clark for the Carnegie Endowment for International Peace. New York (reprint).

Manieri-Elia, Mario. 1983. "Toward an 'Imperial City': Daniel H. Burnham and the City Beautiful Movement." In *The American City: From the Civil War to the New Deal,* ed. Giorgio Ciucci et al. Cambridge, Mass.

Mann, Susan. 1984. "Urbanization and Historical Change in China." *Modern China* 10 (1) (January): 79–113.

Mantetsu fuzokuchi keiei enkaku zenshi 滿鐵附屬地經營沿革全史 (History of the South Manchurian Railway's management of its annexed land). 1939. Dairen.

Mao Dun 茅盾. 1986. *Mao Dun quan ji* 茅盾全集 (Complete works of Mao Dun). Beijing.

Martin, Brian G. 1996. *The Shanghai Green Gang: Politics and Organized Crime, 1919–1937.* Berkeley.

McClain, James L., John M. Merriman, and Ugawa Kaoru, eds. 1994. *Edo and Paris: Urban Life and the State in the Early Modern Era.* Ithaca, N.Y.

Miller, Michael R. 1981. *The Bon Marché: Bourgeois Culture and the Department Store, 1869–1920.* Princeton.

Minguo renwu da cidian 民國人物大詞典 (Dictionary of famous persons in the republican era). 1991. Shijiazhuang.

Minshi ribao 民視日報 (Gaze of the people daily). 1921–1929. Chengdu.

Mitchell, Timothy. 1991. *Colonising Egypt.* Berkeley.

Mori Etsuko 森悦子. 1988. "Tenshin totō gamon ni tsuite," 天津都統衙門について (On the Tianjin provisional government). *Tōyōshi kenkyū* 東洋史研究 67 (2) (September): 314–343.

Mortensen, Esther Tappert. Papers. China Records Project, Day Missions Library. Yale Divinity School, New Haven, Conn.

Mosse, George L. 1975. *The Nationalization of the Masses: Political Symbolism and Mass Movements in Germany from the Napoleonic Wars through the Third Reich.* Ithaca, N.Y.

Mote, F. W. 1973. "A Millennium of Chinese Urban History: Form, Time, and Space Concepts In Soochow." *Rice University Studies* 59 (4) (fall): 35–65.

———. 1977. "The Transformation of Nanking, 1350–1400." In Skinner, ed., 101–153.

Mumford, Lewis. 1961. *The City in History: Its Origins, Its Transformations, and Its Prospects.* New York.

Murphey, Rhoads. 1953. *Shanghai: Key to Modern China.* Cambridge, Mass.

———. 1974. "The Treaty Ports and China's Modernization." In Elvin and Skinner, eds., 17–72.

Myers, Ramon. 1989. "Japanese Imperialism in Manchuria: The South Manchurian Railway Company, 1906–1933." In Duus, Myers, and Peattie, eds., 100–132.

Nanking Woman's Club. 1933. *Sketches of Nanking.* Nanjing.

Naquin, Susan, and Chün-fang Yü, eds.. 1992. *Pilgrims and Sacred Sites in China.* Berkeley.

Nathan, Carl F. 1967. *Plague Prevention and Politics in Manchuria, 1910–1931.* Cambridge, Mass.

Nedostup, Rebecca. Forthcoming. "Religion, Superstition and Governing Society in Nationalist China." Ph.D. dissertation, Columbia University.

Ni Xiying 倪錫英. 1936. *Guangzhou* 廣州 (Canton). Guangzhou.

Nishikawa Yasuhiko 西川太彥. 1995. "Manshūkoku no kensetsu jigyō" 滿洲國の建設事業 (Construction work in Manchukuo). In Yamamoto, ed., 377–461.

North China Daily News. 1893. *"The Jubilee of Shanghai, 1843–1893—Shanghai: Past and Present, and a Full Account of the Proceedings on the 17th and 18th of November, 1893."* Shanghai.

Olsen, Donald J. 1986. *The City as a Work of Art: London, Paris, Vienna.* New Haven, Conn.

Osborne, Peter. 1995. *The Politics of Time: Modernity and Avant-Garde.* London.

Ozouf, Mona. 1988. *Festivals and the French Revolution.* Trans. Alan Sheridan. Cambridge, Mass.

Pahl, R. E. 1968a. "A Perspective on Urban Sociology." In *Readings in Urban Sociology,* ed. R. E. Pahl. Oxford.

———. 1968b. "The Rural-Urban Continuum." In *Readings in Urban Sociology,* ed. R. E. Pahl. Oxford.

Pan, Ling (Lynn Pan). 1982. *In Search of Old Shanghai.* Hong Kong.

Pannell, Clifton. 1981. "Recent Growth and Change in China's Urban System." In *Urban Development in Modern China,* ed. Laurence J. C. Ma and Edward W. Hanten. Boulder, Colo.

Panyuxian xuzhi 番禺縣續誌 (Supplementary gazetteer of Panyu County). 1931.

Pearl, Cyril. 1967. *Morrison of Peking.* Sydney.

Peck, Graham. 1950. *Two Kinds of Time.* Boston.

The Peking and Tientsin Times. 1894–1904. Tianjin.

Perrot, Philippe. 1994. *Fashioning the Bourgeoisie: A History of Clothing in the Nineteenth Century.* Trans. Richard Bienvenu. Princeton.

Perry, Elizabeth J. 1993. *Shanghai on Strike: The Politics of Chinese Labor.* Stanford.

Perry, Elizabeth J., and Jeffrey N. Wasserstrom, eds. 1993–1994. *Shanghai Social Movements,* special issue of *Chinese Studies in History* 27 (1–2) (fall–winter).

Pi Mingxiu 皮明庥. 1985. *Wuhan jinbainian shi* 武漢近百年史: 1840–1949 (One-hundred-year history of Wuhan, 1840–1949). Wuhan.

———. 1993. *Jindai Wuhan chengshi shi* 近代武漢城市史 (Modern history of the city of Wuhan). Beijing.

Pi Mingxiu, ed., with Yang Pulin 楊蒲林. 1990. *Wuhan chengshi fazhan guiji* 武漢城市發展軌跡 (Collected essays on the developmental path of the city of Wuhan). Tianjin.

Pott, F. L. Hawks. 1928. *A Short History of Shanghai.* Shanghai.

Qi Rushan 齊如山.1964. *Qi Rushan quanji* 齊如山全集 (A complete collection of Qi Rushan's work). Taibei.

Qiu Jie 邱捷. 1983. "Guangdong shangren yu xinhai geming" 廣東商人與辛亥革命 (The Guangdong merchants and the 1911 Revolution). In *Jinian xinhai geming qishi zhounian xueshu taolunhui lunwenji* 紀念辛亥革命七十週年學術討論會論文集 (Conference essays commemorating the seventieth anniversary of the 1911 Revolution), vol. 1, 362–396. Beijing.

Quanguo yinhang nianjian 全國銀行年鑒. 1934. (All China bank yearbook). Shanghai.

———. 1935. (All China bank yearbook). Shanghai

———. 1936. (All China bank yearbook). Shanghai.

Rabinow, Paul. 1989. *French Modern: Norms and Forms of the Social Environment.* Cambridge, Mass.

Rasmussen, O. D. 1925. *Tientsin: An Illustrated Outline History.* Tianjin.

Ravetz, Alison. 1986. *The Governance of Space: Town Planning in Modern Society.* London

Ren Jianshu 任建樹 and Zhang Quan 張銓. 1985. *Wusa yundong jianshi* 五卅運動簡史 (A short history of the May Thirtieth Movement). Shanghai.

Reps, John W. 1979. *Cities of the American West: A History of Frontier Urban Planning.* Princeton.

Reynolds, Douglas R. 1993. *China 1898–1912: The Xinzheng Revolution and Japan.* Cambridge, Mass.

Robinson, O. F. 1992. *Ancient Rome: City Planning and Administration.* London.

Rogaski, Ruth. 1996. "From Protecting Life to Defending the Nation: The Emergence of Public Health in Tianjin, 1859–1953." Ph.D. dissertation, Yale University.

Rou Bing 柔冰. 1924. *Hangfang ganjiu shi* 杭防感舊詩 (Nostalgic poetry on the Hangzhou bannermen garrison). Shanghai.

Rowe, William T. 1984. *Hankow: Commerce and Society in a Chinese City, 1796–1889.* Stanford.

———. 1989. *Hankow: Conflict and Community in a Chinese City, 1796–1895.* Stanford.

———. 1993a. "Introduction." In Johnson, ed., 1–15.

———. 1993b. "Wuhan and Its Region, 1736–1938." Unpublished paper.

Rozman, Gilbert. 1973. *Urban Networks in Ch'ing China and Tokugawa Japan.* Princeton.

———. 1982. *Population and Marketing Settlements in Ch'ing China.* Cambridge.

Ruan Yicheng 阮毅成. 1974. *San ju bu li ben "Hang"* 三句不離本 "杭" (I can hardly speak without mentioning my city Hangzhou). Taibei.

Schiffrin, Harold Z. 1980. *Sun Yat-sen, Reluctant Revolutionary.* Boston.

Schinz, Alfred. 1989. *Cities in China.* Berlin.

Schipper, Kristofer M. 1977. "Neighborhood Cult Associations in Traditional Tainan." In Skinner, ed., 651–676.

Schoppa, R. Keith. 1982. *Chinese Elites and Political Change: Zhejiang Province in the Early Twentieth Century.* Cambridge, Mass.

Schwartz, Benjamin I. 1993. "Culture, Modernity, and Nationalism—Further Reflections." *Daedalus* 122 (3) (summer): 207–226.

Scott, James C. 1998. *Seeing Like a State: How Certain Schemes to Improve the Human Condition Have Failed.* New Haven, Conn.

Seidensticker, Edward. 1983. *Low City, High City: Tokyo from Edo to the Earthquake.* New York.

Sennett, Richard. 1994. *Flesh and Stone: The Body and the City in Western Civilization.* New York..

Service, John, ed. 1989. *Golden Inches: The China Memoir of Grace Service.* Berkeley.

Shang Qixu 尙其煦. 1935. *Chengshi jianshe zhi yanjiu* 城市建設之研究 (Study of urban planning). Nanjing.

Shanghai Mercury. 1893. *1843—Shanghai—1893: The Model Settlement. Its Birth. Its Youth. Its Jubilee.* Shanghai.

Shanghai Municipal Tourism Administration and Hong Kong China Tourism Press, eds. 1995. *Focus on Shanghai.* Hong Kong.

Shanghai yanjiu zhongxin 上海研究中心 and Shanghai renmin chubanshe 上海人民出版社 (Shanghai Research Center and Shanghai People's Press), eds. 1991. *Shanghai 700 Nian (1291–1991)* 上海 700 年 (1291–1991) (Shanghai's 700 years, 1291–1991). Shanghai.

Shanghai Yongan gongsi de chansheng, fazhan he gaizao 上海永安公司的產生, 發展和改造 (The establishment, development, and transformation of the Shanghai Yongan [Wing On] Company). 1981. Shanghai.

Shangwu ribao 商務日報 (Commercial daily news). Chongqing.

Shao, Qin. 1994. "Making Political Culture: The Case of Nantong, 1894–1930." Ph.D. dissertation, Michigan State University.

Sheehan, Brett. 1996. "Strange Bedfellows: Warlords, Warlord Capital and Professional Bankers in Tianjin China, 1916–1921." Presented at the annual meeting of the Association for Asian Studies.

———. 1997. "The Currency of Legitimation: Banks, Bank Money and State-Society Relations in Tianjin, China, 1916–1938." Ph.D. dissertation, University of California–Berkeley.

Shi Keshi 石克士. 1934. *Xin Hangzhou daoyou* 新杭州導游 (A new tour guide to Hangzhou). Hangzhou.

Shi, Mingzheng. 1993. "Beijing Transforms: Urban Infrastructure, Public Works, and Social Change in the Chinese Capital, 1900–1928." Ph.D. dissertation, Columbia University.

———. 1998. "From Imperial Gardens to Public Parks: The Transformation of Urban Space in Early Twentieth-Century Beijing." *Modern China* 24 (3) (July): 219–254.

Shi Tuo 師陀. (1935) 1997. "Shisha hai yu xiao shimin" 什刹海與小市民 (Shisha hai and city dwellers). In *Rumeng ling* (Time of dreams). Beijing.

Shiba, Yoshinobu. 1977. "Ningbo and Its Hinterland." In Skinner, ed., 391–439.

Shina shōbetsu zenshi 支那省別全誌 (Gazetteer of the Chinese provinces). 1917–1920. 18 vols. Tokyo.

Shinkyō annai 新京案內 (Guide to Xinjing). 1940. Dairen.

Shiyebu guoji maoyiju 實業部國際貿易局, ed. 1933. *Zhongguo shiyezhi: Zhejiang sheng* 中國實業志: 浙江省 (Gazetteer of Chinese industry: Zhejiang province). Shanghai.

Shizheng pinglun 市政評論 (Review of city administration). 1934–1937. Beiping.

Shizheng quanshu 市政全書 (A complete book of city administration). 1928. Ed. Lu Danlin 陸丹林. Shanghai.

"Shoudu guomin zhengfu waijiao bu ban'gong dalou ji guanshe" 首都國民政府外交部辦公大樓暨官舍 (Capital city national government Ministry of Foreign Affairs main building and official residence). 1935. *Zhongguo jianzhu* 3 (3) (August): 4–16.

Shoudu jianshe 首都建設 (Capital construction). October 1928 – July 1930.

"Shoudu weida jianzhu wu" 首都偉大建築物 (Great works of architecture in the capital city). 1937. In Ma Chaojun, ed. Nanjing.

Shu Xincheng 舒新城. 1934. *Shuyou xinying* 蜀游心影 (Heart-felt reflections on a trip to Sichuan). Shanghai.

Sichuan yuebao 四川月報 (Sichuan monthly review).

Sickman, Laurence, and Alexander Soper. 1960. *The Art and Architecture of China.* Baltimore.

Sit, Victor F. S. 1995. *Beijing: The Nature and Planning of a Chinese Capital City.* New York.

Skinner, G. William. 1964–1965. "Marketing and Social Structure in Rural China." *Journal of Asian Studies* 24 (1, 2, and 3): 3–43, 195–228, and 363–399.

———. 1976. "Mobility Strategies in Late Imperial China: A Regional Systems Analysis." In *Regional Analysis,* ed. Carol Smith, 327–364. New York.

———, ed. 1977. *The City in Late Imperial China.* Stanford.

Speer, Albert. 1970. *Inside the Third Reich.* Trans. Richard and Clara Winston. New York.

Spencer, J. E. 1939. "Changing Chungking: The Rebuilding of an Old Chinese City." *The Geographical Review* 29 (January): 46–60.

Stapleton, Kristin. 1996. "Urban Politics in an Age of 'Secret Societies': The Cases of Shanghai and Chengdu." *Republican China* 22 (1) (November): 23–64.

———. Forthcoming. *Civilizing Chengdu: Chinese Urban Reform, 1895–1937.* Cambridge, Mass.

Steinhardt, Nancy Shatzman. 1990. *Chinese Imperial City Planning.* Honolulu.

Stoler, Ann. 1989a. "Making Empire Respectable: The Politics of Race and Sexual Morality in Twentieth-Century Colonial Cultures." *American Ethnologist* 16 (4) (November): 634–660.

———. 1989b. "Rethinking Colonial Categories: European Communities and the Boundaries of Rule." *Comparative Studies in Society and History* 31 (1) (January): 134–161.

———. 1995. *Race and the Education of Desire: Foucault's History of Sexuality and the Colonial Order of Things.* Durham, N.C.

Storch, Robert D. 1976. "The Policeman as Domestic Missionary: Urban Discipline and Popular Culture in Northern England, 1850–1880." *Journal of Social History* 9 (4) (June): 481–509.

Stranahan, Patricia, ed. 1994–1995. *The Communist Party in Shanghai,* special issue of *Chinese Studies in History* 28 (2) (winter).

Strand, David. 1989. *Rickshaw Beijing: City People and Politics in the 1920s.* Berkeley.

———. 1995a. "Historical Perspectives." In *Urban Spaces in Contemporary China,* eds. Deborah Davis, et. al., 394–426. New York.

———. 1995b. "A High Place Is No Better than a Low Place: The Modern City in the Making of Urban China." Paper presented to a conference on "Becoming Chinese: Passages to Modernity and Beyond, 1900–1950," Center for Chinese Studies, University of California–Berkeley, June 2–4.

Strassberg, Richard E. 1994. *Inscribed Landscape: Travel Writing from Imperial China.* Berkeley.

Su, Gin-djih. 1964. *Chinese Architecture: Past and Contemporary.* Hong Kong.

Su Yun-feng 蘇雲峰. 198l. *Zhongguo xiandaihua quyu yanjiu: Hubei sheng, 1860–1916* 中國現代化區域研究: 湖北省, 1860–1916 (Regional studies of China's modernization: Hubei Province, 1860–1916). Taibei.

Sun Ke 孫科 (Sun Fo).1919. "Dushi guihua lun" 都市規畫論 (On urban planning). *Jianshe* 建設 1 (5): 1–17.

Sun Yat-sen. 1953. *The International Development of China.* Taibei (reprint).

Sun Zhongshan 孫中山 (Sun Yat-sen). 1981–1986. *Sun Zhongshan quanji* 孫中山全集 (Collected works of Sun Yat-sen). Beijing.

Tafuri, Manfredo, and Francesco Dal Co. 1986. *Modern Architecture.* Trans. Robert Erich Wolf. New York.

Takahashi Kōsuke 高橋孝助 and Furuya Tadao 古厩忠夫, eds. 1995. *Shanhai shi* 上海史 (*The History of Shanghai*). Tokyo.

Takekoshi Yosaburo. 1907. *Japanese Rule in Formosa.* London.

Tang Zhenchang 唐振常, ed. 1993. *Jindai Shanghai fanhua lu* 近代上海繁華錄 (The prosperity of modern Shanghai). Hong Kong.

———. 1994. *Jindai Shanghai tansuo lu* 近代上海探索錄 (A record of explorations of modern Shanghai). Shanghai.

Tao Liangsheng 陶亮生. n.d. (c. 1978). "Wanqing zhi Minguo zhi mo Wulao Qixian qinling ji" 晚清至民國之末五老七賢親靈記(A personal account of the Five Elders and Seven Sages from the late Qing to the end of the Republic). Manuscript.

Tenshin kyoryū mindan jimu hōkoku 天津居留民團事務報告 (Tianjin Japanese settlement corporation annual report). 1928. Tianjin.

Tenshin kyoryū mindan jimu hōkokushu, eiseibu 天津居留民團事務報告書, 衛生部 (Tianjin Japanese settlement corporation annual reports, sanitary department). 1908–1943. Tianjin.

Tenshin kyoryū mindan nijū shūnen kinenshi 天津居留民團二十週年紀念史 (Tianjin Japanese settlement corporation twentieth anniversary report). 1930. Tianjin.

Thongchai, Winichakul. 1994. *Siam Mapped: A History of the Geo-Body of a Nation.* Honolulu.

Tianjin Dutong yamen huiyi jiyao 天津都統衙門會議記要 (Minutes of the meetings of the Tianjin provisional government). 1900–1902. Chinese translation of the original French, handwritten manuscript, Tianjin Academy of Social Sciences, Institute of History.

Tianjin jingcha zazhi 天津警察雜誌 (Tianjin police magazine). 1915–1917. Tianjin.

Tianjin renwu lu 天津人物錄 (Record of Tianjin personages). 1987. Tianjin.

Tianjin shanghui dang'an huibian 天津商會檔案彙編 (Collected archival documents from the Tianjin Chamber of Commerce). 1989. Ed. Tianjin shehui kexueyuan lishi yanjiusuo. Tianjin.

Tianjin shi dang'an guan, ed. 1992. *Tianjin zujie dang'an xuanbian* (Collected archival documents from the Tianjin concessions). Tianjin.

Tianjin yinhang gonghui 天津銀行公會 (Tianjin Bankers' Association) Archives. Tianjin Municipal Archives.

Tomes, Nancy. 1997. "American Attitudes toward the Germ Theory of Disease: Phyllis Allen Richmond Revisited." *Journal of the History of Medicine and Allied Sciences* 52 (1) (January): 17–50.

———. 1998. *The Gospel of Germs: Men, Women, and the Microbe in American Society.* Cambridge, Mass.

Tong Longfu 童隆福. 1993. *Zhejiang Hangyun shi* 浙江航運史 (History of navigation and water transportation in Zhejiang). Beijing.

"Toupiao Qiying dimu zhe zhuyi" 投票旗營地畝者注意 (Attention, bidders on the land at the bannermen garrison). 1913. *Zhejiang ribao* 浙江日報 (November 7).

Touraine, Alain. 1995. *Critique of Modernity*. Trans. David Macey. Oxford.

Tsao (Cao) Yu. 1978. *Sunrise*. Trans. A. C. Barnes. Beijing.

Tsin, Michael. 1997. "Imagining 'Society' in Early Twentieth-Century China." In *Imagining the People: Chinese Intellectuals and the Concept of Citizenship, 1890–1920*, eds. Joshua Fogel and Peter Zarrow, 212–231. Armonk, N.Y.

Tsuzuki, J. 1904. "Bericht uber meine epidemioligischen Beobachtungen und Forschundgen wahrend der Cholera-epedemie im Nordchina im Jahre 1902" (Report on my epidemiological observations and researches during the cholera epidemic of 1902 in North China). In *Archiv fur Schiffs und Tropen Hygiene* (Archives for naval and tropical hygiene). Leipzig.

Turner, John A. 1894. *Kwang Tung or Five Years in South China*. London.

Tyau, Min-Ch'ien T. Z., ed. 1930. *Two Years of Nationalist China*. Shanghai.

U.S. Department of State. 1960. *Records of the Department of State Relating to the Internal Affairs of China, 1910–1929*. Washington, D.C.

Uchimi Shiego 内海重夫, ed. 1937. *Daishinkyō keizai gaikan* 太新京經濟概觀 (Survey of the Xinjing economy). Xinjing.

Vale, Lawrence J. 1992. *Architecture, Power, and National Identity*. New Haven, Conn.

Vance, James E. Jr. 1990. *The Continuing City: Urban Morphology in Western Civilization*. Baltimore.

Vaughn, Megan. 1991. *Curing Their Ills: Colonial Power and African Disease*. Cambridge, Mass.

Wakeman, Frederic, Jr. 1985. *The Great Enterprise: The Manchu Reconstruction of Imperial Order in Seventeenth-Century China*. Berkeley.

———. 1993. "The Civil Society and Public Sphere Debate: Western Reflections on Chinese Political Culture." *Modern China* 19 (2) (April): 108–138.

———. 1995a. *Policing Shanghai, 1927–1937*. Berkeley.

———. 1995b. "Licensing Leisure: The Chinese Nationalists' Attempt to Regulate Shanghai, 1927–49." *Journal of Asian Studies* 54 (1) (February): 19–42.

Wakeman, Frederic, Jr., and Yeh Wen-hsin, eds. 1992. *Shanghai Sojourners*. Berkeley.

Wang Di 王笛. 1993. *Kuachu fengbi de shijie: Changjiang shangyou quyu shehui yanjiu, 1644–1911* 跨出封閉的世界: 長江上游區域社會研究, 1644–1911 (Out of a closed world: Research on society in the upper Yangzi macroregion, 1644–1911). Beijing.

Wang Huatang 王華棠, ed. 1990. *Tianjin—yige chengshi de jueqi* 天津一個城市的崛起 (Tianjin—the rise of a city). Tianjin.

Wang Jingyu 汪敬虞, ed. 1957. *Zhongguo jindai gongyeshi ziliao* 中國近代工業史資料 (Source materials on the history of modern Chinese industries), vol. 2, part 1 (1895–1914). Beijing.

Wang Liping. 1996. "Creating a National Symbol: The Sun Yatsen Memorial in Nanjing." *Republican China* 21 (2) (April): 23–63.

———. 1997. "Paradise for Sale: Urban Space and Tourism in the Social Transformation of Hangzhou, 1589–1937." Ph.D. dissertation, University of California–San Diego.

Wang Nengwei 王能偉 et al., eds. 1993. *Nanjing jiuying* 南京舊影 (Old photos of Nanjing). Beijing.

Wang Shiren 王世仁 and Zhang Fuhe 張复合. 1993. "Beijing jindai jianzhu gaishuo" 北京近代建築概說 (A brief introduction to modern architecture in Beijing). In *Zhongguo jindai jianzhu zonglan: Beijing pian* 中國近代建築綜覽: 北京篇 (A review of modern architecture in China: Beijing), 1–26. Beijing.

Wang Shuigong 王水公. 1920. "Xin he jiu" 新和舊 (New and old). *Dongfang zazhi* 東方雜誌 17 (3) (February 10).

Wang Yinnong 王隱農. 1943. "Liluan xing" 離亂行

(Travelling from chaos). *Wenxun* 文訊 (Literary news) 4 (nos. 6, 7) (July): 46–56.

Wasserstrom, Jeffrey N. 1991. *Student Protests in Twentieth-Century China: The View from Shanghai.* Stanford.

———. 1996. "Comparing 'Incomparable' Cities: Post-modern L.A. and Old Shanghai." *Contention: Debates in Society, Culture, and Science* 15 (Spring): 69–90.

Wei, Julie Lee et al. 1994. *Prescriptions for Saving China: Selected Writings of Sun Yat-sen.* Stanford.

Wei Shudong 魏樹東. (1934) 1977. *Beipingshi zhi dijia dizu fangzu yu shuishou* 北平市之地價地租房租與稅收 (Beiping's land price, land rent, house rent, and taxation). Taibei (reprint).

Wei Yingtao 隗瀛濤, ed. 1991. *Jindai Chongqing chengshi shi* 近代重慶城市史 (Urban history of modern Chongqing). Chengdu.

The West China Missionary News. 1901–1935. Chengdu.

Westney, D. Eleanor. 1987. *Imitation and Innovation: The Transfer of Western Organizational Patterns to Meiji Japan.* Cambridge, Mass.

White, Lynn, and Li Cheng. 1993. "China Coast Identities: Regional, National, and Global." In *China's Quest for National Identity,* eds. Lowell Dittmer and Samuel S. Kim, 154–193. Ithaca, N.Y.

White, Theodore. 1978. *In Search of History: A Personal Adventure.* New York.

Wilbur, C. Martin. 1983. *The Nationalist Revolution in China, 1923–1928.* Cambridge.

Wohl, Anthony S. 1983. *Endangered Lives: Public Health in Victorian Britain.* London.

Wolff, David. 1991. "To The Harbin Station: City Building in Manchuria, 1898–1914." Ph.D. dissertation, University of California–Berkeley.

Woodhead, H. G. W. 1931. *The Yangtze and Its Problems.* Shanghai.

Wright, Arthur F. 1977. "The Cosmology of the Chinese City." In Skinner, ed., 33–73.

Wright, Gwendolyn. 1991. *The Politics of Design in French Colonial Urbanism.* Chicago.

Wright, Mary C., ed. 1968. *China in Revolution: The First Phase, 1900–1913.* New Haven, Conn.

Wu Hung. 1995. *Monumentality in Early Chinese Art and Architecture.* Stanford.

Wu Jingzi 吳敬梓. 1986. *Rulin waishi* 儒林外史 (The scholars). Hefei.

Wu Jisheng 吳濟生 (1939) 1978. *Xindu jianwen lu* 新都見聞錄 (Record of things seen and heard in the new capital). Taipei (reprint).

Wu Tingxie 吳廷燮, ed. 1990. *Beijingshi zhigao* 北京市志稿 (Beijing gazetteer), vol. 1. Beijing.

Wu Yu 吳虞. 1986. *Wu Yu riji* 吳虞日記 (Diary of Wu Yu). 2 vols. Chengdu.

Wu Zhezheng 吳哲征. 1988. "Huiguan" 會館 (Guilds). In *Beijing wangshi tan* 北京往事談 (Talks on past events in Beijing). Beijing.

Wuhan daxue xiaoshi 武漢大學校史 (History of Wuhan University). 1993. Wuhan.

Wuhan kangzhan shi 武漢抗戰史 (History of Wuhan during the Anti-Japanese War). 1995. Wuhan.

Wuhan kangzhan shiliao xuanbian 武漢抗戰史料選編 (Selected materials on Wuhan during the Anti-Japanese War). 1985. Wuhan.

Wuhan wenshi ziliao 武漢文史資料 (Materials on the history and culture of Wuhan). 1981–1992. Wuhan.

Xi Wuyi 習五一 and Deng Yibing 鄧亦兵. 1995. *Beijing tongshi* 北京通史 (A general history of Beijing), vol. 9. Beijing.

Xia Yan 夏衍. 1943. "Xiajiangren yu" 下江人語 (Words of downriver people). *Tianxia wenzhang* 天下文章 (World essays) 1 (March): 62.

Xiao Bing 肖兵. 1992. *Nuozha zhi feng: Changjiang liuyu zongjiao xiju wenhua* 儺蠟之風: 長江流域宗教戲劇文化 (Nuo and zha: Religious opera culture in the Yangzi valley). Nanjing.

Xiao Fanbo蕭汎波. 1981. "Guangzhou Xianshi gongsi saduonian de shengshuai" 廣州先施公司卅多年的盛衰 (The rise and decline of the Xianshi [Sincere] Company in over thirty years). *Guangzhou wenshi ziliao* 廣州文史資料 (Source materials on the history and culture of Guangzhou) 23: 126–152.

Xin Shubao 新蜀報 (New Sichuan news). 1921–1948. Chongqing.

Xin Sichuan 新四川 (New Sichuan). 1928. Nanjing.

Xinji tushushe 鑫記圖書社. 1916. *Xihu zhinan* 西湖指南 (Guide to West Lake). Hangzhou.

Xinmin Bao 新民報 (New people's news). 1929–1949. Chongqing.

Xu Heyong 徐和雍, Zheng Yunshan 鄭雲山, and Zhao Shipei 趙世培. 1983. *Hangzhou yu Xihu shihua* 杭州與西湖史話 (History of Hangzhou and West Lake). Hangzhou.

Xu Junming 徐俊鳴 et al. 1984. *Guangzhou shihua* 廣州史話 (A history of Canton). Shanghai.

Xu Ke 徐珂. 1923. *Zengding Xihu youlan zhinan* 增訂西湖游覽指南 (An updated guide to sight-seeing on West Lake). Shanghai.

Xu Youchun 徐友春, ed. 1991. *Minguo renwu da cidian* 民國人物大詞典 (Dictionary of republican personages). Shijiazhuang.

Xue Dubi 薛篤弼. 1925. *Jingzhao gongyuan jishi* 京兆公園記實 (A record of the Jingzhao Park). Beijing. Unpaginated manuscript, Beijing University Library.

Xue Shaoming 薛紹銘. (1937) 1986. *Qian-Dian-Chuan luxingji* 黔滇川旅行記 (A record of travels in Guizhou, Yunnan, and Sichuan). Chongqing (reprint).

Yamamoto Yūzo 山本有造, ed. 1995. *Manshūkoku no kenkyū* 滿洲國の研究 (Studies of Manchukuo). Tokyo.

Yan Qiang 嚴强. 1990. "Hangzhou diyi mian fangzhi chang" 杭州第一棉紡織廠 (The Hangzhou number one cotton mill). In *Hangzhou laozihao (Hangzhou wenshi ziliao di shisi ji)* 杭州老字號 (杭州文史資料第十四輯) (Old shops of Hangzhou), 264–277. Hangzhou.

Yan Renzong 嚴仁宗, ed. 1990. *Yan Xiu xiansheng nianpu* 嚴修先生年譜(The chronological biography of Mr. Yan Xiu). Jinan.

Yang Bingde 楊秉德, ed. 1993. *Zhongguo jindai chengshi yu jianzhu* 中國近代城市與建築 (Cities and architecture of modern China). Beijing.

Yang Kuan 楊寬. 1993. *Zhongguo gudai ducheng zhidushi yanjiu* 中國古代都城制度史研究 (A study of urban systems in premodern China). Shanghai.

Yang Sen jiangjun jinian ji 楊森將軍紀念集 (Collected writings in memory of General Yang Sen). 1979. Editorial Committee of the Yang Sen Jiangjun Commemorative Volume. Taibei.

"Yang Sen xiansheng fangwen jilu." 楊森先生訪問記錄 (Transcript of 1963 oral history interview with Yang Sen). Archives of the Modern History Institute, Academia Sinica, Taiwan.

Yang Yulian 楊余練 et al. 1991. *Qingdai dongbei shi* 清代東北史 (A history of the Northeast in the Qing period). Shenyang.

Yang Zhaoyuan 楊照沅, Du Lei 杜磊, and Qi Yong 戚勇. 1993. "Sha-E Riben xianhou qinzhan de xinxing chengshi Dalian" 沙俄日本先後侵佔的新興城市大連 (The newly rising city of Dalian, occupied first by the Czarist Russians and then by the Japanese). In Yang Bingde, ed., 225–245.

Ye Shaoqing. 1992. "Shanghai before Nationalism." *East Asian History* 3 (June): 33–52.

Yeh, Wen-hsin. 1992. "Progressive Journalism and Shanghai's Petty Urbanites: Zou Daofen and the *Shenghuo Weekly,* 1926–1945." In Wakeman and Yeh, eds., 186–238.

———. 1995. "Corporate Space, Communal Time: Everyday Life in Shanghai's Bank of China." *American Historical Review* 100 (1) (February): 97–122.

———. 1997. "Shanghai Modernity: Commerce and Culture in a Republican City." *China Quarterly* 150 (July): 375–394.

Yanye yinhang, Tianjin fenhang 鹽業銀行, 天津分行 (Tianjin Branch of the Salt Bank) Archives. Tianjin Municipal Archives.

Yeoh, Brenda S. A. 1996. *Contesting Space: Power Relations and the Urban Built Environment in Colonial Singapore.* Kuala Lumpur.

Yeung, Yue-Man, and Sung Yun-wing, eds. 1996. *Shanghai: Transformation and Modernization under China's Open Policy.* Hong Kong.

Yeung, Yue-man, and Xu-wei Hu, eds. 1992. *China's Coastal Cities: Catalysts for Modernization.* Honolulu.

Yip, Ka-che. 1995. *Health and National Reconstruction in Nationalist China: The Development of Modern Health Services, 1928–1937.* Ann Arbor, Mich.

Young, Ernest P. 1968. "Yuan Shih-k'ai's Rise to the Presidency." In Mary C. Wright, ed., 419–442.

Young, Louise. 1996. "Imagined Empire: The Cultural Construction of Manchukuo." In Duus et al., eds., 71–96.

———. 1998. *Japan's Total Empire: Manchuria and the Culture of Wartime Imperialism.* Berkeley.

Yü Chün-fang. 1992. "P'u-t'o Shan: Pilgrimage and the Creation of the Chinese Potala." In Naquin and Yu, eds., 190–245.

———. 1994. "Baojuan wenxue zhong de Guanyin yu minjian xinyang" 寶卷文學中的觀音與民間信仰 (Guanyin in the Baojuan literature and its relationship with popular religion). In *Minjian xinyang yu Zhongguo wenhua guoji taolunhui lunwen ji* 民間信仰與中國文化國際討論會論文集 (Essays from the international conference on popular religion and Chinese culture), 333–351. Taibei.

Yu Dafu 郁達夫. 1982. *Yu Dafu wenji* 郁達夫文集 (Collection of Yu Dafu works). Hong Kong.

Yu Heping 虞和平. 1993. *Shanghui yu Zhongguo zaoqi xiandaihua* 商會與中國早期現代化 (Chambers of commerce and the early modernization of China). Shanghai.

Yu Shouzhen 喻守真, Ge Suicheng 葛綏成, and Zhou Baidi 周白棣. 1926. *Quanguo duhui shangbu luxing zhinan* 全國都會商埠旅行指南 (A travel guide to metropolitan cities and treaty ports in the whole country). Shanghai.

Yuan Jicheng 袁繼成. 1987. "Kangzhan chuqi Wuhan de baozhi kanwu" 抗戰初期武漢的報紙刊物 (Wuhan's press during the early period of the Anti-Japanese War). *Hubei xinwen shiliao huibian* 湖北新聞史料匯編 (Collection on the history of journalism in Hubei) 11: 25–128.

Yuan Liang 袁良. 1935. "Beiping shizheng baogao" 北平市政報告 (A report on Beiping city administration). *Shizheng pinglun* 市政評論 (Review of city administration) 3 (10) (May): 17–21.

Zhang Dachang 張大昌. 1972. *Hangzhou baqi zhufangying zhilue* 杭州八旗駐防營志略 (Gazetteer of the Hangzhou eight banner garrison). Taibei.

Zhang Haipeng 張海鵬 and Zhang Haiying 張海瀛, eds. 1993. *Zhongguo shi da shangbang* 中國 十大商幫 (The ten great commercial *bang* in China). Hefei.

Zhang Henshui 張恨水. 1946. "Chongqing lu ganlu" 重慶旅感錄 (A sentimental record of travels to Chongqing). In *Shuxing manji* 蜀行漫記 (Diffuse notes on travels through Sichuan), ed. Feng Shizhu 馮石竹, 5–21. Shanghai.

Zhang Hongxiang 張洪祥. 1993. *Jindai Zhongguo tongshang kou'an yu zujie* 近代中國通商口岸與租界 (Modern China's treaty ports and concession areas). Tianjin.

Zhang Jishun. 1993–1994. "On Student Groups in the Political Movement in Shanghai (1925–1927)." In Perry and Wasserstrom, eds., 65–83.

Zhang Tao 張燾. (1884) 1986. *Jinmen zaji* 津門雜記 (Miscellaneous records of Tianjin). Tianjin (reprint).

Zhang, Xiaobo. 1995. "Merchant Associational Activism in Early Twentieth Century China: The Tianjin General Chamber of Commerce, 1904–1928." Ph.D. dissertation, Columbia University.

Zhang Yingjin. 1996. *The City in Modern Chinese Literature & Film: Configurations of Space, Time, and Gender.* Stanford.

Zhang Youxin 張又新. 1934. "Beipingshi zhi quedian jiqi jiuji 北平市之缺點及其救濟 (Beiping's shortcomings and their correction). *Shizheng pinglun* 市政評論 (Review of city administration) 1 (June): 5–8.

Zhang Zhongli 張仲禮et al., eds. 1990. *Jindai Shanghai chengshi yanjiu* 近代上海城市研究(Studies of modern Shanghai). Shanghai.

Zhao Gang 趙岡 . 1995. *Zhongguo chengshi fazhanshi lunji* 中國城市發展史論集 (Essays on the history of Chinese urban development). Taibei.

Zhejiang sheng sheke yanjiusuo 浙江省社科研究所, ed. 1984. *Zhejiang renwu jianzhi*浙江人物簡志 (Brief biographies of prominent Zhejiang people). Hangzhou.

Zhong Maoxuan 鍾茂烜. 1984. *Liu Shiliang waizhuan* 劉師亮外傳. (An unofficial history of Liu Shiliang). Chengdu.

Zhong Yulong 鍾毓龍. 1983. *Shuo Hangzhou* 說杭州 (Speaking of Hangzhou). Hangzhou.

Zhongguo jianzhu 中國建築 (Chinese architecture). July 1932–July 1936. Shanghai.

Zhongguo jinrong shi 中國金融史 (A history of Chinese finance). 1993. Chengdu.

Zhongguo luxingshe 中國旅行社. 1963. *Zhongguo luxingshe jianshi* 中國旅行社簡史 (A brief history of the China Travel Agency). Taibei.

Zhongguo zhongyao yinhang zuijin shi nian yingye gaikuang yanjiu 中國重要銀行最近十年營業概況研究 (An analysis of the accounts of the principal Chinese banks, 1921–1931). 1933. Ed. Zhongguo yinhang zong guanlichu jingji yanjiu shi 中國銀行總管理處經濟研究室 (The Bank of China Research Department). Shanghai.

Zhou Enlai zhenglunxuan 周恩來政論選 (Selected political works of Zhou Enlai). 1993. 2 vols. Beijing.

Zhou Feng 周峰, ed. 1990. *Yuan Ming Qing mingcheng Hangzhou* 元明清名城杭州 (Hangzhou, the famous city in the Yuan, Ming, and Qing dynasties). Hangzhou.

———. 1992. *Minguo shiqi Hangzhou* 民國時期杭州 (Hangzhou during the republican period). Hangzhou.

Zhou Junqi 周俊旗. 1994. "Guanyu jindai quyu chengshi xitong yanjiu de jige wenti" 關於近代區域城市系統研究的幾個問題 (Some problems in the study of regional urban systems in the modern period). *Tianjin shehui kexue* 天津社會科學 (Tianjin social science) 5.

Zhou Kaiqing 周開慶. 1972a and 1974. *Minguo Chuanshi jiyao* 民國川史紀要 (Chronicle of Sichuan events during the Republic). 2 vols. Taibei.

———. 1972b. *Sichuan jingji zhi* 四川經濟志 (Sichuan economic annals). Taibei.

Zhou Shoujuan 周瘦鵑, ed. 1929. *Hu shang* 湖上 (On the lake). Shanghai.

Zhou Yonglin 周永林. 1991. "Huashuo 'jingshen baolei,'" 話說精神堡壘 (A few words about the 'spiritual fortress'). In *Chongqing zhanshi jishi, xubian* 重慶戰時記事續編 (Continuation of the history of wartime Chongqing), 61–64. Chongqing.

Zhu An 銖庵 (pseud.: Qu Xuanying 瞿宣穎). 1936a. "Bei you lu hua" 北游錄話 (Recorded conversation on a northern tour). *Yuzhou feng* 宇宙風 (Wind of the universe) 26 (October): 107–108.

———. 1936b. "Wenhua cheng de wenhua" 文化城的文化 (Culture in the city of culture). *Yuzhou feng* 29 (November): 280–283.

———. 1936c. "Beiping de yunming" 北平的運命 (Beiping's fate). *Yuzhou feng* 31 (December): 362–363.

Zhu Dingzhang 祝鼎章. "Nanjing de jinkuang" 南京的近況 (Recent affairs in Nanjing). *Dongfang zazhi* (Eastern miscellany) 21 (4) (February 25, 1924).

Zhu Renxun 諸仁遜. n.d. *Wenjian lu* 聞見錄 (Recollections). Handcopied manuscript. Tianjin Academy of Social Sciences.

"Zhuang Ke" 壯克 (pseud.). 1934. "Beiping shi de teshu xing" 北平市的特殊性 (The special conditions of

Beiping). *Shizheng pinglun* 市政評論 (Review of city administration) 1 (June): 2–3.

Zhuyuan conghua 竹園叢話. 1923–1926. (Complete talks from the bamboo garden). Tianjin.

Zito, Angela. 1993. "Ritualizing *li:* Implications for Studying Power and Gender." *positions: East Asia Cultures Critique* 1 (2): 321–348.

Contributors

David D. Buck is professor of history and former director of the Institute of World Affairs at the University of Wisconsin-Milwaukee. He has published books on modern Chinese urban history and the Boxer movement.

Madeleine Yue Dong is assistant professor in the Jackson School of International Studies at the University of Washington. She has published articles on local communities' experiences of social and cultural transformation in the late nineteenth and early twentieth centuries. She is currently finishing a book on the history of republican Beijing.

Joseph W. Esherick is professor of history and Hwei-chih and Julia Hsiu Professor of Chinese Studies at the University of California, San Diego. He has published books on the 1911 Revolution, the Boxer Uprising, Chinese local elites, and Chinese archives.

Stephen R. MacKinnon is professor of history and former director of the Center for Asian Studies at Arizona State University. He has written books on late Qing politics and Agnes Smedley (co-author), and U.S. reporting on China. He is currently working on a book on the ten months in 1938 when Wuhan was the de facto capital of wartime China.

Lee McIsaac is assistant professor of history at the University of Vermont. Her research interests include urban history, labor history, and gender. She is currently completing a book on the social identities of workers in Chongqing during the War of Resistance against Japan.

Charles D. Musgrove is a Ph.D. candidate at the University of California, San Diego. He is currently working on a dissertation on architecture and urban planning in Nanjing, 1927–1937.

Ruth Rogaski is assistant professor of history at Princeton University. Her research interests include urban history, gender, and the history of science and medicine in East Asia. She is currently completing a book on hygiene and public health in twentieth-century China.

Brett Sheehan is assistant professor of history at the University of Wisconsin, Madison. He has published articles on money and banking in China, and is currently preparing a book manuscript on the role of banks and money in state-society relations in Tianjin during the republican period.

Kristin Stapleton teaches East Asian history at the University of Kentucky. Her study of urban planning and social change in late-Qing and republican Chengdu will be published by the Harvard University Asia Center. She is beginning work on a book on the historical background of Ba Jin's novel *Family*.

David Strand is professor of history and political science at Dickinson College. He is the author of *Rickshaw Beijing: City People and Politics in the 1920s* and co-editor of *Reconstructing Twentieth-Century China: State Control, Civil Society, and National Identity*. He is currently writing a history of public speaking in China.

Michael Tsin teaches Chinese history at Columbia University, and is author of *Nation, Governance, and Modernity in China: Canton, 1900-1927* (Stanford, 1999). He is currently working on a cultural history of the prison in twentieth-century China.

Liping Wang is assistant professor of history at the University of Minnesota. She has published articles on the construction of national symbols in the early twentieth century, and the Nationalist military campaigns against the Japanese during the War of Resistance. She is currently completing a book on Qing and republican Hangzhou.

Jeffrey N. Wasserstrom is associate professor of history at Indiana University. His books and articles cover topics ranging from the history of Chinese student protests to the gendered dimensions of revolutions to competing understandings of human rights. He is currently working on the Shanghai volume for a Routledge book series on global cities of Asia.

Index